HEALTH CARE FOR WOMEN

PSYCHOLOGICAL, SOCIAL, AND BEHAVIORAL INFLUENCES

EDITED BY

SHERYLE J. GALLANT,

GWENDOLYN PURYEAR KEITA,

AND RENEÉ ROYAK-SCHALER

AMERICAN PSYCHOLOGICAL ASSOCIATION
WASHINGTON, DC

Published by
American Psychological Association
750 First Street, NE
Washington, DC 20002-4242

Copies may be ordered from
APA Order Department
P.O. Box 92984
Washington, DC 20090-2984

In the UK and Europe, copies may be ordered from
American Psychological Association
3 Henrietta Street
Covent Garden, London
WC2E 8LU England

Typeset in Century by EPS Group Inc., Easton, MD

Printer: United Book Press, Inc., Baltimore, MD
Cover Designer: Minker Design, Bethesda, MD.
Cover Photograph by Dennis Deloria, © 1981 by Liz Lerman Dance Exchange.
Technical/Production Editor: Susan Bedford

Library of Congress Cataloging-in-Publication Data
Health care for women : psychological, social, and behavioral influences / edited
  by Sheryle J. Gallant, Gwendolyn Puryear Keita, Reneé Royak-Schaler.
        p.   cm.
    Includes bibliographical references and index.
    ISBN 1-55798-422-0 (alk. paper)
    1. Women—Health and hygiene.   2. Women—Mental health.
3. Clinical health psychology.   4. Women—Health and hygiene—
Sociological aspects.   I. Gallant, Sheryle J.   II. Keita,
Gwendolyn Puryear.   III. Royak-Schaler, Reneé, 1946–
    [DNLM: 1. Women's Health Services.   2. Socioeconomic Factors.
3. Life Style.   4. Health Promotion.   WA 309 H4341 1997]
RA564.85.H3985   1997
362.1'082—dc21
DNLM/DLC
for Library of Congress   97-10813
                                                                            CIP

British Library Cataloguing-in-Publication Data
A CIP record is available from the British Library.

Printed in the United States of America
First Edition

Contents

iii

Contributors

Nancy E. Adler, PhD, University of California, San Francisco, CA

Ami B. Becker, PhD, National Institute for Occupational Safety and Health, Taft Laboratories, Cincinnati, OH

Susan J. Blalock, PhD, University of North Carolina, Chapel Hill, Chapel Hill, NC

Susan J. Blumenthal, MD, MPA, U.S. Public Health Service/Office on Women's Health, Washington, DC

Charlotte Brown, PhD, Western Psychiatric Institute and Clinic, University of Pittsburgh, Pittsburgh, PA

Edith A. Burns, MD, University of Wisconsin School of Medicine

Helen L. Coons, Health Federation of Philadelphia, Philadelphia, PA

Marilee Coriell, PhD, University of California, San Francisco, CA

Royda Crose, PhD, Ball State University, Muncie, IN

Susan Czajkowski, PhD, National Heart, Lung and Blood Institute, Bethesda, MD

Sharon Danoff-Burg, PhD, University of Kansas, Lawrence, KS

Carol A. Derby, PhD, Memorial Hospital of Rhode Island, Pawtucket, RI

Paula S. Derry, PhD, Baltimore, MD

Brenda M. DeVellis, PhD, University of North Carolina, Chapel Hill, NC

M. Robin DiMatteo, PhD, University of California, Riverside, CA

Christine Dunkel-Schetter, PhD, University of California, Los Angeles

Mary Ann Dutton, PhD, George Washington University Medical Center and George Washington University Law Center, Washington, DC

Gigi El-Bayoumi, MD, George Washington University Medical Center, Washington, DC

Sheryle J. Gallant, PhD, University of Kansas, Lawrence, KS

Judith A. Hall, PhD, Northeastern University, Boston, MA

Marie R. Haug, PhD, Case Western Reserve University, Cleveland, OH

Yolanda Haywood, MD, George Washington University Medical Center, Washington, DC

Vicki S. Helgeson, PhD, Carnegie Mellon University, Pittsburgh, PA

Kenneth A. Holroyd, PhD, Ohio University, Athens, OH

Katherine L. Kahn, MD, The RAND Corporation, Santa Monica, CA

Gwendolyn Puryear Keita, PhD, American Psychological Association, Washington, DC

Michaela Kiernan, PhD, Stanford Center for Research in Disease Prevention, Palo Alto, CA

Abby C. King, PhD, Stanford University, Palo Alto, CA

Mary Lou Klem, PhD, Western Psychiatric Institute and Clinic, University of Pittsburgh, Pittsburgh, PA

Sarah S. Knox, PhD, National Heart, Lung and Blood Institute, Bethesda, MD

Kate L. Lapane, PhD, Memorial Hospital of Rhode Island, Pawtucket, RI

Elaine A. Leventhal, MD, PhD, UMDNJ/RWJ Medical School, New Brunswick, NJ

Gay L. Lipchik, Ohio University, Athens, OH

Nancy L. Marshall, EdD, Center for Research on Women, Wellesley College, Wellesley, MA

Vickie M. Mays, PhD, University of California, Los Angeles

Robin J. Mermelstein, PhD, Department of Psychology and Prevention Resource Center, University of Illinois at Chicago

Robert Michielutte, PhD, Bowman Gray School of Medicine, Winston-Salem, NC

Patricia J. Morokoff, PhD, University of Rhode Island, Kingston, RI

Ann O'Leary, PhD, Rutgers University, New Brunswick, NJ

Lauri A. Pasch, PhD, University of California, San Francisco

Electra D. Paskett, PhD, Bowman Gray School of Medicine, Winston-Salem, NC

Kathleen M. Pike, PhD, Columbia Presbyterian Medical Center, New York, NY

Chaya S. Piotrkowski, PhD, Fordham University, New York, NY

Betsy A. Polley, MS, Western Psychiatric Institute and Clinic, University of Pittsburgh, Pittsburgh, PA

Tracey A. Revenson, PhD, Graduate School of the City University of New York, New York, NY

Debra L. Roter, DrPh, Johns Hopkins University, Baltimore, MD

Reneé Royak-Schaler, PhD, School of Public Health, Allegheny University of the Health Sciences, Philadelphia, PA, and Lineberger Comprehensive Cancer Center, University of North Carolina at Chapel Hill

Herbert C. Schulberg, PhD, Western Psychiatric Institute and Clinic, University of Pittsburgh, Pittsburgh, PA

Annette L. Stanton, PhD, University of Kansas, Lawrence, KS

Elaine J. Stone, PhD, MPH, National Heart, Lung and Blood Institute, Bethesda, MD

Ruth H. Striegel-Moore, PhD, Wesleyan University, Middletown, CT

Naomi G. Swanson, PhD, National Institute for Occupational Safety and Health, Cincinnati, OH

Nancy D. Vogeltanz, PhD, University of North Dakota School of Medicine and Health Sciences, Grand Forks, ND

Sharon C. Wilsnack, PhD, University of North Dakota School of Medicine and Health Sciences, Grand Forks, ND

Rena R. Wing, PhD, Western Psychiatric Institute and Clinic, University of Pittsburgh, Pittsburgh, PA

Marilyn A. Winkleby, PhD, Stanford University, Palo Alto, CA

Susan F. Wood, PhD, U.S. Public Health Service/Office on Women's Health, Washington, DC

Nancy F. Woods, RN, PhD, FAAN, University of Washington, Seattle, WA

Foreword

Historically, the central role assigned to women's emotions and hormonal activity in understanding their health and well-being has limited the scope of women's health research. A popular medical textbook from the 19th century, for example, informed medical students that "it appears that the process of child-bearing is essentially necessary to the physical health and long life, the mental happiness, the development of the affections and whole character of women. Woman exists for the sake of the womb" (Holbrook, 1871, pp. 13–14).

Although shocking to present-day readers, that maxim expresses what was an accepted assumption of the medical profession for many years: that women's lives were defined by maternity, and women's health was defined by their reproductive system. Other issues in women's health—conditions that affect both men and women, for example—were defined primarily in terms of male anatomy and male models of prevention and treatment, with scant attention given to possible sex and gender differences in prevalence, onset, progression, and treatment of diseases common to women and men. When women's differences from the male model of health and disease were acknowledged, they were often viewed in an unflattering light.

Fortunately, today, this myth is beginning to yield to reason. During the past 25 years, as the roles played by women in American society have expanded and as women have gained a foothold in positions of economic and political power, there has been a growing recognition that women's health issues are deserving of and require special attention. There is also a new and ever-broader acceptance of the idea that physical and mental health are influenced by many factors, including an individual's culture, society, personal behavior, and lifestyle choices, as well as genetic and biological heritage.

As a result of this shift in consciousness concerning women's health and human health in general, resources are now being directed by the federal government to pursue important questions in women's health through an integrated agenda for biomedical and biobehavioral research. In 1990, the National Institutes of Health (NIH) established the Office of Research on Women's Health (ORWH) to serve as a focal point for women's health research conducted and supported by the NIH. The ORWH emphasizes the importance of psychosocial, behavioral, and biological factors as it seeks to improve the health of women through research aimed at expanding scientific knowledge and health professionals' understanding of sex and gender differences in disease and health across the entire life span, from childhood through maturity and the later years of life.

The ORWH serves as a catalyst within the NIH to redress gender inequities in medical research as it fulfills the following tripartite mandate through programs in collaboration with the NIH's constituent institutes and centers: (a) to identify gaps in knowledge and to develop and implement a research agenda on women's health; (b) to ensure that women are appropriately represented in biomedical and biobehavioral research studies, especially clinical trials, that are supported by the NIH; and (c) to take direct initiatives to increase opportunities for women in biomedical and biobehavioral careers.

Among its earliest undertakings, the ORWH convened a series of meetings and workshops that brought together women's health advocates, policymakers, members of the general public, and members of the biomedical and behavioral science communities to develop a national agenda for research on women's health issues. At one of the public hearings that contributed to the formulation of the ORWH's research agenda on women's health, Gwendolyn Puryear Keita of the American Psychological Association (APA) observed that

> dramatic improvements in health and health care historically have been associated with innovative ways of thinking about health and illness. New approaches, such as the germ theory of disease, have led to major advances in public health and the control of communicable diseases, such as cholera and tuberculosis. Our nation is poised to make similar dramatic advances if we are willing to view health not only as a biomedical, but as a social and psychological phenomenon. Psychology has an extensive knowledge base and has, in many areas, expertise relevant to health.[1]

This sage advice is reflected in the resulting research agenda, which states that "neither behavioral scientists nor those in basic research can, in isolation, adequately address the vast array of issues in women's health. . . . The behavioral and social context in which women lead their daily lives must serve as a subject for research" (Office of Research on Women's Health, 1992, p. 40). The agenda further states that "the distinction between behavior and biology is artificial. All future research efforts should aim at merging these two areas whenever it is appropriate. . . . Future research on women's health must be interdisciplinary" (p. 89).

The ORWH's efforts to foster a multidisciplinary, coherent approach to the study of women's health issues have been invigorated by the integration into the NIH of the National Institute on Drug Abuse, the National Institute on Alcohol Abuse and Alcoholism, and the National Institute of Mental Health in 1993. This integration has created new opportunities for collaborations among researchers in the biobehavioral and social sciences with those working in basic biological science. The establishment of the new, congressionally mandated Office of Behavioral and Social Science Research at NIH has also enhanced efforts to integrate biological and be-

---

[1]G. P. Keita, Testimony on behalf of the American Psychological Association for the National Institutes of Health Public Hearing on Opportunities for Research on Women's Health, Bethesda, MD, June 12–13, 1992.

havioral and psychosocial approaches to women's health research in a broader, more collaborative manner.

Because behavior has a far-reaching influence on health, a major aim of women's health research is to discover effective strategies for encouraging women to adopt behaviors to preserve their health, even into the later years of life. The ORWH is supporting efforts to expand the medical community's understanding of the factors that influence health-related decision making among women of diverse ethnic and racial backgrounds. The recruitment and retention of women of diverse backgrounds into clinical studies is a high priority, and many NIH-supported studies and programs focus specifically on finding effective ways to recruit women of diverse backgrounds into clinical trials and to sustain their participation.

Many of the areas identified by the ORWH as high priorities for research have also been cited in the APA's recently published *Research Agenda for Psychological and Behavioral Factors in Women's Health*. These include autoimmune diseases such as arthritis, cardiovascular disease, eating disorders, depression, HIV and AIDS; the health of women as they grow older; substance abuse; violence against women; and occupational and environmental influences on health. In fact, the NIH and APA research agendas augment and complement each other, with many shared areas of research emphasis and a commitment to ensuring that knowledge of women's health is incorporated into the training of all health professionals.

The challenge of truly improving the physical and mental health and well-being of women of all ages can be met only through concerted efforts by those in the biomedical and biobehavioral sciences working collaboratively with health professionals and others on the front lines of health care delivery. The initiatives of the NIH involve the fostering of such multidisciplinary collaborations in research, as there can be little doubt that the fragmentation of medical care among specializations and disciplines has resulted in the neglect of many areas of women's health.

It is imperative that researchers and practitioners gain a complete understanding of what areas of knowledge are still lacking and the obstacles that they face in filling in those knowledge gaps concerning women's health. With the NIH and APA research agendas serving as resource documents to provide guidance, investigators in the biomedical, behavioral, and social science communities today enjoy unprecedented opportunities to improve women's physical, mental, and emotional health.

This book offers a comprehensive overview of salient issues in women's health and highlights important areas for future collaboration between those in the biomedical and behavioral sciences. It embodies the joint commitment of the NIH and the APA to improving women's total, lifetime health through an integration of talents and expertise to address the health of the mind, the body, and the spirit.

VIVIAN W. PINN, MD
Associate Director for Research on Women's Health
Director, Office of Research on Women's Health
National Institutes of Health

References

Holbrook, M. L. (1871). *Parturition without pain: A code of directions for escaping the primal curse.* New York: Wood & Holbrook.

Office of Research on Women's Health. (1992). *Opportunities for research on women's health* (NIH Publication No. 92-3457).

Preface

This book was designed to explore the factors in women's lives that affect their health. It was developed with the recognition that women are a diverse group, and that women from different ethnic and socioeconomic backgrounds bring different life histories, cultural and health beliefs and practices, and concerns to the health care setting.

The importance of a psychosocial perspective was the focus of a conference convened by the American Psychological Association (APA) in May 1994 to address the major psychosocial and behavioral determinants of chronic disease and disability among women and to identify how factors influencing health may differ for men and women. This volume grew out of conference discussions emphasizing the need among health care practitioners for information about health behaviors, their relationships to lifestyle diseases in women, and the process of promoting health through behavior change.

The national focus on women's health has greatly intensified during the past decade. The collaborative efforts of scientists, clinicians, and legislators since the mid-1980s have investigated, evaluated, and promoted the health care needs of women. In September 1995, the Council on Graduate Medical Education (CGME) issued its "Fifth Report: Women and Medicine," focusing on the importance of training female physicians and the training of all physicians in women's health. The report emphasizes that physician education should prepare health professionals to recognize how women access medical care and to understand women's roles in society, their communication methods, and their relationship to the medical system.

This volume supports the goals of the CGME's report and provides critical information for physicians in understanding the psychosocial and behavioral factors most pertinent to health care, health promotion, and disease prevention for women in medical and health settings. For example, several chapters address the importance of understanding the relationship of behaviors (e.g., smoking, diet) and emotional and personality factors (e.g., hostility, depression) to cardiovascular disease and cancer, the two leading causes of death in the United States. The authors also address the ways in which psychosocial factors may influence responses to life cycle challenges that can pose a significant threat to women throughout the life span.

Our goal is to present information on research in women's health that facilitates an understanding of the interplay of psychosocial, behavioral, and physiological functioning, and to synthesize from current knowledge practical applications for health care providers. We hope to reach a broad range of practitioners, including physicians, psychologists, physicians' assistants, nurses, and medical social workers. Our intended audience particularly includes educators and students in these fields. This volume has been developed for use as a source book and textbook, and for general information.

The development of this book would not have been possible without the efforts of our many contributing authors. They were asked to draw upon their areas of expertise in psychosocial research and address the important findings most relevant to the current health care needs of women. We also gratefully acknowledge the helpful assistance provided by those who served as reviewers for various chapters.

We especially want to thank Kenneth A. Wallston and Michele Salisbury, who made several important recommendations during a review of the entire original manuscript.

Finally, we have been fortunate throughout to have the support of the staff of the APA's Women's Programs Office, particularly Tanya Burrwell, and of the APA editorial staff.

Introduction

The past several decades have revolutionized the field of women's health. Thinking has changed dramatically on the importance of promoting the health of women and the methods for reducing their risk of chronic disease and disability. There is now a considerable body of knowledge about psychosocial factors and health, and more is known now than in the past about behavior change. Concern about issues in women's health has grown within the scientific community and the general public, as has the demand for more investigation of the diseases, disorders, and conditions that affect women.

In this book, the authors were asked to synthesize and translate relevant research findings dealing with women's health behaviors, lifestyle factors, and psychosocial circumstances for medical and health care settings. In this introduction, we provide an overview of some of the individual and social factors and aspects of behavior change that are important for promoting health and preventing disease in women.

Approaches to Understanding Health Behavior in Women

Since the early 1970s American health professionals, researchers, policymakers, and the general public have been increasingly concerned with the relationship between health practices and longevity. A survey conducted from 1965 to 1974 among approximately 5,000 residents of Alameda County, California, indicated that individual health behaviors were stable and that adult men and women who followed seven health practices (i.e., sleeping 7–8 hr daily, eating breakfast, rarely eating between meals, maintaining desirable weight, never smoking cigarettes, moderate or no alcohol use, and regular physical activity) had lower mortality rates (Breslow & Enstrom, 1980). Men who followed these seven health practices had mortality rates 28% lower than those who followed fewer than three of the health practices. The pattern for women was equally dramatic and revealed a 43% lower mortality rate (Breslow & Enstrom, 1980).

In 1979 *Healthy People: The Surgeon General's Report on Health Promotion and Disease Prevention* appeared, identifying the importance of health promotion and disease prevention in reducing death and disability in the United States. For the first time a publication delineated national goals for improving the health of the American people during the 1980s. Since then, numerous annual publications have addressed these issues, including *Healthy People 2000*, which provides a framework to significantly reduce preventable death and disability, to enhance the quality of life, and to reduce disparities in the health status of special populations in American society (U.S. Department of Health and Human Services [USDHHS], 1995). Many of the priority areas for *Healthy People 2000* address health behaviors that are critical for preventing disease and promoting the health of women, such as physical activity; nutrition over the life span; tobacco, alcohol, and drug use; mental health; and violent and abusive behavior.

Approaches to preventing disease and promoting health, whether individual or community-based, are founded on the idea that behaviors and lifestyle choices that contribute to an individual's risk profile are influenced by his or her social and physical milieus. Behavioral theories suggest that the ability to adopt healthy behaviors is a function of knowledge and skills as well as confidence in one's ability to succeed (Bandura, 1986). In addition to personal factors, an individual's behaviors are influenced by the attitudes, values, and practices of family and friends and the geopolitical environment of policies and regulations at the community and national levels (Carleton, Lasater, Assaf, Feldman, & McKinlay, 1995). The complexities of individual behavior change and the models that guide health behavior research and interventions are discussed in several chapters in this volume. Smoking cessation is a good example of the difficulties health professionals can experience in making effective recommendations to help their women patients change health-impairing behaviors. This is an area of compelling concern in women's health. Despite a downward trend in cigarette smoking since the U.S. Surgeon General's (1964) report *Smoking and Health* (33.5% of people older than 18 smoked in 1979, 30.1% in 1985, and 26.5% in 1992), the incidence of lung cancer in both Black and White women is increasing faster than any other major type of cancer (USDHHS, 1990). In smoking cessation, as in other areas, it is important for providers to understand and tailor their recommendations specifically to women's concerns (e.g., fear of weight gain, pregnancy).

Community-based intervention programs to date have demonstrated that community involvement in health promotion is both feasible and effective. Although all segments of the U.S. population have benefited from health promotion initiatives in recent years, not all groups have benefited equally. Levels of cardiovascular risk factors, for example, are no longer decreasing steadily in less educated and less affluent groups, and the socioeconomic gap in health behaviors and cardiovascular mortality is increasing (G. A. Kaplan & Keil, 1993; National Heart, Lung, and Blood Institute, 1994).

Factors in Behavior Change

Although a number of factors influence whether people undertake particular health behaviors, research has shown that two are critical: the belief that a given behavior will produce an outcome they desire and the confidence that they are capable of performing the behavior. For example, a woman may begin a walking exercise program because she believes this will reduce her risk of both heart disease and osteoporosis; to successfully carry out the program, however, she must believe she is capable of doing so. According to Bandura (1977), her sense of being capable comes from four major sources: (a) past performance in other exercise programs; (b) vicarious experience through observing others (e.g., when a friend successfully maintains a walking program, she is more likely to feel she can as well); (c) verbal persuasion from both herself and others that she can successfully initiate and maintain the walking program; and (d) emotional and physiological messages from within about how she is coping with the exercise regimen (e.g., being calm and relaxed, enjoying the walking, and experiencing its benefits enhances one's sense of success).

Perceptions of capability and self-efficacy affect every phase of the behavior change process, including the decision to change health habits, the level of effort expended after choosing to change, the extent to which people are able to change, and how well they maintain the changes they achieve (Bandura, 1990).

For both women and men, individual perceptions and belief in one's ability to quit smoking are better predictors of smoking abstinence and relapse than physiological dependence, coping history, motivation to quit, confidence in treatment, and expectancies concerning the rewards of smoking. This appears to be the case regardless of treatment methods, methods of measuring self-efficacy, and the populations being studied (Condiotte & Lichtenstein, 1981; DiClemente, 1981; DiClemente, Prochaska, & Gilbertini, 1985; Lawrance & McLeroy, 1986; Marlatt & Gordon, 1980). Self-efficacy also predicts who will successfully manage eating and weight and overcome eating disorders (Chambliss & Murray, 1979). Strong beliefs in one's ability to manage pain increases pain tolerance during dental treatment and childbirth and in response to tension headaches (Holroyd et al., 1984; Klepac, Dowling, & Hauge, 1982; Manning & Wright, 1983). Finally, the belief in one's ability to affect one's health increases adherence to medical regimens, maintenance of dental regimens to combat periodontal disease, and walking programs for patients with chronic obstructive pulmonary disease (Beck & Lund, 1981; R. M. Kaplan, Atkins, & Reinsch, 1984).

Successful and lasting behavior change is most likely to occur when individuals believe that they can control their motivation, behavior, and social environments. Suggestions for practitioners to effectively facilitate behavior change in female patients while addressing their specific needs are provided throughout this book.

Sociocultural Issues in Women's Health

In the United States it is recognized that lifestyle and environmental factors are major determinants of chronic disease and disability (USDHHS, 1995). For women, coronary heart disease, stroke, lung cancer, and breast cancer are the leading causes of death and disability (Wenger, Speroff, & Packard, 1993). Many of the risk factors identified for these diseases are a function of health behaviors acting in concert with genetic and environmental factors (Luepker, 1994).

Socioeconomic status (SES) is associated with health, and this occurs at all levels of the SES hierarchy (Adler, Boyce, Chesney, Folkman, &

Syme, 1993). Lower SES places women in a vulnerable position in terms of risk of morbidity and mortality. Education and income are two important factors in determining women's access to medical care; those with more education and higher income are more likely to receive immunizations, have regular physical examinations when they have no symptoms, obtain preventive dental care, get Pap smears, and respond to breast cancer screening programs (Kirscht, 1983).

Women who are poor and uneducated are at greater risk for cancer incidence and mortality. The percentage below poverty level accounts for racial differences observed in breast and cervical cancer survival according to data from the National Cancer Institute's (NCI's) Surveillance, Epidemiology, and End Results program, conducted from 1978 to 1982 (McWhorter, Schatzkin, Horm, & Brown, 1989). Women of lower SES have 25% higher death rates from breast cancer and 2.8 times higher cervical cancer mortality rates than do women of higher SES (USDHHS, 1990). SES is a clear risk factor for disease and should be part of an assessment of a patient's profile of risk factors.

In January 1995 the NCI announced the largest short-term decline in breast cancer deaths in 40 years. However, this decline was not experienced by all groups. For White women breast cancer mortality had decreased by 5%, but for African American women death rates actually increased 3% between 1989 and 1992. Further, once again, lower 5-year survival rates were identified in minority women despite a 20% higher breast cancer incidence in White women. Although many of the health differences often attributed to race or ethnicity are accounted for by SES, race or ethnic group membership is an important factor in understanding women's and men's health.

Women from different ethnic and socioeconomic backgrounds bring different life histories, cultural and health beliefs and practices, and concerns to the health care setting. Moreover, they bring different experiences of situational stress and resources for coping with these stressors. For example, results from a recent study (Krieger & Sidney, 1996) indicated that racial discrimination shapes patterns of blood pressure among the U.S. Black population and differences in Black–White blood pressure.

It is especially important that health professionals not let their assumptions and beliefs about different groups of women influence the treatment they provide. For example, as noted by Hawkins (1987), beliefs that Blacks are "just violent people" seriously affects the responsiveness of formal help sources, including health care providers to women victimized by violence.

Violence against women is a significant risk factor for injury and death that health care practitioners should include in their assessment of adult female patients. Violence received national attention as a health issue in 1985 when Surgeon General C. Everett Koop called it the Number 1 health problem facing women in the United States. Although numerous medical organizations and government agencies recommend routine screening of women to prevent, identify, and care for victims of violence, there is still

a critical need to assist health care professionals in recognizing, understanding, and treating the health consequences of violence in their female
patients.

Plan for This Book

This book was developed to provide health professionals with a comprehensive understanding of the role of psychosocial factors in women's
health, their responses to illness, and use of the health care system. The
authors use contextual, life cycle, and disease-specific perspectives in their
discussions of major issues in women's health to accomplish three important goals: (a) to describe the ways in which attitudes and behaviors influence women's health; (b) to examine how attitudes and behaviors interact with physiological processes to influence the health and functioning
of women; and (c) to describe how psychosocial conditions affect health
risk and practices.

In each chapter selected psychosocial and behavioral research is reviewed, and examples, discussions, and applications (whenever possible)
of behaviors, attitudes, and coping patterns encountered by health care
providers in their daily interactions with female patients are presented.
The overall goal is to provide information critical to promoting the health
of women.

Part I: Women's Health in Context

Part I highlights the importance of understanding contextual factors that
structure the experience of women's lives and affect women's health.
These factors include federal policies and initiatives, SES, violence and
victimization, gender differences in communication in the health care setting, personality factors, stress, social networks, and coping strategies.
The importance of the relationships among mental health, physical
health status, and health behaviors in women also are discussed in Part
I. Examples illustrate the impact of health beliefs, such as personal control
and self-efficacy, on health practices and outcomes for women and ways
in which primary care providers can facilitate active coping in their patients.

In chapter 1, Blumenthal and Wood provide a brief historical perspective on the focus on women's health in the United States. They begin
with the early struggle to give women control over their reproduction and
then discuss the legislation passed to include women in clinical research
studies, the Women's Health Equity Act of 1990, and the more recent legislative proposals and programs on breast and cervical cancer, contraception and infertility, and violence against women. They also discuss some
of the mechanisms put into place to ensure continued attention to women's
health in the future.

In chapter 2, Adler and Coriell provide clear evidence of the strong relationship between SES and health and suggest that the health effects of SES are more pervasive and potent than has previously been realized. Using breast cancer as an example, they present data showing the critical importance of SES for mortality as well as morbidity and discuss the implications for practitioners with respect to prevention, screening, and treatment. The authors conclude with suggestions for SES-sensitive services.

Women are different from men in the kinds of stressful events they experience, and the ways they cope with them. In chapter 3 O'Leary and Helgeson describe these differences, along with the beneficial effects that social networks, coping strategies, and perceptions of control have on reducing the harmful effects of stress. They discuss the health benefits associated with stress-resistant personality traits (e.g., optimism) and the health risks associated with stress-prone traits (e.g., Type A behavior pattern) and provide general guidelines for health care practitioners regarding the experience of stress in their female patients.

Violence against women is examined by Dutton, Haywood, and El-Bayoumi in chapter 4. They present evidence of the impact of violence on women's health, focusing on injury, systemic health problems, pregnancy-related issues, and mental health consequences. Dutton et al. provide practical information on how to identify women who have been victimized by violence and how to assess the risk and harm caused by the violence. They also provide a variety of interventions for practitioners working with victims of violence.

The physician–patient interaction is the context explored by Roter and Hall in chapter 5. Drawing on the literature and some of their own studies, they present evidence that there is a particular conversational style in interactions with female physicians that involves more positive talk, partnership building, question asking, and information giving. They discuss the positive effects of this for female patients and the implications for clinical practice and physician training.

Part II: Lifestyle Factors and Health

Part II addresses five lifestyle areas that are central health concerns for women: alcohol abuse, eating disorders, obesity, exercise, and work and occupational stress. These five areas were selected for inclusion because each is recognized as posing special challenges for women and for health care providers in their efforts to reduce the risks to women's health or, as in the case of exercise, to increase health benefits and well-being. Each of these areas has been the focus of extensive research that has increased knowledge of their etiologies and strategies to promote effective coping and change.

Vogeltanz and Wilsnack, in chapter 6, note that at least one in four of those in the United States with alcohol problems are women and that there has been a tremendous recent expansion of knowledge important to treatment and prevention. They review epidemiological data on the inter-play of biological and social variables in the genesis of alcohol problems in women and the serious adverse psychosocial and health consequences of abuse. They also present evidence of important determinants of problem drinking that affect women in particular as well as gender-specific barriers to women receiving effective treatment. Given that a significant proportion of problem drinking in women goes undetected, the information provided on strategies for identifying alcohol problems in women is important to physicians and other health professionals.

Strategies for identifying symptomatic individuals and addressing barriers to treatment of eating disorders are addressed in chapter 7 by Pike and Striegel-Moore. Although it is widely acknowledged that eating disorders are a problem for an increasing portion of the female population, the authors identify resistance to seeking help as a problem that often goes unrecognized. Because the modal onset of eating disorders occurs in adolescence and young adulthood, it is especially important for health pro-fessionals who care for this population to gather information about eating behavior as part of routine health care. The authors also present guide-lines for questions that can be asked in history taking.

In chapter 8 Wing and Klem address the role of lifestyle factors in the development and treatment of obesity. They discuss periods in women's lives when the risk of weight gain is increased and provide guidelines for the treatment of obesity in the primary care setting. Two groups of women are identified as requiring specialized weight control interventions: those with binge eating disorders and overweight middle-aged African American women. Wing and Klem view the prevention of obesity as an important goal for health care providers, emphasizing that the single best predictor of long-term weight loss and maintenance is adoption of an exercise pro-gram.

Regular physical activity is associated with improved physical and psychological functioning and the easing of disease symptoms in women with chronic health problems. Despite these benefits, 75% of American women remain underactive. In chapter 9 King and Kiernan provide a com-prehensive discussion of the prevalence of physical inactivity among women and its health-related consequences. They discuss critical periods in women's lives for natural reductions or increases in physical activity and recommend that health professionals encourage physical activity in their female patients by attending to their past experiences with exercise, their individual preferences for types of activity, social and environmental support, and enjoyability and convenience factors.

Given the number of women in the workforce, an examination of the impact of work on women's health is critical. In chapter 10 Swanson, Pio-trkowski, Keita, and Becker reveal that the "classic job stressors" (e.g., lack of job control) are predictive of health problems for women. However, they also show the deleterious health effects of job stressors of particular concern to women (e.g., sexual harassment). Using case studies, the au-thors provide a guide to the evaluation and treatment of occupational stress in health settings. Especially helpful is their list of sample questions for practitioners to use in assessing occupational stress.

Part III: Responses to Life Cycle Challenges

This section focuses on several health issues likely to be experienced by women of different ages and particular life stages. The three topic areas represented—the stress of combining work and family roles, reproductive-related life events (childbirth, infertility, premenstrual syndrome, and menopause), and the health issues of aging women—address issues of central importance at different points in a woman's life.

The majority of women in the United States both work and have families, and this combination has definite health effects on women. In chapter 11 Marshall provides an overview of current theories about work and family issues and summarizes research showing both positive and negative effects on health of combining work and family. To help health practitioners identify women who may be at risk for work–family strains and related health problems, Marshall reviews the literature on risk factors and provides a list of questions practitioners should ask to assess whether a patient's symptoms may be a consequence of work–family strains.

In chapter 12 DiMatteo and Kahn address the challenging experience of giving birth. Literature is reviewed on the psychological effects of cesarean delivery, which today occurs in nearly 25% of hospital births. An interesting feature of the chapter is the analysis of personal narratives from new mothers; the narratives are informative about the significant effects of "routine" obstetrical and childbirth technology. Five themes emerge, each underscoring that an appreciation of the psychosocial aspects of childbirth is an important issue in patient care. The authors discuss the themes and make recommendations for improving childbirth outcomes.

Given the relatively large number of infertile couples, recent medical advances that can significantly increase couples' chances of conception are often viewed as a godsend. However, as Pasch and Dunkel-Schetter make clear in chapter 13, the new medical technology also presents many couples with challenging issues and potential stressors. Heightened emotional distress in response to infertility and related treatments is not uncommon. The authors suggest that physicians and other health professionals will be best able to help couples if they adopt a stress and coping framework for understanding the effects of infertility. Research is reviewed from this perspective, and recommendations are made for ways that practitioners can assist couples in managing psychological distress, making treatment decisions, and identifying when psychological interventions may be needed.

In chapter 14, Derry, Gallant, and Woods address two additional important aspects of women's reproductive life: premenstrual syndrome and menopause. Particular attention is given in the discussion of premenstrual syndrome to the difficulties inherent in diagnosis. Similarly, issues that have spurred controversy in the literature on menopause, including questions related to menopausal depression and the risks and benefits of hormone replacement therapy, are examined. The important role of health care professionals in providing information to women is highlighted. They emphasize that there is a strong need for individualized assessment of patients and a willingness to consider a broad range of interventions.

In chapter 15 Crose, Haug, Leventhal, and Burns address another life cycle stage: aging. Women outlive men, with a gender gap in life expectancy of 4–10 years, so the world of older people is made up predominantly of women. More of clinical practice in the future will be directed toward the care of older women with chronic and disabling disease. The authors provide important information to help professionals understand the biological and psychosocial processes that underlie senescence and senility and the special challenges facing older women (e.g., caregiving). They also discuss relevant health issues such as osteoporosis, urinary incontinence, sexuality, abuse and neglect, mental health, and social support and give recommendations for health care providers to improve the care they provide to older women.

Part IV: Selected Life-Threatening and Chronic Conditions

Lifestyle and environmental factors are major determinants of chronic disease and disability in the United States (USDHHS, 1991). Chronic stressors and coping mechanisms are factors that affect both lifestyle and psychological well-being. Depression and anxiety can cause serious impairment in social and physical functioning and are associated with increased morbidity and mortality from medical illness. Contributors to the fourth section examine depression and anxiety and the psychosocial, behavioral, and socioeconomic factors important in several life-threatening and chronic conditions that are significant in terms of mortality, morbidity, pain, and suffering among women. Preference is given to topics for which there is important psychosocial and behavioral information that is relevant to the comprehensive assessment, diagnosis, and treatment of women with these conditions.

In chapter 16 Brown and Schulberg provide information about the epidemiology of depression and anxiety, which are the most common psychiatric disorders among primary care patients. They provide detailed information about the diagnosis of depression, generalized anxiety disorder, and panic disorder, and recommendations for their treatment, which addresses both psychosocial and pharmacological approaches. Brown and Schulberg also provide excellent information on differential diagnosis and issues of comorbidity.

In chapter 17 Knox and Czajkowski review the evidence demonstrating that women who develop coronary heart disease fare less well than men and discuss the mechanisms by which psychosocial and behavioral factors promote cardiovascular health, slow disease progression, and enhance treatment outcome. The authors emphasize that it is important for physicians and other health care providers to facilitate the timely detection and treatment of coronary heart disease in women and to foster their recovery by encouraging them to attend cardiac rehabilitation programs.

Waging a successful prevention battle against the continued spread of HIV in women is as much about the social conditions that allow the disease to spread as the biological mechanisms that govern its progress. Morokoff, Mays, and Coons, in chapter 18, discuss the psychological issues in HIV diagnostic testing and screening for diverse groups of women and use case examples to highlight factors affecting women's decisions to obtain screening and issues in pre- and posttest counseling. The authors provide guidelines for identifying women at risk and reducing high-risk behaviors and discuss the challenge of structuring systems of service delivery for women that integrate medical, psychological, and social services needs.

Breast cancer is the most common cancer among women in every major ethnic group in the United States (Kelsey & Horn-Ross, 1993). In chapter 19, Royak-Schaler, Stanton, and Danoff-Burg examine issues of socioeconomic diversity in breast cancer risk, screening, diagnosis, and treatment. They highlight psychosocial and behavioral strategies that promote accurate risk perception, routine screening, and prompt diagnosis and treatment. This chapter offers clear suggestions for office discussions by providers that address socioeconomic barriers and deliver information about screening, symptom care, diagnosis, and treatment using tailored, culturally relevant formats.

In chapter 20, Paskett and Michielutte present effective individual and community-based interventions that address psychosocial factors in promoting gynecological health. They identify factors placing women at risk for developing cervical, endometrial, and ovarian cancer, emphasizing the important role SES plays in high-risk behaviors and limited access to detection and treatment facilities. The authors present strategies to improve screening for gynecological cancers, including health care system interventions, community-based programs, and environmental initiatives.

As noted by DeVellis, Revenson, and Blalock in chapter 21, arthritis presents special challenges for women since the most serious forms occur two to five times more often in women than men. This chapter reviews the psychosocial and behavioral challenges related to rheumatoid arthritis, systematic lupus erythematosus, and fibromyalgia syndrome. All of these are chronic conditions in which pain and the risks of disability, depression, and the loss of important roles and support systems are often present. The authors offer many creative suggestions for addressing important patient concerns. Special emphasis is given to the pattern of physician–patient communication and the importance of perceptions of physician caring and sensitivity in relation to adherence. Several interventions developed to help boost the coping efficacy of patients with arthritis are discussed, including the well-known Arthritis Self Management Program.

In chapter 22 on maintaining glycemic control, Polley and Wing point out that although many of the challenging issues of diabetes management are not unique to women, they must be considered carefully with female diabetic patients to foster optimal management. The new techniques for self-monitoring of blood glucose and more efficient medication present special monitoring behavior challenges. Polley and Wing discuss this issue and other psychosocial and behavioral concerns that can significantly affect diabetes management. Of special importance for women with diabetes are weight control issues. The authors discuss results of some of their own research on the effectiveness of various interventions. Finally, the special concerns of gestational diabetes are reviewed, and the need for achieving glycemic control before pregnancy is emphasized.

Although many people often think of headaches as a minor physical problem, the data reviewed by Holroyd and Lipchik on tension-type and migraine headache disorders, both of which disproportionately affect women, make clear that each can have serious deleterious effects on women's lives. They also discuss the problems of drug-induced headache and transformed migraine that are particularly relevant to women and present challenges in terms of effective management for health care providers. A primary focus of the chapter is on evidence implicating reproductive hormones in the genesis and severity of headache problems and the clinical implications. The authors also highlight the need to increase women's awareness of behavioral and pharmacological therapies available for headache problems because a majority of women who suffer with these problems do not receive treatment.

Part V: New Directions in Health Promotion and Disease Prevention

Parts I–IV clarify the importance of health promotion and disease prevention in reducing death and disability and improving the well-being of women. Part V focuses on individual and community-based approaches to prevention and the behaviors and lifestyle choices that determine an individual's risk profile. The two chapters in this section discuss the complexities of the process of individual behavior change and the models that guide health behavior research and interventions.

Using the example of smoking cessation, Mermelstein outlines in chapter 24 the necessary ingredients and steps for successful behavior change in quitting smoking and other health practices and comprehensively reviews the major models of health-related behavior change that guide individually oriented interventions. These models include the health belief model, social learning theory, the theory of planned behavior, the theory of triadic influence, and the transtheoretical model. She discusses the importance of motivation in all stages of behavior change, of identifying personal barriers to change, and of promoting successful intervention through tailoring according to a patient's stage of receptivity and gender.

Primary prevention aims to reduce the incidence of disease, secondary prevention aims to reduce the prevalence of disease, and tertiary prevention addresses the prevention of complications. In chapter 25, Derby, Winkleby, Lapane, and Stone describe public health approaches to prevention relevant for women's health. They provide background for community approaches to prevention and highlight the contributions of three large community-based cardiovascular disease interventions: the Stanford Five City Project, the Minnesota Heart Health Program, and the Pawtucket Heart Health Program. After describing the knowledge base and materials generated by these studies, they discuss implications for practitioners and their female patients, for program planning and implementation, and for future studies within communities.

Advancing the health and well-being of women through community-based efforts will require the combined efforts of a range of health professionals, including physicians, psychologists, nurses, social workers, and health educators. Providers must be equipped with information to facilitate informed healthcare decisions by their patients in the areas of prevention, screening, and chronic illness management throughout the life cycle.

Our vision for this book was to present comprehensive information, strategies, and recommendations based on state-of-the-art psychosocial and behavioral research. Translating this knowledge into practice and community-based settings will serve as an integrated foundation for promoting the health and well-being of all women.

References

Adler, N. E., Boyce, T., Chesney, M. A., Folkman, S., & Syme, S. L. (1993). Socioeconomic inequalities in health: No easy solution. *Journal of the American Medical Association, 269*, 3140–3145.

Bandura, A. (1977). *Social learning theory*. Englewood Cliffs, NJ: Prentice Hall.

Bandura, A. (1986). *Social foundations of thought and action: A social cognitive theory*. Englewood Cliffs, NJ: Prentice Hall.

Bandura, A. (1990). Perceived self-efficacy in the exercise of control over AIDS infection. *Evaluation and Program Planning, 13*, 9–17.

Beck, K. H., & Lund, A. K. (1981). The effects of health threat seriousness and personal efficacy upon intentions and behavior. *Journal of Applied Social Psychology, 11*, 401–415.

Breslow, L., & Enstrom, J. E. (1980). Persistence of health habits and their relationship to mortality. *Preventive Medicine, 9*.

Carleton, R. A., Lasater, T. M., Assaf, A. R., Feldman, H. A. & McKinley, S. (1995). The Pawtucket Heart Health Program: Community changes in cardiovascular risk factors and projected disease risks. *American Journal of Public Health, 85*, 777–785.

Chambliss, C. A., & Murray, E. J. (1979). Efficacy attribution, locus of control and weight loss. *Cognitive Therapy and Research, 3*, 349–353.

Condiotte, M. M., & Lichtenstein, E. (1981). Self-efficacy and relapse in smoking cessation programs. *Journal of Consulting and Clinical Psychology, 49*, 648–658.

DiClemente, C. C. (1981). Self-efficacy and smoking cessation maintenance: A preliminary report. *Cognitive Therapy and Research, 5*, 175–187.

DiClemente, C. C., Prochaska, J. O., & Gilbertini, M. (1985). Self-efficacy and the stages of self-change of smoking. *Cognitive Therapy and Research, 9*, 181–200.

Hawkins, D. F. (1987). Devalued lives and racial stereotypes: Ideological barriers to the prevention of family violence among blacks. In R. L. Hampton (Ed.), *Violence in the*

Black family: Correlates and consequences (pp. 189–205). Lexington, MA: Lexington Books.

Holroyd, K. A., Penzien, D. B., Hursey, K. G., Tobin, D. L., Rogers, L., Holm, J. E., Marcille, P. J., Hall, J. R., & Chila, A. G. (1984). Change mechanisms in EMG biofeedback training: Cognitive changes underlying improvements in tension headache. *Journal of Consulting and Clinical Psychology, 52,* 1039–1053.

Kaplan, G. A., & Keil, J. E. (1993). Socioeconomic factors and cardiovascular disease: A review of the literature. *Circulation, 88,* 1973–1998.

Kaplan, R. M., Atkins, C. J., & Reinsch, S. (1984). Specific efficacy expectations mediate exercise compliance in patients with COPD. *Health Psychology, 3,* 223–242.

Kelsey, J. L., & Horn-Ross, P. L. (1993). Breast cancer: Magnitude of the problem and descriptive epidemiology. *Epidemiologic Reviews, 15,* 7–16.

Kirscht, J. P. (1983). Preventive health behavior: A review of research and issues. *Health Psychology, 2,* 277–301.

Klepac, R. K., Dowling, J., & Hauge, G. (1982). Characteristics of clients seeking therapy for the reduction of dental avoidance reactions to pain. *Journal of Behavior Therapy and Experimental Psychiatry, 13,* 293–300.

Krieger, N., & Sidney, S. (1996). Racial discrimination and blood pressure: The CARDIA Study of young black and white adults. *American Journal of Public Health, 86,* 1370–1378.

Lawrance, L., & McLeroy, K. R. (1986). Self-efficacy and health education. *Journal of School Health, 56,* 317–321.

Luepker, R. V. (1994). Community trials. *Preventive Medicine, 23,* 602–605.

Manning, M. M., & Wright, T. L. (1983). Self-efficacy expectancies, outcome expectancies, and the persistence of pain control in childbirth. *Journal of Personality and Social Psychology, 45,* 421–431.

Marlatt, G. A., & Gordon, J. R. (1980). Determinants of relapse: Implications for the maintenance of behavior change. In P. Davidson & S. Davidson (Eds.), *Behavioral medicine: Changing health lifestyles* (pp. 424–452). New York: Brunner/Mazel.

McWhorter, W. P., Schatzkin, A. G., Horm, J. W., & Brown, C. C. (1989). Contribution of socioeconomic status to black/white differences in cancer incidence. *Cancer, 63,* 982–987.

National Heart, Lung, and Blood Institute. (1994). *Report of The Task Force on Research in Epidemiology and Prevention of Cardiovascular Diseases.* Bethesda, MD: National Institutes of Health.

U.S. Department of Health and Human Services. (1990). *National Center for Health Statistics: Health, United States, 1989* (DHHS Publication No. PHS 90–1232). Washington, DC: U.S. Government Printing Office.

U.S. Department of Health and Human Services. (1995). *Healthy People 2000: Review 1994.* Rockville, MD: U.S. Public Health Service.

U.S. Surgeon General's Advisory Committee on Smoking and Health, U.S. Department of Health, Education, and Welfare, Public Health Service. (1964). *Smoking and health: Report of the Advisory Committee to the Surgeon General of the Public Health Service.* Washington, D.C.: U.S. Government Printing Office.

Wenger, N. K., Speroff, L., & Packard, B. (1993). Cardiovascular health and disease in women. *New England Journal of Medicine, 329,* 247–256.

Part I

Women's Health in Context

1

Women's Health Care: Federal Initiatives, Policies, and Directions

Susan J. Blumenthal and Susan F. Wood

Over the past century, American society has witnessed enormous changes in women's roles, economic and educational opportunities, and health care status. In 1900, women died on average at the age of 48. Today, women on average live to age 79. This dramatic change resulted from public health knowledge and practices that have improved both the quality and quantity of women's lives. In the early 1900s, women died too frequently in childbirth. Margaret Sanger's work to provide birth control to women gave many women their first opportunity to control their reproduction. The women's self-help movement of the 1970s, epitomized by the book *Our Bodies, Ourselves* (Boston Women's Health Book Collective, 1971) challenged many of the assumptions of the medical system, broadened the very definition of women's health beyond women's health care, and educated women to become informed consumers when making their health care decisions. Additionally, over the past decade, attention has been focused on inequities in the conduct of medical research and in access to health care that has placed the health of American women at risk. In 1989, policymakers both in Congress and within the executive branch of the federal government made women's health an important priority when developing and evaluating health programs, policies, and initiatives. Today, policymakers, health practitioners, scientists, and women's health advocates are working together to identify and address women's health needs and the behaviors that affect them in many areas, including breast cancer, reproductive health issues, domestic violence, HIV and AIDS, and mental illness.

This recent awakening of the federal government in 1990 to women's health issues began when female scientists, working with the female members of Congress and the media, brought attention to the fact that women often were excluded from clinical research studies. This exclusion has led to the unfortunate reality that much less is known about the major killers of women, such as heart disease, than should be. Similarly, many other conditions that threaten the health and lives of women have not received adequate research attention, and there is a dearth of information about gender differences in the causes, prevention, and treatment of disease.

3

The public became aware of this discrepancy when the General Accounting Office (GAO) released a study in June 1990 showing that the National Institutes of Health (NIH) had not implemented its own policy established in 1986 that encouraged the inclusion of women in clinical research trials (General Accounting Office, 1990). The GAO report, requested by the Congressional Caucus for Women's Issues and the chairman of the Health and Environment Subcommittee of the House Energy and Commerce Committee, acted as the spark in igniting a firestorm around women's health issues. The next few years saw a flurry of action, both legislative and programmatic, designed to correct past problems and to proactively ensure that women's health needs would be addressed comprehensively in the future. What follows are some examples of legislative branch and executive branch actions taken in recent years to improve women's health through funding for research and health care services. The successful implementation of these initiatives depends on their translation into primary care practice.

Legislative Proposals and Programs

At the congressional level, the Women's Health Equity Act (WHEA) of 1990 was the first comprehensive attempt to propose legislative remedies to the many health needs of women. This omnibus piece of legislation was introduced by the Congressional Caucus for Women's Issues and included a number of individual bills concerning women's health. By placing them into a single bill, a comprehensive agenda on women's health issues was created to focus attention on the broad spectrum of health concerns facing women and to create the necessary momentum to address them. Several of the provisions within the 1990 WHEA relating to women's health research, such as the mandate to include women in clinical research trials, were incorporated into the NIH legislation that was moving through the legislative process at the time and was signed into law in 1993. Additionally, other individual provisions contained in the bill also were passed into law within the next few years. This model of establishing a legislative agenda on women's health has continued during each successive Congress and remains a successful way of focusing public and congressional attention on the health needs of women.

Breast and Cervical Cancer

Several key legislative victories have occurred, including increased research funding directed at eliminating or reducing the epidemic of breast cancer, a disease that will be experienced by one of every eight women in their lifetime. Today, more than $600 million is being spent each year on breast cancer programs within the federal government, compared with less than $100 million in 1990. Additionally, the Breast and Cervical Cancer Mortality Prevention Program at the Centers for Disease Control and

Prevention (CDC) was first established in 1990 by legislation introduced by Representative Henry Waxman and by Senator Barbara Mikulski as part of the 1990 WHEA. This program, now established in 50 states, 3 territories, the District of Columbia, and 9 Native American tribal organizations, provides grants to states for mammograms and Pap smears for low-income women, who cannot afford these lifesaving early detection health care services.

Another key achievement in the area of breast cancer in 1990 was the restoration of Medicare coverage of mammograms for older women. Preventive services traditionally have not been covered under Medicare. However, mammography coverage had been briefly covered by Medicare in 1988 under legislation that subsequently was repealed in 1989. Representative Mary Rose Oakar led a successful fight on the House of Representatives floor during the 1990 budget battle to restore this hard-won benefit. This lifesaving screening, now covered by Medicare, is being championed by First Lady Hillary Rodham Clinton because many older women are not aware that it is available to them under Medicare. Working with the U.S. Public Health Service (PHS) Office on Women's Health and the Health Care Financing Administration, an educational campaign designed to encourage women to take advantage of mammography screening was undertaken in 1995. Primary care physicians play an important role in this effort by encouraging their older patients to have mammograms.

Legislation to ensure that all mammograms are high quality, safe, and reliable was introduced in 1990 and signed into law in 1992. This legislation, known as the Mammography Quality Standards Act and introduced by Representatives Patricia Schroeder and Marilyn Lloyd and by Senators Barbara Mikulski and Brock Adams, established strict quality standards to be implemented by the Food and Drug Administration for mammography facilities, technicians, and health professionals. The FDA has developed a certification program for facilities providing mammography services, and today it is illegal to operate without this FDA "seal of approval."

Contraception and Infertility

Other important legislative initiatives have focused on a variety of critical women's health issues. The NIH Revitalization Act of 1993 expanded research on contraception and infertility, an area of research that had withered during the 1980s because of the politicalization of women's reproduction. The NIH legislation called for the establishment of six contraception and infertility research centers, as well as for the establishment of an intramural gynecology research program at NIH.

The Infertility Prevention Act also was passed into law in 1992, which created a new program at the CDC to reduce the incidence of STDs that lead to infertility in women, primarily chlamydia and gonorrhea. By providing screening services at places where sexually active young women are more likely to go (i.e., family planning clinics), this program should be successful in lowering the incidence of chlamydia (which is estimated to be more than 4 million new cases each year) and in reducing its serious medical sequelae, such as infertility or ectopic pregnancy. The CDC program has now been expanded to 4 of the 10 PHS regions and has continued to receive increased funding each year from Congress. In 1996, the CDC issued guidelines recommending that sexually active women, particularly those under age 25, be routinely screened for chlamydia.

Violence

Violence against women is finally being recognized as an issue that must be addressed by both the health care and criminal justice systems. Passage of the Violence Against Women Act in 1994, which included programs on rape prevention and education, a national domestic abuse hotline, and community-based domestic violence programs, among others, has provided the mandate for federal involvement in addressing this public health problem. In response, the Department of Health and Human Services has established the Steering Committee on the Prevention of Violence Against Women to oversee these programs and to ensure that domestic violence is included in all training activities supported by the department. Additionally, the Department of Health and Human Services and the Department of Justice have established the National Advisory Council on Violence Against Women, with representatives including health care professionals, legislators, law enforcement personnel, and media and sports figures to develop innovative strategies, partnerships, and solutions to this pervasive problem.

A Women's Health Focus Within the Department of Health and Human Services

One mechanism to improve women's health policies and programs was the creation of offices devoted to women's health programs and activities within the PHS agencies. The first office created was the Office of Research on Women's Health at the NIH. This office was proposed as part of the first WHEA of 1990 by Representatives Patricia Schroeder and Olympia Snowe, co-chairs of the Congressional Caucus for Women's Issues, in response to the GAO report. Other offices on women's health have been established within many of the PHS agencies, including the CDC, the Food and Drug Abuse Administration, and the Substance Abuse and Mental Health Administration (also mandated by legislation). In 1991 the PHS's Office on Women's Health was established by the Bush Administration to address women's health at the departmental level. This office, created within the Office of the Assistant Secretary for Health, has the important role of working with all of the PHS agencies to coordinate women's health activities and programs being undertaken by each agency independently. Before 1993, it worked primarily with the PHS Coordinating Committee on Women's Health to develop an Action Plan on Women's Health (U.S. Public Health Service, 1991) that addressed cross-cutting objectives for the Department of Health and Human Services to advance women's health nationally. In 1993 this office and its mission were expanded when the Clinton Administration made women's health a top priority and appointed the first Deputy Assistant Secretary for Women's Health within the Department of Health and Human Services. In 1995 the office was elevated to be part of the Office of the Secretary to strengthen collaborations both within the department and with other agencies of government. The office now works to identify gaps in women's health activities and to address them through initiatives that cut across disciplines and agencies and that link the public and private sectors in its common goal to improve women's health. The National Centers of Excellence in Women's Health, National Action Plan on Breast Cancer, and the NIH Women's Health Initiative are among these initiatives underway within the Department.

The recently established National Centers of Excellence in Women's Health will serve as models for the integration of health care services, research, public education, and health care professional training focused on women's health. While many institutions around the country have developed one or more of these areas, the goal of the National Centers of Excellence program is to foster Centers that have a coordinated program linking together all of these key aspects of women's health across disciplines and across programs. Over time, these Centers will be able to provide information and mechanisms for implementation that can be used by other academic health centers across the nation.

The NIH Women's Health Initiative is an example of the increased focus on women's health. When a major study on the link between dietary fat and breast cancer was first proposed in the 1980s, the NIH declined to fund it, in part based on findings from earlier studies on men that changes in diet were difficult if not impossible to achieve for the purposes of the trial. In fact, preliminary studies (Henderson et al., 1990) on women had yielded much different results: Women do the majority of shopping and food preparation for the family and therefore can modify their diet more easily. With the new attention given to lack of research on women's health issues in 1990—and with its first female director, Bernadine Healy, appointed in 1991—the NIH took another look at the proposed research on dietary fat and breast cancer. With Healy's leadership, the study was expanded to include the effects of hormone replacement therapy and dietary supplements on colon cancer and heart disease. In 1991, the NIH launched the largest clinical research trial in NIH history, the Women's Health Initiative. This study, budgeted at more than $600 million and scheduled to last 16 years, will provide important information on the major killers of women and on how to prevent them.

The National Action Plan on Breast Cancer exemplifies the important ways that the public and private sectors can and should work together to tackle a national public health problem. This strategic plan, called for by President Clinton after he was presented with a petition containing 2.6 million signatures of breast cancer survivors and their friends and families, is a public–private partnership involving representatives of the federal government, breast cancer advocates, scientists, health professionals, the media, and private industry. The Plan is being implemented by the PHS Office on Women's Health. The Plan currently has six priority areas: information dissemination, national biological resource banks, consumer involvement, breast cancer etiology, increased access to clinical trials, and hereditary susceptibility. In 1995, approximately $9 million was awarded to support 100 innovative new research and demonstration projects in these six areas, and in 1996 the Plan catalyzed a wide variety of projects targeted at the eradication of breast cancer.

Mobilizing other federal agencies to work with the Department of Health and Human Services has also been an important new strategy to improve women's health. Through its initiative known as From Missiles to Mammograms: New Frontiers in Breast Imaging, the PHS Office on Women's Health has brought together scientists from the National Cancer Institute, the Department of Defense, the Central Intelligence Agency, and the National Aeronautics and Space Administration to apply intelligence, defense, and space technologies to improve the early detection of breast cancer. A federal interagency Task Force on Women's Health and the Environment has also been established by the PHS Office on Women's Health to assess the current state of knowledge in this field and to create an inventory of activities being carried out governmentwide in areas ranging from the effects of toxic chemicals on women's health to occupational hazards—including workplace stress—that can adversely affect women's health.

Establishing and maintaining healthy behaviors is critical to the long-term improvement of women's health because lifestyle and behavioral factors are major contributors to all 10 of the leading causes of death for women. Several initiatives have been undertaken to address these concerns. Two public–private partnerships have been established by the PHS Office on Women's Health focusing on improving young women's health by encouraging healthy behavior. A video and educational guide, "Get Real: Straight Talk on Women's Health," was developed and is targeted to college-aged women. It speaks to the health issues facing young women, such as alcohol and tobacco use, diet, violence, and prevention of STDs, including HIV. A second public–private initiative focuses on developing an educational campaign on eating disorders, illnesses that affect 2% of young women and that have grave health consequences.

The education of health professionals, so that they can appropriately address women's health needs, is vital to improving the health of women now and in the future. Working collaboratively, the NIH, the Health Resources and Services Administration, and the PHS Office on Women's Health have assessed the women's health content of current medical school curricula and are developing a model women's health curriculum to assist medical schools in improving their educational programs. In addition, the PHS Office on Women's Health has developed a directory of women's health graduate fellowship and residency programs at academic medical centers around the country.

Future Directions

Information is critical in all of the initiatives discussed earlier, regardless of whether it is research data, public or health care provider education, or knowledge of services and programs available to women in their communities. Within both the federal government and the private sector, there is a wealth of information that could benefit women, researchers, and health care providers, yet often this information is difficult to identify or obtain. The PHS Office on Women's Health, in collaboration with the Department of Defense, is developing a state-of-the-art national clearinghouse for information on women's health. This National Women's Health Information Center will be accessible through a toll-free telephone number as well as through the Internet. By taking advantage of new computer technology and linking information from all agencies of the Department of Health and Human Services, other federal departments, and the private sector, women, health care providers, and scientists will have access to information ranging from the latest research results, to preventive health messages, to federal and private sector women's health resources.

Bringing women's health information and services to women at the regional, state, and community levels is a key goal of federal women's health programs. Regional women's health coordinators have been appointed by the PHS Office on Women's Health and provide the necessary link to women's health activities being carried out by state and local governments, as well as by local women's health organizations.

Addressing women's health needs is not limited to the specific programs targeted at women. In fact, two programs currently facing major changes by the Congress are important women's health programs: Medicare and Medicaid. Women constitute the majority of the users of these programs (National Center for Health Statistics, 1996) because they predominate in the elderly and poor populations. Changes made in these programs have the potential to dramatically reduce women's access to health care. An increase in Medicare copayments, for example, could reduce the use by women of needed medical services. A recent study (Blustein, 1995) has shown that women without supplemental insurance to cover the current Medicare copayment receive screening mammograms much less frequently than women who do not have to make the copayment. Reductions in Medicaid funding, which provides health care services to poor women and dependent children as well as being the primary payer for nursing home care for older people and those with disabilities, could lead to states reducing health care to these vulnerable populations. By lifting any requirements that states provide minimum benefits, the federal government will lose the assurance that services such as family planning, preventive screenings, and prenatal care will be provided. As changes to these major health care programs proceed, those who wish to promote women's health need to remain vigilant and to monitor the impact of the changes, because women's health may be at risk as well.

Conclusion

Policies and programs addressing women's health have improved dramatically over the recent past. Much of that change has come about because of the convictions and actions taken by female scientists, policymakers, and women's health advocates. It is also important to remember that improving women's health will improve the health of all. Knowledge about the similarities and differences in health conditions that face both men and women has the potential to provide scientific breakthroughs that benefit both sexes. Additionally, because women often are the primary caregivers within families, improving women's health and access to services can lead to the improved health of children and other family members. As women adopt healthy behaviors leading to reduced heart disease, cancers, and STDs, so, too, will their families be more likely to develop lifestyles that promote good health.

Continuing the progress that has been made in women's health policy at the federal level may be difficult but makes sense for the future health of all Americans. The commitment and infrastructure for improving women's health has been put in place within the federal government and will remain strong. However, to continue the advances that have been made over the past few years, the commitment and the voices of women across the country must continue to be heard to safeguard their health and to ensure that the new national focus on women's health remains a national priority.

References

Blustein, J. (1995). Medicare coverage, supplemental insurance, and the use of mammography by older women. *The New England Journal of Medicine, 332*, 1138–1143.

Boston Women's Health Book Collective. (1971). *Our bodies, ourselves.* New York: Touchstone.

General Accounting Office. (1990). *National Institutes of Health: Problems in Implementing Policies on Women in Study Populations.*

Henderson, M. M., Kushi, L. H., Thompson, D. J., Gorbach, S. L., Clifford, C. K., Insull, W., Moskowitz, M., & Thompson, R. S. (1990). Feasibility of a randomized trial of low-fat diet for the prevention of breast cancer: Dietary compliance in the Women's Health Trial Vanguard Study. *Prevention Medicine, 19*, 115–133.

U.S. Department of Health and Human Services—National Center for Health Statistics. (1996, September). *Health, United States, 1995* (DHHS Pub. No. 96-1232). Hyattsville, MD: Public Health Service.

U.S. Department of Health and Human Services—Public Health Service. (1991, September). *Action plan for women's health* (DHHS Pub. No. 91-50214). Washington, DC: U.S. Public Health Service's Office on Women's Health.

2

Socioeconomic Status and Women's Health

Nancy E. Adler and Marilee Coriell

Socioeconomic status (SES) has a powerful influence on health (Adler, et al., 1994). Ironically, as is true for gender, SES is so central that psychologists and health researchers rarely address it. Rather, it is used as a control variable or is controlled away through selection of homogeneous populations so that the other variables will not be swamped by its effects. In research, SES "is generally included with as much regularity but with as little thought as is gender" (Marmot, Kogevinas, & Elston, 1987, p. 111). Similarly, although SES is a strong predictor of disease risk, rarely do clinicians explicitly take it into account in assessing patients' risk factors for disease.

Only by understanding how SES influences health can we be effective in reducing social inequalities in health status—both those among women and those between men and women—that now characterize the world. In this chapter we examine the evidence linking SES and health in general and for women in particular, looking at the associations of SES with common diseases of women. A thorough review is beyond the scope of this chapter, so we selected one disease—breast cancer—and consider the implications of the findings regarding the health effects of SES.

SES and the Health Gradient

Most people are aware that SES affects health; it comes as no surprise that the poor, unemployed, and poorly educated are in relatively poor health compared with those with adequate resources. What is less well-known is that the association of SES and health does not occur only at the bottom of the SES hierarchy but also at all levels. As one ascends the SES ladder, health improves and this improvement continues right up to the top (Adler, Boyce, Chesney, Folkman, & Syme, 1993).

The linear association of SES and health suggests that the health effects of SES are pervasive and raises questions about the mechanisms

Preparation of this chapter was supported by the John D. and Catherine T. MacArthur Foundation Planning Initiative on Socioeconomic Status and Health.

by which SES influences health. These mechanisms are likely to include psychological, physiological, behavioral, and environmental factors (Adler et al., 1994). Reducing health inequalities associated with socioeconomic differences requires identifying how these factors are influenced by SES and how they determine health.

SES and Mortality

The SES–health gradient is perhaps most clearly demonstrated in the Whitehall studies of British civil servants. The original Whitehall studies followed more than 17,000 civil servants in nine employment levels (Marmot, Shipley, & Rose, 1984). Over 10 years, those in the lowest employment grade had a relative risk of mortality of 2.7 compared with the top administrators. Less strong but more surprising was the finding that the relative risk of mortality for the professional-executive grade compared

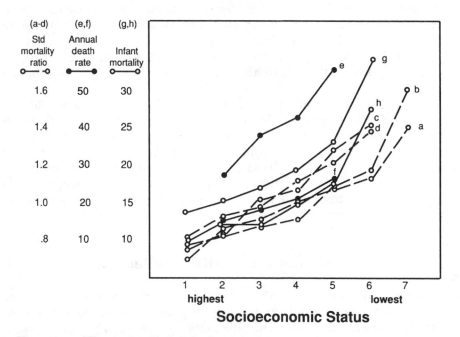

a. Kitagawa and Hauser (1973). Standardized mortality ratio (observed to expected deaths), male.
b. Kitagawa and Hauser (1973). Standardized mortality ratio (observed to expected deaths), female.
c. Adelstein (1980). Standardized mortality ratio (observed to expected deaths), male.
d. Adelstein (1980). Standardized mortality ratio (observed to expected deaths), female.
e. Feldman et al. (1989). Annual death rate per 1,000, male.
f. Feldman et al. (1989). Annual death rate per 1,000, female.
g. Susser, Watson, and Hopper (1985). Infant mortality per 1,000 live births, male.
h. Susser, Watson and Hopper (1985). Infant mortality per 1,000 live births, female.

Figure 1. Mortality by socioeconomic status. Reprinted with permission from Adler et al. (1994).

with the top administrators was 1.6. Individuals at the professional-executive grade had good access to health care, adequate housing, and adequate nutrition. Despite this, they had a significantly higher risk of dying over the course of a decade than did their immediate superiors.

This effect is not peculiar to the British Civil Service. Figure 1, taken from Adler et al. (1994), is a composite of four studies of mortality across several levels of SES. Because this figure summarizes studies that used different indicators, the absolute values of points on the axis are not comparable, but the pattern is clear. No matter what the absolute level, the higher one goes on SES, the lower the risk of mortality. In these studies, the slopes are relatively comparable for both men and women.

SES, Morbidity, and Risk Factors

The SES–health gradient also emerges in morbidity. Figure 2, also taken from Adler et al. (1994), shows SES differences in the prevalence of chronic diseases in general and of osteoarthritis, hypertension, and cervical cancer in particular. There is a graded relationship: With each step up the SES ladder, the prevalence of disease decreases.

The gradient also emerges in risk factors. Winkleby, Fortmann, and

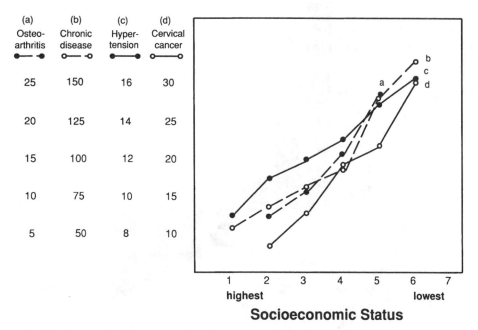

a. Cunningham and Kelsey (1984). Percent diagnosed osteoarthritis.
b. Townsend (1974). Relative prevalence of chronic disease.
c. Kraus, Borhani, and Franti (1980). Prevalence of hypertension.
d. DeVesa and Diamond (1980). Rate of cervical cancer per 100,000.

Figure 2. Morbidity by socioeconomic status. Reprinted with permission from Adler et al. (1994).

Barrett (1990) examined six risk factors for cardiovascular disease: health knowledge, cigarette smoking, hypertension, height (which may reflect benefits conferred by childhood SES), body mass, and cholesterol. Adjusted for age, each risk factor decreased as the level of education, income, or occupation increased.

What Does the Gradient Look Like for Women?

Although the SES–health gradient is roughly linear, it is not a perfectly linear relationship in each instance. A few studies that evaluated the gradient for women have shown smaller health benefits at the upper versus the lower end of education. For example, Figure 3 shows data from Kitagawa and Hauser (1973) as represented in Adler et al. (1993) on women's age-adjusted mortality ratios by education levels. A mortality ratio of 1.0 indicates that the group experienced the number of deaths that would be expected for women of that age in the United States; values above and below 1.0, respectively, indicate greater and lesser mortality than would

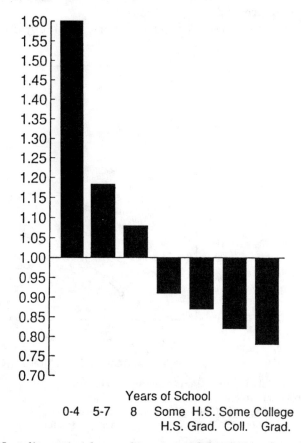

Figure 3. Mortality ratio (observed to expected death) by education. From Adler et al. (1993) based on data from Kitagawa and Hauser (1973).

be expected. Figure 3 indicates that the beneficial effects of additional years of education at the upper end were less than additional years at the bottom. Relative mortality for women with 4 years or less of school was 1.60 and dropped dramatically to 1.18 for those with 5–7 years of schooling. In contrast to this substantial mortality decline, there was a linear gradient of education and mortality ratios, with a gentle slope and no discontinuity from 5 to 7 years on up.

Major Causes of Mortality for Women

The leading causes of death for women are coronary heart disease (CHD), followed by stroke, lung cancer, and breast cancer (Wenger, Speroff, & Packard, 1993). AIDS is the fourth leading cause of death for women aged 25–44 years (Centers for Disease Control [CDC], 1993).

CHD and Stroke

CHD has a strong, graded inverse relationship with SES. Rogot, Sorlie, Johnson, and Schmitt (1992) found the highest standard mortality ratios for CHD among women with primary school education, which decreased at each higher level of education. However, SES was not clearly related to mortality from stroke. Lower cardiovascular mortality has been attributed, at least in part, to changes in lifestyle including reductions in smoking, increased exercise, and lower fat diets. These changes have not been universal and have occurred more frequently at higher levels of SES (Pappas, Queen, Hadden, & Fisher, 1993). Higher SES is associated with fewer risk factors for cardiovascular disease and stroke, including cigarette smoking, hypertension, body mass, cholesterol, diet, and physical activity (Matthews, Kelsey, Meilahn, Kuller, & Wing, 1989; Winkleby et al., 1990).

Compared with men, women delay longer than men in getting treatment for symptoms (Meischke, Eisenberg, & Larsen, 1993), have more myocardial infarctions that go unrecognized (Wenger et al., 1993), and are treated less aggressively (Ayanian & Epstein, 1991). To our knowledge, no studies have addressed CHD, SES, and treatment of CHD for women. It seems likely that less education, income, and lower occupational status would further exacerbate the bias toward later diagnosis and treatment of CHD for women.

Lung Cancer

Lung cancer mortality is not currently related to SES for women in the United States (Rogot et al., 1992), but a British study indicated that women who owned their residence had better survival than those who did not (Kogevinas, Marmot, Fox, & Goldblatt, 1991). The greatest risk factor for lung cancer is cigarette smoking, but current mortality reflects historical risk. In the past, smoking was not seen as a health-risk, and cigarettes were used by women across the SES hierarchy. As information became public on the health risks of cigarettes, higher SES individuals were quicker to quit smoking. Smoking patterns differ by gender, SES, and ethnicity. More women than men begin smoking and more fail to quit (Chesney, 1991). Smoking prevalence is greatest among women with a high school education or less and those who live in poverty (CDC, 1993). African American women are less likely to smoke than are White women (Fiore et al., 1989). Given the current SES gradient in smoking among women, one would expect future emergence of a gradient of SES and lung cancer.

AIDS

Within the United States, HIV infection is more prevalent in low-SES environments (Diaz et al., 1994), and it is growing most rapidly among low-income minority women (O'Leary, Jemmott, Suarez-Al-Adam, AlRoy, & Fernandez, 1993). AIDS is the leading cause of death for women of childbearing age in some urban centers (Chesney, 1994). The relatively greater risk of HIV infection for lower SES women arises both from the fact that they are relatively more likely to engage in risk behaviors (e.g., unprotected sex, injection drug use) and because they reside in areas where HIV prevalence is greater so their risk of exposure is greater. Although individual health care providers need to evaluate the risk status of their patients relative to HIV and to counsel them about actions they can take to reduce their risk of exposure, community-based programs are particularly important (Holtgrave, Valdiserri, & West, 1994).

Breast Cancer: A Complicated Relationship With SES

Although mortality among women is now greater from lung cancer than from breast cancer, breast cancer has a higher incidence and may be more salient to women. Breast cancer has a complicated association with SES and provides some insights into how SES may influence disease incidence and survival. Breast cancer does not show an inverse gradient of incidence with SES. In fact, rates of breast cancer appear to be higher among higher SES women (Baquet, Horm, Gibbs, & Greenwald, 1991). This positive association between SES and breast cancer incidence mirrors the negative association for cervical cancer. Table 1 shows data from Finland on incidence ratios by educational level for breast and cervical cancer standardized by age (Hakama, Hakulinen, Pukkala, Saxen, & Teppo, 1982). Incidence ratios for breast cancer were lowest in women with a primary school education and increased at each level of additional years of education; the reverse was true for cervical cancer.

Behavioral factors associated with SES may contribute to the SES association for both cervical and breast cancer. The inverse gradient of cervical cancer and SES may be partially due to differential risk of STDs. A major risk factor for cervical cancer is a prior STD (Becker et al., 1994), and STD rates are inversely related to SES (Ellen, Kohn, Bolan, Shiboski,

Table 1.   Standardized Incidence Ratios of Breast and Cervical Cancer in Finnish Women Aged 30–69 Years

Education	Breast cancer	Cervical cancer
Primary	90	113
Secondary	115	75
High school	137	59
College or university	172	35

Note. From "Risk Indicators of Breast Cancer and Cervical Cancer on Ecologic and Individual Levels," by M. Hakama, T. Hakulinen, E. Pukkala, E. Saxen, and L. Teppo, 1982, *American Journal of Epidemiology, 116*, pp. 990–1000. Reprinted with permission.

& Krieger, 1995). Relative to breast cancer, delayed childbearing, specifically not having given birth before the age of 30, is a risk factor for breast cancer (Manton & Stallard, 1992), and this is more common among higher SES women.

Although the incidence of breast cancer shows a direct association with SES, survival once breast cancer is diagnosed shows the more familiar inverse gradient (Berg, Ross, & Latourette, 1977): Higher SES women are more likely to get breast cancer, but of those diagnosed with the disease, lower SES women are more likely to die from it. However, the relationship of SES and mortality risk differs by age. For example, Karjalainen and Pukkala (1990) found that the relatively longer survival of higher SES women in Finland was far stronger for women over age 44 than for younger women. This could be due to cohort effects, to differences in the biology of breast cancer in pre- versus postmenopausal women, or to age differences in SES-related behavioral factors such as delay in seeking treatment.

A study done in the United States also showed differences by age in the association of SES with breast cancer. Wagener and Schatzkin (1994) compared breast cancer mortality rates in high- versus low-income counties over three time periods: 1969–1972, 1979–1982, and 1987–1989. Overall, higher income counties had greater breast cancer mortality rates. The gap in mortality rates between richer and poorer counties narrowed over time, but this narrowing occurred in different ways for younger, middle-aged, and older women. Mortality rates dropped across the three time periods for women aged 25–44 years, and declines were greater for women in more affluent counties; by 1987–1989 there were no significant differences in mortality between more and less affluent counties. Mortality rates for women aged 45–64 decreased over time in affluent counties but increased in poorer counties. Finally, mortality increased for all women over the age of 65, but the increase was sharper for women in poorer counties. Mortality rates reflect a variety of factors, including initial incidence of disease, detection, and treatment. It is not clear the extent to which these patterns reflect changes in incidence in the various groups, changes in treatment and survival, or both. It will be important to differentiate these because they have different implications for policy and treatment.

Ethnicity also has a complex association with breast cancer. Breast cancer survival is lower for African American than for White women (Bain, Greenberg, & Whitaker, 1986), although incidence is higher among White women when controlling for SES (Baquet et al., 1991). Richardson et al. (1992) examined ethnicity and SES in relation to stage of diagnosis and treatment seeking among White, African American, and Hispanic women diagnosed with breast cancer. SES was assessed in terms of median income and education in the census tract in which the patients resided. Both SES and ethnicity contributed to late-stage diagnosis. Compared with non-Hispanic White women, both African American and Hispanic women had higher rates of late-stage disease, as did women in lower SES census tract areas. Both ethnicity and SES showed significant associations with late-stage diagnosis when both were included in a predictive equation. SES and ethnicity also showed a significant interaction, such that "the risk of late-stage diagnoses for Black and Hispanic women seems to be compounded by poverty" (Richardson et al., 1992, p. 927).

Implications of Research on SES and Health

Lower SES women have a greater risk of morbidity and mortality; their disadvantages may be cumulative, reflecting differences in health-promoting versus health-risking behaviors, use of screening and early detection, access to care, and treatment received. In each of these areas, services and interventions need to be designed that will be effective for women at every level of the SES hierarchy. Special attention needs to be paid to women who are poorer, less educated, and in jobs with lower status, because they are less likely to be able to avail themselves of the benefits of health interventions and services.

One practical approach to reducing SES inequality for individual clinicians is to allot more time to lower SES patients. Additional time may be needed for an adequate discussion of ways to overcome obstacles to engaging in preventive behaviors, early diagnosis, and treatment. Ironically, the higher a woman is on the SES hierarchy, the more time she is likely to receive from a provider. Lower SES women rely more on emergency rooms and clinics, where there is little individualized attention. The health care system is changing; health systems increasingly are becoming responsible for maintaining the health of given populations rather than simply treating individuals for specific medical problems. Thus, there may be more opportunities for developing procedures that allow for more attention to those lower on the SES hierarchy. However, there also is a risk that lower SES women may get left out of capitated plans that provide the best care.

Prevention

In discussing preventive behavior, providers need to be aware of the constraints on a woman's life related to her SES that may influence her ability to follow recommendations. For example, a frequent suggestion is that patients get more exercise and lower the fat in their diets. However, lower SES individuals may need to have stronger motivation to follow these suggestions than those of higher SES if they are to make such changes. Implementing those recommendations is harder to do in lower SES environments, and the harder it is to implement a regimen, the greater one's motivation must be to accomplish it. For example, at the upper end of the SES hierarchy, it may not be as difficult to engage in exercise. Higher SES individuals generally have more control over their time, have easier access to exercise facilities, and can even have a personal trainer to provide support and motivation. Similarly, it may not be difficult to find health food stores or supermarkets that have low-fat foods. As one goes down the SES hierarchy, these resources are more difficult to obtain. Sooman, Macintyre, and Anderson (1993) compared the accessibility and prices of a "healthy" basket of food in two areas of Glasgow, Scotland, one of which was more affluent. Fewer stores in the poorer area stocked healthy food items, and such foods cost more in the poorer area. Thus, not only do poorer individuals have less disposable income for healthy foods, but those foods are harder to find and are more expensive than for those in more affluent areas. In addition, healthy foods were more expensive relative to less healthy foods within the same market, adding further disincentives to purchasing such foods.

Providers need to do more than just provide equal treatment and access across the SES hierarchy, because the problems faced by lower SES women are more difficult and require more resources. As noted earlier, it may not be helpful simply to suggest that a patient get more exercise or eat a lower fat diet. Providers may need to spend additional time helping lower SES patients think through how they can implement this suggestion. Community-level solutions (e.g., increased availability of exercise facilities, healthy food in poorer areas) also will be important in breaking down barriers facing individuals who are trying to achieve healthier behaviors. Health systems and even individual providers may want to work toward these changes because they would facilitate their patients' health behaviors.

Screening and Treatment

Problems of access to care associated with SES contribute to differences in early detection of disease. There is evidence that lower SES women are more likely to present to providers with more advanced disease. Delay in seeking care may be a function of health attitudes and behaviors or access to care. Ayanian, Kohler, Abe, and Epstein (1993) found that women who lacked insurance coverage or who had Medicaid coverage had more advanced breast cancer at diagnosis and poorer survival than those with private health insurance.

A key behavior in relation to breast cancer is obtaining screening by mammography. Lower SES women and those residing in neighborhoods characterized by low SES are less likely to have mammography screening (Katz & Hofer, 1994). One concrete obstacle for lower SES women may be physical access; women living farther away from screening sites are less likely to have mammograms (Hurley, Huggins, Jolley, & Reading 1994). Distance may be particularly problematic for lower SES women who have to rely on public transportation. Among low-SES women, mammogram use is greater for those who have publicly funded health centers in their neighborhoods (Lane, Polednak, & Burg, 1992). McCoy et al. (1994) found a shift from later to earlier stage breast cancer in low-SES minority women who had access to health care centers in their communities. The use of mobile vans that bring services into lower SES neighborhoods may be helpful in overcoming this obstacle. Beyond access, the cost of screening may be an impediment to use (Stein, Fox, & Murata, 1991). Lowering the costs of mammography should be especially effective for lower SES women, for whom costs are likely to be most salient.

SES differences in breast cancer survival may derive from differential access to care and differential treatment, as well as from differences in non-care-related factors that influence disease course. Dayal, Power, and Chiu (1982) studied breast cancer patients who were treated at a single teaching hospital. Within the same setting, and controlling for age and stage of disease, both SES and ethnicity was related to survival, with poorer women and African American women having poorer survival. In this sample, the difference between ethnic groups became nonsignificant once SES was controlled, suggesting that poorer survival of African American women was due to factors associated with lower SES. Dayal (1987) posited a number of mechanisms that could account for the poorer survival of lower SES women. These include differences in treatment offered to women at different levels of SES, differences in acceptability and choice of treatment, and differences in adherence to treatments that are selected. Each of these mechanisms merits examination in research as well as attention in providing services.

SES-Sensitive Services

SES is a clear risk factor for disease and should be part of an assessment of a patient's profile of risk factors. In addition, interventions and treatments need to be designed with an understanding of the person's life circumstances that are likely to be associated with SES. Health care providers need to make special efforts for lower SES patients to ensure that they have sufficient access to both information and resources to help them to avoid risk, obtain early diagnosis, and follow prescribed treatments. In addition to interventions at the individual level, social policies also are important to reduce the health burden associated with lower SES. The substantial health disadvantages of women at the bottom of the SES hierarchy suggest that education and income-related policies targeting this group are particularly important.

In conclusion, SES is a potent force that contributes substantially to social inequalities in health status. In attempts to understand and improve women's health, researchers need to keep the SES-health relation in mind in the domains we explore. These effects will occur not only at the very bottom of the SES hierarchy, but at every level of SES. However, the nature of the association may vary for different diseases. It will be particularly important for us to establish what the mechanisms are by which socioeconomic factors exert their effects on health; such information is key to developing policies and interventions that will diminish these effects. Researchers need to identify what it is about SES that has protective or adverse influences on women's health so that the inequalities that now exist can be reduced.

References

Adelstein, A. M. (1980). Life-style in occupational cancer. *Journal of Toxicology and Environmental Health, 6*, 953–962.

Adler, N. E., Boyce, T., Chesney, M. A., Cohen, S., Folkman, S., Kahn, R. L., & Syme, S. L. (1994). Socioeconomic status and health: The challenge of the gradient. *American Psychologist, 49*, 15–24.

Adler, N. E., Boyce, T., Chesney, M. A., Folkman, S., & Syme, S. L. (1993). Socioeconomic inequalities in health: No easy solution. *Journal of the American Medical Association, 269*, 3140–3145.

Ayanian, J. Z., & Epstein, A. M. (1991). Differences in the use of procedures between women and men hospitalized for coronary heart disease. *New England Journal of Medicine, 325*, 221–225.

Ayanian, J. Z., Kohler, B. A., Abe, T., & Epstein, A. M. (1993). The relation between health insurance coverage and clinical outcomes among women with breast cancer. *New England Journal of Medicine, 329*, 326–331.

Bain, R., Greenberg, R., & Whitaker, J. (1986). Racial differences in survival of women with breast cancer. *Journal of Chronic Disease, 39*, 631–642.

Baquet, C. R., Horm, J. W., Gibbs, T., & Greenwald, P. (1991). Socioeconomic factors and cancer incidence among Blacks and Whites. *Journal of the National Cancer Institute, 83*, 551–557.

Becker, T. M., Wheeler, C. M., McGough, N. S., Stidley, C. A., Parmenter, C. A., Dorin, M. H., & Jordan, S. W. (1994). Contraceptive and reproductive risk for cervical dysplasia in southwestern Hispanic and non-Hispanic White women. *International Journal of Epidemiology, 23*, 913–922.

Berg, J. W., Ross, R., & Latourette, H. B. (1977). Economic status and survival of cancer patients. *Cancer, 39*, 467–477.

Centers for Disease Control. (1993). Cigarette smoking among adults: United States, 1991. *Morbidity and Mortality Weekly Report, 42*, 230–233.

Chesney, M. A. (1991). Women, work-related stress and smoking. In M. Frankenhauser, U. Lundberg, & M. A. Chesney (Eds.), *Women, work, stress and health* (pp. 139–155). New York: Plenum.

Chesney, M. A. (1994). Prevention of HIV and STD infections. *Preventive Medicine, 23*, 655–660.

Cunningham, L. S., & Kelsey, J. L. (1984). Epidemiology of musculoskeletal impairments and associated disability. *American Journal of Public Health, 74*, 574–579.

Dayal, H. H. (1987). Cancer etiology, management, and outcome: Does it matter who you are? *Progress in Clinical and Biological Research, 248*, 245–254.

Dayal, H., Power, R. N., & Chiu, C. (1982). Race and socioeconomic status in survival for breast cancer. *Journal of Chronic Disease, 35*, 675–683.

DeVesa, S. S., & Diamond, E. L. (1980). Association of breast cancer and cervical cancer incidences with income and education among Whites and Blacks. *Journal of the National Cancer Institute, 65*, 515–528.

Diaz, T., Chu, S. Y., Buehler, J. W., Boyd, D., Checko, P. J., Conti, L., Davidson, A. J., Herman, P., Herr, M., Levy, A., Shields, A., Sorvillo, F., Mokotoff, E., Wythe, B., & Hersch, B. (1994). Socioeconomic differences among people with AIDS: Results from a multistate surveillance project. *American Journal of Preventive Medicine, 10*, 217–222.

Ellen, J. M., Kohn, R. P., Bolan, G. A., Shiboski, S., & Krieger, N. (1995). Socioeconomic differences in STD morbidity rates among black and white adolescents, San Francisco, 1990 to 1992. *American Journal of Public Health, 85*(11), 1546–1548.

Feldman, J. J., Makuc, D. M., Kleinman, J. C., & Cornoni-Huntley, J. (1989). National trends in educational differentials in mortality. *American Journal of Epidemiology, 129*, 919–933.

Fiore, M. C., Novotny, T. E., Pierce, J. P., Hatziandreu, E. J., Patel, K. M., & Davis, R. M. (1989). Trends in cigarette smoking in the United States: The changing influence of gender and race. *Journal of the American Medical Association, 261*, 49–55.

Hakama, M., Hakulinen, T., Pukkala, E., Saxen, E., & Teppo, L. (1982). Risk indicators of breast cancer and cervical cancer on ecologic and individual levels. *American Journal of Epidemiology, 116*, 990–1000.

Holtgrave, D. R., Valdiserri, R. O., & West, G. A. (1994). Quantitative economic evaluations of HIV-related prevention and treatment services: A review. *Risk: Health, Safety, and Environment, 29*, 529–547.

Hurley, S. F., Huggins, R. M., Jolley, D. J., & Reading, D. (1994). Recruitment activities and sociodemographic factors that predict attendance at a mammographic screening program. *American Journal of Public Health, 84*, 1655–1658.

Karjalainen, S., & Pukkala, E. (1990). Social class as a prognostic factor in breast cancer survival. *Cancer, 66*, 819–826.

Katz, S. J., & Hofer, T. P. (1994). Socioeconomic disparities in preventive care persist despite universal coverage: Breast and cervical cancer screening in Ontario and the United States. *Journal of the American Medical Association, 272*, 530–534.

Kitagawa, E. M., & Hauser, P. M. (1973). *Differential mortality in the United States: A study in socioeconomic epidemiology.* Cambridge, MA: Harvard University Press.

Kogevinas, M., Marmot, M. G., Fox, A. J., & Goldblatt, P. O. (1991). Socioeconomic differences in cancer survival. *Journal of Epidemiology and Community Health, 45*, 216–219.

Kraus, J. F., Borhani, N. O., & Franti, C. E. (1980). Socioeconomic status, ethnicity, and risk of coronary heart disease. *American Journal of Epidemiology, 111*, 407–414.

Lane, D. S., Polednak, A. P., & Burg, M. A. (1992). Breast cancer screening practices among users of county-funded health centers vs. women in the entire community. *American Journal of Public Health, 82*, 199–203.

Manton, K. G., & Stallard, E. (1992). Demographics (1950–1987) of breast cancer in birth cohorts of older women. *Journal of Gerontology, 47*, 32–42.

Marmot, M. G., Kogevinas, M., & Elston, M. A. (1987). Social/economic status and disease. *Annual Review of Public Health, 8*, 111–135.

Marmot, M., Shipley, S., & Rose, G. (1984). Inequalities in death: Specific explanations of a general pattern? *The Lancet, 1*, 1003–1006.

Matthews, K. A., Kelsey, S. F., Meilahn, E. N., Kuller, L. H., & Wing, R. R. (1989). Educational attainment and behavioral and biologic risk factors for coronary heart disease in middle-aged women. *American Journal of Epidemiology, 129*, 1132–1144.

McCoy, C. B., Smith, S. A., Metsch, L. R., Anwyl, R. S., Correa, R., Bankston, L., & Zavertnik, J. J. (1994). Breast cancer screening of the medically underserved: Results and implications. *Cancer Practice, 2*, 267–274.

Meischke, H., Eisenberg, M. S., & Larsen, M. P. (1993). Prehospital delay interval for patients who use emergency medical services: The effect of heart-related medical conditions and demographic variables. *Annals of Emergency Medicine, 22*, 1579–1601.

O'Leary, A., Jemmott, L. S., Suarez-Al-Adam, M., AlRoy, C., & Fernandez, M. I. (1993). Women and AIDS. In S. Matteo (Ed.), *American women in the nineties: Today's critical issues* (pp. 173–192). Boston: Northeastern University Press.

Pappas, G., Queen, S., Hadden, M. A., & Fisher, G. (1993). The increasing disparity in mortality between socioeconomic groups in the United States, 1960 and 1986. *New England Journal of Medicine, 329,* 103–109.

Richardson, J. L., Langholz, B., Bernstein, L. Burciaga, C., Danley, K., & Ross, R. K. (1992). Stage and delay in breast cancer diagnosis by race, socioeconomic status, age and year. *British Journal of Cancer, 65,* 922–926.

Rogot, E., Sorlie, P. D., Johnson, N. J., & Schmitt, C. (1992). *A mortality study of 1.3 million persons.* Washington, DC: National Institutes of Health, National Heart, Lung, and Blood Institute.

Sooman, A., Macintyre, S., & Anderson, A. (1993). Scotland's health—A more difficult challenge for some? The price and availability of healthy foods in socially contrasting localities in the west of Scotland. *Health Bulletin, 51,* 276–284.

Stein, J. A., Fox, S. A., & Murata, P. J. (1991). The influence of ethnicity, socioeconomic status, and psychological barriers on use of mammography. *Journal of Health and Social Behavior, 32,* 101–113.

Susser, M., Watson, W., & Hopper, K. (1985). Social class and disorders of health. In M. Susser, W. Watson, & K. Hopper (Eds.), *Sociology in medicine* (3rd ed., pp. 213–259). Oxford, England: Oxford University Press.

Townsend, P. (1974). Inequality and the health service. *The Lancet, 1,* 1179–1189.

Wagener, D. K., & Schatzkin, A. (1994). Temporal trends in the socioeconomic gradient for breast cancer mortality among U.S. women. *American Journal of Public Health, 84,* 1003–1006.

Wenger, N. K., Speroff, L., & Packard, B. (1993). Cardiovascular health and disease in women. *New England Journal of Medicine, 329,* 247–256.

Winkleby, M. A., Fortmann, S. P., & Barrett, D. C. (1990). Social class disparities in risk factors for disease: Eight-year prevalence patterns by level of education. *Preventive Medicine, 19,* 1–12.

3

Psychosocial Factors and Women's Health: Integrating Mind, Heart, and Body

Ann O'Leary and Vicki S. Helgeson

It is often argued that the most challenging modern-day problems in medicine are ones for which psychosocial factors are prominent in both etiology and treatment. Although "magic bullets" such as antibiotic medication and vaccination have reduced the impact of infectious disease on morbidity and mortality, the leading causes of death at the end of the 20th century are chronic diseases for which lifestyle factors are critical. For example, cardiovascular disease and cancer, the two leading causes of death in the United States, are both affected by behaviors (e.g., smoking, diet) and by emotional and personality factors (e.g., hostility, depression; Contrada, Leventhal, & O'Leary, 1990). Furthermore, a growing body of evidence indicates that psychosocial factors may play a role in the immunological defense against infectious illness, autoimmune disease, and cancer (Herbert & Cohen, 1993).

The impact of psychosocial factors on health may differ for men and women. As the causes of death shifted from infectious disease to chronic disease over the 20th century, sex differences in health widened. For example, in 1920 women lived on average 1 year longer than men, whereas in 1990 women's life expectancy was 7 years longer than men's. Although men have higher mortality rates than women, women have higher morbidity rates than men. Women suffer more nonfatal chronic illnesses and more acute illnesses than men. Women are more likely to develop hypertension, kidney disease, and autoimmune diseases, such as rheumatoid arthritis and systemic lupus erythematosus (Litt, 1993). Sex differences exist for some immune parameters, which appear to be mediated by sex hormones (Schuurs & Verheul, 1990). This may account for some of these immune-related sex differences in disease prevalence. Women also have twice the rate of depression as men (Nolen-Hoeksema, 1987). By contrast, young men are more likely to suffer injuries, commit suicide, and be vic-

Work on this chapter was facilitated by National Institute of Mental Health Grants MH48013 and MH48662. We wish to thank Richard Dienstbier for helpful comments on a draft of this chapter and Michael Luongo for assisting with the background research.

tims of violence. Men are considerably more prone to heart disease than women, particularly during their younger years, when women are protected against heart disease by estrogen. Men also are more prone to hostility than women, which may play a role in their enhanced likelihood of cardiovascular disease. Yet, differences in disease prevalence or prognosis do not alone account for women's longer life expectancy (Litt, 1993).

It is important to evaluate the influence of psychosocial factors in women's health because women have different social roles than men and are likely to differ from men on many of the psychological and social variables linked to health. In this chapter, we review the role of psychosocial factors in health, with a particular focus on women. We begin by describing the study of stress. We then describe stress buffers, or psychosocial factors, that reduce the deleterious effects of stress, specifically social networks, coping strategies, and perceived control. We also describe stress-resistant and stress-prone personalities. For each domain, we present a brief overview of the literature, describe its relevance to women's health, and provide some recommendations for health care providers. In the last section, we discuss two pathways by which psychosocial variables might influence health: behavioral and physiological. We discuss the relevance of gender to each of these pathways. We conclude with some general guidelines that health care practitioners might consider when addressing women.

Psychosocial Factors and Health

Emotions and stress have been thought to affect physical health since ancient times. A few decades ago, certain diseases were deemed to be "psychosomatic" because they were believed to be caused or exacerbated by psychological factors (e.g., unconscious conflict). In more recent research using sophisticated methods for assessing disease-related processes, illnesses such as cardiovascular disease, cancer, and autoimmune and infectious diseases have been studied and found to have affective input, usually referred to as "stress" (reviewed by Contrada et al., 1990).

Stress

Stress occurs when the demands of the environment outweigh one's personal resources (Lazarus & Folkman, 1984). The environmental demands are referred to as stressors. Stressors may be acute, such as the death of a loved one, or chronic, such as a demanding job or a difficult marriage. Researchers study reactions to stress by either examining how a group of people cope with the same stressor (e.g., bereavement, unemployment) or how individuals are affected by several environmental events (e.g., death of a loved one, losing a job) that have occurred in the recent past. This latter measure may be a mere summation of the number of events experienced or the weighted sum of these events, taking individuals' appraisals of how stressful each event was into account.

Women. In general, there are not differences in the number of stressful life events that men and women report, but there are differences in the kinds of stressors men and women experience. There are a number of stressors that women clearly are more likely to experience than men. Women in American society suffer greater stress from childbirth, rape and domestic violence, sexism and sexual discrimination, lower pay or status work, concern about weight, and the strain of dividing attention between competing roles (e.g., those of mother and worker). Poverty is more prevalent among women than men. In a survey of more than 2,000 people in the United States, women's greater economic hardships and less paid labor accounted for a portion of their health disadvantage compared with men (Ross & Bird, 1994). There also are some stressors men face more often than women, such as the stress associated with high-responsibility, physically taxing, or hazardous occupations.

There is one additional kind of stressor that women report more than men that may have implications for women's health. Adult and adolescent women report a greater number of relationship stressors, stressors that involve or afflict loved ones (Helgeson & Fritz, 1996). Kessler and McLeod (1984) found in five epidemiological studies that women reported more stressful events that involved network members and that the association of those events to psychological distress was stronger among women than men. Women's greater vulnerability to the effects of relationship stressors accounted for sex differences in depression in those studies. Using a somewhat novel approach, Bolger, DeLongis, Kessler, and Schilling (1989) asked married couples to record their mood and any stressful events experienced on a daily basis for 6 weeks. Women's moods were more strongly related to relationship stressors, such as arguments with network members, than were men's moods.

Implications. Health care professionals should consider a wide array of stressful life events when assessing women's exposure to recent stressors. In trying to determine whether there are psychosocial factors that may account for some of a patient's symptoms or that may detract a patient from taking care of himself or herself, one would need to ask about recent events that have happened to the patient's network members as well as to the patient himself or herself. Practitioners also should be sensitive to financial concerns that women may not articulate. Financial difficulties may impede women from making health behavior changes (e.g., enrolling in an exercise program) or complying with physician instructions (e.g., taking medication).

Stress Buffers

Stressful life events alone account for a small proportion of the variance in health. According to the stress and coping perspective, it is necessary to consider one's appraisal of stressful life events. Appraisals depend on resources. Resources, or stress "buffers," can increase one's resistance to stressors, whereas the lack of resources may increase one's vulnerability to stressors. We discuss three stress buffers: social networks, ways of coping, and perceived control.

Social networks. Social networks have been studied in terms of the number of contacts provided, a quantitative measure, as well as in terms of the resources provided, a functional measure. Both quantitative and functional measures of support have been found to be related to health (Reifman, 1995). Marital status is the most commonly studied quantitative measure of support. Qualitative measures distinguish among three primary functions: emotional support (i.e., love, caring, empathy), instrumental assistance (e.g., running errands, providing transportation), and informational support (i.e., guidance). Among these three kinds of support, researchers have considered emotional support to be the most effective (House, 1981).

WOMEN. The literature is not clear about whether there are sex differences in quantitative support (e.g., network size) or even levels of support functions. Some studies have shown that women perceive and receive more support than men (Burda, Vaux, & Schill, 1984), but there are studies in which no sex difference was found (Flaherty & Richman, 1989). When the type of support is examined, it appears that women are more likely than men to receive emotional support but not other types of support (Stokes & Wilson, 1984).

There are differences in the nature of men's and women's relationships that may have implications for social support. Throughout the life course, women have a greater involvement in their relationships (Chodorow, 1978). Women are more likely than men to have a confidant, and women's friendships are viewed as being more intimate than those of men (Belle, 1987). Interactions that involve a woman are reported to be more meaningful than interactions that involve a man (Wheeler, Reis, & Nezlek, 1983).

It is not clear whether social support has the same effect on health for women and men. In a review of the literature on social support and health, Shumaker and Hill (1991) concluded that the relation of social support to health is weaker and more complex among women than men. They noted that some studies have shown a mortality disadvantage for women with social support.

The reason for the more complicated and sometimes negative relationship between social support and health among women, almost all authors agree, is that social ties are a double-edged sword for women. Relationships mean the provision as well as the receipt of support for women. Women are more likely than men to provide support, and both men and women prefer to turn to women for emotional support (Belle, 1987). Women are more likely than men to assume caretaking responsibilities, not only of their children but also of their elderly parents (Belle, 1987). In addition, women are more likely to have occupational roles that involve support provision (e.g., teacher, nurse, social worker). Thus, relationships have costs as well as benefits for women.

There is one social tie that clearly has less positive health consequences for women than men: marriage. Women derive fewer physical and
mental health benefits from marriage than men (Belle, 1987; Gove, 1972).
In addition, women recover more quickly and suffer less adverse health
consequences on widowhood than men (Stroebe & Stroebe, 1983). One explanation for the latter finding is that women have alternative sources of
emotional support (i.e., friends) when they lose a spouse, whereas men
often lose their sole source of emotional support (Belle, 1987). Wives are
men's primary confidants, but men are not always wives' primary
confidants.

Finally, within close relationships, there may be sex differences in the
types of support men and women provide. In a popular book, *You Just
Don't Understand*, Tannen (1990) suggested that women are more likely
to provide empathy or emotional support, whereas men are more likely to
provide advice. Empirical data addressing this issue are lacking, however.
If true, it would explain why women's relationships are closer than those
of men, why both men and women seek out women for emotional support,
and why both men and women prefer to self-disclose to a woman rather
than a man. It also could explain why interactions with women are more
health beneficial than interactions with men (i.e., Wheeler et al., 1983)
and why marriage confers greater benefits to men than women (Gove,
1972). Evaluative interactions, which would include advice giving, increase cardiovascular reactivity (Allen, Blascovich, Tomaka, & Kelsey,
1991), whereas more supportive interactions (e.g., empathy) decrease cardiovascular reactivity (Kamarck, Manuck, & Jennings, 1990). Thus, relationships with men and women may have different physiological effects.

IMPLICATIONS. Health care professionals should assess the dimensions
of patients' social networks and determine which network members are
supportive. Although the spousal relationship is clearly an important one
in women's lives, health care professionals should not hesitate to include
other network members in treating women and should not presume that
a spousal relationship is supportive. Whenever possible, practitioners
should invite patients to bring a supportive other, whether it is for treatment or for a discussion of treatment options. The support person may not
only reduce a patient's distress during a treatment or procedure but also
can provide a second set of ears to hear physician instructions.

Health care professionals should be sensitive to women's roles as support providers and consider the social constraints on women's health behavior. Women's care for others may prevent them from complying with
physician instructions. Thus, it is important for the practitioner to discern
whether there are obstacles to women's self-care so that alternative routes
to accomplishing the same goal can be developed. For example, a physician
who recommends that a female cardiac patient attend a cardiac rehabilitation program for exercise may not realize that caretaking responsibilities will prevent the patient from attending a 9:00 a.m. to 5:00 p.m. program. If the physician were aware of the constraints, alternative ways of
exercise or alternative programs could be discussed.

To the extent that men and women provide different types of support, a potential conflict may occur when male physicians are treating female patients. Presumably, female patients want information and advice about their health, but physicians may underestimate the importance of empathy and emotional support. Health care practitioners need to be sensitive to patients' desires to self-disclose and share feelings about their illness. Patients who do not feel comforted and understood by their physician may be less likely to disclose important health-relevant information. Patients are more likely to adhere to recommended regimens and return for follow-up when they feel comfortable with their physician (Korsch & Negrete, 1972).

Ways of coping. The term *coping* refers to the marshaling of efforts to ameliorate the effects of potentially stressful events. The ways individuals cope with specific stressors often are divided into two categories: problem-focused coping and emotion-focused coping (Lazarus & Folkman, 1984). Problem-focused coping involves changing the actual stressful situation, whereas emotion-focused coping involves attempts to palliate the distress reaction. Examples of problem-focused coping would be studying for an examination, finding a new job, and divorcing a spouse. Emotion-focused coping strategies include relaxation, distraction, positive reappraisal (i.e., finding something positive in a negative experience), and escape through the use of drugs or alcohol. In general, problem-focused coping is more beneficial in controllable situations, whereas emotion-focused coping is more beneficial in uncontrollable situations (Folkman, 1984).

Cognitive processing of a stressful experience also may be considered a coping style. Pennebaker (1993) suggested that it is important to disclose, in some fashion, feelings about stressful life events. He found that inhibition of affect and nondisclosure of personally upsetting experiences produces negative health consequences and that disclosure produces positive ones. Emotional inhibition also has been found (albeit somewhat controversially) to enhance the likelihood of cancer (see Contrada et al., 1990).

WOMEN. Although the results of some studies support the notion that women have a greater tendency to use emotion-focused coping strategies and men have a greater tendency to use problem-focused coping strategies, Thoits (1991) found in her review of the literature that sex differences in coping styles cut across the problem-focused/emotion-focused distinction. She found that women's ways of coping were more expressive (e.g., expressing feelings, seeking social support) and that men's ways of coping were more rational and stoic (e.g., accepting the situation, engaging in exercise). Across a wide array of studies, one sex difference in coping is clear: Women are more likely than men to seek support (Thoits, 1991).

One reason that sex differences in emotion-focused and problem-focused coping are not always clear is that the categories are too broad. There are different kinds of problem-focused coping and different kinds of emotion-focused coping. In the case of emotion-focused coping, there are clearly healthy types (e.g., positive reappraisal) and clearly unhealthy types (e.g., distraction with substance abuse). Two kinds of emotion-focused coping have been examined relative to gender: rumination and distraction. Nolen-Hoeksema (1987) found that women are more likely than men to ruminate about a stressful event, whereas men are more likely than women to distract themselves from the stressor. She argued that these differences in coping styles contribute to the development and maintenance of sex differences in depression. Women's propensity to ruminate about problems interferes with efforts to resolve the problem (i.e., problem-focused coping) and increases the propensity to have other depressive cognitions.

Taken collectively, the literature on gender and coping suggests positive and negative implications for women. On the negative side, women may be more likely to ruminate to excess about stressful events. On the positive side, women are more likely to seek support and express themselves. Social support buffers the impact of ruminations on distress (Lepore, Silver, Wortman, & Wayment, 1996).

IMPLICATIONS. Given the health benefits of self-disclosure and women's willingness to engage in self-disclosure as well as seek social support, health care professionals should evaluate whether women have available social support and provide access to alternative resources (e.g., support groups). One sign of inadequate sources for ventilation of feelings is intrusive thoughts about the event or ruminations. Patients who are experiencing intrusive thoughts about a chronic illness (e.g., cancer) or chronic loss (e.g., bereavement) may benefit from an opportunity to self-disclose in either an individual or group context.

Health care providers should not hesitate to make referrals. Health care practitioners should gauge how much information patients desire. Providing too much information to information avoiders can heighten their anxiety, whereas providing too little information to information seekers can exacerbate their distress.

Perceived control. People need to feel that they have control over their environment (Thompson, 1981). Environmental events, or stressors, challenge people's perceptions of control. One way to successfully adjust to these events is to regain a sense of control (Taylor, 1983). For example, someone who has had a heart attack may feel a loss of control because his or her daily activities are restricted and health is threatened. One way the patient can restore control is to take actions to prevent future heart problems. Perceived control has been related to better adjustment to a wide array of illnesses, including heart disease, breast cancer, and rheumatoid arthritis (see Taylor, Helgeson, Reed, & Skokan, 1991, for a review).

Several important distinctions have been made about what types of control are adaptive. One distinction is between primary control (i.e., influencing the environment to meet one's needs) and secondary control (i.e., the self accommodating to the environment; Rothbaum, Weisz, & Snyder, 1982). Although primary control is preferred, secondary control is particularly important when the stressful event is uncontrollable (e.g., the death of a loved one). Examples of secondary control are acceptance and positive reappraisal (i.e., finding some positive meaning in the aversive experience). This distinction resembles the one between problem-focused coping and emotion-focused coping. Another distinction that has been made is between control over the central event and control over the event consequences. For example, when faced with a terminal illness, it may be more realistic to attempt to control the consequences of the event (i.e., the pain and symptoms from treatment) than the central event, the disease course. In a study of men and women with cancer, control over the consequences of the event (i.e., treatment symptoms, emotional reactions to the illness) were more strongly related to adjustment than control over the central event (i.e., disease course; Thompson, Sobolew-Shubin, Galbraith, Schwankovsky, & Cruzen, 1993). The underlying theme appears to be that perceptions of control are adaptive when the appraisal is based in reality (Helgeson, 1992). It is more adaptive to perceive control over controllable situations and relinquish control over uncontrollable situations (Folkman, 1984).

WOMEN. It is not clear whether there are sex differences in tendencies to perceive control over outcomes. It is certainly true that "control" is part of the male gender role, with men being socialized to take control and to always be in control. Thus, it may be that women are more receptive to secondary control strategies than men and subsequently better able to adjust to stressors that are uncontrollable. Empirical data on this issue are lacking, however.

IMPLICATIONS. Health care professionals should help patients distinguish among the controllable and uncontrollable aspects of their health. For example, physicians may acknowledge that patients' family history places them at risk for heart disease but also should emphasize the ways in which patients can exert control to prevent the development of heart disease (e.g., through exercise and diet). Health care professionals should emphasize the link between patients' behaviors and health.

Pointing out the relation between a control behavior and health, however, may not be enough to get patients to adopt the behavior. For example, providing women with information about the health hazards of smoking may not be sufficient to get them to quit smoking. Health care professionals need to assess patients' perceptions of their capabilities. Women may know that they should quit smoking or change their diet but not have the skills or resources to make these health behavior changes. Health care practitioners may need to provide information about how to change health behavior in addition to information that it is important to do so.

Stress-Prone and Stress-Resistant Personalities

Some other factors of an ongoing, dispositional nature may affect one's response to stressful life events as well as one's overall health. As we discuss these personality characteristics, we note whether they have been related to gender.

The most widely studied stress-prone personality is the Type A behavior pattern, which has been shown to predict coronary heart disease (see Matthews & Haynes, 1986, for a review). Although Type A behavior is often referred to as a personality characteristic, the cardiologists who discovered the pattern describe it as a predisposition to respond to environmental challenges in a certain way: with impatience, hostility, competitiveness, and aggression (Friedman & Rosenman, 1974). Thus, the behavior pattern is elicited by the combination of a personality predisposition and a challenging environment. The challenges range from minor stressors, such as waiting in line, to major stressors, such as losing a job. Today, it is recognized that the most toxic component of the Type A behavior pattern is hostility (see Contrada, 1994, for a review).

Women are traditionally less hostile than men and less likely to be classified as having a Type A behavior pattern (Matthews et al., 1992). Thus, it seems that this behavior pattern is less relevant to women's health, on average, then men's health. As discussed in chapter 17 in this volume, factors predicting cardiovascular disease in women are somewhat different from those predicting it in men.

A personality factor that may be implicated in women's health is unmitigated communion. Unmitigated communion is a focus on others to the exclusion of the self (Bakan, 1966; Helgeson, 1994). It is an unhealthy form of communion and more commonly found in women than men. Unmitigated communion has been related to reporting greater upset over relationship stressors (Helgeson & Fritz, 1996) and a tendency to get overinvolved in others' problems. In a laboratory study, female college students who scored high on unmitigated communion were more distressed on hearing a stranger disclose a problem and reported greater intrusive thoughts about the problem 2 days later (Fritz & Helgeson, 1996). Unmitigated communion is related to the provision of support but not necessarily the receipt of support, suggesting that these individuals have unbalanced relationships (Helgeson & Fritz, 1996). People who score high on unmitigated communion may be so concerned with taking care of others that they neglect their own health. In one study of cardiac patients, those who scored high on unmitigated communion had greater difficulties adjusting to the illness, partly because they were less likely to reduce household activities as instructed by their physician (Helgeson, 1994). In a study of adolescents with diabetes, unmitigated communion was associated with increased distress and poor metabolic control, partly because these individuals had relationship stressors (Helgeson & Fritz, 1996).

There also is a set of stress-resistant personality factors. Generalized optimism, or the expectation that one will experience good outcomes, has been shown to affect health outcomes, including recovery from bypass surgery and reduced distress after surgery for breast cancer (Carver et al., 1993; Scheier & Carver, 1992). One reason that optimistic people seem to enjoy better health and adjust more successfully to illness is that they engage in more adaptive coping strategies (Carver et al., 1993). A related construct, pessimistic attributional style, also has been related to health outcomes. People who tend to attribute failure to internal, stable, and global factors (i.e., something about oneself that is never going to change and will affect everything one does) have a pessimistic attributional style.

In a study of Harvard alumni, a pessimistic explanatory style during college predicted poor health 35 years later (Peterson, Seligman, & Vaillant, 1988). This style may have implications for gender because women are more likely than men to attribute success to unstable factors (e.g., luck) and failure to stable factors (e.g., lack of ability; Dweck, Davidson, Nelson, & Enna, 1978).

Hardiness is another personality construct that has been shown to buffer the effects of stressful events (Kobasa, 1979). It is composed of three components: (a) control, or the generalized belief that one has control over events; (b) commitment, having a sense of purpose in the activities and people with whom one is involved; and (c) challenge, the tendency to view change as the potential for positive growth. Obviously, these features overlap with constructs previously discussed: perceived control and positive reappraisal. In an early study, executives who scored high on a measure of stressful life events and high on hardiness were less likely than their low-hardiness counterparts to experience illness (Kobasa, 1979). To our knowledge, sex differences have not been found in any of these constructs. Thus, there is no reason to believe that they have unique effects on women's health.

Implications. Obviously, it is difficult to change people's personalities. However, knowledge about the aforementioned dispositional variables can be used to discern which people might be at risk for adverse outcomes and require more attention. Patients who appear to have features of Type A behavior, unmitigated communion, or a pessimistic attributional style and people who lack optimism or hardiness might be more vulnerable to the development of health problems as well as to poor adjustment to existing health problems. These people may be less able to cope effectively with illness and less likely to comply with physician instructions. Health care professionals can educate or provide access to information that will help people with specific personality predispositions. People who appear to lack optimism and hardiness may benefit from coping skills classes or support groups of others with their medical conditions.

There are two personality styles that may make women more vulnerable. With respect to unmitigated communion, health care professionals should be alerted to the possibility that some women's caretaking obligations may interfere with their own health care. Attributional styles also may be important determinants of women's responses to their illness. Women with health problems may be more likely to blame themselves for an illness (internal, stable attribution) and become depressed. When health problems improve, women may be less likely to take credit and attribute improvements to "luck," an unstable, external factor. Health care professionals can model alternative attributional styles.

Mechanisms

There are two primary pathways by which psychosocial factors may influence health. First, psychosocial variables may alter people's behavior. Second, psychosocial variables may alter physiology. We discuss both possibilities and address the issue of gender when relevant.

Behavioral Pathways

Psychosocial variables may influence health behaviors. One health behavior with clear-cut health consequences is substance use. Alcohol consumption is more common among men than women, and men suffer more severe problems with alcohol use, although there is concern that drinking among women is increasing and may be more difficult to detect (see chapter 6 in this volume). Similarly, men smoke more cigarettes than women, although the sex differential is decreasing, as is the overall prevalence (see Mermelstein & Borrelli, 1995). The size of women's mortality advantage began to decrease in the 1980s, and smoking may account for the decrement (Waldron, 1995). During the mid-20th century, smoking became more acceptable among women, and men's rates of smoking decreased more than those of women.

A health behavior that may partially account for women's longevity advantage is their greater use of health care services (Verbrugge, 1979). This phenomenon cannot be explained solely by use of services connected to reproductive health, such as contraception and pregnancy.

By contrast, women are far more frequently prescribed psychotropic medications, such as tranquilizers and antidepressants, than men (Ashton, 1991). This is because of a combination of factors that include women's more frequent reports of distress as well as potential biases on the part of many providers. When more than 200 family physicians were presented with descriptions of common patient complaints, men's illnesses were attributed to different causes depending on the presenting symptom, whereas women's illnesses were more likely to be attributed to psychosomatic causes regardless of the symptom (Bernstein & Kane, 1981).

Physiological Mechanisms

There are physiological pathways by which psychosocial factors may influence health. Perceived stress is associated with activation of a number of physiological systems that have the potential to affect health.

Sympathetic nervous system. Activation of the sympathetic nervous system (SNS), which occurs under conditions of acute emotion (e.g., anger, fear), is associated with neural activation and the release of catecholamines. These have immunomodulating effects (reviewed in O'Leary, 1990), contribute to asthma and some pain conditions, and appear to be the basis for the effects of the Type A personality on cardiovascular disease. Type A individuals have been found to exhibit elevated SNS responses to laboratory stressors. SNS activity appears to contribute to the development of cardiovascular disease via its effects on blood pressure and arterial scarring; lipid mobilization into the bloodstream; and, acutely, increased oxygen demand by the heart (reviewed by Contrada et al., 1990). By contrast, social support may have a positive effect on SNS activity. In one study, the presence of a supportive person reduced cardiovascular reactivity to laboratory challenges (Kamarck et al., 1990).

Women may differ from men in their stress-related neuroendocrine activity. Largely because cardiovascular reactivity has been linked to heart disease, many researchers have examined autonomic or hormonal changes produced by laboratory stressors. In studies in which urinary catecholamine secretion was examined, men typically exhibit larger responses than women (reviewed by Polefrone & Manuck, 1987). Heart rate responses to brief stressors are similar for women and men; differences that have been identified are mixed in direction (Polefrone & Manuck, 1987). There is some indication, however, that the type of task used in laboratory studies and their relevance to men versus women influences arousal. Tasks have been cognitive ones, such as mental arithmetic and reaction time tasks. It has been argued that these tasks tap traditionally male achievement goals. Furthermore, when tasks are used that are not so related to achievement, sex differences are reduced or even reversed. For example, in a study of parents bringing their children to a hospital for testing, mothers exhibited greater norepinephrine release than fathers (Lundberg, de Chateau, Winberg, & Frankenhaeuser, 1981).

Women seem to be relatively protected from cardiovascular disease until they reach menopause. Thus, some researchers have examined effects of female sex hormones on cardiovascular reactivity to elucidate their role in this sex difference. Research paradigms have involved comparing pre- and postmenopausal women, studying women at different stages of the menstrual cycle, and exploring the effects of exogenous sex hormones (reviewed by Polefrone & Manuck, 1987). In general, results are mixed, with numerous negative findings as well as methodological difficulties. Thus, there are not yet definitive answers to this question.

Immune function. Another physiological system that is activated during stress is the hypothalamic–pituitary–adrenocortical system. Stressors that are severe, prolonged, and overwhelming to the organism (e.g., depression) are associated with activity in this system, and this activity has immunosuppressive effects. Suppressed immune function has been associated with loneliness, or the perceived lack of support (Kiecolt-Glaser, Garner, Speicher, Penn, & Glaser, 1984), and marital disharmony (Kiecolt-Glaser et al., 1993). Disclosure of traumas, by contrast, appears to enhance immune function (Esterling et al., 1994).

It is clear that there is still much to learn about the physiological mechanisms by which psychosocial factors influence health. Most of the psychological processes described in this chapter do not map neatly onto these physiological systems. The growing sophistication of techniques for elucidating biological processes will shed more light on this area in the future.

Implications of Stress Theory and Research
for Clinical Practice

Health providers, particularly ones who work with populations likely to be facing stressors, either due to demographic characteristics (e.g., poverty) or the illness for which treatment is sought (chronic, terminal, or painful illness), should be careful to assess patients' psychological functioning. Prescribing psychotropic medications such as antidepressants and tranquilizers, although probably useful and appropriate in many cases, should not be an automatic response to patients' distress. The person may be coping with objectively difficult circumstances (including the presenting illness) that may be amenable to other approaches. When a patient's resources are not adequate to meet the demands of the environment, psychological intervention may be indicated. Support groups, ranging from peer discussion with similar others to educational or coping skills training, may be helpful to patients. Interestingly, such interventions may actually improve the medical condition itself. In a study of women with metastatic breast cancer, those receiving supportive or expressive group psychotherapy had survival periods twice as long as those randomized to a control group (18 vs. 36 months; Spiegel, Bloom, Kraemer, & Gottheil, 1989). In a study of women with rheumatoid arthritis, those receiving a pain and stress management intervention had improved joint counts and reductions in pain and distress (O'Leary, Shoor, Lorig, & Holman, 1988); this intervention is now part of the Arthritis Foundation's self-help program. A stress management intervention for people with diabetes resulted in improved glucose tolerance relative to a comparison group (Surwit & Feinglos, 1983).

For some patients, stressful life conditions may be amenable to correction. Social workers may be able to help patients obtain health care reimbursement, unemployment benefits, and legal services. Domestic violence is a severe stressor that affects many American women and may be detected via sensitive interviewing so that appropriate referrals can be made (see chapter 4, this volume). For women with children, the welfare of those children may constitute their greatest source of concern, and, again, sensitive providers will be aware of services available in their communities and be ready to refer their patients to those services.

Conclusion

In this chapter we have provided a brief overview of psychosocial factors and their relevance to health and the provision of health care. In summary, women appear to differ from men in terms of the types of stressful life events experienced, the nature and impact of their social networks, coping strategies, substance use and use of health services, and some aspects of their biology. Although some contribution from each of these domains is likely to contribute to women's longer life expectancy and to their unique health concerns, researchers clearly have much further to go in understanding how the interactions among personal, social, biological, and environmental aspects of women's lives affect their health. The field of behavioral medicine is still young, and widespread application of its theories to women's health is younger still. Numerous health problems have not yet been explored from a psychosocial perspective, particularly ones that affect primarily women, such as human papillomavirus infection, interstitial cystitis, and vulvodynia. Numerous behavioral issues must be confronted as the results of human genome research lead to diagnostic tests and treatments for genetically related diseases; a recent example would be the identification of the BRCA1 gene, which causes some types of breast cancer and ovarian cancer (Lerman, Audrain, & Croyle, 1994). Of utmost importance is the development of psychosocial interventions both for behavior change and for reduction of distress as they might affect physical and mental health outcomes.

References

Allen, K. M., Blascovich, J., Tomaka, J., & Kelsey, R. M. (1991). Presence of human friends and pet dogs as moderators of autonomic responses to stress in women. *Journal of Personality and Social Psychology, 61*, 582–589.

Ashton, H. (1991). Psychotropic-drug prescribing for women. *British Journal of Psychiatry, 158*(Suppl. 10), 30–35.

Bakan, D. (1966). *The duality of human existence*. Chicago: Rand McNally.

Belle, D. (1987). Gender differences in the social moderators of stress. In R. C. Barnett, L. Biener, & G. K. Baruch (Eds.), *Gender and stress* (pp. 257–277). New York: Free Press.

Bernstein, B., & Kane, R. (1981). Physicians' attitudes toward female patients. *Medical Care, 19*, 600–608.

Bolger, N., DeLongis, A., Kessler, R. C., & Schilling, E. A. (1989). Effects of daily stress on negative mood. *Journal of Personality and Social Psychology, 57*, 808–818.

Burda, P. C., Vaux, A., & Schill, T. (1984). Social support resources: Variation across sex and sex role. *Personality and Social Psychology Bulletin, 10*, 119–126.

Carver, C. S., Pozo, C., Harris, S. D., Noriega, V., Scheier, M. F., Robinson, D. S., Ketcham, A. S., Moffat, F. L., & Clark, K. C. (1993). How coping mediates the effect of optimism on distress: A study of women with early stage breast cancer. *Journal of Personality and Social Psychology, 65*, 375–390.

Chodorow, N. (1978). *The reproduction of mothering*. Berkeley: University of California Press.

Contrada, R. J. (1994). Personality and anger in cardiovascular disease: Toward a psychological model. In A. W. Siegman & T. W. Smith (Eds.), *Anger, hostility, and the heart* (pp. 149–171). Hillsdale, NJ: Erlbaum.

Contrada, R. J., Leventhal, H., & O'Leary, A. (1990). Personality and health. In L. A. Pervin (Ed.), *Handbook of personality: Theory and research* (pp. 638–669). New York: Guilford Press.

Dweck, C. S., Davidson, W., Nelson, S., & Enna, B. (1978). Sex differences in learned helplessness: II. The contingencies of evaluative feedback in the classroom. *Developmental Psychology, 14*, 268–276.

Esterling, B. A., Antoni, M. H., Fletcher, M. A., Margulies, S., & Schneiderman, N. (1994). Emotional disclosure through writing or speaking modulates latent Epstein-Barr virus antibody titers. *Journal of Consulting and Clinical Psychology, 62*, 130–140.

Flaherty, J., & Richman, J. (1989). Gender differences in the perception and utilization of social support: Theoretical perspectives and an empirical test. *Social Science and Medicine, 28*, 1221–1228.

Folkman, S. (1984). Personal control and stress and coping processes: A theoretical analysis. *Journal of Personality and Social Psychology, 40,* 839–852.

Friedman, M., & Rosenman, R. H. (1974). *Type A behavior and your heart.* New York: Fawcett Columbine.

Fritz, H. L., & Helgeson, V. S. (1996, March). *Over-involvement in other people's problems: Exploring the link between unmitigated communion and distress.* Paper presented at the meeting of the Society of Behavioral Medicine, Washington, DC.

Gove, W. (1972). Sex, marital status, and mental illness. *Social Forces, 51,* 34–55.

Helgeson, V. S. (1992). Moderators of the relation between perceived control and adjustment to chronic illness. *Journal of Personality and Social Psychology, 63,* 656–666.

Helgeson, V. S. (1994). Relation of agency and communion to well-being: Evidence and potential explanations. *Psychological Bulletin, 116,* 412–428.

Helgeson, V. S., & Fritz, H. (1996). Implications of unmitigated communion and communion for adolescent adjustment to Type I diabetes. *Women's Health: Research on Gender, Behavior, and Policy, 2,* 163–188.

Herbert, T. B., & Cohen, S. (1993). Stress and immunity in humans: A meta-analytic review. *Psychosomatic Medicine, 55,* 364–379.

House, J. S. (1981). *Work stress and social support.* Reading, MA: Addison-Wesley.

Kamarck, T. W., Manuck, S. B., & Jennings, J. R. (1990). Social support reduces cardiovascular reactivity to psychological challenge: A laboratory model. *Psychosomatic Medicine, 52,* 42–58.

Kessler, R. C., & McLeod, J. D. (1984). Sex differences in vulnerability to undesirable life events. *American Sociological Review, 49,* 620–631.

Kiecolt-Glaser, J. K., Garner, W., Speicher, C. E., Penn, G., & Glaser, R. (1984). Psychosocial modifiers of immunocompetence in medical students. *Psychosomatic Medicine, 46,* 7–14.

Kiecolt-Glaser, J. K., Malarkey, W. B., Chee, M., Newton, T., Caccioppo, J. T., & Glaser, R. (1993). Negative behavior during marital conflict is associated with immunological down-regulation. *Psychosomatic Medicine, 55,* 395–409.

Kobasa, S. C. (1979). Stressful life events, personality, and health: An inquiry into hardiness. *Journal of Personality and Social Psychology, 37,* 1–11.

Korsch, B. M., & Negrete, V. F. (1972). Doctor-patient communication. *Scientific American, 227,* 66–74.

Lazarus, R. S., & Folkman, S. (1984). *Stress, appraisal, and coping.* New York: Springer.

Lepore, S. J., Silver, R. C., Wortman, C. B., & Wayment, H. A. (1996). Social strains, intrusive thoughts, and depressive symptoms among bereaved mothers. *Journal of Personality and Social Psychology, 70,* 271–282.

Lerman, C. E., Audrain, J., & Croyle, R. T. (1994). DNA testing for heritable breast cancer risk: Lessons from traditional genetic counseling. *Annals of Behavioral Medicine, 16,* 327–333.

Litt, I. F. (1993). Health issues for women in the 1990's. In S. Matteo (Ed.), *American women in the nineties: Today's critical issues* (pp. 139–157). Boston: Northeastern University Press.

Lundberg, U., de Chateau, P., Winberg, J., & Frankenhaeuser, M. (1981). Catecholamine and cortisol excretion patterns in three-year-old children and their parents. *Journal of Human Stress, 7,* 3–11.

Matthews, K. A., & Haynes, S. G. (1986). Type A behavior pattern and coronary disease risk. *American Journal of Epidemiology, 123,* 923–960.

Matthews, K. A., Woodall, K. L., Engebretson, T. O., McCann, B. S., Stoney, C. M., Manuck, S. B., & Saab, P. G. (1992). Influence of age, sex, and family on Type A and hostile attitudes and behaviors. *Health Psychology, 11,* 317–323.

Mermelstein, R. J., & Borrelli, B. (1995). Women and smoking. In A. L. Stanton & S. J. Gallant (Eds.), *The psychology of women's health* (pp. 309–348). Washington, DC: American Psychological Association.

Nolen-Hoeksema, S. (1987). Sex differences in unipolar depression: Evidence and theory. *Psychological Bulletin, 101,* 259–282.

O'Leary, A. (1990). Stress, emotion, and human immune function. *Psychological Bulletin, 108,* 363–382.

O'Leary, A., Shoor, S., Lorig, K., & Holman, H. (1988). A cognitive-behavioral treatment for rheumatoid arthritis. *Health Psychology, 7,* 527–544.

Pennebaker, J. W. (1993). Putting stress into words: Health, linguistic, and therapeutic implications. *Behaviour Research and Therapy, 31,* 539–548.

Peterson, C., Seligman, M. E. P., & Vaillant, G. E. (1988). Pessimistic explanatory style is a risk factor for physical illness: A thirty-five-year longitudinal study. *Journal of Personality and Social Psychology, 55,* 23–27.

Polefrone, J. M., & Manuck, S. B. (1987). Gender differences in cardiovascular and neuroendocrine response to stressors. In R. C. Barnett, L. Biener, & G. K. Baruch (Eds.), *Gender and stress* (pp. 13–38). New York: Free Press.

Reifman, A. (1995). Social relationships, recovery from illness, and survival: A literature review. *Annals of Behavioral Medicine, 17,* 124–131.

Ross, C. E., & Bird, C. E. (1994). Sex stratification and health lifestyle: Consequences for men's and women's perceived health. *Journal of Health and Social Behavior, 35,* 161–178.

Rothbaum, F., Weisz, J. R., & Snyder, S. S. (1982). Changing the world and changing the self: A two-process model of perceived control. *Journal of Personality and Social Psychology, 42,* 5–37.

Scheier, M. F., & Carver, C. S. (1992). Effects of optimism on psychological and physical well-being: Theoretical overview and empirical update. *Cognitive Therapy and Research, 16,* 201–228.

Schuurs, A. H., & Verheul, H. M. (1990). Effects of gender and sex steroids on the immune response. *Journal of Steroid Biochemistry, 35,* 157–172.

Shumaker, S. A., & Hill, D. R. (1991). Gender differences in social support and physical health. *Health Psychology, 10,* 102–111.

Spiegel, D., Bloom, J. R., Kraemer, H. C., & Gottheil, E. (1989). Effect of psychosocial treatment on survival of patients with metastatic breast cancer. *The Lancet, 2,* 888–891.

Stokes, J. P., & Wilson, D. G. (1984). The inventory of socially supportive behaviors: Dimensionality, prediction, and gender differences. *American Journal of Community Psychology, 12,* 53–69.

Stroebe, M. S., & Stroebe, W. (1983). Who suffers more? Sex differences in health risks of the widowed. *Psychological Bulletin, 93,* 279–301.

Surwit, R. S., & Feinglos, M. N. (1983). The effects of relaxation on glucose tolerance in non-insulin-dependent diabetes. *Diabetes Care, 6,* 176–179.

Tannen, D. (1990). *You just don't understand: Women and men in conversation.* New York: Ballantine Books.

Taylor, S. E. (1983). Adjustment to threatening events: A theory of cognitive adaptation. *American Psychologist, 38,* 1161–1173.

Taylor, S. E., Helgeson, V. S., Reed, G. M., & Skokan, L. A. (1991). Self-generated feelings of control and adjustment to physical illness. *Journal of Social Issues, 47,* 91–109.

Thoits, P. A. (1991). Gender differences in coping with emotional distress. In J. Eckenrode (Ed.), *The social context of coping* (pp. 107–138). New York: Plenum.

Thompson, S. C. (1981). Will it hurt less if I can control it? A complex answer to a simple question. *Psychological Bulletin, 90,* 89–101.

Thompson, S. C., Sobolew-Shubin, A., Galbraith, M. E., Schwankovsky, L., & Cruzen, D. (1993). Maintaining perceptions of control: Finding perceived control in low-control circumstances. *Journal of Personality and Social Psychology, 64,* 293–304.

Verbrugge, L. M. (1979). Female illness rates and illness behavior: Testing hypotheses about sex differences in health. *Women and Health, 4,* 61–79.

Waldron, I. (1995). Contributions of changing gender differences in behavior and social roles to changing gender differences in mortality. In D. Sabo & D. F. Gordon (Eds.), *Men's health and illness* (pp. 22–45). Thousand Oaks, CA: Sage.

Wheeler, L., Reis, H., & Nezlek, J. (1983). Loneliness, social interaction, and sex roles. *Journal of Personality and Social Psychology, 45,* 943–953.

4

Impact of Violence on Women's Health

Mary Ann Dutton, Yolanda Haywood, and Gigi El-Bayoumi

Women are exposed to violence in the community, in the workplace, and in their homes (Koss et al., 1994). In 1985, former Surgeon General C. Everett Koop stated that the Number 1 health problem facing women in the United States was violence (Koop, 1985). Since that time, numerous medical organizations and government agencies, including the American College of Obstetrics and Gynecology, the American Medical Association, the American College of Emergency Physicians, and the Centers for Disease Control and Prevention, have recommended routine screening of women to help prevent, identify, and care for victims of violence.

The overall purpose of this chapter is to assist health care professionals in working with women and their health problems related to experiences with violence. In this chapter we use the term *violence* to refer to the intentional use of aggressive physical and verbal behaviors regardless of whether injury is actually incurred. Violence includes behaviors such as hitting, punching, slapping, beating up, inappropriate sexual touch or sexual touch that is unwelcomed or resisted, and verbal threats or violence and other forms of intimidation and coercion. First, we discuss the impact of violence on women's health with a focus on injury, systemic health problems, pregnancy-related issues, and the mental health consequences of violence and abuse. Second, we discuss dealing with violence against women. Finally, we address health care, health promotion, and disease prevention by delineating specific steps essential for working with women and violence.

The Impact of Violence on Women's Health

Injury

One of the most obvious consequences of violence against women is the physical injury suffered. A study of 833 female patients at two teaching emergency departments, two hospital walk-in clinics, and one private hospital showed a lifetime prevalence rate of domestic violence of 54.2% and a 1-year incidence rate of 15.3% (Abbott, Johnson, Koziol-McLain, & Lowenstein, 1995).

Injury is more common among victims of violence when the assailant is known to them. Results from the National Crime Victim Survey (Bachman, 1994) showed that injuries resulted from 59% of violent crimes committed by intimates but only 27% committed by strangers. The rate of serious injury, however, was comparable across assailant types. This pattern was reversed for female rape victims, however, such that 43% of victims of nonstranger rapes sustained physical injuries other than the rape compared with 60% of stranger rape victims (Bachman, 1994). These results are limited, however, by the self-report nature of the study, in which respondents were required first to acknowledge that they were victimized by a crime. Many battered women do not label the violence by their intimate partners in this way. Recurrent episodes of violence (Langan & Innes, 1986) make the identification of injuries in multiple stages of healing a valuable tool in suggesting violence victimization, especially by an intimate, as the etiology.

Any type of injury may be sustained as a result of partner violence. Although there may be certain patterns or sites of injury that occur more frequently from domestic violence situations, there are no distinct features of injuries related to battering. Thus, practitioners are strongly encouraged to consider the possibility of domestic violence as being relevant to any identified injury. Injury may not be the direct result of physical assault (e.g., punching, kicking) but the result of attempts to escape or avoid it, such as in the case of a fall (e.g., when running away from a batterer, jumping from a moving vehicle to escape violence) or car crash (e.g., when hurriedly fleeing from a batterer). Finally, some injuries result when women fight back against the attacker. Thus, the health care professional should always rule out that any injury is violence related. Finally, injury is not the hallmark of domestic violence, even when victims seek medical care, because domestic victims often experience health-related problems other than injury.

In some cases, women also use violence against men (and women) in the process of which they are sometimes injured. The use of violence by women does not necessarily mean that it is the woman who is the primary aggressor, although that may be the case. In heterosexual relationships, it is more likely that the woman has used violence to protect herself from her partner's violence or to retaliate against it or the threat of it (Saunders, 1986). In either case—when the woman is the aggressor or when she is responding to violence in kind—the use of violence represents a clear danger both to herself and her partner. The mere fact of a woman's use of violence should neither negate the need for identification and interventions for violence victimization nor lead to an assumption that it is she who is the primary offender.

Health Problems Associated With Violence

Women as victims of violence are not only seen in emergency departments but also in primary care settings. In one study of 394 women seeking medical care from a community practice, 23% reported having been physically assaulted by their partner within the past year; the lifetime prevalence rate was 38.8% (Hamberger, Saunders, & Hovey, 1992). However, in a recent visit, only 6 of these patients had ever been asked by their physicians about abuse. Another study using the same sample indicated that neither demographic nor health factors could accurately predict who among these adult female patients had been victimized (Saunders, Hamberger, & Hovey, 1993). Women who have been victimized by violence have more health problems, use the health care system more frequently, and rate their health problems as being worse more often than those women who have not been abused (Koss, 1994; Koss, Woodruff, & Koff, 1990). They may present to the emergency department, obstetrician, or primary care provider with various symptoms.

The victim herself may be unaware that her symptoms are in any way related to the abuse that she has experienced (Drossman, Leserman, & Nachman, 1990). The health care practitioner can play an important role in exploring the possibility of that link. That is, the practitioner is in a unique position to help the victim of violence understand that her health may be related to her experience with violence. It is important to understand that these health concerns are potentially related not only to actual physical violence but also to stress caused by pervasive emotional and psychological abuse. For many women in battering relationships, emotional abuse is the ongoing backdrop against which physical abuse occurs. Therefore, battered women's symptoms may reflect the stress of dealing with repetitive verbal aggression, humiliation, threats, and social isolation. As such, some presenting complaints can be vague and more chronic in nature. Accordingly, these complaints often are overlooked by health care providers as being potentially linked to domestic violence.

Coping with issues related to an ongoing violent and abusive situation, such as battering (e.g., safety for children or other family members, maintaining a job in spite of frequent interruptions or absences, fear of losing children if she attempts to leave) or sexual harassment (e.g., concerns over maintaining employment, reporting abuse), also increases stress and may lead to health problems. Furthermore, some attempts to cope with the stress (e.g., increase alcohol or drug use, working long hours to remain out of the house, purchasing a gun) may increase health risks.

A battered woman for whom no organic basis for physical complaints can be determined, and especially when she is not identified as battered, may more readily be negatively labeled as "neurotic," "hysterical," or "hypochondriacal" (Stark, Flitcraft, & Frazier, 1979). Conceptualizing the problem in this way suggests that the etiology is psychological and thus that it is "all in her head." Therefore, it is not surprising that abused women are often prescribed painkillers and minor tranquilizers (Stark et al., 1981) for their complaints. This practice may serve to further alienate the victim from the health care system and to reinforce the message that she hears from her batterer: that she is unworthy and that she in fact is the one who is the "real" problem. Furthermore, with medication the battered woman may be more numbed to the effects of violence and to the danger surrounding her, mimicking the practice of self-medication found with excess alcohol and street drugs. Although she may be less anxious as a result either of self- or prescribed medication, increased sedation can increase the physical risks she and her children, if present, face due to a decreased ability to think clearly or to act quickly.

Another potential risk of readily prescribing medication to victims of violence against women is that it may increase the likelihood of suicide. Because suicidality is a risk among battered women (Gondolf, 1988), adult survivors of child abuse (Courtois, 1988), and rape victims (Calhoun & Atkeson, 1991), providing the means to actualize suicidal thoughts can potentially increase that risk. In the absence of close monitoring, recognition of the violence history, and an opportunity for the patient to sort out her options, prescribing medication as a means of dealing with the sometimes vague and diffuse problems presented to the health care practitioner may effectively shut the door to help.

Domestic violence may have public health consequences that are not readily apparent. A growing body of research has shown that women with a history of childhood or adulthood sexual or physical violence are more likely to engage in behaviors that place them at high risk for HIV (Zierler et al., 1991). Furthermore, women with HIV or AIDS may be at increased risk for subsequent abuse from an intimate partner. For example, a simple act of requesting that a sexual partner use a condom may lead to violence against her (Weissman, 1991). Counseling women about safe sex and the risk of HIV and AIDS, without an understanding of the dynamics of power and control between them and their male partners, is irresponsible in that it does not account for the possible risks incurred from following such advice. Accordingly, some women's realities preclude their being able to follow their health care practitioner's advice. In fact, repeated noncompliance with safe sex instructions should be considered a signal that other factors are at play, and domestic violence should be considered one such possibility.

Partner notification of a woman's HIV-positive status also can result in battering. The batterer may believe that his partner's HIV status resulted from a sexual encounter with someone else, that she may hold him responsible for having transmitted the disease to her, or he may be fearful that she may have transmitted it to him. These or other reactions may increase the woman's risk when her partner has information about her HIV-positive status. Partner notification may discourage women from being screened and hence delay treatment for their disease (North & Rothenberg, 1993). Thus, policies are needed that facilitate practitioners' ability to identify women at high risk for HIV without endangering women's safety, thus promoting the intended effect of greater identification and treatment of HIV.

Pregnancy-Related Problems

Unique health-related problems are a risk for pregnant women. Younger, rather than older, pregnant women are at especially high risk of violence (McFarlane, 1991). The prevalence of physical or sexual abuse during pregnancy has been estimated to be 15.6% in a nationally representative sample (Gelles, 1990). Seventeen percent of a sample of pregnant women seeking prenatal care (McFarlane, Parker, Soeken, & Bullock, 1992) reported violence during their pregnancy, and 26% of this sample reported violence having occurred during the previous year. However, there is little or no evidence of increased violence due to pregnancy per se. Rather, the increased reporting of violence against pregnant women has been attributed to age: Younger women are more likely to become pregnant than are older women (Gelles, 1990). One exception is that men's report of violence is greater toward their pregnant, compared with nonpregnant, wives over the age of 25 years (Gelles, 1990).

Ethnic differences in violence victimization have been found among pregnant women. Berenson, Strglich, Wilkinson, and Anderson, (1991) found prevalence rates to be 3.5 times higher among pregnant White women than among pregnant Hispanic or African American women. Although McFarlane (1993) found that African American and White women had the same prevalence of abuse before and during pregnancy, the frequency and severity of abuse was worse among White women. For example, a significantly higher percentage (32.6%) of White women abused during pregnancy reported that their male partner had threatened to kill them, compared with African American (12.7%) and Hispanic (23.1%) women.

Battering during pregnancy can have significant health consequences to both the mother and the fetus. Women commonly report violence directed to the abdomen, especially during pregnancy. This results in significant morbidity and mortality to both mother and infant. These injuries can result in placental separation, antepartum hemorrhage, fetal fractures, rupture of the uterus, preterm labor, and low birth weight (Parker, McFarlane, & Soeken, 1994). The risks of battering to pregnant women obviously extend to the unborn child as well. Miscarriage is an event that can signal to the health care practitioner the presence of violence in a woman's life.

Violence toward women also is a factor in the level of prenatal care. A study of women seeking prenatal care indicated that those who were abused were twice as likely to delay prenatal care into the third trimester as those who were not abused (McFarlane et al., 1992). This delay, as well as the ongoing, recurrent abuse that they experience, may be one reason explaining increased rates of miscarriage, stillbirth, and low-birth-weight babies among these women. Without direct inquiry, violence as a risk factor for pregnancy-related health problems may go undetected.

Mental Health Problems

Even though victims of violence are more likely to seek medical than mental health treatment (Koss et al., 1990), mental health problems associated with violence against women have been more commonly recognized among professionals than have somatic complaints (Koss, 1994). Nevertheless, many women victimized by violence do not develop psychological symptoms. Some women's reactions can best be characterized as expected, normal, and healthy responses to violence (e.g., anger, fear, sadness). A variety of factors (e.g., violence-related factors such as the nature, severity, and circumstances of the violence; the nature of recovery environment; and individual factors) are thought to explain why some women experience more severe psychological reactions to violence than do others and why some appear to be more resistant to these long-lasting detrimental effects (Dutton & Goodman, 1994; Kemp, Green, Hovanitz, & Rawling, 1995).

Symptoms of psychological distress or dysfunction associated with violence against women have included posttraumatic stress disorder (Kemp et al., 1995; Kilpatrick & Resnick, 1994; Saunders, 1994); dissociation (Foa & Riggs, 1995); depression, low self-esteem, suicide, and grief (J. C. Campbell, 1989); anxiety and phobic reactions (Trimpey, 1989); sexual dysfunction (Apt & Huelbert, 1993); and substance abuse problems (Kilpatrick, 1990). Any of these symptoms should signal concern for the possibility of violence in the patient's life, either historically or contemporaneously.

These and other (Herman, 1993) psychological effects of violence may be played out in the dynamics of the relationship between the health care professional and the patient. Thus, they have particular relevance to the medical setting, especially when the physician or other health care worker fails to recognize the variety of psychological indicators (e.g., suspiciousness, hopelessness, or low self-worth) as being potentially influenced by the patient's history of violence. It should be clear that attention to the health and mental health impact of violence in the lives of women requires a broad lens. A focus broader than on injury, or even physical symptoms alone, is necessary to understand and then effectively provide health care to victims of violence.

Practitioner-Related Issues

The Role of the Health Care Professional

Many potential barriers prevent primary care providers from routinely screening their patients for the increasingly recognized problem of violence (Sugg & Inui, 1992). The provider's own lack of knowledge about domestic violence and myths about who at-risk patients are may result in inadequate identification. For example, victimization among patients from a higher socioeconomic status or who are professional colleagues may go undetected because of assumptions about who typically is and is not a victim of violence. Fear of offending a patient, uncertainty about what to do with the information obtained, frustration with the outcome, lack of support staff, and time constraints often are cited as reasons why screening for violence is neglected (Sugg & Inui, 1992).

Another constraint in working with victims of intimate violence can be the professional orientation of the health care worker. The biomedical model, especially as used by physicians and other health care professionals, tends to focus on the elicitation of physical complaints and their treatment (Mishler, 1981). As mentioned earlier, the problem of intimate violence requires a shift in orientation by the provider to a more integrative model that incorporates the psychological and physical aspects of the patient in the cultural, economic, and social contexts defining the battered woman's experience.

A common frustration experienced by health care providers is the reluctance of the battered woman to take their advice or direction. It is the patient herself, not the practitioner, who has control over her decision making. It is she who must decide whether she wants to leave the abusive partner, what this decision's impact on her family might be, and when it is safe to do so if she decides that is what she wants to do. This stance of assuming the battered woman's self-determination can be difficult, especially in instances of severe violence and injury or when the risk to children is apparent. The health care provider often must combat the inclination to "rescue" the battered woman by telling her what to do. Furthermore, failing in this effort, some practitioners may give up trying to be of assistance in the battered woman's struggle and direct their resulting anger or frustration toward the patient. The health care practitioner's role with regard to intimate violence can best be fulfilled by validating the battered woman's experience and educating the patient about her options and their implications.

In short, involvement of the health care professional in finding solutions to the problem of violence against women requires a role that attends to the victim of violence as a whole human being in a context in which the provider is willing to collaborate with her in working toward both safety and health for all family members. Furthermore, to have an impact on violence against women, the health care professional must be informed about domestic violence, its health consequences, community resources, and the local laws governing both criminal and civil remedies for battered women. Effective solutions to violence against women require involvement with other institutions (e.g., shelters, criminal justice, law enforcement). Furthermore, creating a discipline of informed health care practitioners competent to meet the enormous challenge that violence against women presents to the health care community requires thoughtful training beginning at the earliest levels and continuing throughout the professional life span.

Secondary Traumatic Stress

The secondary impact on professionals of violence and other forms of trauma resulting from their work with trauma victims recently has gained attention (Pearlman & Saakvitne, 1995). Such distress can negatively affect health care professionals' work with patients, as well as their interpersonal relationships with family and friends (Dutton & Rubinstein, 1995).

Recognizing that working with victims of violence can produce distress among health care professionals is an essential first step in responding effectively to it. Developing supportive work and personal environments that validate such reactions and provide emotional nurturance are avenues for intervention. Maintaining a balance between work and a personal life also is important for buffering one from negative secondary traumatic effects of violence. Critical-incident stress debriefing (Hiley-Young & Gerrity, 1994) has been an important intervention for front-line rescue workers and other medical personnel confronted not only with major disasters but also with violent events. Although this intervention has yet to be validated empirically, it shows promise for workplace interventions.

Health Care, Health Promotion, and Prevention

The U.S. Public Health Service has called for the screening and detection of the problem of domestic violence in its Healthy People 2000 national health promotion objectives (Public Health Service, 1991). The health care cost to America associated with the failure to develop mechanisms for preventing violence is enormous. Research has demonstrated the increased health costs (Cohen, Miller, & Rossman, 1994; Koss, 1994), as well as additional costs to the community (e.g., through lost worker productivity; Stets & Straus, 1990), associated with violence against women. By necessity, the health care system must play a role in the prevention and treatment of violence.

Attention to the differences that describe women's lives (e.g., language, ethnicity, cultural background, immigration status, age, sexual orientation) is essential for both an understanding of the impact of violence on women's health and for the development of interventions. Additional barriers often face battered women of color, including African American (D. Campbell, 1993; Sullivan & Rumptz, 1994), Native American (Bohn, 1993), Hispanic (Kantor, Jasinski, & Aldarondo, 1994), and Asian American (Ho, 1990) women. Recent female immigrants (Rodriguez, 1993) face barriers of language, immigration status, and acculturation. Among other obstacles, older battered women (Jones, Dougherty, Scheible, & Cunningham, 1988) face the obstacle of invisibility when health care professionals fail to acknowledge that partner abuse can also occur among this group. Battered lesbians (Kanuha, 1990; Renzetti, 1992) face obstacles that may make identification of intimate violence difficult. Sensitivity to these differences in the development of protocols for identification, assessment, and interventions in the health care system influence the extent to which these efforts to combat violence against women are effective.

Identification

Health care professionals' identification of women who have been victimized by violence is a necessary first step in providing appropriate prevention and treatment interventions. As mentioned earlier, routine screening has been recommended by a number of medical associations and the U.S. Public Health Service. In this section, we discuss several considerations for instituting routine screening for violence victimization in medical settings.

1. *Ask about violent behavior.*   Do not require the patient to label her violent experiences. Rather, ask about the violent or abusive behaviors specifically, such as whether the patient has ever been hit, punched, or choked. This approach to identification does not require victims of violence to identify themselves as such and thus allows less opportunity for distortion. Sometimes battered victims or rape victims do not identify violence against them as "violence" or "rape" even when it is severe. Thus, questions such as "Have you ever been raped?" or "Have you ever been a victim of domestic violence?" fail to identify some women who do not think of themselves as being in these categories but whose experience would nevertheless be consistent with these labels. Some victims report that they begin to label their experiences as abuse only after having escaped the violence and having reflected on their experience through support groups or with the help of friends.

2. *Inquire about sexual and physical violence or abuse.*   In partner relationships, sexual abuse may occur in the absence of other forms of physical abuse (Russell, 1982). Thus, questions concerning physical violence, only, will miss patients whose assault has been primarily sexual. Furthermore, it is important to be sensitive to the possibility of violence or abuse across the life span, especially because some childhood victims of abuse are at greater risk for victimization during adulthood. Finally, for some women who have experienced both physical and sexual abuse, it is the sexual abuse that has the most intense impact. Recognizing only physical abuse may fail to identify a woman who is at high risk on the basis of sexual, rather than nonsexual, violence or abuse.

3. *Inquire about the patient's fear of being hurt by an intimate partner.*   In addition to asking about actual acts of prior violence, it also is useful to ask patients specifically about their fears of being hurt by an intimate partner in the future. Such questions identify situations in which serious forms of actual physical abuse may have not yet occurred but for which patients may nevertheless be at high risk (e.g., the batterer has made threats to kill; has used severe violence toward previous partners, even if the violence has not yet become serious in the current relationship).

4. *Inquire about verbal aggression and psychological abuse.*   Empirical data support the link between verbal aggression in relationships and subsequent physical violence (Murphy & O'Leary, 1989). The pattern of actual violence may be episodic, but psychologically abusive behaviors (e.g., emotional abuse, intimidation, and threats), against the backdrop of a credible threat of violence (e.g., previous violent behavior), nevertheless maintain the dynamic of the batterer's power and control over the patient. Furthermore, screening that involves psychologically abusive behaviors can identify patients who are at high risk for violence but who have not yet

been actually physically assaulted. This is especially important when the focus is on secondary, not merely tertiary, prevention.

5. *Do not exempt patients from screening on the basis of assumption of risk.*   Regardless of whether the screening is brief or more detailed, it is important that no patients be exempt because of an assumption that they are not at risk. There is no socioeconomic, professional, cultural, age, gender, or language group in which domestic violence does not occur.

Assessment of Intimate Violence in the Health Care Setting

Identification of victims of violence is merely the first step in the health care worker's response to violence. Physical assessment should include a full body examination, noting both current and previous injuries. The remainder of the discussion focuses on assessment of risk and harm attributable to the violence.

1. *Determine the level of current or anticipated danger to the patient and her family.*   An adequate assessment of current danger for battered women includes inquiry about a variety of factors that have been empirically or clinically associated with severe violence or homicide (Saunders, 1995). Several salient factors associated with homicide of a battered woman or by a battered woman toward the abuser have been incorporated into a danger assessment instrument (J. Campbell, 1995). These include increased frequency and severity of violence; the presence of high-risk violent behaviors (e.g., choking), such as the batterer's history of sexual assault, use of alcohol or drugs, threat of suicide, access to weapons, abuse during pregnancy, jealousy, and violence toward children or toward others outside the home; and the battered woman's risk of suicide.

2. *Assess the risk to children and other family members.*   When a positive identification of domestic violence is made, the physician or health care practitioner should routinely determine the potential risks that also confront children and other family members, including elders. The overlap between the occurrence of domestic violence and child abuse (McKibben, De Vos, & Newberger, 1991; Straus & Gelles, 1990), for example, underscores the necessity for such assessment. Furthermore, assessment of the negative effects of violence should not be limited to the direct risks of violence victimization and should also consider the effects of violence that result from a child's attempting to protect the mother, hearing the violence through bedroom walls, and seeing the aftermath of violence (e.g., the mother's black eye), that is, from being an innocent bystander. Although the child is usually battered by the same person who is abusive to the mother, the child also can be victimized by the mother herself (Straus & Gelles, 1990).

3. *Assess the level of emotional distress.*   Having evaluated the level of danger, the medical practitioner also should assess the patient's level of psychological or emotional distress related to violence to determine whether a more comprehensive mental health assessment and intervention is necessary. Acute distress requires an immediate response by the

health care professional. An adequate assessment provides a map for needed interventions. The following is a brief discussion of prevention and treatment interventions available in the medical setting.

Interventions for Intimate Violence

A variety of interventions for domestic violence are possible within a health care setting. Described next, these include emotional support and mental health intervention, safety planning, patient education, legal advocacy, referral, and documentation.

  1. *Emotional support and mental health intervention.* One of the most important interventions a health care practitioner can provide is support and alliance with the woman who is being battered (Dutton, 1992; Schechter, 1987). Even when there is little else that a battered woman wants or accepts from a practitioner, support and alliance are resources that can be carried with her as she attempts to deal with her situation. The potential impact of this intervention can be underestimated by health care professionals. We have observed both supportive and negative encounters between violence victims and health care providers that have had a particularly powerful impact. For example, a health care practitioner's inability to make eye contact with a battered woman with obvious physical injuries, an off-hand comment that minimizes the danger to the patient and her children, or a dominant and coercive effort to get a battered woman to report her victimization to police can further isolate the patient.

  Mental health interventions can be delivered by specially trained health care practitioners. For example, critical-incident stress debriefing (Ragaisis, 1994) and rape crisis counseling have been adapted for use in a medical setting. The goal of such interventions is to provide the patient with an opportunity to "debrief" from a violent incident, to "normalize" potentially distressing and puzzling psychological reactions by providing information about the normal course of traumatic stress responses, and to develop an opportunity for referral and follow-up when needed. These interventions have been commonly provided in medical settings for rape victims, but intervention models for other types of violence victims (e.g., battered women) are less common.

  2. *Safety planning.* Safety planning is perhaps one of the most important of the interventions in the health care setting. It is a process in which the health care practitioner assists the battered woman both in identifying danger and in developing strategies to respond to it. Different types of plans are needed depending on whether the danger exists within the context of remaining in an abusive relationship, leaving an abusive relationship, or remaining out of a relationship the battered woman has already left. For example, safety plans for battered women who are still in an abusive relationship may include strategies for survival and resistance, whereas those for battered women remaining outside the relationship may include strategies for avoidance and escape.

  A safety plan should be built on the foundation of information about the battered woman's actual experience with violence, her prior strategies for dealing with the violence and their outcomes, her perceptions of current danger, and the resources available to her. It requires time, support, and encouragement to assist a battered woman in considering the actions she may take to increase her own (and her children's) safety.

An important caveat is in order. A safety plan should never be used to persuade a battered woman that she is safer than she believes herself to be. It should not be used to encourage her to remain in an abusive situation. Nevertheless, even when a battered woman has decided to remain in an abusive relationship, discussing a safety plan to protect her against recurrent violence is important.

The process of developing a safety plan is perhaps even more useful than the actual plan, which may require frequent changes to accommodate the batterer's unpredictable violence and abuse. Through a discussion between the health care practitioner and patient identifying signals of danger, strategies that have previously proved to be successful or unsuccessful, and existing options and current resources, both the practitioner and the battered woman herself can gain a new perspective. On the basis of this new vantage point, new options may become apparent or old ones may appear more feasible. Furthermore, options that appeared to be feasible may no longer seem so after deliberate consideration.

One measure of success of a safety plan is whether it develops an increased sense of empowerment for the patient, not that it gives her control over the batterer's behavior but over her own stance against it. A safety plan is not intended to be a road map for solving all the problems in a patient's life. It can, however, be a vehicle for decreasing feelings of isolation, powerlessness, or immobility in the patient's effort to deal with her violent situation. Most important, a safety plan can be the factor that makes the difference between acting quickly in a threatening situation because of planning and preparation (e.g., extra car keys available, arrangements for emergency housing made, important papers and cash available) versus being paralyzed by the intense feelings that accompany violence.

3. *Patient education.*   Intimate violence affects all members of the family unit. Various models exist to help prevent violence among families. For example, Elliott (1993) developed one model based on the family life cycle for organizing violence prevention in a primary care practice. Using brochures, posters, videos, and other patient education materials is another route to domestic violence prevention. Making such material available in waiting rooms, bathrooms, and examining rooms captures an important opportunity for patient education.

4. *Legal advocacy.*   Providing information about the legal system to women who are victims of violence is an important intervention, even for patients not intent on using the legal system at the current time. Such information can provide the patient with options useful for a later time. Greater awareness of available legal remedies (e.g., civil protection orders, criminal prosecution, civil litigation) and the procedures necessary to ac-

cess them (e.g., where to go, what to do, how long it takes) can increase access to the legal system for those who may need it.

5. *Referral*.   Establishing and maintaining ongoing contact with referral sources (e.g., rape crisis centers, battered women's shelters, prosecutor's offices) is important in providing a network of referral services that can truly provide a safety net to battered women. It is especially important to maintain regular contact with the local battered women's shelters because they are often able to provide an immediate resource to battered women leaving the medical setting.

6. *Documentation*.   Documentation, in a way that does not depersonalize or objectify the victim, is a key issue in health care involving violence against women (Warshaw, 1993). Precise documentation of physical abuse is frequently lacking in the medical record (e.g., identification of offender), especially when the perpetrator is an intimate partner. Vague language (e.g., "hit by fist") fails to convey information about who was responsible for engaging in hitting behavior and under what circumstances. Records should contain a complete medical history using the patient's words to describe the chief complaint or the patient's statement in cases in which she may not refer to violence as the presenting problem. The history should recount the events that led to injury or illness. The use of weapons should be specifically recorded. Documentation of past medical history should include reference to previous episodes of abuse, what injuries were sustained, and whether medical attention was sought. A description of injuries that is as detailed as possible is most useful, including the type, number, size, and location of injuries. The use of a drawing or body map is helpful, as are photographs. When photographs are used they should be taken with color film before medical treatment. The patient's face should be included in at least one picture. To illustrate the size of an injury, a coin or ruler may be held next to the injured area. If the police are involved, the name of the investigating officer should be included in the record. A psychosocial history, including the presence of children in the home and previous suicide attempts, also should be included. The medical record may prove invaluable when victims of violence seek legal remedies against their abusers or when they face charges related to their own protection.

Conclusion

Violence against women is a serious health care issue. Recognition of the multiple avenues by which violence may affect women's health and well-being, followed by the implementation of multidisciplinary interventions geared to the various needs of a diverse population of victimized women within different types of health care settings, are necessary steps in a comprehensive approach to medical intervention. Breaking existing social barriers to effective medical interventions requires institutionalization of values that do not tolerate violence against women as an invisible shield between the patient and her health care provider. The cost to individual women's lives, to the health care system in America, and to society at large is simply too great to do otherwise.

References

Abbott, J., Johnson, R., Koziol-McLain, J., & Lowenstein, S. R. (1995). Domestic violence against women: Incidence and prevalence in an emergency department population. *Journal of the American Medical Association, 273,* 1763–1767.

Apt, C., & Huelbert, D. F. (1993). The sexuality of women in physically abusive marriages: A comparative study. *Journal of Family Violence, 8,* 57–69.

Bachman, R. (1994). *Violence against women: A national crime victimization survey report* (Publication No. NCJ-145325). Washington, DC: U.S. Department of Justice.

Berenson, A., Strglich, N., Wilkinson, G., & Anderson, G. (1991). Drug abuse and other factors for physical abuse in pregnancy among White non-Hispanic, Black, and Hispanic women. *Americal Journal of Obstetrics and Gynecology, 164,* 491–499.

Bohn, D. K. (1993). Nursing care of Native American battered women. *AWHONNS Clinical Issues in Perinatal and Women's Health Nursing, 4,* 424–436.

Calhoun, K. S., & Atkeson, B. M. (1991). *Treatment of rape victims: Facilitating psychosocial adjustment.* Elmsford, NY: Pergamon Press.

Campbell, D. (1993). Nursing care of African-American battered women: Afrocentric perspectives. *AWHONNS Clinical Issues in Perinatal and Women's Health Nursing, 4,* 407–415.

Campbell, J. (1995). Prediction of homicide of and by battered women. In J. D. Campbell (Ed.), *Assessing dangerousness* (pp. 96–113). Thousand Oaks, CA: Sage.

Campbell, J. C. (1989). A test of two explanatory models of women's responses to battering. *Nursing Research, 38,* 18–24.

Cohen, M. A., Miller, T. R., & Rossman, S. B. (1994). The costs and consequences of violent behavior in the United States. In A. J. Reiss, Jr., & J. A. Roth (Eds.), *Understanding and preventing violence: Vol 4. Consequences and control* (pp. 67–166). Washington, DC: National Academy Press.

Courtois, C. (1988). *Healing the incest wound.* New York: Norton.

Drossman, D. A., Leserman, J., & Nachman, G. (1990). Sexual and physical abuse in women with functional or organic gastrointestinal disorders. *Annals of Internal Medicine, 113,* 828–833.

Dutton, M. A. (1992). *Empowering and healing the battered woman.* New York: Springer.

Dutton, M. A., & Goodman, L. A. (1994). Posttraumatic stress disorder among battered women: Analysis of legal implications. *Behavioral Sciences and the Law, 12,* 215–234.

Dutton, M. A., & Rubinstein, F. L. (1995). Working with people with PTSD: Research implications. In C. R. Figley (Ed.), *Compassion fatigue: Coping with secondary traumatic stress disorder in those who treat the traumatized* (pp. 82–100). New York: Brunner/Mazel.

Elliott, B. A. (1993). Prevention of violence. *Primary Care: Clinics in Office Practice, 20*(2), 277–288.

Foa, E. B., & Riggs, D. S. (1995). Posttraumatic stress disorder following assault: Theoretical considerations and empirical findings. *Current Directions in Psychological Science, 4*(2), 61–65.

Gelles, R. J. (1990). Violence and pregnancy: Are pregnant women at greater risk of abuse? In M. A. Straus & R. J. Gelles (Eds.), *Physical violence in American families: Risk factors and adaptations to violence in 8,145 families* (pp. 279–286). New Brunswick, NJ: Transaction Books.

Gondolf, E. W. (1988). *Battered women as survivors: An alternative to treating learned helplessness.* Lexington, MA: Lexington Books.

Hamberger, L. K., Saunders, D. G., & Hovey, M. (1992). Prevalence of domestic violence in community practice and rate of physician inquiry. *Family Medicine, 24,* 283–287.

Herman, J. L. (1993). Sequelae of prolonged and repeated trauma: Evidence for a complex posttraumatic syndrome (DESNOS). In J. R. T. Davidson & E. B. Foa (Eds.), *Posttraumatic stress disorder: DSM-IV and beyond* (pp. 213–235). Washington, DC: American Psychiatric Press.

Hiley-Young, B., & Gerrity, E. T. (1994). Critical incident stress debriefing (CISD): Value and limitations in disaster response. *NCP Clinical Quarterly, 4*(2), 17–19.

Ho, C. K. (1990). An analysis of domestic violence in Asian American communities: A multicultural approach to counseling. In L. S. Brown & M. P. P. Root (Eds.), *Diversity and complexity in feminist therapy* (pp. 129–150). New York: Harrington Park Press.

Jones, J., Dougherty, J., Scheible, D., & Cunningham, W. (1988). Emergency department protocol for the diagnosis and evaluation of geriatric abuse. *Annals of Emergency Medicine, 17,* 1006–1015.

Kantor, G. K., Jasinski, J. L., & Aldarondo, E. (1994). Sociocultural status and incidence of marital violence in Hispanic families. *Violence and Victims, 9,* 207–222.

Kanuha, V. (1990). Compounding the triple jeopardy: Battering in lesbian of color relationships. In L. S. Brown & M. P. P. Root (Eds.), *Diversity and complexity in feminist therapy* (pp. 169–184). New York: Harrington Park Press.

Kemp, A., Green, B. L., Hovanitz, C., & Rawlings, E. I. (1995). Incidence and correlates of posttraumatic stress disorder in battered women: Shelter and community samples. *Journal of Interpersonal Violence, 10,* 43–55.

Kilpatrick, D. G. (1990, August). *Violence as a precursor of women's substance abuse: The rest of the drugs-violence story*. Paper presented at the 98th Annual Convention of the American Psychological Association, Boston.

Kilpatrick, D. G., & Resnick, H. S. (1994, September). *Victimization and posttraumatic stress disorder*. Paper presented at the Drug Addiction Research and Health of Women Meeting, Washington, DC.

Koop, C. E. (1985). *The Surgeon General's workshop on violence and public health*. Washington, DC: Government Printing Office.

Koss, M. P. (1994). The negative impact of crime victimization on women's health and medical use. In A. J. Dan (Ed.), *Reframing women's health: Multidisciplinary research and practice* (pp. 189–200). Thousand Oaks, CA: Sage.

Koss, M. P., Goodman, L. A., Browne, A., Fitzgerald, L. F., Keita, G. P., & Russo, N. F. (1994). *No safe haven: Male violence against women at home, at work, and in the community*. Washington, DC: American Psychological Association.

Koss, M. P., Woodruff, W. J., & Koss, P. G. (1990). Relation of criminal victimization to health perceptions among women medical patients. *Journal of Counseling and Clinical Psychology, 58,* 147–152.

Langan, P. A., & Innes, C. A. (1986). *Preventing domestic violence against women* (Bureau of Justice Statistics special report). Washington, DC: U.S. Department of Justice.

McFarlane, J. (1991). Violence during teen pregnancy: Health consequences for mother and child. In B. Levy (Ed.), *Dating violence* (pp. 136–141). Seattle, WA: Seal Press.

McFarlane, J. (1993). Abuse during pregnancy: The horror and the hope. *AWHONNS Clinical Issues in Perinatal and Women's Health Nursing, 4,* 350–362.

McFarlane, J., Parker, B., Soeken, K., & Bullock, L. (1992). Assessing for abuse during pregnancy: Severity and frequency of injuries and associated entry into prenatal care. *Journal of the American Medical Association, 267,* 3176–3178.

McKibben, L., De Vos, E., & Newberger, E. H. (1991). Victimization of mothers of abused children: A controlled study. In R. L. Hamptom (Ed.), *Black family violence: Current research and theory* (pp. 75–84). Lexington, MA: Lexington Books.

Mishler, E. (1981). Viewpoint: Critical perspectives on the biomedical model. In E. Mishler (Ed.), *Social contexts of health, illness and patient care* (pp. 1–19). Cambridge, MA: Harvard University Press.

Murphy, C. M., & O'Leary, K. D. (1989). Psychological aggression predicts physical aggression in early marriage. *Journal of Consulting and Clinical Psychology, 57,* 579–582.

North, R. S., & Rothenberg, K. H. (1993). Partner notification and the threat of domestic violence against women with HIV infection. *New England Journal of Medicine, 329,* 1194–1196.

Parker, B., McFarlane, J. U., & Soeken, K. (1994). Abuse during pregnancy: Effects on maternal complications and birth weight in adult and teenage women. *Obstetrics and Gynecology, 84*, 323–328.

Pearlman, L., & Saakvitne, K. W. (1995). *Trauma and the therapist.* New York: Norton.

Public Health Service. (1991). *Healthy People 2000—National health promotion and disease prevention objectives: Full report, with commentary* (DHHS Publication No. PHS-91-50212, pp. 237–238). Washington, DC: U.S. Department of Health and Human Services.

Ragaisis, K. M. (1994). Critical incident stress debriefing: A family nursing intervention. *Archives of Psychiatric Nursing, 8*, 38–43.

Renzetti, C. M. (1992). *Violent betrayal: Partner abuse in lesbian relationships.* Newbury Park, CA: Sage.

Rodriguez, R. (1993). Violence in transience: Nursing care of battered migrant women. *AWHONNS Clinical Issues in Perinatal and Women's Health Nursing, 4*, 437–440.

Russell, D. E. H. (1982). *Rape in marriage.* New York: Macmillian.

Saunders, D. G. (1986). When battered women use violence: Husband-abuse or self-defense? *Violence and Victims, 1*, 47–60.

Saunders, D. G. (1994). Posttraumatic stress symptom profiles of battered women: A comparison of survivors in two settings. *Violence and Victims, 9*, 125–138.

Saunders, D. G. (1995). Prediction of wife assault. In J. C. Campbell (Ed.), *Assessing dangerousness: Violence by sexual offenders, batterers, and child abusers* (pp. 68–95). Thousand Oaks, CA: Sage.

Saunders, D., Hamberger, K., & Hovey, M. (1993). Indicators of woman abuse based on a chart review at a family practice center. *Archives of Family Medicine, 1993, 2*, 537–543.

Schechter, S. (1987). *Guidelines for mental health practitioners in domestic violence cases.* Washington, DC: National Coalition Against Domestic Violence

Stark, E., Flitcraft, A., & Frazier, W. (1979). Medicine and patriarchal violence: The social construction of a "private" event. *International Journal of Health Services, 9*, 461–493.

Stark, E., Flitcraft, A., Zuckerman, D., Grey, A., Robison, J., & Razier, W. (1981). *Wife abuse in the medical setting: An introduction for health personnel* (Monograph No. 7). Washington, DC: Office of Domestic Violence.

Stets, J., & Straus, M. A. (1990). Gender differences in reporting marital violence and its medical and psychological consequences. In M. A. Straus & R. J. Gelles (Eds.), *Physical violence in American families: Risk factors and adaptations in 8,145 American families* (pp. 151–166). New Brunswick, NJ: Transaction Books.

Straus, M., & Gelles, R. (1990). How violent are American families? Estimates from the National Family Violence Resurvey and other studies. In M. A. Straus & R. J. Gelles (Eds.), *Physical violence in American families: Risk factors and adaptations to violence in 8,145 families* (pp. 113–131). New Brunswick, NJ: Transaction Publishers.

Sugg, N. K., & Inui, T. (1992). Primary care physicians' response to domestic violence. *Journal of the American Medical Association, 267*, 3157–3160.

Sullivan, C. M., & Rumptz, M. H. (1994). Adjustment and needs of African-American women who utilized a domestic violence shelter. *Violence and Victims, 9*, 275–286.

Trimpey, M. L. (1989). Self-esteem and anxiety: Key issues in an abused women's support group. *Issues in Mental Health Nursing, 10*, 297–308.

Warshaw, C. (1993). Domestic violence: Challenges to medical practice. *Journal of Women's Health, 2*, 73–80.

Weissman, G. (1991). AIDS prevention for women at risk: Experience from a national demonstration research project. *Journal of Primary Prevention, 12*, 49–52.

Zierler, S., Feingold, L., Laufer, D., Velentgas, P., Krantrowitz-Gordon, I., & Mayer, K. (1991). Adult survivors of childhood sexual abuse and subsequent risk of HIV infection. *American Journal of Public Health, 81*, 572–575.

5

Gender Differences in Patient–Physician Communication

Debra L. Roter and Judith A. Hall

The past decade has broadened definitions of quality in medical care from adherence to narrow technical standards to include providers' interpersonal skills in all aspects of the medical interview (Lipkin, Quill, & Napodano, 1984). Attracting the most speculation as a likely source of gender differences in the quality of care is the nature of doctor–patient communication. There has been long-standing debate on whether the content and quality of communication from female physicians provide a different therapeutic milieu from that of male physicians, one that would allow for more open exchange and ultimately more comprehensive diagnosis and treatment (Weisman & Teitelbaum, 1989). The consequences of these differences may be considerable. Recent evidence of disparities in the use of major diagnostic and therapeutic interventions for women compared with men, particularly in terms of coronary artery disease, may be a reflection of failed communication between patients and their physicians that might be partly attributable to gender (Steingart et al., 1991; Verbrugge & Steiner, 1981).

The purpose of this chapter is to summarize the literature related to gender and health care communication between patients and physicians and to explore the relevance of these findings to medical practice. The potential clinical implication of these studies for individual patients is significant in terms of satisfaction, compliance with therapeutic recommendations, and, ultimately, morbidity and mortality (Roter & Hall, 1992). Although relative newcomers to the mainstream of medicine, women currently make up nearly 50% of those entering medical school. Long-standing patterns of practice and even the very philosophy of medicine, which has almost by definition been male medical practice, can be expected to change.

Although this chapter is limited to research on gender and its role in patient–physician communication during routine medical visits, we hope that the discussion will encourage work on other variables likely to affect patient–physician communication, such as race or ethnicity and social class.

Attitudes, Biases, and Stereotypes in the Medical Encounter

In general, the interpersonal style of women compared with men is more engaging, warm, and immediate (Hall, 1984, 1987). There are gender differences in the use of smiling, facial expressiveness, gazing, interpersonal distance, body posture, touch, and bodily gestures, with women in each case showing a behavior pattern that suggests more accessibility and friendliness. Women often find it easier to disclose information about themselves in conversation (Aries, 1987) and encourage and facilitate others to talk to them more freely and in a warmer and more immediate way (Hall, 1984). Women both decode the meanings of nonverbal cues (e.g., facial expressions, tone of voice) better than men do, and women express emotions more accurately through nonverbal cues than men do (Hall, 1984). There is also evidence that women are more egalitarian in their social relations, taking greater pains to downplay their own status in an attempt to equalize status with a partner, in contrast to men's tendency to assert status differences (Eagly & Johnson, 1990).

Despite clear gender differences in routine conversation, there is some question about whether "female-linked" conversational styles would be evident in medical students or, if present, whether such styles would survive the long medical training process. Both selection of medical students and the educational process, it is argued, act to equalize differences in the personal characteristics of physicians (Kurtz & Chalfant, 1991). The kinds of students selected into the highly competitive world of medicine are characterized by their task orientation, single-mindedness, narrow focus, and quantitative skills, attributes that are associated with both "maleness" and the middle class (Mechanic, 1978). These selection criteria continue to be in place despite the sevenfold increase in female medical students since the 1960s (Jonas & Etzel, 1988).

The experience of medical education further shapes values and styles. The effect of personal characteristics may give way under the pressures of training in "physician-appropriate" attitudes and behaviors. Physician-appropriate attitudes and behaviors, however, are not gender neutral; they are masculine in nature. In describing her experiences as a medical student at Harvard in the 1980s, Klass (1987) found that she was challenged to think and act in terms she described as "macho." The heart of machismo, Klass maintained, is a view of medicine as conquest. It is the doctor against the patient, the doctor against any other expert consultant, and, ultimately, the doctor against disease itself. The effect of this culture is to turn both male and female medical students into macho doctors valuing "winning" rather than partnership and collaboration (Klass, 1987).

Finally, physicians, like others in American society, are influenced by prejudice and stereotypes. The range of physicians' political and ideological beliefs indicates a broad spectrum of responses to patient groups (Waitzkin, 1985). Physicians generally have scored about the same as nonphysicians in surveys reflecting negative attitudes toward elderly, poor, and physically unattractive people (Marshal, 1981; Nordholm, 1980; Price, Desmond, Snyder, & Kimmel, 1988). Furthermore, physicians (at least male physicians) have reported liking male patients better than they like female patients, even when controlling for age, education, income, and occupation (Hall, Epstein, DeCiantis, & McNeil, 1993).

These findings may not be wholly applicable to the most recent medical cohorts, which are increasingly female. Female physicians have a reputation for being less egotistical and more humanistic, sensitive, and altruistic than their male counterparts (Day, Norcini, Shea, & Benson, 1989). Female physicians also have reported liking their patients more than male physicians did (Hall et al., 1993).

Patients may bring prejudices and stereotypes to the medical encounter, just as physicians do. Because male physicians are the traditional norm, patients may equate "professionalism" and expertise with the male characteristics of dominance and task orientation. To the extent that a patient believes a doctor is by definition male or "malelike," the patient may be hypercritical of female doctors regardless of what they do. The role demands of medicine—exerting professional authority, minimizing psychological immediacy, and emphasizing task orientation—are at odds with the "female" role, which implies partnership and affiliation, emotional responsiveness, and a process orientation. Female physicians are caught between two opposing roles with conflicting expectations to "act like a woman" and "act like a doctor." Complicating the role conflicts even more is that, at this time in history, many patients will be considerably older than the female physician, resulting in an even greater challenge for her to appear authoritative.

Research in Doctor–Patient Communication

Typical studies of doctor–patient communication will have ample numbers of male and female patients, but the physician sample is usually small and predominantly male (Roter, Hall, & Katz, 1988). Therefore, the crucial question of how physician and patient gender both contribute to shaping the process of care is hard to address and is studied infrequently. Predictably, the majority of studies have focused on the effect of patient gender on the care process, with too few female physicians included to do more than generalize broadly to patients' experience with male physicians.

Although there are relatively few direct observational studies that have addressed physician gender issues in doctor–patient communication, it is well documented that visits with male and female physicians differ in terms of time spent with patients. Nationwide data from the National Ambulatory Medical Care Survey (NAMCS), reflecting office-based visits, showed that female physicians spent more time on average with patients than did male physicians (23.5 vs. 18.7 min, respectively; Cypress, 1980). Moreover, female physicians spent more time with female compared with male patients, whereas male physicians showed an opposite trend, resulting in as much as a 6-min differential in visit length. Female physicians in the NAMCS also reported providing psychotherapy or therapeutic listening to their primary care patients more often than did male physicians. Particularly for female physicians in practice for several years and those over the age of 35, the rate of therapeutic listening was more than double that for male physicians of the same age (Cypress, 1980).

Similar but much more detailed results were reported by Bensing, Van den Brink-Muinen, and de Bakker (1993) in a Dutch study of gender differences in general practitioners' care of patients with psychosocial problems. Analysis was based on 161 physicians keeping detailed report logs on all patients seen over a 3-month period. The investigators found that female physicians spent more time with their patients, engaged in more counseling and listening, were less likely to write prescriptions, and were less interventionist in their recommendations. The authors concluded that female physicians were more caring than curing, more passively guiding than actively intervening, and more open to discussing the psychosocial context of the patient's health problems than were male physicians.

Because office logs are based on recall and self-report rather than observation, one does not know how visits with male and female physicians might differ with regard to the communication content or process. Such insight is provided by direct observation studies. Analysis of verbal content has revealed that the visits with female doctors are more positive, more attentive and nondirective (Meeuwesen, Schaap, & Van Der Staak, 1991), more likely to involve the expression of feelings, and more likely to include empathy (Scully, 1980; Wasserman, Inui, Barriatura, Carter, & Lippincott, 1984). In a similar vein, Shapiro (1990) found that the female residents were judged significantly higher than male residents on a range of psychosocially pertinent communication skills, including awareness of nonverbal cues, discussing the impact of the disease on patient and family, eliciting the patient's rationale for the visit, and avoiding criticism.

Male and female physicians also may differ in how they convey instructions to patients. West (1993) found that male physicians were more likely to speak in an authoritative manner, using explicit commands when giving instructions to patients, than female physicians. By contrast, female physicians were more likely to cast their instructions and directives as proposals, engaging the patient in a more balanced partnership than would the male physicians. Meeuwesen et al. (1991) also noted that male general practitioners were more directive and informative than female general practitioners.

Limiting their sample to new patients, and randomly assigning patients without a stated preference for a particular physician to male and female residents, Bertakis, Helms, Callahan, Azari, and Robbins (1995) added several new insights into the understanding of gender dynamics. Unlike other studies, little difference was found in length of visit by physician gender. The authors suggested that when patient gender and health status are controlled, both male and female physicians spend equivalent amounts of time in their first medical visits with patients. Despite little difference in time of visit, several areas of communication differed. Female physicians spent a greater proportion of the visit on preventive services and in discussion of family information than their male colleagues, whereas male physicians devoted more of the visit to history taking.

Studies of Physician Gender

We have conducted two observational studies of physician gender differences in communication during medical encounters. The first study was a multisite national study of communication dynamics (Roter, Lipkin, & Korsgaard, 1991). A total of 537 medical visits were audiotaped for the study, 104 visits with the study's 26 female physicians and 423 visits with the study's 101 male physicians.

The audiotapes were content coded by trained coders using the Roter Interaction Analysis System (RIAS). This system codes each statement or complete thought expressed during the visit, by either patient or physician, into mutually exclusive and exhaustive categories (Roter & Hall, 1989). For summary purposes, the content categories can be combined into larger categories that share common meaning across studies. There are 12 physician and 8 patient categories of this type, and each category was calculated separately for the history, examination, and concluding segments of the visits. The categories included in this analysis are shown in Table 1.

The findings of the study were consistent with those of the NAMCS as well as several other observational studies (Bensing et al., 1993; Blanchard et al., 1983; Gray, 1982; Meeuwesen et al., 1991) in showing that female physicians spent several minutes more with their patients, especially female patients, than did their male colleagues. Much of the difference in length of visit could be attributed to talk during the history-taking segment of the visit, in which female physicians talked about 40% more than male physicians. However, they certainly did not do all the talking. When with female physicians, both male and female patients talked about 58% more than when with male physicians. The patient's gender affected physicians' talk: Both male and female doctors talked more (about 15%) to male than to female patients. However, patient gender did not affect the patient's own talk patterns much.

Not only did female physicians talk more, but their talk also fell into particular categories of interaction. Female physicians engaged in significantly more positive talk, partnership building, question asking, and information giving, both biomedical and psychosocial. Patients, both male and female, engaged in significantly more positive talk and more partnership talk and were more likely to ask questions, give substantially more biomedical information, and engage in almost twice as much psychosocial talk when with female rather than male physicians. Roter et al. (1991) also found that the ratio of physician-to-patient talk differed, with female physicians tending to have more even exchanges (an average ratio of 1.28:1) than male physicians (an average ratio of 1.38:1). This effect was especially evident when female doctors were with female patients (an average ratio of 1.23:1), in contrast to male physicians with male patients (an average ratio of 1.41:1).

It was striking that the differences evident in the content of the visit were most marked during the history-taking segment. These differences may indicate that female physicians were more attuned to early-visit

Table 1. Studies Examining Gender Effects in Medical Communication

Communication variables	Studies documenting differences	
	Physician	Patient
Socioemotional aspects of communication		
Laughter, agreements, approval	Stewart (1983) Meeuwesen et al. (1991) Roter et al. (1991) Hall et al. (1994a)	Hall and Roter (1995) Stewart (1983) Meeuwesen et al. (1991)
Disagreements and criticisms	Shapiro (1990)	Hall and Roter (1995)
Express tension		Stewart (1983)
Feelings or emotions, concern	Hooper et al. (1982) Roter et al. (1991)	Stewart (1983) Meeuwesen et al. (1991)
Empathy, reassurance	Scully (1980) Wasserman et al. (1984) Meeuwesen et al. (1991)	Hooper et al. (1982) Hall and Roter (1995)
Asking for understanding or opinion, paraphrase, interpretation, establishing partnership	Roter et al. (1991) Hall et al. (1994a) Hall et al. (1994b)	Stewart (1983)
Prompters of active listening		
Attentiveness	Meeuwesen et al. (1991) Hall et al. (1994a)	
Nondirectiveness, authoritative manner	Meeuwesen et al. (1991) West (1993)	
Disclosures	Meeuwesen et al. (1991) Candib (1987)	

Smiles	Hall et al. (1994a)	
Nods	Hall et al. (1994a)	
Voice quality		
Friendliness	Hall et al. (1994a)	Hall and Roter (1995)
Anxiety	Hall et al. (1994a)	Hall and Roter (1995)
Interest	Hall et al. (1994a)	
Awareness of nonverbal cues	Shapiro (1990)	
Technical aspects of communication Questions across all topics	Roter et al. (1991) Bertakis et al. (1995)	Wallen et al. (1979) Pendleton and Bochner (1980)
Information and counseling on medical condition or therapeutic regimen	Roter et al. (1991) Meeuwesen et al. (1991) Hall et al. (1994a)	Wallen et al. (1979) Pendleton and Bochner (1980) Hooper et al. (1982) Waitzkin (1985) Meeuwesen et al. (1991)
Psychosocial counseling regarding emotional issues and prevention, lifestyle	Shapiro (1990) Roter et al. (1991) Bensing et al. (1993)	Bertakis et al. (1995)
Length of visit	Cypress (1980) Blanchard et al. (1983) Meeuwesen et al. (1991) Roter et al. (1991) Bensing et al. (1993) Hall et al. (1994a) Bertakis et al. (1995)	

negotiation and more patient centered in their interviewing styles than male physicians. The large differences in patient talk with female physicians, particularly the high frequency of psychosocial talk and partnership building, also suggest that these visits were more patient centered and mutually participatory for both male and female patients.

In the second study, both nonverbal and verbal communication were examined using videotape analysis (Hall, Irish, Roter, Ehrlich, & Miller, 1994a). In this study, a sample of 25 male and 25 female physicians were each videotaped with a male and female patient during routine outpatient visits ($N = 100$). The sample included physicians at all levels of experience (first- through third-year residents, fellows, junior, and senior staff).

Assessment of verbal communication included the same RIAS categories mentioned earlier and a separate measure of active listening and facilitation (backchannel usage; i.e., uh-huh, yeah, go on, okay, right). The use of technical jargon also was assessed. Nonverbal behaviors were coded or rated for smiles, nods, and voice quality. Voice quality was rated by groups of judges after listening to short excerpts of audiotape that had been electronically filtered to mask the verbal content but to preserve the qualities of speech that convey affect (Rosenthal, Hall, DiMatteo, Rogers, & Archer, 1979).

Again, visits with female physicians were different from those with male physicians: Visits to female physicians were more talkative for both the physician (by 24%) and patient (by 40%). Female physicians engaged in more positive talk, partnership statements, and questions, both biomedical and psychosocial. Patients of female physicians expressed more partnership statements and gave more medical information to their doctors. Hall et al. (1994a) found that female physicians were much more likely to "listen actively" by giving facilitating backchannel cues to the patient.

Inspection of the physician-to-patient talk ratios found the same pattern as in the first study (Roter et al., 1991), but there were even more dramatic differences between male and female doctors. The talk ratio indicated an almost even distribution of speech between female physicians and their patients (an average ratio of 1.10:1, with the lowest ratios evident with female patients, 1.04:1), whereas less even distributions were evident in visits of male physicians (an average ratio of 1.23:1, with the highest ratios in visits with male patients, 1.27:1).

The nonverbal exchanges also demonstrated a significantly different pattern for male and female physicians. Female physicians smiled and nodded more than male physicians and created a more responsive and positive atmosphere during the visit. Voice tone also differed, but not in the way one might expect based on the verbal analysis. Female doctors were judged as sounding more anxious and interested throughout the visit and less friendly late in the visit. Thus, female physicians' voice tone seems to convey more negativity, relative to male physicians, than their verbal exchanges and body language indicate. This was especially evident when female doctors were with male patients.

The seeming discrepancy between voice tone and verbal and body cues is similar to findings in the earliest filtered speech study (Hall et al., 1981). Hall et al. found that medical visits in which the physician was judged as having an angry and anxious voice tone, combined with positive words, was associated with greater patient satisfaction and appointment keeping. The combination may be interpreted as conveying simultaneous warmth, professionalism, and concern—a message of "I'm on your side, I'm competent to take care of you, and I take your problems very seriously."

Patient Gender

In contrast to a strong pattern of findings evident in the studies of physician gender, patient effects appear to be less strong and less consistent. Waitzkin (1985) found that female compared with male patients were given more information and that the information was given in a more comprehensible manner (i.e., technical explanations also were clarified or reworded in simpler language; Waitzkin, 1985). In an analysis of the same data set, it was demonstrated that the greater information directed at women was largely in response to women's tendency to ask more questions in general and to ask more questions after the doctor's explanation (Wallen, Waitzkin, & Stoeckle, 1979). Highly similar findings emerged in an English study of general consultations (Pendleton & Bochner, 1980).

Several other investigators have reported that female patients receive more positive talk and more attempts to include them in discussion than male patients. Stewart's (1983) analysis of approximately 140 audiotapes of primary care practice indicated that physicians were more likely to express positive "tension release" (laughter mainly) with female patients and also were more inclined to ask them about their opinions or feelings. Female patients were more likely to express tension and ask for help than were male patients, but male patients appeared to be more likely to take the initiative by being more assertive in presenting suggestions and opinions and more negative in presenting disagreements and antagonisms.

A direct observational study of approximately 150 patient visits similarly showed that female patients had more positive experiences with their physicians than did male patients (Hooper, Comstock, Goodwin, & Goodwin, 1982). Information giving was significantly higher, and there was greater use of empathy with female than male patients. Physicians also were less likely to interrupt the visit by leaving the room when with female than male patients. In a similar vein, Meeuwesen et al. (1991) found in a Dutch patient sample that women were more likely to be affectively engaged with their physician, both agreeing and disagreeing more than male patients.

In the two studies designed to explore patient and physician gender effects on communication, described earlier, it was found that patient gender effects were dwarfed by the much greater magnitude and frequency of physician effects (Hall et al., 1994a; Roter et al., 1991). The patient gender effects that were found were largely for socioemotional variables, whether verbal (as reflected in content coding) or nonverbal (as in the filtered speech analysis).

A separate study conducted with 69 primary care physicians and more than 600 patients in community practices in the greater Baltimore metropolitan area indicated that women sent and received more verbal statements related to emotional concerns, more positive talk, and more disagreements (Hall & Roter, 1995). Female patients used a more interested and more anxious voice tone, as reflected in filtered speech. Women also expressed a greater preference for a feeling-oriented physician on the postvisit questionnaire. Moreover, the physicians (more than 90% of whom were male) were less aware of the satisfaction level of female than male patients. Because male patients' satisfaction was more clearly revealed through their verbal and nonverbal behavior than was female patients' satisfaction, physicians' reduced sensitivity to the satisfaction of women could have been due partly to a failure of the women to clearly communicate their satisfaction.

Inspection of Table 1 suggests that findings relating communication to gender in the affective domain are more often reported and more consistent than those in the technical or task domain, although clearly both types of effects are evident. On the whole, we would agree with Hooper et al. (1982) in concluding that communication differences attributable to gender are certainly present in medical encounters and that these differences may be to the advantage of female patients. Female patients appear to have a more positive experience than is typical for male patients.

Summary of Patient Outcomes Related to Communication

A meta-analysis of 41 videotape or audiotape studies of medical visits showed consistent relationships between patient outcomes and physicians' interviewing skills (Hall, Roter, & Katz, 1988; Roter et al. 1988). In this analysis, three dimensions of patient-centered communication—informativeness, interpersonal rapport, and partnership building—were consistently associated with patient satisfaction, recall of medical information, compliance, and health outcomes. All three of these dimensions are characteristic of female medical exchanges, suggesting that the patients of female rather than male physicians are more likely to reap these benefits as a result of their medical visit.

Conclusion

In integrating our findings, we suggest several conclusions about gender and patient–physician communication. First, female physicians conduct medical visits differently than male physicians, especially during the history-taking segment. The opening of the interview has been identified as a critical time for negotiation regarding which problems and concerns are important and will be included in the visit's agenda (Beckman & Frankel, 1984). This negotiation process addresses several key tasks, as identified by Frankel and Beckman (1989), including defining the patient's specific concerns, understanding the concerns in the patient's life context, developing rapport, creating a therapeutic alliance, and using time efficiently. All these tasks, as well as the specific aspects of communication characteristic of female physicians, may be seen as being consistent with a type of interviewing that best facilitates use of the biopsychosocial model (Morgan & Engel, 1969) and reflects patient-centered interviewing (Stewart et al., 1995).

Second, patients (both male and female) talk more, and appear to participate more actively, in the medical dialogue when with a female physician. Thus, patients appear to take advantage of the opportunity afforded by female doctors to truly engage in the medical dialogue by fully telling their story. Relatedly, status-equalizing behaviors are evident in female physicians' visits with both their male and female patients. It was found that female physicians downplay their professional status in two ways: They use more partnership talk and they are less likely to dominate the visit verbally, as evidenced by a more equal doctor-to-patient talk ratio. Weisman and Teitelbaum (1989) suggested that status congruence would enhance mutual participation in the medical visit and that same-gender encounters would evidence the highest status congruence. We think that they were partially right. Mutual participation in medical visits is enhanced when status congruence is greatest, but congruence is not dependent on participants being of the same gender. Rather, congruence is highest when the gap between professional and lay status is narrowed, as reflected in the female physicians' visits.

Barsky (1981) noted that although psychosocial issues are important concerns for patients in primary care, patients' reluctance to voice these problems early in the visit (or at all) creates a "hidden agenda" of patient concerns. This suggests that there may be less hiding or delay of psychosocial concerns when patients are with female physicians.

Third, the few findings attributed to main effects of patient gender were outweighed by the many effects of physician gender. Female patients appear to be more emotionally engaged in the visits than their male counterparts: They are more positive and sometimes more negative, they disclose more emotional concerns, and they receive more empathy and reassurance. They are also likely to ask more questions and receive more information than male patients.

Fourth, there is a suggestion that female patients especially benefit from exchanges with female physicians because of longer and more affectively positive visits.

Hall et al. (1994a) found that positive statements, nodding, and verbal facilitators were most frequent in female–female combination. Moreover, the ratio of physician-to-patient talk reflected the most equal distribution of talk in the female–female dyads. It seems that in the female–female cell, there was a special priority given to eliciting and hearing the patient's story. Heightened patient disclosure in this cell is consistent with findings from the self-disclosure literature (Aries, 1987; Dindia & Allen, 1992) and anecdotal observations by female physicians concerning their tendency to share personal experience with patients (especially female patients) and have these reciprocated (Candib, 1987). These visits were longer than others by several minutes.

Fifth, female physicians have a particularly complex pattern of communication with male patients.

In the Hall et al. (1994a) study, it seemed that visits of female physicians with male patients were psychologically demanding for both participants. During these visits physicians smiled the most and used the most negative voice tone. Negative voice tone, we believe, conveys seriousness and conscientiousness, and in this case may reflect a special attempt to convey a professional demeanor. It also is possible that discrepant communication could signify role strains felt by female physicians (particularly when faced with male patients who were often considerably older than themselves), producing anxious discomfort and leading to negative cues in the voice as well as high levels of anxious smiling (Hall & Halberstadt, 1986).

Sixth, more needs to be learned about the relation of physician and patient gender to satisfaction. Research suggests that although patients clearly value communication behaviors more common with female physicians and reflecting patient centeredness (Hall et al., 1988), patient satisfaction is often no greater with female than with male physicians, and it is sometimes significantly worse (Hall, Irish, Roter, Ehrlich, & Miller 1994b). Indeed, it was found that patients showed markedly lower satisfaction ratings when with younger female physicians. Perhaps shedding some light on this finding, Fennema, Meyer, and Owen (1990) concluded that patients with a preference for a male physician regarded humaneness as a male physician trait, whereas patients preferring a female physician saw humaneness as a female physician trait. Preference often was based on one's own gender.

Several factors may be involved in reaching an understanding of the satisfaction findings, including prejudice, unmeasured communication differences, differences in technical quality, and unfulfilled expectations on the part of patients.

In conclusion, the results presented throughout this chapter do not imply that all female physicians are good communicators, or better than male physicians, or that there are not many excellent male communicators. A clear and practical implication of these findings is in terms of the need for physician training and curriculum development in the area of communication for all physicians, those in training as well as in practice. It has been found that practicing physicians can be effectively trained to use more patient-centered skills and, once trained, that these skills are evident in their routine practice (Levinson & Roter, 1993; Roter et al., 1995).

Many have argued that medicine is in transition. The traditional biomedical model is giving way to a more patient-centered, biopsychosocial model. With growing numbers of women in the medical workforce and in leadership positions in academic medicine, it is reasonable to predict that the coming transformation in medicine will carry a female signature.

References

Aries, E. (1987). Gender and communication. *Review of Personality and Social Psychology,* *7,* 149–176.

Barsky, A. J. (1981). Hidden reasons some patients visit doctors. *Annals of Internal Medicine, 94,* 492–498.

Beckman, H. B., & Frankel, R. M. (1984). The effect of physician behavior on collection of data. *Annals of Internal Medicine, 101,* 692–696.

Bensing, J., Van den Brink-Muinen, A., & de Bakker, D. (1993). Differences between male and female general practitioners in the care of psychosocial problems. *Medical Care, 31,* 219–229.

Bertakis, K. D., Helms, L. J., Callahan, E. J., Azari, R., & Robbins, J. A. (1995). The influence of gender on physician practice style. *Medical Care, 33,* 407–416.

Blanchard, C. G., Ruckdeschel, J. C., Blanchard, E. B., Arena, J. G., Saunders, N. L., & Malloy, E. D. (1983). Interactions between oncologists and patients during rounds. *Annals of Internal Medicine, 99,* 694–699.

Candib, L. M. (1987). What doctors tell about themselves to patients: Implications for intimacy and reciprocity in the relationship. *Family Medicine, 19,* 23–30.

Cypress, B. K. (1980). *Characteristics of visits to female and male physicians* (Vital and Health Statistics, Series 13, No. 49). Hyattsville, MD: U.S. Department of Health and Human Services.

Day, S. C., Norcini, J. J., Shea, J. A., & Benson, J. A. (1989). Gender differences in the clinical competence of residents in internal medicine. *Journal of General Internal Medicine, 4,* 309–312.

Dindia, K., & Allen, M. (1992). Sex differences in self-disclosure: A meta-analysis. *Psychological Bulletin, 112,* 106–124.

Eagly, A. H., & Johnson, B. T. (1990). Gender and leadership style: A meta-analysis. *Psychological Bulletin, 108,* 233–256.

Fennema, K., Meyer, D. L., & Owen, N. (1990). Sex of physician: Patients' preferences and stereotypes. *Journal of Family Practice, 30,* 441–445.

Frankel, R., & Beckman, H. (1989). Evaluating the patient's primary problem(s). In M. Stewart & D. Roter (Eds.), *Communicating with medical patients* (pp. 86–98). Newbury Park, CA: Sage.

Gray, J. (1982). The effect of the doctor's sex on the doctor-patient relationship. *Journal of Royal College of General Practitioners, 32,* 167–169.

Hall, J. A. (1984). *Nonverbal sex differences: Communication accuracy and expressive style.* Baltimore: Johns Hopkins University Press.

Hall, J. A. (1987). On explaining gender differences: The case of nonverbal communication. *Review of Personality and Social Psychology, 7,* 177–200.

Hall, J. A., Epstein, A. M., DeCiantis, M. L., & McNeil, B. J. (1993). Physicians' liking for their patients: More evidence for the role of affect in medical care. *Health Psychology, 12,* 140–146.

Hall, J. A., & Halberstadt, A. G. (1986). Smiling and gazing. In J. Hyde & M. C. Linn (Eds.), *The psychology of gender: Advances through meta-analysis* (pp. 136–158). Baltimore: Johns Hopkins University Press.

Hall, J. A., Irish, J. T., Roter, D. L., Ehrlich, C. M., & Miller, L. H. (1994a). Gender in medical encounters: An analysis of physician and patient communication in a primary care setting. *Health Psychology, 13,* 384–392.

Hall, J. A., Irish, J. T., Roter, D. L., Ehrlich, C. M., & Miller, L. H. (1994b). Satisfaction, gender, and communication in medical visits. *Medical Care, 32,* 1216–1231.

Hall, J. A., & Roter, D. L. (1995). Patient sex and communication with physicians: Results of a community-based study. *Women's Health, 1,* 77–95.

Hall, J. A., Roter, D. L., & Katz, N. R. (1988). Meta-analysis of correlates of provider behavior in medical encounters. *Medical Care, 26,* 657–675.

Hall, J. A., Roter, D. L., & Rand, C. S. (1981). Communication of affect between patient and physician. *Journal of Health and Social Behavior, 22,* 18–30.

Hooper, E. M., Comstock, L. M., Goodwin, J. M., & Goodwin, J. S. (1982). Patient characteristics that influence physician behavior. *Medical Care, 20,* 630–638.

Jonas, H. S., & Etzel, S. (1988). Undergraduate medical education. *Journal of the American Medical Association, 260,* 1063–1071.

Klass, P. (1987). *A not entirely benign procedure: Four years as a medical student.* New York: Signet Books.

Kurtz, R. A., & Chalfant, H. P. (1991). *The sociology of medicine and illness* (2nd ed.). Boston: Allyn & Bacon.

Levinson, W., & Roter, D. (1993). The effects of two continuing medical education programs on communication skills of practicing primary care physicians. *Journal of General Internal Medicine, 8,* 318–324.

Lipkin, M., Jr., Quill, T. E., & Napodano, R. J. (1984). The medical interview: A core curriculum for residencies in internal medicine. *Annals of Internal Medicine, 100,* 277–284.

Marshal, V. W. (1981). Physician characteristics and relationships with older patients. In M. R. Haug (Ed.), *Elderly patients and their doctors* (pp. 94–118). New York: Springer.

Mechanic, D. (1978). *Medical sociology.* New York: Free Press.

Meeuwesen, L., Schaap, C., & Van Der Staak, C. (1991). Verbal analysis of doctor-patient communication. *Social Science & Medicine, 32,* 1143–1150.

Morgan, W. L., & Engel, G. L. (1969). *The clinical approach to the patient.* Philadelphia: W. B. Saunders.

Nordholm, L. A. (1980). Beautiful patients are good patients: Evidence for the physical attractiveness stereotype in first impressions of patients. *Social Science & Medicine, 14A,* 81–83.

Pendleton, D. A., & Bochner, S. (1980). The communication of medical information in general practice consultations as a function of patients' social class. *Social Science and Medicine, 14A,* 669–673.

Price, J. H., Desmond, S. M., Snyder, F. F., & Kimmel, S. R. (1988). Perceptions of family practice residents regarding health care and poor patients. *Journal of Family Practice, 27,* 615–621.

Rosenthal, R., Hall, J. A., DiMatteo, M. R., Rogers, P. L., & Archer, D. (1979). *Sensitivity to nonverbal communication: The PONS Test.* Baltimore: Johns Hopkins University Press.

Roter, D., & Hall, J. A. (1989). Studies of doctor-patient interaction. *Annual Review of Public Health, 10,* 163–180.

Roter, D. L., & Hall, J. A. (1992). *Doctors talking to patients/ patients talking to doctors: Improving communication in medical visits.* Westport, CT: Auburn House.

Roter, D. L., Hall, J. A., & Katz, N. R. (1988). Patient-physician communication: A descriptive summary of the literature. *Patient Education and Counseling, 12,* 99–119.

Roter, D. L., Hall, J. A., Kern, D. E., Barker, L. R., Cole, K. A., & Roca, R. P. (1995). Improving physicians' interviewing skills and reducing patients' emotional distress: A randomized clinical trial. *Archives of Internal Medicine, 155,* 1877–1884.

Roter, D., Lipkin, M., Jr., & Korsgaard, A. (1991). Sex differences in patients' and physicians' communication during primary care medical visits. *Medical Care, 29,* 1083–1093.

Scully, D. (1980). *Men who control women's health: The miseducation of obstetrician-gynecologists.* Boston: Houghton Mifflin.

Shapiro, J. (1990). Patterns of psychosocial performance in the doctor-patient encounter: A study of family practice residents. *Social Science and Medicine, 31,* 1035–1041.

Steingart, R. M., Packer, M., Hamm, P., et al. (1991). Sex differences in the management of coronary artery disease. *New England Journal of Medicine, 325,* 226–330.

Stewart, M. (1983). Patient characteristics which are related to the doctor-patient interaction. *Family Practice, 1,* 30–35.

Stewart, M., Brown, B. J., Weston, W. W., McWhinney, I., McWilliam, C. L., & Freeman, T. R. (1995). *Patient-centered medicine: Transforming the clinical method.* Thousand Oaks, CA: Sage.

Verbrugge, L. M., & Steiner, R. P. (1981). Physician treatment of men and women patients: Sex bias or appropriate care? *Medical Care, 19,* 609–632.

Waitzkin, H. (1985). Information-giving in medical care. *Journal of Health and Social Behavior, 26,* 81–101.

Wallen, J., Waitzkin, H., & Stoeckle, J. D. (1979). Physician stereotypes about female health and illness. *Women and Health, 4,* 135–146.

Wasserman, R. C., Inui, T. S., Barriatua, R. D., Carter, W. B., & Lippincott, P. (1984). Pediatric clinicians' support for parents makes a difference: An outcome-based analysis of clinician-parent interaction. *Pediatrics, 74,* 1047–1053.

Weisman, C. S., & Teitelbaum, M. A. (1989). Women and health care communication. *Patient Education and Counseling, 13,* 183–199.

West, C. (1993). Reconceputalizing gender in physician-patient relationships. *Social Science and Medicine, 36,* 1047–1052.

Part II

Lifestyle Factors and Health

6

Alcohol Problems in Women: Risk Factors, Consequences, and Treatment Strategies

Nancy D. Vogeltanz and Sharon C. Wilsnack

Until recently, most scientific knowledge about alcohol use disorders was based on clinical studies of men, and generally, alcoholism was considered a "male" disorder. Since the early 1970s, research on women's drinking has increased dramatically, but important questions about the etiology, characteristics, and treatment of women's alcohol use problems remain unanswered. Approximately 10–15% of women in the United States report some type of drinking-related problem, and about 4%, or 4 million, women will meet diagnostic criteria for alcohol abuse or dependence. In addition to the large numbers of women with primarily alcohol-related problems, it is clear that heavy drinking is implicated in a wide range of women's physical and psychological problems.

In the first part of this chapter, we present an overview of patterns of use, etiology, correlates, and consequences of women's alcohol problems. Although the prevalence of drinking and drinking problems in women varies considerably by age and other sociodemographic characteristics, overall, rates have remained relatively stable over recent decades. The etiology of alcohol use disorders is multidetermined and may involve complex interactions between biological and environmental variables. Although it is likely that some etiological factors may be common to women and men (e.g., genetic risk), several psychosocial and demographic variables associated with problem drinking in women appear to be distinct from the correlates of men's alcohol problems. It is clear that women who drink heavily are at serious risk for a number of adverse biomedical and psychosocial consequences. However, some recent research suggests that moderate drinking may have potential health benefits for some women.

In the last half of the chapter, we provide health professionals with information on ways to identify and treat alcohol use disorders and problem drinking in women. Evidence suggests that physicians and other

The national longitudinal survey reported in this chapter was supported by Research Grant R37 AA04610 from the National Institute on Alcohol Abuse and Alcoholism of the National Institutes of Health.

health professionals in non-alcohol-specific treatment settings may serve as a "front line" for identifying female problem drinkers and that more efforts to screen for problem drinking in women should occur in these settings. Significant barriers to women's alcohol treatment exist, and suggestions are made for increasing treatment utilization. Although there is no "best" treatment for alcohol problems generally, recommendations are offered about possible treatment strategies that may increase retention and treatment effectiveness in women.

A 1990 report by the Institute of Medicine declared that the large majority of alcohol problems are not created by "alcoholics" but by people with a broad range of maladaptive problem drinking behaviors. Reflecting the need for a broader understanding of alcohol problems, this chapter is not directed primarily at understanding women's "alcoholism" or alcohol use disorders. Instead, it is concerned with a wide range of alcohol involvement and emphasizes the need for proper assessment and interventions for women with less serious alcohol problems. Because of space limitations, and because alcohol is clearly the largest single drug of abuse among American women, our chapter focuses primarily on issues related to women's use and abuse of alcohol while recognizing that many women abuse alcohol as part of a broader pattern of multiple substance abuse (Graham, Carver, & Brett, 1995; S. C. Wilsnack, 1995).

Patterns of Alcohol Use and Alcohol Problems in Women

Prevalence of Women's Drinking and Alcohol Disorders

The majority of adult women in the United States drink alcohol at least occasionally. However, the percentage of female drinkers varies considerably by age. A 1991 general population survey of women's drinking indicated the following distribution of drinkers by age: 74% of women aged 21–34; 65% of women aged 35–49; 52% of women aged 50–64; and 29% of women aged 65 and older (S. C. Wilsnack, Vogeltanz, Diers, & Wilsnack, 1995). The prevalence of alcohol use disorders among women also varies by age. In the 1992 National Longitudinal Alcohol Epidemiologic Survey (Grant et al., 1994), 12-month prevalence estimates of alcohol abuse and dependence disorders (fourth edition of the *Diagnostic and Statistical Manual of Mental Disorders* [*DSM–IV*; American Psychiatric Association, 1994]) for women were 9.8% for ages 18–29; 4.0% for ages 30–44; 1.5% for ages 45–64; and 0.3% for ages 65 and older. Overall, about 4% of women met diagnostic criteria for alcohol abuse or dependence. In comparison, approximately 11% of men were diagnosed with a *DSM–IV* alcohol use disorder, resulting in a male-to-female ratio of almost 3:1. Prevalence estimates were slightly higher in the National Comorbidity Survey, in which 14.1% of men and 5.3% of women aged 15–54 years had a *DSM–III-R* (American Psychiatric Association, 1987) diagnosable alcohol use disorder (Kessler et al., 1994).

Women's Problem Drinking

Drinking behavior falls on a wide continuum with alcohol abuse or dependence at one extreme. Between any drinking (nonabstention) and diagnosable alcohol disorders is problem drinking. Problem drinking can be defined as drinking behavior that results in adverse physiological, psychological, or social consequences but that does not result in a diagnosable alcohol disorder. Some definitions include heavy drinking as "problem" drinking because of its strong association with problem consequences and the potential for adverse consequences (Dawson, Grant, & Harford, 1995). Rates of problem drinking are considerably higher than rates of alcohol disorders. In a 1991 national survey (S. C. Wilsnack et al., 1995), one or more drinking-related problems in the 12 months before the interview was reported by 26% of women aged 21–30; 17% of women aged 31–40; 10% of women aged 41–50; 7% of women aged 51–60; and 3% of women aged 61–70. The percentages of women reporting at least one symptom of alcohol dependence ranged from 22% of the youngest women to 1% of the women aged 61–70 years.

Despite concerns about an "epidemic" in women's drinking in the past two decades, data from 15 U.S. population surveys conducted between 1971 and 1991 indicate that the prevalence of drinking and heavy drinking in women has remained relatively stable over this 20-year period, with slight increases in the 1970s, followed by modest decreases in the 1980s (S. C. Wilsnack, Wilsnack, & Hiller-Sturmhofel, 1994).

Etiological Factors in the Development of Alcohol Problems in Women

Accounting for Gender Differences in the Prevalence of Alcohol Use Disorders

When prevalence rates of a disorder vary greatly between genders, etiological hypotheses may be generated by studying these differences. The causes of alcohol abuse and dependence are complex, but it is generally believed that once an individual begins drinking, a pattern of heavy use and then prolonged heavy use leads to the social and physiological consequences that characterize alcohol abuse and dependence. As discussed earlier, men drink more heavily than women. In addition, although presumably some heavy drinkers do not experience adverse consequences of their drinking, most studies have shown a relationship between heavy consumption and alcohol problems. For example, Dawson et al.'s (1995) analyses of data from the 1988 National Health Interview Survey found that men were much more likely to drink heavily and that heavy drinking among both men and women was strongly associated with adverse consequences of drinking. The adverse-consequence domain most strongly associated with heavy drinking was impaired control over drinking, followed by continued drinking despite problems and hazardous drinking (e.g., driving while intoxicated). The weakest association was between heavy drinking and tolerance or withdrawal, suggesting that for both women and men, considerable alcohol-related impairment in functioning occurs either before or in the absence of symptoms of physiological dependence. As discussed later, if assessment of alcohol problems relies heavily on questions about physiological withdrawal and tolerance symptoms (i.e., end-stage or severe alcohol problems), earlier stage or less severe problem drinking may go underdetected.

Heavier drinking in men may help to explain gender differences in the prevalence of alcohol use disorders, but this does not explain why men drink more heavily than women. As discussed later in this chapter, a biological explanation proposes that the greater bioavailability of alcohol in women makes them more sensitive to the effects of alcohol and thus may allow women to better moderate alcohol use. Psychosocial explanations focus on the relative social consequences of heavy drinking in women compared with men. According to these explanations, society is generally not as accepting of women's heavy drinking, and women may moderate their drinking to avoid violating societal norms (Blume, 1991; Gomberg, 1988). If this theory is correct, women who drink heavily should experience an equal or higher level of negative consequences of their drinking than men. In support of this view, several studies have indicated that at equal levels of heavy drinking, women and men experienced about the same level of drinking-related problems (Hilton, 1987) or that women experienced more drinking-related problems than men (Knupfer, 1984). Dawson et al. (1995) reported that heavy-drinking women reported more problems than men in almost all *DSM–IV* alcohol dependence problem domains (including social and occupational impairment), and at least one study showed that heavy-drinking women were more likely than men to experience problems related to fighting with spouses, friends, or family (S. C. Wilsnack, Wilsnack, & Klassen, 1986).

By contrast, the results of a large national survey showed that, after controlling for frequency of intoxication and for uncontrolled behavior while drinking, women were less likely than men to report that friends and family had told them they should cut down on their drinking (Robbins & Martin, 1993). In the same study, women reported less frequent intoxication than men, and, controlling for the frequency of intoxication, women reported less uncontrolled behavior (e.g., aggressive feelings and arguments, rapid drinking, memory loss) while drinking than did men.

It is possible that these gender differences in drinking styles (i.e., women less aggressive and more "controlled") somewhat reduce or mitigate the negative social reactions that otherwise might be expected based on greater societal disapproval of women's drinking. It may be that women's perceptions of societal disapproval or stigma modify their behavior more than actual experiences of criticism or rejection from friends and family. In our 1991 national survey (S. C. Wilsnack, 1996), for example, although female respondents themselves were more disapproving of intoxication in women (65% said they strongly disapproved of a woman getting drunk at a party, whereas 58% strongly disapproved of a drunken man), these differences were considerably larger for women's perceptions of how other people would judge the same behavior (50% felt other people would strongly disapprove of a woman getting drunk at a party versus 30% perceiving strong disapproval of a drunken man; all $ps < .001$). This same self-imposed stigma, shame, and embarrassment about drinking may help explain why women are reluctant to seek treatment for alcohol use problems and why women more often choose health and mental health settings than substance abuse settings for assistance (Duckert, 1987).

Genetic and Learning Models

There is evidence for a genetically transmitted contribution to alcohol use disorders in both women and men, although some (McGue & Slutske, 1996) but not all (Heath, Slutske, & Madden, 1997) researchers believe that the genetic contribution may be weaker in women than men. Much of the variance in women's alcohol problems is likely due to environmental factors or to the interaction between inherited vulnerabilities and environmental factors. Learning theories postulate that alcohol problems derive from learned maladaptive uses of alcohol that result from the positively reinforcing aspects of drinking (e.g., pleasant physiological and social effects), the negatively reinforcing aspects (e.g., tension reduction and coping), or modeling (e.g., peer or partner pressure). Cognitive theories emphasize that problem drinking may result from positive expectations and beliefs that drinking will result in beneficial effects.

Demographic and Psychosocial Risk Factors

Regardless of the specific learning or cognitive mechanisms involved, several correlates or predictors of women's alcohol problems have been identified that support the role of environmental influences. Some of the most consistent and significant sociodemographic and psychosocial correlates of women's alcohol problems are reviewed next.

Age, ethnicity, employment, and marital status. Age is a potent predictor of alcohol use and alcohol problems in women, with women in their 20s and 30s consistently reporting higher rates of alcohol disorders and problem drinking than women in older age groups (Grant et al., 1994). Women over age 65 report the lowest rates of drinking, problem drinking, and alcohol disorders of any age group, but older women's drinking may be more risky because of their greater vulnerability to the physiological effects of alcohol, their decreased total body water content, and the greater likelihood that they may be using prescription drugs (Graham et al., 1995; S. C. Wilsnack et al., 1995).

White women are most likely to report problem drinking and alcohol use disorders, followed by Hispanic women; African American women are the least likely (Grant et al., 1991; Williams & DeBakey, 1992). One of the strongest predictors of heavier drinking among ethnic minority women is acculturation, the process by which an immigrant population acquires the attitudes, values, and behavior of a new culture (Gilbert & Collins, 1997). Studies examining the relationship between women's drinking and employment status have shown that women who are employed outside the home do not differ in rates of problem drinking from homemakers (Shore, 1992). However, women who have fewer social roles and responsibilities (e.g., being unmarried or unemployed) are more likely to report problem drinking than are women with multiple roles (R. W. Wilsnack & Cheloha, 1987), and women who work with predominantly male coworkers are likely to drink more than women with predominantly female coworkers (Hammer & Vaglum, 1989).

The relationship between marital status and women's problem drinking is complex. Most surveys have indicated higher rates of problem drinking among divorced or separated women, compared with married women, but a 1991 national survey showed that cohabiting women were the most likely of all marital status groups to report heavy drinking, drinking problems, and alcohol dependence symptoms (S. C. Wilsnack, 1995). One study showed that married women were less likely than unmarried women to report heavy and problem drinking but that those married women who did drink heavily were more likely than unmarried heavy-drinking women to experience problem consequences (Lozina, Russell, & Mudar, 1995).

Partner's drinking. The finding that heavy-drinking married women were more likely than unmarried women to experience problem consequences may reflect complex interactions between a woman's drinking behavior and that of her husband or partner. Numerous studies have shown strong positive associations between women's drinking and their partner's drinking, with recent evidence suggesting that each partner probably influences the drinking behavior of the other (Roberts & Leonard, 1997). The mechanisms involved are not clearly understood, but it seems likely that modeling, social pressures, changes in drinking opportunities, and more generalized relationship conflict and distress make having a problem-drinking spouse or partner an important risk factor for women's problem drinking. It also has been found that discrepant drinking patterns between women and their partners (i.e., infrequent-drinking husband with a heavy-drinking wife or vice versa) are associated with increased drinking problems and marital distress (R. W. Wilsnack & Wilsnack, 1990).

Childhood victimization. Childhood sexual abuse has been associated with alcohol abuse in women in several clinical and nonclinical studies (see B. A. Miller, Downs, & Testa, 1993). In a nationally representative survey that collected personal interview data on childhood sexual abuse, a history of childhood sexual abuse was strongly associated with several problem-drinking indicators after controlling for several demographic variables (S. C. Wilsnack, Vogeltanz, Klassen, & Harris, 1997). The relationship of childhood victimization to subsequent development of alcohol problems was recently evaluated with a sample of women and men who had experienced substantiated occurrences of childhood neglect, abuse (including both physical and sexual abuse), or both between 1967 and 1971. Although no relationship was found between alcohol problems and childhood victimization for men, a significant relationship was found for women after controlling for family history of alcohol or drug problems, poverty, race, and age (Widom, Ireland, & Glynn, 1995).

Although it seems clear that a history of childhood sexual abuse or other forms of childhood victimization puts women at risk for later alcohol problems, the path by which this develops is unclear. Possible paths include the use of alcohol to cope with sexual dysfunction or with negative affectivity resulting from sexual abuse in childhood, or excessive alcohol use as part of a nonconventional or maladaptive lifestyle that also includes early and active sexual behavior.

Adult violent victimization. Women's risks for physical and sexual assault are increased when the perpetrator of the assault has been drinking or when the woman herself has been drinking, is a problem drinker, or both (Martin, 1992). Moreover, a recent national survey indicated that women who experienced violent victimizations in adulthood, including rape, sexual assault, or homicide of a family member or close friend, were four times as likely as nonvictims to report two or more serious alcohol-related problems after their violent experiences (Kilpatrick, Edmonds, & Seymour, 1992). Thus, alcohol abuse appears to be both a risk factor for and a potential consequence of violent victimization in adult women.

Sexual dysfunction. Women in treatment for alcohol use problems have reported higher rates of sexual dysfunction than women in the general population (Schaefer & Evans, 1987). In a 1981 general population survey, heavier-drinking women were more likely to report sexual dysfunction than moderate-drinking women (Klassen & Wilsnack, 1986). Heavy or problematic drinking may cause sexual dysfunction because of physiological impairment, a decreased ability to form intimate relationships, or both (N. S. Miller & Gold, 1988). In addition, sexual dysfunction may cause or contribute to alcohol abuse if alcohol is used as a way to cope with impaired sexual functioning. Longitudinal data suggest that sexual dysfunction may be a robust predictor of women's continued (nonremitting) problem drinking over time (S. C. Wilsnack, Klassen, Schur, & Wilsnack, 1991).

Depression and anxiety. The most common comorbid disorders occurring in women with alcohol use disorders are depression and anxiety disorders, whereas the most common comorbid disorders in alcoholic men are antisocial personality disorder and other substance use disorders (Helzer & Pryzbeck, 1988). Longitudinal analyses from several national surveys suggest that depression may be both a risk factor and a consequence of alcohol abuse in women (Hartka et al., 1991). Similarly, Kushner, Sher, and Beitman's (1990) review of the literature on anxiety disorders among women with alcohol problems concluded that agoraphobia and social phobia most often precede alcohol problems (i.e., women may use alcohol to self-medicate their anxious symptoms) but that panic disorder may more often be a consequence of pathological drinking.

Regardless of whether depression and anxiety precede or follow problem drinking, several studies suggest that alcoholics with comorbid depression or anxiety have more severe problems and worse treatment outcomes (Johnston, Thevos, Randall, & Anton, 1991). However, many of these studies had samples mostly composed of men. Treatment studies have shown both better and worse outcomes for problem-drinking women with comorbid depression (Hesselbrock & Hesselbrock, 1997), but a recent 20-year longitudinal study of mortality risk factors among women with alcohol use disorders indicated that a comorbid diagnosis other than antisocial personality disorder (83% had depression) significantly reduced mortality risks when compared with a diagnosis of alcoholism without comorbid depression (Smith, Lewis, Kercher, & Spitznagel, 1994).

Adverse Physical Consequences of Alcohol Use and Abuse

Gender Differences in Alcohol-Related Mortality and Diseases

It is well documented that prolonged heavy drinking increases the risk of physical illness and death. It appears that women may have even greater risks than men for certain negative physiological effects of heavy drinking, most likely because of differences in the way women and men metabolize ethanol. Because women have lower levels of body water in which to distribute ethanol, women experience higher blood alcohol levels than men after equivalent doses of ethanol even when body weight is controlled (York & Welte, 1994). There also is evidence that more ethanol may pass into the bloodstream in women because of lower levels of gastric alcohol dehydrogenase, a gastric enzyme that provides a "first-pass" metabolism of ethanol in the stomach (Seitz et al., 1993).

Perhaps as a result of women's increased bioavailability of ethanol, women who drink heavily have higher mortality rates than heavy-drinking men (Lindberg & Agren, 1988; Smith, Cloninger, & Bradford, 1983). A recent mortality study estimated that in women, heavy drinking (defined as six or more drinks per day) increased the risk of death by 160% compared with light drinking (more than one drink per month but less than one drink per day), whereas heavy-drinking men's risks were only 40% greater than light-drinking men's risks (Klatsky, Armstrong, & Friedman, 1992).

When drinking levels are held constant, women are more likely than men to develop alcoholic cirrhosis and hepatitis, to develop these problems with shorter drinking histories (i.e., with a lower cumulative dose of alcohol), and to remain at higher risk of liver disease progression after abstinence (Seitz et al., 1993). Furthermore, although there is still disagreement about the effects of alcohol at very low levels of consumption on risk for breast cancer, studies have shown an increased risk for breast cancer in women drinking two (Longnecker, Berlin, Orza, & Chalmers, 1988) or three (Katsouyanni et al., 1994) drinks per day. Finally, the cardiovascular benefits of moderate alcohol use in men may not be as evident for women as the risks of liver disease and breast cancer begin to outweigh the possible benefits of alcohol use at fairly low consumption levels (Fuchs et al., 1995). Heavy-drinking women also may be more vulnerable than their male counterparts to the toxic effects of alcohol on striated muscle and cardiac muscle (Urbano-Marquez et al., 1995).

Reproductive Health

Even small amounts of alcohol (one to two drinks per day) have been associated with increased fetal abnormalities, particularly decreased birth weight, growth abnormalities, and in some studies behavioral decrements (Jacobson & Jacobson, 1994). There currently is no consensus about how much alcohol can be safely consumed during pregnancy, and abstinence during pregnancy is recommended by the U.S. Surgeon General as the only truly safe choice (Institute of Medicine, 1996). Although studies of moderate drinking and pregnancy loss have not been entirely consistent, some studies have shown increased risks of spontaneous abortion and stillbirth at relatively low levels of alcohol consumption (Armstrong, McDonald, & Sloan, 1992), and one study reported that women with a history of alcohol abuse who did not drink during pregnancy had lower-birthweight babies than a nonalcoholic comparison group (Little, Streissguth, Barr, & Herman, 1980). To our knowledge, there is no information on how long a woman should abstain before conceiving, but a history of abusive drinking should be considered a risk factor in pregnancy independent of alcohol use during pregnancy (Little & Ervin, 1984).

Identification of Alcohol Problems in Women

Early Identification and Screening for Alcohol Problems

The identification of alcohol problems in women may be hampered by gender-insensitive diagnostic criteria (Dawson & Grant, 1993), underreporting by women for fear of stigmatization, and the reluctance of women's significant others to identify problem drinking (Lane, Burge, & Graham, 1992). Identification may occur by the problem drinker herself, her family, her workplace, the legal system, or in general health and medical settings. Because women are more likely than men to seek assistance for non-alcohol-related problems and more often seek services in mental health and medical settings, physicians and other health professionals can be primary sources of early identification and referral for alcohol problems (Weisner & Schmidt, 1992). Unfortunately, women's drinking problems tend to be underrecognized in these settings (Moore et al., 1989), and more

training of professionals in health care settings is needed to properly identify and refer women for alcohol treatment services. Health professionals
should routinely screen not only for alcohol use disorders but also for less
severe or earlier-stage alcohol problems. A number of brief questionnaires
have been developed to assist in this process, and some may be especially
useful in detecting women's alcohol problems.

One frequently used instrument, the Michigan Alcoholism Screening
Test (Selzer, 1971), was developed and tested with hospitalized alcoholic
men. Because the questionnaire has items relating to end-stage alcoholic
behaviors (e.g., past treatment history), it may not be sensitive in detecting earlier-stage problem drinking in women. Instruments more sensitive
to earlier-stage alcohol use problems include the CAGE and the Alcohol
Use Disorders Identification Test (AUDIT; Russell, Chan, & Mudar, 1997).
CAGE is an acronym for key words from the four questions: (a) Have you
ever felt you should *cut* down on your drinking? (b) Have people *annoyed*
you by criticizing your drinking? (c) Have you ever felt *guilty* about your
drinking? and (d) Have you ever had a drink first thing in the morning
(*eye-opener*) to steady your nerves or get rid of a hangover? Although
Ewing (1984) recommended that a score of 2 or more be considered highly
suggestive of alcohol problems, Russell et al. (1997) observed that a cut-
point of 1 or more greatly increases the CAGE's sensitivity to problem
drinking in women. An advantage of the CAGE questions is that health
professionals can easily incorporate these questions into routine history-
taking procedures. The CAGE questions are not related to any particular
time frame, and therefore the clinician should ask when the problems occurred (G. R. Jacobson, 1989). Russell et al. (1997) found that adding a
question on alcohol tolerance to various combinations of CAGE questions
increases their sensitivity to women's drinking: A response of three or more
drinks to the question "How many drinks does it take to make you feel
high?" is considered a positive indication of increased alcohol tolerance.

The AUDIT is a 10-item questionnaire that reliably detects heavy
drinkers who have not yet experienced problem consequences as well as
individuals with more severe drinking problems (Babor, Kranzler, &
Lauerman, 1989). Advantages of the AUDIT include its questions about
the frequency and quantity of drinking, as well as questions about adverse
psychological consequences of drinking. Another screening instrument
that may be sensitive to women's risk of alcohol use problems is the 4 Ps
(Burke & Caldwell, in press). The 4 Ps asks about alcohol problems in the
past, in the *present*, in the woman's *parents*, and in her *partner*. Because
women's risks for alcohol problems appear to be strongly related both to
family history of alcohol problems and to their partner's alcohol problems,
assessing these risk factors may be important.

If it is not possible to administer brief screening questionnaires such
as the AUDIT, health professionals should nonetheless ask currently
drinking women the CAGE questions about their alcohol consumption patterns. When assessing alcohol use, two domains should be examined: (a)
the average weekly frequency of drinking, the typical quantity consumed
per drinking day or occasion, and the duration of current consumption

levels; (b) the occurrence and frequency of heavy episodic drinking for women (usually 3 or more drinks per day). If a woman gives one or more positive responses to the CAGE for experiences that occurred in the past year, or reports current consumption of more than 7 drinks per week or more than 3 drinks per occasion, the nature and extent of any alcohol-related problems should be determined. Impairment in interpersonal, occupational, or health domains should be assessed as well as any family history of alcohol-related problems (for a review of alcohol assessment procedures for health-care professionals, see NIAAA, 1995). Assessing the current and past use of other drugs, including both prescription and illicit drugs, is also important in light of the high rates of multiple substance abuse among women with alcohol problems. Results of a recent study (Caetano & Weisner, 1995) suggest that comorbid use of drugs may be more likely among problem-drinking women who are younger, unemployed, or heavier drinkers and those who report fewer symptoms of alcohol dependence. Clearly, considerable caution is needed in prescribing potentially addictive psychoactive drugs to women with any history of alcohol or other drug misuse.

Although some women may deny heavy drinking or drinking problems, health professionals should routinely ask about alcohol problems; ask in nonthreatening, nonjudgmental ways; and educate women about the potential risks of alcohol misuse. When health professionals do detect problem drinking, they may be hesitant to make a treatment referral or they may not be sure if treatment is appropriate. Studies have shown that physicians may refer female problem drinkers for treatment less often than men (Beckman, 1984). It is extremely important that physicians and other health professionals make appropriate referrals for problem-drinking women even though this process may seem uncomfortable. Familiarity with local treatment and self-help resources that are gender sensitive (even if not women specific) can increase the health professional's confidence and competence in identifying and confronting alcohol problems in women.

As discussed next, brief interventions conducted on the spot with women who present at medical settings for alcohol or health problems may be an effective and economical strategy that health professionals can use with women who have less severe alcohol problems. Beyond brief interventions, there are treatment considerations and modalities that may enhance women's success in reducing or eliminating alcohol problems.

Treatment Considerations

Barriers to Alcohol Treatment for Women

Although the proportion of alcohol treatment clients who are female has increased somewhat in recent years—from 22% in 1982 to 28% in 1990 (Schmidt & Weisner, 1993)—women are still substantially underrepresented in many alcohol and drug abuse treatment settings. Treatment services for certain subgroups of women, in particular pregnant substance abusers, are especially limited (Institute of Medicine, 1996). Barriers to care are factors that make women unlikely or less likely to use alcohol treatment services and may include both client barriers and program barriers (Vannicelli, 1984). Women may be less likely than men to recognize that their drinking is the source of impaired functioning, which may decrease their treatment seeking. For example, Thom (1986) found that the majority of men but only a small percentage of women entering treatment for alcoholism felt that their main problem was alcohol related. Although the men in this study thought alcohol caused impairment in several life areas (e.g., legal, financial, family, and work), the women were more likely to identify anxiety, depression, and difficulties in daily living as the problems that caused their drinking.

Other barriers involve characteristics of women's social environments and of the treatment system itself. The stigma surrounding female alcoholism may make women reluctant to seek treatment (Gomberg, 1988). Compared with men, women receive less encouragement to seek treatment and experience more denial of their drinking problems by partners, family, and friends (Thom, 1987). A lack of appropriate child care during treatment, and the fear that they may be considered unfit mothers if they receive treatment services, present significant barriers to treatment for many women with alcohol-related problems.

Gender Differences in Treatment Outcome

Although a variety of therapeutic approaches have been used in treating alcohol problems, treatment outcome research indicates that there is currently no "best" treatment for all individuals. In fact, when treatment effectiveness is averaged across a diverse treatment population, success appears limited (W. R. Miller & Hester, 1986). There is, however, a belief that certain treatments may work best with certain clients, and the alcohol abuse treatment field is currently moving toward this concept of *treatment matching* as a way of increasing the efficacy of alcohol interventions (Donovan & Mattson, 1994).

The need for treatment matching based on gender, although intuitively appealing, has not been empirically established. However, most treatment outcome studies have been conducted with men: Vannicelli (1984) reviewed 530 treatment studies from 1952 to 1980 and found that about 11% of the studies used both men and women and reported gender-specific results. Only 2% of the studies used female-only participants. Of the studies that did report outcome by gender, the majority showed no significant gender differences (Toneatto, Sobell, & Sobell, 1992).

Jarvis (1992) used meta-analysis to measure sex differences in 20 treatment outcome studies conducted between 1953 and 1991. The results showed that at 6- and 12-month follow-up periods, women had better treatment outcomes than men. In the long-term follow-up period (more than 12 months), however, men appeared to have slightly better outcomes than women. Jarvis noted that the majority of studies that reported better long-term results for men were from inpatient programs that included milieu therapy, psychotherapy, and Alcoholics Anonymous (AA) with or without drug therapy. Conversely, most of the programs that reported better results for women used behavioral therapies. Similarly, in a bibliotherapy outcome study designed to reduce heavy drinking (Sanchez-Craig, Spivak, & Davila, 1991), clients were given three sessions of advice on how to use a step-by-step manual for achieving abstinence or moderate drinking, three sessions of more detailed instructions about how to use the manual, or an indefinite number of therapist sessions in which application of the manual was the focus. Women were much more likely than men to achieve moderate drinking in both the advice and instructions conditions. Men, however, were more likely than women to achieve moderation under the therapist condition.

The most comprehensive alcohol treatment outcome study to date—Matching Alcoholism Treatments to Client Heterogeneity (Project MATCH Research Group, 1997)—examined the treatment matching hypothesis for a number of client attributes, including gender, across three different alcoholism treatments (cognitive–behavioral coping skills therapy, 12-step facilitation, and motivational enhancement therapy). Results indicated that only one client attribute, degree of psychopathology, significantly interacted with treatment modality to affect treatment outcomes. Although it had been predicted that cognitive–behavioral treatment would be a superior treatment for women, the study found no gender differences in treatment outcomes. The study did find that both women and men were significantly improved on drinking outcomes at 1-year posttreatment, regardless of treatment modality, and among aftercare participants, women had a higher percentage of abstinent days than men.

Although it appears that Project MATCH has established no clear advantage for outpatient treatment matching based on gender, it should be noted that all three treatments were conducted at the individual level instead of in the most commonly provided group format. The treatments were delivered by well-trained therapists and were rigorously monitored to assure the quality of treatment. Additionally, several thorough follow-up sessions were conducted during the 1-year posttreatment period. Treatment for women may not be as effective when delivered in the more common group format (often mixed-sex groups) and/or without extensive follow-up. A study in Sweden compared women treated in a "women-only" specialized program with women treated in a traditional mixed-sex program (Dahlgren & Willander, 1989). Women with serious alcohol use problems such as cirrhosis, dementia, psychotic symptoms, or a previous history of treatment were excluded. During a 2-year follow-up period, the women treated at the specialized facility had better outcomes—reduced alcohol consumption and improved social functioning—relative to the control group. The authors concluded that a primary benefit of specialized treatment programs that take into account women's need for a broader range of services is the increased likelihood that women will seek services before their alcohol problems become severe. In further support of the need for specialized services for women, a study that compared predictors of treatment dropout for women found that lesbians, women with dependent children, and women with a history of childhood sexual assault were less likely to drop out of treatment if they participated in a specialized women's program compared with a mixed-sex treatment program (Copeland & Hall, 1992).

Effective Treatments for Problem-Drinking Women

As discussed earlier, because women often have different needs than men, treatment programs that take these needs into consideration are likely to experience greater success. Services such as child care, assessment and treatment for mood and anxiety disorders, and skills training for increasing social, parental, and marital or relationship functioning appear to be important for women, as well as assistance with practical issues such as employment, housing, and health care (Finkelstein, 1993). As a result of increased awareness of women's specialized treatment needs, treatment facilities have begun to include more services for women. About 53% of public and private treatment facilities for drug and alcohol problems currently offer some type of women's services. Although the percentage of women-only substance abuse programs made up only 6% of total substance abuse treatment options in 1992, this percentage was up from 3% in 1982 (Schmidt & Weisner, 1995). These women-only units have tended to de-emphasize traditional medically oriented inpatient alcoholism treatments while focusing on a self-help outpatient mode of treatment. On the basis of the empirical findings reviewed earlier, the following treatment approaches appear to be a good "match" for women.

   Brief interventions. Following the identification of women with alcohol problems in the community (e.g., in medical settings), it may be determined that the severity of problems does not warrant a referral to a specialized alcohol treatment program. Given the stigma attached to alcohol treatment for women (e.g., physicians may be reluctant to refer and some women will be reluctant to accept treatment), a brief intervention in the health care setting may be an effective intervention strategy (Babor, 1990). Research has shown that brief interventions can be highly effective and economical (Holder, Longabaugh, Miller, & Rubonis, 1991) and may consist of a single session conducted by an experienced nurse or other health professional or several outpatient sessions conducted in a mental health facility.

   The overall goal of brief intervention is to convince the woman that reduction or elimination of alcohol use is necessary to reduce or prevent alcohol problems. This is usually achieved through (a) feedback about the woman's individual risks from drinking; (b) emphasizing the woman's responsibility in change, giving clear advice for change and a selection of options for achieving change; and (c) providing a high level of empathy and enthusiasm to increase self-efficacy and motivation for change in the woman (W. R. Miller & Rollnick, 1991). Research has shown that brief interventions are more effective than no interventions; often are equally effective as longer, more intensive treatment; and can enhance the overall effectiveness of any subsequent longer-term treatment (Bien, Miller, & Tonigan, 1993). There has been some suggestion in the literature, however, that men may benefit more than women from brief interventions (Anderson & Scott, 1992).

Cognitive–behavioral interventions. Cognitive–behavioral treatments for alcohol problems are based on the theory that alcohol use disorders are learned behaviors that can be changed with behavior modification techniques such as skills training, marital and family therapy, relapse prevention skills, and a variety of strategies aimed at increasing self-efficacy, motivation for change, and adaptive social functioning. Cognitive–behavioral interventions often are conducted as brief interventions, and clients often are allowed to choose their own goals for modifying their drinking problems (i.e., moderation or abstinence). For this reason, cognitive–behavioral approaches often are called "controlled drinking" approaches, although abstinence goals are easily accommodated with this approach. One example of a cognitive–behavioral approach is behavioral self-control training (BSCT), which involves setting limits on consumption, self-monitoring of drinking behavior, learning drink refusal skills, learning which cues in the environment reliably predict drinking or the desire to drink, learning alternative methods of coping with stress, and setting up a reward system for the achievement of goals (Hester & Miller, 1989).

Because women often report drinking in response to stress or negative affective states, this type of approach may be especially helpful. BSCT has been empirically evaluated more than any other alcohol intervention in the field, and its long-term efficacy and cost-effectiveness have been demonstrated (Holder et al., 1991). Combining BSCT with other behavioral skills training (e.g., assertiveness, parenting training, marital communications skills, and relapse prevention training) should enhance overall treatment retention and outcome.

Another similar alcohol program based on cognitive–behavioral principles is guided self-change therapy (Sobell, Sobell, & Gavin, 1995). Treatment usually consists of a detailed assessment followed by four structured treatment sessions. Clients select their own goals regarding their alcohol use and are given several readings and homework assignments to enhance overall treatment efficacy. After the brief treatment, two aftercare phone calls are provided by the therapist at 1 and 3 months and either treatment is concluded or the client may determine that additional sessions are needed. Results of a treatment outcome study of guided self-change therapy indicated that both men and women showed significant reductions in drinking 1 year after treatment.

AA and other women's self-help groups. Although AA and other self-help programs are not usually considered formal alcohol treatment programs, AA was attended more often than any other type of alcohol program from 1979 to 1990 by both women and men (Weisner, Greenfield, & Room, 1995). There are relatively few outcome studies of women in AA, but Beckman (1993) reported that some female alcoholics have better treatment outcomes if they attend AA after formal treatment and that women experience higher abstention rates than men in AA. Special women-only AA groups available in many communities seem particularly helpful for women problem drinkers who also have a history of sexual abuse or other issues that may make discussion in mixed-gender groups more difficult. However, women with serious alcohol problems may have significant problems with self-esteem, stigma, and feelings of helplessness, and some authors believe that AA's emphasis on confrontation and acceptance of powerlessness over drinking may be antithetical to such women's needs (Beckman, 1993). Also, because women are more likely than men to attribute their drinking problems to a number of life stressors, AA's primary focus on alcoholism may not adequately help women resolve difficulties surrounding other problems or disorders (e.g., depression, anxiety, and relationship or marital problems).

Conclusion

The marked increase in scientific knowledge about women's alcohol use and abuse in the past two decades can inform treatment and prevention efforts in several ways. First, epidemiological data on the extent and characteristics of women's alcohol problems have demonstrated clearly that alcohol use disorders are not an exclusively male domain. Knowing that one fourth or more of adults with alcohol use disorders in the United States are women should encourage health professionals and other practitioners to have a high "index of suspicion" for alcohol problems among both the female and male clients whom they serve. Second, emerging knowledge about biological and genetic, sociodemographic, individual–psychological, and social–environmental risk factors can help to identify subgroups of women who may be particularly at risk for alcohol problems, encouraging special attention to early identification of problems within these high-risk subgroups. Third, the multitude of physical, psychological, and environmental problems that appear linked to women's alcohol abuse—as antecedents, consequences, or both—mean that a large variety of practitioners have opportunities to detect and intervene in women's alcohol problems, among them health professionals, mental health practitioners (including marital and sexual therapists), workplace professionals, legal and criminal justice system personnel, educators and child services specialists, and other social service agency personnel. Empirical findings can be used to educate professionals in these diverse settings about the important linkages between women's alcohol use and abuse and the problems with which they are primarily concerned.

In attempting to show a wide range of diverse practitioners how they can be gatekeepers, assisting women to gain help for their alcohol problems, in this chapter we have defined alcohol problems in a deliberately broad way. Learning to identify and intervene in a broad range of maladaptive drinking behaviors ("problem drinking"), rather than solely with more severe alcohol use disorders, maximizes the chances of earlier and more effective intervention with milder alcohol-related problems.

As knowledge about risk factors for alcohol abuse in women continues to accumulate, a priority for the future will be to translate this knowledge into prevention strategies for empirical testing. For example, evidence that childhood sexual abuse or heavy-drinking partners are risk factors for women's alcohol abuse suggests that there may be preventive benefits from early intervention programs for sexually abused girls and adolescents and from preventive education and skills training for women with heavy-drinking partners. Research linking women's alcohol abuse with a lack of social roles, nontraditional employment, acculturation, depression, anxiety, or sexual dysfunction could be used to design alcohol education and prevention modules for women undergoing role transitions (e.g., unemployment, divorce or separation, children leaving home) or rapid acculturation, women in nontraditional workplaces, and women seeking help for mood or anxiety disorders or sexual dysfunctions.

Empirical evaluation of such prevention and early intervention strategies is likely to become increasingly important in an environment of concern about health care costs and growing emphasis on health promotion and disease prevention. Ultimately, systematic evaluation of research-based approaches to both prevention and treatment, within subgroups of women and for women compared with men, can help to improve the matching and the effectiveness of alcohol abuse prevention and intervention for both women and for men.

References

American Psychiatric Association. (1987). *Diagnostic and statistical manual of mental disorders* (3rd ed., rev.). Washington, DC: Author.

American Psychiatric Association. (1994). *Diagnostic and statistical manual of mental disorders* (4th ed.). Washington, DC: Author.

Anderson, P., & Scott, E. (1992). Effect of general practitioners' advice to heavy drinking men. *British Journal of Addiction, 87,* 891–900.

Armstrong, B. G., McDonald, A. D., & Sloan, M. (1992). Cigarette, alcohol, and coffee consumption and spontaneous abortion. *American Journal of Public Health, 82,* 85–87.

Babor, T. F. (1990). Brief intervention strategies for harmful drinkers: New directions for medical education. *Canadian Medical Association Journal, 143,* 1070–1076.

Babor, T. F., Kranzler, H. R., & Lauerman, R. J. (1989). Early detection of harmful alcohol consumption: Comparison of clinical, laboratory, and self-report screening procedures. *Addictive Behaviors, 14,* 139–157.

Beckman, L. J. (1984). Analysis of the suitability of alcohol treatment resources for women. *Substance and Alcohol Actions/Misuse, 5,* 21–27.

Beckman, L. J. (1993). Alcoholics Anonymous and gender issues. In B. S. McCrady & W. R. Miller (Eds.), *Research on Alcoholics Anonymous: Opportunities and alternatives* (pp. 233–248). New Brunswick, NJ: Rutgers Center of Alcohol Studies.

Bien, T. H., Miller, W. R., & Tonigan, J. S. (1993). Brief interventions for alcohol problems: A review. *Addiction, 88,* 315–336.

Blume, S. B. (1991). Sexuality and stigma: The alcoholic woman. *Alcohol Health and Research World, 15,* 139–146.

Burke, N., & Caldwell, D. (in press). *Maternal substance use assessment methods reference manual: A review of screening and clinical assessment instruments for examining maternal use of alcohol, tobacco, and other drugs.* Providence, RI: CSAP National Resource Center.

Caetano, R., & Weisner, C. (1995). The association between *DSM-III-R* alcohol dependence, psychological distress and drug use. *Addiction, 90,* 351–359.

Copeland, J., & Hall, W. (1992). A comparison of predictors of treatment drop-out of women seeking drug and alcohol treatment in a specialist women's and two traditional mixed-sex treatment services. *British Journal of Addiction, 87,* 883–890.

Dahlgren, L., & Willander, A. (1989). Are special treatment facilities for female alcoholics needed? A controlled 2-year follow-up study from a specialized female unit (EWA) versus a mixed male/female treatment facility. *Alcoholism: Clinical and Experimental Research, 13,* 499–504.

Dawson, D. A., & Grant, B. F. (1993). Gender effects in diagnosing alcohol abuse and dependence. *Journal of Clinical Psychology, 49,* 298–307.

Dawson, D. A., Grant, B. F., & Harford, T. C. (1995). Variation in the association of alcohol consumption and five *DSM-IV* alcohol problems domains. *Alcoholism: Clinical and Experimental Research, 19,* 66–74.

Donovan, D. M., & Mattson, M. E. (1994). Alcoholism treatment matching research: Methodological and clinical issues. *Journal of Studies on Alcohol* (Suppl. 12), 5–14.

Duckert, F. (1987). Recruitment into treatment and effects of treatment in female problem drinkers. *Addictive Behaviors, 12,* 137–150.

Ewing J. A. (1984). Detecting alcoholism: The CAGE questionnaire. *Journal of the American Medical Association, 252,* 1905–1907.

Finkelstein, N. (1993). Treatment programming for alcohol and drug-dependent pregnant women. *International Journal of the Addictions, 28,* 1275–1309.

Fuchs, C. S., Stampfer, M. J., Colditz, G. A., Giovannucci, E. L., Manson, J. E., Kawachi, I., Hunter, D. J., Hankinson, S. E., Hennekens, C. H., Rosner, B., Speizer, F. E., & Willett, W. C. (1995). Alcohol consumption and mortality among women. *New England Journal of Medicine, 332,* 1245–1250.

Gilbert, M. J., & Collins, R. L. (1997). Ethnic variations in women's and men's drinking. In R. W. Wilsnack & S. C. Wilsnack (Eds.), *Gender and alcohol: Individual and social perspectives* (pp. 357–378). New Brunswick, NJ: Rutgers University Center of Alcohol Studies.

Gomberg, E. S. L. (1988). Alcoholic women in treatment: The questions of stigma and age. *Alcohol and Alcoholism, 23,* 507–514.

Graham, K., Carver, V., & Brett, P. J. (1995). Alcohol and drug use by older women: Results of a national survey. *Canadian Journal on Aging, 14,* 769–791.

Grant, B. F., Harford, T. C., Chou, P., Dawson, D. A., Stinson, F. S., & Noble, J. (1991). Epidemiologic Bulletin No. 27: Prevalence of *DSM-III-R* alcohol abuse and dependence. United States, 1988. *Alcohol Health and Research World, 15,* 91–96.

Grant, B. F., Harford, T. C., Dawson, D. A., Chou, P., Dufour, M., & Pickering, R. (1994). Epidemiologic Bulletin No. 35: Prevalence of *DSM-IV* alcohol abuse and dependence: United States, 1992. *Alcohol Health and Research World, 18,* 243–248.

Hammer, T., & Vaglum, P. (1989). The increase in alcohol consumption among women: A phenomenon related to accessibility or stress? A general population study. *British Journal of Addiction, 84,* 767–775.

Hartka, E., Johnstone, B. M., Leino, V., Motoyoshi, M., Temple, M., & Fillmore, K. M. (1991). A meta-analysis of depressive symptomatology and alcohol consumption over time. *British Journal of Addiction, 86,* 1283–1298.

Heath, A. C., Slutske, W. S., & Madden, P. A. F. (1997). Gender differences in the genetic contribution to alcoholism risk and to alcohol consumption patterns. In R. W. Wilsnack & S. C. Wilsnack (Eds.), *Gender and alcohol: Individual and social perspectives* (pp. 114–149). New Brunswick, NJ: Rutgers University Center of Alcohol Studies.

Helzer, J. E., & Pryzbeck, T. R. (1988). The co-occurrence of alcoholism with other psychiatric disorders in the general population and its impact on treatment. *Journal of Studies on Alcohol, 49,* 219–224.

Hesselbrock, M. N., & Hesselbrock, V. (1997). Gender, alcoholism, and psychiatric comorbidity. In R. W. Wilsnack & S. C. Wilsnack (Eds.), *Gender and alcohol: Individual and social perspectives* (pp. 49–71). New Brunswick, NJ: Rutgers University Center of Alcohol Studies.

Hester, R. K., & Miller, W. R. (1989). Self-control training. In R. K. Hester & W. R. Miller (Eds.), *Handbook of alcoholism treatment approaches: Effective alternatives* (pp. 141–149). Elmsford, NY: Pergamon Press.

Hilton, M. (1987). Demographic characteristics and the frequency of heavy drinking as predictors of self-reported drinking problems. *British Journal of Addiction, 82,* 913–925.

Holder, H. D., Longabaugh, R., Miller, W. R., & Rubonis, A. V. (1991). The cost-effectiveness of treatment for alcohol problems: A first approximation. *Journal of Studies on Alcohol, 52,* 517–540.

Institute of Medicine. (1990). *Broadening the base of treatment for alcohol problems.* Washington, DC: National Academy Press.

Institute of Medicine. (1996). *Fetal alcohol syndrome: Diagnosis, epidemiology, prevention, and treatment.* Washington, DC: National Academy Press.

Jacobson, G. R. (1989). A comprehensive approach to pretreatment evaluation: I. Detection, assessment, and diagnosis of alcoholism. In R. K. Hester & W. R. Miller (Eds.), *Handbook of alcoholism treatment approaches: Effective alternatives* (pp. 17–53). Elmsford, NY: Pergamon Press.

Jacobson, J. L., & Jacobson, S. W. (1994). Prenatal alcohol exposure and neurobehavioral development: Where is the threshold? *Alcohol Health and Research World, 18,* 30–36.

Jarvis, T. J. (1992). Implications of gender for alcohol treatment research: A quantitative and qualitative review. *British Journal of Addiction, 87,* 1249–1261.

Johnston, A. L., Thevos, A. K., Randall, C. L., & Anton, R. F. (1991). Increased severity of alcohol withdrawal in inpatient alcoholics with co-existing anxiety. *British Journal of Addiction, 86,* 719–725.

Katsouyanni, K., Trichopoulou, A., Stuver, S., Vassilaros, S., Papadiamantis, Y., Bournas, N., Skarpou, N., Mueller, N., & Trichopoulos, D. (1994). Ethanol and breast cancer: An association that may be both confounded and causal. *International Journal of Cancer, 58,* 356–361.

Kessler, R. C., McGonagle, K. A., Zhao, S., Nelson, C. B., Hughes, M., Eshleman, S., Wittchen, H., & Kendler, K. S. (1994). Lifetime and 12-month prevalence of DSM-III-R psychiatric disorders in the United States: Results from the National Comorbidity Survey. *Archives of General Psychiatry, 51,* 8–19.

Kilpatrick, D. G., Edmonds, C. N., & Seymour, A. K. (1992). *Rape in America: A report to the nation.* Arlington, VA: National Victim Center.

Klassen, A. D., & Wilsnack, S. C. (1986). Sexual experience and drinking among women in a U.S. national survey. *Archives of Sexual Behavior, 15,* 363–392.

Klatsky, A. L., Armstrong, M. A., & Friedman, G. D. (1992). Alcohol and mortality. *Annals of Internal Medicine, 117,* 646–654.

Knupfer, G. (1984). The risks of drunkenness (*or Ebrietas Resurrecta*): A comparison of frequent intoxication indices and of population sub-groups as to problem risks. *British Journal of Addiction, 79,* 185–196.

Kushner, M. G., Sher, K. J., & Beitman, B. D. (1990). The relation between alcohol problems and the anxiety disorders. *American Journal of Psychiatry, 147,* 685–695.

Lane, P. A., Burge, S., & Graham, A. (1992). Management of addictive disorders in women. In M. F. Fleming & K. L. Barry (Eds.), *Addictive disorders* (pp. 260–269). St. Louis, MO: Mosby Year-Book.

Lindberg, S., & Agren, G. (1988). Mortality among male and female hospitalized alcoholics in Stockholm 1962–1983. *British Journal of Addictions, 83,* 1193–1200.

Little, R. E., & Ervin, C. H. (1984). Alcohol use and reproduction. In S. C. Wilsnack & L. J. Beckman (Eds.), *Alcohol problems in women: Antecedents, consequences, and intervention* (pp. 155–188). New York: Guilford Press.

Little, R. E., Streissguth, A. P., Barr, H. M., & Herman, C. S. (1980). Decreased birthweights in infants of alcoholic women who abstained during pregnancy. *Journal of Pediatrics, 96,* 974–976.

Longnecker, M. P., Berlin, J. A., Orza, M. J., & Chalmers, T. C. (1988). A meta-analysis of alcohol consumption in relation to risk of breast cancer. *Journal of the American Medical Association, 260*, 652–656.

Lozina, C., Russell, M., & Mudar, P. (1995). Correlates of alcohol-related problems in African-American and White gynecologic patients. *Alcoholism: Clinical and Experimental Research, 19*, 25–30.

Martin, S. E. (1992). The epidemiology of alcohol-related interpersonal violence. *Alcohol Health and Research World, 16*, 230–237.

McGue, M., & Slutske, W. (1966). The inheritance of alcoholism in women. In J. M. Howard, S. E. Martin, P. D. Mail, M. E. Hilton, & E. D. Taylor (Eds.), *Women and alcohol: Issues for prevention research* (National Institute on Alcohol Abuse and Alcoholism Research Monograph No. 32, NIH Publication No. 96-3817, pp. 65–91). Washington, DC: U.S. Government Printing Office.

Miller, B. A., Downs, W. R., & Testa, M. (1993). Interrelationships between victimization experiences and women's alcohol use. *Journal of Studies on Alcohol* (Suppl. 11), 109–117.

Miller, N. S., & Gold, M. S. (1988). The human sexual response and alcohol and drugs. *Journal of Substance Abuse Treatment, 5*, 171–177.

Miller, W. R., & Hester, R. K. (1986). The effectiveness of alcoholism treatment: What research reveals. In W. R. Miller & N. Heather (Eds.), *Treating addictive behaviors: Processes of change* (pp. 121–174). New York: Plenum.

Miller, W. R., & Rollnick, S. (1991). *Motivational interviewing: Preparing people to change addictive behavior.* New York: Guilford Press.

Moore, R. D., Bone, L. R., Geller, G., Mamon, J. A., Stokes, E. J., & Levine, D. M. (1989). Prevalence, detection, and treatment of alcoholism in hospitalized patients. *Journal of the American Medical Association, 261*, 403–407.

National Institute on Alcohol Abuse and Alcoholism. (1995). *The physician's guide to helping patients with alcohol problems* (DHHS Publication No. 95-3769). Washington, DC: U.S. Government Printing Office.

Project MATCH Research Group. (1997). Matching alcoholism treatments to client heterogeneity: Project MATCH posttreatment drinking outcomes. *Journal of Studies on Alcohol, 58*, 7–29.

Robbins, C. A., & Martin, S. S. (1993). Gender, styles of deviance, and drinking problems. *Journal of Health and Social Behavior, 34*, 302–321.

Roberts, L. J., & Leonard, K. E. (1997). Gender differences and similarities in the alcohol and marriage relationship. In R. W. Wilsnack & S. C. Wilsnack (Eds.), *Gender and alcohol: Individual and social perspectives* (pp. 289–311). New Brunswick, NJ: Rutgers University Center of Alcohol Studies.

Russell, M., Chan, A. W. K., & Mudar, P. (1997). Gender and screening for alcohol-related problems. In R. W. Wilsnack & S. C. Wilsnack (Eds.), *Gender and alcohol: Individual and social perspectives* (pp. 417–444). New Brunswick, NJ: Rutgers University Center of Alcohol Studies.

Sanchez-Craig, M., Spivak, K., & Davila, R. (1991). Superior outcome of females over males after brief treatment for the reduction of heavy drinking: Replication and report of therapist effects. *British Journal of Addictions, 86*, 867–876.

Schaefer, S., & Evans, S. (1987). Women, sexuality and the process of recovery. In E. Coleman (Ed.), *Chemical dependency and intimacy dysfunction* (pp. 91–120). New York: Haworth Press.

Schmidt, L., & Weisner, C. (1993). Developments in alcoholism treatment. In M. Galanter (Ed.), *Recent developments in alcoholism: Vol. 11: Ten years of progress* (pp. 369–396). New York: Plenum.

Schmidt, L., & Weisner, C. (1995). The emergence of problem-drinking women as a special population in need of treatment. In M. Galanter (Ed.), *Recent developments in alcoholism: Vol. 12: Alcoholism and women* (pp. 309–334). New York: Plenum.

Seitz, H. K., Egerer, G., Simanowski, U. A., Waldherr, R., Eckey, R., Agarwal, D. P., Goedde, H. W., & von-Wartburg, J. P. (1993). Human gastric alcohol dehydrogenase activity: Effect of age, sex, and alcoholism. *Gut, 34*, 1433–1437.

Selzer, M. L. (1971). The Michigan Alcoholism Screening Test: The quest for a new diagnostic instrument. *American Journal of Psychiatry, 127,* 1653–1658.

Shore, E. R. (1992). Drinking patterns and problems among women in paid employment. *Alcohol Health and Research World, 16,* 160–164.

Smith, E. M., Cloninger, C. R., & Bradford, S. (1983). Predictors of mortality in alcoholic women: A prospective follow-up study. *Alcoholism: Clinical and Experimental Research, 7,* 237–243.

Smith, E. M., Lewis, C. E., Kercher, C., & Spitznagel, E. (1994). Predictors of mortality in alcoholic women: A 20-year follow-up study. *Alcoholism: Clinical and Experimental Research, 18,* 1177–1186.

Sobell, M. B., Sobell, L. C., & Gavin, D. R. (1995). Portraying alcohol treatment outcomes: Different yardsticks of success. *Behavior Therapy, 26,* 643–669.

Thom, B. (1986). Sex differences in help-seeking for alcohol problems: I. The barriers to help-seeking. *British Journal of Addiction, 81,* 777–788.

Thom, B. (1987). Sex differences in help-seeking for alcohol problems: II. Entry into treatment. *British Journal of Addictions, 82,* 989–997.

Toneatto, A., Sobell, L. C., & Sobell, M. B. (1992). Gender differences in the treatment of abusers of alcohol and other drugs. *Journal of Substance Abuse, 4,* 209–218.

Urbano-Marquez, A., Estruch, R., Fernandez-Sola, J., Nicolas, J. M., Pare, J. C., & Rubin, E. (1995). The greater risk of alcoholic cardiomyopathy and myopathy in women compared with men. *Journal of the American Medical Association, 274,* 149–154.

Vannicelli, M. (1984). Treatment outcome of alcoholic women: The state of the art in relation to sex bias and expectancy effects. In S. C. Wilsnack & L. J. Beckman (Eds.), *Alcohol problems in women: Antecedents, consequences, and intervention* (pp. 369–412). New York: Guilford Press.

Weisner, C., Greenfield, T., & Room, R. (1995). Trends in the treatment of alcohol problems in the U.S. general population, 1979–1990. *American Journal of Public Health, 85,* 55–60.

Weisner, C., & Schmidt, L. (1992). Gender disparities in treatment for alcohol problems. *Journal of the American Medical Association, 268,* 1872–1876.

Widom, C. S., Ireland, T., & Glynn, P. J. (1995). Alcohol abuse in abused and neglected children followed-up: Are they at increased risk? *Journal of Studies on Alcohol, 56,* 207–217.

Williams, G. D., & DeBakey, S. F. (1992). Changes in levels of alcohol consumption: United States, 1983–1988. *British Journal of Addiction, 87,* 643–648.

Wilsnack, R. W., & Cheloha, R. (1987). Women's roles and problem drinking across the lifespan. *Social Problems, 34,* 231–248.

Wilsnack, R. W., & Wilsnack, S. C. (1990). *Husbands and wives as drinking partners.* Paper presented at the 16th Annual Alcohol Epidemiology Symposium of the Kettil Bruun Society for Social and Epidemiological Research on Alcohol, Budapest, Hungary.

Wilsnack, S. C. (1995). Alcohol use and alcohol problems in women. In A. L. Stanton & S. J. Gallant (Eds.), *Psychology of women's health: Progress and challenges in research and application* (pp. 381–443). Washington, DC: American Psychological Association.

Wilsnack, S. C. (1996). [Women's perceptions about the social acceptability of women's versus men's drinking]. Unpublished raw data, University of North Dakota School of Medicine and Health Sciences.

Wilsnack, S. C., Klassen, A. D., Schur, B. E., & Wilsnack, R. W. (1991). Predicting onset and chronicity of women's problem drinking: A five year longitudinal analysis. *American Journal of Public Health, 81,* 305–318.

Wilsnack, S. C., Vogeltanz, N. D., Diers, L. E., & Wilsnack, R. W. (1995). Drinking and problem drinking in older women. In T. P. Beresford & E. S. L. Gomberg (Eds.), *Alcohol and aging* (pp. 263–292). London: Oxford University Press.

Wilsnack, S. C., Vogeltanz, N. D., Klassen, A. D., & Harris, T. R. (1997). Childhood sexual abuse and women's substance abuse: National survey findings. *Journal of Studies on Alcohol, 58,* 264–271.

Wilsnack, S. C., Wilsnack, R. W., & Hiller-Sturmhofel, S. (1994). How women drink: Epidemiology of women's drinking and problem drinking. *Alcohol Health and Research World, 18,* 173–181.

Wilsnack, S. C., Wilsnack, R. W., & Klassen, A. D. (1986). Epidemiological research on women's drinking, 1978–1984. In National Institute on Alcohol Abuse and Alcoholism, *Women and alcohol: Health-related issues* (NIAAA Research Monograph No. 16, DHHS No. ADM 86-1139, pp. 1–68). Washington, DC: U.S. Government Printing Office.

York, J. L., & Welte, J. W. (1994). Gender comparisons of alcohol consumption in alcoholic and nonalcoholic populations. *Journal of Studies on Alcohol, 55,* 743–750.

7

Disordered Eating and Eating Disorders

Kathleen M. Pike and Ruth H. Striegel-Moore

Disordered eating and eating disorders constitute problematic resolutions to significant issues intrinsic to growing up female in today's society. Anorexia nervosa (AN), bulimia nervosa (BN), and binge eating disorder (BED) are the three major eating disorders acknowledged in the field today. In addition, partial eating disorder syndromes are much more common than the more narrowly defined syndromes of AN, BN, and BED. Most often, the eating disturbances of individuals with partial syndromes are qualitatively the same as those with the full syndromes, with the primary distinction being one of severity or frequency of disturbed eating behavior.

As reflected by the epidemiology data reviewed in this chapter, the continuum from disordered eating to eating disorders sweeps across a major sector of the female population. In turn, the implications of these eating disturbances for women's health are broad and significant. For the health care professional, the secondary symptoms of eating disturbances, such as swollen parotid glands in the case of BN and oligomenorrhea or amenorrhea in the case of AN, can serve as potential indicators that such eating disturbances exist. Except for extreme weight deviations, many symptoms secondary to an eating disorder are either not obviously linked to disturbances in eating or are unobservable and intentionally kept secret because of shame. Therefore, knowledge of the broad implications of these problems may facilitate both the early detection of eating problems and delivery of services to more individuals whose problems are severe enough to warrant treatment.

Eating disorders are multidetermined; theories of biological and environmental influence have been articulated and, to a lesser extent, investigated empirically (Brownell & Fairburn, 1995). Although issues of etiology are critical for improving both the understanding of these disorders and their prevention, for health care providers the challenge is to identify and provide appropriate treatment for symptomatic individuals. Thus, in this chapter we describe the patterns of eating disorder symptoms from the most specific eating disorders of AN, BN, and BED to the less

We acknowledge the excellent assistance provided by Claire Haiman.

severe but more widespread patterns of disordered eating. After this review, we discuss ways in which disordered eating affects other domains of
health. In particular, we briefly review specific medical, psychological, and
social and interpersonal correlates of eating disturbances. Finally, we discuss barriers to treatment and the need for general health care practitioners to act as educated gatekeepers in detecting eating problems and
directing individuals to appropriate treatment.

The Eating Disorders

Anorexia Nervosa

Clinical features. AN is the most life threatening of the eating disorders, because it has numerous severe physical as well as psychological complications. The core feature of AN is the relentless pursuit of thinness, resulting in severe emaciation and, in women, amenorrhea. The diagnostic
criteria described in the fourth edition of the *Diagnostic and Statistical
Manual of Mental Disorders* (*DSM–IV*; American Psychiatric Association
[APA], 1994) include refusal to maintain a weight above a minimally normal
level for age and height (operationalized as 85% of ideal body weight); intense fears of gaining weight or becoming fat; body image disturbance such
as denial of the seriousness of the current low body weight or undue influence of weight and shape on self-evaluation; and, finally, in postmenarcheal
women, the absence of at least three consecutive menstrual cycles. There
are two clinical subtypes of AN: the restricting type and the binge-eating/
purging subtype. Those individuals with the restricting subtype of AN use
dieting, fasting, and excessive exercise as a means of losing weight, whereas
individuals with the binge-eating/purging subtype of AN regularly engage
in binge eating or purging behavior (e.g., self-induced vomiting, laxative
abuse, and diuretics). Women with the binge-eating/purging subtype have
been found to report more problems with impulsivity than women with the
restricting subtype (Halmi et al., 1991).

Epidemiology. Girls or women account for more than 90% of the reported cases of AN. Among female adolescents and young adults, the prevalence of AN is approximately 1% (Walters & Kendler, 1995). Recently,
childhood-onset AN has been recognized as an important subgroup (Lask
& Bryant-Waugh, 1992). Moreover, research has shown that a subset of
children who fail to thrive evidence a clinical syndrome (infantile anorexia)
that is similar in many respects to AN (Chatoor, 1989). More typically,
however, the disorder emerges between puberty and 17 years of age, and
adult onset is rare (APA, 1994).

Studies of family epidemiology, although sparse, have shown an increased occurrence of AN among biological relatives with the disorder
(Strober, 1992). To date, sample sizes in twin studies have been too small
to permit testing the hypothesis that AN is genetically transmitted or that

it is due to shared environmental factors (Walters & Kendler, 1995). Several community-based studies of AN have shown increased prevalence of the disorder among higher socioeconomic status groups (Walters & Kendler, 1995). However, studies of other cultures indicate that socioeconomic status and urbanization are not correlated with the incidence of AN (Hoek, 1993), suggesting that modern, thin, beauty ideals may be less central to the etiology of AN than other eating disorders. In the United States, research has yet to examine rates of AN in women from varying ethnic or racial backgrounds. However, preliminary data show that women of color who seek treatment for AN have lower admission weights than White women, suggesting that AN may go undetected or untreated longer in ethnic minority women than in White women (Silber, 1986).

Course of illness. The course and prognosis of AN are variable; however, it has been suggested that the onset of the illness during early adolescence may be associated with better prognosis than childhood or adult onset (Herzog, Deter, & Vandereycken, 1992). It is estimated that 40% of individuals with AN recover, approximately 30% show improvement, and for 20%, the illness is chronic (Steinhausen, Rauss-Mason, & Seidel, 1991). Weight restoration, the most immediate goal of therapy, often requires lengthy hospital stays (10–15 weeks). It is unclear whether rates of weight gain vary by subtype (Attia, 1995; Neuberger, Rao, Weltzin, Greeno, & Kaye, 1995; Salisbury, Levine, Crow, & Mitchell, 1995).

Naturalistic follow-up studies have shown that, despite various treatment interventions, approximately 40–50% of patients with AN are chronically underweight at follow-up and continue to experience menstrual irregularities or amenorrhea (Deter & Herzog, 1994). Relatedly, eating behavior often remains chronically problematic; for example, excessive dietary restraint, binge eating, and vomiting often are unremitting, and approximately 50% of individuals with AN require repeated hospitalizations (cf. Hsu, 1990). A small but significant number of individuals die either because of the physical complications arising from self-starvation or because of suicide: Mortality attributable to AN, as measured at long-term follow-up, lies somewhere between 10% and 20% (Crisp, Callender, Halek, & Hsu, 1992). Definitive treatments for AN are not yet established, although several studies are currently under way that evaluate the efficacy of cognitive–behavioral therapy, fluoxetine (Prozac), and the combination of these treatments in the relapse prevention of AN.

Bulimia Nervosa

Clinical features. BN is characterized by recurrent episodes of binge eating followed by extreme behaviors aimed at controlling body weight and shape, such as self-induced vomiting; the abuse of laxatives, diuretics, or enemas; extreme dieting or fasting; or excessive exercise. Additionally, individuals with BN report a persistent overconcern with thinness, judging their self-worth excessively in terms of body shape and weight. To meet

DSM–IV criteria for BN, the individual must binge eat and make use of inappropriate compensatory behaviors, on average, a minimum of twice a week for 3 months (APA, 1994). Similar to AN, BN has two subtypes: the purging type and the nonpurging type. Individuals with the purging sub-type of BN regularly self-induce vomiting or abuse laxatives, diuretics, or enemas. Individuals with the nonpurging subtype of BN regularly use other inappropriate compensatory behavior, such as restrictive dieting, fasting, or excessive exercise.

The *DSM–IV* stipulates that an episode of binge eating is character-ized by eating, in a discrete period of time (defined arbitrarily as 2 hr), an amount of food that is considered definitely larger than what most people would eat during a similar period of time and under similar circumstances. During this period of time the person must experience a sense of loss of control (i.e., a feeling that one cannot stop eating or control what or how much is eaten). There is still a controversy about the size of a binge, and, although *DSM–IV* criteria require the amount of food to be large, to our knowledge there are no published data to support a distinction between large and small amounts. However, there are data to suggest that loss of control is a key feature of binge eating (Beglin & Fairburn, 1992; Rossiter & Agras, 1990).

Epidemiology. Young adult females make up the overwhelming ma-jority of patients with BN, with males accounting for one tenth of the BN cases. Epidemiological studies for BN report prevalence rates of 1–2% of adult females (Fairburn & Beglin, 1990; Hoek, 1993; Kendler et al., 1991). It appears that a cohort shift has occurred, with females born after 1960 having a higher risk for BN than those born earlier (Kendler et al., 1991). BN, like AN, is typified as a disorder of White, affluent Western cultures, yet eating-related problems in general, and perhaps more specifically BN, also are present and possibly increasing in non-White groups, including African Americans (Striegel-Moore & Smolak, 1996) and women in devel-oping non-Western cultures (Pate, Pumariega, Hester, & Garner, 1992). Additionally, particular subgroups of the population, such as certain ath-letes (e.g., gymnasts), models, and dancers may be more susceptible to BN because of the increased pressures to conform to certain ideal weight and body shape standards (Brownell, Rodin, & Wilmore, 1992).

Course of illness. BN usually begins in late adolescence or early adult-hood (Woodside & Garfinkel, 1992). The binge eating frequently begins during or after a period of dieting. BN, once established, seems to be self-perpetuated through a vicious cycle of restriction, binge eating, and vom-iting, although it may wax and wane in severity. Individuals with BN are extraordinarily sensitive to changes in weight and body shape and are both cognitively and behaviorally preoccupied with eating and weight con-cerns (e.g., constantly thinking about food and weight and frequently weighing themselves).

Highly variable results have been found in the treatment outcome of BN, with cognitive–behavioral therapy demonstrating the greatest and most enduring therapeutic benefit for individuals with BN. Psychiatric medications also have been of use, particularly desipramine and more recently fluoxetine. However, across the range of studied treatments, rates of full recovery from BN range from a low of 13% to a high of 71% (for a review, see Keller, Herzog, Lavori, Bradburn, & Mahoney, 1992). Furthermore, relapse rates are high among successfully treated patients. For example, Olmsted, Kaplan, and Rockert (1994) found that approximately one third of women who had achieved complete recovery were found to relapse within 2 years.

Binge Eating Disorder

Clinical features. BED is a newly defined eating disorder, introduced in the *DSM–IV* (APA, 1994) as one example of an eating disorder not otherwise specified (EDNOS). BED is characterized by recurrent episodes of binge eating (i.e., eating an unusually large amount of food accompanied by a feeling of loss of control) without regular attempts to engage in the extreme compensatory weight control practices found in BN, such as purging or fasting. In addition to recurrent binge eating, behavioral indicators also must be present, such as eating faster than normal; eating until uncomfortably full; eating a large amount of food when not physically hungry; eating alone because of social embarrassment about the amount of food eaten; and feeling disgust, depression, or guilt after overeating. Diagnosis further requires marked distress regarding the binge eating.

To meet diagnostic criteria for BED, the binge eating must occur, on average, at least 2 days per week for a minimum of 6 months. The frequency of binge eating for BED is determined on the basis of the number of days instead of discrete episodes because of practical considerations. In particular, the duration of binge-eating episodes can vary greatly, and many individuals with BED have difficulty identifying discrete episodes of binge eating that occur on the same day. However, such individuals usually have little difficulty recalling whether binge eating occurred on a given day (Rossiter, Agras, Telch, & Bruce, 1992). Thus, to promote reliability in the assessment of BED, the method of determining the frequency of binge eating for BED is based on the number of days of binge eating per week instead of the number of discrete episodes. Future research is needed to provide a more empirical basis for this criterion.

Epidemiology. Initial data suggest that in the community, 2% of the adult female population meet criteria for BED (Bruce & Agras, 1992; Spitzer et al., 1992). BED is found across all weight groups (Devlin, Walsh, Spitzer, & Hasin, 1992), although initial reports of community-based samples suggest that about half of those with BED are obese. Although the prevalence of BED among obese people is uncertain, preliminary data suggest that BED affects 5–10% of obese individuals in the community and about 30% of obese individuals who participate in university-based weight control programs (Yanovski, 1993). The relationship between binge eating and obesity is not well understood, and future research is needed to clarify the ways in which binge eating may be linked causally to obesity and vice versa. Individuals with BED make up a diverse group, varying more widely across categories of gender, age, and race than is the case with the other eating disorders. Data suggest that among patients attending weight loss programs, BED is only slightly more common among women than men (a ratio of 3:2; Spitzer et al., 1993). Moreover, Black women and White women appear to be at equal risk for BED (Marcus, 1995).

Course of illness. Because BED has been defined only recently, little is known about its clinical course. Initial data suggest that the onset of BED occurs in young adulthood compared with AN or BN, which typically begin in adolescence. Specifically, in a clinic-based sample of individuals with BED, the mean age of onset of the first binge-eating episode was 18 years; however, the mean age by which patients had established a regular pattern of binge eating was 26 years (Mussell et al., 1995). Two distinct patterns of development of the disorder have been identified. In approximately half the cases dieting preceded the onset of BED, whereas in the remaining number of cases binge eating began in the absence of dieting to lose weight (Berkowitz, Stunkard, & Stallings, 1993; Mussell et al., 1995). Among clinical cases, the course appears to be chronic (Yanovski, 1993).

Treatment for BED is still in the developmental stages because of the recent recognition of the disorder. Cognitive–behavioral treatment has been found to be the most successful (Smith, Marcus, & Kaye, 1992; Wilfley et al., 1993). Treatments using both psychotherapy and psychiatric medication, specifically desipramine and fluoxetine, also have demonstrated efficacy (Agras et al., 1994; Marcus et al., 1990a).

Disordered Eating

Symptoms of eating disorders occur on a severity continuum, and the criteria established to define eating disorders are arbitrary in that no objective data exist to determine the threshold at which a symptom (or constellation of symptoms) is severe enough to warrant a medical diagnosis (Striegel-Moore & Marcus, 1995). Many women and young girls do not meet criteria for AN, BN, or BED, yet they experience significant problems concerning body image, eating, or both (Shisslak, Crago, & Estes, in press). Among adolescent girls, it has been estimated that 2–13% meet criteria for EDNOS (Childress, Brewerton, Hodges, & Jarrell, 1993; Whitaker, 1992) and that among adult women, partial eating disorder syndromes are estimated to occur at a rate of 3–5% (Kendler et al., 1991). Both subthreshold AN and subthreshold BN may be associated with equally high levels of psychiatric disorder and social impairment as have been reported for individuals with full-syndrome AN or BN (Bunnell, Shenker, Nussbaum, Jacobson, & Cooper, 1990; Herzog, Hopkins, & Burns, 1993; Williamson, Gleaves, & Savin, 1992).

Finally, an even larger percentage of women and adolescent girls experience subjective distress because of disordered eating despite never meeting strict criteria for any formal eating disorder diagnosis. Studies indicate that approximately two thirds to three quarters of high school girls in the United States report dieting to lose weight despite their being normal weight or underweight (Pike, 1995). Rates of binge eating reflect borderline-to-clinical levels of severity in approximately 15% of adolescent girls (Pike, 1995), and between 5–15% of adolescent girls engage in more extreme weight control efforts such as self-induced vomiting and laxative and diuretic abuse (Phelps, Andrea, Rizzo, Johnston, & Main, 1993).

From the perspective of a clinical service provider, the presence of key behavioral symptoms of eating disorders such as severely restrictive dieting, recurrent binge eating, and recurrent purging warrant therapeutic intervention for several reasons. First, these symptoms often progress to a full syndrome presentation over time. Second, even if the symptoms do not escalate, they often take a chronic course (Herzog et al., 1993). Third, these symptoms are associated with serious medical complications, psychological comorbidity, and social and interpersonal problems, as discussed next.

Impact of Eating Disturbances on Health and Adjustment

Medical Complications

In this section we highlight the medical problems associated with the range of eating disorders. (For more in-depth reviews, see Brotman, Rigotti, & Herzog, 1985; Goldbloom & Kennedy, 1995; Hsu, 1990; Mitchell, Seim, Colon, & Pomeroy, 1987.)

Menstrual and reproductive problems. The absence of menses for 3 consecutive months in postmenarcheal women is a defining criterion for AN. Although not a core diagnostic feature of BN, menstrual dysfunction also is common in BN; for example, about one third of bulimic women report secondary amenorrhea (Mitchell et al., 1987). Seemingly inexplicable problems with fertility also can be traced to eating disturbances. Compared with a normal population, twice as many women with eating disorders present for treatment to infertility clinics. After gaining weight, approximately 75% of these women resume menstruation and are able to conceive spontaneously (Stewart, 1992). Although some women experience significant improvement of their bulimic symptomatology during pregnancy, most resume their disturbed eating habits after delivery (Lacey & Smith, 1987). Preliminary data suggest that women who exhibit acute symptoms of AN during pregnancy are more likely to miscarry, have difficult labors, experience surgical deliveries, and develop hypertension (Franko & Walton, 1993). These women also experience a greater number of fetal problems during their pregnancy, and their children exhibit increased rates of premature birth, low birth weight, and perinatal mortality (Stewart, 1992).

Bone problems. Among individuals with eating disorders, bone problems are most commonly reported for individuals with AN, due to amenorrhea and severe weight loss. Low bone-mineral density is associated with an increased risk of developing stress fractures, crush fractures, and osteoporosis (Putukian, 1994). Adolescent girls are at particular risk for osteopenia because they often have not achieved peak skeletal mass before the onset of amenorrhea associated with their eating disorder (Seeman, Szmukler, Formica, Tsalamandris, & Mestrovic, 1992). It is unclear whether bone-mineral density normalizes on recovery from AN because the reversibility of these changes has not been adequately studied.

Gastrointestinal problems. Vomiting associated with eating disorders results in various problems of the gastrointestinal tract, ranging from the benign and common swelling of the parotid glands to complaints of constipation, bloating, and gastric discomfort to the rare and possibly fatal rupture of the stomach or esophagus (Palla & Litt, 1988). Disruptions of normal colon functioning also are common, especially for laxative abusers, and may result in long-term disability of the colon that requires surgical repair (Mitchell et al., 1987). Although it is rare, individuals with AN and BN occasionally develop gastric and duodenal ulcers and dilatation (Hsu, 1990).

Cardiovascular problems. Cardiovascular abnormalities, such as bradycardia and hypotension, are present in many patients with AN (Brotman et al., 1985) and should be monitored routinely. Also, individuals with BN often experience symptoms of hypotension (Mitchell et al., 1987). With weight gain and resolution of the eating disorder, the cardiovascular system resumes normal functioning, providing that there has not been extensive abuse of Syrup of Ipecac, which can cause irreversible damage to the heart and other muscular tissue (Brotman et al., 1985; Mitchell et al., 1987).

Dental problems. In addition to swelling of the parotid glands, regular vomiting also is associated with severe dental erosion, greater prevalence of dental decay, increased tooth sensitivity, and periodontal disease (Altshuler, Dechow, Waller, & Hardy, 1990). Additionally, tooth size may be diminished, and the surface of the teeth may appear "moth-eaten" or ragged.

Fluid and electrolyte imbalance. Electrolyte imbalance is most common among individuals with bulimic symptoms. About 50% of this group experience some sort of electrolyte abnormality. Metabolic alkalosis and hypokalemia are seen among individuals who vomit regularly because of depletion of body fluids lost through vomiting. Those abusing laxatives frequently exhibit the opposite phenomenon of metabolic acidosis, or acidic blood, which also is due to a depletion of the body's fluids. Both vomiting and laxative abuse may contribute to low levels of sodium chloride (hypochloremia) because of the dehydration associated with purging (Palla & Litt, 1988).

Obesity. Because BED is associated with increased adiposity, the medical consequences of obesity constitute the core medical complications associated with BED. In particular, obese individuals with BED are at increased risk for diabetes mellitus, hypertension, cardiovascular disease, stroke, gallbladder disease, and certain types of cancer (for a review, see Pi-Sunyer, 1995).

Associated Psychopathology

Eating disorders are often associated with comorbid psychological disturbances. A major limitation of the data on comorbidity is that they are almost exclusively based on clinical cases, and similar data are not available for community samples. Nonetheless, the data document consistently that the eating disorders are associated with significant psychiatric comorbidity.

Depression. Across the spectrum of eating disorders, rates of depression are higher among individuals with AN, BN, and BED compared with rates observed in the general population. Approximately 45% of individuals with AN (Santonastaso, Pantano, Panarotto, & Silvestri, 1991), 43–88% of individuals with BN (Kendler et al., 1991), and approximately 32–50% of obese binge eaters (Yanovski, Nelson, Dubbert, & Spitzer, 1993) have a lifetime history of affective disorder. Interestingly, studies suggest that the phenomenology of the eating disorder and depressive disorder may follow independent courses in terms of onset and response to treatment (Walsh, Hadigan, Devlin, Gladis, & Roose, 1991), suggesting that these are clearly related but distinct phenomena. Also, for individuals with BED, it appears that the associated depression is linked to the binge eating rather than to overweight status (Marcus et al., 1990b). By contrast, weight status is significantly associated with depressive phenomenology for individuals with AN. Specifically, underweight status is associated with higher rates of depressive symptoms, which diminish for many individuals as weight normalizes.

Anxiety and obsessive–compulsive disorders. Although simple phobias, agoraphobia, and panic disorders do not appear to be more common among individuals with eating disorders than would be expected in the general population, social phobias and obsessive–compulsive disorder are disproportionately associated with the entire range of the eating disorders (Halmi et al., 1991; Schwalberg, Barlow, Alger, & Howard, 1992). The association between obsessive and compulsive behavior and the eating disorders has led to the hypothesis that there are shared disturbances in the brain neurotransmitter systems among these disorders, particularly for individuals with AN (e.g., Kaye, Gwirtsman, George, & Ebert, 1991).

Substance abuse. Although consensus in the field is that the eating disorders are not addictive disorders, it also is clear that patients with eating disorders consistently report higher rates of past and current substance abuse than would be expected in the general population (Braun, Sunday, & Halmi, 1994; Strasser, Pike, Walsh, & Wilson, 1992). The most commonly reported substance of abuse is alcohol. Although several mechanisms have been posited linking the eating disorders with substance abuse, imputing genetic, biological, and behavioral models, the underlying association has yet to be articulated (Wilson, 1995).

Social and Interpersonal Functioning

Problems in the realm of social and interpersonal functioning are common for individuals across the range of eating disturbances. However, the degree of impairment and the extent to which such problems are readily apparent vary considerably. Problems in these areas of functioning are not pathognomonic signs of an eating disturbance; however, they can serve as cues that a potential eating disturbance may be at play that would warrant further inquiry on the part of the primary health care provider. Of particular relevance, three areas of social functioning that have been studied most extensively are discussed next.

Family systems. Individuals with eating disorders tend to have more problems in conflict management and expression of negative affect in their families of origin, and their families tend to be less supportive and place less emphasis on assertiveness and autonomy (Strober, 1992). Such problems also are correlated with eating disturbances in nonclinical samples (Pike, 1995). In addition, overconcern with weight and shape in the family also is associated specifically with higher rates of eating disturbances in adolescent daughters (Attie & Brooks-Gunn, 1992; Pike & Rodin, 1991).

Parenting. Recent studies of child rearing among individuals with eating disturbances indicate that women with eating disturbances are at greater risk for providing inadequate nutrition to their children (Stein, 1995). Compared with women without eating disturbances, women with eating disturbances tend to be more intrusive with their infants during play and meal times by being more critical and demonstrating more negative affect during mealtimes, often expressing anxiety and disgust regarding the "mess" that their children make while eating (Stein, Woolley, Cooper, & Fairburn, 1994). Moreover, eating disturbances among adolescent girls appear to be associated with increased criticalness about weight and appearance by their mothers (Pike & Rodin, 1991).

Peer network. Social anxiety and public self-consciousness are significant problems for many individuals with eating disorders that appear to be associated with problems in building intimate and meaningful relationships and with impairment in the friendship network (Grilo, Wilfley, Jones,

Brownell, & Rodin, 1994; Schwalberg et al., 1992; Striegel-Moore, Silber-stein, & Rodin, 1993). Specifically, problems of social isolation, lack of social support, and poor conflict management are common in this population (Grissett & Norvell, 1992; Herzog, Keller, Lavori, & Ott, 1987; Pike, 1995).

Barriers to Treatment

Despite the serious medical complications, emotional distress, and interpersonal problems experienced by individuals with eating disorders, only a minority seek treatment for their eating disorder. For example, in the United States, a community-based study of adolescents showed that only 28% of individuals with eating disorders ever mentioned the problem to their physician (Whitaker, 1992).

Although the weight deviations associated with AN and BED make these individuals more noticeable to health care practitioners, it nonetheless appears that many of these individuals are not in treatment despite significant symptomatology. Individuals with AN are notoriously resistant to treatment; however, what is striking is that in a community study, Hoek (1991) reported that less than half the community cases of AN were detected by primary care practitioners. Similarly, our own clinical experience suggests that many individuals with BED seek medical care for problems such as hypertension and diabetes and pursue a multitude of commercial weight loss programs without ever disclosing their eating disorder. Relatedly, until recently, health care providers have focused primarily on weight loss due to the medical complications of obesity rather than the behavioral eating disturbances. As a result, although individuals with BED make up the largest eating disorder group, they are only recently being referred for treatment specifically aimed at their eating disorder. Studies have yet to be conducted to understand more fully why so few women seek out treatment specifically for their eating disorder. Our clinical experience, based on women who eventually did end up at facilities specializing in the treatment of eating disorders, suggests a number of internal and external barriers that interfere with seeking treatment for an eating disorder.

First, having an eating disorder often is the source of tremendous shame and self-loathing. We have worked with patients who were in previous types of therapies for years without ever disclosing that they had an eating disorder. We also have encountered patients who have undergone medical procedures without ever reporting to their physicians the eating disorder that they believed was at the core of the medical problem. Paradoxically, we find that most patients are nonetheless relieved when they finally disclose their problem; typically, patients also find comfort in learning that they are not alone and that specialized treatments are available.

A second internal barrier to treatment relates to fears that successful treatment will result in weight gain. Except for AN, in which weight restoration is a key aspect of successful treatment, neither the treatment of BN or BED results in significant weight change. Rather, regulating one's eating patterns promotes weight stabilization for the majority of people with BN and BED (Agras et al., 1994; Walsh et al., 1991; Wilfley et al., 1993). Once in treatment, these individuals appear to benefit from education linking weight, dieting, regulation of hunger and satiety, and sound nutritional practices as provided in cognitive–behavioral therapy (Fairburn, Marcus, & Wilson, 1993). Across the spectrum of eating disorders, reduction of the importance of weight and shape in determining self-worth is critical to lasting therapeutic benefit.

Another potential barrier to treatment is the often-held misconception that the eating disorder will go away on its own. In the absence of community-based studies of nonclinical samples, it is unclear whether eating disorders remit spontaneously for a significant number of individuals. On the basis of clinic samples, eating disorders appear to take a chronic course and therefore warrant intervention. Moreover, the duration of illness appears to be inversely correlated with better outcome, particularly for patients with AN (Herzog et al., 1992).

A significant external barrier to treatment is economic. Despite clear evidence of the often profoundly negative physical and psychological sequelae of eating disorders, insurance coverage for eating disorders treatment is limited. This is problematic not only because it results in poor distribution of services but also because it ignores the fact that individuals with eating disorders may use extensive other diagnostic and clinical treatment for problems related to the eating disorder without ever addressing the core problem.

Another important external barrier is lack of knowledge about appropriate referral sources. The National Institute of Mental Health publishes a brochure that includes a listing of self-help organizations, which, in turn, maintain referral directories for specialized treatment centers and health care providers. A professional organization, the Academy for Eating Disorders, also maintains a roster of members, all of whom have expertise in the field of eating disorders. Finally, the APA has developed standards of care that provide details regarding parameters in the treatment of eating disorders. In addition, self-help books may be useful tools for facilitating the entry into treatment for some individuals (Wells, Garvin, Dohm, & Striegel-Moore, in press).

Assessment and Referrals

Given these barriers to treatment, well-informed health care professionals can make a tremendous difference in getting treatment to patients. In addition to an awareness of the range of associated symptoms that have been described in this chapter, a set of standard, straightforward questions implemented routinely in the assessment of patients could facilitate early detection and help individuals with eating problems get appropriate treatment. We recommend that the following questions regarding weight, eating behavior, and attitudes toward weight and shape be asked in routine history taking and periodic medical checkups. These questions are especially relevant for adolescent and adult women, given that they appear to be at highest risk for eating disorders; however, we recommend that these questions be asked of all patients regardless of age, race, or gender.

1. *Assess current weight.*   If the individual's weight is more than 15% above or below recommended weight for height, it increases the risk of either AN or BED.

2. *Assess weight fluctuations.*   If the individual's weight has fluctuated more than 5–10 lb in the past year, it may reflect the oscillation between periods of extreme dieting and overeating or binge eating. This would warrant further attention.

3. *Significant weight loss or weight gain.*   If the individual has lost a significant amount of weight (10 lb or more) during the past year, it is worth assessing how the weight was lost, whether the individual is satisfied with his or her current weight, and whether the individual is planning on losing any more weight. Depending on where the individual's current weight is, this weight change may reflect a healthy adjustment in eating habits and exercise. However, if the weight loss was achieved by extreme dieting, it may reflect increased risk for AN and possibly BN if the individual cannot sustain the dieting and starts binge eating and purging. If the individual has gained a significant amount of weight over the past year, it may reflect problems with binge eating. This should be assessed further.

4. *Inquire about general eating habits.*   Simple specific questions about daily eating habits will provide much information. Skipping meals, eating alone most of the time, not eating much until dinnertime, and avoiding a lot of foods are some important behaviors that suggest dysregulation of eating. If any of these behaviors occur routinely, it could indicate that the individual has some kind of eating disturbance and should be evaluated further.

5. *Inquire about binge eating.*   Although many individuals will not volunteer that they have a problem with binge eating, direct inquiry will give them the opportunity to disclose the problem, and asking about this problem in a matter-of-fact health screening will potentially help relieve some of the associated shame. Thus, we recommend that health care professionals ask directly whether the individual has problems controlling his or her eating, has a problem with overeating, or has a problem binge eating. Using several probes will help find the term that most closely describes the specific problem for a given individual.

6. *Inquire about specific efforts to control weight or lose weight.* Again, a few simple and straightforward questions will provide important information. We recommend that the health care professional ask the individual what he or she does as a means of weight contol. In addition, asking explicitly whether the individual ever engages in fasting, vomiting, or extreme exercise to affect weight will offer individuals an outlet for discussing serious problems. Some individuals use illegal drugs such as cocaine to control their weight and may benefit from drug counseling.

7. *Inquire about attitudes toward weight and shape.*   The health care professional can learn a lot about an individual's risk for an eating disorder simply by asking about feelings regarding current weight and shape.

Health care professionals should expect some "normative discontent" among adult women in particular; however, either significant distress or significant discrepancy between current and ideal weight (10 lb) should raise concerns about the possible increased risk for eating disorders. If an individual reports marked distress or dissatisfaction with current weight, it may be part of an existing eating disorder, or it may put an individual at risk for developing one. In either case, the health care professional can provide important educational information and direct individuals to appropriate treatment if necessary.

8. *Referral for expert evaluation and treatment.* Once it has been determined that an individual requires either further evaluation or treatment, we recommend that health care professionals refer patients to specialized treatment centers or to experts in the treatment of eating disorders. Clinical interventions for eating disorders are actively under study, and experts in the field will be most up to date in their knowledge of treatments and their efficacy. Currently, cognitive–behavioral therapy is the gold standard for the treatment of BN, and, as described earlier, cognitive–behavioral therapy also has demonstrated efficacy in the treatment of BED. In addition, interpersonal psychotherapy has demonstrated efficacy in the treatment of these disorders, and currently studies are under way to assess whether different patient characteristics would make one treatment or the other more appropriate for a given individual. It is possible that cognitive–behavioral therapy and interpersonal psychotherapy will prove to be effective in the treatment of AN, although currently we can recommend cognitive–behavioral therapy on the basis of only preliminary pilot data. As noted earlier, several studies of medication interventions in the treatment of BN and BED indicate that antidepressant medication is significantly better than placebo, although the long-term effects tend not to be as promising as psychotherapy interventions. Nonetheless, the combination of cognitive–behavioral therapy and medication may result in an incremental benefit in terms of reduction of the specific symptoms of the eating disorder, associated depression and anxiety, or both. Many medication interventions for AN have been evaluated with minimal reported benefit. However, some preliminary data on the efficacy of fluoxetine in the relapse prevention of AN suggest that some benefit may accrue.

Taken together, these data emphasize the evolving nature of the knowledge base regarding treatment for eating disorders. Thus, again, we recommend that health care professionals refer patients to experts in the field who will be able to provide state-of-the-art treatment.

Conclusion

Eating disorders and disordered eating are widespread problems for a large segment of the female population. Despite associated problems across medical, emotional, and interpersonal domains of functioning, many individuals with eating disorders nonetheless fail to seek treatment. The primary health care provider can play a critical role in facilitating entry into treatment. Because many individuals with eating disorders are not forthcoming about their problem, it is extremely important that the gatekeepers of the medical system be aware of the range of eating disturbances and associated problems. Early detection of eating disturbances and directing individuals to appropriate services greatly enhance the quality of life for many women who otherwise run the risk of struggling alone with chronic problems that can be treated.

References

Agras, W. S., Telch, C. F., Arnow, B., Eldredge, K., Wilfley, D. E., Raeburn, S. D., Henderson, J., & Marnell, M. (1994). Weight loss, cognitive-behavioral, and desipramine treatments in binge eating disorder: An additive design. *Behavior Therapy, 25,* 225–238.

Altshuler, B., Dechow, P., Waller, D. & Hardy, B. (1990). An investigation of the oral pathologies occurring in bulimia nervosa. *International Journal of Eating Disorders, 9,* 191–199.

American Psychiatric Association. (1994). *Diagnostic and statistical manual of mental disorders* (4th ed.). Washington, DC: Author.

Attia, E. (1995, May). *Inpatient treatment of anorexia nervosa.* Paper presented at the meeting of the American Psychiatric Association, Miami.

Attie, I., & Brooks-Gunn, J. (1992). Developmental issues in the study of eating problems and disorders. In J. Crowther, S. Hobfoll, M. Stephens, & D. Tennenbaum (Eds.), *The etiology of bulimia: The individual and familial contexts* (pp. 35–58). Washington, DC: Hemisphere.

Beglin, S. J., & Fairburn, C. G. (1992). What is meant by the term "binge"? *American Journal of Psychiatry, 149,* 123–124.

Berkowitz, R., Stunkard, A. J., & Stallings, V. A. (1993). Binge eating disorder in obese adolescent girls. *Annals of the New York Academy of Sciences, 29,* 200–206.

Braun, N. L., Sunday, S. K., & Halmi, K. A. (1994). Psychiatric comorbidity in patients with eating disorders. *Psychological Medicine, 24,* 859–867.

Brotman, A., Rigotti, N., & Herzog, D. (1985). Medical complications of eating disorders: Outpatient evaluation and management. *Comprehensive Psychiatry, 26,* 258–272.

Brownell, K. D., & Fairburn, C. G. (Eds.). (1995). *Eating disorders and obesity.* New York: Guilford Press.

Brownell, K. D., Rodin, J., & Wilmore, J. H. (1992). *Eating, body weight, and performance in athletes.* Philadelphia: Lea & Febiger.

Bruce, B., & Agras, W. S. (1992). Binge eating in females: A population based investigation. *International Journal of Eating Disorders, 12,* 365–373.

Bunnell, D. W., Shenker, I. R., Nussbaum, M. P., Jacobson, M. S., & Cooper, P. (1990). Subclinical versus formal eating disorders: Differentiating psychological features. *International Journal of Eating Disorders, 9,* 357–362.

Chatoor, J. (1989). Infantile anorexia nervosa: A developmental disorder of separation and individuation. *Journal of the American Academy of Psychoanalysis, 17,* 43–64.

Childress, A. C., Brewerton, T. D., Hodges, E. L., & Jarrell, M. P. (1993). The Kids' Eating Disorders Survey (KEDS): A study of middle school students. *Journal of the American Academy of Child and Adolescent Psychiatry, 32,* 843–850.

Crisp, A. H., Callender, J. S., Halek, C., & Hsu, G. L. (1992). Long-term mortality in anorexia nervosa: A 20-year follow-up on the St. George's and Aberdeen cohorts. *British Journal of Psychiatry, 161,* 104–107.

Deter, H. C., & Herzog, W. (1994). Anorexia nervosa in a long-term perspective: Results of the Heidelberg-Mannheim study. *Psychosomatic Medicine, 56,* 20–27.

Devlin, M. J., Walsh, B. T., Spitzer, R. L., & Hasin, D. (1992). Is there another binge eating disorder? A review of the literature on overeating in the absence of bulimia. *International Journal of Eating Disorders, 11,* 333–340.

Fairburn, C. G., & Beglin, S. J. (1990). Studies of the epidemiology of bulimia nervosa. *American Journal of Psychiatry, 147*, 401–408.

Fairburn, C. G., Marcus, M. D., & Wilson, G. T. (1993). Cognitive-behavioral therapy for binge-eating and bulimia nervosa: A comprehensive treatment manual. In C. G. Fairburn & G. T. Wilson (Eds.), *Binge-eating nature, assessment and treatment* (pp. 361–404). Guilford: New York.

Franko, D. L., & Walton, B. E. (1993). Pregnancy and eating disorders: A review and clinical implications. *International Journal of Eating Disorders, 13*, 41–48.

Goldbloom, D. S., & Kennedy, S. H. (1995). Medical complications of anorexia nervosa. In K. D. Brownell & C. G. Fairburn (Eds.), *Eating disorders and obesity* (pp. 266–270). New York: Guilford Press.

Grilo, C. M., Wilfley, D. E., Jones, A., Brownell, K. D., & Rodin, J. (1994). The social self, body dissatisfaction, and binge eating. *Obesity Research, 2*, 24–27.

Grissett, N. I., & Norvell, N. K. (1992). Perceived social support, social skills, and quality of relationships in bulimic women. *Journal of Consulting and Clinical Psychology, 60*, 293–299.

Halmi, K. A., Eckert, E., Marchi, P., Sampugnaro, V., Apple, R., & Cohen, J. (1991). Co-morbidity of psychiatric diagnoses in anorexia nervosa. *Archives of General Psychiatry, 48*, 712–718.

Herzog, W., Deter, H. C., & Vandereycken, W. (1992). *The course of eating disorders: Long-term follow-up studies of anorexia and bulimia nervosa.* New York: Springer-Verlag.

Herzog, D. B., Hopkins, J. D., & Burns, C. D. (1993). A follow-up study of 33 subdiagnostic eating disordered women. *International Journal of Eating Disorders, 14*, 261–267.

Herzog, D. B., Keller, M. B., Lavori, P. W., & Ott, I. L. (1987). Social impairment in bulimia. *International Journal of Eating Disorders, 6*, 741–747.

Hoek, H. W. (1991). The incidence and prevalence of anorexia nervosa and bulimia nervosa in primary care. *Psychological Medicine, 21*, 455–460.

Hoek, H. W. (1993). Review of the epidemiological studies of eating disorders. *International Review of Psychiatry, 5*, 61–74.

Hsu, L. K. (1990). *Eating disorders.* New York: Guilford Press.

Kaye, W. H., Gwirtsman, H. E., George, D. T., & Ebert, M. H. (1991). Altered serotonin activity in anorexia nervosa after long-term weight restoration: Does elevated CSF 5-HIAA correlate with rigid and obsessive behavior? *Archives of General Psychiatry, 48*, 556–562.

Keller, M. B., Herzog, D. B., Lavori, P. W., Bradburn, I. S., & Mahoney, E. M. (1992). The naturalistic history of bulimia nervosa: Extraordinary high rates of chronicity, relapse, recurrent, and psychosocial morbidity. *International Journal of Eating Disorders, 12*, 1–9.

Kendler, K. S., Maclean, C., Neale, M., Kessler, R., Heath, A., & Eaves, L. (1991). The genetic epidemiology of bulimia nervosa. *American Journal of Psychiatry, 148*, 1627–1637.

Lacey, J. H., & Smith, G. (1987). Bulimia nervosa: The impact of pregnancy on mother and baby. *British Journal of Psychiatry, 150*, 777–781.

Lask, B., & Bryant-Waugh, R. (1992). Early onset anorexia nervosa and related eating disorders. *Journal of Child Psychology and Psychiatry, 33*, 281–300.

Marcus, M. D. (1995). Binge eating and obesity. In K. D. Brownell & C. G. Fairburn (Eds.), *Eating disorders and obesity* (pp. 441–444). New York: Guilford Press.

Marcus, M. D., Wing, R. R., Ewing, L., Kern, E., Gooding, W., & McDermott, M. (1990a). A double-blind placebo-controlled trial of fluoxetine plus behavior modification in the treatment of obese binge eaters and non-binge eaters. *American Journal of Psychiatry, 147*, 876–881.

Marcus, M. D., Wing, R. R., Ewing, L., Kern, E., Gooding, W., & McDermott, M. (1990b). Psychiatric disorders among obese binge eaters. *International Journal of Eating Disorders, 9*, 69–77.

Mitchell, J., Seim, H., Colon, E., & Pomeroy, C. (1987). Medical complications and medical management of bulimia. *Annals of Internal Medicine, 107*, 71–77.

Mussell, M. P., Mitchell, J. E., Weller, C. L., Raymond, N. C., Crow, S. J., & Crosby, R. D. (1995). Onset of binge eating, dieting, obesity, and mood disorders among subjects seeking treatment for binge eating disorder. *International Journal of Eating Disorders, 17,* 395–401.

Neuberger, S. K., Rao, R., Weltzin, T. E., Greeno, C., & Kayer, W. H. (1995). Differences in weight gain between restrictor and bulimic anorectics. *International Journal of Eating Disorders, 17,* 331–335.

Olmsted, M. P., Kaplan, A. S., & Rockert, W. (1994). Rate and prediction of relapse in bulimia nervosa. *American Journal of Psychiatry, 151,* 738–743.

Palla, B., & Litt, I. (1988). Medical complications of eating disorders in adolescents. *Pediatrics, 81,* 613–623.

Pate, J., Pumariega, A., Hester, C., & Garner, D. (1992). Cross-cultural patterns in eating disorders: A review. *Journal of the American Academy of Child and Adolescent Psychiatry, 31,* 802–809.

Phelps, G. C., Andrea, R., Rizzo, F. G., Johnston, L., & Main, C. M. (1993). Prevalence of self-induced vomiting and laxative/medication abuse among female adolescents: A longitudinal study. *International Journal of Eating Disorders, 14,* 375–378.

Pi-Sunyer, F. X. (1995). Medical complications of obesity. In K. D. Brownell & C. G. Fairburn (Eds.), *Eating disorders and obesity* (pp. 401–405). New York: Guilford Press.

Pike, K. M. (1995). Bulimic symptomatology in high school girls: Toward a model of cumulative risk. *Psychology of Women Quarterly, 19(3),* 373–396.

Pike, K. M., & Rodin, J. (1991). Mothers, daughters, and disordered eating. *Journal of Abnormal Psychology, 100,* 198–204.

Putukian, M. (1994). The female triad: Eating disorders, amenorrhea, and osteoporosis. *Medical Clinics of North America, 78,* 345–356.

Rossiter, E. M., & Agras, W. S. (1990). An empirical test of the *DSM-III-R* definition of binge. *International Journal of Eating Disorders, 9,* 513–518.

Rossiter, E. M., Agras, W. S., Telch, C. F., & Bruce, B. (1992). The eating patterns of nonpurging bulimic subjects. *International Journal of Eating Disorders, 11,* 111–120.

Salisbury, J. J., Levine, A. S., Crow, S. J., & Mitchell, J. E. (1995). Refeeding, metabolic rate, and weight gain in anorexia nervosa: A review. *International Journal of Eating Disorders, 17,* 337–345.

Santonastaso, P., Pantano, M., Panarotto, L., & Silvestri, A. (1991). A follow-up study on anorexia nervosa: Clinical features and diagnostic outcome. *European Psychiatry, 6,* 177–185.

Schwalberg, M. D., Barlow, D. H., Alger, S. A., & Howard, L. J. (1992). Comparison of bulimics, obese binge eaters, social phobics, and individuals with panic disorder on comorbidity across *DSM-III-R* anxiety disorders. *Journal of Abnormal Psychology, 101,* 675–681.

Seeman, E., Szmukler, G., Formica, C., Tsalamandris, C., & Mestrovic, R. (1992). Osteoporosis in anorexia nervosa: The influence of peak bone density, bone loss, oral contraceptive use and exercise. *Journal of Bone and Mineral Research, 7,* 1467–1474.

Shisslak, C. M., Crago, M., & Estes, L. S. (1995). The spectrum of eating disturbances: A literature review. *International Journal of Eating Disorders, 18(3),* 209–219.

Silber, T. (1986). Anorexia nervosa in Blacks and Hispanics. *International Journal of Eating Disorders, 5,* 121–128.

Smith, D. E., Marcus, M. D., & Kaye, W. (1992). Cognitive-behavioral treatment of obese binge eaters. *International Journal of Eating Disorders, 12,* 257–262.

Spitzer, R. L., Devlin, M. J., Walsh, B. T., Hasin, D., Wing, R. R., Marcus, M. D., Stunkard, A., Wadden, T. A., Yanovski, S., Agras, W. S., Mitchell, J., & Nonas, C. (1992). Binge eating disorder: A multisite field trial for the diagnostic criteria. *International Journal of Eating Disorders, 11,* 191–203.

Spitzer, R. L., Yanovski, S., Wadden, T., et al. (1993). Binge eating disorder: Its further validation in a multisite trial. *International Journal of Eating Disorders, 13(2),* 137–153.

Stein, A. (1995). Eating disorders and childrearing. In K. D. Brownell & C. G. Fairburn (Eds.), *Eating disorders and obesity* (pp. 188–195). New York: Guilford Press.

Stein, A., Woolley, H., Cooper, S. D., & Fairburn, C. G. (1994). An observational study of mothers with eating disorders and their infants. *Journal of Child Psychology and Psychiatry, 35,* 733–748.

Steinhausen, H. C., Rauss-Mason, C., & Seidel, R. (1991). Follow-up studies of anorexia nervosa: A review of research findings. *Psychological Medicine, 3,* 239–249.

Stewart, D. (1992). Reproductive functions in eating disorders. *Annals of Medicine, 24,* 287–291.

Strasser, T., Pike, K. M., Walsh, B. T., & Wilson, G. T. (1992). The impact of prior substance abuse on treatment outcome for bulimia nervosa. *Addictive Behaviors, 17,* 387–393.

Striegel-Moore, R. H., & Marcus, M. D. (1995). Eating disorders in women: Current issues and debates. In A. L. Stanton & S. J. Gallant (Eds.), *Women's health book* (pp. 445–487). Washington, DC: American Psychological Association.

Striegel-Moore, R. H., Silberstein, L. R., & Rodin, J. (1993). The social self in bulimia nervosa: Public self-consciousness, social anxiety, and perceived fraudulence. *Journal of Abnormal Psychology, 102,* 297–303.

Striegel-Moore, R. H., & Smolak, L. (1996). The role of race in the development of eating disorders. In L. Smolak, M. Levine, & R. H. Striegel-Moore (Eds.), *The developmental psychopathology of eating disorders: Implications for research, treatment, and prevention* (pp. 259–284). Hillsdale, NJ: Erlbaum.

Strober, M. (1992). Family-genetic studies. In K. Halmi, (Ed.), *Psychobiology and treatment of anorexia nervosa and bulimia nervosa* (pp. 61–76). Washington, DC: American Psychiatric Press.

Walsh, B. T., Hadigan, C. M., Devlin, M. J., Gladis, M., & Roose, S. P. (1991). Long-term outcome of antidepressant treatment for bulimia nervosa. *American Journal of Psychiatry, 148,* 1206–1212.

Walters, E. E., & Kendler, K. S. (1995). Anorexia nervosa and anorexic-like syndromes in a population-based female twin sample. *American Journal of Psychiatry, 152,* 64–71.

Wells, A. M., Garvin, V., Dohm, F. A., & Striegel-Moore, R. H. (in press). Telephone based guided self-help for binge eating disorder: A feasibility study. *International Journal of Eating Disorders.*

Whitaker, A. H. (1992). An epidemiological study of anorectic and bulimic symptoms in adolescent girls: Implications for pediatricians. *Pediatric Annals, 21,* 752–759.

Wilfley, D. E., Agras, W. S., Telch, C. F., Rossiter, E. M., Schneider, J. A., Cole, A. G., Sifford, L., & Raeburn, S. D. (1993). Group cognitive-behavioral therapy and group interpersonal psychotherapy for the nonpurging bulimic: A controlled comparison. *Journal of Consulting and Clinical Psychology, 61,* 296–305.

Williamson, D. A., Gleaves, D. H., & Savin, S. S. (1992). Empirical classification of eating disorder not otherwise specified: Support for DSM-IV changes. *Journal of Psychopathology and Behavioral Assessment, 14,* 201–216.

Wilson, G. T. (1995). Eating disorders and addictive disorders. In K. D. Brownell & C. G. Fairburn (Eds.), *Eating disorders and obesity* (pp. 165–170). New York: Guilford Press.

Woodside, D. B., & Garfinkel, P. E. (1992). Age of onset in eating disorders. *International Journal of Eating Disorders, 12,* 31–36.

Yanovski, S. Z. (1993). Binge eating disorder: Current knowledge and future directions. *Obesity Research, 1,* 305–324.

Yanovski, S. Z., Nelson, J. E., Dubbert, B. K., & Spitzer, R. L. (1993). Binge eating is associated with psychiatric co-morbidity in the obese. *American Journal of Psychiatry, 150*(10), 1472–1479.

8

Obesity

Rena R. Wing and Mary Lou Klem

Despite all the publicity about healthy eating and exercise, the prevalence of obesity in the United States is increasing. Whereas 10 years ago 25% of the American population was overweight, now 33%, or 58 million, of Americans are overweight (Kuczmarski, Fiegal, Campbell, & Johnson, 1994). Thus, obesity is becoming a major health problem in the United States.

Obesity is of special relevance to the health care of women. Thirty-one percent of men aged 20–74 years are overweight compared with 35% of women (Kuczmarski et al., 1994). The prevalence of obesity is even higher in minorities; more than 50% of middle-aged African American and Mexican American women are overweight. Moreover, the prevalence of being overweight is increasing over time.

In addition, more than half of all women (52%) feel that they are overweight (Horm & Anderson, 1993), and two large national surveys have shown that approximately 40% of women (vs. 24% of men) are currently dieting to lose weight (Horm & Anderson, 1993; Serdula et al., 1993). Thus, many women who are not in fact overweight perceive themselves to be and are dieting to try to lose weight. Women in minority populations tend to be less concerned about their weight and view plumpness as a sign of health and prosperity (Brown, 1993).

Lifestyle factors, namely diet and exercise, play a major role in the development and treatment of obesity. In this chapter we review these behavioral aspects of obesity and focus on those issues regarding obesity that are particularly relevant to women's health.

Defining Obesity

Obesity technically means "overfat" and should be assessed with measures of body fatness, as can be obtained through underwater weighing or by measuring skinfold thickness with calipers. However, for most individuals, body weight and body fat are highly related. Consequently, obesity is usually assessed by measuring an individuals' body weight and considering their weight in relation to their height. Although many people still use the Metropolitan Life Insurance norms to define obesity, it has become more common to compute the body mass index (BMI), which is a person's weight (in kilograms) divided by their height (in meters) squared. A BMI of 19–24 corresponds to "ideal" body weight, a BMI of 25–29 is considered moderately overweight (approximately 15–30% over ideal weight), and a BMI of more than 31 is considered severely obese (more than 40% over ideal body weight).

Causes of Obesity

Obesity is a multifactorial disease involving a combination of genetic, environmental, and behavioral determinants. Although there is no evidence that these determinants differ for men and women, it is important that health care professionals be knowledgeable about these determinants so that they are able to appropriately counsel their overweight female patients.

Twin studies and adoption studies clearly show a strong genetic component to obesity, with genetic factors explaining approximately 20–40% of the variance in body weight. In one well-known study, the weight of adults who had been adopted as infants was more similar to those of their biological parents than to the parents who had reared them (Stunkard et al., 1986). Recent research has identified specific genes that are related to obesity (Zhang et al., 1994).

However, behavioral and environmental factors also are important in the development of obesity. There are numerous examples of individuals of similar genetic background who live in different parts of the world and have markedly different body weights (Hodge & Zimmet, 1994). For example, Japanese individuals who live in Japan remain thinner than those who move to Hawaii, who in turn remain thinner than those who move to the mainland United States (Curb & Marcus, 1991). These differences in body weight presumably reflect cultural differences in diet and exercise behavior.

Key behavioral determinants of body weight are physical activity and diet composition. There have been numerous studies showing that obese individuals are less active than normal-weight individuals, and this difference appears to be a cause, rather than a consequence, of obesity (Shah & Jeffery, 1991). Women have particularly low levels of physical activity. Thirty percent of women report no leisure physical activity, and an additional 31% report only irregular physical activity (Caspersen, Christenson, & Pollard, 1985). In addition, consumption of a high-fat diet appears to be related to the development of obesity. The diet of American adults currently contains about 34% fat, 34.1% in men and 33.8% in women (Centers for Disease Control, 1994). This represents a decrease in fat intake from 10 years ago but still is clearly above the recommended 30% fat intake. Such high-fat diets may increase the number of calories consumed and contribute to the development of obesity.

It is important that health care professionals consider both genetic and behavioral determinants of obesity in counseling overweight patients. Patients with a strong family history of obesity should be encouraged to set realistic weight goals for themselves. In addition, all patients should be helped to recognize that modification of their dietary intake, physical activity, or both will result in weight loss.

In contrast to the evidence of genetic and behavioral determinants of obesity, to our knowledge there are no data to support the hypothesis that certain psychological characteristics predispose individuals to obesity (Wadden & Stunkard, 1993). In fact, studies comparing normal-weight and overweight individuals have shown no differences between these two groups on measures of depressive symptomatology, general psychopathology, assertiveness, or self-consciousness. There are some obese individuals who are depressed or anxious or who have other psychiatric symptoms, but there are just as many normal-weight individuals with these problems.

Likewise, although many individuals report that they gain weight during periods of stress, there is little evidence to support this assertion. Animal models of stress-induced obesity have been developed, but the relevance of this to humans is unclear (Greeno & Wing, 1994). We could find only one study of stress-induced eating that specifically compared men and women (Grunberg & Straub, 1992). In that study, college-aged participants were provided with sweet, salty, or bland snacks while watching either a stressful or relaxing video. Unstressed men had the greatest consumption; they ate about twice as much as any of the other groups. Women who watched the stressful video increased their sweet intake but decreased other foods, so that the total consumption by stressed and nonstressed women did not differ.

Consequences of Obesity

There are numerous physical and psychosocial adverse consequences of obesity. Obesity increases the risk of developing hypertension, hyperlipidemia, and Type 2 (or non-insulin-dependent) diabetes. The risk of developing coronary heart disease (CHD) and certain forms of cancer (e.g., cancer of the gallbladder, breast, uterus, cervix, and ovaries in women) also is increased in obese women. The Nurses' Health Study, a study of more than 100,000 women aged 30–55 years who were followed for 8 years, showed that women with a BMI of less than 21 (95% of ideal weight) had the lowest risk of developing CHD (Manson et al., 1990). In those with a BMI of 21–25 (usually considered average weight), the risk was increased 30%; in those with a BMI of 25–29, the risk was increased 80%; and in those with a BMI of more than 29, the risk was increased 200%. Thus, even modest amounts of overweight may contribute to the development of CHD.

There also are profound psychosocial consequences of obesity. Unfortunately, these adverse effects are particularly pronounced in women. A recent prospective study of young adults indicated that overweight women were less likely to marry, had higher rates of household poverty, and lower annual incomes than those who were of normal weight (Gortmaker, Must, Perrin, Sobol, & Dietz, 1993). Compared with normal-weight individuals, those who are overweight have not been shown to have increased rates of depression or other types of psychopathology, an important finding given the stigma associated with being overweight (Wadden & Stunkard, 1993).

Body Fat Distribution

As discussed earlier, obesity has marked effects on morbidity and mortality. In addition, the way in which body fat is distributed influences the impact that it will have on health. The "apple" shape (android obesity), in which weight is distributed in the abdominal area, has been found to be much more detrimental to health than the "pear" shape (gynoid obesity), in which the weight is mainly on the hips. Android obesity has been shown to increase the risk of diabetes, CHD, and all-cause mortality independent of the degree of overall obesity (Lapidus et al., 1984). Men typically have android obesity, whereas women may have either android or gynoid obesity.

There is a strong genetic component to body fat distribution, and studies with monozygote twins have shown strong associations between twin pairs (Price & Gottesman, 1991). However, there also are psychosocial and behavioral determinants of android obesity, including smoking, low exercise, obesity, high-fat diets, and stress (Wing, Matthews, Kuller, Meilahn, & Plantinga, 1991a). Modifying these factors (e.g., increasing exercise) can decrease abdominal obesity.

On the basis of this research, it is important that health care providers begin to measure abdominal obesity in their patients. This typically is done by simply measuring the circumference of the waist (at the umbilicus) and the circumference of the hips (at the widest part) with a tape measure. The ratio of waist-to-hips defines upper body fat or abdominal obesity; ratios of more than 1.0 and 0.8 for men and women, respectively, are considered health risks. Patients with waist-to-hip ratios greater than these values should be helped to modify the behaviors that affect their overall obesity and body fat distribution.

Basic Guidelines for the Treatment of Obesity

Identifying Individuals Who Should Lose Weight

One of the important roles of the health care provider is to identify people needing to lose weight and encourage them to adopt healthier eating and exercise habits. In identifying those who need to lose weight, it is important to consider (a) the patient's degree of obesity; (b) whether the patient has obesity-associated health consequences (e.g., hypertension or diabetes), a family history of these diseases, or both; and (c) whether the patient has android obesity (i.e., by measuring waist to hip ratio). Research done in other areas, such as smoking cessation, suggests that physicians can markedly influence health behaviors by simply discussing these issues with patients and proposing specific strategies for habit change. Although we know of no similar studies in the area of obesity, it would appear that raising and discussing this issue with overweight individuals also may influence these habits. The health care professional should be certain to treat obese patients with respect and to recognize that obesity is a disease, not simply a problem of willpower (Stunkard, 1993).

Selecting a Weight Loss Goal

Overweight individuals should be encouraged to lose modest amounts of weight (15–20 lb) and to maintain this weight loss rather than attempting to achieve "ideal" body weight. Modest weight losses have been shown to be sufficient to reduce blood pressure, to improve glycemic control in those with diabetes, and to improve lipid levels (Blackburn & Read, 1984; Wing et al., 1987). Moreover, those with a family history of obesity should be helped to set a realistic weight goal that takes their genetic predisposition into consideration.

Selecting a Weight Control Program

It remains unclear whether overweight patients who wish to lose weight should be encouraged to try to accomplish this on their own or to seek professional help. Unfortunately, there are few data available on the number of individuals who try to lose weight on their own and their results. For individuals who wish to lose weight on their own, the role of the health care provider may be mainly one of support and encouragement. It also may be possible to recommend appropriate nutrition and exercise changes to patients and to encourage them to purchase a self-help book for guidance, such as *The LEARN Program for Weight Control* by Brownell (1991) or *Learning to Eat* by Ferguson (1975).

Individuals who want more professional help might be encouraged to meet one on one with a registered dietitian or behavioral psychologist, to join a commercial weight loss program or support group (e.g., Jenny Craig, Weight Watchers, or Take Off Pounds Sensibly), or to participate in a university research program. In selecting such programs, it is important to consider (a) the qualifications of the therapist (e.g., is the therapist a trained professional or a peer?); (b) the type of diet prescribed (e.g., is it a balanced healthy diet that people can eat for the rest of their life?); (c) whether exercise is recommended as part of the program; (d) whether behavior modification strategies are taught to help people modify their lifestyle; (e) whether there is ongoing group or therapist support; (f) the cost of the program (higher cost does not necessarily mean a "better" program); and (g) the results that have been obtained to date by this program. Many of these components are discussed in more detail later.

Results to Anticipate From Weight Loss Programs

The most effective weight control programs are programs that combine diet, exercise, behavior modification, and continued contact. In such programs, weight losses average 20–30 lb at the end of approximately a 20-week program; participants in these programs maintain a weight loss of 10–15 lb at 1 year. As noted earlier, weight losses of this magnitude are sufficient to reduce cardiovascular risk factors. Recent programs have sometimes included very-low-calorie diets (VLCDs) as part of the initial treatment. With VLCDs, initial results are increased to approximately 40 lb, but results at 1-year follow-up are not improved (Wadden, 1993; Wing, Marcus, et al., 1991).

Recently, there has been increased interest in pharmacological treatment of obesity. Serotonergic drugs, such as fluoxetine and fenfluramine, have been used alone and in combination with catecholaminergic drugs such as phentermin (Bray, 1992, 1993; Weintraub, 1992). Often these drugs are used along with lifestyle intervention. Treatment with such drugs appears to have a modest effect on weight loss, with the greatest weight losses observed at 6 months. Chronic drug treatment is required because weight is regained as soon as the drugs are terminated (Bray, 1992).

Psychological Consequences of Weight Loss

The widespread prevalence of dieting to lose weight has prompted health professionals to examine closely the psychological consequences of these efforts. Research has primarily focused on the incidence of depression and disordered eating among individuals receiving treatment for weight loss. Although early retrospective studies have suggested that patients were likely to experience depression as a result of treatment, later prospective studies have consistently demonstrated a positive effect of treatment, with most patients experiencing a decrease in depression during the course of a program (Wadden & Stunkard, 1993). Initial studies of the relationship between weight loss treatment and binge eating likewise suggested that dieting might lead to an increase in binge eating (Telch & Agras, 1993). However, a more recent study (Yanovski, Gormally, Leser, Gwirtsman, & Yanovski, 1994) showed that weight loss decreased the frequency and severity of binge eating in patients diagnosed with binge eating disorder (BED) and had no adverse impact on eating behaviors in patients without BED. Thus, it appears that there are positive psychological effects of weight loss in obese individuals.

Weight Cycling

As noted earlier, weight loss treatments are only moderately successful, and some individuals who lose weight in these programs will subsequently regain their weight. Consequently, concern has been raised about possible adverse consequences of such weight cycling. Concern has focused on possible metabolic consequences, psychological consequences, and morbidity and mortality.

The majority of studies to date do not support the hypothesis that weight cycling has adverse effects on metabolism. Most animal studies on this issue and the several prospective studies that have been conducted with humans do not show any evidence that weight cycling affects metabolic rate, body composition, body fat distribution, or the ability to lose weight on subsequent weight loss efforts (National Task Force on the Prevention and Treatment of Obesity, 1994; Wing, 1992).

Results of several epidemiological studies have suggested that individuals with the greatest weight variability have an increased risk of cardiovascular disease and mortality (Blair, Shaten, Brownell, Collins, & Lissner, 1993; Lissner et al., 1991). Unfortunately, it is difficult to interpret these studies because they did not distinguish between voluntary and involuntary weight loss; variability in body weight may reflect involuntary weight loss due to illness rather than intentional efforts to lose weight. Evidence supporting this possibility comes from the finding that the risks of weight variability are greatest in those who are thinnest (Blair et al., 1993). In addition, the mechanisms by which weight cycling might affect mortality in humans remain unclear. Research has found no evidence that weight cycling affects cardiovascular risk factors, such as cholesterol or blood pressure. Rather, researchers found that the key determinant of risk factor change was the magnitude of weight loss that was maintained: Participants who had lost 30 lb and regained 20 lb were similar to those who had lost 10 lb and maintained it, and both had lower CHD risk factors than those who had lost no weight.

Finally, little is known about the psychological consequences of weight cycling. In one of the few studies on this topic, Venditti, Wing, Jakicic, Butler, and Marcus (1996) compared the responses of individuals who differed in their self-reported histories of weight cycling on a large battery of psychological questionnaires. The only consistent difference between cyclers and noncyclers was on a measure of binge eating, with weight cyclers reporting higher rates of binge eating. It remains unclear, however, whether weight cycling increases binge eating or whether binge eating increases weight cycling.

Thus, there has been little documentation of adverse effects of weight cycling attributable to intentional weight loss and regain. Given this, and the strong negative health consequences of obesity, it is important that concern about weight cycling not prevent overweight individuals from embarking on weight loss efforts. However, every effort should be made to help these individuals lose weight and retain it over time.

Components of Behavioral Weight Loss Programs

Behavioral treatments, involving diet, exercise, behavior modification, and ongoing social support, are the most common treatment for mild-to-moderate obesity. The various aspects of these programs are discussed next.

Changing Dietary Intake

Modest reduction of caloric intake, as well as reduction in the amount of calories consumed in the form of fats, is the cornerstone of any healthy dietary intervention. The daily calorie goal is usually set at 1,000–1,500 calories per day, depending on the patient's initial body weight. The daily fat goal is typically to consume 20–30% of calories in the form of fats and is often expressed as the number of fat grams allowed per day.

To monitor attainment of dietary goals, patients are provided with books listing the caloric and fat content of commonly consumed foods (Bellerson, 1993; Kraus, 1991) and asked to record their daily calorie and fat gram intake. Self-monitoring of food intake provides both patient and practitioner with valuable information on current dietary habits, as well as information on specific situations or circumstances that may make compliance with dietary goals difficult.

The emphasis in weight loss programs on limiting fat intake to 20–30% of calories is relatively new and comes from recent evidence suggesting that low-fat/high-carbohydrate diets are more satisfying to patients and require greater energy expenditure for digestion than higher fat diets (Hill, Drougas, & Peters, 1993). Women who have been placed on low-fat diets as a means of preventing breast cancer have been found to lose weight on these diets even though weight loss was not encouraged (Henderson et al., 1990).

Several recent studies have used VLCDs to help patients increase their initial weight loss (Wadden & Stunkard, 1986; Wing, Marcus, et al., 1991). VLCDs are diets of less than 800 kcal/day, which are usually consumed as liquid formula or in the form of lean meat, fish, and fowl. VLCDs produce excellent short-term weight losses, but these losses are usually rapidly regained. Combining VLCDs with behavior modification strategies is more successful than using VLCDs alone. However, the combination of VLCD plus behavior modification is not more successful for long-term weight loss than behavior modification alone (with a 1,000–1,500 kcal/day diet). Thus, at present, most patients with mild obesity (BMI of less than 30) should be treated with balanced low-calorie diets. VLCDs may sometimes be useful for patients who have more weight to lose (BMI of more than 30) because they produce large initial weight losses, which can be motivating to patients.

Increasing Physical Activity

The single best predictor of long-term weight loss and maintenance is adoption of an exercise habit. Kayman, Bruvold, and Stern (1990) interviewed three groups of women: a group of women who had lost weight and regained it; a group who had lost weight and maintained it; and a group of normal-weight control participants. She found that these groups clearly differed in their exercise habits. Thirty-four percent of the regainers reported exercising for at least 30 min/day at least 3 days/week versus 86% of the other two groups. Controlled clinical trials comparing diet, exercise, and the combination of diet plus exercise also strongly support this (Pronk & Wing, 1994); the best long-term results have been found for programs that combine calorie restriction and exercise.

To help patients increase their exercise, an initial goal of expending just 250 calories/week in exercise often is recommended. Over the course of treatment, the patient is encouraged to gradually increase weekly expenditure, with the eventual goal of expending 1,000 calories per week in physical activity (this translates into walking roughly 2.5 miles five times a week). The best type of exercise for weight loss and maintenance is a low-intensity, long-duration activity such as walking or bicycling.

As with modification of dietary intake, patients may benefit from monitoring of their weekly physical activity. Charting of calories expended through physical activity (or miles walked or number of minutes of exercise) provides many patients with immediate positive feedback on their progress in the program.

Using Behavioral Strategies to Promote Long-Term Habit Change

Achieving long-term weight loss requires making permanent changes in diet and exercise behavior. To help patients accomplish this, behavioral strategies are included as an important component of most current weight control programs. Behavioral strategies are designed to help patients change the environmental antecedents and consequences controlling their behavior. Many programs also use cognitive–behavioral techniques and help patients change their thoughts about weight, food, and eating.

One of the most effective behavior change techniques is self-monitoring. As noted earlier, treatment outcome can be enhanced by monitoring of food intake and physical activity. Patients also may benefit from monitoring the antecedents and consequences of eating and exercise behaviors. For example, a patient may notice that she eats appropriately when at home but overeats in social situations such as parties or at restaurants. Likewise, a previously sedentary patient may note that her mood improves after a brisk walk and worsens when she skips a scheduled exercise session.

The information gathered through self-monitoring can serve as the basis for instruction in problem solving, a systematic method of understanding and coping with barriers encountered when working toward treatment goals. Patients are taught to (a) recognize that problems or barriers are a natural part of any behavior change program; (b) define problems in specific behavioral terms; (c) generate, or "brainstorm," a number of possible strategies to deal with these problems; (d) select and implement one of these strategies; and (e) review the effectiveness of the implemented strategy. Problem solving allows the health care provider to individualize treatment because each patient will identify different types of problems and find different solutions to be the most effective.

A more recent addition to standard behavioral treatment programs has been training in relapse prevention strategies. Patients are taught to discriminate between a lapse (i.e., a single episode of overeating or the missing of one planned exercise bout) and a relapse (i.e., a complete return to a sedentary, high-fat lifestyle). Perhaps most important, patients are taught that the occurrence of a lapse does not inevitably lead to relapse. Emphasis is placed on developing a thorough understanding of high-risk situations in which a lapse is likely to occur (e.g., at a social event or when in a bad mood) and on developing strategies that either prevent the lapse from occurring or facilitate recovery from it. Several studies (Drapkin, Wing, & Stiffman, 1995; Grilo, Shiffman, & Wing, 1989) have documented that prevention of relapse is associated with patients' ability to (a) keep a reasonable perspective about the lapse that has occurred; (b) use the lapse as a means of gaining a better understanding of the factors that influence their eating or exercise behaviors; and (c) get back "on track" as quickly as possible after the lapse.

Providing Continued Contact and Support

It is becoming increasingly clear that obesity is a chronic disease requiring ongoing care and treatment. Thus, any weight loss program should include plans not only for weight loss but also for weight maintenance. Continued contact, in the form of ongoing individual or group meetings, should focus on maintenance of the lifestyle changes achieved during the treatment phase of the program as well as development of coping strategies for new barriers that may arise. Patients also may be offered periodic "booster sessions," which are time limited and offer intensive instruction on one topic (e.g., eating out at ethnic restaurants, exercising for cardiovascular fitness). Perri et al. (1988) found that continued contact with patients significantly improved long-term weight maintenance; the nature of the contact (whether it focused on exercise, social support, etc.) was less important than the contact per se.

Identifying Subgroups of Individuals Requiring Specialized Weight Control Interventions

For the most part, weight control programs have not considered individual differences among obese participants. All overweight patients enrolling in a program are given the same treatment regardless of their individual behavioral problems. Proposals have been developed for matching specific types of programs to the degree of obesity in the patients (e.g., using VLCDs for those with a BMI of more than 30). In addition, there has been recent interest in developing specialized treatment programs for overweight people with BED (Marcus, 1993) and for overweight African American women.

Binge Eating Disorders

BED has been included in the fourth edition of the *Diagnostic* and *Statistical Manual of Mental Disorders* as a special case of eating disorder not otherwise specified (EDNOS). Individuals meeting this diagnosis report recurrent episodes of binge eating (at least 2 days/week for 6 months) and a sense of lack of control over eating, but they do not use inappropriate compensatory behaviors such as purging. BED occurs most frequently among overweight individuals; 5–8% of obese individuals in the community and 30% of individuals in obesity treatment programs meet diagnostic criteria for BED (Spitzer et al., 1992). BED appears to occur more commonly in women in weight control programs than in men (32% vs. 21%, respectively; Spitzer et al., 1992) and thus is of special concern to health professionals treating overweight women.

Obese women with BED report high levels of eating disorder pathology (Marcus, 1993). In fact, patients with BED score similarly to individuals with bulimia nervosa on most measures of eating pathology, except on measures of dietary restraint (in which those with BED have lower scores). Moreover, obese binge eaters differ markedly from equally overweight non-binge-eaters, with binge eaters scoring higher on measures of depressive symptomatology, symptoms of personality disorders, and psychiatric symptomatology in general.

Patients with BED appear to do poorly in behavioral weight control programs, often dropping out of treatment or losing weight initially and then rapidly regaining (Marcus, 1993). Consequently, efforts have been made recently to develop treatments for obese patients with BED that focus on disordered eating rather than on weight loss. These programs, which are modeled on programs for normal-weight patients with bulimia nervosa, have used cognitive–behavioral treatment and antidepressants. Both approaches have been found to be helpful in reducing binge eating among patients with BED. However, patients in these programs have not lost weight. Therefore, several investigators are now exploring ways to combine an intervention focused on disordered eating with modest degrees of caloric restriction and exercise in an effort to develop a more effective program for both the obesity and the eating pathology observed in these patients.

African American Women

More than 50% of middle-aged African American women are overweight, but the majority of participants in university-based research studies on weight control are White. In addition, in most studies, African Americans lose less weight than White women (Kumanyika, Obarzanek, Stevens, Hebert, & Whelton, 1991). Whether this difference in weight loss reflects differences in adherence to the program or differences in physiological or metabolic parameters remains unclear. To develop more effective interventions for African American women, behavioral researchers have attempted to make the treatment programs more culturally sensitive and to address issues of particular concern to African American participants (e.g., McNabb, Quinn, & Rosing, 1993).

Identifying High-Risk Periods for Weight Gain in Women

In addition to encouraging those who are already overweight to lose modest amounts of weight, health care providers also are in a good position to try to prevent the development of obesity. Research identifying high-risk periods for major weight gain may be helpful in anticipating and developing strategies for prevention of obesity. Women are most likely to experience major weight gain between 25 and 34 years of age (Williamson, Kahn, Remington, & Anda, 1990). Eight percent of women will gain more than 30 lb during this 10-year interval. Predictors of significant weight gain in women include race, socioeconomic status, and marital status; Black women, those in the lowest socioeconomic status groups, and those who are recently married are the most likely to gain significant amounts of weight during this interval.

Pregnancy

Pregnancy also appears to create a risk for major weight gain in a subset of women. Cross-sectional studies suggest that women who have had four or more children are heavier than those with fewer children, but on average women with zero, one, two, or three children do not differ in BMI. In a review of seven studies of pregnancy and weight gain, Rookus, Rokebrand, Burema, and Deurenberg (1987) estimated that the weight gain attributable to childbearing (independent of aging) was 1–5 lb. However, these average data obscure a great deal of heterogeneity. Twenty-five percent of women report a weight loss from their prepregnancy weight to 1 year postpregnancy, but another 25% report a weight gain of 10 lb or more (Keppel & Taffel, 1993). The best predictor of significant weight retention after pregnancy is the amount of weight gained during pregnancy. Black women also are more likely than White women to experience a significant weight gain from prepregnancy to 1 year postpregnancy. To date, we know of no efforts to prevent or treat excessive weight gain during or after pregnancy.

Smoking Cessation

Another time period in which an effort to prevent weight gain in women is warranted is the time after smoking cessation. Women are now as likely to smoke as men, but their quit rates are lower than those of men and their relapse rates are higher (Pirie, Murray, & Luepker, 1991). The poor rates of smoking cessation in women appear to derive from women's greater concern about weight gain after quitting. Almost 80% of those who stop smoking will gain weight (an average weight gain of 8–10 lb), and women tend to gain more weight than men (Nides et al., 1994). Female smokers who relapse are highly likely to report that weight gain was a cause of their relapse (Pirie et al., 1991; Sorenson & Pechacek, 1987).

Behavioral and pharmacological interventions have been used to try to prevent weight gain after smoking cessation (see Perkins, 1994, for a review). To date, none of these programs have succeeded in reducing cessation-associated weight gain in healthy ex-smokers. Moreover, in several of these studies, smokers who were given weight control training as part of their cessation efforts were actually more likely to relapse than those who did not receive the weight control intervention. These studies suggest that efforts to prevent weight gain after smoking cessation may actually be counterproductive in terms of smoking and have no effect in terms of weight gain and future obesity. Further research is needed to better understand the association between smoking cessation and weight gain and to develop more effective ways to deal with this issue.

Menopause

There continues to be a slow, steady weight gain throughout the entire menopausal period in women. Researchers at the University of Pittsburgh have been studying this by following 540 women through menopause (Wing, Matthews, Kuller, Meilahn, & Plantinga, 1991b). The women were studied first at 42–50 years of age, when all were premenopausal. They then were followed for 7 years, with regular assessments of weight, eating and exercise behavior, and CHD risk factors. The women gained an average of 9 lb over this 7-year follow-up. Forty percent gained 10 lb or more, whereas only 7% lost 10 lb or more. The best predictor of weight gain was a change in physical activity; women who increased their activity gained the least weight. To date, there has been no evidence that hormone therapy affects the rate of weight gain; women who remained premenopausal, those who experienced menopause but did not use hormone therapy, and those who started on exogenous hormones all experienced comparable weight gain. Moreover, weight gain in this age group was associated with a worsening in lipids and blood pressure.

On the basis of these findings, efforts are now being made to prevent weight gain in women during this menopausal period. A randomized clinical trial is under way at the University of Pittsburgh, studying the effects of a low-fat, reduced calorie diet and increased physical activity on changes in lipids and body weight at the time of the menopause.

To date, there has been little research on the prevention of weight gain. It would seem that encouraging a low-fat dietary intake, a slight restriction of calories, and an increase in physical activity would be the most successful approach to weight gain prevention.

Conclusion

The following conclusions should be kept in mind by care providers dealing with the problem of obesity in women:

1. It is important to consider genetic, environmental, and behavioral determinants of an individual's body weight.
2. Obesity is a risk factor for hypertension, diabetes, cardiovascular disease, and mortality in women; it also has important psychosocial consequences.
3. It is important to measure abdominal obesity because the amount of abdominal obesity may be the primary determinant of the health consequences of obesity.
4. Patients should be encouraged to lose modest amounts of weight (15–20 lb) and to maintain this weight loss. Concern about weight cycling should not stop health care providers from encouraging patients to try to lose weight. However, the focus should be on weight loss and maintenance.
5. The most effective treatment programs are those that include diet, exercise, behavior modification, and continued contact.
6. Self-monitoring of food intake provides both patient and provider with valuable information on current dietary habits and information on specific situations or circumstances that may make compliance with dietary goals difficult.
7. The single best predictor of long-term weight loss and maintenance is adoption of an exercise habit.
8. Prevention of obesity may be the most important goal for health care providers. Key times for prevention efforts in women are in young women (aged 25–34 years), at the time of pregnancy, during smoking cessation, and at menopause.

References

Bellerson, K. J. (1993). *The complete & up-to-date fat book: A guide to the fat, calories, and fat percentages in your food.* Garden City Park, NY: Avery Publishing.

Blackburn, G. L., & Read, J. L. (1984). Benefits of reducing revisited. *Postgraduate Medical Journal, 60,* 13–18.

Blair, S. N., Shaten, J., Brownell, K., Collins, G., & Lissner, L. (1993). Body weight change, all-cause and cause-specific mortality in the multiple risk factor intervention trial. *Annals of Internal Medicine, 119,* 749–757.

Bray, G. A. (1992). Drug treatment of obesity. *American Journal of Clinical Nutrition, 55*(Suppl. 2), 538S–544S.

Bray, G. A. (1993). Use and abuse of appetite-suppressant drugs in the treatment of obesity. *Annals of Internal Medicine, 119,* 707–713.

Brown, P. J. (1993). Cultural perspectives on the etiology and treatment of obesity. In A. J. Stunkard & T. A. Wadden (Eds.), *Obesity: Theory and therapy* (2nd ed., pp. 179–193). New York: Raven Press.

Brownell, K. D. (1991). *The LEARN program for weight control.* Dallas, TX: American Health Publishing.

Caspersen, C. J., Christenson G. M., & Pollard, R. A. (1985). Status of the 1990 physical fitness and exercise objective: Evidence from NHIS 1985. *Public Health Reports, 101,* 587–592.

Centers for Disease Control. (1994). Daily dietary fat and total food-energy intakes: Third National Health and Nutrition Examination Survey, Phase 1. *Morbidity and Mortality Weekly Report, 43,* 116–125.

Curb, J. D., & Marcus E. B. (1991). Body fat and obesity in Japanese Americans. *American Journal of Clinical Nutrition, 53*(Suppl. 1), 1552S–1555S.

Drapkin, R. G., Wing, R. R., & Shiffman, S. (1995). Responses to hypothetical high risk situations: Do they predict weight loss in a behavioral treatment program or the context of dietary lapses? *Health Psychology, 14,* 427–434.

Ferguson, J. M. (1975). *Learning to eat: Behavior modification for weight control.* Palo Alto, CA: Bull Publishing.

Gortmaker, S. L., Must, A., Perrin, J. M., Sobol, A. M., & Dietz, W. H. (1993). Social and economic consequences of overweight in adolescence and young adulthood. *New England Journal of Medicine, 329,* 1008–1012.

Greeno, C. G., & Wing, R. W. (1994). Stress-induced eating. *Psychological Bulletin, 115,* 444–464.

Grilo, C. M., Shiffman, S., & Wing, R. R. (1989). Relapse crises and coping among dieters. *Journal of Consulting and Clinical Psychology, 57,* 488–495.

Grunberg, N. E., & Straub, R. O. (1992). The role of gender and taste class in the effects of stress on eating. *Health Psychology, 11,* 97–100.

Henderson, M. M., Kushi, L. H., Thompson, D. J., Gorbach, S. L., Clifford, C. K., Insull, W., Jr., Moskowitz, M., & Thompson, R. S. (1990). Feasibility of a randomized trial of a low-fat diet for the prevention of breast cancer: Dietary compliance in the Women's Health Trial Vanguard Study. *Preventive Medicine, 19,* 115–133.

Hill, J. O., Drougas, H., & Peters, J. C. (1993). Obesity treatment: Can diet composition play a role? *Annals of Internal Medicine, 119,* 694–697.

Hodge, A. M., & Zimmet, P. Z. (1994). The epidemiology of obesity. In I. D. Caterson (Ed.), *Bailliére's clinical endocrinology and metabolism: International practice and research* (pp. 577–599). London: Baillière Tindall.

Horm, J., & Anderson, K. (1993). Who in America is trying to lose weight? *Annals of Internal Medicine, 119,* 672–676.

Kayman, S., Bruvold, W., & Stern, J. S. (1990). Maintenance and relapse after weight loss in women: Behavioral aspects. *American Journal of Clinical Nutrition, 52,* 800–807.

Keppel, K. G., & Taffel, S. M. (1993). Pregnancy-related weight gain and retention: Implications of the 1990 Institute of Medicine guidelines. *American Journal of Public Health, 83,* 1100–1103.

Kraus, B. (1991). *Calorie guide to brand names and basic foods.* New York: Signet Books.

Kuczmarski, R. J., Fiegal, K. M., Campbell, S. M., & Johnson, C. L. (1994). Increasing prevalence of overweight among U.S. adults: The National Health and Nutrition Examination Surveys, 1960 to 1991. *Journal of the American Medical Association, 272,* 205–211.

Kumanyika, S. K., Obarzanek, E., Stevens, V. J., Hebert, P. R., & Whelton, P. K. (1991). Weight-loss experience of Black and White participants in NHLBI-sponsored clinical trials. *American Journal of Clinical Nutrition, 53,* 1631–1638.

Lapidus, L., Bengtsson, C., Larsson, B., Pennert, K., Rybo, E., & Sjostrom, L. (1984). Distribution of adipose tissue and risk of cardiovascular disease and death: A 12 year follow-up of participants in the population study of women in Gothenburg, Sweden. *British Medical Journal, 289,* 1261–1263.

Lissner, L., Odell, P. M., D'Agostino, R. B., Stokes, J., Kreger, B. E., Belanger, A. J., & Brownell, K. D. (1991). Variability of body weight and health outcomes in the Framingham population. *New England Journal of Medicine, 324,* 1839–1844.

Manson, J. E., Colditz, G. A., Stampfer, M. J., Willett, W. C., Rosner, B., Monson, R. R., Speizer, F. E., & Hennekens, C. (1990). A prospective study of obesity and risk of coronary heart disease in women. *New England Journal of Medicine, 322,* 882–889.

Marcus, M. D. (1993). Binge eating in obesity. In C. G. Fairburn & G. T. Wilson (Eds.), *Binge eating: Nature, assessment, and treatment* (pp. 77–96). New York: Guilford Press.

McNabb, W. L., Quinn, M. T., & Rosing, L. (1993). Weight loss program for inner-city black women with non-insulin-dependent diabetes mellitus: PATHWAYS. *Journal of the American Dietetic Association, 93,* 75–77.

National Task Force on the Prevention and Treatment of Obesity. (1994). Weight cycling. *Journal of the American Medical Association, 272,* 1196–1202.

Nides, M., Rand, C., Dolce, J., Murray, R., O'Hara, P., Voelker, H., & Connett, J. (1994). Weight gain as a function of smoking cessation and 2-mg nicotine gum use among middle-aged smokers with mild lung impairment in the first 2 years of the Lung Health Study. *Health Psychology, 13,* 354–361.

Perkins, K. A. (1994). Issues in the prevention of weight gain after smoking cessation. *Annals of Behavioral Medicine, 16,* 46–52.

Perri, M. G., McAllister, D. A., Gange, J. J., Jordan, R. C., McAdoo, W. G., & Nezu, A. M. (1988). Effects of four maintenance programs on the long-term management of obesity. *Journal of Consulting and Clinical Psychology, 56,* 529–534.

Pirie, P. L., Murray, D. M., & Luepker, R. V. (1991). Smoking and quitting in a cohort of young adults. *American Journal of Public Health, 81,* 324–327.

Price, R. A., & Gottesman, I. I. (1991). Body fat in identical twins reared apart: Roles for genes and environment. *Behavior Genetics, 21,* 1–7.

Pronk, N. P., & Wing, R. R. (1994). Physical activity and long-term maintenance of weight loss. *Obesity Research, 2,* 587–599.

Rookus, M. A., Rokebrand, P., Burema, J., & Deurenberg, P. (1987). The effect of pregnancy on the body mass index 9 months postpartum in 49 women. *International Journal of Obesity, 11,* 609–618.

Serdula, M. K., Collins, M. E., Williamson, D. F., Anda, R. F., Pamuk, E., & Byers, T. E. (1993). Weight control practices of U.S. adolescents and adults. *Annals of Internal Medicine, 119,* 667–671.

Shah, M., & Jeffery, R. W. (1991). Is obesity due to overeating and inactivity, or to a defective metabolic rate? A review. *Annals of Behavioral Medicine, 13,* 73–81.

Sorenson, G., & Pechacek, T. F. (1987). Attitudes toward smoking cessation among men and women. *Journal of Behavioral Medicine, 10,* 129–137.

Spitzer, R. L., Devlin, M., Walsh, B. T., Hasin, D., Wing, R., Marcus, M., Stunkard, A., Yanovski, S., Agras, S., Mitchell, J., & Nonas, C. (1992). Binge eating disorder: A multisite field trial of the diagnostic criteria. *International Journal of Eating Disorders, 11,* 191–203.

Stunkard, A. J. (1993). Talking with patients. In A. J. Stunkard & T. A. Wadden (Eds.), *Obesity: Theory and therapy* (2nd ed., pp. 355–363). New York: Raven Press.

Stunkard, A. J., Sorensen, T. I. A., Hanis, C., Teasdale, T. W., Chakraborty, R., Schull, W. J., & Schulsinger, F. (1986). An adoption study of human obesity. *New England Journal of Medicine, 314,* 193–198.

Telch, C. F., & Agras, W. S. (1993). The effects of a very low calorie diet on binge eating. *Behavior Therapy, 24,* 177–193.

Venditti, E. M., Wing, R. R., Jakicic, J., Butler, B., & Marcus, M. D. (1996). Weight cycling, psychological health, and binge eating in obese females. *Journal of Consulting and Clinical Psychology, 64,* 400–405.

Wadden, T. A. (1993). The treatment of obesity: An overview. In A. J. Stunkard & T. A. Wadden (Eds.), *Obesity theory and therapy* (pp. 197–218). New York: Raven Press.

Wadden, T. A., & Stunkard, A. J. (1986). Controlled trial of very low calorie diet, behavior therapy, and their combination in the treatment of obesity. *Journal of Consulting and Clinical Psychology, 54,* 482–488.

Wadden, T. A., & Stunkard, A. J. (1993). Psychosocial consequences of obesity and dieting: Research and clinical findings. In A. J. Stunkard & T. A. Wadden (Eds.), *Obesity: Theory and therapy* (pp. 163–177). New York: Raven Press.

Weintraub, M. (1992). Long-term weight control study. *Clinical Pharmacology and Therapeutics, 51,* 581–646.

Williamson, D. F., Kahn, H. S., Remington, P. L., & Anda, R. F. (1990). The 10-year incidence of overweight and major weight gain in U.S. adults. *Archives of Internal Medicine, 150,* 665–672.

Wing, R. R. (1992). Weight cycling in humans: A review of the literature. *Annals of Behavioral Medicine, 14,* 113–119.

Wing, R. R., Koeske, R., Epstein, L. H., Nowalk, M. P., Gooding, W., & Becker, D. (1987). Long-term effects of modest weight loss in type II diabetic patients. *Archives of Internal Medicine, 147,* 1749–1753.

Wing, R. R., Marcus, M. D., Salata, R., Epstein, L. H., Miaskiewicz, S., & Blair, E. H. (1991). Effects of a very-low-calorie diet on long-term glycemic control in obese type 2 diabetic subjects. *Archives of Internal Medicine, 151,* 1334–1340.

Wing, R. R., Matthews, K. A., Kuller, L. H., Meilahn, E. N., & Plantinga, P. (1991a). Waist to hip ratio in middle-aged women: Associations with behavioral and psychosocial factors and with changes in cardiovascular risk factors. *Arteriosclerosis and Thrombosis, 11,* 1250–1257.

Wing, R. R., Matthews, K. A., Kuller, L. H., Meilahn, E. N., & Plantinga, P. L. (1991b). Weight gain at the time of menopause. *Archives of Internal Medicine, 151,* 97–102.

Yanovski, S. Z., Gormally, J. F., Leser, M. S., Gwirtsman, H. E., & Yanovski, J. A. (1994). Binge eating disorder affects outcome of comprehensive very-low-calorie diet treatment. *Obesity Research, 2,* 205–212.

Zhang, Y., Proenca, R., Maffei, M., Barone, M., Leopold, L., & Friedman, J. M. (1994). Positional cloning of the mouse obese gene and its human homologue. *Nature, 372,* 425–432.

9

Physical Activity and Women's Health: Issues and Future Directions

Abby C. King and Michaela Kiernan

Over the last half of this century, a wealth of scientific evidence has been accumulated underscoring the importance of regular physical activity— defined as "any bodily movement produced by skeletal muscles that results in energy expenditure" (Caspersen, Powell, & Christenson, 1985, p. 129) —for the ongoing health and functioning of both women and men (Bouchard, Shephard, & Stephens, 1994). The benefits of physical activity and exercise (typically defined as "planned, structured, and repetitive bodily movement undertaken to improve or maintain one or more components of physical fitness"; Caspersen et al., 1985, p. 129) have been documented across a range of important health areas, including chronic disease prevention and control, mental health, and daily functioning and health-related quality of life (Bouchard et al., 1994). Among the health benefits of regular physical activity participation that have been most strongly documented is its role in the prevention of cardiovascular disease (CVD), hypertension, and obesity. In addition, promising evidence supporting the efficacy of physical activity in the prevention of non-insulin-dependent diabetes mellitus (NIDDM) and osteoporosis, as well as its positive influence in the mental health arena, has emerged. As in many health areas, although the scientific evidence related to the importance of physical activity in women lags behind that which has been collected on men, the data strongly suggest that women can benefit from engaging in regular physical activity in a manner similar to that of their male counterparts.

Although the association between physical inactivity and the development of CVD, hypertension, and other chronic diseases has been known for some time (McGinnis, 1992), full recognition of the important, independent role that physical activity plays in both the prevention of disease and its control has occurred relatively recently. The American Heart As-

The writing of this chapter was supported in part by Public Health Service (PHS) Grant AG12358 from the National Institute on Aging awarded to Abby C. King. Michaela Kiernan was supported in part by PHS individual National Research Service Award (1 F32 HL09380) and PHS institutional National Research Service Award (5 T32 HL07034) from the National Heart, Lung, and Blood Institute (NHLBI). Portions of this chapter were presented at the NHLBI Conference on Women, Behavior, and Cardiovascular Disease held in September 1991, Washington, DC.

sociation's recent position paper identifying physical inactivity as the fourth independent risk factor for CVD (Fletcher et al., 1992), based on the cumulative weight of several decades worth of epidemiological, clinical, and laboratory evidence, marks a new era for scientific investigation of this important but currently understudied health behavior.

In this chapter we present a summary of current literature on the health risks and benefits associated with levels of physical activity and the determinants of physical activity patterns, focusing on issues of particular importance for women. We highlight research needed to further understand physical activity's effects on women and offer explicit guidelines for health professionals in making recommendations to women concerning physical activity.

Physical Inactivity and Cardiovascular Risk

CVD remains the Number 1 killer of both women and men in the United States (Eaker, Packard, & Thom, 1988). As the scientific focus surrounding diseases of the heart has widened in recent years to more explicitly include women, it has become increasingly clear that the relatively limited amount of data available with respect to women and other CVD risk factors extends to the physical activity arena as well. In both epidemiological and biobehavioral arenas, physical activity remains among the most understudied CVD risk factors for women (King et al., 1992; Powell, Thompson, Caspersen, & Kendrick, 1987).

These limitations notwithstanding, the studies that are available provide evidence for the link between physical inactivity and cardiovascular morbidity and mortality in women. For instance, in a 7-year follow-up of a random population sample of 3,978 men and 3,688 women aged 35–59 years from two counties of eastern Finland, a significant association was found between low levels of physical activity at work and a higher risk of acute myocardial infarction (AMI) in both women and men after controlling for other major CVD risk factors (the relative risk of AMI was 2.4 [90% confidence interval = 1.5–3.7] for women and 1.5 [90% confidence interval = 1.2–2.0] for men). Individuals with a history of myocardial infarction, angina, or cerebral stroke in the 12-month period preceding the baseline survey were excluded from the study analyses. Physical inactivity both at work and in leisure time also was significantly associated with an increased risk of death due to any disease in women and men (Salonen, Puska, & Tuomilehto, 1982).

Although these results are compelling, more longitudinal data evaluating the link between physical activity levels and CVD end points in women clearly are needed. Although more than 50 epidemiological studies in this area have been reported to date, only five have presented separate results for women (Powell et al., 1987). Of these five, three reported significant associations between physical inactivity and rates of angina, myocardial infarction, and coronary heart disease (CHD) death, whereas two reported no association. Because the vast majority of the physical activity measures used in such epidemiological studies were developed and validated primarily on men, inconsistent results reported thus far may be due, at least in part, to the relative insensitivity of the physical activity measures to the types of lighter intensity activities (e.g., walking) more frequently undertaken by women (Blair et al., 1989).

Blair et al. (1989) presented data from a longitudinal study using a more objective measure of physical fitness (i.e., a maximal treadmill exercise test) rather than reported physical activity in investigating the relationship between physical exercise and all-cause and cardiovascular-specific disease mortality rates. In that study, 10,224 men and 3,120 women attending a preventive medicine clinic were followed-up for an average of 8 years. Significant relationships between low levels of physical fitness and all-cause mortality were found for both sexes after adjustment for the other major CVD risk factors, including age, smoking, cholesterol level, systolic blood pressure, fasting blood glucose level, and parental history of CHD. Relative risks were noted to be 4.65 for women (95% confidence interval = 2.22–9.75) and 3.44 for men (95% confidence interval = 2.05–5.77). A similar strong gradient across fitness groups for women and men was noted for CVD-specific death rates as well as for cancer-specific rates. The relative risks for the low-fitness groups were similar in both women and men to those for other major CVD risk factors. These results underscore the importance of regular participation in moderate endurance exercise, which should be sufficient in most women and men to produce beneficial fitness levels (Blair et al., 1989).

Physical Inactivity and Other Chronic Diseases and Conditions

In addition to its independent relationship to CVD risk, regular physical activity affects a large number of other risk factors for CVD as well as other important chronic diseases and conditions in both women and men. These include blood pressure, glucose tolerance and insulin sensitivity, platelet aggregation and fibrinolysis, the lipid profile, bone density, and body weight and composition. Physical activity has been shown to influence both the development of many of these health conditions and their amelioration or control.

There also is some evidence, albeit inconsistent, that regular exercisers or more fit individuals may have less physiological reactivity to psychological stressors relative to their less active counterparts (Crews & Landers, 1987). Few studies in this area, however, have specifically evaluated women. Increased levels of cardiovascular and neuroendocrine reactivity may, over time, contribute to a range of pathophysiological processes and conditions implicated in the development of CHD and other chronic conditions (Matthews et al., 1986). In light of the increased levels of physiological reactivity reported in postmenopausal relative to premenopausal women (Saab, Matthews, Stoney, & McDonald, 1989) and the greater amount of CVD risk occurring after menopause, this is an area that deserves further study.

Although the association between physical activity levels and cancer risk is less well studied than its relationship with CVD risk, the few studies that are available in women are suggestive, indicating that occupational and leisure-time physical inactivity may be associated with increased risk of colorectal and breast cancers (Pinto & Marcus, 1994). There also is preliminary evidence of the potential role that increases in physical activity may play in the rehabilitation of some groups of cancer patients (Winningham, MacVicar, Bondoc, Anderson, & Minton, 1989), although, clearly, these areas require much more systematic investigation.

Appropriately structured physical activity regimens also may provide an effective means for reducing health risks among cigarette smokers (Blair et al., 1989), as well as providing a means of controlling negative affect and weight-related concerns both before and during the quitting process (King, Taylor, & Haskell, 1993; Marcus et al., 1994). As shown in the study by Blair et al. (1989) of healthy women, current smokers who were moderately fit cut their risk of early death by more than half. Notably, ex-smokers who were moderately fit cut their risk by 78%. In fact, in this study, a fit smoker was at the same risk as an unfit nonsmoker. Unfortunately, smokers and the overweight, two groups who could most benefit from becoming more active, typically are the least likely either to adopt or adhere to a physical activity regimen (King et al., 1992).

Physical Activity and Psychological Health and Quality-of-Life Outcomes

A growing literature attests to the utility of physical activity in promoting psychological well-being in women and men (Plante & Rodin, 1990). In particular, recent evidence suggests that women may be able to achieve both acute and chronic decreases in rated stress and anxiety through participation in the more moderate-intensity forms of exercise (e.g., brisk walking) that many women prefer (King et al., 1993; Steptoe & Cox, 1988). Similarly, the few currently available studies suggest that both women and men who become more active in moderate- or high-intensity activities can experience enhancements in an array of perceived daily functioning and quality-of-life outcomes, including physical functioning, current health perceptions, and bodily pain. It appears from such studies that the extent and frequency of physical activity participation, rather than the format or the intensity of the physical activity, may be of particular value in the mental health and quality-of-life arenas. In a similar vein, the utility of physical activity as a healthful means to control weight throughout the life span has important implications for self-esteem, well-being, and related factors that can have a powerful impact on day-to-day quality of life independent of disease prevention issues (King & Tribble, 1991).

Physical Activity and Physical Functioning

In addition to the aforementioned areas, it has been increasingly acknowledged that many of the decrements in physical and physiological functioning typically associated with aging are in fact a consequence of disuse and deconditioning. Regular physical activity has been associated with improved physical functioning in at least two major longitudinal studies of older adults (LaCroix, Guralnik, Berkman, Wallace, & Satterfield, 1993; Mor et al., 1989) and has been shown to be beneficial in easing disease symptoms among those women and men who already have a chronic health problem (Buchner, Beresford, Larson, LaCroix, & Wagner, 1992). Furthermore, exercise regimens focused on strength training have been shown to improve physical and daily functioning outcomes even among the oldest (greater than 80 years of age) and most frail groups (Fiatarone et al., 1990).

Physical Activity in the Rehabilitation Process

In addition to the documented benefits of regular physical activity for the prevention of chronic diseases associated with aging, physical activity participation has been found to be useful in the control of a variety of diseases once they have emerged. For instance, since the 1970s, exercise rehabilitation has become increasingly commonplace for patients with CHD (American College of Sports Medicine, 1993). Although the majority of exercise rehabilitation programs for cardiac patients are offered in class formats in either clinical or community settings, growing evidence supports the utility of nontraditional approaches to exercise participation in this patient population (Houston-Miller, 1993). These include the development of telephone-supervised, home-based training programs for cardiac patients, which allow patients the convenience and flexibility to choose when and where they exercise while maintaining safety through trans-telephonic electrocardiographic monitoring and related techniques. The safety and effectiveness of such home-based programs have been documented through several studies undertaken with this population (Houston-Miller, 1993). Safety issues and guidelines related to exercise programming with cardiac patients have been described by the American Association of Cardiovascular and Pulmonary Rehabilitation (1991) and other medical organizations (Houston-Miller, 1993).

Similarly, over the past three decades, a growing amount of research has supported the role of a regular regimen of physical activity in the management of *arthritis*, the major reason cited for activity limitations among those over the age of 65 (Minor, 1991). In contrast to earlier assumptions, more recent evidence suggests that weight-bearing exercises such as walking, if undertaken in a gradually progressive fashion, can achieve significant improvements in a variety of parameters, including exercise endurance, trunk flexibility, depression, walking speed, and self-reported pain (Minor, Hewett, Webel, Anderson, & Kay, 1989). Among the

factors found to be related to long-term (i.e., 24-month) exercise maintenance in this patient population were initial fitness levels, anxiety and
depression, and amount of reported social support for exercise (Minor,
1991).

Current evidence also supports the potential effectiveness of physical
activity in the treatment of disorders related to carbohydrate metabolism.
Such disorders, including glucose intolerance, insulin resistance, and
NIDDM, represent major health problems among older Americans (Laws
& Reaven, 1991). Training studies have demonstrated that a regular regimen of endurance exercise in patients with impaired glucose tolerance
and NIDDM can lead to significant improvements in fasting glucose and
in glucose and insulin responses to oral glucose tolerance testing; however,
improvement in such variables depends on the proximity of the exercise
sessions to the oral glucose tolerance test (Laws & Reaven, 1991). These
results suggest that it is the acute impact of physical activity on carbohydrate metabolism that is the critical factor, underscoring the need for
developing programs that will facilitate regular and frequent participation
in endurance activities.

Prevalence of Physical Inactivity in Women

Despite the current findings indicating the prominent role that regular
physical activity plays in relation to physical and psychological health and
functioning among women, researchers are dangerously ignorant of the
most effective methods of reliably increasing regular physical activity
among the 75% or more of American women who are underactive. It has
been estimated that fewer than 10% of the American adult population
exercise at the level recommended in the Surgeon General's 1990 Objectives for the Nation (Public Health Service, 1980). This recommended level
entails engaging in sustained large-muscle activities at least three times
per week at an intensity sufficient to increase heart rate to a moderate
level or greater. Furthermore, only 22% of women and men aged 18 years
and older report engaging in light-to-moderate physical activity for at least
30 min five times or more per week. This amount of moderate activity,
akin to brisk walking or similar activities, is deemed to be well within the
capabilities of most adults, has been shown to confer health benefits, and
thus has been given greater emphasis in the *Healthy People 2000 National
Health Promotion and Disease Prevention Objectives* (Public Health Service, 1990) and in the most recent U.S. Centers for Disease Control and
Prevention–American College of Sports Medicine recommendations for
the nation (Pate et al., 1995). Such activities, including brisk walking and
yardwork, are more likely to be adopted and maintained and less likely to
lead to injury than more intensive activities (King et al., 1992).

Current observational data suggest that levels of physical activity are
generally lower for women than for similarly-aged men and become progressively lower as women age (Caspersen, Christenson, & Pollard, 1986).
It remains unclear, however, how much if any of the sex differential in

physical activity is related to measurement insensitivity with respect to assessing more moderate-intensity activities (e.g., walking) that often are more strongly preferred by women. In addition, although comparisons by race and ethnicity remain scarce and are confounded by socioeconomic status, African American women and other ethnic minority populations have been found to be less active than White women (King et al., 1992, Pate et al., 1995), with this ethnic disparity being greater for women than for men (Pate et al., 1995). With respect to intensity issues, it has been reported that men are more likely than women to engage in vigorous exercise and sports (King et al., 1992), with low- to moderate-intensity physical activities more likely to be continued than high-intensity activities for both sexes.

The current prevalence of inactivity in women is especially sobering in light of the much-touted "fitness boom" occurring during the 1970s and 1980s. Unfortunately, little actual progress occurred during that time with respect to physical activity participation rates; recent indicators suggest that only 4 of the 11 physical activity objectives for the year 1990 contained in *Promoting Health/Prevention Disease: Objectives for the Nation* were accomplished (McGinnis, 1992). Failure to make progress in a number of the targeted areas related to physical activity participation, such as decreasing the proportion of adults with a sedentary lifestyle, along with the importance of regular physical activity to the health of all Americans, likely influenced the decision to place physical activity as the first of the 22 priority areas listed in *Healthy People 2000* (McGinnis, 1992). In addition, notable failures to reach targeted reductions in areas such as the prevalence of obesity among women have heightened attention on women as an important target for continued research and intervention in the physical activity area.

The substantial prevalance of physical inactivity across the American adult population as a whole and women in particular has serious public health implications with respect to rates of CVD and other chronic diseases in the United States. For example, as a consequence of the large prevalence of inactivity and lack of fitness in their study population, Blair et al. (1989) found that the population-attributable risk (i.e., the percentage of risk that might be spared in a community or population if community members were to become more fit) for both the unfit women and men in their longitudinal study was comparable to or greater than that of the other major CVD risk factors, including cigarette smoking, hypertension, and serum cholesterol level. The rates for women were particularly alarming. The population-attributable risk for women in the lowest fitness quintile compared with the more fit quintiles was calculated to be 15.3%; the next largest population-attributable risk in women was 7.1% for elevated serum cholesterol level.

In summary, a significant proportion of American women will experience a plethora of health problems as they age, including CVD, osteoporosis, and diabetes mellitus, that could be ameliorated substantially or in some cases eliminated by moderate increases in physical activity. This fact, combined with the number of other positive benefits associated with physical activity and the substantial prevalence of inactivity among American women, provides strong justification for an increasing public health focus on physical activity among women.

Determinants and Correlates of Physical Activity in Women

A growing number of variables have been identified as potentially important determinants of physical activity patterns in both women and men. The available data suggest several points: First, factors associated with initial exercise adoption may differ to some extent from those related to ongoing exercise maintenance. Second, these factors may differ depending on a person's age or life stage. Third, at least some of these factors may differ by sex.

Exercise Adoption Versus Maintenance

Factors found in women and men to be associated with initial exercise adoption include (a) knowledge of and belief in the health benefits of physical activity (i.e., those who understand and believe in the benefits that can accrue to them individually through a program of regular physical activity are more likely to be successful in adopting a physical activity regimen); (b) perceptions of being in poor health, which is associated with less participation; and (c) exercise intensity and exertional factors, (i.e., how difficult the person perceives the physical activity to be in terms of physical work; King et al., 1992). With respect to exercise intensity parameters, men may be more likely to begin vigorous exercise and women more likely to adopt moderate activities across a 1-year period (Sallis et al., 1986). If the physical activity is deemed to be difficult or is perceived to require uncomfortable levels of physical exertion (e.g., jogging as opposed to walking), women in particular may be less likely to participate in the activity, particularly over an extended period of time. Women also differ from men in the specific types of activities that they prefer. Although both groups have been found to consistently rate walking highly, women have reported stronger preferences for aerobic dance and videotaped exercise programs than men (King, Taylor, Haskell, & DeBusk, 1990). Other factors influencing exercise adoption in women include the complexity and convenience of the physical activity regimen, monetary and psychological costs (e.g., embarrassment), and regimen structure and flexibility (King et al., 1992).

Self-efficacy, or one's confidence in being able to successfully perform a specific behavior, has been associated with the adoption of moderate activity for both women and men and more vigorous activity in men (Sallis et al., 1986), as well as the longer term maintenance of moderate activity for women and men in both supervised and free-living settings (King et al., 1992).

Similar to self-efficacy, social support has been found to be an important correlate of both exercise adoption and subsequent maintenance in women and men (King et al., 1992). Current evidence indicates that effective support can derive from a number of different sources (e.g., family, friends, program staff) and can be delivered through a variety of channels (e.g., face to face, by telephone; King, Haskell, Taylor, Kraemer, & DeBusk, 1991). In addition, results of a recent study suggest that for both women and men, the type of support that is most influential in enhancing exercise adherence may vary depending on what phase of the exercise program participants are in (i.e., early vs. later phases; Oka, King, & Young, 1995). The amount of initial support desired from exercise staff was found to be the most powerful predictor of exercise adherence during the initial 6 months of the program. By contrast, the strongest predictor of adherence during the second 6-month period was the level of support the person reported obtaining from family members and friends. In addition, being either divorced or separated put both women and men at added risk for poor exercise adherence during the initial 6-month period. This finding has particular implications for women, given that a significantly higher proportion of women in this sample were in the divorced or separated category relative to same-aged men.

Other variables of particular importance in the maintenance phase of a physical activity regimen include the perceived convenience of facilities; perceptions of a lack of time, which may reflect a lack of interest or commitment to physical activity; and the ability to use self-regulatory skills such as self-monitoring of progress, goal setting, self-reinforcement, and relapse prevention strategies to sustain physical activity participation (King et al., 1992). Women have been shown to use such skills as effectively as men in maintaining their physical activity programs.

Despite the relatively large number of potentially important variables that have been identified, little is known about how these variables interrelate, the nature of the pathways (e.g., causal vs. indirect) linking them with subsequent exercise behavior, and the most effective methods for incorporating them into intervention programs to enhance both physical activity adoption and maintenance. In addition, most of these variables have been studied within the context of programmed leisure time activity. Much less is known about their influences on the more routine levels of daily activity that may provide important sources of energy expenditure for women.

Life Stage and Physical Activity

Evidence suggests that there may be specific "critical periods," or developmental milestones, that occur throughout a woman's life that could set the stage for natural reductions or increases in physical activity. For example, although prepubescent girls have been observed to be as physically active as their male counterparts, a noticeable decrease in energy expenditure among girls appears to occur in early to midadolescence (Fitness Profile in American Youth, 1983). Unfortunately, it is unlikely that the types of physical education curricula currently offered in many school systems throughout the United States will be able to sufficiently counteract such trends. For instance, observations of elementary school children attending school physical education classes revealed that the children moved continuously for an average of only about 2 min per class period (Parcel et al., 1987).

In light of such statistics, some researchers have turned their attention to identifying the factors associated with natural levels of physical activity occurring outside school. In a study of 324 adolescent girls and 356 adolescent boys (aged 15–16 years) followed across a 16-month period, several factors associated with changes in natural levels of physical activity participation during this time period were identified (Reynolds et al., 1990). For boys, the only significant predictor of increases in physical activity from baseline to 4 months was their baseline levels of physical activity; baseline ratings of self-efficacy were marginally significant. For girls, in addition to baseline physical activity level, rated intentions to exercise, less reported stress, and amount of social influence related to whether the girl's family and friends exercised regularly at baseline were significantly associated with increases in physical activity at 4 months.

Initial ratings of self-efficacy were positively related to exercise participation at 16 months in girls but not boys. Of note, initial body mass index was inversely related to exercise participation at 16 months only in girls. These results suggest that psychosocial variables may be differentially related to natural levels of physical activity in adolescent girls and boys and underscore the increasing influence of body weight for girls during this period of development.

A related developmental milestone of potential importance for women appears to occur during one's early 20s, when individuals typically enter the workforce. It is during this time when notable increases in body weight have been reported to occur across the U.S. population of women (Williamson, Kahn, Remington, & Anda, 1990). Similarly, marriage and the addition of children into the family unit may well have important effects on health behaviors such as physical activity that are not currently well understood. For instance, in at least one community-based study of the effects of changes in marital status on physical activity participation, it was found that women who during a 10-year period went from being single to married were more physically active during this time period than women who made the transition from being married to single (King, Oman, Kraemer, & Lin, 1994).

Another potentially important developmental period for women occurs around the time of the menopause. In a longitudinal study of the biological and behavioral effects of menopause that tracked middle-aged women across a 3-year period, it was found that during this time period body weight and several other CVD risk factors (e.g., blood pressure, levels of total and low-density lipoprotein cholesterol, triglycerides, insulin) rose and that high-density lipoprotein cholesterol levels decreased significantly (Owens, Matthews, Wing, & Kuller, 1992). Of note, however, was the observation that women who maintained or increased their physical activity levels during this period in general evidenced the smallest increases in weight and tended to have the smallest decreases in high-density lipoprotein cholesterol. The changes in lipids related to physical activity were largely independent of body weight changes. In addition, women who reported increases in physical activity levels showed less of an increase in depressed affect and reported stress across the 3-year period relative to other women. These results also were independent of body weight. The data indicate, however, that women's reported physical activity levels may be highly stable across this time period, suggesting that women may not naturally increase their physical activity levels despite clear health reasons to do so (Owens et al., 1992).

Older women often face special challenges related to having to fulfill the role of an informal family caregiver to a sick or frail relative (Stone, Cafferata, & Sangl, 1987). Although physical activity represents a potentially important means for maintaining their physical and psychological functioning during what is usually an extremely distressing and demanding ordeal—as well as being a health behavior that female caregivers have voiced a preference for relative to other types of activities (Gallagher-Thompson, Lovett, & Rose, 1991)—few family caregivers are able to regularly attend physical activity classes in their community. The advent of supervised home-based physical activity training programs provides a potentially promising alternative for women who, because of situational demands, cannot attend organized groups or programs. Preliminary data suggest that such home-based approaches may be effective, practical means for facilitating physical activity among this hard-to-reach population of older women (King & Brassington, 1995).

These results suggest the importance of targeting these and other potentially influential life stages or milestones for further systematic study. They underscore the utility of considering physical activity in a developmental context, particularly in light of the fact that, for optimal health, regular exercise should occur across the breadth of a woman's life. By taking this perspective, it is more likely that researchers will be able to achieve not only significant reductions in health-related risk but also simultaneously improve women's day-to-day functioning and quality of life, two outcomes that are important at all stages of a woman's life.

Physical Activity, Women, and Health: Future Directions

Primary care settings are a potentially effective setting for reaching middle-age and older women, as well as women of different ethnic and socioeconomic backgrounds. It is clear that health professionals can serve as powerful role models for their female clients, yet relatively few physicians report that they routinely counsel their patients on physical activity (Mullen & Tabak, 1989). Although the few systematic attempts to train physicians to effectively counsel patients on physical activity have been encouraging (Lewis & Lynch, 1993; Long et al., 1996), more comprehensive evaluations of the best strategies for doing this are needed.

We recommend that health professionals pay particular attention to the patient's past experiences (or lack of experience) with physical activity, individual preferences related to physical activity type (e.g., walking, swimming, bicycling) and format (e.g., class vs. home based), types of social support (e.g., from family members, coworkers, neighbors) that can be tapped to encourage physical activity increases in the person's environment, and other environmental factors (e.g., proximity to safe areas for walking) that could facilitate or hinder efforts to become more active. Enjoyability and convenience factors related to physical activity appear to be particularly important and should be explored with each individual. In light of the severe time constraints that many health professionals often are faced with, the best use of their time may be in providing patients with an unequivocal message about the importance of regular physical activity for their health and functioning, followed by a referral to relevant agencies or organizations found in most communities throughout the United States (e.g., local parks and recreation departments, senior centers, Young Men's Christian Associations, or Young Women's Christian Associations; King et al., 1992).

In summary, there is now a promising body of literature suggesting that (a) regular physical activity is an important determinant of health and functioning in women and (b) a substantial proportion of women of all ages are interested in becoming more active. The challenge remains to identify the best methods for facilitating regular physical activity in different subgroups of women.

References

American Association of Cardiovascular and Pulmonary Rehabilitation. (1991). *Guidelines for cardiac rehabilitation programs*. Champaign, IL: Human Kinetics Books.

American College of Sports Medicine. (1993). *ACSM's resource manual for guidelines for exercise testing and prescription* (2nd ed.). Philadelphia: Lea & Febiger.

Blair, S. N., Kohl, H. W., III, Paffenbarger, R. S., Jr., Clark, D. G., Cooper, K. H., & Gibbons, L. W. (1989). Physical fitness and all-cause mortality: A prospective study of healthy men and women. *Journal of the American Medical Association, 262*, 2395–2401.

Bouchard, C., Shephard, R. J., & Stephens, T. (Eds.). (1994). *Physical activity, fitness, and health: International proceedings and consensus statement*. Champaign, IL: Human Kinetics Books.

Buchner, D. M., Beresford, S. A. A., Larson, E. B., LaCroix, A. Z., & Wagner, E. H. (1992). Effects of physical activity on health status in older adults: II. Intervention studies. *Annual Review of Public Health, 13*, 469–488.

Caspersen, C. J., Christenson, G. M., & Pollard, R. A. (1986). Status of the 1990 physical fitness and exercise objectives: Evidence from NHIS 1985. *Public Health Reports, 101*, 587–592.

Caspersen, C. J., Powell, K. E., & Christenson, G. M. (1985). Physical activity, exercise, and physical fitness: Definitions and distinctions for health-related research. *Public Health Reports, 100*, 126–130.

Crews, D. J., & Landers, D. M. (1987). A meta-analytic review of aerobic fitness and reactivity to psychosocial stressors. *Medicine and Science in Sports and Exercise, 19*(Suppl. 5), S114–S120.

Eaker, E. D., Packard, B., & Thom, T. J. (1988). Epidemiology and risk factors for coronary heart disease in women. *Cardiovascular Clinics, 26*, 129–145.

Fiatarone, M. A., Marcks, E. C., Ryan, N. D., Meredith, C. N., Kipsitz, L. Q., & Evans, W. J. (1990). High-intensity strength training in nonagenarians. *Journal of the American Medical Association, 263,* 3029–3034.

Fitness Profile in American Youth. (1983). *A report on 1981–83 fitness tests involving more than 4 million boys and girls in over 10,000 schools.* East Hanover, NJ: Nabisco Brands.

Fletcher, G. F., Blair, S. N., Blumenthal, J., Caspersen C., Chaitman, B., Epstien, S., Falls, H., Froelicher, E. S., Froelicher, V. F., & Pina, I. L. (1992). AHA medical/scientific statement on exercise—Benefits and recommendations for physical activity programs for all Americans: A statement for health professionals by the Committee on Exercise and Cardiac Rehabilitation of the Council on Clinical Cardiology, American Heart Association. *Circulation, 86,* 340–344.

Gallagher-Thompson, D., Lovett, S., & Rose, J. (1991). Psychotherapeutic interventions for stress in family caregivers. In W. A. Myers (Ed.), *New techniques in the psychotherapy of older patients* (pp. 61–78). Washington, DC: American Psychiatric Press.

Houston Miller, N. (1993). Home exercise training for coronary patients. In *American College of Sports Medicine's resource manual for guidelines for exercise testing and prescription* (2nd ed., pp. 350–355). Philadelphia: Lea & Febiger.

King, A. C., Blair, S. N., Bild, D. E., Dishman, R. K., Dubbert, P. M., Marcus, B. H., Oldridge, N. B., Paffenbarger, Jr., R. S., Powell, K. E., & Yeager, K. K. (1992). Determinants of physical activity and interventions in adults. *Medicine and Science in Sports and Exercise, 24*(Suppl. 6), S221–S236.

King, A. C., & Brassington, G. (1995). Can exercise improve functioning in family caregivers? A randomized study. *The Gerontologist, 35,* 117.

King, A. C., Haskell, W. L., Taylor, C. B., Kraemer, H. C., & DeBusk, R. F. (1991). Group-vs. home-based exercise training in healthy older men and women. *Journal of the American Medical Association, 266,* 1535–1542.

King, A. C., Oman, R., Kraemer, H. C., & Lin, J. (1994). Effects of life transitions on physical activity levels in a community. *Third International Congress of Behavioral Medicine Proceedings,* p. 33.

King, A. C., Taylor, C. B., & Haskell, W. L. (1993). The effects of differing intensities and formats of twelve months of exercise training on psychological outcomes in older adults. *Health Psychology, 12,* 292–300.

King, A. C., Taylor, C. B., Haskell, W. L., & DeBusk, R. F. (1990). Identifying strategies for increasing employee physical activity levels: Findings from the Stanford/Lockheed exercise survey. *Health Education Quarterly, 17,* 269–285.

King, A. C., & Tribble, D. (1991). The role of exercise in weight regulation in nonathletes. *Sports Medicine, 11,* 331–349.

LaCroix, A. Z., Guralnik, J. M., Berkman, L. F., Wallace, R. B., & Satterfield, S. (1993). Maintaining mobility in later life: II. Smoking, alcohol consumption, physical activity, and body mass index. *American Journal of Epidemiology, 137,* 858–869.

Laws, A., & Reaven, G. M. (1991). Physical activity, glucose tolerance, and diabetes in older adults. *Annals of Behavioral Medicine, 13,* 125–132.

Lewis, B. S., & Lynch, W. D. (1993). The effect of physician advice on exercise behavior. *Preventive Medicine, 22,* 110–121.

Long, B. J., Calfas, K. J., Wooten, W., Sallis, J. F., Patrick, K., Goldstein, M., Marcus, B. H., Schwenk, T. L., Chenoweth, J., Carter, R., Torres, T., Palinkas, L. A., & Heath, G. (1996). A multisite field test of the acceptability of physical activity counseling in primary care: Project PACE. *American Journal of Preventive Medicine, 12,* 73–81.

Marcus, B. H., Emmons, K. M., Simkin, L. R., Albrecht, A. E., Stoney, C. M., & Abrams, D. B. (1994). Women and smoking cessation: Current status and future directions. *Medicine, Exercise, Nutrition, and Health, 3,* 17–31.

Matthews, K. A., Weiss, S. M., Detre, T., Dembroski, T. M., Falkner, B., Manuck, S. B., & Williams, R. B. (Eds.). (1986). *Handbook of stress, reactivity, and cardiovascular disease.* New York: Wiley.

McGinnis, J. M. (1992). The public health burden of a sedentary lifestyle. *Medicine and Science in Sports and Exercise, 24*(Suppl. 6), S196–S200.

Minor, M. A. (1991). Physical activity and management of arthritis. *Annals of Behavioral Medicine, 13,* 117–124.

Minor, M. A., Hewett, J. E., Webel, R. R., Anderson, S. K., & Kay, D. R. (1989). Efficacy of physical conditioning exercise in patients with rheumatoid arthritis and osteoarthritis. *Arthritis and Rheumatism, 32*, 1396–1405.

Mor, V., Murphy, J., Masterson-Allen, S., Willey, C., Razmpour, A., Jackson, M. E., Greer, D., & Katz, S. (1989). Risk of functional decline among well elders. *Journal of Clinical Epidemiology, 42*, 895–904.

Mullen, P. D., & Tabak, E. R. (1989). Patterns of counseling techniques used by family practice physicians for smoking, weight, exercise, and stress. *Medical Care, 27*, 694–704.

Oka, R. K., King, A. C., & Young, D. R. (1995). Sources of social support as predictors of exercise adherence in women and men ages 50 to 65 years. *Women's Health: Research on Gender, Behavior, and Policy, 1*, 161–175.

Owens, J. F., Matthews, K. A., Wing, R. R., & Kuller, L. H. (1992). Can physical activity mitigate the effects of aging in middle-aged women? *Circulation, 85*, 1265–1270.

Parcel, G. S., Simons-Morton, B. G., O'Hara, N. M., Baranowski, T., Kolbe, L. J., & Bee, D. E. (1987). School promotion of healthful diet and exercise behavior: An integration of organizational change and social learning theory interventions. *Journal of School Health, 57*, 150–156.

Pate, R. R., Pratt, M., Blair, S. N., Haskell, W. L., Macera, C. A., Bouchard, C., Buchner, D., Caspersen, C. J., Ettinger, W., Heath, G. W., King, A. C., Kriska, A., Leon, A. S., Marcus, B. H., Morris, J., Paffenbarger, R., Patrick, K., Pollock, M. L., Rippe, J. M., Sallis, J., & Wilmore, J. H. (1995). Physical activity and public health: A recommendation from the Centers for Disease Control and Prevention and the American College of Sports Medicine. *Journal of the American Medical Association, 273*, 402–407.

Pinto, B. M., & Marcus, B. H. (1994). Physical activity, exercise and cancer in women. *Medicine, Exercise, Nutrition, and Health, 3*, 102–111.

Plante, T., & Rodin, J. (1990). Physical fitness and enhanced psychological health. *Current Psychology: Research and Reviews, 9*, 3–24.

Powell, K. E., Thompson, P. D., Caspersen, C. J., & Kendrick, J. S. (1987). Physical activity and the incidence of coronary heart disease. *Annual Review of Public Health, 8*, 253–287.

Public Health Service. (1980). *Promoting health / preventing disease: Objectives for the nation*. Washington, DC: U.S. Department of Health and Human Services.

Public Health Service. (1990). *Healthy People 2000: National health promotion and disease prevention objectives* (DHHS Publication No. PHS 91-50212). Washington, DC: U.S. Department of Health and Human Services.

Reynolds, K. D., Killen, J. D., Bryson, S. W., Maron, D. J., Taylor, C. B., Maccoby, N., & Farquhar, J. W. (1990). Psychosocial predictors of physical activity in adolescents. *Preventive Medicine, 19*, 541–551.

Saab, P. G., Matthews, K. A., Stoney, C. M., & McDonald, R. H. (1989). Premenopausal and postmenopausal women differ in their cardiovascular and neuroendocrine responses to behavioral stressors. *Psychophysiology, 26*, 270–280.

Sallis, J. F., Haskell, W. L., Fortmann, S. P., Vranizan, K. M., Taylor, C. B., & Solomon, D. S. (1986). Predictors of adoption and maintenance of physical activity in a community sample. *Preventive Medicine, 15*, 331–341.

Salonen, J. T., Puska, P., & Tuomilehto, J. (1982). Physical activity and risk of myocardial infarction, cerebral stroke and death. *American Journal of Epidemiology, 115*, 526–537.

Steptoe, A., & Cox, S. (1988). Acute effects of aerobic exercise on mood. *Health Psychology, 7*, 329–340.

Stone, R., Cafferata, G. L., & Sangl, J. (1987). Caregivers of the frail elderly: A national profile. *The Gerontologist, 27*, 616–626.

Williamson, D. F., Kahn, H. S., Remington, P. L., & Anda, R. F. (1990). The 10-year incidence of overweight and major weight gain in U.S. adults. *Archives of Internal Medicine, 150*, 665–672.

Winningham, M. L., MacVicar M. G., Bondoc, M., Anderson, J. L., & Minton, J. P. (1989). Effects of aerobic exercise on body weight and composition in patients with breast cancer on adjuvant chemotherapy. *Oncology Nursing Forum, 16*, 683–689.

10

Occupational Stress and Women's Health

*Naomi G. Swanson, Chaya S. Piotrkowski,
Gwendolyn Puryear Keita, and Ami B. Becker*

In the early part of this century, only about one in seven women were employed outside the home. Today, women constitute 46% of the labor force, with 73% of married women with children under the age of 18 and 85% of women without children under the age of 18 employed either full or part time (Fullerton, 1993). One of the consequences for women of this historic change is that most women, like men, are now subject to illnesses, injuries, and diseases resulting from exposure to workplace hazards, including occupational stressors.

Occupational stress is a growing problem in the United States. In the early 1980s, workers' compensation rates involving mental disorders caused by stress more than doubled, accounting for nearly 11% of all occupational claims (National Council on Compensation Insurance, 1985). More recent data indicate that stress remains a growing problem. Compared with 10 years ago, nearly twice as many workers in the United States (30–46%) report experiencing high levels of stress (Galinsky, Bond, & Friedman, 1993; Northwestern National Life, 1991; Silverman, Eichler, & Williams, 1987).

Occupational stress may be a problem of particular magnitude for many employed women, as indicated by the results of several national surveys. Employed women have reported nearly twice the levels of stress-related illness, along with a higher likelihood of "burning out" on the job, than employed men (Northwestern National Life, 1992). In another recent survey of female workers, 60% of the respondents reported that job stress was their Number 1 problem (Reich & Nussbaum, 1994). From these and other studies, it has become increasingly apparent that occupational stress is an important factor in understanding and treating women's health problems.

In this chapter we identify significant job stressors for women and adverse reactions to these stressors. We also provide a brief guide to the assessment and treatment of occupational stress for health practitioners.

An Overview of Occupational Stress

Occupational stressors are working conditions that overwhelm the adaptive capabilities and resources of workers, resulting in acute psychological, behavioral, or physical reactions. Prolonged or chronic exposure to stressful working conditions may lead to illness or disease (Hurrell & Murphy, 1992).

Individual factors such as age, marital status, physical health, and coping strategies can moderate or modify the severity of reactions to occupational stressors to some degree, but occupational stress-related reactions and illnesses result primarily from stressful working conditions. Although we emphasize the influence of job stressors on the worker in this definition, it is important to recognize that the influence of occupational stressors can extend beyond workers to their families and that job stressors can have direct and indirect effects on family members and family functioning (Piotrkowski & Staines, 1991). Job stress also must be understood in its social context (Eckenrode & Gore, 1990) because a worker's social resources—both inside and outside the workplace—also can moderate the impact of stressful job conditions. Resources at work include helpful coworkers; in the family, they include spousal help with housework; and in the community, they include affordable child care.

In general, job stress may stem from job or task demands (e.g., work overload, lack of task control), organizational factors (e.g., unfair management practices), and physical conditions (e.g., noise; Hurrell & Murphy, 1992). To this list could be added stressors resulting from the conflicts between work and family roles and responsibilities, human resource systems (e.g., training and career development issues), and poor organizational climate (e.g., values, communication styles, etc.; Sauter & Swanson, 1996).

Acute stress reactions may be psychological (e.g., affective and somatic responses, job dissatisfaction), behavioral (e.g., sleep problems, absenteeism), or physical (e.g., changes in blood pressure or in stress hormone levels such as catecholamine levels). Chronic health outcomes resulting from prolonged exposure to job stressors may include psychological illnesses, such as depression, and physical illnesses, such as coronary heart disease (CHD). There is individual variation in stress-related responses, so practitioners must be alert to the array of health symptoms that can result from stressors in the workplace.

Classic Job Stressors and Employed Women

Certain job conditions are well-established stressors. These "classic" stressors include heavy workload demands coupled with little control over work; role ambiguity and conflict; lack of job security; poor relationships with coworkers and supervisors; and work consisting of narrow, repetitive, monotonous tasks (Hurrell & Murphy, 1992). Unfortunately, these stressful attributes are prevalent in many predominantly female occupations (e.g., clerical work, caregiving), and studies of occupational stress in these jobs have provided evidence for the deleterious effects of the classic occupational stressors for women. Studies of clerical work have shown that lack of job control, high workload demands, low task clarity, and poor relations with or lack of support from coworkers and supervisors are predictive of various psychological and physical health complaints such as anxiety, depression, headaches, and stomach aches (e.g., Aronsson, Dallner, & Aborg, 1994; Piotrkowski, Cohen, & Coray, 1992) and a greater use of prescription and nonprescription drugs such as sleeping pills, tranquilizers, and laxatives (Billette & Bouchard, 1993).

Studies of nurses have shown that job stressors, such as conflict with coworkers, role conflict, role ambiguity, high workload demands, and lower task variety, are related to burnout (Firth & Britton, 1989) and symptoms of ill health such as insomnia, chronic fatigue, and depression (Service Employees International Union, 1992). Studies of female assembly line workers and sewing machine operators have indicated that high workload demands and low levels of task control are associated with job dissatisfaction, poor psychological health, and higher levels of musculoskeletal complaints (Brisson, Vezina, & Vinet, 1992; Clegg, Wall, & Kemp, 1987). Other studies have shown that physical and psychological symptoms are more common among women who have less opportunity to use their skills, less influence and recognition, less training, and fewer opportunities for advancement (Keenan, Newton, & Logue, 1986; Wright, Bengtsson, & Frankenberg, 1994).

Low levels of job control, coupled with high job demands, have been linked with CHD in men (Karasek, 1979). However, the evidence for women is contradictory. Some studies have shown increased risk for CHD in women experiencing more stressful jobs (Hammar, Alfredsson, & Theorell, 1994), while others have not confirmed this finding (Sorenson et al., 1985).

Poor relations with supervisors, more than with coworkers, are especially significant for health (Repetti, 1993). Female workers who perceive their supervisors as nonsupportive, unfair, not respectful, and so forth also report more frequent physical and psychological symptoms, such as anxiety, depression, and lower self-esteem (Piotrkowski & Love, 1987; Repetti, 1987). The number of supervisors a woman reports to has also been associated with more frequent physical complaints and anxiety, suggesting that multiple supervisors increase job demands and role conflict (Piotrkowski & Love, 1987). The potency of supervisors in affecting health is likely due to their salience, their power, and the relative paucity of effective strategies for coping with hostile or nonsupportive supervisors. Moreover, personal coping strategies that can be used to deal with problems with coworkers, such as expressing anger directly or discussing differences, may be viewed as a dangerous strategy in periods of high unemployment and layoffs.

Job Stressors of Particular Concern to Women

Because research on occupational stress has tended to focus almost exclusively on men, certain gender-specific occupational stressors have received

little attention. These include workplace-based sexual harassment, difficulties combining work and family, certain types of workplace violence,
and the effects of new office technologies.

Sexual Harassment

Sexual harassment in the workplace may involve unwanted sexual attention, sexual coercion, or gender harassment (Gelfand, Fitzgerald, & Drasgow, 1995). It may be one of the most prevalent health hazards for women.
It is estimated that 50% of working women will be harassed at some point
during their academic or professional lives, and, in traditionally male occupations, the percentage of women who encounter sexual harassment can
rise to as much as 80% (Fitzgerald, 1993). No woman is immune because
of race, ethnicity, social status, or age.

Victims of sexual harassment report a variety of psychological, physical, and behavioral symptoms. These may include anxiety, depression,
fearfulness, rage, insomnia, weight change, sexual dysfunction, marital
conflict, headaches, nausea, gastrointestinal problems, and fatigue (Gutek
& Koss, 1993; Hamilton, Alagna, King, & Lloyd, 1987). Symptoms may be
severe and may persist for extended periods of time, even after the actual
harassment has ceased. At the least, a woman encountering sexual harassment is distracted from her work, which may result in diminished
performance and even job loss (Fitzgerald, 1993).

Ethnic minority women, in addition to sexual harassment, also encounter discrimination based on their membership in a racial or ethnic
minority group (James, 1994). Workers who feel discriminated against, or
who feel that their chances for job advancement are limited because of
their ethnic minority status, are more likely to feel burned out by their
jobs and to experience more health problems and higher blood pressure
(Galinsky et al., 1993; James, 1994).

Combining Employment With Family Work

Employed women still have primary responsibility for household work and
the care of dependents (Piotrkowski & Hughes, 1993).[1] Initial concern over
the negative health consequences for women of adding employment to
their jobs in the family has given way to the realization that employment
can have benefits for many women (Repetti, Matthews, & Waldron, 1989),
such as increased financial resources, a sense of achievement, and a reduction in social isolation, all of which may lead to positive health outcomes.

The health benefits of employment, however, are offset to some degree
when women are dissatisfied with their jobs and when they do not have
sufficient help combining maternal responsibilities with employment (Kessler & McRae, 1982; Ross & Mirowsky, 1988). In fact, two thirds of em-

---

[1]For a more complete discussion of the work–family interface, see chapter 11.

ployed women with dependent children report that difficulty balancing work and family and finding affordable child care are key concerns for women (Reich & Nussbaum, 1994). Not surprisingly, women who have difficulty juggling employment and family responsibilities because of overload and role conflict report increased somatic symptoms and feelings of daily stress (Hughes & Galinsky, 1994). Moreover, the classic job stressors, such as excessive job demands, lack of control (especially over one's schedule), and lack of supervisor support, increase the difficulty of combining employment with family responsibilities (Hughes, Galinsky, & Morris, 1994; Katz & Piotrkowski, 1983).

Workplace Violence

Workplace violence is becoming more visible as a workplace stressor of importance for women. Women, particularly health care workers, appear to be primary victims of certain types of violence, such as rape, hitting, kicking, beating, pinching, and scratching (Bureau of Labor Statistics, 1994). Much nonfatal workplace violence and aggression (i.e., physical attacks, threats, harassment) may be perpetrated by fellow workers. For example, Northwestern National Life (1993) data indicate that 27% of attackers, 37% of those making threats, and 86% of harassers were fellow workers.

There are hints that organizational factors and job stressors may increase the incidence of aggression within the workplace. For example, work by Chen and Spector (1992) indicates a linkage between workplace stressors (e.g., role conflict, interpersonal conflict) and aggression or sabotage at work, and Northwestern National Life (1993) data indicate that workplaces with greater work group harmony, higher levels of employee control or autonomy, and coworker–supervisory support had lower rates of workplace violence.

The Role of the Workplace Environment

The physical work environment may interact with job stressors to produce health symptoms. For example, there is increasing evidence of the roles that both physical risk factors (e.g., poor workstation design) and job stressors play in the etiology of musculoskeletal disorders (Sauter & Swanson, 1996). Computerized workplaces that are more stressful have been found to have higher rates of musculoskeletal problems among workers than computerized workplaces that are less stressful (Hopkins, 1990). It is possible that job stressors interact with physical job demands (e.g., typing speed, work postures) to produce health symptoms and conditions. For example, stressors that change the physical demands of the job, such as heavy workload demands, time pressure, and low worker autonomy (i.e., little control over job tasks), have been associated with musculoskeletal problems (e.g., Lim & Carayon, 1993). Additionally, physiological changes resulting from job stressors, such as increases in muscle tension resulting from cognitive demands at work, may exacerbate the effects of physical job demands (Waersted, Bjorklund, & Westgaard, 1991).

Workers sometimes identify the physical environment as causing their symptoms, yet no physical cause can be found. Mass psychogenic illness (MPI) and some indoor air (or environmental) quality (IAQ) outbreaks appear to have a significant job stress component in their etiology (Hurrell, Sauter, Fidler, Wilcox, & Hornung, 1990).

MPI and IAQ outbreaks often are triggered by workplace odors, and the symptoms of both are similar to those characteristic of exposure to an airborne chemical. Symptoms may include fatigue, headaches, nausea, dizziness, irritated throat, itching, burning or watery eyes, shortness of breath, sweating, heart palpitations, trembling, and so on. Many of these symptoms are also characteristic of a psychological reaction to perceived danger, or anxiety (Boxer, 1990).

Both MPI and IAQ workplaces often have been described as having rigid and authoritarian management, poor communication between workers and supervisors, high workload pressures, and boring, monotonous jobs. MPI and IAQ outbreaks also may be correlated with a perceived lack of job security resulting from rapid technological changes or economic changes, such as downsizing, restructuring, or takeovers (Boxer, 1990).

Controlling Occupational Stress

There are two general intervention strategies for controlling occupational stress: (a) intervening with employees themselves to help them more effectively deal with the stress and (b) eliminating the stressors or reducing exposure to them. One type of employee-focused intervention is aimed at preventing adverse health reactions to stressors by increasing workers' resilience and their range of coping strategies (Koeske, Kirk, & Koeske, 1993; Kushnir & Milbauer, 1994). Such techniques may include training in coping strategies, progressive relaxation techniques, and preventive stress management. Because these programs do not eliminate the sources of stress, they should be evaluated for their long-term effectiveness.

More commonly, practitioners are called on to identify and treat occupationally related health problems. Employees sometimes can accurately point to the workplace problems that seem related to their symptoms. At other times, employees misidentify the source of their problems by pointing to physical features of the work environment—such as poor indoor air quality—instead of psychosocial stressors at work. Most commonly, employees are not aware of the link between their physical or psychological symptoms and occupational stressors.

Assessing occupational stress is especially difficult for three reasons: First, there are no recognized occupational stress syndromes. Second, the effects of occupational stressors tend to be nonspecific and to be expressed through psychological, somatic, or behavioral symptoms. Third, health practitioners, including occupational health physicians and nurses, are not trained to recognize occupational stress. As a result, health professionals rarely go beyond noting a patient's occupation as part of the initial assessment.

The first step in assessing occupational stress is to rule out toxic workplace exposures and organic factors as causes of the patient's symptoms. A second step is to assess the patient's exposures to psychosocial stressors, including those in the workplace. The appendix provides a list of questions that can be used to generate information about job stressors. This evaluation must be done sensitively because employees may resent any implication that their symptoms are triggered by psychosocial stressors.

If all organic and other causes are ruled out and the results of the assessment indicate that psychosocial stressors are present at work, appropriate treatment should be initiated. This may include referral for counseling or psychotherapy.

Counseling or psychotherapy for occupational stress has several goals. The first goal is symptom reduction, using medication if needed. The second goal is to reduce shame and self-blame by helping workers understand that their problems are not the result of personal deficits but are related to stress-inducing features of the workplace. This component of treatment is especially important when sexual harassment has been identified as a workplace stressor. The third goal is to increase patients' ranges of coping strategies. This may involve helping them identify resources in their social environments, such as coworkers and spouses. The fourth aim is to support women's own initiatives to reduce the sources of stress in the workplace. Such initiatives may involve convincing an employer to allow job sharing or flextime, trying to rearrange the workload, or confronting a harasser with support from others.

Case Study

The following vignette illustrates the benefits of appropriate assessment and treatment, as well as the limits to individual intervention.

Helen G., a 34-year-old mother of two, complained to her physician of difficulty sleeping, weight loss, loss of energy, backache, and headaches. A complete physical examination revealed no physical basis for her symptoms. An assessment of her work situation ruled out toxic exposures but did reveal some potential psychosocial stressors. Helen worked as a secretary in a small construction firm. She had two children under the age of 5, who were cared for at home by their grandmother. Helen's husband was a long-distance truck driver who was gone for days at a time and could provide only limited help with child care. Recently, her mother's health problems made it difficult for her to continue caring for Helen's active youngsters. Helen found herself having to leave work early to relieve her mother, compounding her workload problems.

Because of a slowdown in construction, Helen's employer had recently laid off the only other secretary. Helen now was responsible for all the office work and reported to four men instead of two. She was finding it difficult to keep up with the work, her computer was constantly crashing after new programs were installed, and one of her new supervisors was making jokes about how lonely she must get when her husband was away. These "jokes" made her very uncomfortable. However, she feared complaining because jobs were scarce in her community, and her income was necessary to help support her family.

Helen's physician identified at least five occupational stressors to which Helen was exposed: inadequate child care resources, work overload, conflicting role demands, sexual harassment, and difficulty with a supervisor. The physician referred her for counseling to a psychologist with special expertise in occupational health psychology. Helen was initially reluctant to accept the referral, insisting that she was not "mental." However, the physician convinced her that she was not weak or ineffectual and that occupational stress is a real problem that affects millions of people.

Counseling focused on reducing symptoms, increasing Helen's coping repertoire, and supporting her efforts to reduce some of the sources of stress by augmenting her resources and options. At first, intervention focused on helping Helen feel more adequate by avoiding self-blame. As her symptoms became less frequent, treatment began to focus on what Helen could do to help herself. First, she was encouraged to identify some additional day-care resources in her neighborhood. As a result, Helen arranged for her children to spend afternoons in a family day-care setting so that her mother cared for the children only in the mornings.

Helen's coping repertoire was expanded by encouraging her to become more assertive at work. Helen identified a new computer as a resource that would help her more effectively manage her workload, and she successfully convinced her boss that a new computer would make her more productive. By not having to leave early and by eliminating computer breakdowns, Helen was able to get more of her work done, reducing her workload somewhat.

Two problems that were more difficult for Helen to solve were conflicting demands from her supervisors and the sexual harassment. Because there was no one to complain to about the sexual harassment, and the supervisor in question was the brother of the owner, she felt she had no alternatives. As a result, she began to search for a new job. Within 6 months she found a job with lower pay but a better working environment. Although this placed additional financial pressure on her family, she took the new job anyway. All her symptoms disappeared soon thereafter. Treatment lasted 20 sessions, with intermittent follow-up over the year.

This vignette illustrates both the positive benefits of individual interventions to deal with occupational stress and their limits. There are many workplace stressors that individuals cannot change. The insecurity associated with downsizing is only one example. Helen G. was fortunate: She had marketable skills and was able to locate a better job, although the reduction in her pay created new economic stresses for her family. In a tight employment market, even this alternative may not be available.

Reducing Job Stress Through Organizational Change and Job Redesign

Because of the limits of interventions focused on individual change, eliminating job stressors through organizational change and job redesign are the best solutions to the problem of occupational stress. Organizational changes that can be particularly beneficial for women include introducing flexible schedules (flextime); dependent care programs and other family supportive programs (Kraut, 1992); and developing clearly articulated, easily accessible policies against sexual harassment that include a formal grievance procedure, education and training of employees and managers, and the appointment of a sexual harassment information officer (Fitzgerald, 1993).

Examples of job redesign include allowing workers to participate in decision making about their jobs and their job tasks through participative management, thereby increasing job control; letting workers do several activities, rather than one, to increase skill utilization (job enlargement); and changing work–rest schedules for workers performing highly repetitive work (Quick & Quick, 1984; Swanson, Sauter, & Chapman, 1989).

In large corporations, employee assistance personnel and human resource staff can work together effectively to pinpoint sources of stress, propose organizational and job design changes to address the identified stressors, and evaluate the effectiveness of the changes (Murphy, 1995). Even small companies with relatively few employees can introduce changes—such as flexible schedules—to reduce occupational stress.

Public and workplace policies that are effectively implemented also can help reduce stressors. Public policies include legislation that makes discrimination illegal and the Family and Medical Leave Act, which provides job-protected leave for the birth or adoption of a child or the serious illness of a family member. Employer-assisted help in finding or paying for child care, although uncommon, is an example of a workplace program that may reduce stressors.

Conclusion

Most women are employed and will be so throughout their adult life. Women work because they want to and because they must. Moreover, for many women, being employed is associated with improved health. Nonetheless, occupational stress is a significant health issue for employed women. Classic stressors include excessive workload, lack of autonomy, and hostile supervisors. Stressors of particular relevance to women include sexual harassment and lack of supportive policies for integrating work and family responsibilites. Women themselves often are unaware that their health problems may be caused by problems at work. It therefore is critical that mental health practitioners, physicians, and nurses be aware that occupational stressors pose a significant threat to the health and well-being of employed women, and they should avail themselves of training opportunities in this important area. Assessing occupational stress needs to be a standard feature of data gathering in all health settings. Finally, health practitioners need to recognize that occupational stress is a public health problem for which prevention is the most effective remedy.

References

Aronsson, G., Dallner, M., & Aborg, C. (1994). Winners and losers from computerization: A study of the psychosocial work conditions and health of Swedish state employees. *International Journal of Human-Computer Interaction, 6*, 17–35.

Billette, A., & Bouchard, R. (1993). Pool size, job stressors, and health problems: A study of data entry clerks. *International Journal of Human-Computer Interaction, 5*, 101–113.

Boxer, P. A. (1990). Indoor air quality: A psychosocial perspective. *Journal of Occupational Medicine, 32*, 425–428.

Brisson, C., Vezina, M., & Vinet, A. (1992). Health problems of women employed in jobs involving psychological and ergonomic stressors: The case of garment workers in Quebec. *Women and Health, 18*, 49–65.

Bureau of Labor Statistics. (1994). Violence in the workplace comes under closer scrutiny. *Issues in labor statistics.* (Bureau of Labor Statistics Summary 94–10). Washington, DC: U.S. Department of Labor.

Chen, P. Y., & Spector, P. E. (1992). Relationships of work stressors with aggression, withdrawal, theft and substance use: An exploratory study. *Journal of Occupational and Organizational Psychology, 65*, 177–184.

Clegg, C., Wall, T., & Kemp, N. (1987). Women on the assembly line: A comparison of main and interactive explanations of job satisfaction, absence and mental health. *Journal of Occupational Psychology, 60*, 273–287.

Eckenrode, J., & Gore, S. (1990). Stress and coping at the boundary of work and family. In J. Eckenrode & S. Gore (Eds.), *Stress between work and family* (pp. 1–16). New York: Plenum.

Firth, H., & Britton, P. (1989). "Burnout": Absence and turnover amongst British nursing staff. *Journal of Occupational Psychology, 62*, 55–59.

Fitzgerald, L. F. (1993). Sexual harassment: Violence against women in the workplace. *American Psychologist, 48*, 1070–1076.

Fullerton, H. N., Jr. (1993, November). Another look at the labor force. *Monthly Labor Review*, pp. 31–39.

Galinsky, E., Bond, J. T., & Friedman, D. E. (1993). *The changing workforce: Highlights of the national study.* New York: Families and Work Institute.

Gelfand, M. F., Fitzgerald, L. F., & Drasgow, F. (1995). The structure of sexual harassment: A confirmatory analysis across cultures and settings. *Journal of Vocational Behavior, 47*, 164–177.

Gutek, B. A., & Koss, M. P. (1993). Changed women and changed organizations: Consequences of and coping with sexual harassment. *Journal of Vocational Behavior, 42*, 28–48.

Hamilton, J. A., Alagna, S. W., King, S. L., & Lloyd, C. (1987). The emotional consequences of gender-based abuse in the workplace: New counselling programs for sex discrimination. In M. Baude (Ed.), *Women, power and therapy* (pp. 155–182). New York: Hawthorne Press.

Hammar, N., Alfredsson, L., & Theorell, T. (1994). Job characteristics and the incidence of myocardial infarction. *International Journal of Epidemiology, 23*, 277–284.

Hopkins, A. (1990). Stress, the quality of work, and repetition strain injury in Australia. *Work and Stress, 4*, 129–138.

Hughes, D. L., & Galinsky, E. (1994). Gender, job and family conditions, and psychological symptoms. *Psychology of Women Quarterly, 18*, 251–270.

Hughes, D., Galinsky, E., & Morris, A. (1994). The effects of job characteristics on marital quality: Specifying linking mechanisms. *Journal of Marriage and the Family, 54*, 31–42.

Hurrell, J. J., Jr., & Murphy, L. R. (1992). Psychological job stress. In W. N. Rom (Ed.), *Environmental and occupational medicine* (2nd ed., pp. 675–684). Boston: Little, Brown.

Hurrell, J. J., Jr., Sauter, S. L., Fidler, A. T., Wilcox, T. G., & Hornung, R. W. (1990, July). *Job stress issues in the Library of Congress/EPA Headquarters Indoor Air Quality and Work Environment study.* Paper presented at Indoor Air 90 (conference), Toronto, Ontario, Canada.

James, K. (1994). Social identity, work stress and minority workers' health. In G. P. Keita & J. J. Hurrell, Jr. (Eds.), *Job stress in a changing workforce* (pp. 127–145). Washington, DC: American Psychological Association.

Karasek, R. A. (1979). Job demands, job decision latitude and mental strain: Implications for job design. *Administrative Science Quarterly, 24,* 285–308.

Katz, M. H., & Piotrkowski, C. S. (1983). Correlates of family role strain among employed Black women. *Family Relations, 32,* 331–339.

Keenan, A., Newton, J., & Logue, C. (1986). Work needs, sex role stereotyping and affective reactions of female professional engineers. *Journal of Occupational Behaviour, 7,* 67–73.

Kessler, R. C., & McRae, J. A., Jr. (1982). The effect of wives' employment on the mental health of married men and women. *American Sociology Review, 47,* 216–226.

Koeske, G. F., Kirk, S. A., & Koeske, R. D. (1993). Coping with job stress: Which strategies work best? *Journal of Occupational and Organizational Psychology, 66,* 319–335.

Kraut, A. I. (1992). Organizational research on work and family issues. In S. Zedeck (Ed.), *Work, families and organizations* (pp. 208–235). San Francisco: Jossey-Bass.

Kushnir, T., & Milbauer, V. (1994). Managing stress and burnout at work: A cognitive group intervention program for directors of day-care centers. *Pediatrics, 94,* 1074–1077.

Lim, S. Y., & Carayon, P. (1993). An integrated approach to cumulative trauma disorders in computerized offices: The role of psychosocial work factors, psychological stress and ergonomic risk factors. In M. J. Smith & G. Salvendy (Eds.), *Human computer interaction: Applications and case studies* (pp. 880–885). Amsterdam: Elsevier Science.

Murphy, L. R. (1995). Managing job stress: An employee assistance/human resource management partnership. *Personnel Review, 24,* 41–50.

National Council on Compensation Insurance. (1985). *Emotional stress in the workplace: New legal rights in the eighties.* New York: Author.

Northwestern National Life. (1991). *Employee burnout: America's newest epidemic.* Minneapolis, MN: Northwestern National Life.

Northwestern National Life. (1992). *Employee burnout: Causes and cures.* Minneapolis, MN: Northwestern National Life.

Northwestern National Life. (1993). *Fear and violence in the workplace.* Minneapolis, MN: Northwestern National Life.

Piotrkowski, C. S., Cohen, B. G., & Coray, K. E. (1992). Working conditions and well-being among women office workers. *International Journal of Human-Computer Interaction, 4,* 263–281.

Piotrkowski, C. S., & Hughes, D. (1993). Dual-earner families. In F. Walsh (Ed.), *Normal family processes* (2nd ed., pp. 185–207). New York: Guilford Press.

Piotrkowski, C. S., & Love, M. (1987). *Quality of supervision and the health and well-being of women office workers* (NIOSH Publication No. 85-35692).

Piotrkowski, C. S., & Staines, G. L. (1991). Job stress and the family. *Business Insights, 7,* 22–27.

Quick, J. C., & Quick, J. D. (1984). *Organizational stress and preventive management.* New York: McGraw-Hill.

Reich, R. B., & Nussbaum, K. (1994). *Working women count! A report to the nation.* Washington, DC: U.S. Department of Labor, Women's Bureau.

Repetti, R. L. (1987). Individual and common components of the social environment at work and psychological well-being. *Journal of Personality and Social Psychology, 52,* 710–720.

Repetti, R. L. (1993). The effects of workload and the social environment at work on health. In L. Goldberger & S. Breznitz (Eds.), *Handbook of stress* (2nd ed., pp. 368–385). New York: Free Press.

Repetti, R. L., Matthews, K. A., & Waldron, I. (1989). Employment and women's health. *American Psychologist, 44,* 1394–1401.

Ross, C. E., & Mirowsky, J. (1988). Child care and emotional adjustment to wives' employment. *Journal of Health and Social Behavior, 29,* 127–138.

Sauter, S. L., & Swanson, N. G. (1996). An ecological model of musculoskeletal disorders in office work. In S. Moon & S. L. Sauter (Eds.), *Beyond biomechanics: Psychosocial factors and musculoskeletal disorders in office work* (pp. 3–21). New York: Taylor & Francis.

Service Employees International Union. (1992). *The national nurse survey.* Washington, DC: Author.

Silverman, M. M., Eichler, A., & Williams, G. D. (1987). Self-reported stress: Findings from the 1985 National Health Interview Survey. *Public Health Reports, 102,* 47–53.

Sorensen, G., Pirie, P., Folsom, A., Luepker, R., Jacobs, D., & Gillum, R. (1985). Sex differences in the relationship between work and health: The Minnesota Heart Survey. *Journal of Health and Social Behavior, 26,* 379–394.

Swanson, N. G., Sauter, S. L., & Chapman, L. J. (1989). The design of rest breaks for video display terminal work: A review of the relevant literature. In A. Mital (Ed.), *Advances in industrial ergonomics and safety I* (pp. 895–898). New York: Taylor & Francis.

Waersted, M., Bjorklund, R. A., & Westgaard, R. H. (1991). Shoulder muscle tension induced by two VDU-based tasks of different complexity. *Ergonomics, 34,* 137–150.

Wright, I., Bengtsson, C., & Frankenberg, K. (1994). Aspects of psychological work environment and health among male and female white-collar and blue-collar workers in a big Swedish industry. *Journal of Organizational Behavior, 15,* 177–183.

Appendix

Sample Questions for Assessing Occupational Stress

This assessment of occupational stress needs to be introduced carefully. The following is a set of questions and probes to gather additional information.

Sample introduction: "I am going to ask you some questions about your job because it is possible that a person's symptoms are related to problems at work. Everything you say, of course, is confidential."

1. Obtain basic information about the employee's job if this information has not yet been obtained: "What is your job title?" "What exactly do you do?" "How long have you been working for your employer?"

2. Inquire about the presence of classic job stressors: "Are there any problems at work now?" "When did they start?" "What shift do you work and what is the pattern of rotation?" (Here the practitioner should look for the frequency and pattern of shift rotation, if any. Certain patterns, such as frequent and irregular changes, are more disruptive than others.) "How many hours per week do you work? Do you work on weekends too? Do you have a second job? How many hours do you work at this job?" (Here the practitioner should assess the overload attributable to excessive hours.) "Do you work under time pressure?" "Do you have too much to do?" "How much say do you have in how you do your job?" "How secure is your job?"

3. Ask about interpersonal relations at work: "To how many people do you report? Is that difficult for you?" "Is your supervisor helpful to you or difficult to work for? If so, what are the difficulties?"

4. Ask about sex discrimination: "Do you feel you are treated fairly with regard to pay and opportunities for advancement?" For ethnic minorities, "Do you feel there is any discrimination toward you because you are _____ ?" (Probe for incidents or examples.)

5. Ask about sexual harassment. Here it is important not to ask about harassment directly but to ask about specific behaviors. Introducing this topic carefully also is important because women feel especially uncomfortable talking about it: "Do you work mostly with men, with women, or with a mixture of men and women?" "Is your immediate supervisor a man or a woman?" If the employee works with many men or in a traditionally male occupation, probe for a hostile work environment: "Is it comfortable for you as a woman to work there? Are women treated with dignity and respect?" "Do things happen that make you uncomfortable as a woman?" (Probe carefully for jokes, degrading sexually charged remarks, pictures, etc.)

Ask about incidents of sexual harassment by introducing the topic carefully. A sample introduction is as follows: "Sometimes things happen to women at work that they feel uncomfortable talking about. I am going to ask you some questions. These are standard questions that I ask all my female patients."

Sample questions are as follows: "Are sexual comments or jokes directed at you that make you uncomfortable?" "Have you ever been propositioned, pressured for dates, touched, kissed, or grabbed or otherwise sexually bothered or made uncomfortable?" (Ask by whom and be especially alert to sexual harassment by a supervisor.) If sexual harassment has occurred, determine how long the harassment was going on, if it is still continuing, and how the patient reacts to it.

6. Inquire about the ease with which the employee integrates work and family responsibilities and the support she has for doing so: "How flexible is your schedule?" "Do you have children? How old are they?" "Who cares for them while you are at work and how is that working out?" "Do you have enough help with child care?" "Many women complain that they have trouble getting everything done at home and at work? How about you? Is anyone helping you?"

7. Inquire about changes in the symptom pattern: "Were there any changes in your job before or at about the time you started experiencing (the symptoms)?" "Do you notice the symptom getting worse or better at times?" (Probe for changes on weekends, during vacations, and in the work situation.)

Part III

Responses to Life Cycle Challenges

11

Combining Work and Family

Nancy L. Marshall

Many women in their child rearing years are combining family responsibilities and employment. In the United States, 60% of women with a child under 6 years of age and 75% of women with school-age children (6–17) are in the labor force (U.S. Department of Labor, 1990). A woman with two children can reasonably expect to spend 20 years or more combining employment and raising a child at home. In addition, about 20% of employed women have some level of responsibility to care for older people. Thus, combining work and family has become the norm for women rather than the exception. In this chapter, we provide an overview of the current theories about, and understanding of, work and family issues. We then discuss the health implications for women of combining work and family. Finally we review specific risk factors and ways to respond to patients or clients with work-related and family-related health problems.

Research on Work and Family

There is a long tradition of research on work and family, including studies of job conditions, parenthood, and marriage. Since the 1960s, there have been increasing numbers of studies that have examined the interface between work and family.

The first stream of research on the work–family interface was based on the premise that individuals have limited time and energy and that adding extra roles and responsibilities necessarily creates tensions between competing demands and a sense of overload and interrole conflict (Goode, 1960). This is referred to as the "scarcity hypothesis." Working long hours, working nonday shifts, extensive work-related travel, stressful job conditions, heavy demands at work and high job involvement, as well as the number and age of children and lack of social support, have all been shown to be related to work–family conflict or strains, although this can vary with individual and family characteristics (Burke, 1988).

The research also has shown that women often report greater work–family strains than men. These gender differences in strains reflect gender differences in job and family roles and responsibilities rather than sex differences per se. Even though women's rate of participation in the labor market has risen dramatically over the past 50 years, women still spend almost twice as many hours as men on household tasks (Coverman, 1983). National time-use studies indicate that in couples, men's share of caring for children and doing housework has increased from about one fifth of the total time spent in the 1960s to about one third of the total time (Pleck, 1993). Even in two-earner couples in which both are employed full time, women continue to maintain primary responsibility for the household in the majority of couples, although about half of the husbands do share the responsibility for supervising the children or staying home with a sick child (Marshall & Barnett, 1995).

The second stream of research on combining work and family has theorized that the rewards that accrue with multiple roles (i.e., greater self-esteem and recognition, greater social involvement) offset the costs of multiple roles (Marks, 1977; Sieber, 1974). This is referred to as the "enhancement hypothesis." The first wave of this research examined the impact of the number of roles that an individual occupied. Generally, the research has shown that individuals with more than one role have better mental and physical health than do individuals with only one role (Voydanoff, 1989). However, the research on parenthood for employed women has generated sometimes-conflicting findings. Although women without children generally have poorer health than women with children, women with many children or with preschool-age children rather than older children often are found to have poorer health than other women with children (Verbrugge, 1986). It generally is argued that this is the case because of the greater workload involved in large families or in the care of young children.

The second wave of "enhancement" research looked at the characteristics or quality of roles, such as job conditions, marital quality, parenting stresses and rewards, and demands at work and at home. Role characteristics have been found to be more strongly related to health than are the number or constellation of roles (Baruch, Biener, & Barnett, 1987).

Overall, the research to date suggests that combining work and family generally has a positive impact on health. However, the research also clearly indicates that women with multiple roles do sometimes experience multiple-role overload and interrole conflict, and this multiple-role strain can be associated with poorer health. These apparently-disparate sets of findings suggest that both the scarcity hypothesis and the enhancement hypothesis are true. Indeed, several studies have shown that multiple roles can be both a source of role gratification as well as a source of strain or conflict (Marshall & Barnett, 1993; Tiedje et al., 1990).

The Health Implications of Combining Work and Family

What, then, are the health implications of combining work and family? For many women, combining work and family is associated with greater self-esteem and better mental health, including reduced depressive symptomatology, anxiety, and psychological distress. Using data on 720 women and men from the New Haven community study, Thoits (1983) found that individuals with more social roles reported significantly fewer psychological and psychosomatic symptoms. Using a sample of 1,086 White members of married couples, Kessler and McRae (1982) found that employed wives, compared with married homemakers, had significantly lower scores on anxiety, depression, and psychological and psychosomatic symptoms and significantly higher self-esteem scores.

Combining work and family also has been associated with better physical health. Verbrugge (1983) asked a sample of 714 White men and women from the Health in Detroit Study about their current health status, health behaviors in the past year, health attitudes, lifestyle behaviors, and anxiety. Of this sample, 589 respondents kept a daily health record for 1–6 weeks. Each day, they answered questions about their general health status, symptoms, health behaviors, mood, and special events. Verbrugge found that the healthiest women were those who were both employed and parents. Verbrugge offered several possible explanations for these findings. She suggested that social involvement (a correlate of employment and participation in family roles) may reduce risks of illness and injury by offering emotional benefits and resources. In addition, individuals who are socially involved may be less likely to perceive symptoms, less likely to view their symptoms as serious, and less likely to seek care.

In a separate analysis of data on health status and disability (e.g., disability days, activity limitation, acute conditions, self-rated health status) from the 1977–1978 wave of the National Health Interview Survey, Verbrugge and Madans (1985) found that, despite significant differences in economic well-being and in health, Black and White women with the same role combinations had similar health profiles and that employment and marriage were associated with fewer health problems for both groups. However, combining parenthood and a job was associated with more health problems for both White and Black single women and Black married women.

Although women who combine work and family often receive a health benefit, for some women combining work and family leads to greater time pressure, an inability to meet the demands of job or family, and other work–family strains or conflicts that can result in increased risk for depression and anxiety, fatigue, more physical symptoms and conditions, and poorer physical health status. In their analysis of women and coronary heart disease (CHD), using data from the Framingham Heart Study, Haynes and Feinleib (1980) found that employment per se was not associated with increased risk for CHD. However, among employed women, CHD rates were highest among women who were or had been married. The risk was especially great for those who had raised three or more children. The increased risk with more children was not observed among housewives. Haynes and Feinleib suggested that the dual roles and demands of employment and raising a family may explain the high incidence of CHD among employed women with several children.

In a study of 828 men and women in police work, Burke (1988) found that individuals with more job stressors, and more nonwork stressors, were more likely to report that their jobs interfered with their family and nonwork lives. Furthermore, those who reported that their jobs interfered with their family and nonwork life reported more psychosomatic symptoms and had higher scores on a negative affective states measure (e.g., anger, depression, insomnia, aggression). In a study of 556 men and women employed in one school system, primarily as teachers, Greenglass, Pantony, and Burke (1989) found that conflict between work and nonwork roles was correlated with depression, anxiety, and somatization, as measured by the Hopkins Symptom Checklist (Derogatis, 1983), for both women and men. In a sample of 300 women in two-earner couples from the Adult Lives Study (Barnett et al., 1994), Marshall (1994) found that women with children, longer work hours, and greater work and nonwork stressors reported more work–family strains (i.e., work's interference with family or family's interference with work). In addition, greater work–family strains were associated with greater depressive symptomatology and greater frequency of, and discomfort from, a range of physical symptoms.

Results of several studies have suggested that combining work and family is particularly likely to lead to poorer health when work–family strains are great enough to counteract the benefits of multiple roles. In a study of 1,026 men and women, Cleary and Mechanic (1983) found that employed married women reported less psychological distress than housewives but that having young children counteracted the advantage of employment. Kessler and McRae (1982) found that the effect of employment on depressive symptoms varied for mothers: Employment was associated with improved mental health for mothers when husbands shared in child care, but the advantages of employment were canceled out for women whose husbands did not share in child care. In the study of women in two-earner couples cited earlier, Marshall (1994) found that having children was associated directly with reduced depressive symptomatology, but, when combining work and children led to work–family strains, it contributed indirectly to greater depressive symptomatology. An individual woman's risk would depend on the balance between the benefits of parenthood and employment as well as the level of work–family strains experienced.

The negative health outcomes of work–family strains can be varied. The specific health outcome may depend on the individual's health history as well as other factors. Health practitioners therefore must consider a range of health symptoms that can be associated with work–family strains.

Risk Factors

Because the purpose of this chapter is to provide information useful to health practitioners whose patients may be experiencing health problems associated with work–family strains, in the rest of the chapter we focus on the possible negative consequences of combining work and family. However, practitioners should be wary of assuming that any woman with multiple roles is at risk for health problems. In fact, the research suggests that certain groups of women are at particular risk, whereas others benefit from the positive effects of multiple roles. To help health practitioners identify individuals who may be at risk for work–family strains and related health problems, we have reviewed the literature on risk factors for work–family strains. These risk factors are cumulative in their impact on health; the more risk factors a women has, the more likely she is to experience work–family strains and poor health.

Workload

One of the hallmarks of work–family strain is too much work and not enough time. Greater workload, as measured by the demands at home or at work, hours spent at work or in child care or other domestic tasks, or by the presence of young children, contributes to greater work–family strain (Voydanoff, 1989).

Work or Family Stress

The quality of one's experiences in work or parenting roles also is predictive of role overload and role strain. In particular, jobs with heavy demands and pressure to work hard and fast, and with limited autonomy and limited challenge, are associated with work–family strains and poorer health in women. Similarly, conflicts with family members, or worries about family members' health or safety, contribute to greater family stress and are associated with greater work–family strains and poorer health for women (Burke, 1988).

Role Commitment

Marks (1977) posited that individuals who were overcommitted to one role were more likely to experience role strains than were individuals who were equally committed to multiple roles. Several studies have provided support for this position. Barnett and Baruch (1985) found that employed women with more education, whom one might expect would be more committed to their work roles, experience more work–family conflict. Greenhaus, Bedeian, and Mossholder (1987) found that an extensive time commitment to work was associated with greater work–family conflict. Marshall and Barnett (1993) found that for parents, women in jobs with greater occupational prestige, which might be expected to require greater work-role commitment, reported more work–family strains.

Other Work Factors

Those working nonday shifts experience higher levels of work–family conflict (Voydanoff, 1989), probably because these work schedules put them "out of sync" with their support networks and societal supports, such as child care. Conversely, employees with flexible work schedules report less work–family conflict and more time for home chores and family, particularly when they can vary their schedule from day to day (Staines, 1990).

Other Nonwork Factors

Lack of social support from family and friends was found to be associated with fewer reported gains from combining work and family in two different samples of employed women (Marshall & Barnett, 1991, 1993). Support from the husband or partner is also crucial. One study indicated that women whose husbands or partners do not approve of their employment reported more multiple-role stress (Elman & Gilbert, 1984). Others have suggested that employed women's greater workload is a function of the limited involvement of husbands in household tasks and child care. When husbands do share in caring for their children, employed women are less likely to be depressed (Ross & Mirowsky, 1988).

Employed women with young children also need child care for their children. When women are dissatisfied with their child-care arrangements, they report greater role strain (Van Meter & Agronow, 1982). Difficulty arranging for child care and concerns about the stability and quality of child-care arrangements also are associated with greater depression and anxiety (Ross & Mirowsky, 1988).

Sex Role Attitudes

Women with traditional sex role attitudes tend to believe that a woman's place is in the home, as a support for her husband, and as a mother for her children. Women with more egalitarian sex role attitudes tend to believe that both women and men should be active both inside and outside the home. Several research studies have indicated that women with traditional sex role attitudes are more likely to experience work–family strains, whereas women with egalitarian attitudes are more likely to experience multiple-role enhancement (Marshall & Barnett, 1993).

Limited Financial Resources

Research also has indicated a relationship between limited financial resources, health, and work–family issues. Haynes and Feinleib (1980) suggested that clerical workers with children, and married to blue-collar workers, have higher rates of CHD because of the economic pressures they experience. Married women in lower prestige occupations report poorer physical health than married women in higher prestige occupations (Marshall, 1994). Moreover, working women with lower family incomes who have children at home are less likely to benefit from the positive impact of multiple roles on depression; their limited financial resources put them at greater risk for depression when combining work and family (Cleary & Mechanic, 1983).

Race and Ethnicity

Much of the work on multiple roles has been conducted on White women (and White men). However, the few studies that have addressed race or ethnicity suggest that although the relationships between multiple roles and health are often similar, women of color are often in poorer quality jobs and face additional nonwork stressors, and therefore would be expected to be at greater risk for work–family strains. In a study of 712 Americans of Mexican descent, Krause and Markides (1987) found that employment and parenthood were associated with less illness for women. Verbrugge and Madans (1985) found that Black women had more short-term disability days each year and more chronic limitation and that they reported worse overall health status than White women, although the links between role occupancy and health were virtually the same for Black and White women. In a study of 229 Black and White women employed as licensed practical nurses (LPNs) and social workers, Marshall and Barnett (1991) found that the Black women reported more concerns about job discrimination on the basis of race or ethnicity. Black LPNs, who were concentrated in the poorest jobs overall, reported less decision authority at work, more dead-end jobs, and more exposure to hazards on the job. In the family arena, both Black and White women reported similar levels of reward and enjoyment from their children. However, Black and White LPNs reported more concerns about their children's health and safety than did their middle-class counterparts, and more concerns about arguments and disagreements with their children, than did the White social workers. Consistent with these differences in job quality and parenting experiences, Black and White LPNs reported working a "double shift," having a heavy workload on the job and at home.

Identifying Women at Risk

The following questions can be used to assess whether a patient's health symptoms may be a consequence of work–family strains. These questions can elicit information to help the health care provider identify women at risk for emotional distress or poor physical health as a consequence of work–family strains. If used with sensitivity, they also can validate a woman's own assessment of the stressors in her life.

First, ask about work–family strains: (a) "Does your family time often seem more pressured because of your job responsibilities?" (b) "Does your work time often seem more pressured because of your family responsibilities?" (c) "Do you often feel that your job interferes with your family life?" (d) "Do you often feel that you have too much to do and cannot get it all done?"

Women who answer yes to one or more of these questions about work–family strains are at risk for depression or physical health problems. Women who appear to be experiencing work–family strains should then be asked a series of questions, to identify the sources of these strains.

The Job

1. "How many hours a week do you work at your job?" (More than 45 hours a week may be a source of strain, particularly for women with heavy family responsibilities.)
2. "Do you find that you have too much to do at work or that you have a lot of deadline pressure?"
3. "Do you enjoy your job?" (Women who enjoy their jobs, particularly if their jobs are challenging or have intrinsic value for the individual woman, are better able to tolerate overload.)
4. "Is your job flexible enough for you to take care of family chores or to do things for yourself?"

The Home

1. "How are things going at home?" (Women with heavy family responsibilities, or who are having problems with children or spouse, are at greater risk for work-family strains.)

Supports and Resources

1. "Do you have someone who regularly helps with the children—your husband, a relative, or friend?"
2. "Do you have someone to talk to about things at work or at home?"
3. "Are you happy with your children's care while you are at work?"

Reducing the Health Consequences of Work–Family Strains

Work–family strain for employed women is most likely to occur when the division of labor within the family, the workplace, and institutional supports for the family such as child care have not kept pace with other changes in the family (Ross & Mirowsky, 1988). Until these societal institutions catch up with the dramatic change in women's employment, and the rising number of single-mother families and two-earner families, women will continue to embody, literally, the strains in United States society.

What can health care providers and clinicians do when faced with a woman whose health is being negatively affected by work–family strains? The first goal should be treatment of the presenting symptoms or conditions, using medication if indicated. Health care providers and clinicians also can recommend activities, such as relaxation techniques, exercise, and increased social support, which can reduce the negative impact of work–family strains on the patient's health. However, it is often most effective to seek ways to empower a woman to address the sources of her work–family strains. Health care providers, in their professional roles, are not expected to be advocates for social change, but it is appropriate for providers to seek to empower women to be their own advocates for changes in their own lives and at the societal level. Recent research suggests that when individuals are effective problem solvers of role-related stressors, they have better health outcomes (Thoits, 1994).

Each situation is different, and solutions need to be tailored to the individual circumstances. The first step is to encourage the woman to identify the specific causes of the stress and strain that she is experiencing; the questions presented earlier can be useful to this end. Once a woman has identified some of the sources of strain, the following ideas may be helpful. These ideas are not meant to be exhaustive but only suggestive of the creative and concrete ways that women may be able to reduce their work–family strains and protect their health. The health professional's empathy and concern is particularly important in this process.

Not Enough Time

Although the reality of not enough time is common for many women who combine work and family, there are some ways to stretch time. For example, some women with many years in the labor force are used to doing everything themselves and set high standards for themselves at work. Other women are returning to work after establishing high expectations for their time investment and performance at home. In both situations, women can be empowered to delegate tasks that were once theirs and to reduce their expectations. This is harder than it sounds: It requires changing not only their behavior and expectations but that of the people around them.

Although it is possible to stretch time sometimes, there are only 24 hours in the day. Women sometimes may need to consider a job change, either with the same employer or with a new employer, to a position that does not require extensive overtime or to one that offers greater flexibility.

Stressful or Bad Job

If a bad or stressful job seems to be contributing to work–family strains, a woman can be empowered to seek support at work, talking with other coworkers who may share her experiences and who may have a perspective that will make it easier to cope. In addition, a woman can be empowered to negotiate or to join with other employees to work for changes in their jobs that will reduce the stress or make the jobs more rewarding. If these approaches are not effective, it may be necessary to change to a less stressful job.

Family Worries

For many women, work–family strains are tied to extra demands or worries at home, such as caring for an infant or dealing with the serious illness of a loved one. The specifics of each situation will partially determine the response. Women with preschool-age children who can combine extra social support, good child care, and a flexible job that does not require more than 40–45 hours a week are the least likely to experience work–family strains. To create these conditions, women with young children might seek out others in their workplace who also have young children and consider some of the other ideas for home and workplace that are mentioned in this section.

Research on combining work and caregiving responsibilities for a seriously ill family member suggests that some women need to reduce or stop their employment (Stone, Cafferata, & Sangl, 1987), but for other women employment can continue to have a positive impact on women's caregiving roles (Stull, Bowman, & Smerglia, 1991). In general, the research on employment status and caring for elderly or disabled individuals indicates that the benefits of combining work and these family responsibilities balances the negative aspects (Moen, Robison, & Dempster-McClain, 1995; Scharlach, 1994). The research is not yet available on who is at risk for health problems when combining employment and caregiving and who benefits from continued employment.

Child Care Worries

When worries about child care are part of the picture, it is important to identify the particular source of the worry. Some women are concerned that leaving their children with someone else will be harmful to the children or to the child's relationship with the mother. The research to date indicates that nonparental child care per se is not damaging to children (Clarke-Stewart, 1992). However, parents should be legitimately concerned about the quality of the care their children receive and with the stability of care. Each individual needs to determine whether his or her child care worries are about unreliable arrangements or whether it is the quality of the care or the cost of the care. Local resources sometimes are available to help identify other child-care options or financial assistance for child care. If quality is the concern, parents need to decide whether they need to find another child-care arrangement or whether they can work with the caregiver to improve the quality of the child care.

Conclusion

A large body of research indicates that women who combine work and family are healthier than women who occupy only one sphere. For some of these women, there are no strains associated with combining work and family. For others, the strains are balanced by the positive gains of combining work and family. However, for some women, the balance is tipped and the work–family strains overwhelm the positive effects. High levels of work–family strains are related to poorer mental and physical health.

Certain women are at greater risk for the high levels of work–family strains that are associated with poor health. In particular, women who work long hours or have non-day-shift hours and women who have stressful jobs with limited flexibility are at risk. Also at risk are women with heavy family demands, such as preschool children or three or more children, and women who have stressful family situations or worries about their child-care arrangements. Finally, women with limited financial resources or inadequate marital or social support are at risk for work–family strains and poorer health.

Health care providers and clinicians can promote better mental and physical health for women by acknowledging the impact of work–family issues on women's health and by empowering individual women to reduce their work–family strains and improve their health.

References

Barnett, R. C., & Baruch, G. K. (1985). Women's involvement in multiple roles and psychological distress. *Journal of Personality and Social Psychology, 49,* 135–145.

Barnett, R. C., Marshall, N. L., & Brennan, R. (1994). Gender and the relationship between marital-role quality and psychological distress: A study of dual-earner couples. *Psychology of Women Quarterly, 18,* 105–127.

Baruch, G. K., Biener, L., & Barnett, R. C. (1987). Women and gender in research on work and family stress. *American Psychologist, 42,* 130–136.

Burke, R. J. (1988). Some antecedents and consequences of work-family conflict. *Journal of Social Behavior and Personality, 3,* 287–302.

Clarke-Stewart, A. K. (1992). Consequences of child care for children's development. In A. Booth (Ed.), *Child care in the 1990s: Trends and consequences* (pp. 63–82). Hillsdale, NJ: Erlbaum.

Cleary, P. D., & Mechanic, D. (1983). Sex differences in psychological distress among married people. *Journal of Health and Social Behavior, 24,* 111–121.

Coverman, S. (1983). Gender, domestic labor time, and wage inequality. *American Sociological Review, 48,* 623–637.

Derogatis, L. R. (1983). *Description and bibliography for the SCL-90-R and other instruments of the psychopathology rating scale series.* Baltimore: Johns Hopkins University School of Medicine.

Elman, M. R., & Gilbert, L. A. (1984). Coping strategies for role conflict in married professional women with children. *Family Relations, 33,* 317–337.

Goode, W. (1960). A theory of strain. *American Sociological Review, 25,* 483–496.

Greenglass, E. R., Pantony, K., & Burke, R. J. (1989). A gender-role perspective on role conflict, work stress and social support. In E. B. Goldsmith (Ed.), *Work and family: Theory, research and applications* (pp. 317–328). Newbury Park, CA: Sage.

Greenhaus, J. H., Bedeian, A. G., & Mossholder, K. W. (1987). Work experiences, job performance, and feelings of personal and family well-being. *Journal of Vocational Behavior, 31,* 200–215.

Haynes, S. G., & Feinleib, M. (1980). Women, work and coronary heart disease: Prospective findings from the Framingham Heart Study. *American Journal of Public Health, 70,* 133–141.

Kessler, R. C., & McRae, J. A., Jr. (1982). The effect of wives' employment of the mental health of married men and women. *American Sociological Review, 47,* 217–227.

Krause, N., & Markides, K. S. (1987). Gender roles, illness, and illness behavior in a Mexican-American population. *Social Science Quarterly, 68,* 102–121.

Marks, S. R. (1977). Multiple roles and role strain: Some notes on human energy, time and commitment. *American Sociological Review, 41,* 921–936.

Marshall, N. L. (1994, May). *The work-family interface and employed women's health*. Paper presented at the American Psychological Association Conference on Women's Health, Washington, DC.

Marshall, N. L., & Barnett, R. C. (1991). Race and class and multiple role strains and gains among women employed in the service sector. *Women and Health, 17*(4), 1–19.

Marshall, N. L., & Barnett, R. C. (1993). Work-family strains and gains among two earner couples. *Journal of Community Psychology, 21*, 64–78.

Marshall, N. L., & Barnett, R. C. (1995, August). *Child care, division of labor and parental well-being among two earner couples*. Paper presented at the meeting of the American Sociological Association, Washington, DC.

Moen, P., Robison, J., & Dempster-McClain, D. (1995). Caregiving and women's well-being: A life course approach. *Journal of Health and Social Behavior, 36*, 259–273.

Pleck, J. H. (1993, February). Remarks to New England Work and Family Association Inaugural Meeting.

Ross, C. E., & Mirowsky, J. (1988). Child care and emotional adjustment to wives' employment. *Journal of Health and Social Behavior, 29*, 127–138.

Scharlach, A. E. (1994). Caregiving and employment: Competing or complimentary roles? *The Gerontologist, 34*, 378–385.

Sieber, S. (1974). Toward a theory of role accumulation. *American Sociological Review, 39*, 567–578.

Staines, G. L. (1990, August). *Flextime and the conflict between work and family life*. Paper presented at the 98th Annual Convention of the American Psychological Association, Boston.

Stone, R. I., Cafferata, G. L., & Sangl, J. (1987). Caregivers of the frail elderly: A national profile. *The Gerontologist, 27*, 616–626.

Stull, D. E., Bowman, K., & Smerglia, V. (1991). *Women in the middle: A myth in the making?* Unpublished manuscript.

Thoits, P. (1983). Multiple identities and psychological well-being. *American Sociological Review, 48*, 174–187.

Thoits, P. (1994). Stressors and problem-solving: The individual as psychological activist. *Journal of Health and Social Behavior, 35*, 143–160.

Tiedje, L. B., Wortman, C. B., Downey, G., Emmons, C., Biernat, M., & Lang, E. (1990). Women with multiple roles: Role compatibility perceptions, satisfaction, and mental health. *Journal of Marriage and the Family, 52*, 63–72.

U.S. Department of Labor, Bureau of Labor Statistics. (1990). *Employee benefits in medium and large firms, 1989* (Bulletin 2363). Washington, DC: U.S. Government Printing Office.

Van Meter, M. J. S., & Agronow, S. J. (1982). The stress of multiple roles: The case for role strain among married college women. *Family Relations, 31*, 131–138.

Verbrugge, L. M. (1983). Multiple roles and physical health of women and men. *Journal of Health and Social Behavior, 24*, 16–30.

Verbrugge, L. M. (1986). Role burdens and physical health of women and men. *Women and Health, 11*, 47–78.

Verbrugge, L. M., & Madans, J. H. (1985). Social roles and health trends of American women. *Milbank Memorial Fund Quarterly, 63*, 691–735.

Voydanoff, P. (1989). Work and family: A review and expanded conceptualization. In E. B. Goldsmith (Ed.), *Work and family: Theory, research and applications* (pp. 1–22). Newbury Park, CA: Sage.

12

Psychosocial Aspects of Childbirth

M. Robin DiMatteo and Katherine L. Kahn

Childbirth represents a major transition in a woman's life and serves as a "rite of passage" into the social institution of motherhood (Eakins, 1986). Birthing a child is challenging both psychologically and physically, and the manner in which a woman experiences birth is likely to affect her adjustment to motherhood, her perceptions of herself and her baby, and the way in which she and her partner bond with their child and adjust to the changes in their relationship (Shearer, 1983). In the United States, childbirth has become intricately involved with the medical care system. Today, nearly all babies are born in the hospital, and nearly one in four is delivered surgically by cesarean section (C-section), which is up from only 4.5% of all births in 1965 (National Center for Health Statistics, 1990; Taffel, Placek, & Kosary, 1992). Therefore, any consideration of the psychological aspects of the management and outcomes of childbirth must consider the effect of medical interventions.

In this chapter we examine several aspects of childbirth, particularly the psychosocial effects of obstetrical routines and technology. We summarize the literature on the psychosocial consequences of cesarean delivery, discuss the results of a focus-group study to highlight important themes characterizing women's experiences of childbirth, and offer explicit recommendations for medical educators and practitioners in fostering healthy childbirth outcomes. We do not examine the psychosocial issues involved in pregnancy, a topic for which readers are referred to several reviews and empirical studies (Cohan, Dunkel-Schetter, & Lydon, 1993; Collins, Dunkel-Schetter, Lobel, & Scrimshaw, 1993; Lobel, Dunkel-Schetter, & Scrimshaw, 1992; O'Hara, 1986, 1995; O'Hara, Varner, & Johnson, 1986).

Obstetrical Interventions in Childbirth

Obstetrical interventions in childbirth are intended to save lives and prevent serious physical and psychosocial morbidities. In some cases, there

This research is part of the Management and Outcomes of Childbirth Patient Outcomes Research Team (PORT), which is supported by a contract to RAND (AHCPR 282-90-0039) from the Agency for Health Care Policy and Research (the co-principal investigators were E. Keller, K. Kahn, and J. Gambone). The views expressed in this chapter are those of the authors and do not reflect the views of RAND or the University of California.

is little question that these interventions are essential to the well-being of mothers and their babies. However, these interventions may have their own associated morbidities. The systematic study of outcomes of obstetrical interventions allows researchers to better understand these morbidities and to weigh the benefits and costs of the use of obstetrical treatments.

One particularly controversial obstetrical intervention is the C-section, which is now the most common major surgery performed in the United States (National Center for Health Statistics, 1990; Rutkow, 1986). Tremendous variation in C-section rates (among physicians, areas of the country, and systems of care) suggests that there is uncertainty about its necessity and that some C-sections may result from nonmedical factors such as physicians' fears of malpractice suits, physicians' preferences and practice patterns, and financial incentives for physicians and hospitals to perform C-sections instead of vaginal deliveries. Research also has suggested that, overall, C-sections have not been clearly associated with an improvement in birth outcomes for either babies or their mothers (Taffel et al., 1992; Van Tuinen & Wolfe, 1992).

Research on the outcomes of various methods of managing childbirth can determine when obstetrical interventions have positive and negative effects on patients' physical and emotional well-being (including maternal and infant health, maternal satisfaction, and cost) and the probabilities of those outcomes. Birth-related decisions that are made by women and their physicians can be informed by this research.

Literature Review of the Psychosocial Outcomes of C-Sections

Published studies of the psychological and social outcomes of C-sections have suggested that C-sections may not only diminish the positive life experience of giving birth but that they also may actually introduce some serious negative psychosocial consequences (Fisher, Stanley, & Burrows, 1990; Fraser, 1983; Oakley, 1983). In C-sections, the potentially disturbing, frightening, and psychologically symbolic experience of surgery (Blacher, 1987; Janis, 1958) is juxtaposed with the expected elation of giving birth to a new life. Resolution of the psychosocial tasks of this important life transition may be impeded by operative delivery.

The research literature suggests that, compared with vaginal delivery, C-sections may be more problematic for certain psychological outcomes (DiMatteo et al., 1996). C-sections have been found to delay the first meeting between mother and infant (Tulman, 1986) and are related to less positive maternal reactions to the newborn soon after birth (Cranley, Hedahl, & Pegg, 1983; Hwang, 1987). C-sections also seem to interfere with the decision to breastfeed. Mothers who had C-sections have been found to be consistently less likely to breastfeed their babies than mothers who deliver vaginally (Cranley et al., 1983; Cummins, Scrimshaw, & Engle, 1988). This may be due to the longer delay in the first meeting between mother and baby and to the inhibiting effects of pain and exhaustion in the mother and anesthesia in both mother and baby. Among women who do decide to breastfeed their babies, the method of delivery does not appear to affect the continuation of breastfeeding once it is begun (Kearney, Cronenwett, & Reinhardt, 1990).

Mothers who had C-sections also have been found to be significantly less satisfied with their birthing experiences than mothers who deliver vaginally (Fawcett, Pollio, & Tully, 1992; Kearney et al., 1990). Birth memories may persist for decades and affect psychological well-being, so this difference may be meaningful (Simkin, 1991). Postpartum depression in mothers in the first 2 months after birth also may be more frequent among those who had C-section than vaginal deliveries, although this difference is somewhat equivocal (Gottlieb & Barrett, 1986; O'Hara, Neunaber, & Zekoski, 1984; O'Hara, Zekoski, Philipps, & Wright, 1990). Given the potentially far-reaching implications of postpartum depression, this is an issue to which clinicians should remain particularly sensitive. Finally, compared with mothers who delivered vaginally, mothers who had C-sections have been found to be less likely to have another child and more likely to undergo voluntary sterilization (Hall, Campbell, Fraser, & Lemon, 1989).

It is important to recognize that research does suggest that cultural beliefs and attitudes may affect women's perceptions of the childbirth experience. Cummins et al. (1988) found that the majority of Latina women giving birth by C-section regarded their surgical delivery as "normal" and that 11% thought they had an advantage having had a C-section. Only 28% of the women having a C-section reported dissatisfaction with the experience. Engle, Scrimshaw, Zambrana, and Dunkel-Schetter (1990) found that Latina women giving birth were more satisfied with and expressed greatest preference for Latina health providers and that their satisfaction depended on good medical explanations and knowledgeable, friendly, and sympathetic health care providers. Norbeck and Anderson (1989) found that social support from the woman's partner or mother was particularly important in reducing gestational complications and prolonged labor or C-section complications among African American women. These findings suggest the importance of including attitudinal assessments in any examination of the psychosocial factors important to childbirth.

There is another methodological complication in this research, however. It is not entirely clear in the literature whether increased psychosocial morbidity associated with C-sections is actually due to the procedure or to increased antepartum morbidity that necessitates the C-section. If pregnancy complications necessitate a C-section, for example, literature reviews such as this limit the ability to determine whether increased morbidity associated with a C-section is truly due to surgical delivery or to the pregnancy complications themselves. Important evidence from the literature suggests, however, that the psychosocial outcomes described earlier are, with some cultural modifications, generally less positive for C-sections than for vaginal deliveries regardless of whether the C-section is emergency or elective.

Patient Outcome Research Teams

The U.S. Agency for Health Care Policy and Research has funded a number of Patient Outcome Research Team (PORT) projects on topics such as prostate disease, cataracts, knee replacement, and childbirth. Each project has sought to examine the outcomes associated with the use of various common medical and surgical interventions. These projects explore the effectiveness of interventions by comparing outcomes across providers and patients after accounting for preexisting conditions. Comparison of severity-adjusted outcomes for individuals who do and do not receive a medical intervention allows the researchers to understand which interventions benefit specific patient groups.

It is important that researchers examine methods of managing childbirth because the outcomes of various obstetrical interventions, particularly C-sections, are not fully known or understood. A PORT study on the management and outcomes of childbirth currently is being conducted with an interdisciplinary team consisting of obstetrical specialists, internists, epidemiologists, statisticians, economists, and social scientists. This research requires the identification of important postpartum outcomes and predictors of those outcomes. Also being studied are the development of reliable and valid measures, an accounting of patients' preexisting conditions through sample selection and statistical adjustments, carefully monitored field research, longitudinal design, and several data collection sources.

This research and related clinical recommendations are based on several underlying assumptions: (a) Two patients (the mother and baby) as well as their relationship must be considered when making childbirth decisions. (b) Outcome data can be useful to both clinicians and patients. (c) Postpartum outcomes (long after the mother has left the hospital) are important to examine. (d) No single data source exists to answer all the research questions. (e) Researchers must use methods that allow differences in outcomes to be correctly attributed to differences in the method of delivery rather than confounded by a condition that contributed to the choice to have a certain method of delivery. (f) Researchers should examine the childbirth experiences of women from different ethnic and socioeconomic backgrounds. (In the PORT study, e.g., in primary data collection, 55% of the women are White, 28% are Latina or Hispanic, 8% are Asian American, and 7% are African American. In the focus groups, approximately one quarter are low-income women from urban and rural locations.)

Women's Narratives of their Birth Experiences

As part of the PORT study on management and outcomes of childbirth, focus groups were conducted with new mothers to explore their experiences of childbirth and adjustment to motherhood (DiMatteo, Kahn, & Berry, 1993). The goal was to learn, by analyzing narratives of the birth experience, more generally about the effects of many types of childbirth routines and obstetrical technology on the lives of new mothers (Perez, 1989). Forty-one English-speaking new mothers, who were 15–22 weeks post-partum, participated in one of six focus groups to discuss their birth experiences. These women varied in education, socioeconomic status, health insurance status (none, Medicaid, or private), age, rural versus urban residence, location of delivery (hospital, birthing center), and difficulty in becoming pregnant. (Although DiMatteo et al. did not systematically collect data on ethnicity, fewer than one quarter were non-White, thus limiting the generalizability of the sample.) The women were recruited from physician and midwife practices and from notices placed in the community. Although the sample was one of convenience, it included a cross-section of new mothers in terms of socioeconomic status. The C-section rate was high (approximately 40%), and most mothers were in their late 20s or early 30s. Throughout the focus-group sessions, which typically lasted about 2 hr, women were encouraged to describe their physical and psychosocial experiences of labor and birth. The narratives were tape-recorded and transcribed, and on review, themes were extracted by the authors.

Mothers described their transition to motherhood as a physically and psychologically transforming experience. The literature has suggested that women may be unwilling to express dissatisfaction with the childbirth process if their baby arrived healthy and that assessing negative reactions after the birth of a healthy baby is a methodological challenge (Oakley, 1985). By contrast, Di Matteo et al. (1993) found that the supportive environment of the focus-group format was particularly helpful in giving women the opportunity to describe problematic aspects of their childbirth experiences. Anecdotally, it appeared that women who had more obstetrical interventions appeared to express greater dissatisfaction and to report more negative reactions about the birth than did those who had few interventions, a finding reported by Oakley (1983) and Simkin (1991). We view the focus-group findings as important statements of the problems and concerns that mothers experience with childbirth. Although the focus-group format may have encouraged women to emphasize their negative experiences, we think it is important to recognize these experiences, to understand them, and to attempt to address them.

Five themes emerged from the analysis. The first involved women's feelings of loss of personal autonomy and control during labor and delivery in hospital environments that did not give them emotional support and physical comfort. Some were particularly distressed because medical providers exerted control over them, both verbally and physically, and, in their vulnerable state, they felt powerless to argue. For example, one mother reported that her glasses were removed and she could not see her baby being born. Another described frustration at being told to lie down throughout labor to facilitate external fetal monitoring when she preferred to move around. Another mother described her baby being taken away immediately after delivery with no explanation and the baby being fed with glucose water when she had indicated that she wanted to breastfeed.

Other mothers reported having had their hands tied during stitching of the abdomen (C-section) or episiotomy. Mothers who complained during delivery felt admonished that the "good of the baby" superseded their preferences. Several mothers felt overly controlled by the medical system. Other researchers, too, have described mothers feeling "controlled" by a medical system during birth (Arms, 1975; Davis-Floyd, 1990; Oakley, 1985). Because control and choice in childbirth tend to contribute to women's greater satisfaction and fulfillment from childbirth and higher subsequent emotional well-being (Green, Coupland, & Kitzinger, 1990), the institution of methods that allow women the benefits of medical care without feeling controlled during birth could make an important contribution.

The second theme involved the primiparous mothers' being surprised at the physical pain of childbirth. Many also were surprised at the postpartum functional limitations they experienced after an operative or instrumental delivery or an episiotomy (Garcia et al., 1985). Many mothers, even those who had attended childbirth preparation classes, felt that they had been poorly prepared for the pain of labor and delivery. They described the pain as a "well-kept secret" for which no one, including their physicians, family members, and childbirth educators, had provided realistic preparation (Chalmers, Enkin, & Keirse, 1989; Hausknecht & Heilman, 1991). More education of women during pregnancy about the realities of childbirth could help to alleviate this concern.

The third theme involved the mothers' unexpected emotional reactions to birthing. Regardless of anesthesia and mode of delivery, most women described their emotions as "raw" and reported feeling disappointment and a surprising sense of sadness rather than the happiness they had expected to feel. A few mothers were surprised at feeling detached from their babies and from their own bodies immediately after birth. Several mothers, whether giving birth vaginally or by C-section, criticized their own "performance" during childbirth. Some women described an inability to control their emotions during the postpartum period and a lack of any preparation for the "postpartum blues." Although their reactions have been documented as normal elements of postpartum adjustment (Fisher et al., 1990), most mothers received no preparation for these feelings and were concerned that their emotions were not "normal." Although many reported dysphoria, each believed that she was unique despite findings that up to 85% of new mothers experience postpartum blues (O'Hara et al., 1990) and that 10–15% experience postpartum depression (Philipps & O'Hara, 1991).

Many mothers compared themselves unfavorably with stereotypes, possibly gleaned from the mass media, of the perfect and perfectly happy new mother. Furthermore, although research has suggested that decreased self-esteem may be an outcome specific to C-section delivery (Cox & Smith, 1982), the research by DiMatteo et al. (1993) suggests that anything short of a quiet, emotionally composed, unassisted vaginal delivery left some women feeling inadequate, as if they had somehow failed themselves, their husband, and their physicians. Their standards appear to have been unrealistic, particularly if they had assumed that their delivery would not be subject to hospital routine and medical technology. Helping birthing mothers to understand the details of their care might help to reduce their stress during the delivery process.

The fourth theme involved the financial pressures of childbirth. Prenatal care and the nature of decisions about managing the birth itself were sometimes constrained by insurance coverage (e.g., delivery by C-section to have insurance coverage). The focus-group analyses added to the understanding of the possible role played by financial factors in the birth experiences of new mothers, even suggesting that because of monetary concerns, optimal decisions about patient care may not always be made.

The fifth theme concerned the role of the support person during labor and delivery. Taking place in the context of an existing relationship (e.g., a marriage), with its own unique history and interactional scripts, the role played by the partner was not always reported by the mother as helpful and stress-free. Whereas some husbands were supportive, others had no prior experience in the hospital setting and were upset and terrified to see their wife in pain. Some women suggested that their partner's reactions to their labor contributed to their having epidural anesthesia or a C-section. Some noted that the ideal coach may be another woman who "has been through it." The role of such a woman, often termed a *doula*, has been supported by clinical research (Kennell, Klaus, McGrath, Robertson, & Hinkley, 1991). For some study women, the support role was filled well by a midwife or nurse who had enough time to attend to her directly and consistently. For many others, hospital routines and the demands of the care of other patients in a busy labor and delivery suite made it difficult for them to obtain adequate attention, assistance, and encouragement.

Additional Goals of the PORT Study

These findings suggest that the psychological support of women during labor and delivery contributes to women's positive experiences of birth. As hospitals and physicians come under increasing pressure to save resources, in-hospital and home-based opportunities to support the essential psychosocial needs of women in labor should be examined carefully.

To examine further the psychosocial outcomes of C-sections, we currently are engaged in a case control study of 2,463 standard-risk mother–infant pairs. Mothers from 30 hospitals in seven cities in two states (California and Iowa) have been asked to participate during their hospital stay. Data collection sources included medical records and mothers' responses to interview questions. The goal is to study the effects of obstetrical intervention on the mother–child relationship; the mother's satisfaction with her labor and delivery; and the mother's energy, fatigue, mental health, sleep patterns, self-esteem, perceptions of her sexuality, evolving mother–child relationship, functional status, return to work and school, and plans for future delivery. Mothers are being interviewed by phone during the postpartum period (4–8 weeks postpartum). We intend to compare the prevalence of preferred and adverse postpartum psychosocial outcomes for mothers with C-sections as compared with vaginal deliveries. What will be most important in this research is the comparison of outcomes by method of delivery after accounting for preexisting conditions.

Recommendations

The research reported here suggests that the psychosocial aspects of childbirth are critically important issues in patient care. The focus groups and literature review demonstrate some broad principles that should be considered by caregivers, childbirth educators, and expectant parents to improve birthing experiences.

Emotions and Self-Control in Childbearing

Childbirth educators should assist birthing women to recognize the difference between personal self-control (e.g., breathing patterns and responses to pain), which may be possible to attain, and situational control (e.g., obstetrical routines), which may not. Physicians, nurses, and midwives need to be encouraged to be responsive to the emotional, informational, and self-determination needs of birthing mothers and to help address their needs and expectations (Simkin, 1991).

Pain of Childbirth

Childbirth preparation should involve realistic preparation for the pain of childbirth. Research on pain perceptions demonstrates that having accurate information about a painful medical procedure helps an individual to feel less pain and anxiety and facilitates coping with pain (Johnson & Leventhal, 1974). If the pain of childbirth is trivialized (e.g., called merely "uncomfortable"), it is likely that the experience of intense pain will be perceived as abnormal, heightening the mother's anxiety, increasing her perceptions of pain, interfering with her coping, and leading her to believe that something may be wrong with her or her baby. Health professionals should be encouraged to learn more about the psychology of pain and to be better prepared to help women in their efforts to cope with pain during labor and delivery (Fordyce, 1988). Prenatal education should realistically prepare women for the pain of childbirth and provide them with mechanisms for communicating their needs and coping with their pain experiences. Cultural differences in pain expression should also be accepted and supported. Prenatal education also should prepare women for postpartum pain and for the challenges that follow the C-section and episiotomy, so that they can be better prepared for difficulties by arranging household and other help and can be more accepting of postpartum physical limitations.

Postpartum Blues

Expectant parents should be prepared for their likely experience of some disturbing emotions in the face of the tremendous exhaustion and life changes that follow the birth of a baby. They should be helped to accept the complexities of their emotions and to recognize when they need to seek psychological support and how to obtain that support. Once having a baby, women should be educated about the likely experience of postpartum blues and the possible occurrence of postpartum depression. The new mother's individual emotional responses should be appreciated and assisted.

Financial Concerns

Health professionals should recognize the effect of financial concerns on the mother's and family's experience of obstetrical care. Whatever caregivers can do to ease the financial burdens associated with giving birth may contribute to a greater capacity by new parents to cope with the physical and emotional rigors of their new roles. In addition, cutbacks in services due to cost considerations (e.g., early hospital discharge after childbirth) should, before being implemented, be examined carefully with regard not only to their physical impact but also to their psychological impact on the new mother and her family.

Childbirth Support and Coaching

Mothers and couples should be helped to choose the most supportive and competent individual to assist, or "coach," during labor and delivery. Without adequate preparation, some fathers may become involved reluctantly or be too overwhelmed by their fears of the medical situation or their empathy for the mother's pain to provide effective labor support. Alternatively, this role can be filled by a doula or professional labor companion (Kennell et al., 1991), even though this may require the presence of an additional person. The father can still be present during labor and birth, but his role will be less directly involved with labor coaching. It also is important to recognize the critical impact that supportive health professionals can have on birthing parents and to recognize the important role played by cultural variations in expectations of and satisfaction with support during the birth experience. It is interesting that women's long-term memories of a helpful nurse or physician during labor and delivery have persisted for as long as 20 years and have had a profound effect on perceptions and recollections of and satisfaction with the entire birth experience (Simkin, 1991). Outcomes also may be improved if childbearing women are helped to discuss their feelings in a supportive environment (e.g., a postpartum support group). It is particularly important to encourage women to appreciate their own efforts during the challenging events of childbirth and to discourage them from holding their own "performance" up to an imagined standard.

Psychosocial Outcomes of Vaginal Versus Cesarean Delivery

Our literature review also has suggested that more negative psychosocial outcomes appear to be associated with C-sections than with vaginal delivery. Perhaps this knowledge can contribute to more accurate attributions of mothers' psychosocial outcomes after delivery as well as more effective clinical care for birthing and postpartum mothers and their babies. Women who have C-sections and other obstetrical interventions should be given additional support to cope with any difficulties they may encounter, particularly impediments to the initiation of breastfeeding. If a C-section or problematic delivery is anticipated, realistic emotional preparation of the mother may facilitate postpartum coping. Certainly, the potential psychosocial consequences of a C-section should be taken into account in cases in which there are no compelling reasons for a C-section and a safe and successful vaginal birth can be achieved. Consumer pressures to avoid "unnecessary or inappropriate" surgical interventions (Consumers Union, 1992) and efforts to reduce unnecessary costs also affect physicians' priorities and practice patterns. In addition, there is a growing interest among many physicians, managed care coordinators, policymakers, cost-containment experts, and patient-consumers in improving patient outcomes.

Conclusion

Current medical, economic, policy, and consumer debates about the process of childbirth and postpartum care need to be informed not only by research on the costs of and physical outcomes of childbirth but also by detailed information about its attendant psychosocial consequences. Understanding and appreciation of the psychosocial aspects of birthing has significant implications for the well-being of mothers and families.

References

Arms, S. (1975). *Immaculate deception*. Boston: Houghton-Mifflin.

Blacher, R. S. (1987). *The psychological experience of surgery*. New York: Wiley.

Chalmers, I., Enkin, M., & Keirse, M. J. (Eds.). (1989). *Effective care in pregnancy and childbirth*. Oxford, England: Oxford University Press.

Cohan, C. L., Dunkel-Schetter, C., & Lydon, J. (1993). Pregnancy decision making: Predictors of early stress and adjustment. *Psychology of Women Quarterly, 17,* 223–239.

Collins, N. L., Dunkel-Schetter, C., Lobel, M., & Scrimshaw, S. C. (1993). Social support in pregnancy: Psychosocial correlates of birth outcomes and postpartum depression. *Journal of Personality and Social Psychology, 65,* 1243–1258.

Consumers Union. (1992). Wasted health care dollars. *Consumer Reports, 7,* 435–449.

Cox, B. E., & Smith, E. C. (1982). Research and practice: The mother's self-esteem after a cesarean section. *Maternal Child Nursing, 7,* 309–314.

Cranley, M. S., Hedahl, K. J., & Pegg, S. H. (1983). Women's perceptions of vaginal and cesarean deliveries. *Nursing Research, 32,* 10–15.

Cummins, L. H., Scrimshaw, S. C., & Engle, P. L. (1988). Views of cesarean birth among primiparous women of Mexican origin in Los Angeles. *Birth, 15*, 164–170.

Davis-Floyd, R. E. (1990). The role of obstetrical rituals in the resolution of cultural anomaly. *Social Science and Medicine, 31*, 175–189.

DiMatteo, M. R., Kahn, K. L., & Berry, S. H. (1993). Narratives of birth and the postpartum: An analysis of the focus group responses of new mothers. *Birth, 20*, 204–211.

DiMatteo, M. R., Morton, S. C., Lepper, H. S., Damush, T. M., Carney, M. F., Pearson, M., & Kahn, K. L. (1996). Cesarean childbirth and psychosocial outcomes: A meta-analysis. *Health Psychology, 15*, 230–241.

Eakins, P. S. (1986). The conduct of birth. In P. S. Eakins (Ed.), *The American way of birth* (pp. 99–103). Philadelphia: Temple University Press.

Engle, P. L., Scrimshaw, S. C., Zambrana, R. E., & Dunkel-Schetter, C. (1990). Prenatal and postnatal anxiety in Mexican women giving birth in Los Angeles. *Health Psychology, 9*, 285–299.

Fawcett, J., Pollio, N., & Tully, A. (1992). Women's perceptions of cesarean and vaginal delivery: Another look. *Research in Nursing and Health, 15*, 439–446.

Fisher, J. R. W., Stanley, R. O., & Burrows, G. D. (1990). Psychosocial adjustment to cesarean delivery: A review of the evidence. *Journal of Psychosomatic Obstetrics and Gynaecology, 11*, 91–106.

Fordyce, W. E. (1988). Pain and suffering: A reappraisal. *American Psychologist, 43*, 276–283.

Fraser, C. M. (1983). Selected perinatal procedures—Scientific basis for use and psychosocial effects: A literature review. *Acta Obstetrica et Gynecologica Scandinavica, 117* (Suppl.), 1–39.

Garcia, J., Anderson, J., Vacca, A., Elbourne, D., Grant, A., & Chalmers, I. (1985). Views of women and their medical and midwifery attendants about instrumental delivery using vacuum extraction and forceps. *Journal of Psychosomatic Obstetrics and Gynaecology, 4*, 1–9.

Gottlieb, S. E., & Barrett, D. E. (1986). Effects of unanticipated cesarean section on mothers, infants, and their interaction in the first month of life. *Journal of Developmental and Behavioral Pediatrics, 7*, 180–185.

Green, J. M., Coupland, B. A., & Kitzinger, J. V. (1990). Expectations, experiences, and psychological outcomes of childbirth: A prospective study of 825 women. *Birth, 17*, 15–24.

Hall, M. H., Campbell, D. M., Fraser, C., & Lemon, J. (1989). Mode of delivery and future fertility. *British Journal of Obstetrics and Gynaecology, 96*, 1297–1303.

Hausknecht, R., & Heilman, J. R. (1991). *Having a cesarean baby* (2nd ed.). New York: Penguin Books.

Hwang, C. P. (1987). Cesarean childbirth in Sweden: Effects on the mother and father-infant relationship. *Infant Mental Health Journal, 8*, 91–99.

Janis, I. L. (1958). *Psychological stress: Psychoanalytic and behavioral studies of surgical patients.* New York: Academic Press.

Johnson, J. E., & Leventhal, H. (1974). Effects of accurate expectations and behavioral instructions on reactions during a noxious medical examination. *Journal of Personality and Social Psychology, 29*, 710–718.

Kearney, M. H., Cronenwett, L. R., & Reinhardt, R. (1990). Cesarean delivery and breast-feeding outcomes. *Birth, 17*, 97–103.

Kennell, J., Klaus, M., McGrath, S., Robertson, S., & Hinkley, C. (1991). Continuous emotional support during labor in a U.S. hospital. *Journal of the American Medical Association, 265*, 2197–2201.

Lobel, M., Dunkel-Schetter, C., & Scrimshaw, S. C. (1992). Prenatal maternal stress and prematurity: A prospective study of socioeconomically disadvantaged women. *Health Psychology, 11*, 32–40.

National Center for Health Statistics. (1990). *Vital statistics of the United States, 1988: Vol. 1. Natality* (DHHS Publication No. PHS-90-1100). Washington, DC: U.S. Government Printing Office.

Norbeck, J. S., & Anderson, N. J. (1989). Psychological predictors of pregnancy outcomes in low-income Black, Hispanic, and White women. *Nursing Research, 38*, 204–209.

Oakley, A. (1983). Social consequences of obstetric technology: The importance of measuring "soft" outcomes. *Birth, 10*, 99–108.

Oakley, A. (1985). Doctors, maternity patients and social scientists. *Birth, 12*, 161–166.

O'Hara, M. W. (1986). Social support, life events, and depression during pregnancy and the puerperium. *Archives of General Psychiatry, 43*, 569–573.

O'Hara, M. W. (1995). Childbearing. In M. W. O'Hara, R. C. Reiter, S. R. Johnson, A. Milburn, & J. Engeldinger (Eds.), *Psychological aspects of women's reproductive health* (pp. 26–48). New York: Springer.

O'Hara, M. W., Neunaber, D. J., & Zekoski, E. M. (1984). Prospective study of postpartum depression: Prevalence, course, and predictive factors. *Journal of Abnormal Psychology, 93*, 158–171.

O'Hara, M. W., Varner, M. W., & Johnson, S. R. (1986). Assessing stressful life events associated with childbearing: The Peripartum Events Scale. *Journal of Reproductive and Infant Psychology, 4*, 85–98.

O'Hara, M. W., Zekoski, E. M., Philipps, L. H., & Wright, E. J. (1990). Controlled prospective study of postpartum mood disorders: Comparison of childbearing and nonchildbearing women. *Journal of Abnormal Psychology, 99*, 3–15.

Perez, P. G. (1989). The patient observer: What really led to these cesarean births? *Birth, 16*, 130–139.

Philipps, H. C., & O'Hara, M. W. (1991). Prospective study of postpartum depression: 4 1/2-year follow-up of women and children. *Journal of Abnormal Psychology, 100*, 151–155.

Rutkow, I. (1986). Obstetric and gynecologic operations in the United States. *Obstetrics and Gynecology, 67*, 755–759.

Simkin, P. (1991). Just another day in a woman's life? Women's long-term perceptions of their first birth experience: Part I. *Birth, 18*, 203–210.

Shearer, E. C. (1983). How do parents really feel after cesarean birth? *Birth, 10*, 91–92.

Taffel, S. M., Placek, P. J., & Kosary, C. L. (1992). United States cesarean section rates 1990: An update. *Birth, 19*, 21–22.

Tulman, L. J. (1986). Initial handling of newborn infants by vaginally and cesarean-delivered mothers. *Nursing Research, 35*, 296–300.

Van Tuinen, I., & Wolfe, S. M. (1992). *Unnecessary cesarean sections: Halting a national epidemic.* Washington, DC: Public Citizens' Health Research Group.

13

Fertility Problems: Complex Issues Faced by Women and Couples

Lauri A. Pasch and Christine Dunkel-Schetter

Approximately 8% of all couples in the United States with a woman of childbearing age experience fertility problems (Mosher & Pratt, 1990). In the past two decades, there have been dramatic advances in medical technology aimed at increasing a couple's chances of having children and in the number of couples who seek medical services for infertility (Office of Technology Assessment [OTA], 1988). Increases in use of services have been attributed to several factors, including the availability of new treatments, increases in public awareness of infertility, and increases in rates of infertility within certain age groups presumably attributable to delayed childbearing, exposure to environmental toxins, and increases in rates of sexually transmitted diseases (STDs; OTA, 1988). Currently, tens of thousands of attempts using in vitro fertilization (IVF) and similar technologies are made every year, resulting in the births of thousands of children.

Infertility is medically defined as the inability to conceive a pregnancy after one year of regular sexual intercourse without contraception (OTA, 1988). Despite the static nature of this medical definition, infertility is not a discrete event but instead an unfolding process. It typically begins unexpectedly, as a period of time of anticipating a pregnancy passes without success. For couples who seek medical treatment, estimates suggest that 50% are successful in achieving a pregnancy by one means or another (OTA, 1988).[1] However, the process can take many years, it may involve extensive procedures and complex decisions, and any given treatment procedure usually has a limited chance of success. Eventually, unsuccessful couples explore options other than having a genetic offspring together, including donor sperm, donor eggs, or a surrogate mother; adopting a child; or not having children. It has become increasingly difficult for couples to know when it is time to accept the loss of their joint reproductive potential because they may feel that each new technological advance renews the possibility of success. Health care professionals who work with

Preparation of this chapter was supported by National Institute of Mental Health Training Grant MH19391.

[1]For a detailed description of diagnosis and treatment procedures for infertility, see Davajan and Israel (1991) or Taymor (1990).

individuals or couples with fertility problems are faced with many complex tasks, including assisting them in dealing with the invasive nature of diagnostic and treatment procedures, helping with decision making regarding treatment options, and identifying and offering counseling to those who experience significant emotional distress.

In this chapter we present an overview of research on (a) the relationship between psychological factors and the etiology of infertility; (b) psychological reactions to infertility; (c) effects of infertility on couples; and (d) psychological issues in the treatment process, with particular attention to assisted reproductive technologies (ARTs). In this overview, we identify some common misperceptions from the research literature. The overview is followed by an attempt to translate research findings into recommendations for clinical practice.

Historically, infertility has been considered mainly a "women's issue." As the medical causes of infertility have been identified, most estimates suggest that the biological origin of infertility is equally likely to be male as female (Speroff, Glass, & Kase, 1983). Although the research literature has focused on women, men who want to be fathers are substantially affected by infertility too. Therefore, throughout this chapter, we consider fertility problems as they affect women, men, and the couple as a unit. Nevertheless, there are still several compelling reasons to consider infertility as an important women's health issue: Women see having children as being more important than men do (Berg, Wilson, & Weingartner, 1991), are more likely to seek treatment and make treatment-related decisions (Greil, Leitko, & Porter, 1988), and are more likely to experience distress (Leiblum, Kemmann, & Lane, 1987). Also, regardless of the biological cause, the vast majority of medical treatments for infertility are aimed at the female partner; thus, they incur the medical risks and physical and emotional pain associated with the patient status more so than do their male partners. Reproductive technologies also become a women's health issue when women seek to conceive as single parents or within lesbian relationships. These women then may face the complex dilemma of seeking medical assistance (i.e., donor insemination) within a sociopolitical system that questions their rights to make use of reproductive technologies (see Golombok & Tasker, 1994).

Research Overview

Psychological Factors and the Etiology of Infertility

As recently as two decades ago, emotional factors were presumed to be the cause of 30–50% of infertility cases (OTA, 1988). Much of the literature generated from these psychogenesis models was highly speculative, and reviews of studies with more rigorous designs have concluded that the preponderance of evidence is not in favor of psychogenesis models (see Edelmann & Connolly, 1986; Stanton & Dunkel-Schetter, 1991). In addition, as medical advances have been made, the number of cases of unexplained infertility (which previously were attributed to psychological causes) has dramatically decreased.

The absence of support for psychogenesis models does not mean that psychological factors are never involved in the etiology of fertility problems. First, there are a few well-known circumstances in which psychiatric problems are related to infertility (i.e., severe anorexia nervosa, certain sexual dysfunctions; see Taymor, 1990). None of these circumstances are permanent, and careful assessment is the key to treating the problem. Second, the presence of a medical factor does not necessarily obviate the possibility that psychological factors such as stress and anxiety are involved in an interactive role with physiological factors (i.e., Barnea & Tal, 1991; Hammond, Kretzer, Blackwell, & Steinkampf, 1990; Harrison, Callan, & Hennessey, 1987). This is an area in need of continued research because results would have strong implications for clinical practice.

Remnants of simplistic psychogenesis theories persist in popular culture and perhaps among some health care professionals. As one woman interviewed by Miall (1985) reported regarding reactions from friends,

> You get it all. My favorite is "It's all in your head; go take a vacation and it will be fine." I think the other phrase that really drove me crazy was "Well, you know, I had this friend who couldn't get pregnant and then adopted a child and do you know what? Seven months later she was pregnant." (p. 392)

The notion that adoption facilitates conception by relieving stress has now been refuted in research that shows no differences in the rates of pregnancy in couples with fertility problems who adopt and those who do not (Seibel & Taymor, 1982). Nonetheless, myths such as these may lead women to retreat from their social networks, and perhaps from receiving desired medical care, to avoid embarrassment and receiving unhelpful advice (see Abbey, Andrews, & Halman, 1991).

Psychological Reactions to Infertility

The heightened emotional distress experienced by many couples with fertility problems is better understood as a consequence rather than as a cause of having a fertility problem. In describing the experience of infertility, some authors have concluded that the experience is so profound that they have conceptualized it as a life crisis (e.g., Berger, 1980; Menning, 1980) and described a series of stages (i.e., shock, denial, anger) through which individuals are expected to pass. The life crisis conceptualization has helped to bring the psychological consequences of infertility into view and has led to the development of support groups aimed at helping couples manage the crisis. However, Stanton and Dunkel-Schetter (1991) have argued that this conceptualization is flawed in two important ways (see also Stanton & Danoff-Burg, 1995). First, crisis models do not fully recognize the substantial interindividual variability. Second, there is no evidence that individuals go through predictable stages in response to stress in general or in response to infertility in particular; instead, it appears that various emotions and reactions are experienced by different people at different points in the coping process (see Wortman & Silver, 1987). On the basis of an extensive review of the empirical and clinical literature, Dunkel-Schetter and Lobel (1991) concluded that although there seems to be a consensus that infertility is almost universally a difficult and emotionally charged experience, "methodologically rigorous research suggests that the majority of people with infertility do not experience clinically significant emotional reactions, loss of self-esteem, or adverse marital and sexual consequences" (p. 50).

Given these findings, Stanton and Dunkel-Schetter (1991) proposed that infertility may best be thought of as an important and ongoing source of stress that affects different people in different ways. They argued that a stress and coping framework (i.e., Lazarus & Folkman, 1984) may be a more useful model for understanding the effects of infertility. Research based on a stress and coping framework has identified certain factors that are associated with psychological adjustment. These include (a) characteristics of the stressor (e.g., length of time attempting to conceive before firm diagnosis; extent of diagnostic tests and treatments; gender of person diagnosed); (b) individual appraisal (e.g., degree of investment in the parent role as a source of self-fulfillment, feeling responsible for the fertility problem, and low perceived control over one's ability to get pregnant); (c) coping resources (e.g., positive reappraisal and seeking-support coping strategies); and (d) social environment (e.g., support from one's spouse, a good marital relationship, social network support). Other factors are under investigation.

Effects of Infertility on Couples

Infertility is unique among stressors because it typically confronts a couple as a unit as well as the individual partners. Medically, it is best treated as a characteristic of the couple regardless of which partner has the etiological factors. When one partner has a fertility problem, both partners find themselves unable to have a child. This is in contrast to many other medical problems, including some described in this book (e.g., cardiovascular disease, diabetes), that, although clearly affecting both partners, basically characterize only the afflicted partner.

There has been much concern that infertility is the cause of significant marital and sexual problems. However, on the basis of a review of the well-designed studies, Stanton and Danoff-Burg (1995) concluded that the evidence consistently reveals no impairment in marital functioning as a result of infertility. In fact, two controlled studies have shown that marital satisfaction is higher in couples who seek treatment for fertility problems than in control couples who have no fertility problem (Callan & Hennessey, 1989; Downey & McKinney, 1992). As with emotional distress, there is substantial variability in the impact of infertility on marital functioning, with some couples reporting significant marital problems and others reporting improvements as a result of "going through this together."

It also is important to put the experience of infertility in the broader context of couples' lives and consider how the experience of infertility compares with the experience of becoming new parents. Abbey, Andrews, and Halman (1994) have shown that compared with women who did not become parents over the 2-year course of the study, women who became parents reported more positive life quality but also less intimacy in their marital relationship. Thus, couples who are not successful in having children may experience less overall life satisfaction than those who have children, but it does not appear that the continued experience of failure to conceive results in significant marital problems. In fact, any negative effect on the marriage appears to be, on average, less than that of becoming parents.

Given the large variability in effects of infertility on marital relationships, an important question is what factors are associated with a greater likelihood of relationship problems. The descriptive literature has suggested that differences between husbands and wives in their responses to a fertility problem are an important source of marital problems (e.g., Mahlstedt, 1985; Salzer, 1991). For example, consider the situation in which one spouse feels that the only way to cope with the pain associated with infertility is to talk about it and share feelings, and the other spouse feels that talking only makes the problem worse. As a result of this difference, communication between partners may be characterized by demanding, stonewalling, blaming, and attacking (see Pasch, 1994). Couples who encounter this type of problem may find that their inability to communicate effectively begins to affect the overall functioning of their relationship, and they may benefit from couples' counseling, as discussed later in this chapter.

Psychological Factors in the Use of ARTs

IVF is the most widely used of the ARTs, with an average success rate (defined as live births) for a given treatment cycle (e.g., ovary stimulation, egg retrieval, fertilization, transfer) of about 15% (Society for Assisted Reproductive Technology, 1994). Research has shown that individuals attempting ARTs tend to overestimate their chances of success and have unrealistic expectations about how they will be affected (Callan & Hennessey, 1988; Johnston, Shaw, & Bird, 1987). This tendency to overestimate likelihood of success and minimize risks has been the cause of significant concern, under the assumption that overly optimistic expectations will lead to a difficult adjustment to failure. Some authors have suggested that this overestimation occurs as a result of the *availability heuristic* (Adler, Keyes & Robertson, 1991; Johnston et al., 1987). Media reports of successful new procedures, plus pictures of babies conceived through IVF posted in physicians' offices, may lead to many more examples of success stories than failures, thus leading couples to overestimate the likelihood that they will be successful. In addition, Adler et al. (1991) have argued that given the emotional and physical demands of these treatments, coupled with the high financial cost, individuals may have a psychological need to bolster hope to justify going through the experience. Physicians and medical staff also may contribute to unrealistic expectations, not so much out of an attempt to intentionally mislead patients, but they may be overly optimistic out of a desire to justify both their work and putting the couple through so much stress and to foster hope in patients who are distressed by continued failure.

What is known about psychological reactions to the stress of undergoing ARTs? There is little doubt that the use of ARTs is highly stressful. Women report that egg retrieval and the waiting period after embryo transfer before it is known whether a pregnancy has occurred are the most stressful components of the treatment (Callan & Hennessey, 1988; Seibel & Levine, 1987). Emotional reactions appear to vary dramatically over the course of treatment (Newman & Zouves, 1991). The psychological process associated with ARTs has been described as an "emotional rollercoaster" because it is characterized by so many different emotions in so short a time (Stewart & Glazer, 1986).

The availability of ARTs also presents couples with a complex dilemma: If they attempt this treatment, it will involve significant disruption of their lives, many office visits, physical pain for the woman, high financial costs, and a high likelihood of failure, whereas if they choose not to attempt it, they may find themselves regretting their decision not to try everything possible and will always wonder whether it would have been successful. Most couples who achieve a pregnancy using one of these procedures do so after more than one treatment cycle. Thus, the decision-making process may occur over a period of months and years, with anticipation and disappointments, followed by the difficult decision of whether to try again.

How individuals react to failed IVF has been a major concern. Evidence has shown that although most men and women seem to cope with the distress adequately and are satisfied with having attempted IVF, a sizable percentage experience short-term but clinically significant depression and anxiety (Baram, Tourtelot, Muechler, & Huang, 1988). Studies that have included men reveal that they are clearly affected, although women tend to be at higher risk for negative reactions to failed IVF than are men, especially those who have no previous children (i.e., Leiblum et al., 1987). The few follow-up studies that exist reveal no long-term negative effects of failed IVF; however, attrition rates make it impossible to draw firm conclusions (Baram et al., 1988).

Translating Research Into Clinical Practice

Given the lack of longitudinal research, researchers do not yet know the long-term impact of continued unsuccessful infertility treatment. Also, researchers know little of the experience of couples with fertility problems

who do not seek treatment at all, either because of lack of financial resources or otherwise, or those who terminate treatment. Furthermore,
there is a clear need to include individuals from ethnic minority groups,
individuals in lower socioeconomic groups, and single and lesbian women
in research on both fertility problems and reproductive technologies.

Attention to the potential for negative psychological effects of the experience of infertility and its treatment, and ways to avoid negative effects,
should be central in the minds of all health care professionals who work
with individuals with fertility problems. Clearly, attending to and implementing ways to avoid negative effects is easier said than done, and even
well-intentioned professionals may have difficulty. For example, consider
the physician who does not acknowledge to patients the stressful nature
of fertility treatment (perhaps because of a belief that it is best to keep
medical and emotional issues separate). This may leave patients feeling
that their emotional reactions are unacceptable or indicative of serious
psychological problems.

The research literature can provide some guidance on how health care
professionals working with individuals with fertility problems can be most
helpful. Broadly, health care professionals must play a delicate balancing
act. Given that researchers know that emotional reactions to the stress of
infertility are common and are not usually indicative of psychological problems, health care practitioners should avoid treating patients as weak and
should not pathologize emotional responses. Instead, emotional responses
can be seen as part of a normal reaction to highly distressing circumstances. Simultaneously, health care practitioners should be continuously
sensitive to their patients' level of vulnerability and should allow patients
the opportunity to bring emotional responses into the realm of treatment
planning yet not require that they do so.

Managing Patient Distress

Emotional responses. It is extremely important to acknowledge to patients from early in the infertility investigation that there are several common emotional responses, such as feeling sadness, anxiety, and feeling out
of control and that there is considerable interindividual variability in the
experience of these. This is particularly important if ovulation-inducing
agents (i.e., Clomid, Pergonal) are prescribed because these drugs have
common mood-altering side effects. Also, the health care professional
should point out that it is typical for a given person to experience fluctuations over time in their emotional responses, with the testing and diagnostic period often involving particularly distressing emotions and the
treatment period possibly being more hopeful. Psychological theory and
research indicates that the patient should never be told to expect predictable stages of emotional response (Wortman & Silver, 1987).

Coping strategies. Although certain coping strategies are associated
with better or poorer adjustment, it is not typically useful to "prescribe"

any strategies or to warn against the use of others. First, it may be that coping strategies are used as a result of the level of distress as opposed to being capable of changing the level of distress. Second, there is little evidence to suggest that an individual's natural coping style can in fact be altered, although it may be useful to offer patients the option of a broader coping repertoire, leaving the choice up to the individual. Furthermore, the consequences of spontaneously implementing a particular coping strategy may be much different from those that result when a coping strategy is adopted at the suggestion of others (Dunkel-Schetter & Stanton, 1991).

Reducing stress. Treatment facilities should focus on reducing the controllable aspects of the stress associated with infertility treatment. First, reducing treatment-related stress may lead to a lower risk of excess psychological distress among patients. Second, stress-induced cognitive processing deficits (see Janis, 1993) may lead couples to make poor treatment-related decisions. Poor decision making, in turn, has many costs, as discussed later in this chapter.

Because loss of control often is cited as a key element in the stress of fertility treatment, treatment programs might focus their efforts to reduce stress on increasing the patient's perceived control. Outlining a diagnostic plan, and later a treatment plan, with both members of the couple is particularly important in this regard, as is explaining what the couple can expect when undergoing various procedures. A reasonable attempt should be made to help couples understand the rationale underlying the treatment plan, and partners should be given the opportunity to ask questions and discuss their feelings. Providing patients with the opportunity to make use of various books, pamphlets, and videotapes pertaining to various aspects of treatment is useful. Patients who do not understand the reasoning behind the treatment plan may be inclined to try to increase their sense of control by going from one doctor to another, attempting various treatments. This is costly, emotionally and physically draining, and wasteful because tests are often repeated and more invasive procedures attempted before less invasive ones.

It also is critical to tailor the evaluation and treatment plan to be responsive to the couple's particular needs. For example, although research has shown that many fertility patients want information and involvement in treatment planning, some patients may prefer to play a less active role and defer to the physician. These individuals may feel overwhelmed by too much information about possible risks and benefits (see Burger, 1992) and may experience undue stress if they are given too much control. Additionally, ethnic and cultural variations may affect the amount of control desired as well as the acceptability of various procedures and treatments. Such factors (i.e., individual, cultural) must be thoroughly considered.

Couples will have an easier time coming to the decision to terminate treatment if a realistic, well-defined, individually tailored treatment plan has been developed (Taylor, 1990). This allows couples who are not successful to have some degree of comfort in concluding that all realistic options have been exhausted in order to begin to pursue other options. Patients who have not progressed through a carefully structured treatment plan may have considerably more difficulty coming to the decision to terminate treatment.

In addition to advocating that treatment facilities adopt a focus on the reduction of stress, we urge that they not place the burden for stress reduction on the patient. This responsibility creates a danger that women (who are typically the patients) will come away with the message that they are responsible for the success of treatment (e.g., "If only I had been less stressed, I would be pregnant by now"). Many patients cite their own level of stress as a reason for their IVF failure (Callan & Hennessey, 1988), and patients who believe they had a role in the failure tend to experience more distress (Litt, Tennen, Affleck, & Klock, 1992).

Working With Couples as a Unit

It is extremely useful for health care professionals to remember that infertility usually affects the couple as a unit as well as the individual patient. For the physician, this means that when an individual seeks help for a fertility problem, diagnostic and treatment plans can be developed in the presence of both partners. Failure to include both partners in treatment planning can lead to a member of the couple participating in a treatment protocol that he or she finds objectionable. It also may lead to nonadherence with the protocol. Unfortunately, eliciting the participation and cooperation of both partners is not always easy. As described earlier, there often are gender differences in responses to infertility, with men on average being somewhat less invested in treatment and less willing to become involved in treatment. The physician and other medical staff can encourage the participation of a partner who shows minimal interest by making it clear, sensitively and nonjudgmentally, that his or her opinions and reactions are as important as the other partner's and that he or she will be included in the decision-making process should he or she choose to participate.

As discussed earlier, although infertility does not usually lead to serious marital problems, some couples experience significant distress. For couples who seek marital counseling, there are well-established techniques for communication skills training that may help the couple reach a mutually acceptable solution (see Jacobson, 1986). However, couples who seek counseling often are experiencing so much conflict that they can no longer openly discuss the problem. In this case, it may be helpful for the counselor to first try to promote acceptance of each other's views (see Christensen, Jacobson, & Babcock, 1995). This can be achieved through detailed discussions of the nature of the conflict and each spouse's point of view. Through these discussions, the counselor can help the couple to see that although their problems may occur as a result of differences between them, each spouse's view is understandable and not originally intended to hurt the other. For example, the counselor might help the husband see that his wife does not continually ask him for support to annoy him and that his lack of responsiveness has made her feel alone. Similarly, the counselor can help the wife to see that her husband does not distance himself from the fertility problem to make her feel alone but instead perhaps because he feels overwhelmed by the enormity of the situation.

Providing Help With Treatment Decision Making

The health care professional must help patients with treatment-related decisions under conditions of extreme uncertainty. In light of evidence that patients tend to overestimate the likelihood of success, we agree with Leiblum et al. (1987) that it is "critical that IVF personnel understand the tendency of couples to display both overoptimism and denial with respect to success probability so that they do not reinforce these feelings and inadvertently contribute to the tremendous disappointment that accompanies failure to conceive" (p. 174). Medical staff should be alert to the manner in which they portray risks, benefits, and success rates and should be aware that how facts are framed (i.e., as likelihood of success vs. failure) can affect how information is used in the decision-making process. Patients should be informed of the success rates for the particular treatment facility and for cases similar to theirs before they consent to treatment.

On the basis of the assumption that overly optimistic expectations will lead to more difficulty coping with failure, some authors have concluded that health care professionals must monitor patients' level of expectations throughout the process and repeatedly remind them of the typically low success rates (Callan & Hennessey, 1988; Leiblum et al., 1987). We argue that it would be inappropriate to intervene in an individual's natural coping process without clear evidence that such interventions would have the desired effect. On the contrary, Adler et al. (1991) have argued that, based on social psychological principles, the appearance of unrealistic expectations may be a reasonable and adaptive stress management technique in some cases. Reformulating one's own estimates of the likelihood of success in one's mind may give one more justification for undergoing such a difficult procedure, making it easier to cope with the stress. This hypothesis was supported by the results of Litt et al. (1992), who found that women who were pessimistic about their chance of success and who were distressed before the IVF were more distressed after failure than women who were optimistic about their chances and less distressed before the IVF.

The following are our tentative conclusions about how to approach patient expectations. Individuals considering ARTs should be given clear, straightforward information regarding success rates and risks. Any misperceptions identified during the evaluation period can be corrected and patients counseled sensitively concerning realistic expectations. However, once a decision has been made, medical staff should not interfere with the psychological process of overoptimism because it may reduce stress. Instead, medical staff should pay special attention to the distress levels of those who appeared pessimistic and distressed at the start of the cycle.

Another major issue is how patients should be helped to decide whether to pursue options such as ARTs after initial options have failed and how to help unsuccessful couples decide to terminate treatment or elect to use donor sperm, an egg donor, or a surrogate mother. Given the complexity and uncertainty of new reproductive options, and the emotional nature of the procedures themselves, there is a need for the development of decision-making aids for couples faced with fertility treatment decisions. This could be achieved using videotapes that provide information regarding particular procedures and outline some of the positive and negative aspects of choosing a procedure. These videotapes might contain the stories of couples who have undergone (and of some who have chosen not to undergo) the procedure, with various outcomes.

Psychological Intervention

Many authors have advocated the provision of professional counseling as a component of infertility treatment programs (i.e., Dennerstein & Morse, 1988), and it is now considered a required component for participation in some IVF programs (Seibel & Levine, 1987). Also, many couples undergoing infertility treatment, particularly IVF, report that they would welcome the opportunity for counseling (Baram et al., 1988), although a small minority make use of services when they are offered on a voluntary basis (Reading, 1991).

Although the availability of counseling in conjunction with treatment is clearly important, research to date does not suggest that psychological counseling is necessary for everyone, nor should all couples making use of ARTs or other fertility treatments be required to have counseling. Yet, offering counseling on a purely voluntary basis can lead to underutilization. Thus, this concern must be balanced with the danger that making counseling a requirement of participation in a treatment program may contribute to an individual's sense of loss of control by forcing him or her into yet another patient role. Women may be at particular risk in this way because they are more often the designated patient and therefore the most likely target of psychological interventions.

The role mental health professionals should play and the best psychological interventions for individuals with fertility problems are major unresolved issues. Pretreatment assessment is one role that psychologists and social workers have been asked to perform in the ART process. There is some ambiguity about whether this is a gatekeeper role, intended to deny access to treatment to certain patients (e.g., because of emotional instability), or simply a support and troubleshooting role, so that efforts can be taken to treat any problems (i.e., major depression) that might result in undue stress over the course of treatment. We believe that mental health professionals should be wary of the gatekeeper role for several reasons. First, there is limited research evidence to guide these decisions, and thus they are likely to result in unfair discrimination (see Humphrey, Humphrey, & Ainsworth-Smith, 1991; Sparks & Hamilton, 1991). Second, as pointed out by Stanton and Danoff-Burg (1995), the psychological consequences of denying access to reproductive technologies to those who desire to use them are not known. In addition, ambiguity about the purpose of the initial assessment may lead patients to hide concerns or emotional problems, fearing that revealing any problems might lead to their rejection from the program. Therefore, when pretreatment assessments are used, we recommend that the purpose be made clear to patients.

Approaches to psychological interventions described in the literature include remnants of the psychogenesis model of infertility (i.e., psychodynamic psychotherapy aimed at uncovering conflicts over the maternal role) as well as treatments such as crisis intervention, grief counseling, supportive counseling, stress management techniques, cognitive–behavioral therapy, and more. Little controlled research has been conducted to assess the usefulness of any type of psychological counseling for patients with fertility problems (however, see Connolly et al., 1993).

There appear to be three key arenas for psychological intervention, each with a different set of goals. First, it appears that the majority of fertility patients could benefit simply from an opportunity to discuss their fears, anxieties, and frustrations with a knowledgeable and supportive person (Adler et al., 1991). The goal of this intervention would be to provide support, access to information, and the opportunity to vent distressing emotions and discuss relationship issues. This intervention may be particularly important for patients undergoing ARTs and can be offered by many health care professionals (e.g., psychologists, social workers, nurses). This supportive function may be achieved through group interventions that are well established (i.e., RESOLVE, a national support group network for individuals facing fertility problems). This type of intervention is distinct from most conceptualizations of psychotherapy, in that there is no assumption that the patient has a psychological problem that must be solved through acceptance of the patient role.

The second arena for psychological intervention is the provision of help with decision making. Here, trained health professionals can work closely with couples in choosing the options that best fit their needs and goals. This function could be similar to that of the genetic counselor, who is adept at presenting information and choices. The third arena for psychological intervention involves those patients (or partners) who present for treatment with preexisting psychiatric disorders or who experience clinically significant levels of psychological distress as a result of coping with treatment. It may be difficult for the health practitioner to identify when a patient's level of distress is so high that intervention is warranted because, as we have indicated, some level of emotional response to infertility is expected in most cases. Some possible indicators of extreme reactions are (a) major depressive reactions (particularly when accompanied by suicidal ideation or social withdrawal); (b) severe relationship problems, particularly those involving physical or psychological abuse, or those involving a stalemate between partners (e.g., one insists on continued treatment and the other refuses to continue); (c) sexual dysfunctions beyond common temporary reactions to the stress of fertility treatment; and

(d) serious ruminative or obsessive reactions, such as preoccupation with getting pregnant leading to going from one doctor to another or trying numerous exploratory treatments. Couples with these responses may need referral to qualified mental health professionals who can work in conjunction with medical staff in treatment planning according to the patient's desire.

Conclusion

The purpose of this chapter has been to focus on psychological issues faced by women and by couples during the period of time defined medically as infertility. Considerable research provides a foundation for drawing several conclusions, discarding some myths, and developing psychological interventions. Nevertheless, more research is needed to better understand and treat psychological responses to infertility in couples and individuals.

Nature, not culture, prescribed that women be childbearers. Thus, it is not surprising that the bulk of responsibility for many reproductive issues, including infertility, falls on women. In all likelihood, women will continue to bear the greater burden of the patient role in infertility treatment. However, they need not be held solely responsible for cause or solution. Health care professionals can have an important, positive influence on the adjustment process by creating an environment in which men feel comfortable being involved in the diagnosis and treatment process. In addition to reducing the emotional burden on women, more equal sharing of the responsibility could result in a greater sense of efficacy and control among men. As understanding of and solutions to infertility continue to grow, we hope that health care professionals can maintain an accepting and not a pathologizing approach in working with individuals with fertility problems.

References

Abbey, A., Andrews, F. M., & Halman, L. J. (1991). The importance of social relationships for infertile couples' well-being. In A. L. Stanton & C. Dunkel-Schetter (Eds.), *Infertility: Perspective from stress and coping research* (pp. 61–86). New York: Plenum.

Abbey, A., Andrews, F. M., & Halman, L. J. (1994). Infertility and parenthood: Does becoming a parent increase well-being? *Journal of Consulting and Clinical Psychology, 62,* 398–403.

Adler, N. E., Keyes, S., & Robertson, P. (1991). Psychological issues in new reproductive technologies: Pregnancy-inducing technology and diagnostic screening. In J. Rodin & A. Collins (Eds.), *Women and new reproductive technology: Medical, psychosocial, legal, and ethical dilemmas* (pp. 111–133). Hillsdale, NJ: Erlbaum.

Baram, D., Tourtelot, E., Muechler, E., & Huang, K. (1988). Psychosocial adjustment following unsuccessful in vitro fertilization. *Journal of Psychosomatic Obstetrics and Gynecology, 9,* 181–190.

Barnea, E. R., & Tal, J. (1991). Stress-related reproductive failure. *Journal of in Vitro Fertilization and Embryo Transfer, 8,* 15–23.

Berg, B. J., Wilson, J. F., & Weingartner, P. J. (1991). Psychological sequelae of infertility treatment: The role of gender and sex-role identification. *Social Science Medicine, 33*, 1071–1080.

Berger, D. M. (1980). Couple's reactions to male infertility and donor insemination. *American Journal of Psychiatry, 137*, 1047–1049.

Burger, J. M. (1992). *Desire for control: Personality, social and clinical perspectives.* New York: Plenum.

Callan, V. J., & Hennessey, J. F. (1988). Emotional aspects and support in in vitro fertilization and embryo transfer programs. *Journal of in Vitro Fertilization and Embryo Transfer, 5*, 290–295.

Callan, V. J., & Hennessey, J. F. (1989). Psychological adjustment to infertility: A unique comparison of two groups of infertile women, mothers and women childless by choice. *Journal of Reproductive and Infant Psychology, 7*, 105–112.

Christensen, A., Jacobson, N. S., & Babcock, J. (1995). Integrative behavioral couple therapy. In. N. S. Jacobson & A. S. Gurman (Eds.), *Clinical handbook of marital therapy* (pp. 31–64). New York: Guilford Press.

Connolly, K. J., Edelmann, R. J., Bartlett, H., Cooke, I. D., Lenton, E., & Pike, S. (1993). An evaluation of counseling for couples undergoing treatment for in vitro fertilization. *Human Reproduction, 8,*, 1332–1338.

Davajan, V., & Israel, R. (1991). Diagnosis and medical treatment of infertility. In A. L. Stanton & C. A. Dunkel-Schetter (Eds.), *Infertility: Perspectives from stress and coping research* (pp. 17–28). New York: Plenum.

Dennerstein, L., & Morse, C. (1988). A review of psychological and social aspects of in vitro fertilisation. *Journal of Psychosomatic Obstetrics and Gynecology, 9*, 159–170.

Downey, J., & McKinney, M. (1992). The psychiatric status of women presenting for infertility evaluation. *American Journal of Orthopsychiatry, 62*, 196–205.

Dunkel-Schetter, C., & Lobel, M. (1991). Psychological reactions to infertility. In A. L. Stanton & C. Dunkel-Schetter (Eds.), *Infertility: Perspectives from stress and coping research* (pp. 29–57). New York: Plenum.

Dunkel-Schetter, C., & Stanton, A. L. (1991). Psychological adjustment to infertility: Future directions in research and application. In A. L. Stanton & C. Dunkel-Schetter (Eds.), *Infertility: Perspectives from stress and coping research* (pp. 197–222). New York: Plenum.

Edelmann, R. J., & Connolly, K. J. (1986). Psychological aspects of infertility. *British Journal of Medical Psychology, 59*, 209–219.

Golombok, S., & Tasker, F. (1994). Donor insemination for single heterosexual and lesbian women: Issues concerning the welfare of the child. *Human Reproduction, 9*, 1972–1976.

Greil, A. L., Leitko, T. A., & Porter, K. L. (1988). Infertility: His and hers. *Gender and Society, 2*, 172–199.

Hammond, K. R., Kretzer, P. A., Blackwell, R. E., & Steinkampf, M. P. (1990). Performance anxiety during infertility treatment: Effect on semen quality. *Fertility and Sterility, 53*, 337–340.

Harrison, K. L., Callan, V. J., & Hennessey, J. F. (1987). Stress and semen quality in an in vitro fertilization program. *Fertility and Sterility, 48*, 633–637.

Humphrey, M., Humphrey, H., & Ainsworth-Smith, I. (1991). Screening couples for parenthood by donor insemination. *Social Science and Medicine, 32*, 273–278.

Jacobson, N. S. (1986). Marital therapy: A social learning-cognitive perspective. In N. S. Jacobson & A. S. Gurman (Eds.), *Clinical handbook of marital therapy* (pp. 29–70). New York: Guilford Press.

Janis, I. L. (1993). Decision-making under stress. In L. Goldberger & S. Brezmitz (Eds.), *Handbook of stress: Theoretical and clinical aspects* (2nd ed., pp. 56–74). New York: Free Press.

Johnston, M., Shaw, R., & Bird, D. (1987). "Test-tube baby" procedures: Stress and judgements under uncertainty. *Psychology and Health, 1*, 25–38.

Lazarus, R. S., & Folkman, S. (1984). *Stress, appraisal, and coping.* New York: Springer.

Leiblum, S. R., Kemmann, E., & Lane, M. K. (1987). The psychological concomitants of in vitro fertilization. *Journal of Psychosomatic Obstetrics and Gynecology, 6*, 165–178.

Litt, M. D., Tennen, H., Affleck, G., & Klock, S. (1992). Coping and cognitive factors in adaptation to in vitro fertilization. *Journal of Behavioral Medicine, 15,* 171–187.

Mahlstedt, P. P. (1985). The psychological component of infertility. *Fertility and Sterility, 43,* 335–346.

Menning, B. E. (1980). The emotional needs of infertile couples. *Fertility and Sterility, 34,* 313–319.

Miall, C. E. (1985). Perceptions of informal sanctioning and the stigma of involuntary childlessness. *Deviant Behavior, 6,* 383–403.

Mosher, W. D., & Pratt, W. F. (1990). Fecundity and fertility in the United States, 1965-88. *Advance Data, 192,* 1–9.

Newman, N. E., & Zouves, C. G. (1991). Emotional experiences of in vitro fertilization participants. *Journal of in Vitro Fertilization and Embryo Transfer, 8,* 322–328.

Office of Technology Assessment, U.S. Congress. (1988). *Infertility: Medical and social choices* (Publication No. OTA-BA-358). Washington, DC: U.S. Government Printing Office.

Pasch, L. A. (1994). *Fertility problems and marital relationships: The effects of appraisal and coping differences on communication.* Unpublished doctoral dissertation, University of California, Los Angeles.

Reading, A. E. (1991). Psychological intervention and infertility. In A. L. Stanton & C. Dunkel-Schetter (Eds.), *Infertility: Perspectives from stress and coping research* (pp. 183–196). New York: Plenum.

Salzer, L. P. (1991). *Surviving infertility.* New York: Harper Perennial.

Seibel, M. M., & Levine, S. (1987). A new era in reproduction technologies: The emotional stages of in vitro fertilization. *Journal of in Vitro Fertilization and Embryo Transfer, 4,* 135–140.

Seibel, M. M., & Taymor, M. L. (1982). Emotional aspects of infertility. *Fertility and Sterility, 37,* 137–145.

Society for Assisted Reproductive Technology, the American Fertility Society. (1994). Assisted reproductive technology in the United States and Canada: 1992 results from the American Fertility Society, Society for Assisted Reproductive Technology Registry. *Fertility and Sterility, 62,* 1121–1128.

Sparks, C. H., & Hamilton, J. A. (1991). Psychological issues related to alternative insemination. *Professional Psychology: Research and Practice, 22,* 308–314.

Speroff, L., Glass, R. H., & Kase, N. G. (1983). *Clinical gynecologic endocrinology and infertility.* Baltimore: Williams & Wilkins.

Stanton, A. L., & Danoff-Burg, S. (1995). Selected issues in women's reproductive health: Psychological perspectives. In A. L. Stanton & S. J. Gallant (Eds.), *The psychology of women's health: Progress and challenges in research and application* (pp. 261–305). Washington, DC: American Psychological Association.

Stanton, A. L., & Dunkel-Schetter, C. (1991). Psychological adjustment to infertility: An overview of conceptual approaches. In A. L. Stanton & C. Dunkel-Schetter (Eds.), *Infertility: Perspectives from stress and coping research* (pp. 3–16). New York: Plenum.

Stewart, S., & Glazer, G. (1986). Expectations and coping in women undergoing in vitro fertilization. *Maternal-Child Nursing Journal, 15,* 103–113.

Taylor, P. J. (1990). When is enough enough? *Fertility and Sterility, 54,* 772–774.

Taymor, M. L. (1990). *Infertility: A clinician's guide to diagnosis and treatment.* New York: Plenum.

Wortman, C., & Silver, R. (1987). Coping with irrevocable loss. In G. R. VandenBos & B. K. Bryant (Eds.), *Cataclysms, crises, and catastrophes: Psychology in action* (pp. 185–235). Washington, DC: American Psychological Association.

14

Premenstrual Syndrome and Menopause

Paula S. Derry, Sheryle J. Gallant, and Nancy F. Woods

Menstruation and the end of menstruation are normal, universal aspects of the female life cycle. Pathological variants of these processes, whether best understood in terms of psychological or physiological processes, are important health problems. Yet, research, clinical practice, and the subjective experience of women are characterized in Western cultures by longstanding controversies about the basic nature of menstrual phenomena. Where health practitioners stand in relation to these controversies can influence what research results are given credence, what interventions seem sensible, and how patient education is conceptualized. We explore these themes by focusing on premenstrual syndrome (PMS) and the health-related factors in menopause.

PMS

PMS refers to a broad range of negative emotional, behavioral, and somatic states reported to occur during the premenstrual phase of the menstrual cycle. It is not uncommon for women to experience some premenstrual changes, but only those who experience symptoms severe enough to impair normal functioning are considered to a have a PMS disorder. There is substantial controversy about the validity of PMS as a syndrome, even though serious attempts have been made to remedy problems of definition and measurement that left many early findings open to question. The standard definition currently in the field derives from criteria from the fourth edition of the *Diagnostic and Statistical Manual of Mental Disorders (DSM–IV*; American Psychiatric Association [APA], 1994) for premenstrual dysphoric disorder (PMDD).

To diagnose PMDD, it must be demonstrated (with prospective daily symptom ratings) that a woman experiences multiple symptoms during the premenstrual phase, predominantly depression, anxiety, anger-irritability, or mood swings, and that symptoms markedly interfere with work, usual social activities, or relationships with others. Symptoms must show a recurrent "on–off" pattern (i.e., present premenstrually but not in the remainder of the cycle). This distinguishes severe PMS from chronic dysphoric states and from cases of premenstrual magnification, in which symptoms are present over the cycle but worsen premenstrually. Women seeking treatment for severe PMS when evaluated carefully often are found to have another psychiatric disorder (e.g., major depression, dysthymia, anxiety) or, in some cases, a medical condition that accounts for their premenstrual complaints.

At first glance, the problem of diagnosing and treating PMS may seem straightforward (i.e., what is needed is an agreed-on definition, a valid and reliable method of assessment and evidence of efficacious treatments). However, even though much attention has been given to each of these areas, issues remain that likely are to be challenging to any practitioner who wants to understand what PMS is, whether one can determine who has it and who does not, and how one can effectively help women who seek treatment for this problem. There are a number of recent, detailed reviews of both biomedical and psychosocial research on PMS (e.g., see Bancroft, 1994). We briefly summarize some of these findings, but our main emphasis is on how they inform or distort understanding of women's premenstrual experience.

Understanding PMS: The Biomedical Perspective

The biomedical view of PMS presumes the centrality of biological factors as causative agents. Research has focused on uncovering the pathophysiology responsible for symptoms, and numerous hypotheses have been investigated, including possible hormonal dysfunctions, neurotransmitter abnormalities, vitamin deficiencies, and many others (Parry, 1994). The overall results provide no strong support for any biological factor: "No abnormalities in basal or stimulated plasma hormone levels have been identified. No neuroendocrine agent related to cyclical ovarian activity has been identified which is able to provoke PMS in symptom-free women" (Schagen van Leeuwen et al., 1993, p. 96). Schmidt et al. (1991), for example, found no differences in timing or intensity of PMS symptoms between experimental groups administered placebo or drugs altering luteal-phase endocrine events. Thus, although many studies have been done, there is still no clear understanding of how, if in any way, premenstrual psychological experience is related to changes in menstrual cycle physiology or pathophysiology. This does not rule out the possibility that biological factors may have a causal role in PMS; however, current evidence is weak, making it likely that such factors cannot account for the significant psychological distress that many women report experiencing.

In the face of so many equivocal and disconfirming results, one might reasonably ask why the search for an endocrinopathology of PMS persists so tenaciously. However, given the complexity of the menstrual cycle and the plethora of potential interactions with other equally complex neuroendocrine systems (peripheral and central), it is not surprising that a biological model of PMS remains seductive or that, despite a lack of supporting data, PMS often is treated with hormonal substances. Rather than being abandoned in the face of disconfirming evidence, endocrine hypotheses have simply gotten more complex, as in a recent hypothesis asserting that normal hormonal fluctuations may affect central neurotransmitters in unusual ways in some women, thereby triggering the experience of distressing premenstrual symptoms. Furthermore, the reproductive cycle has been viewed as a major determinant of women's psychological functioning and behavior for centuries. Continuing the search for a biological cause of PMS is consistent with this age-old search for the supposed negative effect of reproductive functioning on women's well-being.

Finally, women seeking treatment for PMS often conceptualize their problem as one of hormonal imbalance, and this view is supported by reports in the media and popular press that Chrisler and Levy (1990) found to be clearly biased toward emphasizing negative premenstrual changes and treating as scientifically proved the role of biological factors, such as hormones, in PMS.

Although a biological basis for PMS remains unproved, treatment of severe symptoms with certain antidepressants has shown reductions in symptom severity greater than with placebo (Yonkers & Brown, 1996). The most promising results involve serotonergic compounds, particularly fluoxetine, although the benefits may require daily dosing versus luteal phase only, and little is known about the effects of long-term treatment.

Understanding PMS: Psychosocial Approaches

Research on psychosocial factors in PMS has examined the potential importance of psychological variables such as menstrual attitudes, expectations, and attributional patterns; sociocultural factors, including stereotypes; and differences in the life circumstances of women who report severe PMS.

Several lines of research suggest that women report symptoms during the premenstrual phase because of social learning (i.e., they internalize stereotypical beliefs about what women are like premenstrually and so expect to feel this way). Women may be biased toward attributing negative moods experienced premenstrually to their cycle, whereas they might feel the same at other times but interpret it differently (e.g., in terms of the situation; Ruble & Brooks-Gunn, 1979). Expectancy effects have been found in markedly symptomatic samples. Several studies (e.g., Osborn & Gath, 1990) of women with severe PMS who had undergone a hysterectomy (with conservation of the ovaries) have shown that symptoms declined dramatically after surgery despite the continued presence of hormone fluctuations. This would be the expected outcome if symptoms are primarily a product of expectations rather than hormonal variations.

Stress and coping. Responses to stress also have been implicated in PMS. Several studies (e.g., Gallant, Popiel, Hoffman, Chakraborty, &

Hamilton, 1992; Woods, Mitchell, & Lentz, 1995) have shown that women with PMS complaints report a higher degree of life stress than asymptomatic women. The difficulty is that researchers have not found any causal relationship between stress and PMS. For example, Beck, Gevirtz, and Mortola (1990) found that stress ratings increased premenstrually in a sample of women diagnosed with PMS. However, when the stress contributed by the symptoms themselves was statistically removed, stress was not found to be greater premenstrually than in other cycle phases, nor was the frequency of various stressors different premenstrually, and the level of stress in a particular cycle did not predict the severity of PMS experienced. Thus, although stress may exacerbate symptoms or make a woman less able to cope with them, there is no strong evidence that stress causes PMS. An alternative possibility was suggested by Woods et al. (1995). Their findings indicate that women with PMS experience heightened arousal and stress reactivity and that these may interact with stressful life circumstances and with socialization concerning menstruation to promote interpreting premenstrual arousal as negative and in this way account for some of the symptoms that women with PMS report. An alternative explanation is that arousal may be entrained to the menstrual cycle by socialization and expectancy and accentuated by a stressful life.

The possible mediating role of coping responses also has been examined (e.g., Gallant, Popiel, & Hoffman, 1994). Results suggest that women reporting severe symptoms use more indirect coping strategies (e.g., more avoidance coping) that are often less effective in reducing stress. Here again, however, the causal importance of this in PMS remains to be determined.

Recently, interest has focused on the potential role of interpersonal stress because women complaining of PMS often report relationship problems and claim that their symptoms negatively affect their interactions with others, particularly spouses and family members (e.g., Brown & Zimmer, 1986). Research (e.g., Siegel, 1986) suggests an association between PMS and relationships in which there is poor communication and problem solving. However, whether this association represents a causal relationship and the direction of any such relationship is not clear. Despite this ambiguity, the most frequent interpretation in clinical reports is that PMS causes marital and family problems, and this is certainly the most common view taken by PMS sufferers.

From a sociocultural perspective, attention has been drawn to the fact that the recent surge of interest in PMS comes on the heels of dramatic changes in womens' roles in Western societies (e.g., Johnson, 1987). It has been suggested that this is not a coincidence and that PMS facilitates a structural realignment of gender roles without directly threatening the status quo because the stereotype of women as the "weaker" sex is maintained, albeit confined to the premenstrual phase (e.g., Morokoff, 1990). In addition, PMS may provide a "survival strategy" for women, allowing the expression of emotional states and behaviors that violate cultural expectations (e.g., anger, aggression) but that premenstrually are sanctioned in being labeled as PMS and attributed to "raging" hormones.

Although evidence about the role of psychosocial factors in PMS is preliminary, these are issues that should be assessed carefully in evaluating premenstrual complaints. The framework suggested by Woods et al. (1995) may prove useful in providing guidelines for medical professionals. It encompasses stressful life contexts, menstrual socialization, and expectations about symptoms related to menstruation that have been found to differentiate women reporting low-severity symptoms from those presenting with premenstrual syndrome or premenstrual magnification.

PMS diagnosis. In addition to factors that may be related to the etiology of PMS, psychological research has been important in relation to the assessment of symptoms. To be diagnosed with severe PMS (i.e., PMDD), it is necessary that symptoms "markedly" interfere with work, usual social activities, or relationships with others (Criterion b in the *DSM–IV*; APA, 1994). This is meant to distinguish severe PMS from premenstrual symptoms that are distressing but not disruptive. Although researchers have found that women often perceive themselves to function less well premenstrually, there is little objective confirmation of women's poorer performance. For example, in a study in which women completed daily diaries over several menstrual cycles (Gallant et al., 1992), those reporting severe PMS were not found to differ from those reporting no PMS in the frequency of work performance problems, relationship problems with spouse or intimate partner, problems with relatives or friends, or interpersonal problems with coworkers premenstrually, even though they reported a greater decline in their work functioning and less enjoyment of social relationships premenstrually than did the asymptomatic women.

Psychological research also has been important in establishing the need to diagnose PMS on the basis of daily symptom ratings rather than retrospective ratings. The need for such ratings is now considered essential and has been incorporated as part of the PMS diagnosis (Criterion d in the *DSM–IV*; APA, 1994). When daily ratings are used, a woman rates her experience of symptoms each day, and the presence of PMS is determined by comparing her premenstrual ratings with ratings in the remainder of the cycle, typically with ratings in the early follicular phase. The emphasis on prospective ratings grew out of research documenting the unreliability of retrospective symptom reports. Studies have repeatedly shown that recalled symptoms tend to be more severe than those reported prospectively, suggesting that they may be more a reflection of cultural stereotypes than actual experience (Parlee, 1982). Furthermore, many women who claim to experience severe PMS do not show the requisite pattern of symptoms in their daily ratings, and it is only by collecting these ratings that this can be determined (e.g., Hurt, Freeman, Gise, Rivera-Tovar, & Steege, 1992).

To appropriately collect daily symptom ratings, one needs a measure that is psychometrically sound and practically feasible. Research on the dimensionality of moods suggests there are reasons to prefer unipolar scales over bipolar scales, and it can be argued that one ideally would want a woman to rate her symptoms on a daily basis, as free as possible of influence of her previous days ratings, but we do not know for sure what difference this might make because, to our knowledge, no one has compared the effects of different formats.

When comparing premenstrual and early follicular symptom ratings, some method must be used to decide whether a woman's premenstrual ratings increased sufficiently to be symptoms of a disorder. Research studies using several different degree-of-change methods to confirm severe PMS overwhelmingly report that whatever method is used, few women with complaints of severe PMS meet it. The reality is that of all those who present for treatment of severe PMS, perhaps as few as 4% and likely less than 10%, will show a pattern of changes that will get a confirmed diagnosis (e.g., Gallant et al., 1992). Thus, it would seem that the real challenge facing practitioners is not how to diagnose PMS but how to understand the problem of those claiming to experience PMS, most of whom will not qualify as "true" cases.

Furthermore, methods of evaluating symptom change, even the more conservative ones, often do not differentiate between women who identify as having severe PMS and women who report no troubling premenstrual symptoms. One study (Gallant et al., 1992) that examined several methods used to diagnose PMS on the basis of daily symptom ratings showed that none discriminated women reporting severe PMS from women who identified as not having PMS. Similar findings were obtained in a more recent study (McFarlane & Williams, 1994), in which among the women whose ratings showed evidence of premenstrual cyclicity, about half identified themselves as having PMS and about half perceived themselves to be symptom-free.

These findings suggest that fluctuation in moods is normative and that a major difference between women who experience severe PMS and women who do not may be one of identity. That is, the data indicate that some women who experience cyclical changes in moods see themselves as suffering from PMS and have made this a salient way of organizing their life experience, whereas other women who experience moods that are similar do not, and there is little understanding at this point as to why this is the case. At the least, these data suggest that clinicians need to explore with their patients what their premenstrual symptoms mean to them. Furthermore, it seems that researchers will not really understand the psychology of PMS until they know more about the psychological and sociocultural processes by which a woman comes to label aspects of her menstrual experience as symptomatic.

Menopause

Overview

Menopause, like PMS, is characterized by ambiguity and disagreement about basic definitional issues, what constitutes a normal or pathological process, and the usefulness of a biomedical view in which hormones are seen as playing a dominant role. As a physiological process, natural menopause refers to the last menstrual period. However, the menopausal process is not a discrete event but a gradual process that typically occurs over a period of years. There is a gradual decrease in ovulatory cycles, with steadily increasing levels of luteinizing hormone (LH) and follicle-stimulating hormone (FSH) and levels of estrogen that fluctuate but, overall, decrease until menstruation ceases (Gannon, 1990). Among the important markers or transitions of this process are premenopause, when menstruation is regular but hormonal changes may have begun; perimenopause, when estrogen, LH, and FSH cycling have changed enough to result in menstrual irregularities such as changes in the frequency, regularity, or amount of flow; and postmenopause, the time following (usually by 1 year) permanent cessation of menses (S. McKinlay, Brambilla, & Posner, 1992). Although menopause is defined retrospectively, most commonly as when a woman has not had a period for 12 months, 5% of these women may begin menstruating again, and a small number of women without periods may have LH or estrogen levels typical of premenopause (Schmidt & Rubinow, 1991).

Symptoms Associated With Menopause

In menopause, as in PMS, a fundamental question is when normal fluctuations produce symptoms severe enough to warrant calling them pathological. As with PMS, there are strongly held ideas about what symptoms constitute menopausal problems that have proved difficult to validate experimentally. Furthermore, there also is a biomedical view that holds that symptoms are the direct result of physiological changes, especially declining estrogen levels, that similarly have proved difficult to demonstrate experimentally.

Among both professionals and the general public, there is a strongly held view that symptoms typically appear during menopause that are the direct result of changing estrogen levels. Although up to 100 symptoms have been variously attributed to menopause, the "menopausal syndrome" most commonly includes depression, anxiety, joint pain, headaches, insomnia, loss of sexual interest, hot flashes (i.e., subjective feelings of intense heat, sometimes followed by sweating or shivering), and vaginal dryness and atrophy (thinning of the vaginal wall). However, population-based research studies (e.g., see C. Ballinger, 1990) fail to confirm the existence of a menopausal syndrome: Except for hot flashes, night sweats, vaginal atrophy (especially appearing several years after menopause), and perhaps insomnia (which also is related to vasomotor symptoms and stress), symptoms do not increase in frequency during the menopausal years, do not co-occur as a syndrome, and do not respond reliably to hormonal treatment. Even in the case of hot flashes, which clearly are related to menopausal status, the underlying mechanisms are complex, because endogenous hormone levels do not predict hot flash frequency or intensity; flashes are most common during the years surrounding the menopausal transition; and psychosocial factors such as stress, diet, and expectations all appear to play a role. Yet, the menopausal syndrome continues to be treated as fact in both popular books and clinically based professional accounts.

Cross-cultural differences in menopausal symptoms further argue against a universal biological process. Lock (1993), using and modifying when necessary a research instrument also used in the United States and Canada, found that Japanese women were far less likely than Western women to report symptoms such as hot flashes. They also had far lower rates of cardiovascular disease (CVD) and osteoporosis than Western women (notwithstanding that, on average, Japanese bone density was thinner), and women and their physicians both included as symptoms experiences such as stiff shoulders that are not thought of as a menopausal symptom in the West. It is unclear what underlies health differences favoring the Japanese, but possibilities include differences in health behaviors, including a generally more healthy (e.g., low-fat) diet, a diet rich in phytoestrogens (from soy bean products), and life-long habits of exercise; psychological differences, such as an attitude of acceptance towards one's life circumstances and stressors and a socially defined meaning to one's life stage; and other differences, such as unknown biochemical differences.

For menopause, as for PMS, a better understanding of the role of cultural expectations, coping mechanisms, and other factors is needed. How can the conviction that the menopausal syndrome exists be understood and reconciled with population-based research? What role do cultural expectations play in how women understand and cope with their experience? Menopausal women in the United States have been the object of strong, negative stereotypes. Kaufert (1994) described the classical view as that of a depressed woman whose useful life has ended with her ability to reproduce. In Kaufert's view, a more recent stereotype is that of a woman who may be employed but who is devastated by the discovery of her aging, an aging process from which she hopes to be saved by estrogen replacement therapy (ERT). Expectations about menopausal discomforts have been found in many studies to be correlated with symptoms. Matthews (1992), for example, found in her sample of normal middle-aged women that negative expectations (i.e., that they would experience vasomotor symptoms) were associated with having greater numbers of symptoms, whereas positive expectations (i.e., that menopause would have some benefit, that information would facilitate a good experience) were associated with fewer symptoms. She suggested that women with negative expectations may cope less well, becoming depressed when symptoms appear rather than taking positive action. The possible role of life transitions, especially internal psychological transitions associated with adult development or coping with stress, has been largely ignored (Notman, 1990).

Dysphoria During Menopause

The experience of dysphoria provides an arena for examining the complex relationships between hormonal and psychosocial factors. There is a common stereotype that psychological distress, especially depression, is a symptom of menopause. Matthews (1992) found that 80% of the participants in her research on normal midlife women believed that women are likely to become depressed when menopausal, and 55% believed that they themselves were liable to become depressed. Among professionals, depression is included in checklists of menopausal symptoms and presumed to be of etiological importance (e.g., Schmidt & Rubinow, 1991).

However, again, no clear-cut relationship between hormonal changes and mood have been demonstrated (Gannon, 1990). Sherwin (1994), for example, found only small, difficult-to-interpret differences between hormone replacement therapy (HRT) users and nonusers in her experimental studies. Furthermore, a series of well-conducted population-based studies have established that when random samples of community women are examined (e.g., Kaufert, Gilbert, & Tate, 1992; J. McKinlay, McKinlay, & Brambilla, 1987), the rates of depression do not increase when women reach menopause. For the majority of women, menopause is not associated with clinical depression or significant depressive symptomatology.

In the epidemiological studies, what predicted depression was (as is the case for other age groups) psychosocial stressors. Stressors particular to midlife documented in these studies included health problems, responsibility for the care of relatives, and so on. Negative attitudes toward aging and menopause both predicted depression in one study (Woods & Mitchell, 1996). Having a history of depression is an additional risk factor (C. Ballinger, 1990), as is a history of PMS (Woods & Mitchell, 1996). A woman at midlife who complains of depression must be carefully evaluated in terms of whether there are concurrent stressful events in her life or long-standing psychological issues that may be associated with her mood and whether she may be overestimating the likelihood that her menopause and mood are related because of their stereotypical association.

Although natural menopause is not related to an increase in the rates of depression, women who experience surgical menopause and women in perimenopause (C. Ballinger, 1990) are at greater risk. However, it is not clear from the research the degree to which depression in a surgically menopausal woman may best be understood in terms of a rapidly changing hormonal environment, the psychological trauma of surgery, or whether women who are depressed are more likely to be candidates for such operations (J. McKinlay et al., 1987).

During perimenopause, symptoms of distress such as depression increase in frequency (C. Ballinger, 1990), although absolute rates are still low. For example, Matthews (1992) reported a sixfold increase in moderate depression, which still accounted for only 10% of her sample. It is unclear why depression rates increase during perimenopause. However, perimenopause is a period of transition when uncomfortable or confusing physical changes (e.g., hot flashes or menstrual irregularities) and psychological changes (e.g., confronting aging or the possibility of chronic illness) may first appear and coping mechanisms may not yet exist.

The case reports and anecdotal evidence of dramatic experiences of depression, memory loss, or fatigue that begin abruptly with menopause and remit with hormone treatment warrant further research examination of whether a subset of women do experience menopause-related dysphoria. Even though overall rates of depression do not increase at menopause, causes of depression may nevertheless differ at different ages. There is a subgroup of women whose symptoms improve when hormones are prescribed: It remains unclear whether the depression is primary or secondary to symptoms such as severe hot flashes and consequent sleep disturbance, because some data suggest that depression remits only if vasomotor symptoms (such as severe hot flashes that produce severe insomnia) also remit (C. Ballinger, 1990). Regardless of cause, for this subgroup HRT does appear to improve symptoms. Furthermore, as with PMS, negative endocrine findings have resulted in more complex hypotheses rather than disconfirmation: (a) that atypical or subclinical depressions, rather than the major depressions examined in the epidemiological research, are what increases after menopause; (b) that a subgroup of women have an unidentified pathogenic atypical physiological response to estrogen or atypical neurotransmitter receptor response; or (c) that hormonal changes in menopause, as in PMS, result in altered levels of arousal or responses to stress that interact with social variables to increase the likelihood of depression. Even if a subgroup of women who are physiologically different are identified, whether hormones act as independent variables or in interaction with other factors will still need to be understood. For example, does altered hormonal functioning result in greater stress reactivity? What is the relevance of how physiological changes are labeled or coped with?

It is important to address the psychological meaning of dysphoria that may arise coincident with menopause. Many of the symptoms attributed to menopause are those associated with stress, including insomnia, depression, anxiety, palpitations, and so on (S. Ballinger, 1990). Notman (1990) suggested that life experiences and internal processes combine to produce psychological maturation and personality change throughout the life cycle; menopause occurs in a context of personal developmental changes, change in the family and social situation, and internal reevaluation (conscious and unconscious). Both external crises and internal transitions can involve a process of initial confusion or sense of loss, then psychological reevaluation and reorganization (conscious and unconscious), and finally resolution or a new integration. Unwillingness to experience this process can be associated with feelings of "being stuck" and dysphoria. It is possible that a subset of menopausal or perimenopausal women are distressed because they are in conflict or in a developmental transition or because their need to go inward is unacceptable. For example, fears of aging, memories of one's family of origin, or feelings of anger toward one's husband that emerge during an internal transition toward greater autonomy may be unacceptable to some women and cause dysphoria because they violate other internal standards, elicite too much distress, or are simply too time-consuming.

In summary, knowing how to identify depressions best treated as menopause-related and those that are not awaits further research, with the exception that depression that arises in coincidence with vasomotor symptoms can be treated with HRT. Clinicians most likely will be presented with a heterogeneous population, even given similar symptoms, for whom individual evaluation will be necessary.

HRT

If menopause-related symptoms are the direct result of declining or fluctuating estrogen levels, treatment with hormones should alleviate symptoms. ERT and HRT (i.e., estrogen in combination with a progestin) have been prescribed for a wide range of menopausal symptoms. ERT and HRT are effective in decreasing the frequency of hot flashes, night sweats, and urogenital symptoms (e.g., Gannon, 1990). Estrogens also have been prescribed for a broad range of other symptoms, such as wrinkling of skin; while discredited during the 1970s (National Institute of Health, cited in National Women's Health Network, 1993), these claims have nonetheless resurfaced (e.g., Cutler & Garcia, 1992). Most recently, hormones have been prescribed to prevent osteoporosis and CVD, conditions whose incidence increases in midlife. Although encouraged by recent evidence for protective effects, caution pervades discussion of recommendations for use of ERT and HRT for disease prevention. The American College of Physicians (1992) published guidelines for counseling postmenopausal women about preventive hormone therapy, in which it advocated careful and separate consideration of benefits of short-term use of hormone therapy for managing menopausal symptoms and the use of hormone therapy for disease prevention.

HRT and CVD: Pros and Cons

It is in CVD prevention that the greatest controversy about scientific fact, appropriate health practices, and ethical dilemmas exist. We therefore focus the discussion of HRT on its use in this area.

Epidemiological researchers have found that women electing to use ERT had less risk of CVD than women not using hormones (Stampfer & Colditz, 1991), with the most typical reduction in risk of 50% or greater for users relative to ERT nonusers. Because CVD is the Number 1 cause of mortality in middle-aged and elderly women, these findings have led to suggestions that long-term HRT be used prophylactically for heart disease prevention among the general population (Stampfer & Colditz, 1991). Those cautioning against widespread prophylactic use of HRT (e.g., Barrett-Connor & Bush, 1991) argue that hormone use is pharmacological, not a replacement, because estrogen and progestin are restored at different levels and with different chemicals than those normally found in the body. Hormone treatments should therefore be evaluated with clinical trials like any other untested drug before being recommended for widespread and long-term use (Barrett-Connor & Bush, 1991). Although a possible increased risk of breast cancer is the main cost associated with hormone use that is discussed, it is difficult to be convinced at this point that this is the only potential significant cost associated with the use of HRT. Repeatedly in the past, unforeseen negative consequences of hormone use have arisen, such as the occurrences of cancer in ERT users and in users of DES and their children and cardiovascular accidents in users of early high-dose birth control pills.

How to translate the results of epidemiological studies into clinical practice remains unclear. Epidemiologists (e.g., see Lock, 1993) are uncertain how the overall reduction of 50% risk should be applied in specific cases. Most commonly, women at high risk for CVD are not included in these studies. If they do benefit, how long and when should medication be prescribed? If a healthy woman has a good cholesterol profile, what is her benefit? The studies comparing ERT users and nonusers also have been criticized because they were correlational and women who elect hormone treatments are known to differ from those who do not in many ways favoring health, including their higher education and general health (Barrett-Connor & Bush, 1991); more favorable cholesterol profiles before menopause; and health behaviors such as exercise (Matthews, Kuller, Wing, & Meilahn, 1994). It may be that differences in health practices are associated with both a decision to use HRT and lower rates of heart disease.

Information about whether HRT is causally related to, rather than simply correlating with, CVD risk factors (not actual CVD) was gathered in the Postmenopausal Estrogen/Progestin Interventions trials (PEPI Writing Group, 1995). Although ERT was indeed related to levels of high-density lipoproteins (HDLs), low-density lipoproteins, and other markers of CVD risk, HRT using medroxyprogesterone acetate (Provera), the most commonly prescribed progestin, had weaker positive effects on HDLs than did estrogen alone or in combination with micronized progesterone, a product typically not marketed in the United States. (Unopposed estrogen, known to increase the risk of endometrial cancer, in fact produced unacceptable endometrial abnormalities in 34% of the women and a significantly higher rate of hysterectomies during the course of the study.)

CVD is usually conceptualized as being multifactorial. The effect size of estrogens relative to other factors is not known. That is, what is the relative importance of menopausal changes in hormone levels relative to lifestyle factors such as inactivity, poor diet, and smoking? Definitive answers to these questions await the completion of the Women's Health Initiative, a large-scale research project (Rossouw et al., 1995) evaluating the health effects of hormonal treatments and dietary and lifestyle changes. However, Matthews et al. (1994), for example, found that in a population of healthy women, women who engaged in moderate exercise did not develop risk factors after menopause such as a lowering of HDLs. The major determinants of change in levels of HDLs in the healthy-women study were obesity and fat distribution, physical activity, cigarette smoking, and alcohol use rather than estrogen levels. Furthermore, do hormonal changes act independently or in interaction with other factors in CVD? For example, psychological factors may interact with physiological factors to predict CVD vulnerability, as when a greater physiological response to stressors has been found in postmenopausal than in premenopausal women, especially in the response of blood pressure, heart rate, and epinephrine levels (e.g., Matthews, 1989).

Finally, the impact of social factors such as race and class on CVD risk in general and HRT use has been understudied. Lower class and minority women have participated minimally in research investigating CVD risk and HRT use. For lower socioeconomic status women, factors such as poor access to health care may loom larger as risk factors than the use or nonuse of HRT (Lock, 1993). Kaufert (1994) suggested that natural variations in occupational stress and activity levels common to daily life (as opposed to exercise classes) also may be important.

Promoting Informed Decisions About HRT

The controversy about how to assess and apply the available information about HRT raises issues of informed consent, patient education, and ethics. There has been little work directed at understanding how women decide to adopt hormone therapy. Research (e.g., Rothert et al., 1990) currently suggests that women are influenced largely by symptom distress associated with hot flashes and to a lesser extent by the risk of osteoporosis and side effects of hormone therapies. In a subsequent study, groups with different decision-making patterns were sorted into four distinct groups distinguished by several factors: educational level, perceived stress, and attitudes toward menopause and use of medications. Prediction of willingness to take estrogen was related to the perception that hormone treatment might be helpful in controlling menopausal symptoms and knowledge about menopause and its effects on women. Expectations that menopause would be difficult were related to a lower likelihood of taking hormone therapy (Schmitt et al., 1991). Additional studies are in progress to determine whether and how decision aids support women in resolving their questions about using HRT. Of interest is that few efforts address the broader issue of health promotion and prevention of disease among midlife women using a variety of strategies.

Ladd (1993) suggested that in a situation such as the one with HRT, in which definitive information is lacking, physicians should provide information and allow patients to make decisions. Ladd suggested that a personal assessment of costs and benefits, based on accurate available information about state-of-the-art research and risk factors specific to the patient, are needed and that in an area where information is incomplete, personal values also are part of the decision-making equation and should be explicitly articulated. We suggest that the possibility of unforeseen long-term consequences also should be part of counseling women about

HRT. The possibility of "rational noncompliance" should also be examined: If a woman stops using hormones because of uncomfortable side effects or even if a woman prefers the risk of an earlier death or a shorter lifetime than the average in her culture to the risk of a chronic disease such as cancer, it is important to consider that such noncompliance may represent a truly rational choice (Ladd, 1993; Lock, 1993).

Psychoeducational and Other Nonpharmacological Approaches to Menopausal Symptoms

Although not well researched, the surveys that do exist suggest that many women believe they do not have enough information about menopause. Mansfield, Theisen, and Boyer (1992), for example, found that even well-educated women wanted more information about normal changes associated with menopause and wanted to learn new health care activities. Lack of information was related to misinterpreting normal changes as pathological and a sense of uncertainty and lack of control that might be related to distress. Health education should begin during perimenopause because this is when vasomotor symptoms first begin, depression rates do rise temporarily, and health behaviors related to the prevention of chronic disease later in life (e.g., exercise and calcium supplementation) should be discussed.

Although there has been relatively little study of nonpharmacological interventions compared with the number of studies of HRT, there are several therapies that appear promising.

Lifestyle modification interventions appear to be potentially beneficial, particularly those incorporating exercise and dietary modification strategies. Women who exercised regularly had a lower incidence of hot flashes, sweats, and vegetative symptoms of depression than did those who did not participate in organized physical exercise (Hammar, Berg, & Lindgren, 1990). In addition to menopausal status, household activity predicted the frequency of hot flashes and sweats, and occupational leisure activity levels predicted general health symptoms among a midlife sample (Wilbur, Dan, Hedricks, & Holm, 1990). Aerobic exercise for postmenopausal women has been associated with significantly lower blood pressure levels and attenuated blood pressure reactivity to behavioral stressors (Blumenthal et al., 1991).

Dietary modification is a frequent recommendation found in the literature for women coping with menopause. Limiting or eliminating caffeine and alcohol has been frequently suggested, and some studies confirm a relationship between alcohol and caffeine intake and hot flash frequency or occurrence (Gannon, Hansel, & Goodwin, 1987). More recently, studies of plant estrogens (phytoestrogens) such as those contained in soy and wheat flour preparations suggest that diet may be linked to hot flashes. In one study, women in a randomized double-blind trial over 12 weeks reduced their frequency of hot flashes by 25–40% (Murkies et al., 1995).

On the basis of findings that stressful life events were related to menopausal hot flashes (Gannon et al., 1987), stress management interventions, including biofeedback, systematic relaxation, and coping skills therapies, have been explored. Germaine and Freedman (1984) examined the effect of progressive relaxation training on the frequency and intensity of menopausal hot flashes. They found a 60% reduction in symptom frequency in a study using heat stress to stimulate hot flashes. Stevenson and Del Prato (1983) found that biofeedback training for hot flashes produced positive therapeutic results, lowering skin temperature and enhancing one's ability to cope. Their treatment plan included 10 sessions of training in a variety of stress- and temperature-control techniques, incorporating relaxation, self-suggestions of cool imagery, marital contingency contracting, and temperature feedback. Treatment gains were maintained 6 months later at follow-up.

Treatment Suggestions

PMS and menopause are characterized by unresolved issues that complicate setting priorities in patient care. Questions remain about the best way to conceptualize the phenomena involved and where the line should be drawn between pathology and normal variations. Questions remain about the causal role of hormonal variations, the interaction of the endocrine system with other body systems and with psychological and social events, and the potential bidirectional influence of these systems on each other. Questions remain about the roles of social constraints and culture. For example, are menopausal hot flashes a purely physiological phenomenon? If so, how should the fact that cultures vary in the frequency and intensity of flashes (e.g., Lock, 1993) be understood?

We believe it will be beneficial to patient care for practitioners to clarify for themselves where they stand in relation to these issues. Furthermore, although more research is needed on what treatments are best in particular circumstances, some general recommendations can be offered.

First, patients should be given a complete physical examination. A careful evaluation of whether symptoms are in fact temporally related to menstrual events should be made, including, for PMS, a distinction between PMS and PMDD. Symptom severity, especially its impact on functioning, should be evaluated.

Second, the following may contribute to symptomatology: a history of depression; current stressful events and reactivity to stress; and negative expectations, uncertainty, or anxiety about symptoms, menstrual events, or midlife. A woman may be overestimating the likelihood that menstrual phenomena and symptoms such as depression are related because of their stereotypical association. When appropriate, medication should be offered and the effects carefully monitored. Educational materials describing normal changes throughout the menstrual cycle or menopause and about self-help techniques are useful. Information about midlife issues that presents a positive view of menopause and midlife may be important.

Third, for vasomotor symptoms and other menopausal distress, and for PMS, resources or referrals for nonbiomedical techniques that may be helpful should be available to patients, especially stress management, biofeedback, and relaxation techniques; coping skills training or conflict resolution techniques; and dietary practices. When appropriate, information about support groups or psychotherapy for life-stage-related issues should be provided. Lifestyle changes such as exercise and good diet that might help prevent chronic diseases in midlife should be recommended. Written information about risks and benefits of various kinds of treatments is helpful but should not replace face-to-face discussion of these issues.

In conclusion, in the absence of definitive evidence concerning the role of biomedical and psychosocial factors, recognition of the importance of individualized assessment of patients and a willingness to consider a broad range of causes and interventions will be most likely to result in quality patient care.

References

American College of Physicians. (1992). Guidelines for counseling postmenopausal women about preventive hormone therapy. *Annals of Internal Medicine, 117,* 1038–1041.

American Psychiatric Association. (1994). *Diagnostic and statistical manual of mental disorders* (4th ed.). Washington, DC: Author.

Ballinger, C. (1990). Psychiatric aspects of the menopause. *British Journal of Psychiatry, 156,* 773–787.

Ballinger, S. (1990). Stress as a factor in lowered estrogen levels in the early postmenopause. *Annals of the New York Academy of Sciences, 592,* 95–113.

Bancroft, J. (1994). The premenstrual syndrome: A reappraisal of the concept and the evidence. *Psychological Medicine,* monograph supplement 24, pp. 1–47.

Barrett-Connor, E., & Bush, T. (1991). Estrogen and coronary heart disease in women. *Clinical Cardiology, 265,* 1861–1867.

Beck, L. E., Gevirtz, R., & Mortola, J. F. (1990). The predictive role of psychosocial stress on symptom severity in premenstrual syndrome. *Psychosomatic Medicine, 52,* 536–543.

Blumenthal, J., Fredrickson, M., Matthews, K., et al. (1991). Stress reactivity and exercise training in premenopausal and postmenopausal women. *Health Psychology, 10,* 384–391.

Brown, M. A., & Zimmer, P. A. (1986, Jan./Feb.). Personal and family impact of premenstrual symptoms. *Journal of Obstetrical and Gynecological Nursing,* 31–38.

Chrisler, J. C., & Levy, K. B. (1990). The media construct a menstrual monster: A content analysis of PMS articles in the popular press. *Women and Health, 16,* 89–104.

Cutler, W., & Garcia, C. R. (1992). *Menopause: A guide for women and the men who love them.* New York: Norton.

Gallant, S. J., Popiel, D. A., & Hoffman, D. (1994). The role of psychological variables in the experience of premenstrual symptoms—Mind-body rhythmicity: A menstrual cycle perspective. *Proceedings of the Society for Menstrual Cycle Research,* 9th conference (pp. 139–151).

Gallant, S. J., Popiel, D. A., Hoffman, D. M., Chakraborty, P. K., & Hamilton, J. A. (1992). Using daily ratings to confirm premenstrual syndrome/late luteal phase dysphoric disorder: Part II. What makes a "real" difference? *Psychosomatic Medicine, 54,* 167–181.

Gannon, L. (1990). Endocrinology of menopause. In R. Formanek (Ed.), *The meanings of menopause: Historical, medical, and clinical perspectives* (pp. 179–237). Hillsdale, NJ: Analytic Press.

Gannon, L., Hansel, S., & Goodwin, J. (1987). Correlates of menopausal hot flashes. *Journal of Behavioral Medicine, 10,* 277–285.

Germaine, L., & Freedman, R. (1984). Behavioral treatment of menopausal hot flashes: Evaluation of objective methods. *Journal of Consulting and Clinical Psychology, 52,* 409–412.

Hammar, M., Berg, G., & Lindgren, R. (1990). Does physical exercise influence the frequency of postmenopausal hot flash? *Octa Obstetrica Gynaecologica Scandinavia, 69,* 409–412.

Hurt, S. W., Freeman, E., Gise, L., Rivera-Tovar, A., & Steege, J. (1992). Late luteal phase dysphoric disorder in 670 women evaluated for premenstrual complaints. *American Journal of Psychiatry, 149,* 525–530.

Johnson, T. (1987). Premenstrual syndrome as a Western culture-specific disorder. *Culture, Medicine, and Psychiatry, 11,* 337–356.

Kaufert, P. (1994). A health and social profile of the menopausal woman. *Experimental Gerontology, 29,* 343–350.

Kaufert, P., Gilbert, P., & Tate, R. (1992). The Manitoba Project: A re-examination of the link between menopause and depression. *Maturitas, 14,* 143–155.

Ladd, R. (1993). Medical decision-making: Issues concerning menopause. In J. Callahan (Ed.), *Menopause: A midlife passage* (pp. 194–203). Bloomington: Indiana University Press.

Lock, M. (1993). *Encounters with aging: Mythologies of menopause in Japan and North America.* Berkeley: University of California Press.

Mansfield, P., Theisen, S., & Boyer, B. (1992). Midlife women and menopause: A challenge for the mental health counselor. *Journal of Mental Health Counseling, 14,* 73–83.

Matthews, K. (1989). Interactive effects of behavior and reproductive hormones on sex differences in risk for coronary heart disease. *Health Psychology, 8,* 373–387.

Matthews, K. (1992). Myths and realities of the menopause. *Psychosomatic Medicine, 54,* 1–9.

Matthews, K., Kuller, L., Wing, R., & Meilahn, E. (1994). Biobehavioral aspects of menopause: Lessons from the Healthy Women Study. *Experimental Gerontology, 29,* 337–342.

McFarlane, J. M., & Williams, T. M. (1994). Placing premenstrual syndrome in perspective. *Psychology of Women Quarterly, 18,* 339–373.

McKinlay, J., McKinlay, S., & Brambilla, D. (1987). The relative contributions of endocrine changes and social circumstances to depression in middle-aged women. *Journal of Health and Social Behavior, 28,* 345–356.

McKinlay, S., Brambilla, D., & Posner, J. (1992). The normal menopause transition. *Maturitas, 14,* 103–115.

Morokoff, P. J. (1990, March). *Premenstrual syndrome: Representation of a cultural conflict.* Paper presented at the 12th Annual Meeting of the Society of Behavioral Medicine, Washington, DC.

Murkies, A., Lombard, D., Straus, B., Wilcos, G., Burger, H., & Morton, M. (1995). Dietary flour supplementation decreases post-menstrual hot flashes: Effect of soy and wheat. *Maturitas, 21,* 189–195.

National Women's Health Network. (1993). *Taking hormones and women's health: Choices, risks, and benefits.* Washington, DC: Author.

Notman, M. (1990). Menopause and adult development. *Annals of the New York Academy of Sciences, 592,* 149–155.

Osborn, M. F., & Gath, D. H. (1990). Psychological and physical determinants of premenstrual symptoms before and after hysterectomy. *Psychological Medicine, 20,* 565–572.

Parlee, M. B. (1982). The psychology of the menstrual cycle: Biological and physiological perspectives. In R. C. Friedman (Ed.), *Behavior and the menstrual cycle* (pp. 77–99). New York: Marcel Dekker.

Parry, B. L. (1994). Biological correlates of premenstrual complaints. In J. H. Gold & S. K. Severino (Eds.), *Premenstrual dysphorias: Myths and realities* (pp. 47–66). Washington, DC: American Psychiatric Press.

PEPI Writing Group. (1995). Effects of estrogen or estrogen/progestin regimens on heart disease risk factors in postmenopausal women. *Journal of the American Medical Association, 273,* 199–208.

Rossouw, J., Finnegan, L., Harlan, W., Pinn, V., Clifford, C., & McGowan, J. (1995). The evolution of the Women's Health Initiative: Perspectives from NIH. *Journal of the American Medical Women's Association, 50,* 50–55.

Rothert, M., Rover, D., Holmen, M., Schmitt, N., Talarczyk, G., Knoll, J., & Gogato, J. (1990). Women's use of information regarding hormone replacement therapy. *Research in Nursing and Health, 13,* 355–366.

Ruble, D. N., & Brooks-Gunn, J. (1979). Menstrual symptoms: A social cognition analysis. *Journal of Behavioral Medicine, 2,* 171–194.

Schagen van Leeuwen, J. H., te Velde, E. R., Koppeschaar, H. P. F., Kop, W. J., Thijssen, J. H. H., van Ree, J. M., & Haspels, A. A. (1993). Is premenstrual syndrome an endocrine disorder? *Journal of Psychosomatic Obstetrics and Gynecology, 14,* 91–109.

Schmidt, P. J., & Rubinow, D. (1991). Menopause-related affective disorders: A justification for further study. *American Journal of Psychiatry, 148,* 844–852.

Schmitt, N., Gogate, J., Rovner, D., Holmes, M., Talarczyk, G., Given, B., & Kroll, J. (1991). Capturing and clustering women's judgement policies: The case of hormonal therapy for menopause. *Journal of Gerontology: Psychological Sciences, 46*(3), 92–101.

Sherwin, B. (1994). Sex hormones and psychological functioning in postmenopausal women. *Experimental Gerontology, 29,* 423–430.

Siegel, J. P. (1986). Marital dynamics of women with premenstrual tension syndrome. *Family System Medicine, 4,* 358–365.

Stampfer, M., & Colditz, G. (1991). Estrogen replacement therapy and coronary heart disease: A quantitative assessment of the epidemiologic evidence. *Preventive Medicine, 20,* 47–63.

Stevenson, D., & Del Prato, D. (1983). Multiple component self-control programs for menopausal hot flash. *Journal of Behavioral Therapy and Experimental Psychiatry, 14,* 137–140.

Wilbur, J., Dan, A., Hedricks, C., & Holm, K. (1990). The relationship among menopausal status, menopausal symptoms, and physical activity in mid life women. *Family and Community Health, 13*(3), 67–78.

Woods, N., & Mitchell, E. (1996). Patterns of depressed mood among midlife women: Observations from the Seattle Midlife Women's Study. *Research in Nursing and Health, 19,* 111–123.

Woods, N., Mitchel, E., & Lentz, M. (1995). Social pathways to premenstrual symptoms. *Research in Nursing and Health, 18,* 225–237.

Yonkers, K. A., & Brown, W. A. (1996). Pharmacologic treatments for premenstrual dysphoric disorder. *Psychiatric Annuals, 26,* 586–589.

15

The Challenges of Aging

*Royda Crose, Elaine A. Leventhal, Marie R. Haug,
and Edith A. Burns*

Getting older in the 21st century and maintaining a healthy sense of self and well-being has become one of the greatest challenges in America today. The United States has become more urbanized and has many working-parent families. "Traditional," extended, or multigeneration families of the past, seen as the idealized caregiving environment, are increasingly rare. There have been greater economic demands placed on families, and these have been exaggerated by the pressures of an extended life expectancy and an increasingly independent aging population. These "cultural" changes are taking place in a society that worships youth and has a unique angst about being old and an ageist approach to the graying of the population.

Therefore, there is a need for a gerontological approach to professional training that will inform practitioners about the care of an aging population. Getting older in the United States has become colored by fear of illness, dependency, death, and concerns about the increased societal costs of caring for the expanding population of older adults. This American "ageism" has led to some unique strategies for both elderly people and their families and for health providers. Unlike other "isms" (e.g., sexism, racism, anti-Semitism, homophobia) that are aimed at someone different from oneself, ageism is aimed at what people themselves will become. Ageism may create a strong denial of one's own age and foster a sense of separation from people who are aged or physically or mentally frail. By contrast, a "reverse ageism" has motivated many older people to separate themselves into retirement communities committed to keeping residents active, "young," vigorous, and secure. This separation of generations is volitional but may lead many residents, as they become less functional, to feel isolated and even imprisoned.

Health practitioners are not immune to fears about getting old and are at risk of projecting their own beliefs and stereotypes about aging onto their older patients. To equate disease, disability, and terminal illness with the normal processes of aging can lead to misdiagnosis, inappropriate or inadequate treatment, lowered expectations for prognosis, and premature termination of care. If ageism is combined with gender bias, older women are in double jeopardy of discrimination in the health care system. Those who are ethnic minority, lesbian, or disabled have even more challenges in obtaining appropriate health care. In this chapter we attempt to help health care professionals understand more about the biological and psychosocial processes that underlie senescence and senility and to point out the special challenges for older women.

Increased Variability With Age

As growth stops, senescence, or "normal" aging, begins. Senescence is characterized by different cell-, and organ-, and gender-specific rates of decline. Senility, or age-related disease, on the other hand, represents the combination of an individual's innate or intrinsic biological plasticity, changing over time, with the results of extrinsic factors such as behavioral patterns, environmental exposure, and the wide range of injuries, infections, and experiences. Because of individual variability, these add together to produce increasing heterogeneity between individuals as they age. The emotional and behavioral components of illness become as atypical in their presentation in the aging individual as the physical manifestations of illnesses. Therefore, it is important for the health care professional to understand basic senescent processes and senile pathology. This can lead to the development of more effective skills to manage age-related behavioral changes that occur in association with illness and increasing frailty (Leventhal, 1993, 1996).

In the adult years and especially in late life, the individual history, along with a comprehensive examination, becomes the primary method of determining the need for health services and prognosis for outcome. Time spent on getting accurate information about medical, psychosocial, educational, vocational, and family history is necessary for quality health care of all older patients. Assessing lifestyle, intelligence, and personality also should be included. Such a detailed history will reveal much about flexibility, relationships, and resilience in past life experiences for each patient (Crose, Nicholas, Gobble, & Frank, 1992). For example, the health of a highly educated but eccentric woman who has no social supports may be more at risk than the health of a compliant man with minimal education and some cognitive impairment who has strong family supports. On the other hand, an older woman who watches her diet, exercises, and has many friends is more likely to better manage her own health care than is a younger, high-powered, overweight business executive who abrogates all responsibilities for nutrition and social activities to his wife.

Gender Differences in Aging

The chances of reaching the age of 65 has increased from 4% in 1900 to 12% today and is projected to rise to 20% by 2020. More people are living longer, and a greater proportion of these aging Americans are women. Mortality differs by gender and race, with the age-adjusted White male and female death rates in 1991 estimated at 634.4 and 366.3 per 100,000 people, respectively. The gender bias for the Black population was similar, although death rates were higher: 1,048.8 for Black men and 575.1 for Black women per 100,000 people (U.S. Department of Health and Human Services, 1994).

The disparity in death rates becomes more dramatic as women outlive their male partners. Older women have more acute and chronic illnesses but die at a lower rate. The risk for death from coronary heart disease (CHD) is much higher among men, and, although overall patterns of morbidity are similar, the clinical manifestations of CHD vary by gender. Men with CHD present most frequently with acute myocardial infarction. Silent infarcts are more common in women. Women have more hypertension, yet men die more frequently from stroke and hypertensive heart disease. There is a much higher incidence of diabetes in women, but women's mortality rates are only slightly higher than the rates for men for this disease. Women are commonly thought to be more frail and less healthy, but they live longer than men and many will spend a significant portion of their lives alone, coping with the physical and the psychosocial changes of isolation, loss, and aging (Leventhal, 1993).

Although often characterized as the "weaker sex," it appears that women have a biological and psychological robustness that has provided them with a distinct survival advantage, such that throughout the industrialized world there is a gender gap in life expectancy of 4–10 years. They survive through the decades, providing care and succor for their mates, who die from cardiovascular disease and cancer. However, because of this success, when they develop the same illnesses 10 years later, they may no longer have social supports or caregivers. This survival advantage may be related to the cardioprotective effects of estrogen, with women developing cardiac disease a decade later than men when they become estrogen deficient after menopause. Women have more comorbidity and more significant disease at presentation but are treated less aggressively than men, despite similar complaints of anginal pain and reports of greater functional disability (Khan et al., 1990).

If women survive common illnesses such as cardiovascular disease and cancer, they live long enough to develop the devastating illnesses that are unique to the very old: peripheral vascular disease, geriatric malignancies, degenerative joint diseases that are responsible for pain and immobility, and neurological degenerative diseases such as dementia and Parkinson's disease. Thus, the old-old, who reach their 80s or 90s with minimal cardiovascular disease or malignancy and are by definition "elite" survivors of both biological and chronological aging, may have added years that are not healthy years. The cumulative psychological and social changes that occur across the life span, combined with maladaptive illness and health behaviors, can lead to loss of esteem and the onset of frailty and dependency. Maladaptive illness habits and behaviors (e.g, smoking, poor diet), begun early in life and combined with the normal biological changes of aging, have serious implications for adaptation to disease and dysfunction occurring in the mature years. Some of these illness behaviors (e.g., smoking, poor calcium intake) specifically put old women at risk for serious disease such as osteoporosis. The aging woman also has caregiving demands on her from her spouse, children, and parents. She may need to make decisions about institutionalization for those she cannot care for. She needs to cope with dependency behaviors and deal with depression in herself or her family members.

Three Cohorts of Aging Women

Contemporary health care providers encounter three distinct cohorts of older women who have differing needs. The three cohorts include those born between 1929 and 1938 (Cohort A), those born between 1919 and 1928 (Cohort B), and those born in 1918 or earlier (Cohort C). The most recent detailed health data were collected in 1993 when Cohort A was aged 55–64 years (the preretirement years), Cohort B (the young-old) was aged 65–74 years, and Cohort C was aged 75–84 years (the old). Within Cohort C there is a subgroup of those 85 and older, the old-old, that represents the most rapidly growing proportion of the elderly population. There are economic, educational, and political differences among the three cohorts. The historical context of a woman's cohort may influence her understanding of and adaptation to the psychological and physiological changes of aging.

Women in Cohort C were infants during World War I and young adults during the Great Depression. Their educational attainment is considerably below that of younger populations, and few members of this cohort are currently in the labor force. These women are often widowed (67.6%), living alone (49.9%), or with relatives (24.8%) and typically are on insufficient incomes. A large proportion reside in nursing homes. As young women, this cohort had little experience with physicians and relied on home remedies and self-care. They tend to be passive and compliant when participating in the health care system.

Cohort B women were born in the 1920s and were at a prime age for military service during World War II. Women not enlisting in military service became the "Rosie the Riveters" of the war industries, filling traditionally male jobs. Although returning soldiers sent many back to the role of housewife, others continued to work, juggling jobs, homemaking, and children. This cohort has experienced drastic changes in family structure and social networks as a result of mass migration within the country, primarily from South to North as the lure of industrial jobs took rural workers into ghettos in northern cities. These women are likely to have limited incomes because they had little access to pension programs and low social security benefits as a result of interrupted and uneven work histories. Thirty-nine percent are widowed, 35% live alone, and 14% live with relatives. These women have had more experience with physicians and the health care system than earlier generations. Because of the greater availability of health care in the 1940s and 1950s, the discoveries of antibiotics, and widespread introduction to concepts of preventive health behaviors, they are more accepting and comfortable with professional advice and assistance.

Women in Cohort A have had life experiences much different from those of the other two cohorts. They are an advantaged group benefiting from the postwar boom economy. Their direct experiences with the Depression and World War II were minimal. Many of these women entered the professions, reaching maturity at a time when women had begun to combine work with families. The ideas of women's rights and equal pay were being openly debated and discussed, although often they were not realities. Many of these women are now reaching retirement age; although some plan to continue working, some are caring for husbands, parents, or both who have chronic illness. With more education, expanded roles, and increased information about medical decision making, Cohort A women may be more assertive in dealing with health care providers.

On the basis of these life experiences, women from different cohorts will have different needs and different expectations from the health care system. Although most of the oldest-old women in American society continue to live in the community, either independently or with relatives (usually a daughter), long-term-care institutions are filled with women from the 85+ cohort of the oldest-old who are suffering from dementia, osteoporosis, arthritis, incontinence, and other chronic disabling conditions. Most expected to live with family members throughout their lives, as their parents had done. Institutionalized, many are angry that they have been placed in nursing homes, and their families also may feel guilty and distressed. Nursing homes are rarely well equipped to handle these emotional and family issues, and these women may be living with untreated mental disorders and the effects of family dysfunction along with physical disease.

Women in their 70s and 80s, Cohorts B and C, who are in relatively better health than very old women in nursing homes, often are living alone and managing their lives independently for the first time. Because the majority of these women were married homemakers, their independence may not have blossomed until they became widowed. They may be proud of the fact that they can function so well and are resistant to intrusions into their newly experienced independence. If they need help, they rely on family members (usually daughters or daughters-in-law) and want such assistance as home health aides, part-time housekeeping, or home chore help in maintaining their independent living conditions.

Women in Cohort A are the daughters of these older women and are becoming older women in their own right. They may have the responsibility for care of parents and in-laws, spouses, and even teenage children or grandchildren. These preretirement, postmenopausal women may be in good health but are at risk of emotional and energy debilitation from the stressors of caregiving. Disease prevention, health promotion, and stress management are extremely important for these women. Resources such as respite care, day care, and support groups are needed to preserve the health of these caregivers. They are the "hidden patients" whose well-being is too frequently overlooked by their care receivers' physicians (Haug, 1994).

These synopses are obvious generalities, with many differences within as well as overlap between cohorts. The varying life experiences and historical events to which women have been exposed in the 20th century shape their beliefs and behaviors. Thinking in cohort terms can help health professionals understand why the very old women of the 21st century will be significantly different from the very old women of today.

Major Health Care Issues for Older Women

Numerous physical changes accompany normal aging, including graying of the hair, various changes in skin, loss of musculoskeletal mass, fat redistribution, and sensory impairments. Of the obvious signs of aging, changes in the skeleton, muscle mass, and sensory loss directly impair physical function and can also affect cognition. Typically, all functions begin to slow as people get older; mobility is slowed, some thinking processes slow, and emotional experiences appear to be less intense. Although some of these changes may impair quality of life, other changes may actually add to quality of life (e.g., maturity, greater experience with problem solving, less impulsive behavior, greater security and self-esteem). Women in particular appear to become more satisfied with life, assertive, and self-assured as they age (Friedan, 1993).

Living With Disabilities

Although aging is not synonymous with disease and disability, humans become more vulnerable to disease and disability with age. For many older people, poor health and functional loss create a significant loss in quality of life. Because women live longer than men, it is women who more often live many years with chronic, disabling conditions such as osteoporosis, arthritis, sensory and cognitive impairment, poverty, and lack of supportive services.

Functional abilities are commonly measured as the degree of independence in performing (a) activities of daily living (ADLs), which include eating, toileting, bathing, grooming, dressing, walking, and getting in and out of a bed or chair, and (b) instrumental activities of daily living (IADLs), which include meal preparation, shopping, managing money, using the telephone, light or heavy housework, and managing medications. Older women (those 70 or older) living in the community consistently are more likely to have some difficulty in both ADLs and IADLs than are older men (Miller, Prohaska, Mermelstein, & Van Nostrand, 1993). Indeed, with respect to ADLs, only 18% of men aged 65+ had problems, compared with 26% of women (Prohaska, Mermelstein, Miller, & Jack, 1993).

More of clinical practice in the future will be directed toward the care of older women with chronic and disabling disease. It has been well documented that there has been a gender-specific bias in the delivery of health care to older women (Leventhal, 1993) and that the long-term care needs of older women have suffered from a biomedical and societal bias that focuses on testing and the hope of "cure" (Estes & Lee, 1985). It is increasingly important to explore, develop, and promote treatments that aim to maintain function and independence. These include environmental adaptations, nutritional consultation, therapeutic exercise programs, massage, and support groups. These treatment approaches require a collaborative interdisciplinary team and should include close consultation with the patient, family members, and primary caregivers.

Sensory Loss

Some senescent sensory impairments are almost universal. Usually, the earliest to appear is presbyopia, or difficulty with focusing the eyes for sharp near vision. Thus, the early 40s may be the time when many people begin to need reading glasses, if they have not needed corrective lenses before. Presbycusis, or age-related loss in the ability to distinguish high-pitched tones, is common. Loss of taste buds on the tongue and odor-sensing nerves in the nose and brain can result in changing food preferences or, for some, a diminished desire for food altogether. Such sensory loss can make the environment hostile and require either adjustments or adaptations to the limitations, such as the use of glasses or hearing aids.

Health care practitioners should assess patients for sensory loss and compensate for losses during patient interactions by modifying treatment plans, printed materials, and office arrangements. For example, instructions or medical information for older patients should be in large, high-contrast print. The office or hospital should be well lit with limited glare, and background noise should be kept to a minimum. Written instructions are useful for patients and caregivers. Prescriptions for special diets should accommodate patient preferences, ethnic styles, and ability to follow recommendations. Understanding the effects of sensory impairment and the behaviors that result may prevent misdiagnoses of dementia, or unwarranted diagnoses of personality disorders, and avoid resistance to treatment in older patients.

Osteoporosis

Diseases of the autoimmune system (see chapter 21), cardiovascular conditions (see chapter 17), cancer (see chapters 19 and 20), and other illnesses are addressed in other chapters of this book because they are disorders that affect women of all ages. However, one serious, chronic health problem that strikes older women that is not discussed in other chapters is osteoporosis.

Osteoporosis, or a decline in bone mineralization, is a disorder that occurs most frequently in postmenopausal women. Short, smaller boned women of Western European or Asian descent are at greater risk than women with larger frames or from other ethnic backgrounds. Under-mineralized bones become increasingly fragile with age, but a diagnosis of osteoporosis is typically made only after a fracture occurs. It is estimated that 1.2 million fractures per year in the United States are attributable to osteoporosis. The incidence of fracture increases exponentially after the perimenopausal period between the ages of 40–50 years. One third of women aged 65 and older are expected to have at least one vertebral fracture during their lifetime, and 1 of every 3 women who live to extreme old age will experience a hip fracture (Melton & Riggs, 1983). Hip fractures are especially serious because they often result in nursing home placement, permanent loss of mobility, death, or all of these.

The causes of osteoporosis are complex. Estrogen deficiency after menopause is primarily implicated in vertebral body bone loss. Diet, exercise, muscle strength, and body size affect the long bones of the legs and arms. Osteoporosis is best treated preventively in high-risk, premenopausal women. Considering risk factors such as ethnic background, body habitus, estrogen depletion, low calcium intake, low level of physical activity, alcoholism, smoking, excessive protein intake, and a family history of osteoporosis, interventions such as adequate calcium and Vitamin D dietary intake, weight-bearing exercise, and cessation of cigarette and alcohol use may be recommended as prophylactic measures (Chesnut, 1994). There are hormones and drugs that may directly affect bone loss, such as estrogen and progesterone replacement, calcitonin, and bisphosphonates. It also is important to look for secondary causes of bone loss (i.e., medications or other diseases that can accelerate the loss of bone density). Roberto and McGraw (1991) studied the effects of osteoporosis on the self-perceptions of older women and concluded that this disorder, which interferes with mobility, can have psychological effects and that health care professionals should recognize and intervene appropriately.

Stigmatized Health Issues

Older women may be hesitant to talk with health care professionals about some areas of health that are embarrassing to them but that have a significant influence on their quality of life and well-being. Three of these health issues are urinary incontinence, abuse, and sexuality.

Urinary Incontinence

One special health issue for older women is the treatment of urinary incontinence. Because many women do not voluntarily discuss the problem with physicians, it often is ignored and the older woman may not have the opportunity to try available treatment modalities. Research has shown that behavior modification techniques, medication, and surgery are effective treatments for urinary incontinence and that older women can be helped with this problem by education and more aggressive treatment (Ouslander, 1994). Behavioral treatment includes bladder and habit training, prompted voiding, and pelvic muscle exercises (the Kegel regimen).

Additional treatment interventions in conjunction with these are biofeedback, vaginal cone retention, and electrical stimulation (U.S. Department of Health and Human Services, 1992).

Urinary incontinence has a great impact on the older woman's quality of life because it interferes with socializing, mobility, sleep, and eating patterns. Incontinence may be the culminating problem that determines the need for placement in a nursing home, although it is rarely urinary incontinence alone but the combination of urinary with fecal incontinence that pushes caregivers into placement decisions. In the nursing home, care providers too frequently adopt an easy solution: the use of adult diapers. A major complaint of women (and men) in nursing homes is the loss of dignity that comes with being diapered and the humiliation suffered from toileting accidents.

Elder Abuse and Neglect

Although strong support systems are the blessing of many older women, some are left without support and are vulnerable to various forms of abuse, ranging from fraud to violence. Criminals take advantage of older women living alone or victimize them on the street. In dysfunctional families, especially in those experiencing the stress of caregiving, elder abuse and neglect can result (Pillemer & Findelhor, 1989). Likewise, although most nursing homes have good, caring health care workers, some notorious examples exist of maltreatment of frail patients by disreputable administrators or low-paid, untrained staff.

Physicians, case managers, and nurses may be the only people older women have to turn to for help, and they are often too frightened to reveal the abuse. Elder abuse and neglect is a complex issue because adults have the right to privacy, autonomy, and independence to live their lives as they want unless they have been declared incompetent. Therefore, effective intervention depends on the sensitivity, awareness, and skill of the geriatric health care assessment team (Fulmer, 1991). A careful family history will alert the practitioner to family patterns of severe conflict in the past and abuse that may be ongoing. Older adults who are dependent on caregivers may be reluctant to register complaints for fear of being abandoned. Unexplained bruises, broken bones, anxiety, and fear, as well as caution and reticence in giving a family history, may be indicators of elder abuse and are important to explore in depth to help elders obtain protection.

Sexuality

It is generally agreed that sexual behavior does not necessarily diminish with age and is more widespread than younger people realize, even continuing into the 90s and beyond for some people. Postmenopausal women are free to enjoy sexual relations without the fear of unwanted pregnancy, a freedom that can improve sexual pleasure. Some women have reported that they found sex more satisfying and their attitudes about sex more open and positive in their later years (Crose & Drake, 1993). However, the major problem for older heterosexual women is the dearth of available men. Because men die earlier than women on average, and because older men tend to marry younger women, the number of available partners for heterosexual women declines in old age. Some older women who are married report that although they still desire sex, their husbands have lost interest or cannot have erections because of disease or sexual dysfunction.

For women who have a continued interest in sex but have no partners, their lives can be enhanced through sensual exploration and arranging for greater intimacy and affectionate touch in available relationships with family and friends. The use of fantasy, fragrances, music, lotions and oils with masturbation (Dodson, 1987), therapeutic massage, and support groups may help older women meet some of their needs for sensuality, sexuality, and intimacy. Health care professionals can help older female clients by initiating discussions of sexuality and by giving permission and encouragement to express and explore this vital, enriching aspect of life in ways that are available and pleasurable.

Depression and Dementia

The most common form of mental distress among older people is depression, not necessarily clinical depression but more frequently subclinical dysphoric mood. In a study of depressive symptoms using information from the Alameda County Study that covered three cohorts at three data collection points, women were consistently found to have higher rates of dysphoric mood in each age category (Roberts, Lee, & Roberts, 1991). However, the data also showed that these age differences in womens' dysphoric mood were more an effect of their cohort membership and life experiences than of aging per se.

Depression caused by major losses such as illness and death may become chronic when accompanied by other losses over a short period of time. Compression of loss, in which one does not have time to recover from one trauma before another strikes, often is the experience of older people who have outlived their friends, siblings, and sometimes even their children. Yet, these women are extraordinarily resilient, as evidenced by their low suicide rates compared with men. Although studies have indicated that women's depression overall seems to peak at midlife and then declines somewhat with age (McGrath, Keita, Strickland, & Russo, 1990), depression in late life may go undiagnosed or be misdiagnosed as dementia and thus go untreated or be treated in inadequate ways. Older adults often do not experience "classic" symptoms of sleeplessness, fatigue, loss of appetite, feelings of guilt, expressions of depressed mood, and so on. Depression presents with atypical vague complaints in elderly people: malaise, apathy, confusion, dominant somatic symptoms, and cognitive complaints, including denial of dysphoric mood. The absence of such symptoms will lead to underdiagnosis or misdiagnosis and thus the failure to treat dysthymia or depression appropriately and aggressively (Kaszniak & Scogin,

1995). These equivocal symptoms need to be explored as vigorously as more concrete complaints. If a diagnosis of depression fits, the older woman should be treated aggressively, including referral to a mental health professional for more intensive evaluation and treatment. Older people do not tend to seek treatment independently for mental health issues; therefore, it is incumbent on physicians and other medical professionals to encourage and refer them for psychological interventions.

Memory loss or dementia carries an enormous stigma and underlies much of the cultural ageism that is described in this chapter. Fears of dementia are often part of a patient's hidden agenda when presenting with vague symptoms. Reversible causes of progressive cognitive impairment are, unfortunately, rare. The classic symptoms of dementia are the loss of ability to think, use good judgment, remember, and take care of oneself. The manifestations of dementia can be significantly exaggerated by loss of vision and hearing. The sensory deprivation causes misinterpretation or partial understanding of external events and can lead either to withdrawal or paranoia and escalating agitation and confusion. Alzheimer's disease is the most common irreversible and progressive cause of dementia, and, although there are increasing numbers of degenerative diseases being identified, the behavioral features of all are relatively similar, the prognoses are fatal and the management dilemmas universal.

Only about 5–8% of elderly people living outside of institutions have a dementing condition (Kay & Bergmann, 1980). With the feminization of increasing life expectancy, women are at greater risk of developing dementia in very old age. However, the overwhelming impact of dementia on women is that they are often thrust into the role of caregiver to a parent or spouse with a dementing condition.

Caregiving Responsibilities

Caregiving for most older women involves attending to the physical and emotional needs of a physically or cognitively disabled family member who also is old. In many cases, this is the woman's parent or spouse. A 65-year-old woman may be taking care of her father, mother, or in-law who is 85 or older. Because women typically marry older men, there is a higher probability that an older wife will be caring for an even older husband than vice versa. Stone, Cafferata, and Sangl (1987) have estimated that more than 2 million people are providing unpaid care to 1.6 million disabled older people. From these numbers emerges a clear picture of a major challenge faced by many older women in providing care for a close relative who is also old, often very old. There is a great deal of literature on the stresses, strains, and burdens of this caregiving role. Indeed, the cost to the caregiver may be extensive, both in terms of physical and mental well-being, but there are also benefits. Caregivers often express a sense of accomplishment, satisfaction in having fulfilled a family obligation, and pleasure from an old relative's appreciation and affection (Picot, 1995).

Another potential caregiving role for older women is that of grandmother. This involves different challenges and stresses and perhaps greater opportunities and rewards than caregiving for a parent or spouse. This phenomenon of older women raising their children's children is becoming more common. A study by the research department of the American Association of Retired Persons revealed that the median age of grandparent caregivers was 57, with 23% being 65 or older and 7%, 70 or older. For some women this new role is possibly less burdensome than that of caregiving for a disabled older person. Children grow up to be helpful and show affection and support for their grandparent. Being involved in school and sports activities of grandchildren may be stimulating and rewarding. Although caring for grandchildren may bring mixed blessings, this responsibility has the potential to give purpose and relieve loneliness for the older woman who enjoys caring for others.

The implications of such caregiving scenarios for practitioners are that attention must be paid specifically to the caregiver in the treatment of the older patient. Who is taking care of this patient, and what are the health risks to the caregiver? A systems perspective on diagnosis, treatment, and prognosis is needed in determining what is best for each individual (Kreppner & Lerner, 1989). The informal support for the patient is crucial for health care, and, if the caregiving system is not healthy, the patient is at risk and another patient is created because of the stressors of caregiving (Haug, 1994).

Economic Issues

Many older women live on small, fixed incomes and thus have limited economic resources for their health care. Women who were not employed, or worked intermittently in low-paying jobs, may not have pensions or other retirement benefits in their own right. Fifteen percent of older women live below the national poverty rate compared with 9% of older men. In addition, 43% of older women live alone or with nonrelatives, leaving them at greater risk for poverty (American Association of Retired Persons, 1994). The median income of ethnic minority women is even lower, at approximately half that for White women. Women who live on limited incomes with few resources may have to choose between adequate health care, food, or heat and maintenance for their homes. No matter what their choice, their health will be affected.

For health practitioners, these factors must be taken into consideration when prescribing medications, which may be expensive, or making referrals to speciality services that may not be covered by Medicare. Professional case management is an ideal approach to deal with these complex issues, and a comprehensive, multidimensional perspective is necessary for quality treatment of these older women. For those who have economic and family resources, case management is integrated into the available support network and is not as crucial, but for those who are poor and alone, it is vital to the well-being of the older woman.

Importance of a Supportive Health Care System for Older Women

Social support systems are the blessing of many older women. Over a lifetime women typically develop reciprocal and supportive relationships with family and friends that pay off in old age when they need help (Lewittes, 1989). Relationships with health care professionals also become an important part of women's support systems in old age. One problem faced by many older women is that they survive their physicians as well as their ministers and other professional supports. This can be damaging for the continuity of health care of older women. The new, younger physician should be aware of and respect the significance that the physician–patient relationship has for the older woman. As with all patients, spending time getting to know an older patient is extremely important to gaining her trust and confidence. The more she feels that she is known and respected, the more comfortable she will be in discussing issues such as sexuality, loneliness, and mental health concerns. The more confidence she has in the competence and the sincerity of her health care providers, the greater will be her compliance with treatment recommendations.

Helping older women achieve the best quality of life possible can be a rewarding goal that brings as much satisfaction as curing an acute illness, repairing a wound, or removing an inflamed appendix in a younger patient. Care of the older patient requires skill in treating multiple, complex illnesses simultaneously and in knowing how to assess for hidden problems such as incontinence, depression, and elder abuse. The practice of health care requires artistic sensitivity as well as technical skill, so that sustenance and comfort are provided for patients of all ages in their time of need.

References

American Association of Retired Persons. (1994). *A profile of older Americans*. Washington, DC: Author.

Chesnut, C. H., III (1994). Osteoporosis. In W. R. Hazzard, E. L. Bierman, J. P. Blass, W. H. Ettinger, Jr., & J. B. Halter (Eds.), Principles of geriatric medicine and gerontology (3rd ed., pp. 897–910). New York: McGraw-Hill.

Crose, R., & Drake, L. K. (1993). Older women's sexuality. *The Clinical Gerontologist, 12,* 51–56.

Crose, R., Nicholas, D., Gobble, D., & Frank, B. (1992). Gender and wellness: A multidimensional systems model for counseling. *Journal of Counseling and Development, 71,* 149–154.

Dodson, B. (1987). *Sex for one: The joy of selfloving*. New York: Crown Publishers.

Estes, C. L., & Lee, P. R. (1985). Social, political, and economic background of long term care policy. In C. Harrington, R. J. Newcomer, & C. L. Estes (Eds.), *Long term care of the elderly: Public policy issues* (pp. 17–39). Newbury Park, CA: Sage.

Friedan, B. (1993). *The fountain of age*. New York: Simon & Schuster.

Fulmer, T. (1991). Elder mistreatment: Progress in community detection and intervention. *Family and Community Health, 14,* 26–34.

Haug, M. R. (1994). Elderly patients, caregivers and physicians: Theory and research on health care triads. *Journal of Health and Social Behavior, 35,* 1–12.

Kaszniak, A. W., & Scogin, F. R. (1995). Assessment of dementia and depression in older adults. *The Clinical Psychologist, 48*(2), 17–24.

Kay, D. W. K., & Bergmann, K. (1980). Epidemiology of mental disorders among the aged in the community. In J. E. Birren & R. B. Sloane (Eds.), *Handbook of mental health and aging* (pp. 34–56). Englewood Cliffs, NJ: Prentice Hall.

Khan, S. S., Nessim, S., Gray, R., Czer, L. S., Chaux, A., & Matloff, J. (1990). Increased mortality of women in coronary artery bypass surgery: Evidence for referral bias. *Annals of Internal Medicine, 112*, 561–567.

Kreppner, K., & Lerner, R. M. (Eds.). (1989). *Family systems and life-span development.* Hillsdale, NJ: Erlbaum.

Leventhal, E. A. (1993). Gender and aging: Women and *their* aging. In D. M. Reddy, V. J. Adesso, & R. Flemming (Eds.), *Psychological perspectives on women's health* (pp. 11–35). New York: Hemisphere.

Leventhal, E. A. (1996). The aging process: Biological aspects. In J. Sadavoy, L. W. Lazarus, L. F. Jarvik, & G. T. Grossberg (Eds.), *Comprehensive review of geriatric psychiatry: American Association for Geriatric Psychiatry study guide–II* (pp. 81–112). Washington, DC: American Psychiatric Press.

Lewittes, H. J. (1989). Just being friendly means a lot: Women, friendship, and aging. In L. Grau (Ed.), *Women in the later years: Health, social, and cultural perspectives* (pp. 139–159). New York: Harrington Park Press.

McGrath, E., Keita, G. P., Strickland, B. R., & Russo, N. F. (1990). *Women and depression: Risk factors and treatment issues.* Washington, DC: American Psychological Association.

Melton, L. J., III, & Riggs, B. L. (1983). Epidemiology of age-related fractures. In L. V. Avioli (Ed.), *The osteoporotic syndrome* (pp. 1–30). New York: Grune & Stratton.

Miller, B., Prohaska, T., Mermelstein, R., & Van Nostrand, F. (1993). *Vital and health statistics, health data on older Americans: United States, 1992* (Series 3, No. 27). Rockville, MD: U.S. Department of Health and Human Services.

Ouslander, J. G. (1994). Incontinence. In W. R. Hazzard, E. L. Bierman, J. P. Blass, W. H. Ettinger, Jr., & J. B. Halter (Eds.), *Principles of geriatric medicine and gerontology* (3rd ed., pp. 1229–1249). New York: McGraw-Hill.

Picot, S. J. (1995). Rewards, costs, and coping of African American caregivers. *Nursing Research, 44*, 147–152.

Pillemer, K., & Findelhor, D. (1989). Causes of elder abuse: Caregiver stress versus problem relatives. *American Journal of Orthopsychiatry, 59*, 179–187.

Prohaska, T., Mermelstein, R., Miller, B., & Jack, S. (1993). *Vital and health statistics, health data on older Americans: United States, 1992* (Series 3, No. 27). Rockville, MD: U.S. Department of Health and Human Services.

Roberto, K. A., & McGraw, S. (1991). Self-perceptions of older women with osteoporosis. *Journal of Women and Aging, 3*, 59–70.

Roberts, E., Lee, E., & Roberts, C. (1991). Changes in prevalence of depressive symptoms: Alameda County: Age, period, and cohort trends. *Journal of Aging and Health, 3*, 66–86.

Stone, R., Cafferata, G. L., & Sangl, J. (1987). Caregivers of the frail elderly: A national profile. *The Gerontologist, 27*, 616–626.

U.S. Department of Health and Human Services. (1992). *Clinical practice guideline: Urinary incontinence in adults* (AHCPR Publication No. 92-0038). Rockville, MD: Author.

U.S. Department of Health and Human Services. (1994). *Monthly Vital Statistics Report, 42*(13).

Part IV

Selected Life-Threatening and Chronic Conditions

16

Depression and Anxiety Disorders: Diagnosis and Treatment in Primary Care Practice

Charlotte Brown and Herbert C. Schulberg

Epidemiological studies administering standardized diagnostic interviews to primary care patients have reported prevalence rates of psychiatric disorders ranging from 15% to 31% (Schulberg & Burns, 1988). Depression and anxiety, the most common psychiatric disorders among primary medical care patients, are associated with functional disability rivaling or exceeding that found among chronic illnesses (Spitzer et al., 1995). Not surprisingly, they also lead to excessive health care utilization and increased medical costs (Wells et al., 1989).

Women experiencing psychiatric disorders seek help as frequently from their primary care physicians as from mental health specialists (Narrow, Regier, Rae, Manderscheid, & Locke, 1993). This trend will continue and will increase as mental health services are shifted to the general medical sector, where direct costs are one third to one half of those in specialist sectors (Sturm & Wells, 1995). Primary care physicians typically provide pharmacological treatment, and, if the quality level of these interventions are to resemble those of mental health specialists, they will need to become more skilled in diagnosing and treating psychiatric disorders. Therefore, in this chapter we focus on depression and anxiety, two of the most prevalent forms of psychiatric disorders presenting in the primary medical care sector. After describing the epidemiology of these disorders in the general medical sector, we provide principles for diagnosing and treating them in women whose comorbid medical and psychiatric conditions may confound the clinical picture.

Epidemiology of Mood Disorders

Depression is one of the most prevalent psychiatric disturbances affecting women. Epidemiological investigations have estimated point prevalence rates of 1.6–2.9% (Weissman, Bruce, Leaf, Florio, & Holzer, 1991) and 4.9% (Blazer, Kessler, McGonagle, & Swartz, 1994) in community samples. Regarding racial differences in prevalence rates, the findings are mixed.

Epidemiological studies have shown that African American people, compared with White people, have (a) lower rates of current and lifetime major depression and higher rates of minor depression among individuals of lower socioeconomic status (Weissman & Myers, 1978); (b) higher rates of current major and minor depression and lower lifetime prevalence (Vernon & Roberts, 1982); (c) no differences in lifetime or 6-month prevalence rates of major depression (Somervell, Leaf, Weissman, Blazer, & Bruce, 1989); and (d) lower rates of current or lifetime mood disorders (Kessler et al., 1994).

Major depression is at least twice as prevalent among primary care patients (6–8%) as in community samples (Katon & Schulberg, 1992). The rates in primary care practice of milder mood disorders such as dysthymia and minor depression are less well documented. Katon and Schulberg's (1992) review of studies in which structured interview schedules were administered to primary care patients indicated prevalence rates of 2.1–3.7% for dysthymia and 3.4–4.7% for minor depression. The point prevalence of mixed-anxiety depression in primary care centers was 8% (Zinbarg et al., 1994). Of particular importance here is the consistent finding that women's risk for depression exceeded that of men by 2 to 1 (Agency for Health Care Policy and Research [AHCPR] Depression Guideline Panel, 1993a). The difference held for White, Black, and Hispanic women (Russo, Amaro, & Winter, 1987; Russo & Sobel, 1981) and also when income level, education, and occupation were controlled (Ensel, 1982). Gender differences in help seeking or in the willingness of women to report symptoms of mood disorder do not adequately explain their excessive rates (Nolen-Hoeksema, 1990; Weissman & Klerman, 1985). As noted by the American Psychological Association's (APA's) National Task Force on Women and Depression (McGrath, Keita, Strickland, & Russo, 1990), gender differences have been substantiated for some mood disorder subtypes (e.g., major depression and dysthymia), but not for others (e.g., bipolar disorder).

Mood Disorders

The AHCPR clinical practice guidelines for diagnosing depression (AHCPR Depression Guideline Panel, 1993a) describe a mood disorder as a syndrome involving disturbances in emotional, cognitive, behavioral, and somatic regulation. Thus, depressive disorders should not be confused with the normal reaction to distressing life experiences (e.g., losses or disappointments that are transient and generally not associated with impaired functioning). An individual is diagnosed with major depression when at least five of the following symptoms (including either depressed mood or markedly diminished interest or pleasure in most activities) are present nearly every day for at least 2 weeks: significant weight loss or gain, insomnia or hypersomnia, psychomotor agitation or retardation, fatigue or loss of energy, feelings of worthlessness or excessive guilt, impaired concentration or indecisiveness, and recurrent thoughts of death or suicide. The symptoms cause significant distress or impairment in social, occupational, or other important areas of functioning and are not caused by the physiological effects of a drug or a general medical condition.

Dysthymia is characterized by a chronic mood disturbance (sad or depressed mood) present most of the time over a 2-year period, and at least two other concurrent symptoms of depression. The associated functional impairment, although clinically significant, is generally less severe than that associated with major depression. The essential feature of minor depression is one or more periods of depressive symptoms that are identical to major depression in duration but that involve fewer symptoms and less impairment. Thus, an episode of minor depression involves either a sad mood or loss of interest or pleasure in nearly all activities and at least two but less than four additional symptoms.

Finally, reproductive-related events such as menstruation, pregnancy, childbirth, infertility, abortion, and menopause conceivably are related to women's depression, although they do not explain gender-related differences in depression rates (Hamilton, 1984; Weissman & Klerman, 1977). For example, 50–80% of women experience mild postpartum dysphoria, or the "baby blues," which typically occurs 3–7 days after delivery and lasts from 1 to 14 days. The most severe form of postpartum illness is depression, which is now included in the fourth edition of the *Diagnostic and Statistical Manual of Mental Disorders* (*DSM–IV*; American Psychiatric Association, 1994) as a longitudinal course specifier. Postpartum depression is distinguished from the baby blues by its severity and frequency of symptoms, timing of the course of the disorder, and epidemiology. Hamilton (1988) found that prenatal depression predicts postpartum depression. Menopausal symptoms parallel those of depression and include sleep disturbance, fatigue, irritability, and other mood changes. There is some evidence that depressive symptoms may be a precursor rather than a consequence of menopausal difficulties (McKinlay, McKinlay, & Brambilla, 1987). Premenstrual dysphoric disorder, included in the *DSM–IV* Appendix as a mood disorder requiring further research, is characterized by markedly depressed mood, anxiety, and affective lability, as well as decreased interest in activities, regularly occurring during the last week of the luteal phase in most menstrual cycles during the prior year. The diagnosis is considered only when the symptoms markedly interfere with social or occupational functioning and should be distinguished from premenstrual worsening of an existing psychiatric disorder. In its review of risk factors for depression in women, the APA's National Task Force on Women and Depression (McGrath et al., 1990) recommended that clinicians improve their clinical history taking with regard to mood and behavior changes occurring simultaneously with reproductive events. Particular attention should be paid to the relationship between a history of affective disorder and a woman's responses to reproductive-related events over the life cycle.

Differential diagnosis. Although the principal features of depression are similar in psychiatric and primary care populations, depressed primary care patients may be less likely to endorse psychological distress

(Katon, 1987) in their initial complaint and tend to describe more physical symptoms, experience more pain, perceive their health as worse, and exhibit poorer physical functioning (Stewart et al., 1993) than individuals seeking care from mental health facilities. Racial differences also may be evident in symptom presentation. Brown, Schulberg, and Madonia (1996) found African American and White primary care patients similar in severity of depression. However, African American patients exhibited more severe somatic symptoms and poorer self-reported physical functioning, and perceived themselves as having less control over their health status than White patients. Gender differences in expression of symptoms also may influence the physician's clinical judgment. For example, Newmann (1986) found that women were more likely than men to report sadness even when this feeling was unrelated to the depressive syndrome. Thus, if physicians expect women to be more expressive, particularly when distressed, women who report predominantly somatic symptoms may have their mood disorder unrecognized.

The AHCPR Depression Guideline Panel (1993a) noted that many general medical conditions are risk factors for major depression. In fact, 12–16% of patients with a general medical condition have clinically diagnosable depression, and the rates may be higher for particular disorders. The psychiatric diagnosis becomes complex when *DSM–IV* symptoms of depression (e.g., weight loss, sleep disturbances, and low energy) are shared by medical disorders that include endocrinopathies such as diabetes; pituitary, adrenal, or thyroid disorders; certain malignancies; some infections; some neurological disorders; collagen disorders; cardiovascular disease; and vitamin or mineral deficiency, excess states, or both.

When comorbid with medical conditions, depression can amplify physical symptoms (Katon, 1987). For example, Carney et al. (1988) concluded that major depression in patients with coronary artery disease had an additive effect on the individual's level of disability. Major depression also has been linked with poor adherence to cardiac treatment regimens (Blumenthal, Williams, Wallace, Williams, & Needles, 1982; Guiry, Conroy, Hickey, & Mulcahy, 1987) and poor glucose regulation and increased complications in diabetic people because of poor adherence to dietary or medication regimens (AHCPR Depression Guideline Panel, 1993a). Such findings argue strongly for the diagnosis and treatment of major depression in women with these other medical conditions.

When concerned that a concurrent medical disorder is causing the somatic symptoms of depression, the clinician should particularly evaluate cognitive and mood disturbances so that alternative causes of the depressive symptoms can be ruled out. If the depressive symptoms are indeed due to a medical condition, they should be treated first. If the depression persists, however, the mood disorder should be treated independently. Various medications also have been associated with depressive symptoms. Such agents include antihypertensives, various hormones such as corticosteroids and anabolic steroids, histamine-2 receptor blockers, anticonvulsants, levodopa, antibiotics, and antiarrhythmics. If depressive symptoms develop after starting a medication, the drug should be discontinued or changed to determine whether the clinical picture is then altered.

Psychiatric comorbidity is also common among depressed primary care patients (Brown, Schulberg, Madonia, Shear, & Houck, 1996; Schulberg et al., 1995). Substance abuse disorders, eating disorders, or obsessive–compulsive disorder should be treated before the depressive disorder and may necessitate referral to a mental health specialist. However, women presenting with a personality disorder or generalized anxiety disorder (GAD) should receive depression-specific treatment first. In the case of panic disorder (PD), the physician must ascertain which symptoms are primary, or most debilitating, and treat those first.

Epidemiology of Anxiety Disorders

Before 1980, anxiety was considered a unidimensional condition. However, the third edition of the *DSM* established several specific diagnostic categories characterized by specific symptom clusters, with unique etiologies, treatments, and prognostic implications. Numerous anxiety disorders are described in the *DSM–IV*, but the two most prevalent in primary care practice are GAD and PD. As with depressive disorders, GAD and PD are more common in medical than community populations. In fact, primary care physicians rated anxiety disorders as the most common psychiatric problem in their practices (Orleans, George, & Houpt, 1985). The estimated point prevalence of GAD and PD among primary care patients, based on structured clinical interviews, ranges from 1.6% to 9.1%, and 1.4% to 6.7%, respectively (Schulberg Katon, & Shear, in press). Although women and men have similar rates of GAD, women seeking health care are 2.5–3.0 times more likely than men to receive a diagnosis of PD. Regarding racial differences in the prevalence rates of anxiety disorders, epidemiological studies of community-based samples have reported higher lifetime prevalence rates of simple phobia and agoraphobia and 12-month prevalence rates of GAD among African American people compared with White people, but similar rates of PD (Blazer, Hughes, George, Swartz, & Boyer, 1991; Eaton, Dryman, & Weissman, 1991; Horwath, Johnson, & Hornig, 1993). However, the National Comorbidity Survey indicated no differences between the two racial groups in lifetime or 12-month prevalence rates of PD, agoraphobia, simple phobia, or GAD (Kessler et al., 1994).

Medical patients with anxiety disorders also may use health care excessively. Katon et al. (1990) found that among psychologically distressed "high utilizers" of health services, 20% of their sample were assigned the diagnosis of PD and 40% the diagnosis of GAD. The Epidemiological Catchment Area (ECA) Study, which sampled community residents, showed that among people with anxiety disorders, 46% were seen by general medical practitioners (Regier et al., 1993). Fifer et al. (1994) found that in a prepaid health maintenance organization, only 44% of self-reported anxious patients had been recognized and treated for this disorder.

Comorbidity of anxiety disorders with depression is common, and this may be particularly true in primary care settings. Fifer et al. (1994) reported that 70% of patients with untreated anxiety had elevated symptoms of depression. Similarly, Schulberg et al. (1995) found that 75% of patients with a current major depression had a lifetime history of comorbid anxiety disorder. Conversely, Shear, Schulberg, and Madonia (1994) found that 80% of patients who met criteria for current PD or GAD also reported lifetime major depression.

Mixed-anxiety depression also is highly prevalent in primary care settings. A field trial of this syndrome estimated prevalence rates of 8% in primary care settings (Zinbarg et al., 1994). Individuals with this newly defined syndrome have distressing and debilitating mood and anxiety symptoms that fail to meet full diagnostic criteria for either an anxiety or a depressive disorder (Zinbarg et al., 1994). In fact, Fifer et al. (1994) found that mixed-anxiety depression was associated with more impairment than anxiety disorders alone and only slightly less impairment than comorbid anxiety and depressive disorders.

Anxiety disorders are underrecogonized in the primary care setting because clinically anxious individuals often present with physical symptoms rather than psychological distress. Bridges and Goldberg (1985) found that approximately 80% of such patients presented with a somatic symptom or complaints about a chronic physical illness. Physicians correctly diagnosed anxiety and depression in patients who described psychological distress as their presenting complaint. However, only 48% of patients with clinically significant anxiety and depression who presented with somatic complaints or complaints about their chronic medical illness were diagnosed correctly.

PD

Patients with PD frequently present to medical clinics with what they describe as a most frightening autonomic symptom such as chest pain, heart palpitations, or shortness of breath (Katon, 1989). These attacks initially occur suddenly and unexpectedly while the individual is performing everyday tasks. Within a short interval additional symptoms are experienced, such as rapid heart beat, dyspnea, dizziness, chest pain, nausea or abdominal distress, numbness or tingling of hands and feet, trembling or shaking, sweating, choking, or a feeling that they are going to die, go crazy, or do something uncontrolled. Given the overlap in anxiety symptoms and organic disorders, the primary care practitioner must consider several unique features of PD in making a differential diagnosis. The *DSM–IV* classification system requires that the individual experience recurrent, unexpected panic attacks that are characterized by intense apprehension, fear or terror, and at least four somatic symptoms. Furthermore, at least one attack must be followed by persistent concern about future attacks, worry about the attack's implications, or altered behavior.

The chronological development of PD also should be considered (Katon, 1989). Initial attacks are often associated with stressful life events that the person perceives as threatening and unavoidable. Some individuals experience one or more attacks under stress, but they recover uneventfully with education and reassurance about the nature of their attacks. Others move quickly to a second phase, in which the panic attacks become more frequent, anticipatory anxiety develops, and avoidance of events and circumstances associated with the attack occurs. Some individuals progress to a third stage marked by increasing behavioral avoidance and agoraphobia (i.e., a fear of being in places or situations from which escape might be difficult or embarrassing or help might be unavailable in the event of a panic attack). As the agoraphobia worsens, marital and family relations may suffer as the person becomes increasingly dependent, and occupational functioning may decline as work absenteeism or avoidance of certain work activities increases. Visits to physicians also increase during this stage because patients present to physicians with unexplained physical symptoms and hypochondriacal fears.

GAD

According to the *DSM–IV*, individuals with GAD are troubled for at least 6 months by uncontrollable anxiety and worry about one or more life circumstances. The worry is accompanied by at least three of the following six symptoms: restlessness or feeling keyed up or on edge, being easily fatigued, difficulty concentrating or mind going blank, irritability, muscle tension, or sleep disturbance. The anxiety, worry, or physical symptoms must cause the individual clinically significant distress or impairment in social, occupational, or other important areas of functioning. Individuals with GAD also frequently present with other major psychiatric disorders, most commonly PD, major depression, or alcohol abuse (Katon, Vitaliano, Anderson, Jones, & Russo, 1987).

Differential diagnosis. The clinician diagnosing anxiety disorders must consider the possible role of medical illnesses and medications in precipitating anxiety symptoms. Numerous medical disorders cause symptoms that resemble anxiety disorders (e.g., hyperthyroidism, cardiac arrhythmias, mitral valve prolapse [MVP], temporal lobe epilepsy). However, drug toxicity and withdrawal are by far the more common precipitants of PD. Determining whether medical conditions and medications play an etiologic role in the onset of a panic attack is important, but it also should be recognized that PD and medical illness frequently coexist. For example, individuals with medical illness had a 41% higher rate of anxiety disorders than those with no medical illness in the ECA Study (Wells, Golding, & Burnam, 1988). Primary care patients with a chronic medical illness who develop PD frequently experience intensified medical distress, possibly because of sympathetic nervous system arousal from the anxiety disorder, which can lead to physiological worsening of illnesses such as angina pectoris, peptic ulcer, or hypertension (Schulberg et al., in press). If medical conditions remain untreated, the anxiety disorder may be prolonged. Similarly, untreated anxiety disorders may prolong the course and worsen the outcome of medical illness (Shear & Schulberg, 1995).

The co-occurrence of PD and MVP is particularly well studied (Schulberg et al., in press). Although PD is no more prevalent among patients with MVP than patients with other cardiac conditions (Margraf, Ehlers, & Roth, 1988), patients with PD have a higher prevalence of MVP than control patients. However, MVP associated with PD is of questionable clinical significance because it is mild and not associated with thickened mitral valve leaflets or small ventricular size (Gorman et al., 1988). In fact, MVP may originate in the autonomic arousal thought to play a role in the development of panic attacks. The MVP does not affect the response to lactate or the response of panic patients to imipramine; in fact, MVP disappears in some individuals after adequate treatment of panic.

Elevated rates of PD are also found in patients with irritable bowel syndrome (Drossman et al., 1988) and hypertension (Katon, 1986). PD is also occasionally associated with labile hypertension and leads to medical workups for pheochromocytoma, a rare catecholamine-secreting tumor (Schulberg et al., in press). A recent study showed that 40% of those with negative laboratory tests for pheochromocytoma met PD criteria on a structured psychiatric interview compared with only 5% in a hypertensive control group receiving cholesterol workups. Only 1 of 300 laboratory workups for pheochromocytoma was positive in two large hospitals during this same time period (Fogarty, Engel, Russo, Simon, & Katon, 1994).

Diagnosing Mood and Anxiety Disorders in the Medical Setting

Clinical guidelines have been developed by the AHCPR of the U.S. Public Health Service to assist primary care practitioners in the diagnosis and treatment of mood disorders (AHCPR Depression Guideline Panel, 1993a, 1993b). Also, the American Psychiatric Association has developed the *DSM–IV–PC*, a *Diagnostic and Statistical Manual* designed specifically for primary care practitioners (Pincus et al., 1995). Casefinding and diagnostic instruments such as the Primary Care Evaluation of Mental Disorders (Spitzer et al., 1994) and the Symptom Driven Diagnostic System for Primary Care (Broadhead et al., 1995) are also available. Both consist of brief self-report patient screening questionnaires and more extended interview guides designed for use by the physician in gathering additional information about specific diagnostic areas. Once depression or anxiety has been diagnosed, the primary care practitioner can assess the patient's symptomatic status using self-report rating scales such as the Beck Depression Inventory (Beck, 1978), the Anxiety scale of the Self-Rating Scale for Depression (Zung, 1971), or the Hopkins Symptom Checklist (Derogatis, Lipman, Rickels, Uhlenhuth, & Covi, 1975).

The APA National Task Force on Women and Depression (McGrath et al., 1990) considers it essential that the assessment of depressed women not be limited to establishing symptom patterns and identifying risk factors. It is critical that the physician also view the woman's current presenting symptoms within the context of her history and prior experiences. For example, a context-relevant assessment is vital for differentiating symptoms of anxiety and depression from those indicative of acute or post-traumatic stress disorder (McGrath et al., 1990).

Treatment Strategies for Mood and Anxiety Disorders

In deciding how to treat an anxious or depressed woman, the primary care practitioner must first determine whether an active intervention is indicated. In making this decision, Schulberg and Pajer (1994) recommended consideration of the disorder's clinical severity, the degree of social and occupational impairment, the presence of medical and psychiatric comorbidity, and the likelihood of obtaining adequate treatment adherence. When an active treatment is deemed appropriate, the primary care practitioner should decide whether he or she will provide such treatment or whether referral to a mental health specialist is indicated. Although primary care physicians are likely to provide pharmacotherapy, in some instances they will choose to initiate brief counseling. Such counseling is usually generic (e.g., Stuart & Lieberman, 1993). Unlike the depression or anxiety-specific psychotherapies provided by mental health specialists, whose efficacy is well documented, the efficacy of generic counseling provided by generalists is not yet known. The choice of initial treatment is an important clinical decision, and a patient's preference should receive strong consideration by the primary care practitioner. There is, however, persisting controversy about the choice of first line treatment for major depression. The AHCPR Depression Guideline Panel (1993b) found that patients with mild-to-moderate depression who prefer psychotherapy as the initial treatment should be so treated, but pharmacotherapy was recommended for severely depressed patients. However, some clinicians question the appropriateness of AHCPR's practice guidelines that encourage primary care physicians to directly treat their depressed patients in lieu of making a referral to a mental health specialist. Munoz, Hollon, McGrath, Rehm, and VandenBos (1994) were concerned that primary care physicians lack the specific training and expertise needed to treat mental disorders. Others have criticized both the AHCPR and the American Psychiatric Association's guidelines (American Psychiatric Association, 1993) for understating the value of psychotherapy in the treatment of depression, particularly as a first line treatment for more severely depressed outpatients (Persons, Thase, & Crits-Christoph, 1996).

When psychotherapy is the chosen treatment modality, several factors may influence its effective implementation. Psychotherapy may be provided by a mental health specialist within the general health care facility or may involve referral to a specialist setting. The former can enhance continuity of care and possibly result in greater compliance with the referral. In the latter situation, however, treatment compliance is more likely to be influenced by factors such as concerns about stigma associated with mental health treatment as well as insurance deductibles, copayments, and limits on the number of allowable sessions. Thus, although specialist referral potentially improves clinical care (Balestrieri, Williams, & Wilkinson, 1988), these benefits must be balanced against the cost of losing the 20–50% of medical patients who, for various reasons, do not comply with specialist referrals (Matas, Staley, & Griffin, 1992). In light of these factors, new collaborative models that link primary care practitioners with mental health specialty treatment are critical, and such models are being developed and tested empirically (Katon et al., 1995).

Although many episodes of anxiety and depression can be treated effectively by the primary care practitioner, the AHCPR Depression Guideline Panel (1993b) recommended that mental health specialists be actively involved when (a) complexities in the management of antidepressant or anxiolytic medications are evident, such as when the individual is hypersensitive to a drug's side effects or when he or she has serious medical comorbidity; (b) the person exhibits behavioral problems associated with a personality disorder or with current substance abuse; and (c) the individual has only a partial response to the initial treatment or experiences breakthrough symptoms after a positive acute phase response.

The AHCPR Depression Guideline Panel (1993b) also recommended that all treatments (psychosocial, pharmacological, or both) be administered in the context of clinical management. This involves educating the individual (and families when appropriate) about the nature of depression, its course, and the relative benefits and costs of treatment options. Furthermore, it is important that the practitioner and patient collaborate in treatment decision making to increase treatment adherence and its effectiveness. Adherence is a significant problem in the patient's management regardless of whether he or she presents with psychiatric or medical conditions. Among depressed individuals, characteristics and factors associated with nonadherence include the presence of a personality disorder or concurrent substance abuse, lack of acceptance of the diagnosis or treatment plan, and troublesome side effects.

Numerous studies of depressed outpatients have indicated that patient education produces higher rates of treatment adherence (e.g., C. M. Anderson et al., 1986; Peet & Harvey, 1991). Thus, the AHCPR Depression Guideline Panel (1993b) recommended that patients, and their families when appropriate, be provided with the following information about depression: (a) its causes, symptoms and natural history; (b) treatment options, including indications, mechanisms of action, costs, risks, and benefits; (c) anticipated outcomes in terms of symptom relief, functional ability, and quality of life; (d) potential difficulties in complying with treatment and strategies to handle these problems; and (e) early warning signs of relapse or recurrence.

Treatment of Mood Disorders

The efficacy of psychosocial and pharmacological treatments for major depression in psychiatric populations is well documented, but their efficacy in depressed general medical patients is less clear. Nevertheless, the AHCPR Depression Guideline Panel (1993b) concluded that major depression in general medical patients can usually be treated successfully with medication, psychotherapy, or a combination of the two. Indeed, the more recent randomized controlled trials (RCTs), which have shown that psychosocial and pharmacological interventions are equally effective with general medical populations (Katon et al., 1995; Mynors-Wallace, Gath, & Lloyd-Thomas, 1995; Schulberg et al., 1996), support the panel's earlier recommendations. However, virtually no RCTs have been conducted with primary care populations to test the efficacy of interventions for the subclinical conditions of minor depression or mixed-anxiety depression. Miranda and Munoz (1994) found a cognitive–behavioral prevention course superior to no treatment for the former disorder, and Katon et al. (1995) reported that individuals with the latter disorder had good outcomes when treated with low doses of antidepressants and psychotherapy. Finally, previous research on the psychosocial or pharmacological treatment of mood disorders did not address gender differences in clinical outcomes. Therefore, the following discussion of efficacious treatments for these disorders is based on studies that included both men and women in their samples.

The treatment of major depression is now recognized as proceeding through three phases: acute, continuation, and maintenance treatment. Acute phase treatment, which lasts approximately 12 weeks, is designed to alleviate depressive symptoms and restore functioning. Continuation-phase treatment is designed to prevent symptomatic relapse once a therapeutic response has been achieved. Individuals whose symptoms have remitted require an additional 4–6 months of treatment to prevent relapse. Finally, because many patients experience recurrent episodes of depression, maintenance treatment aims at preventing new episodes. The work of Frank et al. (1990) documents the benefits of extending treatment for 3–5 years for individuals who have had at least three depressive episodes or for those who have had two episodes and have a first-degree relative with bipolar or recurrent major depression.

Psychosocial treatments. Most psychotherapies for depression have been developed and validated with psychiatric populations. In a recent review of RCTs conducted in primary care settings, Brown and Schulberg (1995) identified only seven studies in which primary care patients were diagnosed as depressed with a structured clinical interview and the efficacy of a psychosocial intervention evaluated. Despite this limited number of RCTs, the AHCPR Depression Guideline Panel (1993b) generalized from studies of psychiatric populations that cognitive, behavioral, and interpersonal psychotherapies are generally as efficacious as antidepressant medication (50–60% recovery). Furthermore, these depression-specific psychotherapies are generally more similar than different in outcomes despite their varied theoretical principles and therapeutic foci (Imber et al., 1990). However, the relative efficacy of psychotherapy or pharmacotherapy in treating severe depressions is unclear (Persons et al., 1996). Elkin et al. (1995) found that imipramine alone was superior to interpersonal psychotherapy or cognitive–behavioral therapy for psychiatric patients with Hamilton Rating Scale for Depression scores above 19, but this finding has not been replicated with primary care patients. When the general practitioner chooses psychotherapy as the sole treatment, the AHCPR Depression Guideline Panel recommended that it be time-limited and focused on current problems and symptom reduction rather than personality change; the therapist should be experienced and trained in the use of the therapy; and clinical course should be monitored and medication considered for individuals failing to show any improvement by Week 6 or nearly full remission by Week 12.

Pharmacological treatments. Meta-analyses of almost 200 studies with psychiatric outpatients and approximately 10 with primary care patients led the AHCPR Depression Guideline Panel (1993b) to conclude that all antidepressants are equally efficacious. Approximately 50–60% of individuals prescribed an antidepressant will recover with the initial drug; however, no single medication is effective for all patients. There are several classes of antidepressants: tricyclics, heterocyclics, monoamine oxidase inhibitors (MAOIs), and selective serotonin reuptake inhibitors (SSRIs). Among the tricyclics, the secondary amines (e.g., desipramine, nortriptyline) generally have fewer side effects and are as efficacious as the parent tertiary amines (e.g., imipramine, amitriptyline). The newer SSRIs are generally associated with fewer long-term side effects, such as weight gain, than the older tricylic medications.

When pharmacotherapy is the treatment of choice, selection of a specific antidepressant is based on the following: the medication's side effect profile; the patient's history of prior responses to medication; family history of a first-degree relative's responses to an antidepressant; the type of depression; comorbid medical illnesses affecting the drug's safety and toxicity; concurrent use of other medications that can alter the drug's metabolism or increase its side effects; the cost of the medication; the physician's experience with the medication; and the patient's preference. When treating women whose medical condition may be unstable, the physician may find SSRIs preferable to tricyclic or heterocyclic medication because they have a less adverse effect on the heart's conduction system. The side effects associated with antidepressant treatment can be particularly problematic among medical patients, who likely are already experiencing various physical symptoms. Although the SSRIs have a more favorable side effect profile than the tricyclic and heterocyclic antidepressants, and are thus thought to increase treatment adherence (I. Anderson & Tomenson, 1995), they are not completely devoid of side effects. The primary care physician should therefore become familiar with the medication's specific side effects (particularly central nervous system, gastrointestinal, and cardiovascular). Furthermore, because many of the drug's affective and physical side effects resemble existing symptoms of depression, these symptoms should be carefully assessed before initiating pharmacological treatment so that any changes caused by the medication may be evaluated accurately.

Finally, the prescribing of an appropriate dosage is critical to the drug's efficacy. Primary care physicians tend to err on the side of underdosing, using the rationale that medical patients are likely to respond adequately to lower doses and are less tolerant of side effects (Schulberg & Pajer, 1994). However, this practice is not supported by clinical trials, and antidepressants should be prescribed at the full dosages needed to achieve therapeutic efficacy. One exception involves medically fragile patients, who should receive only half the recommended dosage, which should be increased more slowly. The AHCPR Depression Guideline Panel, (1993b) has recommended drug-specific dosages and has developed side effect profiles for these antidepressants as a guide to primary care physicians.

Treatment of Anxiety Disorders

The presentation of complex autonomic or neurovegetative symptoms that are often concurrent with physical illness make anxiety disorders among the most difficult psychiatric disorders to treat among primary care patients. Despite the lack of consensus about basic research conventions applicable to clinical trials (Shear & Maser, 1994), efficacious cognitive, behavioral, and pharmacological treatments have been developed that are specific for each anxiety disorder. However, as with depression, these treatments have not been well studied in primary care settings, and thus their effectiveness with general medical patients is undocumented. Definitive treatment guidelines are not yet available for anxiety disorders. Finally, previous research on the treatment of anxiety disorders did not address gender differences in clinical outcomes. Therefore, the following discussion of efficacious treatments for these disorders is based on studies that included both men and women in their samples.

As with mood disorders, the treatment of anxiety disorders occurs in three phases. The goal of the acute phase is to block spontaneous panic attacks or persistent anxiety symptoms, and it generally lasts 4 months. It is important that patients be encouraged to reenter environments or participate in social situations that were previously avoided in order to reexperience the situation and realize that it no longer need be avoided because the panic attacks have gone away. This often is effective in decreasing avoidance behavior and anticipatory anxiety. Effective treatment also requires that the practitioner understand the patient's beliefs about the illness. As Katon (1989) noted, individuals with PD or GAD are often convinced that they have a cardiac or neurological disorder and that their anxiety is secondary to the physical symptoms. When informed that the diagnosis is of an anxiety disorder, the patient may feel that the practitioner does not believe the symptoms are "real." In this instance, education about biological research findings on PD and GAD may be helpful (e.g., PD results from a dysfunction of the sympathetic nervous system in which bursts of catecholamines are released into peripheral circulation and cause symptoms such as tachycardia, chest pain, and dizziness). Providing educational information about anxiety disorders may also aid the individual in recognizing that the physical symptoms of anxiety are not dangerous even though they are uncomfortable or even distressing.

Once symptoms have remitted, the continuation treatment phase of approximately 4–6 months begins. Its goal is to stabilize and maintain previously attained therapeutic gains. As with patients experiencing chronic or recurrent depression, those with recurring episodes of GAD or PD should be provided maintenance treatment.

Psychosocial treatments. The efficacy of psychosocial treatments for both PD and GAD is well documented. Clum, Clum, and Surls (1993) meta-analyzed treatment efficacy studies for PD and found that relaxation training, cognitive restructuring, and exposure produced clinical outcomes equivalent to antidepressant and benzodiazepine medications. Similarly, Durham and Allen's (1993) meta-analysis of cognitive–behavioral treatments for GAD indicated that they were superior to control conditions and comparable in efficacy to anxiolytics. However, such treatments may be optimal but not always practical because of cost or therapist availability considerations. The use of briefer treatments is particularly applicable to the primary care setting. Interventions such as Barkham's (1989) three-session cognitive–behavioral intervention, White and Keenan's (1990) large-group didactic "course" on anxiety management strategies, brief problem-solving therapy (Mynors-Wallace & Gath, 1992), or one-session psychoeducation and exposure instructions (Swinson, Soulios, Cox, & Kuch, 1992) represent innovative, brief approaches that possibly are feasibly provided to clinically anxious patients in general medical settings. Thus, the primary care practitioner is not limited to pharmacological interventions and may choose from various psychosocial treatments when preferred by the patient and therapists are available.

Pharmacologic treatments. Individuals with anxiety disorders are challenging to treat pharmacologically because of their sensitivity to minor side effects and misinterpretation of these physical symptoms as possibly health endangering or fatal. As was previously indicated with regard to an antidepressant's side effects, physicians should carefully note preexisting symptoms, discuss possible medication side effects with the patient, and assure him or her that such effects will gradually decrease. It also should be emphasized that medication is not to be discontinued without first consulting the physician. Medication should be prescribed so that symptoms of anxiety are completely eliminated, not just reduced.

The four types of medications with demonstrated efficacy in treating PD and GAD are tricyclics, SSRIs, MOAIs, and benzodiadepines (BZDs). The tricyclics are as effective as BZDs and more effective than placebo for treating both GAD and PD (e.g., Lydiard, Roy-Byrne, & Ballenger, 1988;

Rickels, Downing, Schweitzer, & Hassman, 1993). The efficacy of SSRIs in treating PD has been demonstrated in controlled trials (Christiansen et al., 1995; Den Boer & Westenberg, 1990), and the Food and Drug Administration in 1996 approved the use of paroxetine in treating this anxiety disorder. Although controlled studies are still lacking, clinical experience suggests that SSRIs also may be useful for treating GAD (Schulberg et al., in press). The MAOIs, particularly phenelzine, have been shown to be effective in treating PD (Sheehan, Ballenger, & Jacobsen, 1980). However, MAOIs are often considered second- or third-order medications for PD and GAD because of necessary dietary restrictions (patients must adhere to a low-tyramine diet), their adverse interaction with other medications such as decongestants and vasoconstrictors, and their potential for creating a hypertensive crisis. BZDs are frequently used by primary care physicians because they have a rapid onset of action, reduce both somatic and psychic symptoms, and are relatively safe from overdose. Three high-potency BZDs (alprazolam, clonazepam, and lorazepam) have demonstrated efficacy in controlling PD (Ballenger et al., 1988; Tesar & Rosenbaum, 1986). However, primary care physicians are often reluctant to prescribe BZDs because of their potential to create physical or psychological dependence and the difficulty in tapering them after long-term use at therapeutic dosages (Katon, 1994). Such problems can be minimized, however, if BZDs are not prescribed to individuals at high risk for abuse potential (i.e., those with histories of alcohol or substance abuse, chronic pain, personality disorders, and possibly family histories of substance abuse; Katon, 1989).

Conclusion

Mood and anxiety disorders are the most common psychiatric disorders among primary medical care patients and are associated with significant psychological distress, functional disability, and increased use of health services. The presence of comorbid medical and psychiatric conditions often makes the recognition and accurate diagnosis of these disorders difficult. However, a careful assessment that includes a thorough review of the symptom picture, the ruling out of alternative syndromes, and consideration of a woman's social and interpersonal context will lead to an accurate diagnosis. Several screening instruments and diagnostic tools recently have been developed to aid primary care practitioners in this process. Once anxiety or depression is diagnosed, the primary care practitioner can choose from psychosocial or pharmacological treatments, which generally have similar efficacy. Clinical management that educates the patient (and family if appropriate) about the nature and course of the disorder, treatment options, the patient's treatment preference, and the patient and clinician's expectations for symptomatic and functional improvement is a critical component of all treatment. Given the recurring and relapsing nature of both mood and anxiety disorders, treatment of either disorder should proceed through both acute and continuation phases and even maintenance treatment if indicated.

References

AHCPR Depression Guideline Panel. (1993a). *Depression in primary care: Vol. 1. Detection and diagnosis: Clinical practice guideline, No. 5* (AHCPR Publication No. 93-0550). Washington, DC: U.S. Government Printing Office.

AHCPR Depression Guideline Panel. (1993b). *Depression in primary care: Vol. 2. Treatment of major depression: Clinical practice guideline, No. 5.* (AHCPR Publication No. 93-0551). Washington, DC: U.S. Government Printing Office.

American Psychiatric Association. (1993). Practice guideline for major depressive disorder in adults. *American Journal of Psychiatry, 150*(Suppl), 1–25.

American Psychiatric Association. (1994). *Diagnostic and statistical manual of mental disorders* (4th ed.). Washington, DC: Author.

Anderson, C. M., Griffin, S., Rossi, A., Pagonis, I., Holder, D. P., & Treiber, R. (1986). A comparative study of the impact of education vs. process groups for families of patients with affective disorders. *Family Process, 25,* 185–205.

Anderson, I., & Tomenson, B. (1995). Treatment discontinuation with selective serotonin reuptake inhibitors compared with tricyclic antidepressants: A meta-analysis. *British Medical Journal, 315,* 1433–1438.

Balestrieri, M., Williams, P., & Wilkinson, G. (1988). Specialist mental health treatment in general practice: A meta-analysis. *Psychological Medicine, 18,* 711–717.

Ballenger, J., Burrows, G., DuPont, R., Lesser, I., Noyes, R., Pecknold, J., Rifkin, A., & Swinson, R. (1988). Alprazolam in panic disorder and agoraphobia: Results from a multicenter trial. *Archives of General Psychiatry, 45,* 413–422.

Barkham, M. (1989). Brief prescriptive therapy in two-plus-one sessions: Initial cases from the clinic. *Behavioural Psychotherapy, 17,* 161–175.

Beck, A. T. (1978). *Beck Depression Inventory.* (Available from the Center for Cognitive Therapy, Room 602, 133 South 36th Street, Philadelphia, PA 19104)

Blazer, D. G., Hughes, D., George, L. K., Swartz, M., & Boyer, R. (1991). *Generalized anxiety disorder.* In L. N. Robins & D. A. Regier (Eds.), *Psychiatric disorders in America: The Epidemiological Catchment Area Study* (pp. 180–203). New York: Free Press.

Blazer, D., Kessler, R., McGonagle, K., & Swartz, M. S. (1994). The prevalence and distribution of major depression in a national community sample: The National Comorbidity Survey. *American Journal of Psychiatry, 151,* 979–986.

Blumenthal, J. A., Williams, R. S., Wallace, A. G., Williams, R. B., Jr., & Needles, T. L. (1982). Physiological and psychological variables predict compliance to prescribed exercise therapy in patients recovering from myocardial infarction. *Psychosomatic Medicine, 44,* 519–527.

Bridges, K. W., & Goldberg, D. P. (1985). Somatic presentation of *DSM-III* psychiatric disorder in primary care. *Journal of Psychosomatic Research, 29,* 563–569.

Broadhead, W., Leon, A., Weissman, M., Barrett, J., Blacklow, R., Gilbert, T., Keller, M., Olfson, M., & Higgins, E. (1995). Development and validation of the SDDS-PC screen for multiple mental disorders in primary care. *Archives of Family Medicine, 4,* 211–219.

Brown, C., & Schulberg, H. C. (1995). The efficacy of psychosocial treatments in primary care: A review of randomized clinical trials. *General Hospital Psychiatry, 17,* 414–424.

Brown, C., Schulberg, H., & Madonia, M. (1996). Clinical presentations of major depression by African Americans and Whites in primary medical care practice. *Journal of Affective Disorders, 41,* 181–191.

Brown, C., Schulberg, H., Madonia, M., Shear, M. K., & Houck, P. (1996). Treatment outcomes for primary care patients with major depression and lifetime anxiety disorders. *American Journal of Psychiatry, 153,* 1293–1300.

Carney, R. M., Rich, M. W., Freedland, K. E., Saini J., teVelde, A., Simeone, C., & Clark, K. (1988). Major depressive disorder predicts cardiac events in patients with coronary artery disease. *Psychosomatic Medicine, 50,* 627–633.

Christiansen, P., Behnke, K., Ocherberg, S., Borup, A., Severin, B., Soegaard, J., Calberg, H., Judge, R., Ohrstrom, J., & Manniche, P. (1995). Paxoretine in the treatment of panic disorder: A randomized double blind, placebo controlled trial. *British Journal of Psychiatry, 167,* 374–379.

Clum, G., Clum, G., & Surls, R. (1993). A meta-analysis of treatment for panic disorder. *Journal of Consulting and Clinical Psychology, 61,* 317–326.

Den Boer, J., & Westenberg, H. (1990). Serotonin function in panic disorder: A double blind placebo controlled study with fluvoxamine and ritanserin. *Psychopharmacology, 102,* 85–94.

Derogatis, L., Lipman, R., Rickels, K. Uhlenhuth, H., & Covi, L. (1975). The Hopkins Symptom Checklist (HSCL): A self-report symptom inventory. *Behavioral Science, 19,* 1–15.

Drossman, D. A., McKee, D. C., Sandler, R. S., Mitchell, C. M., Cramer, E. M., Lowman, B. C., & Berger, A. L. (1988). Psychosocial factors in the irritable bowel syndrome: A multivariate study of patients and nonpatients with irritable bowel syndrome. *Gastroenterology, 95,* 701–708.

Durham, R., & Allen, T. (1993). Psychological treatment of generalized anxiety disorder. *British Journal of Psychiatry, 163,* 19–26.

Eaton, W. W., Dryman, A., & Weissman, M. M. (1991). *Panic and phobia.* In L. N. Robins & D. A. Regier (Eds.), *Psychiatric disorders in America: The Epidemiologic Catchment Area Study* (pp. 155–179). New York: Free Press.

Elkin, I., Gibbons, R., Shea, M., Sotsky, S., Watkins, J., Pilkonis, P., & Hedeker, D. (1995). Initial severity and differential treatment outcome in the National Institute of Mental Health Treatment of Depression Collaborative Research Program. *Journal of Consulting and Clinical Psychology, 63,* 841–847.

Ensel, W. M. (1982). The role of age and the relationship of gender and marital status to depression. *Journal of Nervous and Mental Disease, 170,* 536–543.

Fifer, S. K., Mathias, S. D., Patrick, D. L., Mazonson, P. D., Lubeck, D. P., & Buesching, D. P. (1994). Untreated anxiety among adult primary care patients in a health maintenance organization. *Archives of General Psychiatry, 51,* 740–750.

Fogarty, J., Engel, C., Russo, J., Simon, G., & Katon, W. (1994). Hypertension and pheochromocytoma testing: The association with anxiety disorders. *Archives of Family Medicine, 3,* 55–60.

Frank, E., Kupfer, D., Perel, J., Cornes, C., Jarrett, D. B., Mallinger, A. G., Thase, M. E., McEachran, A. B., & Grochocinski, V. J. (1990). Three-year outcomes for maintenance therapies in recurrent depression. *Archives of General Psychiatry, 47,* 1093–1099.

Gorman, J., Goetz, R., Fyer, M., King, D., Fyer, A., Liebowitz, M., & Klein, D. (1988). The mitral valve prolapse-panic disorder connection. *Psychosomatic Medicine, 10,* 114–122.

Guiry, E., Conroy, R. M., Hickey, N., & Mulcahy, R. (1987). Psychological response to an acute coronary event and its effect on subsequent rehabilitation and lifestyle change. *Clinical Cardiology, 10,* 256–260.

Hamilton, J. A. (1984). Psychobiology in context: Reproductive-related events in men's and women's lives (review of motherhood and mental illness). *Contemporary Psychiatry, 3,* 12–16.

Hamilton, J. A. (Ed.). (1988). *Report from the Committee on Etiology and Diagnosis, Task Force on Women and Depression.* Washington, DC: American Psychological Association.

Horwath, E., Johnson, J., & Hornig, C. D. (1993). Epidemiology of panic disorder in African-Americans. *American Journal of Psychiatry, 150,* 465–469.

Imber, S., Pilkonis, P., Sotsky, S., Elkin, I., Watkins, J., Collins, J., Shea, M., Leber, W., & Glass, D. (1990). Mode-specific effects among three treatments for depression. *Journal of Consulting and Clinical Psychology, 58,* 352–359.

Katon, W. (1986). Panic disorder: Epidemiology, diagnosis, and treatment in primary care. *Journal of Clinical Psychiatry, 47*(Suppl. 10), 21–27.

Katon, W. (1987). The epidemiology of depression in medical care. *International Journal of Psychiatry in Medicine, 17,* 93–112.

Katon, W. (1989). *Panic disorder in the medical setting.* (DHHS Publication No. ADM 89-1629). Washington, DC: U.S. Govt. Printing Office.

Katon, W. (1994). Primary care-psychiatry panic disorder management module. In B. Wolfe & J. Maser (Eds.), *Treatment of panic disorder* (pp. 41–56). Washington DC: American Psychiatric Press.

Katon, W., & Schulberg, H. (1992). Epidemiology of depression in primary care. *General Hospital Psychiatry, 14,* 237–247.

Katon, W., Vitaliano, P. P., Anderson, K., Jones, M., & Russo, J. (1987). Panic disorder: Residual symptoms after the acute attacks abate. *Comprehensive Psychiatry, 28,* 151–158.

Katon, W., Von Korff, M., Lin E., Walker, E., Simon, G., Bush, T., Robinson, P., & Russo, J. (1995). Collaborative management to achieve treatment guidelines. *Journal of the American Medical Association, 273,* 1026–1031.

Katon, W., Von Korff, M., Lin E., Walker, E., Simon, G., Robinson, P., Bush, T., & Irvin, S. (1990). Distressed high utilizers of medical care. *General Hospital Psychiatry, 12,* 355–362.

Kessler, R. C., McGonagle, K. A., Zhao, S., Nelson, C. B., Hughes, M., Eshleman, S., Wittchen, H.-U., & Kendler, K. S. (1994). Lifetime and 12-month prevalence of *DSM-III-R* psychiatric disorders in the United States: Results from the National Comorbidity Survey. *Archives of General Psychiatry, 51,* 8–19.

Lydiard, R., Roy-Byrne, P., & Ballenger, J. (1988). Recent advances in the psychopharmacological treatment of anxiety disorders. *Hospital and Community Psychiatry, 39,* 1157–1165.

Margraf, J., Ehlers, A., & Roth, W. T. (1988). Mitral valve prolapse and panic disorder: A review of the relationship. *Psychosomatic Medicine, 50,* 93–113.

Matas, M., Staley, D., & Griffin, W. (1992). A profile of the noncompliant patient: A thirty-month review of outpatient psychiatry referrals. *General Hospital Psychiatry, 14,* 124–130.

McGrath, E., Keita, G. P., Strickland, B. R., & Russo, N. F. (Eds.). (1990). *Women and depression: Risk factors and treatment issues.* Washington, DC: American Psychological Association.

McKinlay, J. B., McKinlay, S. M., & Brambilla, D. J. (1987). Health status and utilization behavior associated with menopause. *American Journal of Epidemiology, 125,* 110–121.

Miranda, J., & Munoz, R. (1994). Intervention for minor depression in primary care patients. *Psychosomatic Medicine, 56,* 136–142.

Munoz, R. F., Hollon, S. D., McGrath, E., Rehm, L. P., & VandenBos, G. R. (1994). On the AHCPR depression in primary care guidelines: Further considerations for practitioners. *American Psychologist, 49,* 42–61.

Mynors-Wallace, L. M., & Gath, D. H. (1992). Brief psychological treatments. *International Review of Psychiatry, 4,* 301–305.

Mynors-Wallace, L. M., Gath, D. H., & Lloyd-Thomas, A. R. (1995). Randomised controlled trial comparing problem-solving treatment with amitriptyline and placebo for major depression in primary care. *British Medical Journal, 310,* 441–445.

Narrow, W., Regier, D., Rae, D., Manderscheid, R. W., & Locke, B. Z. (1993). Use of services by persons with mental and addictive disorders. *Archives of General Psychiatry, 50,* 95–107.

Newmann, J. P. (1986). Gender, life strains, and depression. *Journal of Health and Social Behavior, 27,* 161–178.

Nolen-Hoeksema, S. (1990). *Sex differences in depression.* Stanford, CA: Stanford University Press.

Orleans, C., George L., & Houpt, J. (1985). How primary physicians treat psychiatric disorders: A national survey of family practitioners. *Archives of General Psychiatry, 42,* 52–57.

Peet, M., & Harvey, N. S. (1991). Lithium maintenance: 1. A standard education programme for patients. *British Journal of Psychiatry, 158,* 197–200.

Persons, J. B., Thase, M. E., & Crits-Christoph, P. (1996). The role of psychotherapy in the treatment of depression: Review of two practice guidelines. *Archives of General Psychology, 53,* 283–290.

Pincus, H., Vettorello, N., McQueen, L., First, M., Wise, T. N., Zarin, D., & Davis, W. W. (1995). Bridging the gap between psychiatry and primary care: The *DSM-IV-PC. Psychosomatics, 36,* 328–335.

Regier, D. A., Narrow, W. E., Rae, D. S., Manderscheid, R. W., Locke, B. Z., & Goodwin, F. K. (1993). The de facto U.S. mental and addictive disorders service system. *Archives of General Psychiatry, 50,* 85–94.

Rickels, K., Downing, R., Schweitzer, E., & Hassman, H. (1993). Antidepressants for the treatment of generalized anxiety disorder. *Archives of General Psychiatry, 50,* 884–895.

Russo, N. F., Amaro, H., & Winter, M. (1987). The use of inpatient mental health services by Hispanic women. *Psychology of Women Quarterly, 11,* 427–442.

Russo, N. F., & Sobel, S. B. (1981). Sex differences in the utilization of mental health facilities. *Professional Psychology, 12,* 7–19.

Schulberg, H. C., Block, M. R., Madonia, M. J., Scott, C. P., Rodriguez, R., Imber, S. D., Perel, J., Lave, J., & Coulehan, J. (1996). Treating major depression in primary care practice: Eight-month clinical outcomes. *Archives of General Psychiatry, 53,* 913–919.

Schulberg, H. C., & Burns, B. (1988). Mental disorders in primary care: Epidemiologic, diagnostic, and treatment research directions. *General Hospital Psychiatry, 10,* 79–87.

Schulberg, H. C., Katon, W., & Shear, M. K. (in press). The management of mood and anxiety disorders in primary care practice. In A. J. Rush (Ed.), *Current review of mood disorders.* Philadelphia: Current Medicine.

Schulberg, H., Madonia, M., Block, M., Coulehan, J. L., Scott, C. P., Rodriquez, E., & Black, A. (1995). Major depression in primary care practice: Clinical characteristics and treatment implications. *Psychosomatics, 36,* 129–137.

Schulberg, H. C., & Pajer, K. (1994). Treatment of depression in primary care. In J. Miranda, A. Hohmannn, C. Attkisson, & D. Larson (Eds.), *Mental disorders in primary care* (pp. 259–286). San Francisco: Jossey-Bass.

Shear, K. M., & Maser, J. (1994). Standardized assessment for panic disorder research: A conference report. *Archives of General Psychiatry, 51,* 346–354.

Shear, M. K., & Schulberg, H. C. (1995). Anxiety disorders in primary care. *Bulletin of the Menninger Clinic, 59*(Suppl. A), A73–A84.

Shear, M. K., Schulberg, H. C., & Madonia, M. (1994, September). *Panic and generalized anxiety disorder in primary care.* Paper presented at the National Institute of Mental Health International Research Conference On Mental Disorders in the General Health Care Sector, McLean, VA.

Sheehan, D., Ballenger, J., & Jacobsen, G. (1980). Treatment of endogenous anxiety with phobic, hysterical, and hypochondriacal symptoms. *Archives of General Psychiatry, 37,* 51–59.

Somervell, P. D., Leaf, P. J., Weissman, M. M., Blazer, D. G., & Bruce, M. L. (1989). The prevalence of major depression in Black and White adults in five United States communities. *American Journal of Epidemiology, 130,* 725–735.

Spitzer, R., Kroenke, K., Linzer, M., Hahn, S., Williams, J., deGruy, F., Brody, D., & Davies, M. (1995). Health-related quality of life in primary care patients with mental disorders. *Journal of the American Medical Association, 274,* 1511–1517.

Spitzer, R., Williams, J., Kroenke, K., Linzer, M., deGruy, F. V., Hahn, S. R., Brody, D., & Johnson, J. G. (1994). Utility of a new procedure for diagnosing mental disorders in primary care: The PRIME-MD 1000 study. *Journal of the American Medical Association, 272,* 1749–1756.

Stewart, A., Sherbourne, C., Wells, K., Burnam, A., Rogers, W., Hays, R., & Ware, J. (1993). Do depressed patients in different treatment settings have different levels of well-being and functioning? *Journal of Consulting and Clinical Psychology, 61,* 849–857.

Stuart, M. R., & Lieberman, J. A. (1993). *The fifteen minute hour: Applied psychotherapy for the primary care physician* (4th ed.). Westport, CT: Praeger.

Sturm, R., & Wells, K. (1995). How can care for depression become more cost-effective? *Journal of the American Medical Association, 273,* 51–58.

Swinson, R. P., Soulios, C., Cox, B. J., & Kuch, K. (1992). Brief treatment of emergency room patients with panic attacks. *American Journal of Psychiatry, 149*, 944–946.

Tesar, G., & Rosenbaum, J. (1986). Successful use of clorazepam in patients with treatment resistant panic disorder. *Journal of Nervous and Mental Disease, 174*, 477–482.

Vernon, S. W., & Roberts, R. E. (1982). Use of the SADS-RDC in a tri-ethnic community survey. *Archives of General Psychiatry, 39*, 47–52.

Weissman, M., Bruce, M., Leaf, P., Florio, L., & Holzer, C. (1991). Affective disorders. In L. Robins & D. Regier (Eds.), *Psychiatric disorders in America* (pp. 53–80). New York: Free Press.

Weissman, M. M., & Klerman, G. L. (1977). Gender and depression. *Trends in Neurosciences, 8*, 416–420.

Weissman, M. M., & Klerman, G. L. (1985). Sex differences in the epidemiology of depression. *Archives of General Psychiatry, 34*, 98–111.

Weissman, M. M., & Myers, J. K. (1978). Affective disorders in a U.S. urban community. *Archives of General Psychiatry, 35*, 1304–1311.

Wells, K., Golding, J., & Burnam, M. (1988). Psychiatric disorder in a sample of the general population with and without chronic medical conditions. *American Journal of Psychiatry, 145*, 176–181.

Wells, K. B., Stewart, A., Hays, R. D., Burnam, A., Rogers, W., Daniels, M., Berry, S., Greenfield, S., & Ware, J. (1989). The functioning and well-being of depressed patients: Results from the Medical Outcomes Study. *Journal of the American Medical Association, 262*, 914–919.

White, J., & Keenan, M. (1990). Stress control: A pilot study of large group therapy for generalized anxiety disorder. *Behavioural Psychotherapy, 18*, 143–146.

Zinbarg, R., Barlow, D., Liebowitz, M., Street, L., Broadhead, E., Katon, W., Roy-Byrne, L., Lepine, J.-P., Teherani, M., Richards, J., Brantley, P. J., & Kraemer, H. (1994). The *DSM-IV* field trial for mixed anxiety-depression. *American Journal of Psychiatry, 151*, 1153–1162.

Zung, W. (1971). A rating instrument for anxiety disorders. *Psychosomatics, 12*, 371–379.

17

The Influence of Behavioral and Psychosocial Factors on Cardiovascular Health in Women

Sarah S. Knox and Susan Czajkowski

Despite a steadily declining rate of cardiovascular disease (CVD) mortality in the United States, heart disease is still the Number 1 cause of death in American women, killing more women than all malignant neoplasms combined (Kochanek & Hudson, 1994). Women also have a worse prognosis for survival after myocardial infarction (MI) than men (Bell et al., 1993; Fiebach, Viscoli, & Horwitz, 1990; Greenland, Reicher-Reiss, Goldbourt, Behar, & the Israeli SPRINT Investigators, 1991). This can be explained partially by a worse risk factor profile in women at the time of first infarction (Cannistra, Balady, O'Malley, Weiner, & Ryan, 1992; Fiebach et al., 1990). However, the worst prognosis is in Black women (Tofler et al., 1987), the reasons for which are still unclear. There are also different referral patterns in men and women with regard to coronary artery disease (CAD) treatment (Ayanian & Epstein, 1991; Steingart et al., 1991), but the extent to which these differences actually represent treatment biases or appropriate responses to different needs in women is still being debated (Bickell et al., 1992; Laskey, 1992).

CVDs, such as heart disease and cerebrovascular disease, develop progressively over many years through complex interactions of genetic, biological and environmental factors. In its early stages, CVD is usually covert (e.g., atherosclerotic plaque cannot be detected by usual diagnostic tests, and hypertension, which is not associated with standard overt symptoms, can go undiagnosed for years if blood pressure is not measured). For this reason, it is important to track risk factors, such as plasma or serum lipid concentrations, adiposity, blood pressure, and diabetes, which are known to be associated with increased risk. In this respect, behavioral and psychosocial factors also play a crucial role. It is well known that genetic predisposition contributes to many components of cardiovascular health, explaining a significant amount of the variance in major CVD risk factors such as high blood lipids, hypertension, obesity, and diabetes. However, the interaction of these predispositions with the environment determines the extent to which they are expressed. Behavioral and psychosocial factors are important triggers in the gene–environment interaction and may

be critical in prolonging life when fully addressed in primary and secondary prevention. This chapter will review the mechanisms through which
psychosocial, behavioral, and socioeconomic factors function to promote
cardiovascular health, slow disease progression, and enhance treatment
outcomes. Its goal is to provide a practical guide in promoting cardiovascular health at different stages of the life span.

Etiology and Prevention

A healthy lifestyle and feelings of psychological well-being can contribute
greatly to the enhancement of cardiovascular health. Both our general
state of well-being and the lifestyle we choose to adopt are influenced by
our psychosocial environment. Chronic stressors, social contacts, and coping mechanisms are examples of factors that affect both lifestyle and psychological well-being. The two primary pathways through which psychosocial factors can influence the cardiovascular system involve health
behaviors and neuroendocrine mechanisms. Health behaviors such as diet,
smoking, alcohol consumption, and physical activity are extremely important factors in cardiovascular health that can prevent or promote the onset
of disease. However, chronic psychological strain and its opposite, psychological well-being, can also have effects on cardiovascular physiology
through changes that occur in the brain and are transmitted through the
vagal, sympathetic, and hormonal systems to the rest of the body. Due to
the need for brevity in this chapter, the reader is referred to other chapters
for reviews of the importance of health behaviors. This chapter will focus
on the neuroendocrine pathways in primary prevention and treatment
strategies in secondary prevention.

Psychosocial Factors and Neuroendocrine Pathways

Psychosocial factors influence health behaviors, which interact with ath-
erogenic and hemostatic metabolic processes, and, coupled with genetic
predisposition, can promote or reduce the progression of CVD. Psychosocial factors can also influence the cardiovascular system through neuroendocrine effects triggered by positive or negative emotions. Emotions influence cardiovascular risk through processes initiated in the neurochemical
substrate of emotion located in the limbic system, the components of which
are closely interconnected through neurotransmitter systems, and communicate with the rest of the body through vagal, sympathetic–adrenal–
medullary, and hypothalamic–adrenal–cortical pathways. These pathways can be influenced both positively, through regenerative processes
that strengthen and buffer the system against stress, and negatively,
through pathological processes that weaken it and increase risk. The influence of psychosocial factors and neuroendocrine processes most relevant
to the etiology and prevention of cardiovascular disease are described in
the following sections.

Social isolation and social support. Social isolation, which is variously defined as lacking an intimate confidant, having few friends or social activities, or not having access to practical assistance when needed in everyday situations, has been associated with cardiovascular mortality in several epidemiological studies (Berkman & Syme, 1979; House, Robbins, & Metzner, 1982; Orth-Gomer, Rosengren, & Wilhelmsen, 1993; Schoenbach, Kaplan, & Fredman, 1986) and in studies of CAD and post-MI patients (Berkman, Leo-Summers, & Horowitz, 1992; Blumenthal et al., 1987; Case, Moss, Case, McDermott, & Eberly, 1992; Ruberman, Weinblatt, Goldberg, & Chaudhary, 1984; Seeman & Syme, 1987; Williams et al., 1992). In addition, social isolation has been associated with higher blood pressure (Bland, Krogh, Winkelstein, & Trevisan, 1991), a major risk factor for coronary end points. Social support, in conjunction with adaptive coping strategies, has also predicted fewer depressive symptoms after an MI (Holahan, Moos, Holahan, & Brennan, 1995). Although some of the earlier reports indicated a more pronounced effect in men than in women, there is now substantial evidence for the negative effects of social isolation on cardiovascular outcome in women. Some of the earlier inconsistencies may have been due partially to inadequate power for detecting results in women (Seeman & Syme, 1987).

One obvious way in which social support can contribute to cardiovascular health is by providing instrumental assistance. Having a spouse who helps with adherence to a proper diet, accompanies her on walks to improve fitness, or, in the case of patients' recovery from an MI, drives her to doctors' appointments, promotes adherence to a healthy lifestyle. Support can also help in the promotion of good health behaviors, such as smoking cessation (Hanson, Isacsson, Janzon, & Lindell, 1990).

There is also evidence that emotional aspects of social support can influence cardiovascular physiology. Social isolation has been reported in association with resting levels of elevated blood pressure (Knox, 1993) and with correlates of elevated blood pressure such as heart rate and resting plasma adrenalin levels (Knox, Theorell, Svensson, & Waller, 1985). Both of those studies were conducted with men, and the strength of the relationships has yet to be verified in women. However, two studies done only on women reported that social affiliation was associated with attenuated blood pressure response to acute (laboratory) challenge (Gerin, Milner, Chawla, & Pickering, 1995; Kamarck, Annunziato, & Amateau, 1995).

It would seem that social support and social isolation influence the cardiovascular system through multiple mechanisms. The first involves improving compliance with treatment and supporting good health behaviors. The second is hypothesized to occur as a result of neurophysiological changes (i.e., through the limbic system in conjunction with hypothalamic, sympathetic–adrenal–medullary, and possibly vagal pathways) accompanying positive and negative emotional states. Since there is now overwhelming evidence of a relationship between social isolation and CVD, it is important that health care providers emphasize the importance of social networks and that methods for helping people enhance them be integrated into primary and secondary prevention programs.

Hostility. Much has been published concerning Type A behavior, anger coping styles, and hostility as they relate to CVD. The findings concerning Type A behavior have been contradictory (Langeluddecke, Fulcher, Jones, & Tennant, 1988; Shekelle et al., 1985; Silver, Jenkins, Ryan, & Melidossian, 1980; Williams et al., 1988), and the majority of the researchers in this field now believe that hostility is more important. Results of two prospective studies using the Cook-Medley Hostility Scale have shown an association between hostility and increased incidence of coronary heart disease (CHD) after 20 and 25 years of follow-up, respectively (Barefoot, Dahlstrom, & Williams, 1983; Shekelle, Gale, Ostfeld, & Paul, 1983). Also, the negative effects of hostility seem to be mediated through health behaviors as well as neuroendocrine pathways.

Effects of hostility on health behaviors have been demonstrated in the findings that high hostility has been associated with higher caffeine consumption (Siegler, Peterson, Barefoot, & Williams, 1992); more smoking (Scherwitz et al., 1992; Siegler et al., 1992); more marijuana use, increased alcohol intake, and greater caloric intake (Scherwitz et al., 1992); and higher cholesterol consumption and (only in women) higher animal fat intake and lower fiber intake (Musante, Treiber, Davis, Strong, & Levy, 1992).

Neuroendocrine pathways mediating hostility are exemplified in the associations between two commonly used measures of hostility and blood pressure reactivity to provocative laboratory stressors (Suls & Wan, 1993), as well as between hostility and decreased levels of prolactin and increases in epinephrine, norepinephrine, adrenocorticotropin hormone, and growth hormone (but not cortisol) in otherwise healthy people (Malarkey, Kiecolt-Glaser, Pearl, & Glaser, 1994).

In conclusion, hostile personality characteristics can negatively affect cardiovascular health through multiple paths. Behavioral treatment to reduce hostility has been developed (Williams, 1989) and should be seriously considered in cardiac rehabilitation programs for use with people measuring high on this trait. Health care practitioners should be aware of the effects of hostility on preventive health behaviors and integrate this awareness into treatment strategies.

Depression. Recently, depression has been identified as a possible risk factor for CHD mortality. In a meta-analysis, Booth-Kewley and Friedman (1987) found that depression was strongly and significantly associated with CHD for both men and women. In several case-control and retrospective studies, depression and other negative affects have been related to both all-cause mortality (Murphy et al., 1987) and sudden cardiac death (Binik, 1985; Cottington et al., 1980; Kamarck & Jennings, 1991; Talbott, Kuller, Detre, & Perper, 1977; Talbott, Kuller, Perper, & Murphy, 1981) in women. In addition, a large-scale prospective study of 795 initially healthy women found that the severity of depression predicted angina pectoris, but not MI or CHD death, at 12-year follow-up (Haellstrom, Lapidus, Bengtsson, & Edstrom, 1986).

Studies have also shown women to be more depressed than men after an MI (Carney, Freedland, & Jaffe, 1990; Schleifer et al., 1989), and several studies have linked depression with cardiac mortality after an MI in men and women (Ahern et al., 1990; Falgar & Appels, 1982; Schleifer et al., 1989; Stern, Pascale, & Ackerman, 1977). Thus, evidence is accumulating that depression increases the risk of cardiac events and death for women as well as men. The implication of this research is that patients with pronounced depressive symptoms should be referred for psychological evaluation and possible treatment.

Socioeconomic status and racial differences in cardiovascular risk. A consistent pattern of inverse associations between CHD and socioeconomic status (SES) has been established cross-culturally (Ferrario & Cesana, 1993; Luepker et al., 1993; Marmot, Rose, Shipley, & Hamilton, 1978; Theorell, Svensson, Knox, & Ahlborg, 1982; Woodward, Shewry, Smith, & Tunstall-Pedoe, 1992). People with low SES not only have higher mortality (Hypertension Detection and Follow-Up Program Cooperative Group, 1987) but are also less likely to survive out-of-hospital cardiac arrest (Hallstrom, Boutin, Cobb, & Johnson, 1993) and have a worse prognosis among medically treated patients with CAD (Williams et al., 1992). Even the decline in CHD mortality is greatest in higher SES areas (Wing, Barnett, Casper, & Tyroler, 1992).

Within the United States, improvement in life expectancy and rates of illness and death from CHD has not been as great for Blacks as for Whites (National Heart, Lung and Blood Institute [NHLBI], 1994a). The report of the Secretary's Task Force on Black and Minority Health (Heckler, 1985) suggests that "it is not minority status, itself, which leads to poorer health. . . . Rather, it is the association of low SES with minority group membership which has consequences for health." The social class differences in mortality for heart disease are larger than those for race (Navarro, 1990). When income is used as the definition of SES, Blacks are reported to have higher mortality at each level than Whites (Sorlie, Rogot, Anderson, Johnson, & Backlund, 1992); however, when education is used to define SES, racial differences are no longer significant (Keil, Sutherland, Knapp, & Tyroler, 1992). In the United States, the prevalence of hypertension is greater among Blacks than Whites at all ages (Burt et al., 1995; NHLBI, 1994b). However, the prevalence of hypertension in Blacks in sub-Saharan Africa is substantially lower than that of Black Americans (Kaufman, Owoaje, James, Rotimi, & Cooper, 1996). Although research has made it clear that there is a genetic component to hypertension and that hypertension and CHD aggregate in families of African American people (Rotimi, Cooper, Sundarum, & McGee, 1994), the discrepancy between American and African Black people indicates that a genetic explanation is inadequate and that nongenetic (e.g., environmental) factors may play an important role. An overwhelming majority of Black Americans belong to a poorly educated working class with low pay (Navarro, 1990).

In the search for mechanisms to explain the association between low

SES and heart disease, one obvious candidate is health behavior. Education is the most frequently used measure of SES, and it is assumed that higher education increases knowledge about the consequences of proper diet, the hazards of smoking, insufficient exercise, and so on. This has been substantiated by research on SES (see chapter 2 in this book).

Health behavior is not the only aspect of SES that influences morbidity and mortality outcomes. Access to adequate health care also is important. Lack of health care coverage, not surprisingly, is associated with low income (Ries, 1991). In people who are not covered by health insurance, preventive care such as regular physical checkups are less likely to occur. People with low SES also have a greater risk for suffering medical injury due to substandard medical care (Burstin, Lipsitz, & Brennan, 1992). However, the socioeconomic gradient for health exists even in countries where everyone has access to good health care, such as Norway (Holme, Helgeland, Hjermann, Leren, & Lund-Larsen, 1977) and Finland (Nayha, 1977). So this, too, is only a partial explanation. Low SES is also characterized by jobs that have low decision latitude and are highly demanding (Theorell et al., 1984), such as factory and clerical work. Social inequality for people at the lower end of the socioeconomic gradient involves the simultaneous presence of multiple chronic stressors. These include less social support, as defined by stability of the family, size of network, and diversity of relations or closeness of marital bonds (Siegrist, Siegrist, & Weber, 1986), as well as more unemployment, dilapidated housing units, and housing units with a shared bathroom or no bathroom (Haan, Kaplan, & Camacho, 1987). In a recent review, Adler et al. (1994) concluded that low-SES people are more likely to experience stress and to have stressful life events beyond their control than those higher on the gradient. These negative psychosocial stressors are hypothesized to influence CHD end points through neuroendocrine influences on endothelial injury and platelet function (Ruberman, 1992).

In conclusion, low SES affects cardiac end points through multiple mechanisms: health behaviors, access to adequate health care, and psychosocial stress. Differences in CHD mortality are higher for social class than they are for race. A majority of Blacks in the United States are clustered at the lower end of the socioeconomic gradient, and thus associations between race and CHD mortality are inextricably intertwined with SES. This is illustrated in the study by Haan et al. (1987), who found a significant association between race and mortality. When "poverty area residence" was added to the equation, the association was reduced by 26%. For the health care professional, it is helpful to know that educational efforts in the Stanford Five-City Project (Winkleby, Fortmann, & Rockhill, 1992) did show declines in smoking prevalence and levels of blood pressure and cholesterol and demonstrated that people from all educational levels can modify their risk for CVD. However, awareness on the part of the treating physician of the potent stress associated with low SES may help in structuring interventions to meet the needs of individual patients.

Detection, Treatment, and Recovery

CVD is not only the leading cause of death, but an important cause of hospitalization, disability, and reduced quality of life for women. Two and one-half million women will be hospitalized this year in the United States for cardiovascular disorders (Wenger, Speroff, & Packard, 1993). Most women survive an acute CVD event but face physical, emotional, and social challenges as they learn to live with heart disease.

Evidence shows that women who develop CHD fare less well than men (Wenger, 1993). Several studies have documented a higher rate of mortality for women than men following an MI (Greenland et al., 1991; Tofler et al., 1987), and women report poorer health and more days of reduced activity after an MI than do men (Conn, Taylor, & Abele, 1991). Women also have a higher operative mortality during coronary artery bypass graft (CABG) surgery than men; report less improvement in symptoms, mainly angina; and have lower rates of graft patency than men after a CABG (Khan, 1991; Khan et al., 1990).

The poorer prognosis of women following CHD events and procedures may be due to the fact that, on average, women develop heart disease 10 years later than men. Because women are older than men when diagnosed with CHD, they are more likely to have other chronic diseases that can complicate their recovery (Eysmann & Douglas, 1993). However, the poorer medical and risk factor profiles of female CHD patients may not be the only contributors to women's poorer outcomes. Other factors, including the way in which CHD is detected and treated in women, and the poorer psychosocial functioning of female CHD patients relative to men, have been cited as important predictors of recovery in women with CHD.

Detection and Treatment of CHD in Women

Concerns have been raised that women with CHD are managed less aggressively, that is, they are referred for CABG and other invasive procedures later in the course of their disease than men. Women are referred less frequently for angiography, percutaneous transluminal coronary angioplasty, and CABG surgery following hospitalization for MI and angina, even after controlling for age and disease severity (Ayanian & Epstein, 1991; Steingart et al., 1991). It is not clear from the data whether these procedures are underutilized in women or overutilized in men. However, at least one group of authors has speculated that this less aggressive management and later referral may increase women's chances of operative death during CABG (Khan et al., 1990).

The reasons for these gender differences in the management of CHD are unknown. However, evidence suggests that the perception of cardiac symptoms by women and their physicians has a significant impact on diagnostic and treatment strategies. For example, women with coronary disease who experience chest pain may not seek care as frequently as men, and women with severe chest pain wait longer than men before seeking emergency care (Moser & Dracup, 1994). Physicians may refer women less often for invasive interventions because of beliefs about the relative ineffectiveness of some procedures in women; because they believe some diagnostic procedures (e.g., electrocardiography) are less reliable in women than men; or because women's symptoms are not interpreted by physicians as cardiac symptoms as early in the disease process as in men. Regarding the latter hypothesis, results of one study showed that physicians were less likely to refer women for certain medical procedures than men, even when the women presented with the same symptoms as men (McKinlay, Crawford, McKinlay, & Sellers, 1994).

More studies are needed to determine the extent to which psychosocial factors (e.g., misinterpretation of symptoms and delayed care seeking in women, physician beliefs and attitudes about heart disease in women) play a role in the clinical management, and ultimately the poorer prognosis, of women following CHD events and treatments. These studies should include research on the decision-making process used by women in seeking care and by their physicians in ordering diagnostic tests and referring women for invasive procedures.

Given the benefits derived from appropriate identification and treatment, early detection of CHD should become a priority for women and their health care providers. Unfortunately, women are often unaware of the threat posed by CHD to their lives and health. One study found that when asked to identify the most serious health problem faced by women, 76% of the women surveyed said cancer, whereas only 6% identified diseases of the heart, blood vessels, diabetes, and arthritis (Frank & Taylor, 1993). Since CVD is by far the leading cause of death in women, these results reveal a lack of concern on the part of women about the real risks imposed by CVD. This lack of awareness of how common CVD is in women may contribute to a lack of recognition of its symptoms and the failure to seek treatment when symptoms occur.

Physicians and other health care providers can facilitate the timely detection and treatment of CHD in women by providing information to their female patients about the risk of CVD and by emphasizing the importance of modifying risk factors, such as smoking, obesity, and sedentary lifestyle, in preventing CVD. In addition, providers should review the signs and symptoms of CVD for all women, but particularly for their older female patients, and encourage women to take seriously any symptoms and seek care as quickly as possible. Physicians should also make sure they attend to women's concerns regarding possible CVD symptoms and avoid minimizing the meaning of signs and symptoms of CHD reported by their female patients. By fostering an awareness of the importance of CVD as a health threat to women, and emphasizing that women can take control of their health by modifying CVD risk factors and identifying CHD symptoms in a timely manner, health care personnel can play a major role in enhancing the cardiovascular health of their female patients.

Psychosocial Functioning in Women With CHD

Several studies have documented poorer psychosocial functioning in women who survive an MI or undergo CABG surgery relative to men. Following an MI, women return to work less often than men and take longer to recuperate physically (Chirikos & Nickel, 1984; Stern et al., 1977). Women also experience more negative affect and mood disturbance, especially depression, than do men (Conn, Taylor, & Wiman, 1991; Stern et al., 1977), and they experience delays in the resumption of sexual activity relative to men (Boogard & Briody, 1985; Papadopoulos, Beaumont, Shelley, & Larrimore, 1983; Stern et al., 1977). Furthermore, these findings cannot be solely attributed to women's poorer medical status following MI, since at least one study has shown a worse psychosocial profile for women than for men after an MI, even when taking into account women's older age, comorbidities, and medications (Schron, Pawitan, Shumaker, & Hale, 1991).

Women undergoing CABG surgery also show greater decrements in psychosocial functioning than do men. Some studies have shown women have greater anxiety, depression, and sleep disturbance after CABG than men (Stanton, 1987), and women who have had multiple bypasses have poorer psychological functioning than men 1 year after surgery independent of their medical status (Zyzanski et al., 1981). Women forced to retire have poorer psychosocial adjustment than men (Zyzanski, Rouse, & Stanton, 1982), and women report poorer health and fewer benefits of surgery than do men following CABG (Gortner, 1989). There is some evidence that these psychosocial vulnerabilities are present preoperatively, not just following bypass surgery: Women have been found to be more socially isolated (e.g., unmarried, living alone), to have lower incomes, and to have greater impairments in physical, social, and emotional functioning prior to CABG surgery than men (Czajkowski et al., in press).

The fact that women experience more severe psychosocial sequellae after CHD events and treatments is important in several respects. First, the decrements in daily functioning that accompany CHD for women are important in their own right because they take a significant toll on the well-being, productivity, and quality of life of a significant number of women. Second, studies have shown that psychosocial factors, particularly depression and social isolation, are associated with a greater risk of death and recurrent events in both men and women with CHD (Berkman et al., 1992; Case et al., 1992; Frasure-Smith, Lesperance, & Talajic, 1993; Williams et al., 1992). Therefore, the poorer psychosocial functioning of female patients with CHD may contribute to their less favorable outcomes following CHD diagnosis, events, and treatment.

It is important that physicians and other health care providers become aware of the potential difficulties faced by women with CHD and take steps to enhance the recovery process for their female patients. Health care providers should closely monitor the psychosocial functioning of female patients with CHD, especially their emotional status and the availability of social resources. Follow-up office or hospital visits should not only include an assessment of the physical status of the patient but also questions designed to elicit problems in the areas of physical, social, and emotional recovery. For example, women may be asked whether they live alone and whether they have sources of help and support; if a patient reports that she lives alone, the provider may recommend that a family member or close friend stay with her for a period of time during recovery, or, at the least, schedule home care visits if possible. Referrals to mental health professionals, support groups, and other community resources that provide supportive care should be made when deficits in emotional and social functioning are identified or suspected. Ideally, attention to the psychosocial decrements accompanying CHD recovery in women should be as important an aspect of patient care as treatment of its physical effects.

Another important aspect of CHD recovery that is currently underutilized by women is cardiac rehabilitation programs. Women are less likely to participate in formal exercise rehabilitation programs relative to men following an MI or CABG surgery, and have excessive dropout rates from such programs (Ades, Waldmann, Polk, & Coflesky, 1992; Boogard & Briody, 1985; Conn, Taylor, & Abele, 1991; Schuster & Waldron, 1991). However, when they do participate, they derive benefits equivalent to those of men. In one study, although women had poorer risk factor profiles and greater impairments than men prior to entry into a post-MI rehabilitation program, they showed improvements similar to men in exercise duration, oxygen consumption, and depression, with older women (those over the age of 60) showing the greatest improvements in exercise capability (Downing & Littman, 1994).

Given the importance of cardiac rehabilitation programs to women's recovery from CHD, it is disturbing that relatively few women attend and adhere to these programs. Some have suggested that the lower participation rates of women reflect the increased lifestyle constraints imposed on women, especially older women. Women are more likely than men to have caregiving burdens and to have transportation and other practical difficulties in attending formal rehabilitation programs.

Physicians can play a key role in their female patients' recovery by encouraging them to enroll in and attend cardiac rehabilitation programs. In fact, physician attitudes and behaviors have been found to be important determinants of patient participation in these programs. Ades et al. (1992) found physician recommendations to be the most powerful predictor of attendance in these programs. Thus, physicians should emphasize women's enrollment in these programs as an important part of the recovery process and should closely monitor their female patients' attendance in the programs. To the extent possible, these programs should be structured to be flexible and to address women's special needs. Finally, when necessary, health care providers should refer women to appropriate community resources (e.g., programs that provide care for dependents, hospital vans, and other sources of transportation to alleviate logistical difficulties) to enable their attendance in cardiac rehabilitation programs.

Conclusion

In summary, the evidence reviewed above demonstrates the importance of psychosocial factors and health behaviors in the etiology, prevention, and detection of CHD in women and documents gender differences in response to treatment and in recovery from heart disease. It also suggests an important role for health care providers in a variety of areas related to women's health, from emphasizing adoption of health-related behaviors in women, to an emphasis on the timely and accurate identification of CHD symptoms, and finally to facilitating women's enrollment in and adherence to cardiac rehabilitation programs.

References

Ades, P. A., Waldmann, M. L., Polk, D. M., & Coflesky, J. T. (1992). Referral patterns and exercise response in the rehabilitation of female coronary patients aged ≥62 years. *American Journal of Cardiology, 69*, 1422–1425.

Adler, N. E., Boyce, T., Chesney, M. A., Cohen, S., Folkman, S., Kahn, R. L., & Syme, S. L. (1994). Socioeconomic status and health: The challenge of the gradient. *American Psychologist, 49*, 15–24.

Ahern, D., Gorkin, L., Anderson, J., Tierney, C., Hallstrom, A., Ewart, C., Capone, J., Schron, E., Kornfeld, D., Herd, J., Richardson, D., & Follick, M. (1990). Biobehavioral variables and mortality or cardiac arrest in the Cardiac Arrhythmia Pilot Study (CAPS). *American Journal of Cardiology, 66*, 59–62.

Ayanian, J. Z., & Epstein, A. M. (1991). Differences in the use of procedures between women and men hospitalized for coronary heart disease. *New England Journal of Medicine, 325*, 221–225.

Barefoot, J. C., Dahlstrom, W. G., & Williams, R. B. (1983). Hostility, CHD incidence and total mortality: A 25-year follow-up study of 255 physicians. *Psychosomatic Medicine, 45*, 59–63.

Bell, M. R., Holmes, D. R., Jr., Berger, P. B., Garratt, K. N., Bailey, K. R., & Gersh, B. J. (1993). The changing in-hospital mortality of women undergoing percutaneous transluminal coronary angioplasty. *Journal of the American Medical Association, 269*, 2091–2095.

Berkman, L. F., Leo-Summers, L., & Horwitz, R. I. (1992). Emotional support and survival after myocardial infarction. *Annals of Internal Medicine, 117*, 1003–1009.

Berkman, L. F., & Syme, S. L. (1979). Social networks, host resistance, and mortality: A nine-year follow-up study of Alameda County residents. *American Journal of Epidemiology, 109*, 186–204.

Bickell, N. A., Pieper, K. S., Lee, K. L., Mark, D. B., Glower, D. D., Pryor, D. B., & Califf, R. M. (1992). Referral patterns for coronary artery disease treatment: Gender bias or good clinical judgement? *Annals of Internal Medicine, 116*, 791–797.

Binik, Y. M. (1985). Psychosocial predictors of sudden death: A review and critique. *Social Science and Medicine, 20*, 667–680.

Bland, S. H., Krogh, V., Winkelstein, W., & Trevisan, T. (1991). Social network and blood pressure: A population study. *Psychosomatic Medicine, 53*, 598–607.

Blumenthal, J. A., Burg, M. M., Barefoot, J., Williams, R. B., Handy, T., & Zimet, G. (1987). Social support, Type A behavior, and coronary artery disease. *Psychosomatic Medicine, 49*, 331–339.

Boogaard, M., & Briody, M. (1985). Comparison of the rehabilitation of men and women post-myocardial infarction. *Journal of Cardiopulmonary Rehabilitation, 5*, 379–384.

Booth-Kewley, S., & Friedman, H. D. (1987). Psychological predictors of heart disease: A quantitative review. *Psychological Bulletin, 101*, 343–362.

Burstin, H. R., Lipsitz, S. R., & Brennan, T. A. (1992). Socioeconomic status and risk for substandard medical care. *Journal of the American Medical Association, 268,* 2383–2387.

Burt, V. L., Whelton, P., Roccella, E. J., Brown, C., Cutler, J. A., Higgins, M., Horan, M. J., & Labarthe, D. (1995). Prevalence of hypertension in the U.S. adult population: Results from the Third National Health and Nutrition Examination Survey, 1988-1991. *Hypertension, 25,* 305–313.

Cannistra, L. B., Balady, G. J., O'Malley, C. J., Weiner, D. A., & Ryan, T. J. (1992). Comparison of the clinical profile and outcome of women and men in cardiac rehabilitation. *American Journal of Cardiology, 69,* 1274–1279.

Carney, R. M., Freedland, K. E., & Jaffe, A. S. (1990). Insomnia and depression prior to myocardial infarction. *Psychosomatic Medicine, 52*(6), 603–609.

Case, R. B., Moss, A. J., Case, N., McDermott, M., & Eberly, S. (1992). Living alone after myocardial infarction. *Journal of the American Medical Association, 267,* 515–519.

Chirikos, T. N., & Nickel, J. L. (1984). Work disability from coronary heart disease in women. *Women and Health, 9,* 55–71.

Conn, V. S., Taylor, S. G., & Abele, P. B. (1991). Myocardial infarction survivors: Age and gender differences in physical health, psychosocial state and regimen adherence. *Journal of Advanced Nursing, 16,* 1026–1034.

Conn, V. S., Taylor, S. G., & Wiman, P. (1991). Anxiety, depression, quality of life, and self-care among survivors of myocardial infarction. *Issues in Mental Health Nursing, 12,* 321–331.

Cottington, E. M., Matthews, K. A., Talbott, E., & Kuller, L. H. (1980). Environmental events preceding sudden death in women. *Psychosomatic Medicine, 42,* 567–575.

Czajkowski, S. M., Terrin, M., Lindquist, R., Hoogwerf, B., Dupuis, G., Shumaker, S. A., Gray, R., Herd, J. A., Treat-Jacobson, D., Zyzansky, S., & Knatterud, G. L. for the Post CABG Biobehavioral Study Investigators. (in press). Comparison of preoperative characteristics of men and women undergoing coronary artery bypass grafting (The Post Coronary Artery Bypass Graft [CABG] Biobehavioral Study). *American Journal of Cardiology.*

Downing, J., & Littman, A. (1994). Gender differences in response to cardiac rehabilitation. In S. M. Czajkowski, D.R. Hill, & T. B. Clarkson (Eds.), *Women, behavior and cardiovascular disease: Proceedings of a National Heart, Lung and Blood Institute sponsored conference* (NIH Publication No. 94-3309, pp. 353–354). Washington, DC: U.S. Government Printing Office.

Eysmann, S. B., & Douglas, P. S. (1993). Coronary heart disease: Therapeutic principles. In P. S. Douglas (Ed.), *Cardiovascular health and disease in women* (pp. 43–61). Philadelphia: W. B. Saunders.

Falgar, P., & Appels, A. (1982). Psychological risk factors over the life course of myocardial infarction patients. *Advances in Cardiology, 29,* 132–139.

Ferrario, M., & Cesana, G.C. (1993). Socioeconomic status and coronary disease: Theories, research methods, epidemiological evidence and the results of Italian studies. *Medicina del Lavoro, 84,* 18–30.

Fiebach, N. H., Viscoli, C. M., & Horwitz, R. I. (1990). Differences between women and men in survival after myocardial infarction: Biology or methodology? *Journal of the American Medical Association, 263,* 1092–1096.

Frank, E., & Taylor, C. B. (1993). Psychosocial influences on diagnosis and treatment plans of women with coronary heart disease. In N. K. Wenger, L. Speroff, & B. Packard (Eds.), *Cardiovascular health and disease in women* (pp. 231–237). Greenwich, CT: Le Jacq.

Frasure-Smith, N., Lesperance, F., & Talajic, M. (1993). Depression following myocardial infarction: Impact on 6-month survival. *Journal of the American Medical Association, 270,* 1819–1825.

Gerin, W., Milner, D., Chawla, S., & Pickering, T. G. (1995). Social support as a moderator of cardiovascular reactivity in women: A test of the direct effects and buffering hypotheses. *Psychosomatic Medicine, 57,* 16–22.

Gortner, S. R., Rankin, S., Gillis, C. L., Sparacio, P. A., Paul, S. M., Shinn, J. A., & Leavitt, M.B. (1989). Expected and realized benefits from cardiac surgery: An update. *Cardiological Nursing, 25,* 19–24.

Greenland, P., Reicher-Reiss, H., Goldbourt, U., Behar, S., & the Israeli SPRINT Investigators. (1991). In-hospital and 1-year mortality in 1,524 women after myocardial infarction. *Circulation, 83,* 484–491.

Haan, M., Kaplan, G. A., & Camacho, T. (1987). Poverty and health: Prospective evidence from the Alameda County Study. *American Journal of Epidemiology, 125,* 989–998.

Haellstroem, T., Lapidus, L. Bengtsson, C., & Edstrom, K. (1986). Psychosocial factors and risk of ischemic heart disease and death in women: A twelve-year follow-up of participants in the population study of women in Gothenburg, Sweden. *Psychosomatic Research, 30,* 451–459.

Hallstrom, A., Boutin, P., Cobb, L., & Johnson, E. (1993). Socioeconomic status and prediction of ventricular fibrillation survival. *American Journal of Public Health, 83,* 245–248.

Hanson, B. S., Isacsson, S. O., Janzon, L., & Lindell, S. E. (1990). Social support and quitting smoking for good: Is there an association? Results from the population study, "Men Born in 1914," Malmo, Sweden. *Addictive Behaviors, 15,* 221–233.

Heckler, M. M. (1985). *Report of the secretary's task force on Black and minority health* (Vol. II). Rockville, MD: U.S. Department of Health and Human Services.

Holahan, C. J., Moos, R.H., Holahan, C. K., & Brennan, P. L. (1995). Social support, coping and depressive symptoms in a late-middle-aged sample of patients reporting cardiac illness. *Health Psychology, 14,* 152–163.

Holme, I., Helgeland, A., Hjermann, I., Leren, P., & Lund-Larsen, P. G. (1977). Coronary risk factors in various occupational groups: The Oslo study 1977. *British Preventive Society of Medicine, 31,* 96–100.

House, J. S., Robbins, C., & Metzner, H. L. (1982). The association of social relationships and activities with mortality: Prospective evidence from the Tecumseh Community Health Study. *American Journal of Epidemiology, 116,* 123–140.

Hypertension Detection and Follow-up Program Cooperative Group. (1987). Educational level and 5-year all-cause mortality in the Hypertension Detection and Follow-up Program. *Hypertension, 9,* 641–646.

Kamarck, T. W., Annunziato, B., & Amateau, L. M. (1995). Affiliation moderates the effects of social threat on stress-related cardiovascular responses: Boundary conditions for a laboratory model of social support. *Psychosomatic Medicine, 57,* 183–194.

Kamarck, T. W., & Jennings, J. R. (1991). Biobehavioral factors in sudden cardiac death. *Psychological Bulletin, 109,* 42–75.

Kaufman, J. S., Owoaje, E. E., James, S. A., Rotimi, C., & Cooper, R. S. (1996). The determinants of hypertension in West Africa: Contribution of anthropometric and dietary factors to urban-rural and socioeconomic gradients. *American Journal of Epidemiology, 143,* 1203–1218.

Keil, J. E., Sutherland, S. E., Knapp, R. G., & Tyroler, H. A. (1992). Does equal socioeconomic status in Black and White men mean equal risk of mortality? *American Journal of Public Health, 82,* 1133–1136.

Khan, S. S. (1991). Why women have a significantly higher bypass surgery mortality rate. *Cardiology Board Review, 8,* 54–67.

Khan, S. S., Nessim, S., Gray, R., Czer, L. S., Chaux, A., & Matloff, J. (1990). Increased mortality of women in coronary artery bypass surgery: Evidence for referral bias. *Annals of Internal Medicine, 112,* 561–567.

Knox, S. S. (1993). Perception of social support and blood pressure in young men. *Perceptual and Motor Skills, 77,* 132–134.

Knox, S. S., Theorell, T., Svensson, J. C., & Waller, D. (1985). The relation of social support and working environment to medical variables associated with elevated blood pressure in young males: A structural model. *Social Science and Medicine, 21,* 525–531.

Kochanek, K. D., & Hudson, B. L. (1994). Advance report of final mortality statistics, 1992. *Monthly Vital Statistics Report, 43*(6S).

Langeluddecke, P., Fulcher, G., Jones, M., & Tennant, C. (1988). Type A behaviour and coronary atherosclerosis. *Journal of Psychosomatic Research, 32,* 77–84.

Laskey, W. K. (1992). Gender differences in the management of coronary artery disease: Bias or good clinical judgement? *Annals of Internal Medicine, 116,* 869–871.

Luepker, R. V., Rosamond, W. D., Murphy, R., Sprafka, J. M., Folsom, A. R., McGovern, P. G., & Blackburn, H. (1993). Socioeconomic status and coronary heart disease risk factor trends. *Circulation, 88*(Pt. 1), 2172–2179.

Malarkey, W. B., Kiecolt-Glaser, J. K., Pearl, D., & Glaser, R. (1994). Hostility behavior during marital conflict alters pituitary and adrenal hormones. *Psychosomatic Medicine, 56*, 41–51.

Marmot, M. G., Rose, G., Shipley, M., & Hamilton, P. J. S. (1978). Employment grade and coronary heart disease in British civil servants. *Journal of Epidemiology and Community Health, 32*, 244–249.

McKinlay, J. B., Crawford, S., McKinlay, S. M., & Sellers, D. E. (1994). On the reported gender difference in coronary heart disease: An illustration of the social construction of epidemiologic rates. In S. M. Czajkowski, D. R. Hill, & T. B. Clarkson (Eds.), *Women, behavior and cardiovascular disease: Proceedings of a National Heart, Lung and Blood Institute sponsored conference* (NIH Publication No. 94-3309, pp. 223–252). Washington, DC: U.S. Government Printing Office.

Moser, D. K., & Dracup, K. (1994). Gender differences in symptom recognition and health care seeking behavior in acute myocardial infarction. In S. M. Czajkowski, D. R. Hill, & T. B. Clarkson (Eds.), *Women, behavior and cardiovascular disease* (NIH Publication No. 94-3309, pp. 261–278). Washington, DC: U.S. Government Printing Office.

Murphy, J. M., Monson, R. R., Olivier, D.C., et al. (1987). Affective disorders and mortality: A general population study. *Archives of General Psychology, 44*, 473–480.

Musante, L., Treiber, F. A., Davis, H., Strong, W. B., & Levy, M. (1992). Hostility: Relationship to lifestyle behaviors and physical risk factors. *Behavioral Medicine, 18*, 21–26.

National Heart, Lung and Blood Institute. (1994a). Report of the Working Group on *Research in coronary heart disease in Blacks*. Rockville, MD: U.S. Department of Health and Human Services.

National Heart, Lung and Blood Institute. (1994b). Chartbook on Cardiovascular, Lung, and Blood Disease: *Morbidity and Mortality*. Rockville, MD: U.S. Department of Health and Human Services.

Navarro, V. (1990). Race or class versus race and class: Mortality differentials in the United States. *The Lancet, 336*, 1238–1240.

Nayha, S. (1977). Social group and mortality in Finland. *British Journal of Prevention and Social Medicine, 31*, 231–237.

Orth-Gomer, K., Rosengren, A., & Wilhelmsen, L. (1993). Lack of social support and incidence of coronary heart disease in middle aged Swedish men. *Psychosomatic Medicine, 55*, 37–43.

Papadopoulos, C., Beaumont, C., Shelley, S., & Larrimore, P. (1983). Myocardial infarction and sexual activity of the female patient. *Archives of Internal Medicine, 143*, 1528–1530.

Ries, P. (1991). Characteristics of persons with and without health care coverage: United States, 1989. *Vital and health statistics, 201*. Rockville, MD: U.S. Department of Health and Human Services.

Rotimi, C., Cooper, R., Cao, G., Sundarum, C., & McGee, D. (1994). Familial aggregation of cardiovascular diseases in African-American pedigrees. *Genetic Epidemiology, 11*, 397–407.

Ruberman, W. (1992). Psychosocial influences on mortality of patients with coronary heart disease. *Journal of the American Medical Association, 267*, 559–560.

Ruberman, W., Weinblatt, E., Goldberg, J. D., & Chaudhary, B. S. (1984). Psychosocial influences on mortality after myocardial infarction. *New England Journal of Medicine, 311*, 552–559.

Scherwitz, L. W., Perkins, L. L., Chesney, M. A., Hughes, G. H., Sidney, S., & Manolio, T. A. (1992). Hostility and health behaviors in young adults: The CARDIA study. *American Journal of Epidemiology, 136*, 136–145.

Schleifer, S. J., Macari-Hinson, M. M., Coyle, D. A., William, W. R., Kahn, M., Gorlin, R., & Zucker, H. D. (1989). The nature and course of depression following myocardial infarction. *Archives of Internal Medicine, 149*, 1785–1789.

Schoenbach, V., Kaplan, B. H., & Fredman, L. (1986). Social ties and mortality in Evans County, Georgia. *American Journal of Epidemiology, 123*, 577–691.

Schron, E., Pawitan, Y., Shumaker, S. A., & Hale, C. (1991). Health quality of life differences between men and women in a postinfarction study. *Circulation, 84*(Suppl. II), II-976.

Schuster, P. M., & Waldron, J. (1991). Gender differences in cardiac rehabilitation patients. *Rehabilitation Nursing, 16*, 248–253.

Seeman, T. E., & Syme, L. (1987). Social networks and coronary artery disease: A comparison of the structure and function of social relations as predictors of disease. *Psychosomatic Medicine, 49*, 341–354.

Shekelle, R. B., Gale, M., Ostfeld, A. M., & Paul, O. (1983). Hostility, risk of coronary heart disease and mortality. *Psychosomatic Medicine, 45*, 109–114.

Shekelle, R. B., Hulley, S. B., Neaton, J. D., Billings, J. H., Borhani, N. O., Gerace, T. A., Jacobs, D. R., Lasser, N. L., Mitterlmark, M. B., & Stamler, J. (1985). The MRFIT Behavior Pattern Study: II. Type A behavior and incidence of coronary heart disease. *American Journal of Epidemiology, 122*, 559–570.

Siegler, I. C., Peterson, B. L., Barefoot, J. C., & Williams, R. B. (1992). Hostility during late adolescence predicts coronary risk factors at mid-life. *American Journal of Epidemiology, 136*, 146–154.

Siegrist, J., Siegrist, K., & Weber, I. (1986). Sociological concepts in the etiology of chronic disease: The case of ischemic heart disease. *Social Science and Medicine, 22*, 247–253.

Silver, L., Jenkins, C. D., Ryan, T. J., & Melidossian, C. (1980). Sex differences in the psychological correlates of cardiovascular diagnosis and coronary angiographic findings. *Journal of Psychosomatic Research, 24*, 327–334.

Sorlie, P., Rogot, E., Anderson, R., Johnson, N. J., & Backlund, E. (1992). Black-White mortality differences by family income. *The Lancet, 340*, 346–350.

Stanton, B. A. (1987). Psychosocial aspects of coronary heart disease in women: Implications and expectations for rehabilitation. In E. D. Eaker, B. Packard, N. K. Wenger, T. B. Clarkson, & H. A. Tyrolene (Eds.), *Coronary heart disease in women* (pp. 257–263). New York: Haymarket Douma.

Steingart, R. M., Packer, M., Hamm, P., Coglianese, M. E., Gersh, B., Geltman, E. M., Sollano, J., Katz, S., Moye, L., Basta, L. L., Lewis, S. J., Gottlieb, S. S., Bernstein, V., McEwan, P., Jacobson, K., Brown, E. J., Kukin, M. L., Kantrowitz, N. E., & Pfeffer, M. A. (1991). Sex differences in the management of coronary artery disease. *New England Journal of Medicine, 325*, 226–230.

Stern, M., Pascale, L., & Ackerman, A. (1977). Life adjustment post-myocardial infarction. *Archives of Internal Medicine, 137*, 1680–1685.

Suls, J., & Wan, C. K. (1993). The relationship between trait hostility and cardiovascular reactivity: A quantitative review and analysis. *Psychophysiology, 30*, 615–626.

Talbott, E., Kuller, L. H., Detre, K., & Perper, J. (1977). Biologic and psychosocial risk factors for sudden death from coronary disease in White women. *American Journal of Cardiology, 39*, 858–864.

Talbott, E., Kuller, L. H., Perper, J., & Murphy, P. A. (1981). Sudden unexpected death in women: Biologic and psychosocial origins. *American Journal of Epidemiology, 114*, 671–682.

Theorell, T., Alfredson, L., Knox, S., Perski, A., Svensson, J., & Waller, D. (1984). On the interplay between socioeconomic factors, personality and work environment in the pathogenesis of cardiovascular disease. *Scandinavian Journal of Work Environment and Health, 10*, 373–380.

Theorell, T., Svensson, J., Knox, S., & Ahlborg, B. (1982). Blood pressure variations across areas in the greater Stockholm region: Analysis of 74,000 18-year-old men. *Social Science and Medicine, 16*, 469–473.

Tofler, G. H., Stone, P. H., Muller, J. E., Willich, S. N., Davis, V. G., Poole, W. K., Strauss, W., Willerson, J. T., Jaffe, A. S., Robertson, T., Passamani, E., Braunwald, E., & the Milis Study Group. (1987). Effects of gender and race on prognosis after myocardial infarction: Adverse prognosis for women, particularly Black women. *Journal of the American College of Cardiology, 9*, 473–482.

Wenger, N. K. (1993). Coronary heart disease: Diagnostic decision-making. In P. S. Douglas (Ed.), *Cardiovascular health and disease in women* (pp. 25–42). Philadelphia: W. B. Saunders.

Wenger, N. K., Speroff, L., & Packard, B. (1993). Cardiovascular health and disease in women. *New England Journal of Medicine, 329*, 247–256.

Williams, R. (1989). *The trusting HEART: Great news about Type A behavior*. New York: Time Books.

Williams, R. B., Barefoot, J. C., Califf, R. M., Haney, T. L., Saunders, W. B., Pryor, D. B., Hlatky, M. A., Siegler, I. C., & Mark, D. B. (1992). Prognostic importance of social and economic resources among medically treated patients with angiographically documented coronary artery disease. *Journal of the American Medical Association, 267*, 520–524.

Williams, R. B., Barefoot, J. C., Haney, T. L., Harrell, F. E., Blumenthal, J. A., & Pryor, D.B. (1988). Type A behavior and angiographically documented coronary atherosclerosis in a sample of 2,289 patients. *Psychosomatic Medicine, 50*, 139–152.

Wing, S., Barnett, E., Casper, M., & Tyroler, H. A. (1992). Geographic and socioeconomic variation in the onset of decline of coronary heart disease mortality in White women. *American Journal of Public Health, 82*, 204–209.

Winkleby, M. A., Fortmann, S. P., & Rockhill, B. (1992). Trends in cardiovascular disease risk factors by educational level: The Stanford Five-City Project. *Preventive Medicine, 21*, 592–601.

Woodward, M., Shewry, M. C., Smith, W. C. S., & Tunstall-Pedoe, H. (1992). Social status and coronary heart disease: Results from the Scottish Heart Study. *Preventive Medicine, 21*, 136–148.

Zyzanski, S. J., Rouse, B. A., Stanton, B. A., & Jenkins, C. D. (1982). Employment changes among patients following coronary bypass surgery: Social, medical and psychological correlates. *Public Health Reports, 97*, 558–565.

Zysanski, S. J., Stanton, B. A., Jenkins, C. D., & Klein, M. D. (1981). Medical and psychosocial outcomes in survivors of major heart surgery. *Journal of Psychosomatic Research, 25*, 213–221.

18

HIV Infection and AIDS

Patricia J. Morokoff, Vickie M. Mays,
and Helen L. Coons

In this chapter we provide an overview for the health practitioner of the psychosocial aspects of HIV infection and AIDS in women. We focus on prevention and treatment issues of special relevance to women. We begin with a brief epidemiological overview of relevant data and then present information on HIV transmission. We also discuss the provision of HIV and AIDS prevention services, including information about factors affecting women's decisions to obtain serotesting and issues in pre- and posttest counseling. Finally, we discuss the assessment of women's psychosocial needs and secondary prevention for women with HIV infection or AIDS.

Epidemiological Overview

Prevalence and Characteristics of Women With AIDS

In 1985, AIDS cases in women represented only 7% of the total number (Ellerbrock, Bush, Chamberland, & Oxtoby, 1991). By the year ending in June 1996, the proportion of AIDS cases in women had reached 19.5% (Centers for Disease Control and Prevention [CDC], 1996). For cases of HIV infection, reported by states with confidential HIV-infection reporting, women represent 24% of the cumulative total and 29% of the cases reported in the year ending June 1996 (CDC, 1996).

Women diagnosed with AIDS tend to be young women of color. A large percentage of women diagnosed with AIDS (84%) are between the ages of 15 and 44 (CDC, 1993d). More than half of American women with AIDS are classified by the CDC (1996) as Black (not Hispanic; 55%), whereas just under one quarter are White and one fifth are Hispanic. When one considers the rate per 100,000 population, Black women are 16.5 times more likely to be diagnosed with AIDS than White women and 2.4 times more likely than Hispanic women. Hispanic women are 6.8 times more likely to be diagnosed with AIDS than White women (CDC, 1994a). The CDC also classifies AIDS cases in the categories of Asian/Pacific Islander and American Indian/Alaska Native. Cases in these categories make up less than 1% of the total.

The CDC classifies people with AIDS according to category. According to these data (CDC, 1996), the greatest percentage of women are classified as having been exposed through injection drug use (46%). The next most prevalent exposure category is heterosexual contact (38%). Of women infected through heterosexual contact, the most frequent transmission route is sex with an injecting drug user (IDU; 18% of the total). Thus, 64% of women with AIDS were exposed to HIV through injection drug use or having sex with an IDU.

Women are much more likely than men to be exposed to HIV through heterosexual contact. In contrast to the 38% figure cited earlier for women, only 4% of men are in the CDC's heterosexual-contact exposure category. If one looks only at individuals classified as exposed through heterosexual contact, women represent 66% of the total (CDC, 1996). A woman is at greater risk of infection from sex with an infected man than a man is from sex with an infected woman. The risk of transmission during unprotected sex with an infected man is believed to be 12 times greater than the risk to a man of having unprotected sex with an infected woman (Padian, Shiboski, & Jewell, 1990).

Sexual Orientation

Little data are available on the risk of female-to-female transmission (Kennedy, Scarlett, Duerr, & Chu, 1995). Although CDC data categorize only 0.8% of women with AIDS as lesbian (Chu, Buehler, Fleming, & Berkelman, 1990), subgroups of lesbians are likely to be at risk for HIV infection (Mays, Cochran, Pies, Chu, & Erhardt, 1996). These include lesbians who have unprotected sex with men or women at risk, lesbian IDUs who share needles or paraphernalia, lesbians who use unscreened semen for donor insemination, and the unprotected sharing of sex toys (Kennedy et al., 1995). In a study conducted by Magura, Kang, Shapiro, and O'Day (1993), 43% of a prison sample of women were found to be HIV-positive. Of these, 30% identified themselves as exclusively lesbian and another 23% identified themselves as bisexual.

Mortality

HIV infection and AIDS have become major contributors to premature loss of life in young adult women, most notably among young African Americans and Latinas. "Nationally, HIV infection was the fourth leading cause of death in 1993 among women 25–44 years of age" (CDC, 1995). Stratified by race, HIV infection was the leading cause of death for Black women in this age group in 1993 and the third leading cause of death among Hispanic women.

Sexual Networks

Although a woman may be exposed to HIV as a result of sharing drug equipment or sexual activity with an infected person, these behaviors pose no such risk if the other person is not infected. A woman's risk is thus tied to the prevalence of HIV infection in members of her sexual network, defined as the set of her sexual partners and her partners' sexual partners. It may be difficult to determine the risk level associated with a woman's sexual network, especially because surveillance of HIV infection is not mandatory in all jurisdictions. As of June 30, 1996, 26 states had laws or regulations requiring confidential reporting by name of all individuals confirmed with HIV infection (CDC, 1996). Furthermore, there are many impediments, as discussed later, to widespread HIV diagnostic testing. Nevertheless, some idea of relative risk may be obtained from CDC information on AIDS cases in various localities. The higher the incidence of HIV and AIDS in a given locality, the greater the risk associated with failure to engage in appropriate preventive strategies. CDC guidelines allow health care institutions to take into account the HIV seroprevalence in the patient population in deciding whether to routinely offer HIV counseling and voluntary testing services (CDC, 1993b). Of course, even in areas with low rates of AIDS cases (e.g., North Dakota), there is some risk associated with unprotected sexual behaviors or sharing of drug injection equipment.

HIV Transmission

As can be seen from the routes of transmission for HIV infection, the most common sources of exposure to HIV are through injection drug use and sexual behavior with an infected person.

Risk Associated With Drug Injection Equipment

It is important for health care providers to understand changes in drug trends so they can understand women's risks for HIV infection. The four most commonly injected substances are heroin, cocaine, heroin and cocaine combined, and amphetamines. More IDUs have injected cocaine than have injected any other drug (Feucht, Stephens, & Sullivan, 1993).

Women can be exposed to HIV infection by sharing needles and other drug injection paraphernalia. Any equipment that comes in contact with blood, such as drug cookers used to melt heroin in water before use, cotton used to filter drugs, or water used to unclog needles, may transmit infection (Singer, 1991). Women may be especially vulnerable to infection as a result of their patterns of sharing drug injection equipment with a sex partner. The majority of women who inject drugs share drug injection equipment, and this tends to occur in a relational context. Women are more likely than men to have a partner who is an IDU (Feucht, Stephens, & Roman, 1990) and are more likely than men to have only one needle-sharing partner (Brown & Weissman, 1993), who is typically a sex partner. More women than men report sharing drug equipment with a sex partner (Stephens, Feucht, & Gibbs, 1993). Women report using drugs at home more frequently than men (Stephens et al., 1993), again emphasizing the relational context of drug use for women. Women often use drug injection equipment after their male partner (Castro, Valdiserri, & Curran, 1992).

HIV transmission via injection drug use can be prevented if women do not inject drugs or if they clean drug injection equipment. Substance abuse treatment programs may not be readily available to women. Although there has been an increase in programs that accept women, availability is still limited for women who are Medicaid beneficiaries or for women with children. Even more limited are opportunities for substance abuse treatment to pregnant women (Kumpfer, 1991). Women and their partners can be taught to clean their own drug injection equipment with bleach. In some localities, syringe and needle exchange programs (NEPs) are available. As of September 1993, there were 37 active NEPs in the United States (CDC, 1993c). Studies evaluating these programs typically conclude that the NEP is effective in decreasing the rates of HIV drug risk behavior. A recent study of an NEP in San Francisco demonstrated that the program was rapidly accepted by male and female IDUs (Watters, Estilo, Clark, & Lorvick, 1994). It is important to recognize that there may be special barriers to women's use of NEPs. For example, child-care responsibilities may make it difficult for women to travel to the center to exchange syringes and needles.

Risk Associated With Sexual Behavior

Vaginal intercourse is the most common mode of heterosexual transmission of HIV infection worldwide. Research indicates that the co-occurrence of a sexually transmitted disease (STD) that produces genital ulcers is an additional risk factor for both the transmission and acquisition of HIV infection (Moss et al., 1991). Vaginal intercourse involving mucosal trauma further increases the risk of transmission. It is believed that anal intercourse is the riskiest form of heterosexual sex, probably because of mucosal trauma during insertion. Oral sex also is a possible route for infection, especially for the receptive partner when the insertive partner is infected and ejaculates.

One strategy for reducing the risk from sexual behavior is abstinence from sexual activities that could expose people to infectious bodily fluids, such as intercourse. This is the safest approach to preventing HIV infection. An alternative strategy is to begin using condoms during all insertive sexual activity. Condoms have been shown to be efficacious in preventing HIV infection and other STDs (Weller, 1993). It is important for health care providers to give women information on how to obtain and use condoms and how to be sexually assertive with respect to declining unwanted sex or initiating condom use. Women who are using oral contraceptives need to learn the importance of also using condoms to protect themselves from STDs.

However, there are significant barriers to the use of condoms that make it unlikely that providing information alone to women about condoms will increase their use. One barrier may be a monogamous relationship. It may be difficult to ask a steady sex partner to begin using condoms because of the implication that he is not trusted. Women who have multiple partners report a higher rate of condom use (Mosher & Pratt, 1993). A second barrier is that male condoms are a male-controlled method of protection. Because of this, women are in the position of negotiating with a male partner rather than being able to decide on their own when to use male condoms. In some couples (approximately one third according to Osmond et al., 1993), either condom use is never discussed or the male partner is the condom use decision maker. According to a study of condom use among Hispanic men and women (Mikawa et al., 1992), the use of condoms appeared to be a male prerogative rather than a female one, with men being much more likely than women to buy and initiate the use of condoms. If men are the decision makers concerning condom use, they typically decide not to use condoms. Only 12% of couples in which the male partner made condom decisions used condoms more than half the time compared with 32% of couples in which both partners made the decision and 49% of couples in which the woman made the decision herself (Osmond et al., 1993). Assertiveness concerning pregnancy and STD prevention has been found to be inversely related to a history of sexual abuse (Morokoff et al., in press).

A third strategy that could be used is adoption of the female condom. This disease prevention method is female controlled and thus potentially avoids some of the problems just identified. The female condom is a light-weight polyurethane pouch consisting of a soft, loose-fitting sheath and two flexible polyurethane rings. One of the rings is at the closed end of the pouch and is inserted into the vagina. The other ring remains outside the vagina after insertion. This product is marketed by Wisconsin Pharmacal as the Reality Condom. Research indicates that this product provides contraceptive efficacy in the same range as other barrier methods, especially when used consistently and correctly (Farr, Gabelnick, Sturgen, & Dorflinger, 1994; Trussell, Sturgen, Strickler, & Dominik, 1994). Because the female condom is obtrusive, it is apparent to a partner when it is used, and therefore its use may require negotiation with the partner.

From the perspective of female control, the best alternative, which is not currently available, would be a microbicide which could be used as a spray. Such a product could be used unobtrusively and would not require a partner's consent before use. Research is currently underway to develop such a product (Morokoff, Harlow, & Quina, 1995).

Social vulnerability: Race, gender, and poverty. In addition to examining barriers experienced by individual women in negotiating condom use with heterosexual partners, it is worthwhile looking at larger social issues that create conditions in which women have difficulty protecting themselves. The factors of poverty, racism, and gender inequality are fundamental social problems that foster risk taking and create conditions of risk for women both in the United States and worldwide (Population Council, 1994).

Ethnic minority and poor women. Although the rates and risk of HIV infection in ethnic minority women and poor women in inner cities is high, it is important to have accurate information about the nature of this risk. A national study that included a sample drawn from high-risk cities revealed that respondents were more likely to have had multiple sexual partners if they were more highly educated, were male, and were White or African American compared with Hispanic (Catania et al., 1992). Examination of data from women in the same sample revealed that 8% of White women reported multiple partners compared with 7% of Black women and 3% of Hispanic women (Grinstead, Faigeles, Binson, & Eversley, 1993). Only two significant predictors of having a risky sexual partner were reported: income and gender. Individuals with lower incomes were more likely to report a risky partner as were women. It is thus increasingly evident that poor ethnic women are at higher risk, not because their own behaviors are riskier than that of others (i.e., they do not have more sex partners or use condoms less) but because their male partners are riskier (Hobfoll, Jackson, Lavin, Britton, & Shepherd, 1994).

Providing HIV and AIDS Prevention Services

The national health objectives for the year 2000 include increasing to at least 75% the proportion of primary care and mental health care providers who provide age-appropriate counseling on the prevention of HIV and other STDs; increasing the proportion of individuals with HIV infection who have been tested to 80%; and increasing to at least 50% the proportion of primary care clinics that screen, diagnose, treat, counsel, and provide (or refer for) partner notification services for HIV infection and bacterial STDs (Public Health Service, 1991).

The Context of Prevention Interventions

In what contexts should women receive messages concerning prevention of HIV transmission? It is important that information be available and counseling offered in any setting in which women are provided with health and mental health care. This includes (a) routine medical care checkups (e.g., in primary care or obstetrics-gynecology); (b) family planning clinics in conjunction with receiving contraception; (c) prenatal clinics; (d) STD clinics; (e) mental health clinics; and (f) substance abuse treatment facilities, including methadone maintenance clinics. It is recommended that hospitals and associated clinics encourage health care providers to routinely ask patients about their risks for HIV infection and to offer HIV counseling and voluntary testing services to patients at risk (CDC, 1993b). Other health care institutions, including drug treatment centers, mental health facilities, and private medical practitioners, are encouraged to consider offering these services. Furthermore, universal counseling and voluntary testing programs for pregnant women are recommended. Thus,

health care providers should ensure that all pregnant women are counseled and encouraged to be tested for HIV infection. Testing is especially
important for pregnant women because administration of zidovudine (ZDV
[also known as AZT]) early in pregnancy can substantially reduce the risk
for perinatal HIV transmission (CDC, 1995). Because a growing group of
younger and older women are at risk for HIV infection, prevention services
should be offered whenever medical care is provided to women.

Primary care providers should be important sources of HIV prevention
services to their patients. However, according to a survey of primary care
physicians (CDC, 1994b), a substantial portion indicated they would not
"usually" or "always" take sexual history information from a new patient.
These results emphasize the lost opportunities to provide HIV risk counseling during encounters with patients. Furthermore, health care providers frequently do not assess sexual or drug risk behaviors. For example,
only 49% of primary care physicians would usually or always ask about
STDs, 31% about condom use, 27% about sexual orientation, and 22%
about number of sex partners (CDC, 1994b). A barrier to assessment of
such information was the physicians' concern (endorsed by 25% of the
sample) that patients would be offended by questions about their sexual
behaviors. For health care providers to feel more confident in providing
risk assessment counseling, they need to be knowledgeable about HIV infection and its transmission (Gerber et al., 1993) as well as about sensitive
strategies for assessing sexual and drug-related risks.

The CDC provides technical guidance on how counseling for risk assessment should be conducted (CDC, 1993b). It is emphasized that counseling must be client centered (i.e., tailored to the individual). It is specified that counseling be confidential, culturally competent, sensitive to
issues of sexual identity, developmentally appropriate, and linguistically
specific (i.e., presented in terms the client will understand).

Confidentiality. An important component to such assessment is a
guarantee of confidentiality. This means that all information provided by
the client will be kept private. This is especially important when patients
are to be asked about sexual activity and drug use.

Cultural sensitivity. It is crucial to recognize that questions and information concerning transmission of disease are not received in a cultural
vacuum. Individuals will interpret questions and information within the
context of their cultural understanding of disease. For example, a study
of traditional health beliefs among some African American women showed
that most participants believed that there were other ways to acquire HIV
infection besides sex and drugs (Flaskerud & Rush, 1989). Some medical
practices may be seen as a threat to, or in conflict with, cultural or religious beliefs (Health Resources and Service Administration, 1993a, 1993b),
and thus women may delay the use of prescribed medicines until they have
become seriously ill. Health care providers may find it helpful to explore
women's cultural beliefs during the clinical encounter.

Research has indicated that some African American women underestimate the prevalence of AIDS among African Americans (Mays & Cochran, 1995; Quinn, 1993). In addition, some African Americans and Puerto Ricans may be hesitant to participate in clinical trials or engage in a regimen of experimental drugs because of past encounters with federal and local public health officials that have left feelings of mistrust and neglect (Mays & Cochran, 1997; Health Resources Service Administration, 1993a, 1993b; Thomas & Quinn, 1991). Finally, as suggested by Mays and Cochran (1988), for poor ethnic minority women, HIV risk may be a less pressing threat than exposure to the elements, difficulty providing for dependent children, hunger, acute illness, trauma associated with physical or sexual assault, and other dangers.

Sensitivity to issues of sexual identity. As previously discussed, lesbian and bisexual women in some populations represent the majority of HIV infection cases (Magura et al., 1993). Furthermore, sex with bisexual men is a significant risk factor for HIV transmission in women. It is important that health counselors not presume that women are heterosexual, that their partners are heterosexual, or that heterosexuality confers greater risk for HIV infection in women. Health care providers should assess risk for HIV in lesbians or bisexual women in a manner similar to that of other women patients. Women who self-identify as lesbians may engage in sexual activity with men, suffer STDs, inject drugs, or engage in behaviors that may put them at risk for HIV infection. Although the biological mechanisms for female-to-female transmission are not known, for health providers with lesbian or bisexual patients it may be prudent to provide assessment and prevention counseling.

Developmental appropriateness. It also is crucial that risk assessment and risk reduction counseling be age appropriate. A particularly important but difficult group to reach is female adolescents, whose needs may be much different from those of women of other age groups. Girls and boys should be provided with sex education focusing on information about human sexuality, individual rights, and sexual responsibilities. It may, however, be difficult to reach those adolescents in most need of HIV prevention counseling, testing, and treatment services. Many at highest risk are school dropouts, who will not have access to school-based programs. For others without medical insurance or the ability to seek services without parental consent, accessing family planning clinics that have services may present a problem. Although adolescents are generally healthy, some do consult primary care or family practitioners for periodic health checkups. Health practitioners in these settings are encouraged to explore sexual concerns with these young women and to help them develop HIV prevention strategies, even if they are not currently sexually active.

Accuracy of information. Research indicates that the best information can be obtained by asking individuals to remember sexual behaviors with each partner individually rather than asking for a global estimate (Catania, Gibson, Chitwood, & Coates, 1990). It is also crucial to know the risk status of each partner, including the gender of the partner and whether the partner has had multiple partners, has ever engaged in injection drug use, is bisexual, or has been diagnosed with HIV infection. Putting all this information together provides an estimate of the woman's overall level of HIV risk. It is also important to remember that many women may not know the truth of their partners' risk histories (Cochran & Mays, 1990; Mays & Cochran, 1993). Although many women may not know about a partner's risk behavior, others may know or suspect that their partner is not being monogamous or using drugs but not be ready to reveal or confront such information. Thus, health care providers may wish to discuss prevention strategies with women even in the face of no acknowledged risk.

HIV Counseling, Testing, and Referral for Women

The CDC (1994c) has identified several functions of HIV counseling. These include providing information on serostatus; providing prevention counseling to help initiate behavior change; providing referrals for additional prevention, medical care, and other services; and providing prevention services and referrals for sex and needle-sharing partners of HIV-infected individuals. Counseling and testing services offer an opportunity for health care providers to help women accurately understand their risk, to negotiate a relevant risk reduction plan, and to make appropriate referrals. It is crucial, however, that health care providers offer prevention counseling to all patients across the life span, paying particular attention to social class and ethnic group membership.

Most health care settings provide written materials (e.g., pamphlets) containing information on preventing HIV transmission. Research has indicated that this type of information alone rarely facilitates behavior change (e.g., Harlow, Quina, Morokoff, Rose, & Grimley, 1993). Therefore, to change sexual or drug use behavior, additional efforts are needed. These may include videotapes on prevention, individual counseling from a health care provider, or group sessions to discuss strategies for making changes in sexual and drug behaviors. Some research indicates that group sessions can be effective in helping women increase their frequency of protected sex. For example, Kelly et al. (1994) found that a three-session group was effective in increasing condom use among inner-city women from 26% to 56% of the time.

According to the CDC's standards and guidelines, the necessary components of HIV counseling, testing, and referral services include maintenance of confidentiality, risk assessment, prevention counseling, provision of test results, and provision of referrals (CDC, 1994c). Most HIV prevention counseling and testing for women is provided as an integrated part of health settings in which women receive care for their primary and reproductive health needs. A question faced by health care professionals, which is often determined by available resources, is whether primary care providers, clinic nurses, or social workers should provide services or whether there should be a designated pretest–posttest counselor for these activities. Regardless of who performs these clinical interventions, it is important that the person is well trained not just in the biomedical aspects of transmission and risk reduction but also in the roles gender, culture, and social class play in women's abilities to initiate and sustain necessary behavior changes for risk reduction.

According to a national survey (CDC, 1993b), most physicians (66%) indicated that if HIV testing were appropriate for a patient, they would probably provide the test counseling themselves. However, various factors influenced physicians to refer patients for counseling and testing. These included a perception that counseling was too time-consuming (55%), a perception that information was insufficient to enable counseling (45%), and a preference for anonymous testing for their patients (42%).

Pretest counseling. According to CDC guidelines (CDC, 1993b, 1994c), HIV pretest counseling must include a personalized client risk assessment following the guidelines previously discussed. This assessment should lead to prevention counseling and, when appropriate, the development of a personalized plan for the client to reduce the risk of HIV infection and transmission. This plan should focus on barriers to safer behaviors and identify previous successes in making behavior changes. It is important that this plan be developed before test results are determined.

When appropriate, clients should be provided with information about the virus and how it is transmitted. The health counselor should discuss what the test results mean and indicate that there is a need to be retested after discontinuing high-risk behaviors. Anticipated reactions should be assessed and assistance provided in helping individuals to receive support from others.

During pretest counseling, it is important to discuss safer sex practices even if the woman indicates that she plans to become abstinent. It is still important to develop an HIV risk reduction plan in case she should become sexually active. In presenting safer sex practices, it is vital to consider and integrate the woman's religious and cultural practices, her sexual orientation, her individual sex habits, concerns she may have about changing her behavior with a particular partner, and the presence of coercion or physical abuse from that partner (Holman & McTague, 1995).

As discussed in the earlier section on prevention, it may be difficult for an individual woman to introduce the use of condoms to her partner. Discussing partner reactions, offering to counsel or present safer sex information to partners as well, and presenting women with information on alternatives that may provide some protection such as the use of the female condom or spermicidal agents is crucial to enhancing safer sex behaviors (Holman & McTague, 1995). Counselors need to be aware of the difficulty of providing individual options for a dyadic behavior. The more that men can be brought into the counseling process and made aware of their role and responsibilities for contributing to their partner's health, the greater the chance that dyadic options such as condom use will be adopted as a prevention strategy.

Return for posttest counseling. Not everyone who receives HIV testing returns for posttest counseling. Research indicates that overall, only 63% of individuals who received testing returned for posttest counseling (CDC, 1993b). The lowest rates of return were recorded for adolescents, Blacks, and clients served in family planning and STD clinics (Valdiserri et al., 1993). These statistics may reflect difficulties in accessing the health care system for these subgroups. Overall, women were slightly less likely to return for HIV posttest counseling than men. CDC technical guidance indicates that HIV counseling programs should be active in addressing the problem of failure to return for HIV posttest counseling, determining whether specific barriers associated with the facility, such as long waiting times, deter clients. It is recommended that programs contact HIV-positive and high-risk HIV-negative clients who have not returned to learn their test results and who therefore have not received posttest counseling.

Posttest counseling. Posttest counseling, like pretest counseling, should be conducted by a provider who is trained in pre- and posttest counseling as well as gender- and culture-specific issues. In addition, whenever possible, posttest counseling should be conducted by the same provider who conducted the pretest counseling. For the woman who is HIV-negative, posttest counseling is another opportunity to provide and review information about HIV, safer sex practices, and the meaning of a negative test (Holman & McTague, 1995). For the woman who is HIV-positive, Holman and McTague reviewed the seven most important matters to cover during initial posttest counseling: (a) the test results; (b) the meaning of a positive test, review of HIV transmission, and its effects on the immune system; (c) the importance of maintenance of health, monitoring, early medical interventions, and antiviral therapies; (d) review and development of an individualized plan for safer sex and safer needle and drug paraphernalia practices; (e) issues of confidentiality of test results; (f) reproductive issues and pregnancy; and (g) identification of support persons. Additionally, at the time of posttest counseling it is important to provide referrals for whatever additional services might be necessary such as social, legal, psychological, and peer support services. Referrals or appointments for HIV antibody counseling and testing of partners and other family members should be given when appropriate. A follow-up visit should be scheduled within 1–2 weeks following a positive test result for support, continuity, medical treatment when appropriate, and psychosocial care. This visit should be sooner if requested by the client.

It is best to inform an individual of her HIV status at the start of the posttest counseling visit. However, for those who are HIV-positive, shock at the news of learning that she has a life-threatening illness may result in being unable to hear and recall information provided in the posttest counseling session. This can be due to the impact of trauma on short-term memory (Jaccard, Wilson, & Radecki, 1995). Therefore, verbal descriptions about HIV infection, treatment, and transmission should be supplemented with written and visual materials for some individuals. Women who are less likely to read about the disease should be referred to additional services for follow-up.

When counseling an HIV-positive individual, the provider should go over information about the disease and strategies for reducing transmission. Sessions usually last 45–75 minutes when conducted by a dedicated HIV counselor. Much of the care women receive for HIV and AIDS is in the primary care setting, either hospital or community based. In these settings, it may be unrealistic for providers to offer the amount of time necessary for full counseling. Therefore, it is important to schedule a woman for a return visit soon or to refer her to specialized HIV services to follow up with additional information.

Health care providers must not underestimate the difficulty of making changes in women's sexual behaviors, however. Research indicates that the behavioral consequences of HIV counseling and testing are limited (Ickovics, Morrill, Beren, Walsh, & Rodin, 1994). Although the average level of sexual risk was lower for tested than nontested women, there was no change for either group from baseline to 3-month follow-up posttesting.

Some preliminary studies have examined the psychosocial sequelae of notification of HIV status. Data document the existence of depression in women blood donors who had been notified of their HIV-positive status (Cleary et al. 1993). Another study, however, showed that depression, anxiety, hostility, and other symptoms were just as high or higher in an HIV-negative group who had requested testing (Pergami et al., 1993). This result emphasizes that depression may be high among women who perceive themselves to be at risk for HIV infection, even if they turn out to be HIV-negative.

Barriers to HIV counseling and testing. Many barriers exist to serotesting for women. A primary barrier is the reluctance of health care professionals to encourage testing despite the presence of relevant symptoms or risk factors. Physicians often encourage testing for groups that historically have been considered at high risk for HIV infection. In a national survey, 95% of primary care physicians indicated they would encourage gay men and IDUs to be tested. However, only 74% indicated they would encourage testing on the basis of an STD history, 57% on another drug or alcohol history, and only 40% would encourage testing of sexually active adolescents (CDC, 1993b).

A second barrier is that women may not want HIV testing for a variety of reasons, including the lack of perception of risk. Kalichman, Hunter, and Kelly (1992) found that minority women at risk perceived themselves to be less susceptible to HIV infection than nonminority women at risk. On the other hand, women may not want to know their HIV status for fear of having to tell others they are HIV-positive, leading to possible rejection from the family or other types of negative evaluation. Other factors that may inhibit women from seeking testing include fear of discrimination, effects on jobs, effects on children and ability to care for families, or fears about the implications of HIV and AIDS for health (Ethier, Ickovics, & Rodin, 1995). In a nationwide, population-based telephone survey of more than 13,000 men and women, for women aged 21–34 who had had more than 10 partners in their life, only 38% had been tested for HIV (Berrios et al., 1993).

A third barrier is that women may have poor access to testing because of travel expenses or lack of child care, especially test sites and providers offering bilingual services.

Optimizing Health and Mental Health Outcomes in Women With HIV and AIDS

Health care providers can play a significant role in optimizing health and mental health outcomes of women who are HIV-positive or who have AIDS. The clinical and preliminary research literature suggest several strategies that may reduce morbidity as well as adverse psychosocial sequelae associated with HIV and AIDS in women.

Assessment of Psychosocial Stress, Symptoms, and Strengths Across the Disease Spectrum

It is important to assess the psychological and social service concerns of women as they progress along the disease spectrum. This evaluation must take into account the complex relationships between physiology and psychology. Women with HIV may be at greater risk for psychological and relational distress at specific times in the disease course (Coons, Spence, Walch, Harwell, & Striepe, 1995). The first significant stressor occurs at the time of HIV testing, when the individual may learn that she has a life-threatening disease subject to social stigma. Information on HIV status may precipitate depression, anxiety, or suicidal thoughts in some women. However, for other women, the diagnosis of HIV infection may lead them to take better care of themselves and take more control of their lives (e.g., by returning to work or school, stopping drug use, improving health habits).

Subsequent points of stress or anxiety include the development of HIV- and AIDS-related physical symptoms, hospitalizations for opportunistic infections, the diagnosis of opportunistic infections that signal a transition to AIDS, or a decline in daily functioning. As physical problems progress, social, psychological, and economic burdens may increase (Jaccard et al., 1995). It is important to remember that each woman interprets these markers according to her own set of meanings about their consequences. The perceived consequences of the disease will affect not only her own functioning but also the functioning of her family, partner, and children. Providers may find it useful to assess the impact of the disease on a woman's daily living and relationships. Providing information about the course and treatment of HIV infection and AIDS as well as its psychosocial impact will allow women to react on the basis of accurate knowledge rather than fears.

Responding to the Health, Mental Health, and Social Needs of Women With HIV and AIDS

Women coping with HIV and AIDS report a broad range of service needs for themselves as well as their family members (Coons et al., 1993). These concerns are likely to change throughout the course of the disease. Health care professionals can play a key role in referring women to appropriate hospital, community, and peer resources. These may include referral to specialists for medical evaluation and treatment; mental health providers; drug treatment programs; social workers or case managers to respond to housing and financial concerns; or legal aid workers to address custody, marital, property, or criminal issues. Clergy may be a valuable resource in providing support and addressing spiritual concerns. Participation in peer support groups for women living with HIV or AIDS that are sensitive to ethnic or cultural, sexual orientation, or religious concerns can also be encouraged.

Reducing Isolation and Increasing Social Support

Many women have little or no access through their own social networks to information about HIV or AIDS and therefore must rely on the medical setting for this knowledge. Many HIV-positive women may have never met another woman with HIV infection (Chung & McGraw, 1992). Disclosing HIV status, seeking support, and finding referrals for HIV-related problems often are more stressful when a person's social network is not very knowledgeable about HIV.

An important component of obtaining support is a willingness to disclose AIDS or HIV infection. One study of disclosure in women showed that rates were lowest for disclosure to extended family members, somewhat higher for immediate family members, and highest for lovers and friends. Spanish-speaking Latinas were the least likely to disclose their HIV-positive status (Simoni et al., 1995). Simoni et al. speculated that for these unacculturated Latina women, the cultural norms of simpatía and familism may have inhibited disclosure. Health care providers may find it useful to refer women who want to maintain closeness with their parents or other family members to counseling and supportive services that can help them to disclose their HIV status to their family.

Nearly two thirds of women of various ethnic or racial backgrounds in another study expressed a desire for information on how to disclose their HIV status to others (Coons et al., 1993). Furthermore, Simoni et al. (1995) found that women's reasons for not disclosing varied by target of disclosure. Nondisclosure to lovers and friends was attributed to a desire to avoid rejection or maintain privacy. Nondisclosure to parents was often attributed to a desire to protect the parent or concerns about stigmatization. It is clear that there are significant and varied concerns that prevent some women from telling family members and others of their illness and potentially gaining support. Women's perceptions of rejection or even physical abuse if others learn they are HIV-positive or have AIDS also may be realistic. These concerns underscore the need for change in societal attitudes to a more compassionate, less morally judgmental view of HIV and AIDS.

Some preliminary research has demonstrated that support groups for women with HIV or AIDS are helpful. Chung and McGraw (1992) found that a common problem identified by women was isolation. They found that women experienced shame and stigmatization because of their illness. Many believed that the only available support services were designed for gay men. It is important to reduce social isolation among women who have been diagnosed with HIV infection or AIDS. Health care providers can encourage patient participation in peer support groups by providing them with meeting times and contact information. Providing space or other resources at the hospital or community sites also can encourage participation.

Reducing High-Risk Behavior and Enhancing Self-Care

It is important for women with HIV infection to reduce high-risk behavior, including drug use and sexual behaviors, that put them at risk for additional STDs. However, research on the extent to which women modify risky behaviors after learning they are HIV-positive is lacking. For some women, the stress of being diagnosed with a chronic, life-threatening illness may be the precipitant for further risky behavior, especially if a woman tends to cope with stress through the use of drugs, alcohol, or sex. It thus is important for providers to assess drug use and sexual behaviors in women with HIV infection, to inform women about the potentially health-threatening effects of these behaviors, and to encourage training in stress reduction and healthful coping strategies.

It currently is unclear how drug or alcohol use in women with HIV infection affects immune functioning, viral activity, or disease survival, although research suggests adverse effects on these outcomes (Peterson et al., 1993). Furthermore, repeat exposure to HIV infection may lead to co-infection with a distinct HIV strain, a phenomenon that may occur more frequently than previously thought (Hu et al., 1996). Therefore, it is important to help women abstain from both drug use and sexual behaviors that put them at risk of exposure to another strain of the HIV, increased viral load (which could occur through infection by someone in a more advanced stage of HIV disease; Cohn, 1993), or another STD and to prevent the infection of others.

Health professionals can play a significant role in secondary prevention of adverse psychosocial and disease sequelae by providing appropriate counseling, referrals, and encouragement to abstain from drugs and increase safer sex behaviors. These activities, as well as improved nutrition, social support, and healthful coping strategies such as meditation or relaxation may also help women to feel they have increased control over their own health and well-being.

Identifying Women at Risk

The majority of women living with HIV or AIDS demonstrate a high degree of resilience. Many women with HIV infection or AIDS care for dependent children as well as other relatives. They may be working or attending school or participating in a drug recovery program. In addition, they are often coping with the stresses associated with poverty.

However, some women are at risk for more rapid progression of HIV infection toward AIDS. As discussed, research indicates that women who continue to engage in risky behaviors may be at greater risk for a faster progression toward AIDS. Correlates of these risky behaviors include a history of sexual abuse and physical abuse (Harlow et al., 1993). Women who are homeless or those with severe mental illness requiring hospitalization are at increased risk. It has been reported that 6.4% of hospitalized homeless mentally ill patients in New York City (1 in 16) were found to be HIV-positive (Empfield et al., 1993), as were 5.5% of predominantly domiciled patients admitted to two public psychiatric hospitals in New York City (Cournos et al., 1991). Women who are at risk require increased contact with support resources, including medical and mental health practitioners as well as social service and community-based programs. In addition, women who are caring for infected partners or other family members as well as themselves are under increased stress, which puts them at risk for a more rapid disease progression.

Conclusion

Many health care practitioners have learned that care and prevention are two sides of the same coin (Coates, 1994). Prevention of HIV and AIDS requires that HIV and AIDS assessment and intervention prevention services be offered whenever medical services are provided to women. Because there are significant barriers to receiving such services for women, it is important that the way in which services are offered be tailored to meet women's needs.

It is useful to remember that fighting HIV is as much about the social conditions that allow the disease to spread as the biological mechanisms that govern its progression. If researchers are to be successful in the prevention of HIV infection and AIDS, it is crucial that effective prevention, intervention, and treatment strategies are identified that are sensitive to the conditions of women's lives. Such issues range from women's reproductive desires in the face of HIV infection to the possibility that partner notification procedures may result in physical violence. It will be challenging for health care providers to structure care that integrates not only medical but psychological, relational, and social services needs for women at risk for HIV infection, women who are HIV-positive, and those living with AIDS. In providing HIV prevention services, health care providers must remember that women are diverse in their needs with respect to issues such as age, sexual orientation, and ethnicity.

It also is crucial that greater resources be invested in developing prevention methods that women can control. Because the only HIV prevention strategy for sexually active women is the use of condoms, women may not have direct control over their own health protection. Men should also be the target of behavior modification programs so that male norms for condom use are changed.

Health care providers play a crucial role in secondary prevention as well. Health and mental health prevention efforts must continue with women who have already been diagnosed with HIV infection. A growing body of evidence supports the interconnection of stress to immune functioning, emphasizing the need to reduce stress in women's lives associated with poverty and abusive living conditions, as well as the need to teach women healthful coping strategies. Such efforts will have long-lasting effects in promoting the physical as well as emotional well-being of women and their families.

In every phase of intervention, from primary prevention to provision of services to women with AIDS, significant barriers exist to the realization of women's health goals. It is the challenge of health care providers to work toward the elimination of these barriers so that the full goal of prevention of HIV and AIDS in women may be achieved.

References

Berrios, D. C., Hearst, N., Coates, T. J., Stall, R., Hudes, E., Turner, H., Eversley, R., & Catania, J. (1993). HIV antibody testing among those at risk for infection. *Journal of the American Medical Association, 270*, 1576–1580.

Brown, V., & Weissman, G. (1993). Women and men injection drug usrs: An updated look at gender differences and risk factors. In B. S. Brown & G. M. Beschner (Eds.), *Handbook on risk of AIDS: Injection drug users and sexual partners* (pp. 173–194). Westport, CT: Greenwood Press.

Castro, K. G., Valdiserri, R. O., & Curran, J. W. (1992). Perspectives on HIV/AIDS epidemiology and prevention from the Eighth International Conference on AIDS. *American Journal of Public Health, 82*, 1465–1470.

Catania, J. A., Coates, T. J., Stall, R., Turner, H., Peterson, J., Hearst, N., Dolcini, M., Hudes, E., Gagnon, J., Wiley, J., & Groves, R. (1992). Prevalence of AIDS-related risk factors and condom use in the United States. *Science, 258*, 1101–1106.

Catania, J. A., Gibson, D. R., Chitwood, D. D., & Coates, T. J. (1990). Methodological problems in AIDS behavioral research: Influences on measurement error and participation bias in studies of sexual behavior. *Psychological Bulletin, 108*, 339–362.

Centers for Disease Control and Prevention. (1993a). Update: Mortality attributable to HIV infection/AIDS among persons aged 25–44 years—United States, 1981–1991. *Morbidity and Mortality Weekly Report, 42*, 481–486.

Centers for Disease Control and Prevention. (1993b). Recommendations for HIV testing services for inpatients and outpatients in acute-care hospital settings and technical guidance on HIV counseling. *Morbidity and Mortality Weekly Report, 42*, 1–17.

Centers for Disease Control and Prevention. (1993c). *The public health impact of needle exchange programs in the United States and abroad.* Atlanta, GA: Author.

Centers for Disease Control and Prevention. (1993d). Update: Acquired immunodeficiency syndrome—United States, 1992. *Morbidity and Mortality Weekly Report, 42*, 547–557.

Centers for Disease Control and Prevention. (1994a). *HIV/AIDS surveillance report (through December 1994)*. Atlanta, GA: Author.

Center for Disease Control and Prevention. (1994b). HIV prevention practices of primary-care physicians—United States, 1992. *Morbidity and Mortality Weekly Report, 42*, 988–992.

Centers for Disease Control and Prevention. (1994c). *HIV counseling, testing and referral standards and guidelines*. Rockville, MD: U.S. Department of Health and Human Services.

Centers for Disease Control and Prevention. (1995). U.S. Public Health Service recommendations for human immunodeficiency virus counseling and voluntary testing for pregnant women. *Morbidity and Mortality Weekly Report, 44*, 1–13.

Centers for Disease Control and Prevention. (1996). *HIV/AIDS surveillance report (through June 1996)*. Atlanta, GA: Author.

Chu, S. Y., Buehler, J. W., Fleming, P. L., & Berkelman, R. L. (1990). Epidemiology of reported cases of AIDS in lesbians, United States 1980–89. *American Journal of Public Health, 80*, 1380–1381.

Chung, J. Y., & McGraw, M. M. (1992). A group approach to psychosocial issues faced by HIV-positive women. *Hospital and Community Psychiatry, 43*, 891–894.

Cleary, P. D., Van Devanter, N., Rogers, T. F., Singer, E., Shipton-Levy, R. Steilen, M., Stuart, A., Avorn, J., & Pindyk, J. (1993). Depressive symptoms in blood donors notified of HIV infection. *American Journal of Public Health, 83*, 534–539.

Coates, T. (1994). Care and prevention: Hand and hand. *Focus, 9*, 1–4.

Cochran, S. D., & Mays, V. M. (1990). Sex, lies and HIV. *New England Journal of Medicine, 322*, 774–775.

Cohn, J. A. (1993). Human immunodeficiency virus and AIDS: 1993 update. *Journal of Nurse-Midwifery, 38*, 65–85.

Coons, H. L., McCown, W. G., Koffler, S. P., Spence, M. R., Helz, J. W., Walch, S. E., Malloy, C. D., Campbell, E., Striepe, M., & Smith, J. (1993). Psychosocial aspects of HIV and AIDS in women. In P. J. Morokoff (Chair), *Primary and secondary prevention of AIDS in women*. Symposium conducted at the 101st Annual Convention of the American Psychological Association, Toronto.

Coons, H. L., Spence, M. R., Walch, S. E., Harwell, T. S., & Striepe, M. I. (1995, August). Predictors of psychosocial adjustment in women with HIV/AIDS. In H. L. Coons (Chair), *Adjustment in women with HIV/AIDS: Implications for research and practice*. Symposium conducted at the 103rd Annual Convention of the American Psychological Association, New York.

Cournos, F., Empfield, M., Horwath, E., McKinnon, K., Meyer, I., Schrage, H., Durrie, C., & Agosin, B. (1991). HIV seroprevalence among patients admitted to two psychiatric hospitals. *American Journal of Psychiatry, 148*, 1225–1230.

Ethier, K. A., Ickovics, J. R., & Rodin, J. (1995). For whose benefit? Women and AIDS public policy. In A. O'Leary & L. Jemmott (Eds.), *Women and AIDS: The emerging epidemic*. New York: Plenum.

Ellerbrock, T., Bush, T. J., Chamberland, M. E., & Oxtoby, M. J. (1991). Epidemiology of women with AIDS in the United States, 1981 through 1990: A comparison with heterosexual men with AIDS. *Journal of the American Medical Association, 265*, 2971–2975.

Empfield, M., Cournos, F., Meyer, I., McKinnon, K., Horwath, E., Silver, M., Schrage, H., & Herman, R. (1993). HIV seroprevalence among homeless patients admitted to a psychiatric inpatient unit. *American Journal of Psychiatry, 150*, 47–52.

Farr, G., Gabelnick, H., Sturgen, K., & Dorflinger, L. (1994). Contraceptive efficacy and acceptability of the female condom. *American Journal of Public Health, 84*, 1960–1964.

Feucht, T., Stephens, R., & Roman, S. (1990). The sexual behavior of intravenous drug users: Assessing the risk of sexual transmission of HIV. *The Journal of Drug Issues, 20*, 195–213.

Feucht, T. E., Stephens, R. C., & Sullivan, T. S. (1993). Drug use patterns among injection drug users and their sex partners. In B. S. Brown & G. M. Beschner (Eds.), *Handbook on risk of AIDS: Injection drug users and sexual partners*. Westport, CT: Greenwood Press.

Flaskerud, J., & Rush, C. E. (1989). AIDS and traditional health beliefs and practices of Black women. *Nursing Research, 38*, 210–215.

Gerber, A. R., Valdiserri, R. O., Holtgrave, D. R., Jones, T. S., West, G. R., Hinman, A. R., & Curran, J. W. (1993). Preventive services guidelines for primary care clinicians caring for adults and adolescents infected with the human immunodeficiency virus. *Archives of Family Medicine, 2*, 969–979.

Grinstead, O. A., Faigeles, B., Binson, D., & Eversley, R. (1993). Sexual risk for human immunodeficiency virus infection among women in high-risk cities. *Family Planning Perspectives, 25*, 252–256, 277.

Harlow, L. L., Quina, K., Morokoff, P. J., Rose, J. S., & Grimley, D. M. (1993). HIV risk in women: A multifaceted model. *Journal of Applied Biobehavioral Research, 1*, 3–38.

Health Resources and Service Administration. (1993a). *HIV/AIDS work group on health care access for Hispanic Americans: Work group #2 access to Ryan White services by Hispanic Americans* (DHHS Publication No. HRSA RD-SP-93-8). Rockville, MD: U.S. Department of Health and Human Services.

Health Resources and Service Administration. (1993b). *HIV/AIDS work group on health care access for American Indians/Alaska Natives* (DHHS Publication No. HRSA RD-SP-93-6). Rockville, MD: U.S. Department of Health and Human Services.

Hobfoll, S. E., Jackson, A. P., Lavin, J., Britton, P. J., & Shepherd, J. B. (1994). Reducing inner-city women's AIDS risk activities: A study of single, pregnant women. *Health Psychology, 13*, 397–403.

Holman, S., & McTague, B. L. (1995). Providing HIV counseling and testing services to women. In H. L. Minkoff, J. A. DeHovitz, & A. Duerr (Eds.), *HIV infection in women* (pp. 263–277). New York: Raven Press.

Hu, D. J., Dondero, T. J., Rayfield, M. A., George, J. R., Schochetmen, G., Jaffe, H. W., Luo, C.-C., Kalish, M. L., Weniger, B. G., Pau, C.-P., Schable, C. A., & Curran, J. W. (1996). The emerging genetic diversity of HIV: The importance of global surveillance for diagnostic, research, and prevention. *Journal of the American Medical Association, 275*, 210–216.

Ickovics, J. R., Morrill, A., Beren, S. E., Walsh, U., & Rodin, J. (1994). Limited effects of HIV counseling and testing for women. *Journal of the American Medical Association, 272*, 443–448.

Jaccard, J. J., Wilson, T. E., & Radecki, C. M. (1995). Psychological issues in the treatment of HIV-infected women. In H. L. Minkoff, J. A. DeHovitz, & A. Duerr (Eds.), *HIV infection in women* (pp. 87–105). New York: Raven Press.

Kalichman, S. C., Hunter, T. L., & Kelly, J. A. (1992). Perceptions of AIDS susceptibility among minority and nonminority women at risk for HIV infection. *Journal of Consulting and Clinical Psychology, 60*, 725–732.

Kelly, J. A., Murphy, D. A., Washington, C. D., Wilson, T. S., Koob, J. J., Davis, D. R., Ledezma, G., & Davantes, B. (1994). Effects of HIV/AIDS prevention groups for high-risk women in urban primary health care clinics. *American Journal of Public Health, 84*, 1918–1922.

Kennedy, M. B., Scarlett, M. I., Duerr, A. C., & Chu, S. Y. (1995). Assessing HIV risk among women who have sex with women: Scientific and communication issues. *Journal of the American Medical Women's Association, 50*, 103–107.

Kumpfer, K. L. (1991). *Treatment programs for drug-abusing women. The Future of Children, 1*, 50–60. (Available from The David & Lucille Packard Foundation, 300 Second Street, Suite 102, Los Altos, CA 94022).

Magura, S., Kang, S., Shapiro, J., & O'Day, J. (1993). HIV risk among women injecting drug users who are in jail. *Addiction, 88*, 1351–1360.

Mays, V. M., & Cochran, S. D. (1988). Issues in the perception of AIDS risk and risk reduction activities by Black and Hispanic/Latina women. *American Psychologist, 43*, 949–957.

Mays, V. M., & Cochran, S. D. (1993). Ethnic and gender differences in beliefs about sex partner questioning to reduce HIV risk. *Journal of Adolescent Research, 8*, 77–88.

Mays, V. M., & Cochran, S. D. (1995). HIV/AIDS in the African American community: Changing concerns, changing behaviors. In M. Stein & A. Baum (Eds.), *Chronic diseases* (pp. 259–272). Hillsdale, NJ: Erlbaum.

Mays, V. M., & Cochran, S. D. (1997). *Is there a legacy of Tuskegee? AIDS misbeliefs among inner city African Americans and Hispanics*. Manuscript submitted for publication.

Mays, V. M. Cochran, S. D., Pies, C., Chu, S. Y., & Erhardt, A. (1996). The risk of HIV infection for lesbians and other women who have sex with women: Implications for HIV research, prevention, policy, and services. *Women's Health: Research on Gender, Behavior, and Policy, 2 (nos. 1 and 2)*, 119–139.

Mikawa, J. K., Morones, P. A., Gomez, A., Case, H. L., Olsen, D., & Gonzales-Huss, M. J. (1992). Cultural practices of Hispanics: Implication for the prevention of AIDS. *Hispanic Journal of Behavioral Sciences, 14*, 421–433.

Morokoff, P. J., Harlow, L. L., & Quina, K. (1995). Women and AIDS. In A. L. Stanton & S. J. Gallant (Eds.), *The psychology of women's health* (pp. 117–169). Washington, DC: American Psychological Association.

Morokoff, P. J., Quina, K., Harlow, L. L., Whitmire, L., Grimley, D. M., Gibson, P. R., & Burkholder, G. (in press). *The Sexual Assertiveness Scale (SAS) for Women: Development and validation. Journal of Personality and Social Psychology.*

Mosher, W. D., & Pratt, W. F. (1993). *Advance data from vital and health statistics of the National Center for Health Statistics* (Vol. 239). Rockville, MD: U.S. Department of Health and Human Services.

Moss, G. B., Clementson, D., D'Costa, L. J., Plummer, F. A., Ndinya, A., Reilly, M., Holmes, K. K., Piot, P., Maitha, G. M., Hillier, S. L., Kiviat, N. C., & Cameron, C. W. (1991). Association of cervical ectopy with heterosexual transmission of human immunodeficiency virus: Results of a study of couples in Nairobi, Kenya. *Journal of Infectious Diseases, 164*, 588–591.

Osmond, M. W., Wambach, K. G., Harrison, D. F., Byers, J., Levine, P., Imershein, A., & Quadagno, D. M. (1993). The multiple jeopardy of race, class, and gender for AIDS risk among women. *Gender and Society, 7*, 99–120.

Padian, N. S., Shiboski, S. S., & Jewell, N. (1990, June). The relative efficiency of female-to-male HIV sexual transmission. *Proceedings of the VIth International Conference on AIDS*, Abstract No. Th.C.101, p. 159.

Pergami, A., Gala, C., Burgess, A., Durbano, F., Zanello, D., Riccio, M., Invernizzi, G., & Catalan, J. (1993). The psychosocial impact of HIV infection in women. *Journal of Psychosomatic Research, 37*, 687–696.

Peterson, P. K., Gekker, G., Chao, C., Schut, R., Verhoef, J., Edelman, C. K., Erice, A., & Balfour, H. H. (1993). Cocaine amplifies HIV-1 replication in cytomegalovirus-stimulated peripheral blood mononuclear cell cultures. *Journal of Immunology, 149*, 676–680.

Population Council. (1994). *The Population Council annual report, 1994.*

Public Health Service. (1991). *Healthy people 2000: National health promotion and disease prevention objectives—Full report, with commentary* (DHHS Publication No. PHS 91-50212). Rockville, MD: U.S. Department of Health and Human Services.

Quinn, S. C. (1993). AIDS and the African American woman: The triple burden of race, class, and gender. *Health Education Quarterly, 20*, 305–320.

Simoni, J. M., Mason, H. R. C., Marks, G., Ruiz, M. S., Reed, D., & Richardson, J. L. (1995). Women's disclosure of HIV infection: Rates, reasons, and reactions. *Journal of Consulting and Clinical Psychology, 63*, 474–478.

Singer, M. (1991). Confronting the AIDS epidemic among IV drug users: Does ethnic culture matter? *AIDS Education and Prevention, 3*, 258–283.

Stephens, R. C., Feucht, T. E., & Gibbs, B. H. (1993). Needle use behavior. In B. S. Brown & G. M Beschner (Eds.), *Handbook on risk of AIDS* (pp. 116–136). Westport, CT: Greenwood Press.

Thomas, S., & Quinn, S. (1991). The Tuskegee Syphilis Study 1932–1972: Implications for HIV education and AIDS risk reduction programs in the African American community. *American Journal of Public Health, 81*, 1498–1505.

Trussell, J., Sturgen, K., Strickler, J., & Dominik, R. (1994). Comparative contraceptive efficacy of the female condom and other barrier methods. *Family Planning Perspectives, 26*, 66–72.

Valdiserri, R. O., Moore, M., Gerber, A. R., Campbell, C. H., Dillon, B. A., & West, G. R. (1993). A study of clients returning for counseling after HIV testing: Implications for improving rates of return. *Public Health Reports, 108*, 12–18.

Watters, J. K., Estilo, M. J., Clark, G. L., & Lorvick, J. (1994). Syringe and needle exchange as HIV/AIDS prevention for injection drug users. *Journal of the American Medical Association, 271,* 115–120.

Weller, S. C. (1993). A meta-analysis of condom effectiveness in reducing sexually transmitted HIV. *Social Science and Medicine, 36,* 1635–1644.

19

Breast Cancer: Psychosocial Factors Influencing Risk Perception, Screening, Diagnosis, and Treatment

Reneé Royak-Schaler, Annette L. Stanton, and Sharon Danoff-Burg

Breast cancer has a profound psychological impact on American women and their families. It is the Number 1 cause of death in women aged 40–55 years and follows cardiovascular disease as the Number 2 cause for women over 50 (U.S. Department of Health Human Services, 1990). During 1995 approximately 182,000 new cases of breast cancer occurred among women in the United States (American Cancer Society, 1995). It is the most common cancer among women in the United States in every major ethnic group (Kelsey & Horn-Ross, 1993). Despite the 20% higher incidence of breast cancer in White women, the 5-year relative survival rate for Black women diagnosed from 1983 to 1988 was 17% less than in White women. This disparity continued between 1989 and 1992, with death rates for White women declining 5.5% and those for Black women increasing by 2.6% (National Cancer Institute [NCI], 1995).

These differences appear to be related to socioeconomic factors. Minority low-income women are less likely to recognize breast cancer risk factors and the need for early detection than White women of higher incomes (Burack & Liang, 1989). Women with lower-than-median education and incomes are less likely to be screened for breast cancer, delay seeking care in the presence of symptoms, are diagnosed in later disease stages, and have 25% higher death rates from breast cancer than those of higher education and incomes (Hayward, Shapiro, Freeman, & Corey, 1988). They are less likely to participate in psychosocial interventions demonstrated to improve psychological and physical well-being among cancer patients.

It is critical to educate women about breast cancer risk factors, early detection, prompt symptom care, treatment options, and effective intervention programs for dealing with the psychosocial consequences of breast cancer. In this chapter we clarify the role of the medical educator in this process, highlighting the importance of psychosocial and behavioral interventions in facilitating breast cancer screening, symptom care, and treatment. Although the literature is uneven with regard to relevant individual differences (e.g., socioeconomic status [SES], ethnicity) in these realms, we address data on diversity when available.

Breast Cancer Screening in the 1990s

Despite advances in the early detection of breast cancer, many women are not compliant with recommended screening guidelines for breast physical examination and mammography. Data from the National Health Interview Survey of 1987 indicate that more than 80% of women 40 years and older have had a physical breast examination, although only one third reported having had one in the past year and 63% reported having been examined in the past 3 years. Women with higher education and incomes are more likely to have had recent physical breast examinations and mammograms. Twice as many women with family incomes of $20,000 or more reported having had mammograms in 1987 as those with lower incomes (Breen & Kessler, 1994). Income and education, more so than race, explained underscreening among older Hispanic, White, and Black women (Fox & Roetzheim, 1994).

Although 50% of eligible women in the United States have had at least one mammogram, fewer follow American Cancer Society guidelines that recommend yearly mammograms for women 50 and older and screening every 1–2 years for women aged 40–49 years (National Cancer Institute Breast Cancer Screening Consortium, 1990). Surveys indicate that approximately one third of women have regular mammograms. Younger women (aged 40–64 years) are more likely to have had a mammogram than older women (aged 65 and older; NCI Breast Cancer Screening Consortium, 1990). Among low-income, inner-city older women, financial barriers to mammography persist despite Medicare coverage (Kiefe, McKay, Halevy, & Brody, 1994).

Mammography Screening: Developing Guidelines While the Debate Continues

Mammography is a highly effective screening modality in women aged 50–74 years. It reduces breast cancer mortality by 26% regardless of the number of mammographic views per screening, screening interval, duration of screening or follow-up, or addition of clinical breast examination (CBE; Kerlikowske, Grady, Rubin, Sandrock, & Ernster, 1995).

In 1993 the NCI International Workshop on Screening for Breast Cancer concluded that for 40- to 49-year-old women, randomized controlled trials of breast cancer screening showed no benefit 5–7 years after entry and uncertain benefit at 10–12 years (Fletcher, Black, Harris, Rimer, & Shapiro, 1993). Subsequently, the NCI withdrew its support for mammography screening every 1–2 years for 40- to 49-year-old women. The American Cancer Society, the National Medical Association, and several other organizations concluded that there were insufficient new data to change the consensus guidelines, and they continue recommending mammography screening beginning at age 40, every 1–2 years, and once a year after age 50. CBEs are recommended yearly after age 40 and breast self-examinations (BSEs) on a monthly basis beginning at age 20 (Patterson, 1994).

In 1994, the NCI Office of Cancer Communications assessed the responses of women to the controversy in screening guidelines and found that 40- to 49-year-old women wanted the following kinds of information to help them make screening decisions: (a) information on breast cancer risk, including checklists to determine personal risk status; (b) information on mammogram safety over time, including sequelae of false-positives and false-negatives; and (c) guidelines for obtaining good-quality mammograms (D. Bloom, 1994; Sutton, Eisner, & Johnston, 1994).

The debate still continues in the medical community. Recent findings of eight clinical trials document 24% fewer deaths from breast cancer in women who had mammograms in their 40s than those who did not get them until age 50 (Smart, Hendrick, Rutledge, & Smith, 1995). To examine the newly available data from observational studies and randomized trials, NCI and the Office of Medical Applications of Research of NIH convened a 1997 Consensus Development Conference on Breast Cancer Screening for Women ages 40–49. The consensus statement from this conference specified that the available data do not warrant a single recommendation for all women in their forties. It recommended informed decision making by women ages 40 to 49 years, in consultation with their health care providers. These decisions would be based on individual medical histories, perceptions of risks and benefits, and the ability to cope with uncertainty. The consensus panel urged reimbursement by third-party payors and health maintenance organizations for women in their forties who choose to have mammograms (Gordis, 1997).

Primary care providers are critical agents in communicating this information to women and sustaining the increases in screening mammography observed from 1987 to 1990. Part of this process involves acquiring skills to educate women with information that promotes informed screening decisions and strategies to translate these decisions into action. This can be accomplished by (a) using culturally specific strategies to promote screening for early detection; (b) recommending mammograms to all women meeting the risk and age requirements; (c) providing information about low-cost mammography facilities that meet federal quality standards; and (d) promoting national insurance coverage for both mammograms and CBEs (Breen & Kessler, 1994).

Mammography, CBE, and BSE: Complementary Screening Modalities

Mammography, CBE, and BSE are complementary screening modalities. Historical and tumor registry data, observational studies, and randomized trials suggest that the detection of breast cancers at smaller sizes through physical examinations can lead to important reductions in mortality (Foster, Worden, Costanza, & Soloman, 1992; Zapka, 1994). The Health Insurance Plan Study of Greater New York indicated that without mammograms, 30% of breast cancers would not have been detected when they were; without CBE, 45% would have gone undetected. Together, these two methods accounted for 75% of detections (Shapiro, Venet, Strax, & Venet, 1988). The Breast Cancer Detection Demonstration Project, involving 285,000 participants, showed that screening with CBE and mammograms was the least sensitive for women aged 35–39 (60% tumor detection rate) and the most sensitive for women aged 60–74 (81% detection rate; Seidman et al., 1987).

The ability of mammography to detect breast cancer is age dependent; younger women have greater breast tissue density and less breast fat, making X-ray penetration more difficult. Reported rates of false-negative mammograms across women of all ages is 10–22%, with higher rates in younger women (Physician Insurers Association of America [PIAA], 1990). Even though only one third of breast cancers are diagnosed in women under 50 years of age, 70% of claimants in the PIAA study and 84% of indemnity awards were for women in this age group, raising questions about mammography effectiveness in younger women (Brenner, 1992). Significantly, delay in the diagnosis of breast cancer is now the second leading cause of negligence lawsuits filed against physicians and the leading cause of dollar awards issued by third-party carriers (PIAA, 1990).

Despite ongoing questioning of the value of BSE as a screening test, several studies have demonstrated that women who perform BSE have breast cancer detected at earlier stages of disease (Locker et al., 1989). Unfortunately, BSE practice is less than optimal in terms of both the number of women who perform it monthly, only 25–30% of women, and its proficiency (Stefanek & Wilcox, 1990). Black women appear to practice BSE irregularly and to be less aware of its benefits; older Black women tend to practice BSE more frequently than younger women (Nemcek, 1989). Women increase their BSE skill and frequency with adequate training (Jacob, Penn, Kulik, & Spieth, 1992).

BSE practice is associated with increased awareness of breast health and the perception of increased control over one's health (Foster et al., 1992). BSE frequently is performed by women who have had previous biopsies and a history of benign breast disease, are well informed about BSE and screening, demonstrate self-efficacy in relation to the procedure, and perceive themselves to be active partners in controlling their own health (Baines, 1992). When encouraging their patients to perform BSE, medical professionals should be aware that the long-term practice of BSE may require that providers discuss the negative consequences of not performing BSE with their patients as well as the benefits (Meyerowitz & Chaiken, 1987).

The practice of BSE and CBE has been associated with obtaining regular mammograms (Baines, To, & Wall, 1990). It therefore is important for health care providers to emphasize the companion nature of all three screening methods. As with mammograms, there are quality control issues with physical examinations. Women and their physicians must both be urged to practice consistent and thorough patterns of coverage and appropriate palpation techniques (Fletcher, O'Malley, Polgrim, & Gonzalez, 1989).

Facilitating Early Detection Practices

Psychosocial factors that are linked to women participating in CBE and mammography screening include women's perceptions of need; health care providers' perceptions, practices, and recommendations; and social and demographic factors (Smith & Haynes, 1992). The mammography screening barriers most frequently cited by women include cost, lack of insurance coverage, not having any problems with their breasts, and no physician recommendation (Zapka, Stoddard, Costanza, & Greene, 1989). Data from the 1990 National Health Interview Survey indicated that the most frequently reported reason for not having a mammogram was no awareness of need or no breast problems (Breen & Kessler, 1994). Forty-one percent lacked knowledge about the need for breast cancer screening, and 31% reported that physicians had not recommended mammography. Cost was cited by 7% of women as a reason for not having mammograms.

Although recent legislation in many states mandates coverage of screening mammography by insurers and biennial screening mammography by Medicare, Washington State surveys with women aged 50–75 did not find that improved insurance coverage significantly increased the use of screening mammography (Urban, Anderson, & Peacock, 1994). The lack of coverage for preventive office visits, however, limits women's contact with physicians for CBE and mammography referral (Burg, Lane, & Polednak, 1990). Research with low-income Black women in North Carolina emphasizes the important role of CBE in mammography referral. Mammography screening was correlated with CBE for 40- to 49-year-old women (Royak-Schaler et al., 1995). Legislation mandating coverage by private insurers and Medicare could significantly affect physician recommendation and create an important standard of care. If all physicians were to refer women for mammography at the same rates as do gynecologists, mammography screening could increase from 59% to 75% (Urban et al., 1994).

Social Networks, Breast Cancer Screening, and Cancer Prevention

Social networks are important in encouraging breast cancer screening tests, timely follow-up for symptoms, and acceptance of doctors' recommendations (J. Bloom, Grazier, Hodge, & Hayes, 1991). Even after controlling for age, education, health status, type of health insurance, and having a primary care physician, Black women with more social ties are more likely to receive mammograms than those with fewer social ties (Kang, Bloom, & Romano, 1994). Social networks, specifically the number of close friends and traditional attitudes toward family, are important determinants of mammography screening behavior among older, low-income Mexican American women (Suarez, Lloyd, Weiss, Rainbolt, & Pulley, 1994). The absence of social ties and sources of emotional support are associated with late diagnosis and increased breast cancer death rate among Black women (Reynolds et al., 1994).

Health promotion interventions using social ties in church communities have been successful in cancer prevention and control and may successfully promote early detection. Church-based education programs with African American and Hispanic women have increased the rates of mammography, BSE, and cervical cancer screening (Davis et al., 1994; Erwin, Spatz, & Turtuno, 1992). Using African American breast cancer survivors as role models, the "witnessing program" promoted breast cancer detection by addressing existing attitudes, norms, and values regarding BSE and mammography (Erwin et al., 1992). Shared values of participants and Black lay health educators may provide positive experiences with breast cancer survivors, serving to counteract the fatalism, negativism, and low knowledge levels within the African American community regarding cancer.

Physician Communication to Facilitate Screening

Women rely on their physicians to tell them when and if they need CBE and mammograms (Smith & Haynes, 1992). Women aged 65 and older whose physicians recommend and discuss mammography are more likely to have had the test in the past year than women whose doctors have not discussed it. Physicians' enthusiasm about the importance of mammography accounts for significant increases in older patients' screening practices (Fox, Siu, & Stein, 1994).

Mammography follow-up rates to CBE can be improved through letters sent to women by physicians. Printed mammography reminder letters should be tailored to individual women's perceptions about mammography and breast cancer, their breast cancer risk factors, and their mammography screening status (Skinner, Strecher, & Hospers, 1994). Low-income Black women are especially responsive to tailored physician letters; they are more likely to read and remember the letters and obtain mammograms after receiving them.

Although more obstetrician-gynecologists are reported to order screening mammograms for their patients older than 50 than are family physicians, general practitioners, and internists, many women receive preventive care from family practice physicians. Because the context of physician practice and the performance of CBE is associated with ordering mammography, encouraging family practice physicians to screen their patients with CBE and mammography according to current guidelines may increase breast cancer screening rates (Taplin, Taylor, Montano, Chinn, & Urban, 1994).

Breast Cancer Risk: Perceptions, Worry, and Screening Among Women With Family Histories of Breast Cancer

Women having one first-degree relative with breast cancer are two to four times more likely to develop the disease; this risk is even higher for women with more than one affected relative (Claus, Risch, & Thompson, 1993). Family history strongly predicts early fatal breast cancer; women with relatives diagnosed at young ages are at increased risk of developing and dying from the disease at younger ages (Calle, Miracle, Moss, & Health, 1993).

Perceptions of risk for developing breast cancer influence women's screening practices. Accurate knowledge of breast cancer risk, particularly the role of family history, perceptions of personal risk, and beliefs about screening effectiveness, is significantly related to screening behaviors (Royak-Schaler et al., 1995). A study that identified perceptions that promote breast cancer screening in Black women with family histories of breast cancer indicated that the majority of participants had inaccurate knowledge of breast cancer risk factors and that they had not received adequate education about risk by their health care providers. Only 25% identified the risk of family history; one quarter identified factors that have not been demonstrated to increase risk, such as bumping and bruising a breast and smoking. Less than 10% of the women identified other factors known to increase breast cancer risk besides family history according to the Gail model, including current age, age at first live birth, age at menarche, and number of benign breast biopsies (Gail et al., 1989; Royak-Schaler et al., 1995).

Although only 25% of this sample reported being told of their higher risk of developing breast cancer because of family, approximately 50% perceived themselves to be at risk of developing this disease and reported concern and worry about this (Royak-Schaler et al., 1995). Unlike rates of breast cancer concern reported for White middle- and upper-income women with family histories, these low-income Black women did not feel that their concern affected their carrying out daily activities (87%) or their moods (70%). Other researchers, however, have found that anxiety or worry about breast cancer risk interferes with mammography screening among women both with and without family histories of breast cancer, particularly those with limited educations (Kash, Holland, Halper, & Miller, 1992; Lerman & Schwartz, 1993).

Along with being concerned about developing breast cancer, many women with family histories of breast cancer overestimate their own risk. Even after individualized counseling that included feedback on personal risk based on the Gail model (Gail et al., 1989; Royak-Schaler et al., 1995), annual screening recommendations for mammography and CBE, and instruction in BSE and monthly recommendation, almost two thirds of women continued to overestimate their personal risk (Lerman et al., 1995). Black women improved their personal risk comprehension more than White women (60% vs. 22%), perhaps because of their lower levels of breast cancer preoccupation. Breast cancer risk counseling appears to reduce breast-cancer-specific distress more for women with a high school education or less, compared with those with more education (Lerman et al., 1995).

Risk counseling is particularly relevant for women with high levels of breast cancer concern and anxiety, who may be more inclined to seek DNA-based testing for breast cancer susceptibility and consider prevention options. These options might include participation in chemoprevention trials, such as the Breast Cancer Prevention Trial, currently being conducted with 16,000 women at centers throughout the United States and Canada, and prophylactic mastectomy. With managed care, women will increasingly rely on primary health care providers for providing information regarding prevention decisions and results of genetic testing. Developing these protocols is critical.

It is important for providers to acknowledge their influence on the screening practices of women with family histories of breast cancer. Professionals can motivate women to participate in routine screening through office visit discussions that provide accurate information about their risk status and the factors that contribute to personal risk. They can facilitate regular screening by addressing the breast cancer concerns and anxiety of women patients (Royak-Schaler, Cheuvront, Wilson, & Williams, 1996).

Breast Symptoms: Patterns of Seeking Care

Patient delay in seeking help for breast symptoms and provider delay in treating those symptoms combine to decrease breast cancer survival. A meta-analysis of 12 studies on patient delay documented that 34% of women were symptomatic for several months before seeking evaluation and that poor women of color were overrepresented in this number (Facione, 1993). Black women, in particular, have lower survival due to later-stage diagnosis and delay in seeking care (Coates et al., 1992).

It is important for health professionals to address the practices and beliefs of patients and providers that may contribute to delays in seeking help. In women with prior histories of fibrocystic breast disease, for example, breast lumps often are attributed to the benign fibrocystic process by both patients and providers, resulting in delays (Lierman, 1988). Women sometimes decide to monitor their breast symptoms by themselves because they believe the lump will go away, are afraid of treatment, or believe treatment will not help (Timko, 1987). On the other hand, women may seek help immediately because of believing treatment will be less disabling and cure more likely with prompt care. Women who practice BSE have been found to seek help promptly for symptoms (Huguley et al., 1988).

Both providers and patients have a variety of responses to breast symptoms. Providers should be aware of the possible range of their patients' as well as their own responses to symptom discovery. Helping patients identify incorrect beliefs and fears will increase the likelihood that women's decisions to seek help or delay are based on accurate understanding of the consequences associated with their actions (Timko, 1987). Understanding the anxiety that patients experience about their symptoms, potential diagnoses, and procedures can enhance effective communication in the medical encounter and promote effective decision making when dealing with breast symptoms.

Breast Cancer Diagnosis: Psychosocial and Behavioral Factors

To provide effective psychosocial intervention to women receiving a diagnosis of breast cancer, health care providers must become knowledgeable about women's experience. For most women with breast cancer, psychological functioning is indistinguishable from that of physically healthy women 12–24 months after diagnosis if the treatment is complete and the cancer is controlled (Vinokur, Threatt, Caplan, & Zimmerman, 1989). Rather than producing global psychological dysfunction, a cancer diagnosis often produces "islands" of psychosocial disruption (Andersen, Anderson, & deProsse, 1989) that vary across the course of the experience and as a function of medical, intrapersonal, and social contexts. In contrast to the research on cancer detection discussed earlier, research on adjustment to breast cancer indicates little about whether the psychological experience varies as a function of ethnic and cultural factors. It is clear that a breast cancer diagnosis may affect a woman's quality of life in several areas, including the psychological, physical, cognitive, and interpersonal realms.

Psychological Distress and the Need for Support

With regard to the chronology of affective experience, psychological distress (e.g., anxiety, depressed mood, fatigue) typically is elevated as one awaits the diagnostic procedure and increases further at the point of breast cancer diagnosis (Stanton & Snider, 1993). For most, distress decreases once a treatment plan is set, although particular aspects of treatment can be disturbing. Distress may surge at the end of active treatment (Hoffman, 1988), perhaps because of a decreased sense that one is playing an active role in fighting cancer, the loss of frequent contact with health care providers, and the perception by oneself and others that one should now be "well." When cancer recurs, women may experience distress exceeding that at diagnosis, and those who have end-stage disease are at risk for psychological disruption (Andersen, 1993; Hoffman, 1988). Medical professionals can aid women by offering referrals for psychological support at the point of diagnosis, providing information about what to expect over the course of treatment, preparing women for treatment termination, and promoting adequate support for women who face recurrent or terminal disease.

Physical Consequences: Treatment Side Effects and Body Image Concerns

Women with cancer may confront a variety of treatment- and disease-related symptoms. During chemotherapy, it is most commonly reported that 25–35% of cancer patients develop anticipatory nausea and vomiting (e.g., Challis & Stam, 1992), depending on factors such as regimen toxicity, patient anxiety, and the context for treatment administration (Redd, 1990); the introduction of more effective anti-emetic medications and chemotherapy administration regimens has reduced this side effect.

The psychological impact of other somatic consequences, such as hair loss, weight gain, and fatigue, can be significant. For example, breast cancer survivors questioned 4–12 months after treatment cited hair loss as one of the three most stressful aspects of undergoing chemotherapy (Green, Rowland, Krupnick, & Epstein, 1995). Furthermore, pain is a problem at some time for approximately 70% of those with cancer (Portenoy & Foley, 1990). Although it has been suggested that 95% of cancer patients can be free of significant pain, less than 50% of those with pain report adequate relief, indicating undertreatment (Redd et al., 1991).

Concerns about bodily appearance can be significant for women who have had breast surgery. Kiebert, de Haes, and van de Velde (1991), reviewing studies on the effects of mastectomy versus breast-conserving surgery, concluded that the procedures produced equivalent outcomes with regard to emotional adjustment and physical function. A limited effect emerged for the superiority of breast conservation on sexual functioning and body image. Women who seek breast reconstruction in general display sound psychological adjustment and report positive effects after the procedure (e.g., Schover et al., 1995). Comparing women who received breast conservation versus reconstruction, Schover et al. found that the type of surgery performed was less important than other factors (e.g., receipt of chemotherapy, marital dissatisfaction) in predicting quality of life. Women feel unsupported by those who assume that their concern about breast loss supersedes concerns about life threat from breast cancer (Peters-Golden, 1982). Indeed, Zemore, Rinholm, Shepel, and Richards (1989) found that breast loss was not among the greatest concerns of mastectomy patients. Rather, concerns centered around fear of cancer recurrence, problems engaging in physical activity, and receiving optimal medical care.

Clearly, breast cancer and its treatment may produce a broad range of physical consequences. Medical professionals can aid women by offering information about these consequences, assessing and targeting for intervention specific areas of impact for individual women, and maintaining current knowledge of developments directed at improving women's physical and functional quality of life.

Cognitive Concerns: Challenges to Core Beliefs and Decision Making

Cancer can present challenges to women's core beliefs about the controllability and fairness of life, and a search for meaning in their experience may ensue. This search may have positive consequences, as many cancer patients report benefits with regard to meaningfulness of life and interpersonal relationships (Andrykowski, 1992).

Cognitive demands also are placed on women at the point of diagnosis, when they are required during a period of heightened anxiety to make decisions about treatment options. Although some women do not wish to be responsible for treatment decisions, research suggests that a woman's perception that she can make an autonomous decision about treatment predicts positive adjustment (e.g., Fallowfield, 1990). Investigating the treatment decision-making process, Stanton et al. (in press) found that women's expectancies for the consequences of electing mastectomy versus breast conservation, assessed before surgery, successfully discriminated between those who received the two procedures. When women's original expectancies about the consequences of their chosen treatment were violated (i.e., they experienced disappointment in some realm), they became more distressed over the course of the year after diagnosis. Medical personnel can reduce cognitive concerns by providing comprehensive information to promote realistic expectancies and by encouraging careful consideration of treatment options at the point of diagnosis.

Interpersonal Concerns: Functioning in Occupational Roles, Intimate Relationships, and Communications With Health Professionals

The experience of breast cancer may affect a number of social roles. For example, work roles may be compromised by devotion of time to treatment and recovery. For some, "job lock" may result from the necessity to maintain health insurance coverage.

Women with breast cancer report that most of their interpersonal relationships remain satisfying, including their marriages (Andersen, 1993). For example, most women's relationships with their daughters remain strong (Lichtman et al., 1984), and daughters in general appear to cope well when their mothers are diagnosed with breast cancer. When problems do occur in intimate relationships, these often involve interpersonal distance and high levels of distress experienced by significant others (Andersen, 1993). Although sexual dysfunction after a diagnosis of breast cancer is relatively uncommon (Andersen, 1993), a period of adjustment with regard to becoming comfortable in one's sexual relationships certainly is likely.

Maintaining adequate relationships with health care providers also is important in adjusting to breast cancer. Lerman et al. (1993) found that 84% of 97 breast cancer patients reported difficulties in communicating with the medical team, with frequent complaints including difficulties in understanding physicians' communications, expressing feelings, asking questions, and maintaining a sense of control over the medical team. Having such communication problems predicted heightened distress 3 months later.

Predictors of Psychological Adjustment

It is important to identify women who might be the most at risk for problematic psychological adjustment so as to provide effective psychosocial intervention. Andersen (1994) suggested that the empirical literature supports several risk factors for maladjustment that can be identified at the point of cancer diagnosis, including a history of psychological disorder, particularly depression, the presence of comorbid chronic illnesses, the lack of a supportive social network or primary relationship, and low SES. There also is evidence that higher distress is associated with younger age at breast cancer diagnosis (e.g., Vinokur, Threatt, Vinokur-Kaplan, & Satariano, 1990). Once cancer is diagnosed, the extent of disease and treatment also are predictors of psychological and behavioral morbidity, as are psychosocial variables (Andersen, 1994). Both personality attributes and situation-specific coping strategies have been demonstrated in longitudinal studies to predict adjustment to breast cancer. For example, a higher level of general optimism predicts lower distress over time (Carver et al., 1993). Furthermore, coping strategies directed at disengagement (e.g., cognitive and behavioral avoidance) appear to confer risk for maladjustment, and those directed at active engagement with the stressor (e.g., acceptance, seeking social support) appear to be adaptive for breast cancer patients (Carver et al., 1993; Stanton & Snider, 1993).

Psychological Adjustment: Conclusions

Although most women remain psychologically resilient in the face of breast cancer diagnosis, several realms of functioning may be affected at various points during diagnosis and treatment. At this point, little is known about whether psychosocial issues or specific needs for support vary as a function of ethnicity or SES of the affected women. In designing interventions, health care providers need to assess specific areas of psychosocial impact for particular women. Providers can support women by offering information about psychosocial resources to all women confronting a breast cancer diagnosis. Some women at risk for psychological morbidity (e.g., those at a younger age, or coping through disengagement) may warrant specific psychosocial support referral.

Psychological Interventions for Cancer Patients

Many cancer patients cope successfully without the aid of formal psychological intervention and report feeling highly satisfied with the support they receive from others. However, Massie, Holland, and Straker (1990) approximated that at least 25% of cancer patients and their families need additional psychological support, and many well-functioning women actively pursue psychosocial interventions. There is good evidence that psychosocial interventions, such as individual or group supportive therapy, as well as treatments directed at specific cancer-related symptoms (e.g., anticipatory nausea, pain), can significantly ameliorate or prevent the distress associated with cancer and its treatment. Using meta-analytic methods, Meyer and Mark (1995) synthesized the results of 45 randomized, controlled studies of a variety of psychosocial interventions for cancer patients. They found significant beneficial effects with regard to patients' emotional adjustment, functional adjustment (e.g., return to work), and treatment- and disease-related symptoms. Here, we outline the types of psychological interventions available to cancer patients, comment on their effectiveness, and provide information on selected resources.

Types of Interventions

Group therapy. The best known work on group interventions has been conducted by Spiegel and colleagues. Their supportive–expressive group therapy (Spiegel & Spira, 1991) involves encouraging patients to share emotions and discuss topics such as physical problems, communication with physicians, relationships with family, finding meaning in life, and facing death. Spiegel, Bloom, and Yalom (1981) reported that after a weekly, year-long intervention, women with metastatic breast cancer who were randomly assigned to group therapy had significantly less mood disturbance than did control women. Those whose group therapy included hypnosis had less pain than those attending group therapy without hypnosis and had half the pain of those in the control group. Although the intervention was not designed a priori to influence survival and some methodological concerns exist, a 10-year follow-up showed that women in the intervention group lived on average twice as long (36.6 vs. 18.9 months from study entry to death) as women in the control group (Spiegel, Bloom, Kraemer, & Gottheil, 1989). Causal mechanisms for the survival difference were unknown, although the authors suggested social support, compliance with medical regimens, health behavior changes, and neuroendocrine and immune function as potential mediators.

Intriguing results about the effect of psychological intervention on adjustment and survival also have been presented by Fawzy and colleagues. Their 6-week structured intervention includes health education, stress management, and coping skills in a supportive group format. The model was developed with melanoma patients and currently is being extended to breast cancer patients (Fawzy & Fawzy, 1994). Findings for melanoma patients were promising, revealing greater use of active coping, reductions in emotional distress, and a better survival rate after 6 years for intervention participants relative to control participants (Fawzy et al., 1993).

Individual psychotherapy. Mental health professionals conducting psychotherapy with cancer patients commonly use a brief therapy or crisis intervention model, focusing on present concerns related to the patient's illness (Massie et al., 1990). In a review of interventions for cancer patients to enhance quality of life, Andersen (1992) noted that individual and group therapeutic interventions yielded equivalent outcomes. Thus, effectiveness depends more on the content of treatment than the format of delivery.

Coping skills training. Specific behavioral skills such as relaxation have been shown to reduce emotional distress as well as aversive symptoms associated with medical treatment. For example, women with early-stage breast cancer who were trained in relaxation techniques showed less mood disturbance than patients in a control group who were instructed to talk about themselves and their interests (Bridge, Benson, Pietroni, & Priest, 1988). In another study, cancer patients who before chemotherapy underwent one 90-min coping preparation (i.e., tour of the oncology clinic, videotape presentation about chemotherapy, discussion–question–answer session, and a take-home booklet for patients and families) had lower levels of anticipatory nausea and postchemotherapy vomiting relative to patients who before chemotherapy had received relaxation training or routine clinic preparation. Participants in the coping preparation procedure also were less depressed and hostile, more knowledgeable about their cancer and its treatment, and experienced less disruption in their daily lives and at work (Burish, Snyder, & Jenkins, 1991).

Psychopharmacological medication. Cancer patients experiencing severe psychological symptoms or disorders (e.g., depression, anxiety, delirium, or insomnia) may benefit from appropriate psychopharmacological treatment. Psychotropic medications such as antidepressants have been underused in oncology, but physicians are becoming increasingly skilled in effective pharmacological management for this population (Massie & Lesko, 1990).

Psychological Interventions: Conclusions

A number of psychosocial interventions have been shown to improve psychological and physical well-being among cancer patients through various stages of the disease process. When administered early, these approaches also can be effective in preventing distress and treatment-related symptoms. Effective intervention programs for cancer patients include emotional support, information about disease and treatment, cognitive–behavioral coping strategies, and relaxation training (Andersen, 1992). Health care providers can help women with breast cancer by providing information about the resources and options for psychosocial support available in their communities. This includes developing patient referral relationships with experts in psychosocial oncology.

Breast Cancer Support for Providers and Patients

Many national programs exist to offer information and support to those with cancer and the health care providers who serve them. Here we offer information on a few of these.

The American Cancer Society sponsors a variety of programs free of charge to patients. Specific to breast cancer is the Reach to Recovery Program (e.g., Rinehart, 1994). Trained volunteers, who have had breast cancer themselves, visit women newly diagnosed with breast cancer to offer information and support. Also available are programs such as I Can Cope, an 8-week series of educational classes for patients and supporters; Look Good . . . Feel Better, which helps patients adapt to the effects of treatment related to physical appearance; and Road to Recovery, which provides patients with transportation for treatment. In addition, group support programs, which may be specific to breast cancer, are offered in many communities. The American Cancer Society can be contacted through local chapters or at 800-ACS-2345.

The National Cancer Institute offers a Cancer Information Service (800-4-CANCER). The Cancer Service provides information on particular types of cancer, state-of-the-art treatment, and clinical trials. Referrals to local resources are provided, as are free printed materials. Information from the NCI's CANCERLIT database also can be obtained via fax (301-402-5874).

The ENCOREplus Breast and Cervical Cancer Program (202-628-3636) is a national health promotion program of the Young Women's Christian Association. Sites funded by ENCOREplus exist in 25 states, and program components include community outreach (e.g., group support, exercise), breast health education, referral to breast and cervical screening, and advocacy.

The Y-ME National Breast Cancer Organization (800-221-2141) is a nonprofit organization providing peer counseling by telephone for women and men with breast cancer and their partners, education, support groups, and in-service programs for health professionals. Y-ME also runs a wig and prosthesis bank available to women with limited financial resources.

Several additional programs are designed to provide information and support as well as advocacy for women with breast cancer. Among these are the National Alliance of Breast Cancer Organizations (NABCO; 212-719-0154), a nonprofit central resource center for information and advocacy; the National Coalition for Cancer Survivorship (NCCS; 301-650-8868), a nonprofit network for those interested in survivorship and support resources; the Anderson Network of the University of Texas M.D. Anderson Cancer Center (800-345-6324), which provides cancer patients contact with a volunteer who has similar characteristics; and CHEMOcare, a nonprofit program that matches patients beginning chemotherapy or radiation with a trained volunteer who has undergone the same treatment (800-55-CHEMO).

Conclusion

Psychosocial and behavioral strategies that target both women and their health care providers can promote accurate risk perception, routine screening, prompt diagnosis and treatment, and recovery in breast cancer.

One goal for effective intervention is patient–physician communication that enhances decision making while taking into account the patient's perspectives. Office discussions that provide information, skills necessary for decision making, and emotional support enhance women's perceptions of control in screening and treatment decisions. Eliciting women's risk perceptions and providing accurate feedback can help them weigh the balance between the benefits and costs of screening (Harris & Leininger, 1995).

Because risk perception is related directly to screening practices, educating patients about accurate breast cancer risk and their providers about the process of information delivery is critical. Physician recommendation and reinforcement regarding the need for routine mammography for women aged 50+, even in the absence of symptoms, remains one of the most significant factors in screening. Discussions to address socioeconomic barriers and deliver information using tailored, culturally relevant formats are usually the most effective in reaching their target audiences.

Health care professionals can help women diagnosed with breast cancer by providing information about the resources for psychosocial support available in their communities. This type of support and psychosocial interventions that promote well-being during breast cancer treatment and the adjustment period afterward must be made available to all women, including those from diverse socioeconomic and ethnic backgrounds. Women who are at risk for psychological morbidity (e.g., young women and those with limited social support) may need specific kinds of psychosocial support, referral, and follow-up. Providers can facilitate this process by establishing patient referral networks with experts in psychosocial oncology and community-based organizations to help women and their families cope with diagnosis, treatment, and recovery.

References

American Cancer Society. (1995). *Cancer facts and figures: 1995*. Atlanta, GA: Author.

Andersen, B. L. (1992). Psychological interventions for cancer patients to enhance quality of life. *Journal of Consulting and Clinical Psychology, 60*, 552–568.

Andersen, B. L. (1993). Cancer. In C. Niven & D. Carroll (Eds.), *The health psychology of women* (pp. 75–89). Chur, Switzerland: Harwood Academic.

Andersen, B. L. (1994). Surviving cancer. *Cancer, 74*, 1484–1495.

Andersen, B. L., Anderson, B., & deProsse, C. (1989). Controlled prospective longitudinal study of women with cancer: II. Psychological outcomes. *Journal of Consulting and Clinical Psychology, 57*, 692–697.

Andrykowski, M. A. (1992, August). *Positive psychosocial adjustment among cancer survivors: Cancer as a psychosocial transition*. Paper presented at the 100th Annual Convention of the American Psychological Association, Washington, DC.

Baines. C. J. (1992). Breast self-examination. *Cancer* (Suppl.), *69*, 1942–1946.

Baines, C. J., To, T., & Wall, C. (1990). Women's attitudes to screening after participation in the National Breast Screening Study. *Cancer, 65*, 1663–1669.

Bloom, D. (1994). *Focus group on information needs for making decisions about mammography*. (Tech. Rep.) Durham, NC: Duke Comprehensive Cancer Center.

Bloom, J. R., Grazier, K., Hodge, F., & Hayes, W. A. (1991). Factors affecting the use of screening mammography among African American women. *Cancer Epidemiology, Biomarkers and Prevention, 1*, 75–82.

Breen, N., & Kessler, L. (1994). Changes in the use of screening mammography: Evidence from the 1987 and 1990 National Health Interview Surveys. *American Journal of Public Health, 84*, 62–67.

Brenner, R. J. (1992). Evolving medical-legal concepts for clinicians and imagers in evaluation of breast cancer. *Cancer* (Suppl.), *69*, 1950–1953.

Bridge, L. R., Benson, P., Pietroni, P. C., & Priest, R. G. (1988). Relaxation and imagery in the treatment of breast cancer. *British Medical Journal, 297*, 1169–1172.

Burack, R. C., & Liang, J. (1989). The acceptance and completion of mammography by older Black women. *American Journal of Public Health, 79*, 721–726.

Burg, M. A., Lane, D. S., & Polednak, A. P. (1990). Age group differences in the use of breast cancer screening tests: The effects of health care utilization and socioeconomic variables. *Journal of Aging and Health, 2*, 514–530.

Burish, T. G., Snyder, S. L., & Jenkins, R. A. (1991). Preparing patients for cancer chemotherapy: Effect of coping preparation and relaxation interventions. *Journal of Consulting and Clinical Psychology, 59*, 518–525.

Calle, E. E., Miracle, H. L., Moss, R. E., & Health, C. W. (1993). Personal contact from friends to increase mammography usage. Abstract from the American Society of Preventive Oncology 17th Annual Meeting, Tucson, AZ.

Carver, C. S., Pozo, C., Harris, S. D., Noriega, V., Scheier, M. F., Robinson, D. S., Ketcham, A. S., Moffat, F. L., & Clark, K. C. (1993). How coping mediates the effect of optimism on distress: A study of women with early stage breast cancer. *Journal of Personality and Social Psychology, 65*, 375–390.

Challis, G. B., & Stam, H. J. (1992). A longitudinal study of the development of anticipatory nausea and vomiting in cancer chemotherapy patients: The role of absorption and autonomic perception. *Health Psychology, 11*, 181–189.

Claus, E. B., Risch, N., & Thompson, W. D. (1993). Autosomal dominant inheritance of early onset breast cancer: Implications for risk prediction. *Cancer, 73*, 643–651.

Coates, R. J., et al. (1992). Differences between Black and White women with breast cancer in time from symptom recognition to medical consultation. *Journal of the National Cancer Institute, 84*, 938–950.

Davis, D. T., Bustamante, A., Brown, C. P., Wolde-Tsadik, G., Savage, E. W., Cheng, X., & Howland, L. (1994). The urban church and cancer control: A source of social influence in minority communities. *Public Health Reports, 109*, 500–506.

Erwin, D. O., Spatz, T. S., & Turtuno, C. L. (1992). Development of African-American role model interventions to increase breast self-examination and mammography. *Journal of Cancer Education, 7*, 311–319.

Facione, N. C. (1993). Delay versus help seeking for breast cancer symptoms: A critical review of the literature on patient and provider delay. *Social Science and Medicine, 36*, 1521–1534.

Fallowfield, L. J. (1990). Psychosocial adjustment after treatment for early breast cancer. *Oncology, 4*, 89–96.

Fawzy, F. I., & Fawzy, N. W. (1994). A structured psychoeducational intervention for cancer patients. *General Hospital Psychiatry, 16*, 149–192.

Fawzy, F. I., Fawzy, N. W., Hyun, C. S., Elashoff, R., Guthrie, D., Fahey, J. L., & Morton, D. L. (1993). Malignant melanoma: Effects of an early structured psychiatric intervention, coping, and affective state on recurrence and survival 6 years later. *Archives of General Psychiatry, 50*, 681–689.

Fletcher, S. W., Black, W., Harris, R., Rimer, B. K., & Shapiro, S. (1993). Report of the International Workshop on Screening for Breast Cancer. *Journal of the National Cancer Institute, 85*, 1644–1656.

Fletcher, S. W., O'Malley, M. S., Polgrim, C., & Gonzalez, J. (1989). How do women compare with internal medicine residents in breast lump detection. *Journal of General Internal Medicine, 4*, 277–283.

Foster, R. S., Jr., Worden, J. K., Costanza, M. C., & Solomon, L. J. (1992). Clinical breast examination and breast self-examination. *Cancer (Suppl.), 69*, 1992–1998.

Fox, S. A., & Roetzheim, R. G. (1994). Screening mammography and older Hispanic women: Current status and issues. *Cancer, 74*(Suppl.), 2028–2033.

Fox, S. A., Siu, A. L., & Stein, J. A. (1994). The importance of physician communication on breast cancer screening of older women. *Archives of Internal Medicine, 154,* 2058–2068.

Gail, M. H., Brinton, L. A., Byar, D. P., Corle, D. K., Green, S. B., Schairer, C., & Mulvihill, J. J. (1989). Projecting individualized probabilities for developing breast cancer for White females who are being examined annually. *Journal of the National Cancer Institute, 81,* 1879–1886.

Gordis, L. (Panel Chair). (1997). *National Institutes of Health Consensus Development Conference Statement, Breast Cancer Screening For Women Ages 40–49, January 21–23, 1997.* Bethesda, MD: NIH Office of Medical Applications of Research.

Green, B. L., Rowland, J. H., Krupnick, J. L., & Epstein, S. A. (1995, November). *PTSD symptoms after diagnosis and treatment of breast cancer.* Paper presented at the annual meeting of the Academy of Psychosomatic Medicine, Palm Springs, CA.

Harris, R., & Leininger, L. (1995). Clinical strategies for breast cancer screening: Weighing and using the evidence. *Annals of Internal Medicine, 122.*

Hayward, R. A., Shapiro, M. F., Freeman, H. E., & Corey, C. R. (1988). Who gets screened for cervical and breast cancer. *Archives of Internal Medicine, 148,* 1177–1181.

Hoffman, R. S. (1988). The psycho-oncologist in a multidisciplinary breast treatment center. In C. L. Cooper (Ed.), *Stress and breast cancer* (pp. 171–193). New York: Wiley.

Huguley, C. M., Brown, R. L., Greenberg, R. S., & Clark, W. S. (1988). Breast self-examination and survival from breast cancer. *Cancer, 62*(7), 1389–1396.

Jacob, T., Penn, N., Kulik, J., & Spieth, L. (1992). Effects of cognitive style and maintenance strategies on breast self-examination (BSE) practice by African American women. *Journal of Behavioral Medicine, 15,* 589–609.

Kang, S. H., Bloom, J. R., & Romano, P. S. (1994). Cancer screening among African-American women: Their use of tests and social support. *American Journal of Public Health, 84,* 101–103.

Kash, K., Holland, J., Halper, M., & Miller, D. (1992). Psychological distress and surveillance behaviors of women with a family history of breast cancer. *Journal of the National Cancer Institute, 84,* 24–30.

Kelsey, J. L., & Horn-Ross, P. L. (1993). Breast cancer: Magnitude of the problem and descriptive epidemiology. *Epidemiologic Reviews, 15,* 7–16.

Kerlikowske, K., Grady, D., Rubin, S. M., Sandrock, C., & Ernster, V. L. (1995). Efficacy of screening mammography: A meta-analysis. *Journal of the American Medical Association, 273,* 149–154.

Kiebert, G. M., de Haes, J. C. J. M., & van de Velde, C. J. H. (1991). The impact of breast-conserving treatment and mastectomy on the quality-of-life of early-stage breast cancer patients: A review. *Journal of Clinical Oncology, 9,* 1059–1070.

Kiefe, C. I., McKay, S. V., Halevy, A., & Brody, B. A. (1994). Is cost a barrier to screening mammography for low-income women receiving Medicare benefits? A randomized trial. *Archives of Internal Medicine, 154,* 1217–1224.

Lerman, C., Daly, M., Walsh, W. P., Resch, N., Seay, J., Barsevick, A., Birenbaum, L., Heggan, T., & Martin, G. (1993). Communication between patients with breast cancer and health care providers. *Cancer, 72,* 2612–2620.

Lerman, C., & Schwartz, M. (1993). Adherence and psychological adjustment among women at high risk for breast cancer. *Breast Cancer Research and Treatment, 28,* 145–155.

Lerman, C., Schwartz, M., Miller, S., Daly, M., Sands, C., & Rimer, B. (1995). *A randomized trial of breast cancer risk counseling: Interacting effects of counseling, educational level, and coping style.* Unpublished manuscript.

Lichtman, R. R., Taylor, S. E., Wood, J. V., Bluming, A. Z., Dosik, G. M., & Leibowitz, R. L. (1984). Relations with children after breast cancer: The mother-daughter relationship at risk. *Journal of Psychosocial Oncology, 2*(3–4), 1–19.

Lierman, L. M. (1988). Discovery of breast changes. *Cancer Nursing, 11.*

Locker, A., Caseldine, J., Mitchell, A., Blamey, R., Roebuck, E., & Elston, C. (1989). Results from a seven-year programme of breast self-examination in 89,010 women. *British Journal of Cancer, 60,* 401–405.

Massie, M. J., Holland, J. C., & Straker, N. (1990). Psychotherapeutic interventions. In J. C. Holland & J. H. Rowland (Eds.), *Handbook of psychooncology* (pp. 455–469). New York: Oxford University Press.

Massie, M. J., & Lesko, L. M. (1990). Psychopharmacological management. In J. C. Holland & J. H. Rowland (Eds.), *Handbook of psychooncology* (pp. 470–491). New York: Oxford University Press.

Meyer, T. J., & Mark, M. M. (1995). Effects of psychosocial interventions with adult cancer patients: A meta-analysis of randomized experiments. *Health Psychology, 14*, 101–108.

Meyerowitz, B. E., & Chaiken, S. (1987). The effect of message framing on breast self-examination attitudes, intentions, and behavior. *Journal of Personality and Social Psychology, 52*, 500–510.

National Cancer Institute. (1995). *Cancer facts*. Washington, DC: Author.

National Cancer Institute Breast Cancer Screening Consortium. (1990). Screening mammography: A missed clinical opportunity. *Journal of the American Medical Association, 264*, 54–58.

Nemcek, M. A. (1989). Factors influencing Black women's breast self-examination practice. *Cancer Nursing, 12*, 339–343.

Patterson, E. A. (1994). Screening guidelines for African-American women: Looking at the facts and sorting out the confusion. *Journal of the National Medical Association, 86*, 415–416.

Peters-Golden, H. (1982). Breast cancer: Varied perceptions of social support in the illness experience. *Social Science and Medicine, 16*, 482–491.

Physician Insurers Association of America. (1990). *Breast cancer study*. Lawrenceville, NJ: Author.

Portenoy, R. K., & Foley, K. M. (1990). Management of cancer pain. In J. C. Holland & J. H. Rowland (Eds.), *Handbook of psychooncology* (pp. 369–382). New York: Oxford University Press.

Redd, W. H. (1990). Management of anticipatory nausea and vomiting. In J. C. Holland & J. H. Rowland (Eds.), *Handbook of psychooncology* (pp. 423–433). New York: Oxford University Press.

Redd, W. H., Silberfarb, P. M., Andersen, B. L., Andrykowski, M. A., Bovbjerg, D. H., Burish, T. G., Carpenter, P. J., Cleeland, C., Dolgin, M., Levy, S. M., Mitnick, L., Morrow, G. R., Schover, L. R., Spiegel, D., & Stevens, J. (1991). Psychologic and psychobehavioral research in oncology. *Cancer, 67*, 813–822.

Reynolds, P., Boyd, P. T., Blacklow, R. S., Jackson, J. S., Greenberg, R. S., Austin, D. F., Chen, V. W., Edwards, B. K., & the National Cancer Institute Black/White Cancer Survival Study Group. (1994). The relationship between social ties and survival among Black and White breast cancer patients. *Cancer Epidemiology, Biomarkers and Prevention, 3*, 253–259.

Rinehart, M. E. (1994). The Reach to Recovery Program. *Cancer, 74*, 372–375.

Royak-Schaler, R., Cheuvront, B., Wilson, K. R., & Williams, C. M. (1996). Addressing women's breast cancer risk and perceptions of control in medical settings. *Journal of Clinical Psychology in Medical Settings, 3*(3), 185–199.

Royak-Schaler, R., DeVellis, B. M., Wilson, K. R., Sorenson, J. R., Lannin, D., & Emerson, J. W. (1995). Breast cancer in African-American families: Risk perception, cancer worry, and screening practices of first-degree relatives [Monograph]. *Annals of the New York Academy of Sciences, 768*, 281–286.

Schover, L. R., Yetman, R. J., Tuason, L. J., Meisler, E., Caldwell, B. E., Hermann, R. E., Grundfest-Broniatowski, S., & Douden, R. V. (1995). Partial mastectomy and breast reconstruction: A comparison of their effects on psychosocial adjustment, body image, and sexuality. *Cancer, 75*, 54–64.

Seidman, H., Geib, S. K., Silverbert, E., et al. (1987). Survival experience in the Breast Cancer Detection Demonstration Project. *CA-A: Cancer Journal for Clinicians, 37*, 258–290.

Shapiro, S., Venet, W., Strax, P., & Venet, L. (1988). Current results of the Breast Cancer Screening Randomized Trial: The Health Insurance Plan (HIP) of greater New York study. In N. E. Day & A. B. Miller (Eds.), *Screening for breast cancer*. Toronto: Hans Huber.

Skinner, C. S., Strecher, V. J., & Hospers, H. (1994). Physicians' recommendations for mammography: Do tailored messages make a difference? *American Journal of Public Health, 84*, 43–49.

Smart, C. R., Hendrick, R. E., Rutledge, J. H., III, & Smith, R. A. (1995). Benefit of mammography screening in women ages 40 to 49 years. *Cancer, 75*, 1619–1626.

Smith, R. A., & Haynes, S. (1992). Barriers to screening for breast cancer. *Cancer, 69*, 1968–1978.

Spiegel, D., Bloom, J. R., & Yalom, I. (1981). Group support for patients with metastatic cancer: A randomized outcome study. *Archives of General Psychiatry, 38*, 527–533.

Spiegel, D., Bloom, J. R., Kraemer, H. C., & Gottheil, E. (1989). Effect of psychosocial treatment on survival of patients with metastatic breast cancer. *The Lancet, ii*, 888–891.

Spiegel, D., & Spira, J. (1991). *Supportive-expressive group therapy: A treatment manual of psychosocial intervention for women with recurrent breast cancer.* Stanford, CA: Stanford University School of Medicine, Psychosocial Treatment Laboratory.

Stanton, A. L., Estes, M. A., Estes, N. C., Cameron, C. L., Danoff-Burg, S., & Irving, L. M. (in press). Treatment decision-making and adjustment to breast cancer: A longitudinal study. *Journal of Consulting and Clinical Psychology.*

Stanton, A. L., & Snider, P. R. (1993). Coping with a breast cancer diagnosis: A prospective study. *Health Psychology, 12*, 16–23.

Stefanek, M. E., & Wilcox, P. (1990). Breast self-examination among women at increased risk: Assessment of proficiency. *Cancer Prevention, 1*, 79–83.

Suarez, L., Lloyd, L., Weiss, N., Rainbolt, T., & Pulley, L. (1994). Effect of social networks on cancer screening behavior of older Mexican-American women. *Journal of the National Cancer Institute, 86*, 775–779.

Sutton, S. M., Eisner, E. J., & Johnston, C. M. (1994). The mammography guideline controversy: Where does the consumer fit in? *Journal of the American Women's Medical Association, 49*, 53–59.

Taplin, S. H., Taylor, V., Montano, D., Chinn, R., & Urban, N. (1994). Specialty differences and the ordering of screening mammography by primary care physicians. *Journal of the American Board of Family Practice, 7*, 375–386.

Timko, C. (1987). Seeking medical care for breast cancer symptoms: Determinants of intentions to engage in prompt or delay behavior. *Health Psychology, 6*, 305–328.

Urban, N., Anderson, G. L., & Peacock, S. (1994). Mammography screening: How important is cost as a barrier to use? *American Journal of Public Health, 84*, 50–55.

U.S. Department of Health and Human Services. (1990). National Center for Health Statistics. *Health, United States, 1989* (DHHS Publication No. PHS 90-1232). Washington, DC: U.S. Government Printing Office.

Vinokur, A. D., Threatt, B. A., Caplan, R. D., & Zimmerman, B. L. (1989). Physical and psychosocial functioning and adjustment to breast cancer: Long-term follow-up of a screening population. *Cancer, 63*, 394–405.

Vinokur, A. D., Threatt, B. A., Vinokur-Kaplan, D., & Satariano, W. A. (1990). The process of recovery from breast cancer for younger and older patients: Changes during the first year. *Cancer, 64*, 1242–1254.

Zapka, J. (1994). Promoting participation in breast cancer screening [Editorial]. *American Journal of Public Health, 84*, 12–13.

Zapka, J. G., Stoddard, A. M., Costanza, M. E., & Greene, H. L. (1989). Breast cancer screening by mammography: Utilization and associated factors. *American Journal of Public Health, 79*, 1499–1502.

Zemore, R., Rinholm, J., Shepel, L. F., & Richards, M. (1989). Some social and emotional consequences of breast cancer and mastectomy: A content analysis of 87 interviews. *Journal of Psychosocial Oncology, 7*(4), 33–45.

20 _____

Psychosocial Factors
Associated With
Gynecological Cancers

Electra D. Paskett and Robert Michielutte

Gynecological cancers, cancer of the cervix, uterus, and ovaries, account for 75,200 new cancer cases and 25,200 cancer deaths annually in the United States (Wingo, Tong, & Bolden, 1995). Endometrial cancer is the most common female pelvic malignancy, and ovarian cancer is the most lethal. Gynecological cancers not only affect the morbidity and mortality of a significant number of women each year, but they also cause psychosocial problems. In this chapter we examine psychosocial issues among women at risk for the development of gynecological cancers, women who participate in the early detection and screening process, women with premalignant abnormalities, and women who are undergoing treatment for a gynecological cancer. Recommendations are included for addressing and reducing the effects of psychosocial factors for women at each stage.

Risk Factors in Gynecological Cancers

Several factors have been identified as putting women at increased risk for developing each gynecological cancer. The most important risk factors known to be associated with cervical cancer include early age at first intercourse (younger than 15 years of age), multiple sexual partners, sex with a partner who has had multiple sex partners, smoking, history of sexually transmitted diseases (STDs), cervical dysplasia, and lack of a recent (within 5 years) Pap smear. A woman's risk of developing endometrial cancer increases if she is obese; has hypertension, diabetes, a history of infertility, breast cancer, adenomatous uterine hyperplasia, or chronic anovulation; or received long-term estrogen therapy. Women at the highest risk for developing ovarian cancer have a family history of the disease; have had breast, colon, or endometrial cancer; have never had children; or have had pelvic irradiation. Older women are more likely to develop any one of these cancers than younger women. Finally, although not directly a risk factor for these cancers, women of lower socioeconomic status are at higher risk for developing and dying from these cancers. High-risk behaviors (e.g., smoking and obesity) and lower access to detection and treatment facilities are more prevalent among women of lower socioeconomic levels.

Women who are at risk for developing gynecological cancers often have beliefs and attitudes about cancer that act as barriers to their understanding of individual risk. Among many women, the word *cancer* itself often evokes fear and fatalism as general reactions (Wilson, Romano, & Stein, 1985). Gregg and Curry (1994) provided further insight into the beliefs and attitudes about cancer of African American women from lower income and educational-level groups. Many of these women had experience with cancer; however, their experiences had been with friends and family members diagnosed at late stages. Thus, they have watched cancer destroy a loved one's life and doubt there is a cure for cancer. Even if caught in time by a Pap smear, many women believe that the mental pain of knowing about the cancer may cause death more quickly. Treatment itself is sometimes believed to cause more health problems and depletes a family's financial resources, however meager. Finally, a woman's religious faith was mentioned by many as the one sure and powerful treatment alternative available.

These beliefs result in actions such as avoidance (e.g., of physicians or discussions of cancer) or the discounting of dissonant information (e.g., the curability of cancers detected early). Although these reactions are meant to protect the individual from psychological damage, they are medically harmful because attention is turned away from prevention and early detection behaviors (Dignan et al., 1990). Moreover, the risk factors associated with the development of gynecological cancers (e.g. sexual activity) have great potential for being perceived by women as negative, labeling statements (Dignan et al., 1990).

Clinicians can assist in efforts to communicate correct information about cancer and risk status. Health risk appraisals (Dignan et al., 1993) or risk scoring systems (Wilkinson, Peters, Harvey, & Stott, 1992) can be self-administered and easily implemented in a clinic setting. For example, while waiting to be seen by a physician, women can be asked to complete a simple one-page sheet that asks about the presence of each risk factor for cervical cancer. Women are instructed to circle yes or no for each statement. At the bottom of the sheet patients are instructed to add the number of "yes" responses and match that number with a listed risk category. Instructions also include an action statement to motivate the patient to return the sheet to their health care provider and ask for a Pap smear, thus encouraging the patient to take a more active role in her health care. If fears are aroused with the use of this form, the provider can directly address issues during the visit. Once a woman is identified as being "at risk" for a specific gynecological cancer, she should obtain relevant screening examinations. Information about the examinations available for a specific cancer and screening guidelines can accompany risk notification communications as a way of reducing the emotional distress often associated with labeling (Haynes, Sackett, Taylor, Gibson, & Johnson, 1978).

Screening and Early Detection

Cervical Cancer Screening

Reported rates of Pap smear screening indicate that many women at the highest risk for developing cervical cancer underuse this test. Data from the 1992 National Health Interview Survey indicate that 72% of women aged 18–39 years, 54% of women aged 65–74 years, and 36% of women aged 75 and older had had a Pap smear within the past 3 years (Anderson & May, 1995). In terms of racial differences, African American women are screened at similar or higher rates than White women; however, Hispanic women, particularly those who speak only or mostly Spanish and women of other racial groups (e.g., American Indians, women of Asian/Pacific Islander descent) are less likely to be screened (Harlan, Bernstein, & Kessler, 1991; Wilcox & Mosher, 1993). Women of lower socioeconomic levels, regardless of race, underuse Pap smear screening, as do women who never married or who are widowed or who failed to complete high school (Calle, Flanders, Thun, & Martin, 1993; Harlan et al., 1991; Moody-Thomas & Fick, 1994; Weinrich, Coker, Weinrich, Eleazer, & Greene, 1995).

Reasons for the underuse of Pap smears have been examined in several studies. The most frequently reported reasons involve health care system issues. Although most women (90%) regularly visit a health care provider at least once a year, Pap smears are not being done at these visits (National Cancer Institute Cancer Screening Consortium for Underserved Women, 1995; Wilcox & Mosher, 1993). Only half the women surveyed by Moody-Thomas and Fick (1994) indicated that their physician had recommended a Pap smear. Other characteristics of the health care system also have been cited as contributing to negative impressions about and noncompliance with Pap smear screening. Among women who had had recent Pap smear tests, "poor or no explanations of the test" was mentioned by 10%; overall, 37% of the women viewed the Pap smear test experience as negative and 20% had both negative and positive comments (McKie, 1993a). In addition, women who receive care at health maintenance organizations are more likely to receive Pap smear screening, either because of the removal of cost factors or because of the "prevention orientation" of health maintenance organizations (Harlan et al., 1991).

In several studies women who were noncompliant with Pap smear guidelines were asked why they had not had a Pap smear. The most frequently stated reasons for not having had a Pap smear were that they believed it was unnecessary, had no problems, or had just procrastinated. Reasons also varied by income, race, and age groups. Women in upper-income groups cited lack of time as one of the prohibitive factors, women in middle-income groups mentioned the cost of the test as a barrier, and women in lower-income groups reported cost as well as other responses such as "I don't want to go," "No appointment was made," or "I wasn't pregnant" (Moody-Thomas & Fick, 1994). White women tended to cite having had a hysterectomy as the reason for not having a Pap smear more often than African American or Hispanic women, whereas non-White women stated that the test was not recommended by their physician (Harlan et al., 1991). Younger women were more likely to state fear and embarrassment as a reason for noncompliance, whereas older women (aged 60+) cited lack of a physician recommendation as a reason for not having a Pap smear (Harlan et al., 1991).

Misconceptions about the purpose of the Pap smear have been reported by women who have regular Pap smear tests as well as by noncompliant women (McKie, 1993a, 1993b). Among women who had not responded to invitations to obtain Pap smears, the majority (57%) did not know what caused cervical cancer, 37% felt that they would have a Pap smear only if they had symptoms, and almost half (46%) would not be motivated to get a Pap smear for any reason (McKie, 1993b). Half the women who received a Pap smear test when invited to do so did not know the causes of cervical cancer, and knowledge about the meaning of a positive test result was poor.

In summary, women who are at the highest risk for developing cervical cancer also are the women who are less likely to receive adequate Pap smear screening. The most common factors associated with lack of screening involve health care system issues, financial barriers, poor knowledge and negative beliefs about the test and cervical cancer, and fear and embarrassment. Strategies to address these factors have been developed and tested in three areas: health care system interventions, community-based programs, and environmental initiatives.

Strategies to Improve Pap Smear Screening

Because "missed opportunities" for cervical cancer screening have been cited as reasons for low screening rates, especially in older women (Celentano, 1989), a number of interventions directed at the health care system have been tested. Opportunistic screening (i.e., offering a Pap smear when a woman is in the doctor's office for a visit) has been tested in several studies, with promising results. Cockburn, Hirst, Hill, and Marks (1986) found that 50% of women aged 40 and older would agree to screening when asked by their physician. Burack and Liang (1987) found that 69% of women complied with their physician's recommendation to have a Pap smear within an 8-month period when asked. However, Pap smear screening was offered to only 39% of the eligible women. The intensity of the advice for screening during opportunistic encounters was tested by Ward, Boyle, Math, Redman, and Sanson-Fisher (1991). Brief advice (i.e., advising the women of the need for a smear and offering to perform one during that visit) was as effective as maximal persuasion (i.e., exploration of and counseling about barriers) in increasing women's compliance with screening recommendations. Opportunistic screening has great potential for improving Pap smear screening rates among older women. Brett (1992) reported that 73% of women aged 50–70 years received appropriate Pap smear screening when opportunistic screening was initiated during routine surgery consultations.

Prompts, in the form of chart stickers or patient questionnaires about risk factors, have also encouraged physicians to provide Pap smear screening during routine visits. Oleszkowicz, Kresch, and Painter (1994) used chart stickers to help physicians identify women in need of a Pap test. Of 2,321 women who had not had a Pap smear within the past 2 years, only 18% refused a test offered by their physicians when prompted by the chart sticker during a routine visit. Ward et al. (1991) also used patient questionnaires to prompt physicians to inquire about a Pap smear in eligible women. Only 9% of eligible women did not receive an offer for screening.

Call and recall systems have been used in several European countries to provide a systematic method of calling and recalling women for Pap smear screening (Austoker, 1994; Palm et al., 1993; Sigurdsson, 1993). These systems consistently improve screening rates, particularly among older women and women in lower socioeconomic classes who have never had a Pap smear (Elkind, Eardley, Thompson, & Smith, 1990; Palm et al., 1993). Women are more likely to respond to invitations for Pap smear screening if (a) the benefits of the test are explained properly; (b) a specific appointment time is offered rather than an open invitation; (c) reminder phone calls are used; (d) personal contact from health care workers is used to overcome anxiety about the test; and (e) a brochure addressing beliefs, attitudes, and barriers about cervical cancer screening accompanies the invitation letter (Austoker, 1994).

Nurses also can play an important role in promoting compliance with cervical cancer screening. Two studies have examined the efficacy of nurse-delivered intervention to reduce barriers to Pap smear screening in low-income African American women. Ansell, Lacey, Whitman, Chen, and Phillips (1994) found that a nurse-based intervention that included patient recruitment and education directly related to identified barriers, followed by the performance of Pap smear tests, was successful in screening the target population. Mandelblatt, Traxler, Lakin, Kanetsky, and Thomas (1993) found similar results in low-income African American women aged 65 and older using a nurse practitioner to deliver same-day Pap smear screening during routine health care visits at urban public hospital clinics.

Patient health minirecords, booklets that record health problems and physician visits, have been found to be effective in improving cancer screening among geriatric patients (Dietrich & Duhamel, 1989) and as a means of improving patient compliance with several preventive services among family practice patients (Dickey & Petitti, 1992). Patient education, involving distribution of a pamphlet on cervical cancer screening, together with a physician offering a Pap smear, was concluded to be effective in increasing the screening rate of Australian women who had not had a Pap smear in the past 2 years (Cockburn et al., 1986).

Finally, women have voiced concerns about not being notified of Pap smear test results after the receipt of the test. McKie (1993a) found that only 54% of women receiving a Pap smear test were given results of their test. Moreover, the main ways women secured the results of their Pap smear test were by calling the doctor themselves or by asking during the next visit to their physician. Schofield, Sanson-Fisher, Halpin, and Redman (1994) surveyed women who had received Pap smears to identify preferences for notification of test results. Women indicated a preference for written notification from their physician as the most favored method, followed by a phone call and in-person consultations. The use of a systematic notification system of test results also can reduce the anxiety and fear caused by the anticipation of abnormal test results (McKie, 1993a).

Screening for Other Gynecological Cancers

Women 50 years of age or older who are at increased risk for endometrial cancer should undergo screening with endometrial aspiration or curettage at menopause and thereafter at the advice of a physician (American Cancer Society, 1995). Studies are ongoing related to the efficacy of transvaginal sonography as a screening test for endometrial cancer (Gordon, Fleischer, & Reed, 1990; Gruickshank, Randall, & Miller, 1989). Because screening is not recommended for the general population, little is known about the psychosocial effects of screening for endometrial cancer among asymptomatic women (Gordon et al., 1990; Gruickshank et al., 1989). More is known about psychosocial symptoms among women with endometrial cancer and is discussed later.

Women at high risk for developing ovarian cancer (i.e., a family or personal history of ovarian, breast, endometrial, or colon cancer; nulliparous; a history of pelvic irradiation) should receive an annual pelvic examination. Estimates from the 1988 National Survey of Family Growth, a survey of 8,450 women aged 15–44 years, indicate that 62.5% of women had received a Pap smear and pelvic examination within the past 12 months (Wilcox & Mosher, 1993). This examination, however, usually misses smaller curable lesions. Other screening methods such as biomarkers (e.g., CA-125, NB70K, urinary gonadotrophin peptide), transvaginal sonography, and transvaginal color Doppler studies are being investigated but are not recommended for general use. This lack of proved screening tests for ovarian cancer causes severe psychosocial distress among many women at increased risk (Green, Morton, & Statham, 1991).

As part of a study to validate new screening methods for ovarian cancer (Paskett, Phillips, Miller, Hopkins, & Nelson, 1994), 31 participants were asked about their feelings regarding ovarian cancer and early detection methods. All women were at high risk for developing ovarian cancer because of either a personal or family history of breast, colon, or ovarian cancer. Respondents expressed concerns about developing ovarian cancer that would be undetected until it had invaded their entire body. Many women had watched a mother or sister die a painful death from this "silent killer." Several women were considering prophylactic oophrectomy to reduce their risk of developing ovarian cancer because the pelvic examination was not adequate in detecting curable lesions. Reasons given for participating in the research study itself were for "peace of mind" and "being able to see that nothing was wrong with their ovaries."

To reduce concern and worry and enhance well-being in women with family histories of ovarian cancer, health care providers may wish to recommend genetic counseling. This counseling should optimally begin when a woman is in her early 20s, with surveillance beginning in her early 30s. Unfortunately, limited research has been conducted to develop effective interventions for reducing symptoms that occur in high-risk women, such as fear, anxiety, sleeplessness, depression, and reduced sexual functioning. There is evidence, however, that women benefit from receiving information about screening options, genetic counseling options, and prophylactic oophrectomy, when symptoms are severe enough to upset daily activities (Green et al., 1991).

Abnormalities Detected on Screening

For screening to achieve its goal of reducing mortality, appropriate and prompt follow-up of the abnormalities detected must occur. Ensuring adequate follow-up, however, involves (a) the notification process, (b) obtaining the recommended treatment and diagnostic tests, and (c) the tracking of women with abnormalities. At each of these steps, psychosocial reactions are likely, and these reactions must be addressed for full compliance to occur. Because cervical cancer is the only gynecological cancer that has been studied in detail for the psychosocial impact of abnormalities, we focus specifically on cervical abnormalities (i.e., atypia and dysplasia). However, the recommendations discussed may be generalizable to women with abnormalities detected in ovarian and endometrial cancer screenings.

Notification of Test Results

As soon as screening tests are completed, most women become anxious about the results of the test (McKie, 1993a; Schofield et al. 1994). Women should be promptly notified of test results, and the responsibility for notification resides with the physician (or health care provider) who performed the Pap smear. For women with normal results, notification is important because it will (a) help reduce anxiety about possible abnormal test results, (b) provide positive reinforcement for having decided to have the test, and (c) provide an opportunity to encourage future screening. For women with abnormal test results, notification serves as the cue for action in terms of obtaining recommended follow-up tests or treatment.

The most opportune time to reduce psychological symptoms and maximize the probability of compliance with treatment recommendations is at the time a woman is notified of her test result. The usual methods of notification of test results are in writing, over the telephone, and in person. Ideally, multiple forms of notification should be used to ensure that the message has been received (Paskett & Rimer, 1995). Written forms, usually letters or postcards, may not be understandable to the patient because of the reading level of the message or because of the use of terminology that is foreign and not defined clearly (Paskett, Carter, Chu, & White, 1990). For example, women with dysplasia who were interviewed in a pilot study described their frustration at being instructed to obtain a colposcopy examination while not being given a description of a colposcopy examination (Paskett, Carter, et al., 1990). Written communications about abnormal test results may convey multiple and sometimes mixed messages. Women with atypias may be informed they have "cervical abnormalities" but that they do not need to return for up to 6 months. Mixed messages may reduce the importance of proper follow-up and treatment because there is no recommendation for immediate follow-up. Letters should always include instructions to call a specific person in the office as soon as possible.

Telephone contact has strengths and limitations. The telephone permits personal interaction between the patient and provider and the opportunity to clarify information, reinforce the importance of follow-up, and respond to the patient's questions. However, a small proportion of the lowest income population does not have a telephone. Additionally, physicians' offices usually contact patients during daytime hours when working people are not home. These points were demonstrated in a Chicago study, in which 23% of the patients with an abnormal test result could not be notified by telephone (Manfredi, Lacey, & Warnecke, 1990).

In-person notification also has strengths and limitations. The potential exists to tailor information to the needs of the patient and to offer reassurance. The provider can obtain feedback to verify the woman's comprehension. Family members can be included in the process. Moreover, physicians can be trained to become better communicators. Limitations of in-person notification include the communication skills of the physician or provider and the costs, both in terms of finances and time, of the extra visit (Shapiro, Boggs, Melamed, & Graham-Pole, 1992).

Interventions to Improve Adherence With Follow-Up Treatment

Compliance rates for follow-up of abnormal Pap smears range from 20% to 74% in the usual clinic setting (Lane, 1983; Richart et al., 1980; Robertson, Woodend, & Crozier Hutchinson, 1988; Rome, Cahnen, & Pagano, 1987; Soutter, Wisdom, Brough, & Monaghan, 1986). Special intervention clinics, which use phone calls or in-person visits to find and remind women to return for follow-up, obtain compliance rates of 33–95% (Frish, 1986; Hulka & Redmond, 1971; Lerman et al., 1989; Marcus et al., 1992; Michielutte, Diseker, Young, & May, 1985; Paskett et al., 1990; Tavelli, Judson, Hetrick, & Root, 1985; Washington State Department of Social and Health Services, 1978). Two studies conducted among poor African American women found compliance rates of 70% for women with abnormal Pap smears (Lacey et al., 1993; Mandelblatt, Traxler, Lakin, Thomas, et al., 1993).

Reasons given for lack of follow-up among women with abnormal Pap smears include beliefs and facilitating conditions surrounding treatment.

Using multiattribute utility theory, Paskett, Carter, et al. (1990) identified issues related to seeking treatment after an abnormal Pap smear. These issues included the value of the doctor's opinion, the perception of the accuracy or seriousness of the test result, the belief in the importance of early detection, familiarity with the procedure, fear of loss of femininity, the fear of treatment effects, perceived risk of cervical cancer, and fear of developing cervical cancer. Mitchell, Hoy, Temple-Smith, and Quinn (1992) found that women who defaulted from management of an abnormal Pap smear did so because of an identified pregnancy or seeking care elsewhere. McDonald, Neutens, Fischer, and Jessee (1989) reported an effect of a diagnosis of cervical intraepithelial neoplasia on self-esteem and body image. Patients reported concerns about cancer, loss of attractiveness, loss of sexual functioning, and anxiety. These perceptions contributed to noncompliance with treatment recommendations.

Studies conducted in usual clinic settings mainly used routine methods to recall patients within the regular routine of the health care setting. Intervention studies, on the other hand, focused specifically on motivating women with abnormal Pap smears to return for prompt follow-up and treatment. Several studies tested special interventions, including the establishment of a dedicated clinic for cervical abnormalities, specifically designed brochures, and telephone counseling, and a few studies have used in-person home visits (Hulka & Redmond, 1971; Lerman et al., 1992; Marcus et al., 1992; Paskett, Phillips, & Miller, 1995; Paskett, White, Carter, & Chu, 1990; Spitzer, Krumholz, Chernys, Seltzer, & Lightman, 1987; Washington State Department of Social and Health Services, 1978).

Lerman et al. (1989) assessed the anxiety and reactions of women with dysplasia who were referred to a colposcopy clinic for evaluation. Based on the findings of this investigation, a telephone counseling intervention was developed and tested with women referred for colposcopy. Women who received the counseling were significantly more likely to comply with colposcopy referrals and less likely to report fear or misunderstanding of the procedure. Marcus et al. (1992) most recently reported the results of a study that tested three interventions: (a) a personalized follow-up letter and pamphlet, (b) a slide and tape program on Pap smears, and (c) transportation incentives designed to improve compliance with recommendations for abnormal Pap smear follow-up. Transportation incentives and the combined intervention condition of personalized follow-up and slide and tape program resulted in increasing follow-up rates. These studies demonstrate that once barriers (e.g., transportation, cost, beliefs, or anxiety) are eliminated, improvement in compliance rates and reduction of anxiety can occur.

Stewart, Lickrish, Sierra, and Parkin (1993) tested the effectiveness of a mailed educational brochure about abnormal Pap smears on reducing psychological distress and concerns about cancer. Women who received the brochure were less distressed and anxious about their abnormal Pap test result. Women in the intervention group also were more likely to have completed treatment and follow-up (75.4%) than those in the control group (45.8%); (Stewart, Buchegger, Lickrish, & Sierra, 1994). Michielutte, Dignan, Bahnson, and Wells (1994) used a multistrategy approach, including patient and provider education and mailing educational materials with a notification letter to improve the proportion of African American women who returned for follow-up or treatment of an abnormal cervical smear.

Suggestions to assist health care providers in ensuring that efforts are made to reach women with abnormal Pap smear tests have been made by several researchers. Shepard and Moseley (1976) found letter reminders to be more cost-effective than telephone reminders because several attempts were needed to make a single contact. Automated reminder systems supported by computerized medical records may be more cost-effective than manual methods (McDowell, Newell, & Rosser, 1989) once the initial investment is made. However, the effectiveness of any system may depend on the elapsed time between prompt and the scheduled appointment (Roth, Caron, & Hsi, 1971). Reminders delivered within 1 week of the appointment were the most effective (Macharia, Leon, Howe, Stephenson, & Haynes, 1992).

Other strategies that health care providers can use to reduce noncompliance include orientation statements, patient contracts, and physician prompts. Orientation statements consist of assistance from a clerk to make convenient arrangements for follow-up appointments. These statements, as well as patient contracts, are effective because they enhance communication between the health care provider and the patient. The negotiation procedure allows a patient's expectations to be tailored to the clinical setting, arrangements to be fit to the patient's needs, and anxiety and misunderstanding to be reduced (Kleinman, Eisenberg, & Good, 1978).

Summary

Acceptable and effective methods of communication have been developed. The challenge is to integrate them into health care settings. There are several techniques that health care providers can use to help improve the process of notification and reduce the negative psychosocial effects of abnormal Pap test results. These include reducing the time until the referred appointment, providing clear instructions for follow-up recommendations, using triage and tracking systems for monitoring compliance, sharing test results with patients, reducing barriers to compliance within the medical system, and using reminder systems.

Treatment of Gynecological Cancers

In the past decade, many studies have examined the psychological and behavioral outcomes associated with gynecological cancer. A major determinant of quality of life for these women is the extent of disease and treatment. In addition, each woman reacts differently to disease, and some have more difficult posttreatment outcomes than others. Andersen, Anderson, and deProsse (1989a, 1989b) found that sexuality is the area that undergoes the greatest disruption after gynecological cancer. Other reported types of psychological and behavioral morbidity associated with these cancers include worry over the loss of fertility, anxiety, irritability, depression, and reduced activities of daily living and physical activity (Guidozzi, 1993; Marchetti & Romagnolo, 1992; Payne, 1992).

To assist in predicting which woman will have more difficult posttreatment outcomes, Andersen (1993) developed a model that helps identify those who should be referred for specific types of intervention efforts. The model uses both predisposing factors and disease variables to determine the levels of psychological and behavioral morbidity risk. The predisposing factors available at the time of diagnosis include sociodemographic characteristics, prior health status, existing social networks and support, and other life stressors. Sociodemographic variables include age, race, education, and income. Disease variables include the degree of disruptive signs or symptoms produced, the extent of the disease, the treatment, the availability of rehabilitation, and continuing stressors from the disease or treatment.

According to the model, women at greater risk for adjustment difficulties after gynecological cancer is diagnosed include younger patients; non-White women; women with lower education and income; women with prior physical or mental health conditions; unmarried women; women undergoing other life stress events (e.g., divorce or caretaking duties); women with a disease that causes disruptive signs and symptoms (e.g., sexual difficulties, malaise, weight loss, discomfort) early during the course of diagnosis and treatment; women with extensive disease; women with extensive or complicated treatment; women receiving no rehabilitative medical efforts (e.g., reconstructive surgery, hormone replacement therapy); and women with side effects or morbidity associated with treatment (Andersen, 1993). After identification of risk profiles, interventions to reduce predicted distress can be implemented.

Patients who are at high risk for psychological morbidity are characterized by advanced disease at diagnosis, recurrent disease, or disease that rapidly progresses to death. These women usually display elevated levels of anxiety, confusion, depression, and anger, along with facing increasing physical debilitation and problems with pain (Thompson, Andersen, & DePetrillo, 1992). To our knowledge, no intervention studies have been conducted among women with gynecological cancer in this risk group. Studies of patients with other types of cancer suggest that an interdisciplinary crisis intervention program (i.e., supportive group therapy plus patient education), group support programs, and self-hypnosis (Ferlic, Goldman, & Kennedy, 1979; Spiegel & Bloom, 1983; Spiegel, Bloom, & Yalom, 1981) can improve some aspects of quality of life for women in this risk group.

Women with regional disease who are receiving combination therapy and have a 50–50 chance of survival form the group with moderate morbidity risk. One intervention study has been conducted among women with gynecological cancer in this risk group (Cain, Kohorn, Wuinlan, Latimer, & Schwartz, 1986). The intervention provided information and skills in the following areas: (a) cancer causes; (b) the impact of treatment on body image and sexuality; (c) relaxation training; (d) maintaining good dietary and exercise patterns; (e) communication difficulties with medical staff; (f) family communication; (g) setting goals for the future to cope with uncertainty; and (h) fears of recurrence. The program was presented in both individual and group settings. Both formats demonstrated improvements in depression, anxiety, and psychosocial adjustment.

For women with a low risk for psychological distress (i.e., women with localized disease, treatment consisting of one technique, disease with a good prognosis), the types of interventions that have been investigated among women with gynecological cancer include (a) brief crisis-oriented interventions that help women express their feelings about the diagnosis and treatment, provide information about treatment effects, and enhance self-esteem, femininity, and interpersonal relationships (Capone, Good, Westie, & Jacobson, 1980); and (b) peer counseling sessions that emphasize maintaining interpersonal relationships, making positive plans for the future, asking doctors about treatments, side effects, and sexual outcome, and maintaining normal routines (Houts, Whitney, Mortel, & Bartholomew, 1986). These interventions have been found to produce limited improvement, mainly in sexual functioning. However, long-term follow-up of participants receiving these interventions also showed some positive outcomes in emotional distress, coping, or both.

In summary, women with gynecological cancers need assistance to cope with the psychological effects of their disease and its treatment. Programs should address all phases of the disease time line: (a) diagnosis and pretreatment; (b) during and immediately after treatment and recovery; and (c) disseminated disease, death, or both (Andersen, 1993). To accomplish this, programs should be longer (i.e., longer than 10 sessions), which may not be feasible for high-risk women. Some common topics must be included for all patients, whatever their risk. Newly diagnosed patients can benefit from a crisis intervention or brief therapy model that focuses on the trauma of learning about a life-threatening condition. Focused interventions for sexual functioning for women treated for gynecological cancer should include sexuality information, medical interventions (e.g., hormonal therapy), and specific sex therapy suggestions (Andersen, 1993).

Conclusions

Gynecological malignancies are responsible for a significant amount of morbidity and mortality for women. Morbidity includes both physical suffering and psychosocial distress. These events occur with the designation of "at risk," during screening among asymptomatic women, during follow-up and treatment of abnormalities found on screening, and among women with cancer. What adds to the confusion and anxiety of gynecological cancers for women is the high degree of uncertainty about the illness and available health actions (e.g., the lack of validated screening tests for ovarian and endometrial cancer).

Suggestions for health care providers to achieve these efforts include the use of physician-initiated notification; the use of educational materials (e.g., brochures, flyers, handouts) delivered at clinic visits or in mailings; paying attention to the needs of various patients by involving family members, friends, and community agencies as necessary; and monitoring adherence to recommended actions (screening or follow-up), including the initiation of personal contact with noncompliant women as necessary. Only with concerted efforts by health care providers, educators, and researchers in the areas mentioned will an impact be made in reducing the psychosocial effects of gynecological cancer. Once this is achieved, maximum compliance with screening and treatment recommendations will occur, thus moving closer toward the ultimate goal of reduced morbidity and mortality from these cancers and improved quality of life.

References

American Cancer Society. (1995). *Cancer facts and figures*. Atlanta, GA: Author.

Andersen, B. L. (1993). Predicting sexual and psychologic morbidity and improving the quality of life for women with gynecologic cancer. *Cancer, 71*, 1678–1690.

Andersen, B. L., Anderson, B., & deProsse, C. (1989a). Controlled prospective longitudinal study of women with cancer: I. Sexual functioning outcomes. *Journal of Consulting and Clinical Psychology, 57*, 683–691.

Andersen, B. L., Anderson, B., & deProsse, C. (1989b). Controlled prospective longitudinal study of women with cancer: II. Psychological outcomes. *Journal of Consulting Clinical Psychology, 57*, 692–697.

Anderson, L. M., & May D. S. (1995). Has the use of cervical, breast, and colorectal cancer screening increased in the United States? *American Journal of Public Health, 85*, 840–842.

Ansell, D., Lacey, L., Whitman, S., Chen, E., & Phillips, C. (1994). A nurse-delivered intervention to reduce barriers to breast and cervical cancer screening in Chicago inner city clinics. *Public Health Reports, 109*, 104–111.

Austoker, J. (1994). Screening for cervical cancer. *British Medical Journal, 309*, 241–248.

Brett, T. (1992). Opportunistic cervical screening among 50–70 year olds: A prospective study in general practice. *Australian Family Physician, 21*, 1781–1784.

Burack, R., & Liang, J. (1987). The early detection of cancer in the primary-care setting: Factors associated with the acceptance and completion of recommended procedures. *Preventive Medicine, 16*, 739–751.

Cain, E. N., Kohorn, E. L., Wuinlan, D. M., Latimer, K., & Schwartz, P. E. (1986). Psychosocial benefits of a cancer support group. *Cancer, 57*, 183–189.

Calle, E. E., Flanders, D. W., Thun, M. J., & Martin, L. M. (1993). Demographic predictors of mammography and Pap smear screening in U.S. women. *American Journal of Public Health, 83*, 53–60.

Capone, M. A., Good, R. S., Westie, K. S., & Jacobson, A. F. (1980). Psychosocial rehabilitation of gynecologic oncology patients. *Archives of Physical and Medical Rehabilitation, 61*, 128–132.

Celentano, D. (1989). Prevention of cancer in the elderly. In T. V. Zenser & R. M. Coe (Eds.), *Cancer and aging* (pp. 187–209). New York: Springer.

Cockburn, J., Hirst, S., Hill, D., & Marks, D. (1986). Increasing cervical screening in women of more than 40 years of age: An intervention in general practice. *Medical Care, 24*, 904–914.

Dickey, L. L., & Petitti, D. (1992). A patient-held minirecord to promote adult preventive care. *Journal of Family Practice, 34*, 457–463.

Dietrich, A. J., & Duhamel, M. (1989). Improving geriatric preventive care through a patient-held checklist. *Family Medicine, 21*, 195–198.

Dignan, M., Michielutte, R., Blinson, K., Sharp, P., Wells, H. B., & Sands, E. (1993). Cervical cancer prevention. An individual approach. *Alaska Medicine, 35*, 279–284.

Dignan, M., Michielutte, R., Sharp, P., Bahnson, J., Young, L., & Beal, P. (1990). The role of focus groups in health education for cervical cancer among minority women. *Journal of Community Health, 15*, 369–375.

Elkind, A., Eardley, A., Thompson, R., & Smith, A. (1990). How district health authorities organise cervical screening. *British Medical Journal, 301*(6757), 915–918.

Ferlic, M., Goldman, A., & Kennedy, B. J. (1979). Group counseling in adult patients with advanced cancer. *Cancer, 43*, 760–766.

Frish, L. E. (1986). Effectiveness of case management protocol in improving follow-up and referral of Papanicolaou smears indicating cervical intraepithelial neoplasia. *Journal of American College of Health, 35*, 112–115.

Gordon, A. N., Fleischer, A. C., & Reed, G. W. (1990). Depth of myometrial invasion in endometrial cancer: Preoperative assessment by transvaginal ultrasonography. *Gynecologic Oncology, 39*, 321–327.

Green, J., Morton, F., & Statham, H. (1991). Psychosocial issues raised by a familial ovarian cancer register. *Journal of Medical Genetics, 30*, 575–579.

Gregg, J., & Curry, R. H. (1994). Explanatory models for cancer among African-American women at two Atlanta neighborhood health centers: The implications for a cancer screening program. *Social Science and Medicine, 39*, 519–526.

Gruickshank, D. J., Randall, J. M., & Miller, I. D. (1989). Vaginal endosonography in endometrial cancer. *The Lancet, 1*, 445–446.

Guidozzi, F. (1993). Living with ovarian cancer. *Gynecologic Oncology, 50*, 202–207.

Harlan, L. C., Bernstein, A. B., & Kessler, L. G. (1991). Cervical cancer screening: Who is not screened and why? *American Journal of Public Health, 81*, 885–890.

Haynes, R. B., Sackett, D. L., Taylor, D. W., Gibson, E. S., & Johnson, A. L. (1978). Increased absenteeism from work after detection and labeling of hypertensive patients. *New England Journal of Medicine, 299*, 741–744.

Houts, P. S., Whitney, C. W., Mortel, R., & Bartholomew, M. J. (1986). Former cancer patients as counselors of newly diagnosed cancer patients. *Journal of the National Cancer Institute, 76*, 793–796.

Hulka, B. A., & Redmond, C. K. (1971). Factors related to progression of cervical atypias. *American Journal of Epidemiology, 93*, 23–32.

Kleinman, A. M., Eisenberg, L., & Good, B. (1978). Culture, illness, and care: Clinical lessons from anthropologic and cross-cultural research. *Annals of Internal Medicine, 88*, 251–258.

Lacey, L., Whitfield, J., DeWhite, W., Ansell, D., Whitman, S., Chen, E., & Phillips, C. (1993). Referral adherence in an inner city breast and cervical cancer screening program. *Cancer, 72*, 950–955.

Lane, D. S. (1983). Compliance with referrals from a cancer screening project. *Journal of Family Practice, 5*, 811–817.

Lerman, C., Hanjani, P., Caputo, C., Miller, S., Delmoor, E., & Engstrom, P. (1992). Telephone counseling improves adherence to colposcopy among lower-income minority women. *Journal of Clinical Oncology, 10*, 330–333.

Lerman, C., Miller, S. M., Scarborough, R., Hanjani, P., Nolte, S., & Smith, D. (1989). Adverse psychologic consequences of positive cytologic cervical screening. *American Journal of Obstetrics and Gynecology, 165*, 658–662.

Macharia, W. M., Leon, G., Howe, H. R., Stephenson, B. J., & Haynes, B. (1992). An overview of interventions to improve compliance with appointment keeping for medical services. *Journal of the American Medical Association, 267*, 1813–1817.

Mandelblatt, J., Traxler, M., Lakin, P., Kanetsky, P., & Thomas, L. (1993). Breast and cervical cancer screening of poor, elderly, Black women: Clinical results and implications. *American Journal of Preventive Medicine, 9*, 133–138.

Mandelblatt, J., Traxler, M., Lakin, P., Thomas, L., Chauhan, P., Matseoane, S., Kanetsky, P., & the Harlem Study Team. (1993). A nurse practitioner intervention to increase breast and cervical cancer screening for poor, elderly Black women. *Journal of General Internal Medicine, 8,* 173–178.

Manfredi, C., Lacey, L., & Warnecke, R. (1990). Results of an intervention to improve compliance with referrals for evaluation of suspected malignancies at neighborhood public health centers. *American Journal of Public Health, 80,* 85–87.

Marchetti, M., & Romagnolo, C. (1992). Fertility after ovarian cancer treatment. *European Journal of Gynaecological Oncology, 13,* 498–501.

Marcus, A. C., Crane, L. A., Kaplan, C. P., Reading, A. E., Savage, E., Gunning, J., Bernstein, G., & Berek, J. S. (1992). Improving adherence to screening follow-up among women with abnormal Pap smears: Results from a large clinic-based trial of three intervention strategies. *Medical Care, 30,* 216–230.

McDonald, T. W., Neutens, J. J., Fischer, L. M., & Jessee, D. (1989). Impact of cervical intraepithelial neoplasia diagnosis and treatment on self-esteem and body image. *Gynecologic Oncology, 34,* 345–349.

McDowell, I., Newell, C., & Rosser, W. (1989). Computerized reminders to encourage cervical cancer screening in family practice. *Journal of Family Practice, 28,* 420–424.

McKie, L. (1993a). Women's views of the cervical smear test—Implications for nursing practice: Women who have had a smear test. *Journal of Advanced Nursing, 18,* 1228–1234.

McKie, L. (1993b). Women's views of the cervical smear test—Implications for nursing practice: Women who have not had a smear test. *Journal of Advanced Nursing, 18,* 972–979.

Michielutte, R., Dignan, M., Bahnson, J., & Wells, H. B. (1994). The Forsyth County Cervical Cancer Prevention Project: II. Compliance with screening follow-up of abnormal cervical smears. *Health Education Research, 9,* 421–432.

Michielutte, R., Diseker, R. A., Young, O. L., & May, W. J. (1985). Noncompliance in screening follow-up among family planning clinic patients with cervical dysplasia. *Preventive Medicine, 14,* 248–258.

Mitchell, H., Hoy, J., Temple-Smith, M., & Quinn, M. (1992). A study of women who appear normal to default from management of an abnormal Pap smear. *Austrialian and New Zealand Journal of Obstetrics and Gynaecology, 32,* 54–56.

Moody-Thomas, S., & Fick, A. C. (1994). Women's health: Early detection and screening practices for breast and cervical cancer. *Journal of the Louisiana State Medical Society, 146,* 152–158.

National Cancer Institute. (1989). *Annual cancer statistics review, including cancer trends: 1950–1985* (NIH Publication No. 88-2789). Bethesda, MD: National Institutes of Health.

National Cancer Institute Cancer Screening Consortium for Underserved Women. (1995). Breast and cervical cancer screening among underserved women. *Archives of Family Medicine, 4,* 617–624.

Oleszkowicz, K. L., Kresch, M. G., & Painter, J. T. (1994). Pap smear screening in family physicians' offices in rural area with a high cervical cancer rate. *Family Medicine, 26,* 648–650.

Palm, B. T. H. M., Kant, A. C., Van Den Bosch, W. J. H. M., De Beijer, C. W. B., Gerrits, M. E. J., & Van Weel, C. (1993). Implementation of the national cervical cancer screening in general practice and feasibility of a general practice-based call system: The GP's opinion. *Family Practice, 10,* 173–177.

Paskett, E. D., Carter, W. B., Chu, J., & White, E. (1990). Compliance behavior in women with abnormal Pap smears. *Medical Care, 28,* 643–656.

Paskett, E. D., Phillips, K. C., & Miller, M. E. (1995). Improving compliance among women with abnormal Papanicolaou smears. *Obstetrics and Gynecology, 86,* 353–359.

Paskett, E. D., Phillips, K. C., Miller, M. E., Hopkins, J. O., & Nelson, L.H. (1994, March). *Feasibility of screening for ovarian cancer among high-risk women.* Paper presented at 18th Annual Meeting of the American Society for Preventive Oncology, Bethesda, MD.

Paskett, E. D., & Rimer, B. K. (1995). Psychosocial effects of abnormal Pap tests and mammograms: A review. *Journal of Women's Health, 4,* 1–10.

Paskett, E. D., White, E., Carter, W. B., & Chu, J. (1990). Improving follow-up after an abnormal Pap smear: A randomized controlled trial. *Preventive Medicine, 19,* 630–641.

Payne, S. A. (1992). A study of quality of life in cancer patients receiving palliative chemotherapy. *Social Science and Medicine, 35,* 1505–1509.

Richart, R. M., Townsend, D. E., Crisp, W., DePetrillo, A., Ferenczy, A., Johnson, G., Lickrish, G., Roy, M., & Villa Santa, U. (1980). Analysis of "long-term" follow-up results in patients with cervical intraepithelial neoplasia treated by cryotherapy. *American Journal of Obstetrics and Gynecology, 137,* 823–826.

Robertson, J. H., Woodend, B. E., & Crozier Hutchinson, J. (1988). Risk of cervical cancer associated with mild dyskaryosis. *British Medical Journal, 297,* 18–21.

Rome, R. M., Cahnen, W., & Pagano, R. (1987). The natural history of human papillomavirus (HPV) atypia of the cervix. *Australian and New Zealand Journal of Obstetrics and Gynaecology, 27,* 287–290.

Roth, H. P., Caron, H. S., & Hsi, B. P. (1971). Estimating a patient's co-operation with this regimen. *American Journal of Medical Science, 262,* 269–273.

Schofield, M. J., Sanson-Fisher, R., Halpin, S., & Redman, S. (1994). Notification and follow-up of Pap test results: Current practice and women's preferences. *Preventive Medicine, 23,* 276–283.

Shapiro, D. E., Boggs, S. R., Melamed, B. G., & Graham-Pole, J. (1992). The effect of varied physician affect on recall, anxiety, and perceptions in women at risk for breast cancer: An analogue study. *Health Psychology, 11,* 61–66.

Shepard, D. S., & Moseley, T. A. (1976). Mailed versus telephone reminders to reduce broken appointments in a hospital outpatient department. *Medical Care, 14,* 268–273.

Sigurdsson, K. (1993). Effect of organized screening on the risk of cervical cancer. Evaluation of screening activity in Iceland. *International Journal of Cancer, 54,* 563–570.

Soutter, W. P., Wisdom, S., Brough, A. K., & Monaghan, J. M. (1986) Should patients with mild atypia in a cervical smear be referred for colposcopy? *British Journal of Obstetrics and Gynaecology, 93,* 70–74.

Spiegel, D., & Bloom, J. R. (1983). Group therapy and hypnosis reduce metastatic breast carcinoma pain. *Psychosomatic Medicine, 45,* 333–339.

Spiegel, D., Bloom, J. R., & Yalom, I. (1981). Group support for patients with metastatic cancer: A randomized outcome study. *Archives of General Psychiatry, 38,* 527–533.

Spitzer, M., Krumholz, B. A., Chernys, A. E., Seltzer, V., & Lightman, A. R. (1987). Comparative utility of repeat Papanicolaou smears, cervicography, and colposcopy in the evaluation of atypical Papanicolaou smears. *Obstetrics and Gynecology, 69,* 731–735.

Stewart, D. E., Buchegger, P. M., Lickrish, G. M., & Sierra, S. (1994). The effect of educational brochures on follow-up compliance in women with abnormal Papanicolaou smears. *Obstetrics and Gynecology, 83,* 583–585.

Stewart, D. E., Lickrish, G. M., Sierra, S., & Parkin, H. (1993). The effect of educational brochures on knowledge and emotional distress in women with abnormal Papanicolaou smears. *Obstetrics and Gynecology, 81,* 280–282.

Tavelli, B. G., Judson, F. N., Hetrick, A. E., & Root, C. J. (1985). Cost-yield of routine Papanicolaou smear screening in a clinic for sexually transmitted diseases. *Sexually Transmitted Disease, 12,* 110–113.

Thompson, L., Andersen, B. L., & DePetrillo, D. (1992). The psychological processes of recovery from gynecologic cancer. In M. Coppleson, P. Morrow, & M. Tattersall (Eds.), *Gynecologic oncology* (2nd ed., pp. 499–505). Edinburgh: Churchill Livingstone.

Ward, J. E., Boyle, K., Math, B., Redman, S., & Sanson-Fisher, R. W. (1991). Increasing women's compliance with opportunistic cervical cancer screening: A randomized trial. *American Journal of Preventive Medicine, 7,* 285–291.

Washington State Department of Social and Health Services. (1978). *Washington State Cervical Cancer Screening Program: Final report.* Olympia, WA: Author.

Weinrich, S., Coker, A. L., Weinrich, M., Eleazer, P. G., & Greene, F. L. (1995). Predictors of Pap smear screening in socioeconomically disadvantaged elderly women. *Journal of the American Geriatrics Society, 43,* 267–270.

Wilcox, L. S., & Mosher, W. D. (1993). Factors associated with obtaining health screening among women of reproductive age. *Public Health Reports, 108,* 76–86.

Wilkinson, C. E., Peters, T. J., Harvey, I. M., & Stott, N. C. H. (1992). Risk targeting in cervical screening: A new look at an old problem. *British Journal of General Practice, 42*, 435–438.

Wilson, J., Romano, R. M., & Stein, J. (1985). Public perception of cancer risk and prevention: Implications for physicians. *Maryland Medical Journal, 34*, 63–66.

Wingo, P. A., Tong, T., & Bolden, S. (1995). Cancer statistics, 1995. *CA: A Cancer Journal for Clinicians, 45*, 8–30.

21

Rheumatic Disease and Women's Health

Brenda M. DeVellis, Tracey A. Revenson, and Susan J. Blalock

The rheumatic diseases encompass more than 100 different illnesses and conditions and, in general, affect more women than men. The rheumatic diseases include all forms of arthritis, a number of autoimmune diseases (e.g., systemic lupus erythematosus [SLE]), and soft-tissue rheumatism (e.g., fibromyalgia syndrome [FMS]; Silman & Hochberg, 1993). As Verbrugge (1995) noted, despite its great prevalence, arthritis is often overlooked because the tendency of biomedical research is to focus on fatal conditions, even though America's health future will be dominated by chronic nonfatal health conditions. Arthritis is the most common self-reported chronic condition affecting women (Centers for Disease Control, 1995), and many of the more common and more serious forms of rheumatic disease affect two to five times more women than men. Thus, rheumatic disease represents a significant health problem for women. In this chapter we examine the impact of rheumatic disease on physical activity, psychological functioning, and social and marital life and discuss gender issues in treatment, coping, and psychoeducational interventions. We focus on four forms of rheumatic disease that have a higher prevalence among women than men: rheumatoid arthritis (RA), SLE, osteoarthritis (OA), and FMS.

These four rheumatic diseases, although different from each other in many ways, pose common challenges. All are chronic. Pain, potential disability and loss of role functioning, increased risk for developing depression, the need to interact with the health care system and adhere to prescribed regimens, and threats to coping abilities and social support systems are issues that commonly arise. The need to tolerate and cope with uncertainty is an ever-present issue.

RA is a systemic autoimmune disease of unknown cause. Major features include joint inflammation often leading to progressive joint destruction. Its symptoms include joint pain, swelling and deformity, prolonged

We thank Robert DeVellis and JoAnne Jordan, who reviewed an earlier draft of this chapter.

morning stiffness, and fatigue. Between 1% and 2% of adults have RA. Its prevalence increases with increasing age, and, overall, it affects about 2.5 times as many women as men (Schumacher, Klippel, & Koopman, 1993).

SLE also is an autoimmune disease that can involve multiple systems of the body. Symptoms may include malaise; fever; weight loss; joint pain; renal, cardiac, neurological, and liver problems; and skin and mucous membrane problems. The incidence of SLE peaks between the ages 15 and 40, 90% of the cases involve female patients, and its prevalence is significantly higher among African American women (Silman & Hochberg, 1993).

OA, the most common form of arthritis, involves pain in a joint that worsens with activity, stiffness in that joint after periods of not moving it, joint enlargement and instability, and functional impairment. OA can occur in one or multiple joints. The prevalence of OA at all joint sites increases with age. After age 50, women have a higher prevalence and greater incidence of OA than men (Schumacher et al., 1993; Silman & Hochberg, 1993).

FMS is a source of controversy among physicians because frequently there is no identifiable underlying disease process. Symptoms include diffuse achiness, stiffness, fatigue, and, on physical examination, multiple tender points in specific areas of the body. FMS predominates in women. About 10–20% of new patients in rheumatologists' practices and 2–6% of patients in nonspecialist practices have FMS (Wolfe, Ross, Anderson, Russell, & Hebert, 1995). In a study using a community sample, Wolfe et al. found a prevalence rate of 3.4% for women and 0.5% for men. This prevalence increased with age, with 7% of women between the ages of 60 and 79 having FMS. The syndrome tends to be chronic and treatments include reassurance, exercise, and medication to promote good sleep patterns.

Except for SLE, most of these rheumatic diseases pose no immediate life threat. RA is associated with shortened life expectancy, however, particularly among those with more severe disease (Pincus & Callahan, 1992). Although symptoms and disease progression are controllable to some extent, arthritis is not curable. The presence and severity of symptoms and disease progression can be highly variable and unpredictable. Finally, the treatment regimens can involve medications with unpleasant and occasionally life-threatening side effects. Thus, the stresses engendered by rheumatic disease are chronic and require lifelong coping efforts.

Disease Impact

Symptoms

Pain, stiffness, and fatigue are commonly experienced symptoms in rheumatic diseases, and these symptoms often lead to functional limitations.

In a study of gender differences in symptom reporting among people with RA, P. P. Katz and Criswell (1993b) found that when differences between men and women in disease severity and sociodemographic characteristics (e.g., age, income) were not taken into account, women reported more symptoms than men. However, when these factors were taken into account, women reported fewer symptoms than men. This finding suggests that, given comparable disease severity, women do not overreport symptoms.

Physical Health Status and Activity Limitations

Among women age 15 and older, arthritis is the most frequently cited reason for activity limitations (Centers for Disease Control, 1995). About 4.6 million American women experience activity limitations due to arthritis. Women with arthritis have lower labor-force participation, and labor-force participation rates among people with arthritis are declining (Yelin, 1992). The data suggest that arthritis has a more severe effect on employment for women than for men (Yelin, 1992). In addition, the economic impact of women's work disability is underestimated because women's nurturant, teaching, and housekeeping work in the paid labor market is economically undervalued. Finally, the economic value of work that women do at home without pay is undervalued even more (Reisine, Grady, Goodenow, & Fifield, 1989; Yelin, 1992).

Reisine et al. (1989) examined factors associated with work disability among women with RA. Women with the least autonomy over the pace and schedule of work were 36 times more likely to be disabled than women with the most autonomy. The supportiveness of a woman's family and disease severity also contributed to work disability. Women with more supportive family environments and less severe disease were less likely to be disabled.

Many different types of activities are affected by arthritis. Relative to control participants matched for age, sex, and community of residence, people with either OA or RA experienced more limitations in the areas of performing household chores, shopping, and running errands (Yelin, Lubeck, Holman, & Epstein, 1987). In addition, people with RA experienced difficulty participating in leisure and religious activities, visiting family and friends, and using different forms of transportation. In a study of 988 adults with RA, Reisine and Fifield (1992) found that men and women were affected differently in family work roles. More men reported impairment in their abilities to do yardwork and care for the car. More women reported impairment in their abilities to cook, clean, and shop. For women, arthritis also had a striking impact on nurturant activities such as making arrangements for others and taking them places, maintaining social ties by writing or calling, listening, and taking care of sick people. Women who experience these types of limitations are less satisfied with their ability to be a nurturant support provider than unimpaired women (Reisine, Goodenow, & Grady, 1987). Thus, nurturant functions are important parts of the family work role neglected in past research on disability.

In a study of employed women, Reisine and Fifield (1995) found that family demands had a greater effect on depressive symptoms than did paid work demands. Abraido-Lanza (1994), studying a group of Hispanic women with rheumatic disease, and Karasz and Ouellette (in press), studying a group of women with SLE, found that disease severity resulted in psychological distress when it intruded on valued social roles. P. P. Katz and Yelin (1995) found that loss of the ability to perform valued activities was a risk factor for development of depressive symptoms. Thus, to understand the impact of chronic disabling illness, health care providers must examine not just physical limitations but also women's psychological interpretations of the meaning of those limitations.

Psychological Functioning

The most frequently studied effect of rheumatic disease on psychological functioning has been its impact on depression and depressive symptoms. One conclusion from two recent literature reviews on depression in rheumatic diseases (B. M. DeVellis, 1993, 1995) is that depressive disorders and depressive symptoms appear to be more prevalent in people with rheumatic diseases than in people without any serious chronic illness. This conclusion is consistent with the general finding that depression often occurs with greater frequency among people with a serious chronic illness (Rodin, Craven, & Littlefield, 1991; Stewart et al., 1989; Wells, Golding, & Burnam, 1988). It is important to recognize, however, that although a significant minority of people with rheumatic disease may experience depressive disorders and symptoms, most do not. In addition, the definitive study on the prevalence of depressive disorders among people with rheumatic disease has yet to be done.

Depression alone is a devastating condition: Wells et al. (1989) found that people with symptoms of depression, in the of absence any other health problems, had functioning and well-being worse than people with arthritis, angina, hypertension, diabetes, gastrointestinal problems, lung problems, and back problems. More important, when depressive symptoms occurred in combination with any of the other diseases, declines in functioning were additive.

Depression is more prevalent among women than men, with the average female-to-male ratios close to 2:1 (McGrath, Keita, Strickland, & Russo, 1990). Thus, women are not only at greater risk than men for some of the more common and serious rheumatic diseases, but they also are at greater risk for depression. Health practitioners need to be especially alert for depression in female patients with rheumatic diseases so that both the depression and the rheumatic disease are recognized and treated. If depression in women with rheumatic diseases is overlooked, declines in functioning caused by depression could be mistakenly attributed to the rheumatic disease and result in overtreatment. Alternatively, if symptoms of depression are mistakenly assumed to be a natural part of a rheumatic disease process that does not warrant treatment, women may suffer needlessly given the presence of efficacious treatments for depression.

Social and Marital Life

Given the enormous stressors of living with a chronic condition such as arthritis, to what extent do patients experience intrusions into their social lives? A fair amount of research has focused on that closest of relationships, the marital relationship. Early studies investigated rates of divorce among people with rheumatic disease. Many concluded that divorce is more prevalent among people with RA (e.g., Cobb, Miller, & Wieland, 1959), but to our knowledge no U.S. population studies support this point. Furthermore, even in the one study that did indicate higher rates of divorce, the majority of divorces preceded disease onset (Anderson, Bradley, Young, McDaniel, & Wise, 1985). Comparisons of patients with RA with patients suffering from other rheumatic disorders also have produced equivocal findings: One well-cited study (Medsger & Robinson, 1972) showed a greater incidence of divorce among the patients with RA. A more recent study of 7,293 individuals with various rheumatic diseases, however, showed that individuals with RA were no more likely to be currently divorced than individuals with other inflammatory rheumatic disorders but that they were slightly more likely to be currently divorced than people with noninflammatory rheumatic disorders, particularly OA of the hip or knee (Hawley, Wolfe, Cathey, & Roberts, 1991). In both studies, people with RA were less likely to remarry after divorce. Hawley et al. concluded that differences between people with RA and others in current marital status are attributable to decreased remarriage after divorce, not from increased divorce among those with RA. Whether RA itself or the effect it has on one's life deters remarriage is not known.

Studies focused on the consequences of rheumatic disease for other aspects of family life paint a somewhat brighter picture. In one study, individuals with RA rated their close attachment relationships (primarily family) at least as favorably as did other comparison groups (Fitzpatrick, Newman, Lamb, & Shipley, 1988). In a study of the spouses of people with RA (Revenson & Majerovitz, 1990), positive effects on the marriage were as likely to be named as negative ones. When the onset of the illness is later in life, as is often the case with OA, for example, marital and family relationships may be less vulnerable to disruptions caused by the need to adjust to the disease. However, for widowed women, the illness may have even greater costs in terms of reduced sources of support and increased levels of distress (Fitzpatrick, Newman, Archer, & Shipley, 1991).

Relations with friends may be more at risk. People with RA report that they visit others less often (Deyo, Inui, Leininger, & Overman, 1982) and have fewer opportunities for contact with friends and less satisfaction with these relationships (Fitzpatrick et al., 1991). As suggested earlier, reduced mobility and increased pain make social relations outside the home more difficult to maintain. In some cases, social isolation may arise to avoid stigma and embarrassment associated with the condition. However, Majerovitz and Revenson (1993) found that over an 18-month period, 70% of a sample of patients with RA maintained their close relationships.

It also has been suggested that individuals with rheumatic disease may be vulnerable to sexual problems created by both the physical changes of the illness and its attendant emotional distress. Reisine et al. (1987) found that sexual interest and activity were adversely affected for 53% of women. Studies comparing patients with healthy control participants revealed no differences in sexual satisfaction (Blake, Maisiak, Alarcon, Holley, & Brown, 1987; Blake, Maisiak, Koplan, Alarcon, & Brown, 1988; Majerovitz & Revenson, 1994), although patients with arthritis were more likely to report declines in sexual satisfaction over time. Sexual dissatisfaction is greater for those with severe joint involvement or greater functional disability. Blake et al. (1988) found that men were less satisfied with their current sexual relationships than women and that they experienced greater sexual dysfunction than female patients. Majerovitz and Revenson (1994), however, found that women reported greater sexual dissatisfaction than men. A third study (Curry, Levine, Jones, & Kurit, 1993) examined the best combination of predictors of sexual adjustment among a group of 100 women with SLE: Poor general sexual adjustment was predicted by severe disease, older age, being White, poor premorbid sexual relationship, and poor relationship quality.

Sexuality is seldom addressed by health professionals treating people with rheumatic disease, and the literature just cited suggests that men and women may have different concerns about sexuality. Health providers should be sensitive to patients' questions and concerns about sexuality and should discuss these issues openly with both patients and their partners.

Treatment Adherence and the Patient–Physician Relationship

The effectiveness of most treatments depends on patients' carrying out therapeutic recommendations. Treatment may involve taking medication, exercising, wearing splints, and keeping appointments as well as lifestyle changes, such as changing diet or work habits. Risk factors for nonadherence to therapeutic regimens for arthritis and other chronic illnesses include characteristics of the treatment regimen (e.g., duration or complexity, the extent of side effects), patient characteristics (e.g., age, social class, beliefs about treatment efficacy), and characteristics of the social (e.g., family support) and health care setting. To our knowledge, there is no evidence to suggest that these factors differ for men and women. Several excellent literature reviews focus on treatment adherence (e.g., Bradley, 1989; Feinberg, 1988) and techniques for improving adherence among those with arthritis (Daltroy, 1993; Hovell & Black, 1989).

Patient–physician communication may be the single most important variable affecting adherence. For successful communication physicians must present information clearly, and patients must seek clarification and ensure that their concerns are addressed. Time constraints of most medical visits, impersonal health care environments, the inequity in power and status in the patient–physician encounter, and patients' unfamiliarity with medical language all lead to poor communication. Physicians often underestimate how much information patients desire, and patients often fail to inform the physician when they do not understand the information presented. Furthermore, physicians often misperceive their patients' desires regarding the amount, content, and preferred method for obtaining information on arthritis and its treatments (Lorig, Cox, Cuevas, & Britton, 1984; Potts, Weinberger, & Brandt, 1984).

Perceptions of physician friendliness, caring, warmth, sensitivity, concern, interest, and respect also affect adherence. In fact, research suggests that when the physician addresses the arthritis patient's concerns during a visit, satisfaction with care increases (Potts et al., 1984). Unfortunately, physicians may not elicit or discuss psychosocial concerns, believing that they are irrelevant, time-consuming, or outside their expertise (Daltroy, 1993).

Finally, adherence increases when patients feel capable of initiating and maintaining the treatment; this is the concept of self-efficacy. Patients feel less able to carry out therapeutic regimens when the regimens are complex or interfere with other daily routines (Bradley, 1989). Thus, simplifying treatment regimens (e.g., by prescribing daily medication in one dosage instead of multiple administrations or by recommending exercises that can be fit into one's daily schedule) is likely to enhance self-efficacy beliefs and treatment adherence.

Effects of Gender on Treatment

There is little information on whether the use of specific procedures, drugs, or treatment strategies differ for female and male patients with rheumatic disorders. One study showed that women undergo major orthopedic surgery at a more advanced stage in their disease and that this gender difference could not be explained by other medical variables (e.g., disease severity; J. N. Katz et al., 1994). One explanation is that women wait longer for surgery because of family caregiving demands; however, this could not be tested. Another study (P. P. Katz & Criswell, 1993a), however, showed no gender differences across a number of specific drug treatments for RA, even when clinical variables assessing disease severity and progression were controlled statistically.

Researchers need to explore possible gender differences in referral rates and treatment plans and reasons underlying such differences. Physicians may base treatment plans on differential expectations for treatment success (J. N. Katz et al., 1994), and these expectations may be based on stereotyped beliefs about men and women (Revenson, Cameron, & Gibosky, 1992). There is some indication, for example, that gender stereotypes are invoked with FMS; (female) patients are often told that their symptoms are imagined or psychogenic in origin (Goldenberg, 1987).

Coping and Coping Resources

Rheumatic disease engenders a variety of specific stressors with which patients must cope: pain, functional limitations, modifications in role activities, and treatment demands. Efforts can be directed at dealing with the stressful situation itself or at managing psychological distress aroused by the situation. Most stressful situations evoke both types of coping efforts.

Research involving patients with arthritis has shown that wishful thinking (Felton & Revenson, 1984; Manne & Zautra, 1989), self-blame (Parker et al., 1988), and other avoidant and passive coping strategies (Smith & Wallston, 1992) are associated with poorer psychological functioning. This research includes longitudinal studies (e.g., Brown & Nicassio, 1987), increasing the confidence that using these types of coping strategies plays a causal role in the exacerbation of distress. Research also suggests that active coping strategies and strategies such as information seeking (Felton & Revenson, 1984; Manne & Zautra, 1989) and cognitive restructuring (Parker et al., 1988) are associated with better psychological functioning (see Manne & Zautra, 1992, for a critical review of the literature on coping with arthritis).

Marital Coping

Although research has focused primarily on the coping efforts of individuals, a chronic stressor such as illness affects the whole family. Thus, it is important to extend the study of stress, coping, and adaptation. Revenson (1994) studied 113 couples in whom one partner had rheumatic disease to examine dyadic patterns of coping. Dissimilar coping styles used by husbands and wives did not result in greater psychological distress or in lower levels of marital adjustment. In couples in whom an extremely instrumental, problem-focused coping style was shared by patients and their spouses, patients were more depressed and their spouses felt a greater caregiver burden. However, the patients in these couples also had more severe illness and disability, perhaps accounting for their greater level of distress.

Gender Differences in Coping

Few studies have examined gender differences in coping. The most often cited finding is that men use more problem-focused strategies, whereas women use more emotion-focused strategies and seek social support to help them cope to a greater degree (e.g., Shumaker, & Hill, 1991; Thoits, 1991). Felton, Revenson, and Hinrichsen (1984), however, found no gender differences in a study of middle-aged and elderly adults coping with chronic illnesses, including RA. Instead, factors such as the medical controllability of the illness, the patient's perceived control, and the level of disability shaped the choice of coping strategies (Revenson & Felton,

1989). Affleck, Urrows, Tennen, and Higgins (1992) studied 75 individuals with RA over 75 consecutive days and found that women and men differed in the use of only one of seven coping strategies: Women tended to seek social support to a greater degree. Nonetheless, women made more coping efforts overall and used a greater number of coping strategies than men. These findings suggest that women may be more flexible in their coping efforts and have broader coping repertoires.

Social Support as a Coping Resource

The term *social support* refers to interpersonal exchanges that provide information, emotional reassurance, material assistance, and a sense of self-esteem. Because social support can facilitate the use of effective coping strategies, it is often viewed as a coping resource. Research focused on people with rheumatic diseases has shown that those who receive more support exhibit greater self-esteem (Fitzpatrick et al., 1988), psychological adjustment (Affleck, Pfeiffer, Tennen, & Fifield, 1988) and life satisfaction (Smith, Dobbins, & Wallston, 1991), more effective coping skills (Manne & Zautra, 1989), and less depression (Brown, Wallston, & Nicassio, 1989; Goodenow, Reisine, & Grady, 1990; Revenson, Schiaffino, Majerovitz, & Gibofsky, 1991). Several studies also have shown that these effects are more pronounced for individuals facing greater illness-related stress (the stress-buffering hypothesis; e.g., Affleck et al., 1988; Brown et al., 1989).

There also is evidence that different types and amounts of support, from different sources, may be helpful at different points in the illness (Lanza, Cameron, & Revenson, 1995). Early in the disease, when diagnosis is uncertain, there is a strong desire for information. As patients begin to adjust to their illness, emotional support is most helpful. Finally, as illness progresses, patients often have to cope with increasing physical limitations, requiring more tangible assistance with the chores of everyday living as well as continued emotional support. Common types of unhelpful support reported by patients with RA include minimizing illness severity, pessimistic comments, and pity or overly solicitous attitudes (Affleck et al., 1988); such problematic support from friends and family has been related to depression (Revenson et al., 1991). People with RA who reported receiving little positive support and much problematic support were at highest risk for depression. In another study of female patients with RA (Manne & Zautra, 1989), critical remarks made by the husband were related to maladaptive coping.

Social Support and Family Functioning

Marriage provides a fundamental source of support. Married people with RA have less disability and lower rates of disability progression than their unmarried counterparts (Ward & Leigh, 1993). Providing support may be a source of stress for patients' spouses, however. Rheumatic conditions often require spouses to provide continual support to patients coping with pain, increasing disability, and an unpredictable illness course. Over time, patients' needs may adversely affect their partners' psychological well-being. Indeed, in a study of women with RA and their spouses (Revenson & Majerovitz, 1990), several spouses said it was difficult to meet what they perceived as increased demands for support from their wives. Wives, in turn, reported less spousal support and greater marital conflict when their spouses were more depressed.

Support from naturally occurring social ties may help spouses to cope with their partners' illness. Revenson and Majerovitz (1991) found that spouses who received more support outside the marital relationship were able to be more supportive to their ill partner, particularly if their partner's disease was active or had become significantly worse during the past year. Outside support may alleviate some of the burden of providing care or provide a safe outlet for expressing negative feelings about the stresses of living with an ill spouse.

Psychoeducational Interventions and Clinical Implications

A variety of psychological and educational interventions for people with rheumatic disease have been developed. Their aim is to minimize the impact of arthritis on physical, psychological, and social functioning. Although most interventions are hybrids, they usually include one or more of the following components: provision of information about arthritis, instruction in arthritis self-management skills, social support, biofeedback, cognitive–behavioral techniques, and other nonbehavioral psychological techniques (e.g., hypnosis to aid relaxation; R. F. DeVellis & Blalock, 1993). Although there is little evidence that providing information about arthritis by itself has a beneficial effect on outcomes, some of the other intervention modalities appear to be more promising.

The most widely disseminated psychoeducational intervention for people with arthritis is the Arthritis Self-Management Program (ASMP; Lorig, 1986). The ASMP is a 12-hr course taught over a 6-week period in a series of 2-hr sessions. Typically, classes include 15 participants and are conducted by a pair of trained lay leaders. The ASMP teaches basic arthritis self-management skills, such as development of individualized exercise regimens and cognitive pain management strategies. Recent revisions of the ASMP emphasize the enhancement of patients' self-efficacy to manage their arthritis (Lorig & Gonzalez, 1992). Evaluations of the ASMP have demonstrated beneficial effects on pain for as long as 4 years after the intervention (Lorig & Holman, 1993).

Cognitive–behavioral interventions are also promising. These interventions often are multimodal, combining cognitive–behavioral pain management skills, biofeedback, instruction in coping, relaxation, goal setting, and self-rewards with sharing of concerns. These types of interventions can have beneficial effects in terms of decreasing pain (O'Leary, Shoor, Lorig, & Holman, 1988; Radojevic, Nicassio, & Weisman, 1992), disease activity (Bradley et al., 1987), joint swelling (Radojevic et al., 1992), joint impairment (O'Leary et al., 1988), and anxiety (Bradley et al., 1987). They also have been shown to increase self-efficacy (O'Leary et al., 1988) and perceptions of pain control (Parker et al., 1988). Most of these benefits appear to be short-term, however, and dissipate in the months after treatment (R. F. DeVellis & Blalock, 1993). Thus, a challenge in this area is the development of intervention strategies with more long-lasting effects.

Families often participate in multicomponent programs, which tend to be more structured, intense, and longer, possibly accounting for their greater impact on well-being (Lanza & Revenson, 1993). Recognizing that family relationships can be liabilities as well as assets, that social support transactions involve a provider and recipient, and that rheumatic disease affects the well-being of all family members, we suggest several guidelines for the clinician.

First, clinicians should work with family members to encourage patients' coping efforts and offer instrumental help that does not undermine the patient's self-esteem and autonomy. They also may help patients and family members to more positively evaluate the meaning of the illness in their lives. Second, many of the unintended consequences of helping result from miscommunication or misinterpretation of the patient's need for support. Thus, interventions might strengthen communication skills among family members. By focusing on how the illness affects the marriage (rather than either individual), practitioners can help wives and husbands to understand each other's perspective. Discussions could involve how spouses feel about providing and receiving help from each other and how to identify when the help offered might upset or anger the recipient. Third, some intervention strategies might target the spouse. Building support networks outside the marriage can be encouraged both through existing settings, such as neighborhood and work environments, and other avenues, such as organized support groups or telephone helplines. Although these networks may become more critical as the patient's health declines, network building should be encouraged in the early stages of the illness. Finally, the clinician can serve as a source of information concerning community resources and arthritis support groups or patient education programs often available through local chapters of the Arthritis Foundation.

Conclusion

Rheumatic disease represents a significant health problem for women and has profound effects on their functioning and well-being. The costs of arthritis and rheumatic disease to society are high because of medical care expenses, work disability, lost earning power, and role and activity limitations. More research is needed on prevention and treatment. In addition, more research and resources need to be devoted to the prevention and treatment of negative psychological and social sequelae of rheumatic disease. Finally, researchers need to understand more fully the social and psychological factors that are associated with resilience in the face of the severe challenges that the rheumatic diseases pose for women.

References

Abraido-Lanza, A. F. (1994). *Social role identity, social support, competence and psychological well-being among Hispanic women with arthritis.* Unpublished doctoral dissertation, City University of New York, New York, NY.

Affleck, G., Pfeiffer, C., Tennen, H., & Fifield, J. (1988). Social support and psychosocial adjustment to rheumatoid arthritis. *Arthritis Care and Research, 1,* 71–77.

Affleck, G., Urrows, S., Tennen, H., & Higgins, P. (1992). Daily coping with pain from rheumatoid arthritis: Patterns and correlates. *Pain, 51,* 221–229.

Anderson, K. O., Bradley, L. A., Young, L. D., McDaniel, L. K., & Wise, C. (1985). Rheumatoid arthritis: Review of psychological factors related to etiology. *Psychological Bulletin, 98,* 358–387.

Blake, D. J., Maisiak, R., Alarcon, G. S., Holley, H. L., & Brown, S. (1987). Sexual quality of life of patients with arthritis compared to arthritis-free controls. *Journal of Rheumatology, 14,* 570–576.

Blake, D. J., Maisiak, R., Koplan, A., Alarcon, G. S., & Brown, S. (1988). Sexual dysfunction among patients with arthritis. *Clinical Rheumatology, 7,* 50–60.

Bradley, L. A. (1989). Adherence with treatment regimens among adult rheumatoid arthritis patients: Current status and future directions. *Arthritis Care and Research, 2*(Suppl. 3), S33–S39.

Bradley, L. A., Young, L. D., Anderson, K. O., Turner, R. A., Agudelo, C. A., McDaniel, L. K., Pisko, E. J., Semble, E. L., & Morgan, T. M. (1987). Effects of psychological therapy on pain behavior of rheumatoid arthritis patients. *Arthritis and Rheumatism, 30,* 1105–1114.

Brown, G. K., & Nicassio, P. M. (1987). Development of a questionnaire for the assessment of active and passive coping strategies in chronic pain patients. *Pain, 31,* 53–64.

Brown, G. K., Wallston, K. A., & Nicassio, P. M. (1989). Social support and depression in rheumatoid arthritis: A one-year prospective study. *Journal of Applied Social Psychology, 19,* 1164–1181.

Centers for Disease Control. (1995). Prevalence and impact of arthritis among women—United States, 1989–1991. *Morbidity and Mortality Weekly Report, 44,* 329–334.

Cobb, S., Miller, M., & Wieland, M. (1959). On the relationship between divorce and rheumatoid arthritis. *Arthritis and Rheumatism, 2,* 414–418.

Curry, S. L., Levine, S. B., Jones, P. K., & Kurit, D. M. (1993). Medical and psychosocial predictors of sexual outcome among women with systemic lupus erythematosus. *Arthritis Care and Research, 6,* 23–30.

Daltroy, L. H. (1993). Doctor-patient communication in rheumatological disorders. *Balliere's Clinical Rheumatology, 7,* 221–240.

DeVellis, B. M. (1993). Depression in rheumatologic diseases. *Balliere's Clinical Rheumatology, 7,* 241–258.

DeVellis, B. M. (1995). Psychological impact of arthritis: Prevalence of depression. *Arthritis Care and Research, 8,* 284–289.

DeVellis, R. F., & Blalock, S. J. (1993). Psychological and educational interventions to reduce arthritis disability. *Balliere's Clinical Rheumatology, 7,* 397–416.

Deyo, R. A., Inui, T. S., Leninger, J., & Overman, S. (1982). Physical and psychosocial function in rheumatoid arthritis. *Archives of Internal Medicine, 142,* 879–882.

Feinberg, J. (1988). The effect of patient-practitioner interaction on compliance: A review of the literature and application in rheumatoid arthritis. *Patient Education and Counseling, 11,* 171–187.

Felton, B. J., & Revenson, T. A. (1984). Coping with chronic illness: A study of illness controllability and the influence of coping strategies on psychological adjustment. *Journal of Consulting and Clinical Psychology, 52,* 343–353.

Felton, B. J., Revenson, T. A., & Hinrichsen, G. A. (1984). Stress and coping in the explanation of psychological adjustment among chronically ill adults. *Social Science and Medicine, 18,* 889–898.

Fitzpatrick, R., Newman, S., Archer, R., & Shipley, M. (1991). Social support, disability, and depression: A longitudinal study in RA. *Social Science and Medicine, 33,* 605–611.

Fitzpatrick, R., Newman, S., Lamb, R., & Shipley, M. (1988). Social relationships and psychological well-being in rheumatoid arthritis. *Social Science and Medicine, 27*, 399–403.

Goldenberg, D. L. (1987). Fibromyalgia syndrome: An emerging but controversial condition. *Journal of the American Medical Association, 257*, 2782–2787.

Goodenow, C., Reisine, S. T., & Grady, K. E. (1990). Quality of social support and associated social and psychological functioning in women with rheumatoid arthritis. *Health Psychology, 9*, 266–284.

Hawley, D. J., Wolfe, F., Cathey, M. A., & Roberts, F. K. (1991). Marital status in rheumatoid arthritis and other rheumatic disorders: A study of 7,293 patients. *Journal of Rheumatology, 18*, 654–660.

Hovell, M. F., & Black, D. R. (1989). Minimal interventions and arthritis treatment: Implications for patient and physician compliance. *Arthritis Care and Research, 2* (Suppl. 3), S65–S70.

Karasz, A., & Ouellette, S. C. (in press). Role strain and psychological well-being in women with systemic lupus erythematosus. *Women and Health.*

Katz, J. N., Wright, E. A., Guadagnoli, E., Liang, M. H., Karlson, E. W., & Cleary, P. D. (1994). Differences between men and women undergoing major orthopedic surgery for degenerative arthritis. *Arthritis and Rheumatism, 37*, 687–694.

Katz, P. P., & Criswell, L. A. (1993a, November). *Gender differences in disease characteristics and treatment for RA.* Paper presented at annual meeting of the Arthritis Health Professionals Association, San Antonio, TX.

Katz, P. P., & Criswell, L. A. (1993b, November). *Gender differences in RA symptom reporting.* Paper presented at annual meeting of the Arthritis Health Professionals Association, San Antonio, TX.

Katz, P. P., & Yelin, E. H. (1995). The development of depressive symptoms among women with rheumatoid arthritis: The role of function. *Arthritis and Rheumatism, 38*, 49–56.

Lanza, A. F., Cameron, A. E., & Revenson, T. A. (1995). Determinants of helpful and unhelpful support for rheumatic disease patients. *Psychology and Health, 10*, 449–462.

Lanza, A. F., & Revenson, T. A. (1993). Social support interventions for rheumatoid arthritis patients: The cart before the horse? *Health Education Quarterly, 20*, 97–117.

Lorig, K. (1986). Development and dissemination of an arthritis patient education course. *Family and Community Health, 9*, 23–32.

Lorig, K., & Gonzalez, V. (1992). The integration of theory and practice: A 12-year case study. *Health Education Quarterly, 19*, 355–368.

Lorig, K., & Holman, H. (1993). Arthritis self-management studies: A twelve year review. *Health Education Quarterly, 20*, 17–28.

Lorig, K. R., Cox, T., Cuevas, Y., & Britton, M. C. (1984). Converging and diverging beliefs about arthritis: Caucasian patients, Spanish speaking patients, and physicians. *Journal of Rheumatology, 11*, 76–79.

Manne, S. L., & Zautra, A. J. (1989). Spouse criticism and support: Their association with coping and psychological adjustment among women with rheumatoid arthritis. *Journal of Personality and Social Psychology, 56*, 608–617.

Manne, S. L., & Zautra, A. J. (1992). Coping with arthritis: Current status and critique. *Arthritis and Rheumatism, 35*, 1273–1280.

Majerovitz, S. D., & Revenson, T. A. (1993). *Stability and change in social networks and social support among individuals facing a chronic stressor.* Unpublished manuscript.

Majerovitz, S. D., & Revenson, T. A. (1994). Sexuality and rheumatic disease: The significance of gender. *Arthritis Care and Research, 7*, 29–34.

McGrath, E., Keita, G. P., Strickland, B. R., & Russo, N. F. (Eds.). (1990). *Women and depression: Risk factors and treatment issues.* Washington, DC. American Psychological Association.

Medsger, A. R., & Robinson, H. (1972). A comparative study of divorce in rheumatoid arthritis and other rheumatic diseases. *Journal of Chronic Diseases, 25*, 269–275,

O'Leary, A., Shoor, S., Lorig, K., & Holman, H. R. (1988). A cognitive-behavioral treatment for rheumatoid arthritis. *Health Psychology, 7*, 527–544.

Parker, J. C., Frank, R. G., Beck, N. C., Smarr, K. L., Buescher, K. L., Phillips, L. R., Smith, E. I., Anderson, S. K., & Walker, S. E. (1988). Pain management in rheumatoid arthritis: A cognitive-behavioral approach. *Arthritis and Rheumatism, 31*, 593–601.

Pincus, T., & Callahan, L. F. (1992). Early mortality in RA predicted by clinical status. *Bulletin of the Rheumatic Diseases, 41*, 1–4.

Potts, M. K., Weinberger, M., & Brandt, K. D. (1984). Views of patients and providers regarding the importance of various aspects of an arthritis treatment program. *Journal of Rheumatology, 11*, 71–75.

Radojevic, V., Nicassio, P. M., & Weisman, M. H. (1992). Behavioral intervention with and without family support for rheumatoid arthritis. *Behavior Therapy, 23*, 13–30.

Reisine, S. T., & Fifield, J. (1992). Expanding the definition of disability: Implications for planning, policy, and research. *Milbank Quarterly, 70*, 491–508.

Reisine, S. T., & Fifield, J. (1995). Family work demands, employment demands and depressive symptoms in women with rheumatoid arthritis. *Women and Health, 22*, 25–45.

Reisine, S. T., Goodenow, C., & Grady, K. E. (1987). The impact of rheumatoid arthritis on the homemaker. *Social Science and Medicine, 25*, 89–95.

Reisine, S. T., Grady, K. E., Goodenow, C., & Fifield, J. (1989). Work disability among women with rheumatoid arthritis: The relative importance of disease, social, work, and family factors. *Arthritis and Rheumatism, 32*, 538–543.

Revenson, T. A. (1994). Social support and marital coping with chronic illness. *Annals of Behavioral Medicine, 16*, 122–130.

Revenson, T. A., Cameron, A. E., & Gibosky, A. (1992, November). Age and gender stereotyping by physicians: Is there a double standard? In M. G. Ory (Chair), *Current research on the physician-older patient relationship.* Symposium presented at the annual meeting of the Gerontological Society of America, Washington, DC.

Revenson, T. A., & Felton, B. J. (1989). Disability and coping as predictors of psychological adjustment to rheumatoid arthritis. *Journal of Consulting and Clinical Psychology, 57*, 344–348.

Revenson, T. A., & Majerovitz, S. D. (1990). Spouses' support provision to chronically ill patients. *Journal of Social and Personal Relationships, 7*, 575–586.

Revenson, T. A., & Majerovitz, S. D. (1991). The effects of illness on the spouse: Social resources as stress buffers. *Arthritis Care and Research, 4*, 63–72.

Revenson, T. A., Schiaffino, K. M., Majerovitz, S. D., & Gibofsky, A. (1991). Social support as a double-edged sword: The relation of positive and problematic support to depression among rheumatoid arthritis patients. *Social Science and Medicine, 33*, 801–813.

Rodin, G., Craven, J., & Littlefield, C. (1991). *Depression in the medically ill: An integrated approach.* New York: Brunner/Mazel.

Schumacher, H. R., Klippel, J. H., & Koopman, W. A. (1993). *Primer on the rheumatic diseases.* Atlanta, GA: Arthritis Foundation.

Shumaker, S. A., & Hill, D. R. (1991). Gender differences in social support and physical health. *Health Psychology, 10*, 102–111.

Silman, A. J., & Hochberg, M. C. (1993). *Epidemiology of the rheumatic diseases.* Oxford, England: Oxford University Press.

Smith, C. A., Dobbins, C. B., & Wallston, K. A. (1991). The mediational role of perceived competence in psychological adjustment to rheumatoid arthritis. *Journal of Applied Social Psychology, 21*, 1218–1247.

Smith, C. A., & Wallston, K. A. (1992). Adaptation in patients with chronic rheumatoid arthritis: Application of a general model. *Health Psychology, 11*, 151–162.

Stewart, A. L., Greenfield, S., Hays, R. D., Wells, K., Rogers, W. H., Berry, S., McGlynn, E. A., & Ware, J. E. (1989). Functional status and well-being of patients with chronic conditions. *Journal of the American Medical Association, 262*, 907–913.

Thoits, P. A. (1991). Gender differences in coping with emotional distress. In J. Eckenrode (Ed.), *The social context of coping* (pp. 107–138). New York: Plenum.

Verbrugge, L. M. (1995). Women, men, and osteoarthritis. *Arthritis Care and Research, 8*, 212–220.

Ward, M. M., & Leigh, J. P. (1993). Marital status and the progression of functional disability in patients with rheumatoid arthritis. *Arthritis and Rheumatism, 36*, 581–588.

Wells, K. B., Golding, J. M., & Burnam, M. A. (1988). Psychiatric disorder in a sample of the general population with and without chronic medical conditions. *American Journal of Psychiatry, 145,* 976–981.

Wells, K. B., Stewart, A., Hays, R. D., Burnam, A., Rogers, W., Daniels, M., Berry, S., Greenfield, S., & Ware, J. (1989). The functioning and well-being of depressed patients: Results from the Medical Outcomes Study. *Journal of the American Medical Association, 262,* 914–919.

Wolfe, F., Ross, K., Anderson, J., Russell, I. J., & Hebert, L. (1995). The prevalence of fibromyalgia in the general population. *Arthritis and Rheumatism, 38,* 19–28.

Yelin, E. (1992). Arthritis: The cumulative impact of a common chronic condition. *Arthritis and Rheumatism, 35,* 489–497.

Yelin, E., Lubeck, D., Holman, H., & Epstein, W. (1987). The impact of rheumatoid arthritis and osteoarthritis: The activities of patients with rheumatoid arthritis and osteoarthritis compared to controls. *Journal of Rheumatology, 14,* 710–717.

22

Diabetes: The Challenge of Maintaining Glycemic Control

Betsy A. Polley and Rena R. Wing

More than 12 million Americans have diabetes, and slightly more than half are women. Although women are not at increased risk for insulin-dependent diabetes mellitus (IDDM), women and ethnic minorities (e.g., Blacks, American Indians, and Mexican Americans) are at increased risk for non-insulin-dependent diabetes mellitus (NIDDM), the more common form of the disease; about 58% of individuals with NIDDM are women (Cowie & Eberhardt, 1995). In addition, women are subject to a unique form of diabetes that occurs during pregnancy, gestational diabetes mellitus, which usually remits after pregnancy but increases the risk of developing NIDDM in later life.

Individuals with diabetes are at increased risk of blindness, kidney disease, amputations, and coronary heart disease; as a result, diabetes is the sixth leading cause of death in the United States. The Diabetes Control and Complications Trial recently demonstrated that better glycemic control can reduce the risk of developing complications and slow the progression of existing complications (Diabetes Control and Complications Trial Research Group [DCCTRG], 1993). Therefore, most individuals with diabetes are now encouraged to maintain strict control of their blood glucose levels. The availability of quick and easily used blood glucose meters, and increasing use of multiple insulin injections, sliding insulin dosages, and the insulin infusion pump, have made it easier for people with diabetes to achieve better control of their glucose levels, but maintaining glycemic control remains a daunting task for the patient with diabetes.

In this chapter we review the behavioral demands in diabetes self-management and discuss how diabetes interacts with life events such as pregnancy, stress, and depression. Behavioral and psychosocial issues that are clearly relevant to women are addressed (e.g., reproductive issues, weight control, and eating disorders), as are psychological and behavioral concerns that are not specific to women (e.g., difficulties with self-management, interactions of diabetes with stress and depression), because we think that all these issues should be considered in the care of women with diabetes.

Self-Management of IDDM

The goal of the person with IDDM is to maintain normal blood glucose levels, and this task includes self-monitoring of glucose levels, injecting insulin, and adjusting diet and exercise. Diabetes management is a lifetime chore, and it is unlikely that patients will always be able to carry out all areas of diabetes care successfully, nor should it be expected. Overall, there are lower rates of adherence to diet and exercise regimen. than to insulin administration (Ary, Toobert, Wilson, & Glasgow, 1986; Orme & Binik, 1989), but for an individual patient adherence to any given behavior varies over time (Glasgow, McCaul, & Schafer, 1987). Thus, it is rarely useful to label patients as "adherent" or "nonadherent"; it is more helpful to discuss which behaviors are most difficult at a given time and to work together to determine why they are difficult.

In this section, we focus on specific research related to adherence in four diabetes care behaviors: self-monitoring of blood glucose (SMBG), insulin administration, exercise, and eating. Although there is little research on gender differences in adherence, we point out the ways that these issues may be different for or more relevant to women.

SMBG

The information from SMBG is a cornerstone of intensive therapy. On the basis of the information about current blood glucose level, the person with diabetes can fine-tune insulin administration or diet to maintain good glycemic control. Adherence to self-monitoring involves both doing the recommended number of tests and accurately recording the results. Results of some studies show that participants perform SMBG at least as often as their physicians recommend (Gonder-Frederick, Julian, Cox, Clarke, & Carter, 1988), but in studies in which more frequent SMBG is recommended (e.g., four to eight tests per day), patient adherence to the testing schedule decreases. Thus, the increased testing demanded by intensive therapy may be difficult for patients to adhere to. In addition, studies have shown significant differences between the values recorded in participants' monitoring diaries and the values recorded in the meter's memory; Gonder-Frederick et al. (1988) found that the majority of their participants added or omitted (or both) values from their diaries.

It is important that individuals with diabetes understand that the goal of frequent monitoring is not to evaluate them; rather, the goal is to provide information for adjusting other aspects of the regimen. In investigating why a patient finds it difficult to self-monitor, some of the following barriers should be considered: the pain and inconvenience of testing, development of calluses or bruises on fingertips, lack of privacy for testing in public places, and feeling that test results are a report card rather than useful information (i.e., who wants to fill out their own report card when they know it will not be all As?). Finally, people with diabetes may hesitate to test if they know they will get negative feedback (i.e., when they perceive their blood glucose levels to be above or below their goal; Cox & Gonder-Frederick, 1992). The cost of strips used for monitoring also is a real barrier to frequent testing. Patients who test but do not record may need help in selecting a self-monitoring record that is easy and convenient to use.

Adherence to SMBG can be monitored easily with current blood glucose meters that have computerized memories. These allow the diabetes care team to evaluate whether the patient is checking blood glucose levels as often as needed and whether the patient is accurately recording blood glucose results.

Frequent SMBG is useless unless it forms the basis for adjusting the regimen (e.g., insulin dosage; Davidson, 1986). To our knowledge, there have been no studies that have examined whether patients use SMBG results to make appropriate regimen adjustments, but this aspect of SMBG deserves increased attention. Finally, we know of no research on gender differences in the frequency or accuracy of SMBG, in the reasons for nonadherence to SMBG schedules, or the extent to which SMBG is used to adjust the treatment regimen.

Insulin Administration

Insulin must be administered in carefully titrated dosages and times, and even small changes may have a significant impact on blood glucose levels. However, patients with IDDM report that they take their insulin as instructed only 78.3% of the time on average (Ary et al., 1986), and, with intensive therapy, the demands of insulin administration are even greater. However, adherence to insulin administration is not simply whether the patient takes his or her shots. Particularly in intensive therapy, adherence to insulin administration involves injecting as many as four or more times per day and timing insulin injections so that insulin action peaks when food is eaten (e.g., it is often recommended that injections be given 30 min before meals, with an even longer delay if blood glucose is elevated). In addition, the correct dosage must be calculated using a sliding scale that takes into account current blood glucose levels, planned variations in diet and activity, or both. Although these steps increase the demands of insulin therapy, they also increase freedom, allowing patients to maintain good glycemic control even with variations in diet and exercise.

To our knowledge, gender differences in adherence to insulin administration have not been investigated. However, two barriers to appropriate insulin administration may be particularly relevant to women: fear of weight gain and fear of hypoglycemia.

Weight gain and insulin omission. Several studies have shown that tight glycemic control is associated with weight gain (Wing, Klein, & Moss, 1990), primarily because of more efficient use of the food that is eaten. For example, in the DCCT, patients' body weights increased from 101.6% of ideal body weight at baseline to 109.2% after 1 year of intensive treatment

(DCCTRG, 1988). This weight gain may be especially upsetting to women and lead them to manipulate their insulin dosages (e.g., reduce or omit dosages), to intentionally induce glycosuria, the loss of calories in the urine.

Manipulation of insulin to produce weight loss was first noted in women with IDDM and eating disorders. However, recent studies have indicated that insulin misuse also is prevalent in women with IDDM who do not have an eating disorder. One recent study showed that 31% of women with diabetes omitted insulin, with half reporting that the omission was for weight control purposes (Polonsky et al., 1994) and that women who omitted insulin had worse glycemic control than those who did not.

Interestingly, one study showed that patients who omitted insulin were more likely to report being dishonest with their physicians than patients who did not omit insulin (Biggs, Basco, Patterson, & Raskin, 1994), and this may make it more difficult to identify patients who are misusing insulin. When high glucose levels are accompanied by weight loss, health care professionals should examine possible explanations, including insulin misuse as one possibility. Researchers have found that it is often sufficient to simply ask their patients how often they take less insulin than they should and whether they omit insulin so they can overeat without gaining weight (Polonsky et al., 1994). It may be possible to prevent insulin misuse by watching carefully for weight gain during the initiation of intensive therapy and explaining to patients on intensive therapy why they may need fewer calories to maintain their weight.

Hypoglycemia. Another barrier to appropriate insulin administration is fear of hypoglycemia (low blood sugar). In people with diabetes, blood glucose levels may drop below normal, causing symptoms such as trembling, sweating, and fatigue. If untreated, glucose levels continue to drop and can result in mental confusion, seizures, or unconsciousness. Hypoglycemia is not only physically aversive, but it can be dangerous (e.g., if it occurs while driving) or embarrassing (e.g., if it occurs during a business meeting or date). To avoid the effects of hypoglycemia, patients may intentionally keep their glucose levels higher than desirable. In fact, many practitioners consider fear of hypoglycemia the biggest obstacle to maintaining good glycemic control.

Mild hypoglycemia can be treated by consuming a quick source of carbohydrates. However, many patients "overtreat" hypoglycemia by eating until the aversive symptoms subside (i.e., minimally 15 min), which may considerably increase calories. Women who are worried about their weight may be particularly concerned about having to consume extra calories to treat hypoglycemia and may intentionally keep their blood glucose in a higher range.

The problem of hypoglycemia may be increased by intensive therapy. The DCCT indicated that intensive therapy increased the risk of severe hypoglycemia (DCCTRG, 1993). Furthermore, in patients with better glycemic control, hypoglycemia may be less likely to elicit symptoms (i.e., hypoglycemia unawareness), allowing blood glucose levels to drop to dangerously low levels before the patient is aware of any problems, sometimes leading to unconsciousness (Clarke, Gonder-Frederick, Richards, & Cryer, 1991). Thus, the increased risk of severe hypoglycemic reactions may intensify fears of hypoglycemia in patients undergoing intensive therapy (Cox, Irvine, Gonder-Frederick, Nowacek, & Butterfield, 1987). Fear of hypoglycemia is related to the number and severity of past hypoglycemic episodes, and even one aversive experience may increase worry about hypoglycemia and behaviors to avoid it (Irvine, Cox, & Gonder-Frederick, 1991).

There is some evidence of gender differences in the experience of hypoglycemia. In a recent study, men showed more deterioration in performance of cognitive and motor tasks than women while they were mildly hypoglycemic, but both women and men had similar declines in performance during moderate hypoglycemia (Gonder-Frederick, Cox, Driesen, Ryan, & Clarke, 1994). Thus, women may be less likely to detect mild hypoglycemia and thus may be at greater risk for severe hypoglycemia, although this has not been examined that we know of.

Fear of hypoglycemia results in poorer glycemic control because of avoidance behaviors such as intentionally keeping glucose levels high and eating large bedtime snacks (Cox et al., 1987). When fear of hypoglycemia interferes with glycemic control, patients may be taught to monitor their glucose levels more frequently to prevent hypoglycemia, particularly if they have episodes of hypoglycemia unawareness. Behavioral training has been used to effectively enhance patient awareness of blood glucose levels, but it has not been found to decrease the fear of hypoglycemia (Cox et al., 1991).

Exercise

Exercise is an important component of diabetes management for several reasons. First, exercise has been shown to improve insulin sensitivity and may result in improved glycemic control. Second, it is important for cardiovascular fitness. This is of particular relevance for women with diabetes because diabetes removes the "protection" from cardiovascular disease usually afforded premenopausal women. However, one study has shown that women with diabetes are less likely than nondiabetic women to exercise regularly (Ford & Herman, 1995), whereas diabetic and nondiabetic men are equally likely to exercise regularly. One barrier to exercise is that there is an increased risk of hypoglycemia both during exercise, as muscles burn more glucose, and in the hours after exercise, as glucose is diverted to replenish glycogen stores. Thus, patients may avoid exercise to avoid hypoglycemia, and women who exercise for the purpose of weight control may be discouraged by the necessity of consuming extra calories to treat exercise-induced hypoglycemia. There are several behavioral strategies that may help patients avoid exercise-induced hypoglycemia, including more frequent SMBG or adjusting insulin dosages to accommodate exercise.

Diet

The traditional diet for treating diabetes is the "exchange diet," in which foods are divided into categories on the basis of macronutrient content (e.g., starches and breads, meats) and exchanges within a category are allowed. Meal plans prescribe the number of exchanges that can be eaten for each meal and the time of day the meal is to be eaten. It is important not only to eat the correct foods in the correct amounts but also at the right time of day. Even small deviations in intake may affect blood glucose levels in patients with diabetes; for a woman of average weight, 15 g of carbohydrates (e.g., one slice of bread) can be expected to raise blood glucose levels by about 60 mg/dl. Clearly, even one extra (or omitted) bread exchange may have adverse effects on blood glucose levels. Unfortunately, results of a recent study showed that only 10% of patients with IDDM adhered to their planned exchanges as much as 90% of the time (Christensen, Terry, Wyatt, Pichert, & Lorenz, 1983). On average, patients added or deleted one exchange for every four exchanges in their diet.

Carbohydrate counting. Dietary adherence may become less of a problem with intensive therapy, which allows patients to adjust insulin to accommodate smaller or larger meals. For example, there is increasing use of carbohydrate counting, a simple, flexible alternative to the exchange system. With carbohydrate counting, patients calculate the amount of glucose produced by foods they plan to eat and use an algorithm to determine the appropriate amount of insulin. This system allows greater flexibility in meal plans and provides a mechanism for preventing blood glucose spikes from the consumption of "extra" food.

Eating disorders. It has been suggested that the strict diabetic diet places women with IDDM at an increased risk of developing eating disorders, such as bulimia nervosa or anorexia nervosa. However, recent well-designed studies have indicated no differences in the prevalence of clinical eating disorders or in subclinical symptoms of eating disorders between patients with IDDM and control participants (Fairburn, Peveler, Davies, Mann, & Mayou, 1991; Peveler, Fairburn, Boller, & Dunger, 1992). Of greater concern is the high prevalence of subclinical eating problems, such as binge eating. As many as 85% of women with IDDM report occasional binge eating (La Greca, Schwarz, & Satin, 1987), and it has been reported that 17% binge eat at least once per week (Stancin, Link, & Reuter, 1989). These rates are no different from that found in nondiabetic women, but for women with IDDM, binge eating has a dramatic impact on glycemic control. Indeed, higher levels of disordered eating are associated with poorer glycemic control and increased diabetic complications (La Greca et al., 1987).

It may be difficult to identify eating disorders or disordered eating in diabetic women. Women with diabetes may be reluctant to "admit" to deviations from their meal plan, and it may be difficult to distinguish eating disorder symptomatology from diabetes-related symptoms or attitudes.

Many eating disorder questionnaires ask about preoccupations with food and about avoiding certain foods, such as those with sugar (Wing, Nowalk, Marcus, Koeske, & Finegold, 1986); women with diabetes may endorse these items as part of good diabetes management.

If an eating disorder is suspected, patients should be referred to a psychologist with expertise in treating eating disorders. For both anorexia and bulimia, cognitive–behavioral therapies are recommended, with in-patient treatment for anorexia and outpatient treatment for bulimia. For the patient with diabetes, care should be coordinated with her diabetes care team because regaining glycemic control is a priority (Peveler & Fairburn, 1989, 1992). In addition, professional treatment may be warranted for subclinical eating disorders in women with diabetes because of the negative effects on glycemic control.

It is possible that the recent emphasis on glycemic control may exacerbate concern with dietary intake and promote eating pathology. Conversely, the increased dietary flexibility that comes with intensive therapy and sliding insulin dosages may reduce eating disturbances in women with IDDM.

Dealing With Nonadherence

Warning patients about the prospect of complications is rarely a useful method of increasing adherence, nor is it helpful if the patient feels that poor glycemic control is her "fault." Rather than willful disobedience, most difficulties with self-care are caused by social, environmental, or even psychological barriers, and the solution lies in identifying the barriers to good self-care and developing strategies for dealing with difficult situations. Social and environmental barriers to adherence include factors such as the cost of testing materials and supplies, irregular work schedules, and the lack of private places to perform testing when in public. There also are psychological factors, such as not wanting to identify oneself as having a chronic illness, or denial of the importance of adherence. Finally, it is important that clinicians help their patients realize that it is common to have problems following a diabetes regimen over the long-term and to provide patients with an opportunity to discuss barriers to self-care with a nurse, physician, or psychologist who can help them discover solutions.

Obesity and NIDDM

NIDDM usually occurs in individuals over the age of 45, although in some ethnic minority groups, NIDDM is commonly diagnosed at an earlier age (i.e., 30–45 years of age). The strongest risk factor for NIDDM is obesity, and 60–90% of NIDDM patients are overweight. A family history of diabetes also is a strong risk factor for NIDDM. The prevalence of diabetes is particularly great in several ethnic minority populations within the United States. Approximately 6% of Whites have NIDDM, compared with

10% of African Americans, 13% of Mexican Americans, and up to 49% of American Indians (Harris, 1991). It is unknown why ethnic minorities are at higher risk for developing NIDDM, but both genetic and behavioral factors (e.g., ethnic differences in diet) may be important. Results of some studies have suggested that women are at higher risk for NIDDM than men, but this is not true across all communities and ethnic groups. When gender differences are observed in the prevalence of NIDDM, these may reflect differences in obesity, access to medical care, and the frequency of screening (Wing, Nowalk, & Guare, 1988).

The cornerstone of treatment for patients with NIDDM is weight loss. Weight loss improves glycemic control, reduces insulin resistance, and improves coronary heart disease risk factors. Other aspects of treatment may include diet, exercise, oral medications, or insulin. Although the DCCT did not include individuals with NIDDM, the findings from that study (DCCTRG, 1988) are assumed to also apply to NIDDM patients. Thus, it is extremely important to try to improve glycemic control in NIDDM patients, although it is common for NIDDM to be considered "less severe" than IDDM by the general public. Most studies show that individuals with NIDDM often have poor glycemic control, and a recent study documented higher blood sugar levels in African Americans with NIDDM than in Whites (Weatherspoon, Kumanyika, Ludlow, & Schatz, 1994). It is common now for NIDDM patients to be treated with a stepped-care approach, beginning with dietary treatment, progressing to oral medications, and finally to insulin treatment as needed. It is unknown whether improved glycemic control can be achieved with improved adherence to diet and exercise programs or whether insulin therapy should be initiated more aggressively.

Weight Control in NIDDM

The approach to weight control in individuals with NIDDM is similar to that recommended for the treatment of obesity in general (see chapter 8 in this book). The majority of participants in behavioral weight control programs for individuals with NIDDM are women, as is seen in the general treatment of obesity. Successful treatments for these individuals should include diet, exercise, behavior modification, and ongoing contact.

Wing and colleagues have been studying behavioral weight control programs for individuals with diabetes and have reached several conclusions from this research (Wing, 1993). First, the combination of diet plus exercise is more effective for weight loss and glycemic control in people with NIDDM than is diet alone (Wing, Epstein, et al., 1988). Not only does the combination of diet plus exercise increase the magnitude of short- and long-term weight loss, but also after adjusting for the amount of weight lost, individuals treated with diet plus exercise experience greater improvements in glycemic control than individuals treated with diet alone.

Second, there appear to be several benefits to including very-low-calorie diets (VLCDs) in the treatment program. In one study, a year-long treatment program that used a balanced low-calorie diet throughout was compared with a program that alternated between 12 weeks on VLCDs (400 kcal/day of lean meat, fish, or fowl), 12 weeks of refeeding and balanced diet, and 12 weeks on a VLCD (Wing, Blair, Marcus, Epstein, & Harvey, 1994). The program that incorporated the VLCDs improved weight loss, but this benefit resulted primarily from differences for women in the study. Women treated with the intermittent VLCD lost 14.1 kg over the course of the year-long study, whereas those treated with the low-calorie diet lost 8.6 kg ($p < 03$). By contrast, men achieved the same weight loss on the VLCD and balanced low-calorie regimens (15.4 vs. 15.5 kg). Thus, VLCDs may be of particular interest to consider as a treatment approach for women with NIDDM.

VLCDs also may be helpful for treating patients with NIDDM because they may increase insulin secretion. Wing and colleagues found that use of a VLCD as part of a behavioral treatment program improved glycemic control through a 1-year follow-up (Wing, Marcus, Salata, et al., 1991). Interestingly, this improvement in glycemic control occurred despite the facts that those in the VLCD and low-calorie diet conditions both regained weight over the year of follow-up and that no differences were seen in weight loss from baseline to 1-year follow-up.

Finally, Wing and colleagues have studied the effect of spouse support in the treatment of obese patients with NIDDM (Wing, Marcus, Epstein, & Jawad, 1991). Overweight patients and their overweight spouses were recruited to participate in the study. Half the couples were randomly assigned to be treated together, with both the patient and the spouse targeted for weight loss. The other half were assigned to be treated alone, with just the patient allowed to participate in the weight loss program. Weight loss of patients in the alone and together conditions did not differ at posttreatment (9.0 vs. 8.7 kg) or at 1-year follow-up (5.3 vs. 3.2 kg). However, there was a significant Treatment × Gender interaction. Women did better when treated with their spouses, whereas men did better when treated alone. Although it is unclear why this interaction effect was observed, the clinical impression was that men who were treated with their spouse completed fewer of the behavioral assignments by themselves, often delegating these tasks to their spouse. By contrast, for women it was helpful to include the spouse because he was then more supportive of his wife's efforts. Heitzmann and Kaplan (1984) likewise found that satisfaction with social support was associated with better glycemic control in women but poorer control in men.

Thus, for patients with NIDDM, the emphasis is often on producing weight loss as a means to improve glycemic control. The use of VLCDs, exercise, and spousal support may be helpful in the treatment of these individuals.

Stress, Depression, Pregnancy, and Diabetes

Stress, clinical depression, and pregnancy occur both in women with and without diabetes. These life events are successfully negotiated by most women. However, for the woman with diabetes, these events may hinder efforts to maintain glycemic control, and diabetes may contribute to these events or make them more difficult to negotiate.

Psychological Stress

With the current norm for women to maintain multiple roles in society (e.g., working and mothering), women may encounter a great deal of psychological stress. Although high stress levels have become a cultural norm, they may be detrimental for women with diabetes. Indeed, having diabetes is an additional stressor, especially if it is poorly controlled. Delamater, Kurtz, Bubb, White, and Santiago (1987) found that when asked to describe a recent stressor, children with poorly controlled diabetes were more likely to describe a diabetes-related stressor, whereas children with better controlled diabetes were more likely to describe academic stress.

For the patient with diabetes, stress may contribute to poor control. Stress may directly increase blood glucose levels by producing physiological changes that elevate glucose levels; stress hormones act to increase blood glucose, even in people without diabetes (reviewed by Goetsch, 1989). However, most studies of patients with diabetes find that, on average, there is not an increase in blood glucose after a laboratory stressor (Kemmer et al., 1986), suggesting that the effect of stress on glycemic control may not be attributable to direct physiological effects. In individual patients, though, dramatic rises in blood glucose have been documented (Gonder-Frederick, Carter, Cox, & Clarke, 1990); these patients appear to be particularly susceptible to the physiological effects of stress.

Stress also may influence glycemic control by affecting adherence to the regimen (i.e., eating patterns, activity levels, time schedules, motivation to monitor blood glucose levels and make appropriate adjustments in the treatment plan). Indeed, most questionnaire studies document an association between chronic stress and poor glycemic control (Frenzel, McCaul, Glasgow, & Schafer, 1988) and between stress and poor adherence (Frenzel et al., 1988). However, here too, there is large individual variability. In particular, Balfour, White, Schiffrin, Dougherty, and Dufresne (1993) found that in patients who failed to adhere to their diet during stress, stress was associated with poor control, whereas there was no association between stress and control for patients who maintained dietary adherence. In a study of women with diabetes, one third of the women had higher blood glucose levels on days when they reported more daily hassles (Aikens, Wallander, Bell, & McNorton, 1994), again suggesting that real-world stress may indeed affect glycemic control in some patients.

Stress management training has not been found to improve glycemic control for patients with IDDM (Boardway, Delamater, Tomakowsky, & Gutai, 1993), but relaxation training is highly effective in patients with NIDDM (Surwit & Feinglos, 1984). It is unclear how best to treat stress in patients with IDDM.

Depression

Not only is depression more common in people with diabetes, depression also is twice as common in women than in men. Thus, depression may be a significant problem for women with diabetes. About 18% of people with diabetes are clinically depressed (Lustman, Griffith, Gavard, & Clouse, 1992) compared with 4% of the general population. However, it is not uncommon for rates of depression to be high in patients with other chronic illnesses, suggesting that there may be something about dealing with a chronic disease that increases rates of depression rather than diabetes itself. In addition, depression in people with diabetes tends to be recurrent (Lustman, Griffith, & Clouse, 1988).

Physicians often fail to diagnose depression in their patients with diabetes because the depressive symptoms are seen as appropriate in coping with a chronic disease and because it may be difficult to determine whether symptoms such as weight loss are attributable to diabetes or to depression (Lustman & Harper, 1987). There is overwhelming evidence that depression is associated with poor glycemic control (Lustman et al., 1988; Von Dras & Lichty, 1990), probably through disruptions in self-care. Health care providers should be alert to symptoms such as sadness, irritability, and lack of interest or pleasure in daily activities and physiological symptoms such as changes in sleep or eating patterns, weight changes, and fatigue. Patients suspected of having a depressive disorder should be referred to a qualified psychotherapist.

Pregnancy

Women with diabetes may be anxious about pregnancy because in the past, women with diabetes were more likely to have babies who were especially large or had birth defects. However, current research has linked these complications to poor glycemic control during pregnancy. Birth defects are associated with poor control, particularly in the early weeks of pregnancy, when vital organs are formed; women with diabetes who attain good glycemic control before conceiving significantly reduce the chance of having a baby with birth defects (Kitzmiller et al., 1991; Steel, Johnstone, Hepburn, & Smith, 1990). In fact, the rate of birth defects in the babies of women with diabetes who have good glycemic control throughout pregnancy is similar to that of women in the general population (i.e., less than 2.0%; Freinkel, Dooley, & Metzger, 1985).

Thus, it is essential that women with diabetes plan ahead for their pregnancies and work with their health care team to attain excellent glycemic control before becoming pregnant. However, in a recent 5-year study of young women with diabetes, most pregnancies were unplanned; 78% of 23 pregnancies were unplanned, compared with 48% of the pregnancies among nondiabetic control women (St. James, Younger, Hamilton, & Waisbren, 1993). It is appropriate and essential that diabetes care providers ask about contraception use and reproductive plans in women and teenagers of childbearing age, and, beginning in early adolescence all women with diabetes should be counseled about appropriate contraception and the necessity of excellent glycemic control before becoming pregnant. In a recent study, women with diabetes who were not counseled before pregnancy were found to have less education, were less likely to be living with their partner, were less likely to be receiving regular diabetes care, and were less likely to have been encouraged to seek pre-conception care by a health care provider (Janz et al., 1995).

On the other hand, the incidence of macrosomia can be significantly decreased by good glycemic control in later pregnancy (Combs, Gunderson, Kitzmiller, Gavin, & Main, 1992; Jovanovic-Peterson et al., 1991). Although most patients with diabetes are accustomed to monitoring blood glucose before meals, during pregnancy postprandial blood glucose levels appear to be even more important in influencing the incidence of macrosomia. Poor glycemic control in later pregnancy also may increase the risk that the fetus' pancreas will produce too much insulin, which may lead to neonatal hypoglycemia in the baby.

A huge burden is placed on the woman with diabetes during her pregnancy; tight glycemic control is essential for the health of her baby. At the same time, metabolic changes during pregnancy also affect glucose levels (i.e., vomiting during the first trimester, insulin resistance in later pregnancy). During pregnancy, it is particularly important to avoid any implications that high glucose levels are the woman's fault. In addition, women with diabetes should be reminded that even with perfect control, they may still experience pregnancy complications and that they are not to blame; malformations are not completely eliminated by good glycemic control (Mills et al., 1988)

Conclusion

Individuals with diabetes are required to maintain many difficult behavior changes, and this task may be particularly difficult for women. Education may not be sufficient to improve adherence to the regimen. Rather, patients with diabetes may need opportunities to discuss psychosocial issues that make it difficult to perform self-care behaviors and help in dealing with these issues. To facilitate these interactions with their patients, health care professionals may find it useful to read several of the many books on psychological interviewing (Leon, 1989; Shea, 1988) and behavior change techniques (Watson & Tharp, 1992), which provide guidelines for effective patient interactions. In addition, it may be helpful to have resource information available to patients on topics such as eating disorders, insulin manipulation, stress, and weight control. The American Diabetes Association's Advanced Information Series covers many of these topics. Patients may be more open to discussing such topics if they realize that they are also problems for other people and that their health care provider is willing to discuss these issues. Finally, identification of such problems is only a first step. Resolving these problems may require referrals to behavior change therapists, who should collaborate with the diabetes care providers in formulating a treatment plan.

References

Aikens, J. E., Wallander, J. L., Bell, D. S. H., & McNorton, A. (1994). A nomothetic-idiographic study of psychological stress and blood glucose in women with Type I diabetes mellitus. *Journal of Behavioral Medicine, 17,* 535–548.

Ary, D. V., Toobert, D., Wilson, W., & Glasgow, R. E. (1986). Patient perspective on factors contributing to nonadherence to diabetes regimen. *Diabetes Care, 9,* 169–172.

Balfour, L., White, D. R., Schiffrin, A., Dougherty, G., & Dufresne, J. (1993). Dietary disinhibition, perceived stress, and glucose control in young, Type 1 diabetic women. *Health Psychology, 12,* 33–38.

Biggs, M. M., Basco, M. R., Patterson, G., & Raskin, P. (1994). Insulin withholding for weight control in women with diabetes. *Diabetes Care, 17,* 1186–1189.

Boardway, R. H., Delamater, A. M., Tomakowsky, J., & Gutai, J. P. (1993). Stress management training for adolescents with diabetes. *Journal of Pediatric Psychology, 18,* 29–45.

Christensen, N. K., Terry, D., Wyatt, S., Pichert, J. W., & Lorenz, R. A. (1983). Quantitative assessment of dietary adherence in patients with insulin-dependent diabetes mellitus. *Diabetes Care, 6,* 245–250.

Clarke, W. L., Gonder-Frederick, L. A., Richards, F. E., & Cryer, P. E. (1991). Multifactorial origin of hypoglycemic symptom unawareness in IDDM: Association with defective glucose counterregulation and better glycemic control. *Diabetes, 40,* 680–685.

Combs, C. A., Gunderson, E., Kitzmiller, J. L., Gavin, L. A., & Main, E. K. (1992). Relationship of fetal macrosomia to maternal postprandial glucose control during pregnancy. *Diabetes Care, 15,* 1251–1257.

Cowie, C. C., & Eberhardt, M. S. (1995). In National Diabetes Data Group (Eds.), *Diabetes in America* (NIH Publication No. 95-1468, 2nd ed., pp. 85–101). Washington, DC: National Institutes of Health.

Cox, D. J., & Gonder-Frederick, L. (1992). Major developments in behavioral diabetes research. *Journal of Consulting and Clinical Psychology, 60,* 628–638.

Cox, D. J., Gonder-Frederick, L., Julian, D., Cryer, P., Lee, J. H., Richards, F. E., & Clarke, W. (1991). Intensive versus standard blood glucose awareness training (BGAT) with insulin-dependent diabetes: Mechanisms and ancillary effects. *Psychosomatic Medicine, 53,* 453–462.

Cox, D. J., Irvine, A., Gonder-Frederick, L., Nowacek, G., & Butterfield, J. (1987). Fear of hypoglycemia: Quantification, validation, and utilization. *Diabetes Care, 10,* 617–621.

Davidson, M. B. (1986). Futility of self-monitoring of blood glucose without algorithms for adjusting insulin doses. *Diabetes Care, 9,* 209–210.

Delamater, A. M., Kurtz, S. M., Bubb, J., White, N. H., & Santiago, J. V. (1987). Stress and coping in relation to metabolic control of adolescents with Type 1 diabetes. *Developmental and Behavioral Pediatrics, 8,* 136–140.

Diabetes Control and Complications Trial Research Group. (1988). Weight gain associated with intensive therapy in the Diabetes Control and Complications Trial. *Diabetes Care, 11,* 567–573.

Diabetes Control and Complications Trial Research Group. (1993). The effect of intensive treatment of diabetes on the development and progression of long-term complications in insulin-dependent diabetes mellitus. *New England Journal of Medicine, 329,* 977–986.

Fairburn, C. G., Peveler, R. C., Davies, B., Mann, J. I., & Mayou, R. A. (1991). Eating disorders in young adults with insulin dependent diabetes mellitus: A controlled study. *British Medical Journal, 303,* 17–20.

Ford, E. S., & Herman, W. H. (1995). Leisure-time physical activity patterns in the U.S. diabetic population. *Diabetes Care, 18,* 27–33.

Freinkel, N., Dooley, S. L., & Metzger, B. E. (1985). Care of the pregnant woman with insulin-dependent diabetes mellitus. *New England Journal of Medicine, 313,* 96–101.

Frenzel, M. P., McCaul, K. D., Glasgow, R. E., & Schafer, L. C. (1988). The relationship of stress and coping to regimen adherence glycemic control of diabetes. *Journal of Social and Clinical Psychology, 6,* 77–87.

Glasgow, R. E., McCaul, K. D., & Schafer, L. C. (1987). Self-care behaviors and glycemic control in Type I diabetes. *Journal of Chronic Disease, 40,* 399–412.

Goetsch, V. L. (1989). Stress and blood glucose in diabetes mellitus: A review and methodological commentary. *Annals of Behavioral Medicine, 11,* 102–107.

Gonder-Frederick, L. A., Carter, W. R., Cox, D. J., & Clark, W. L. (1990). Environmental stress and blood glucose change in insulin-dependent diabetes mellitus. *Health Psychology, 9,* 503–515.

Gonder-Frederick, L. A., Cox, D. J., Driesen, N. R., Ryan, C. M., & Clarke, W. L. (1994). Individual differences in neurobehavioral disruption during mild and moderate hypoglycemia in adults with IDDM. *Diabetes, 43,* 1407–1412.

Gonder-Frederick, L. A., Julian, D. M., Cox, D. J., Clarke, W. L., & Carter, W. R. (1988). Self-measurement of blood glucose: Accuracy of self-reported data and adherence to recommended regimen. *Diabetes Care, 11,* 579–585.

Harris, M. I. (1991). Epidemiological correlates of NIDDM in Hispanics, Whites, and Blacks in the U.S. population. *Diabetes Care, 14,* 639–648.

Heitzmann, C. A., & Kaplan, R. M. (1984). Interaction between sex and social support in the control of Type II diabetes mellitus. *Journal of Consulting and Clinical Psychology, 52,* 1087–1089.

Irvine, A. A., Cox, D., & Gonder-Frederick, L. (1991). Methodological issues in examination of fear of hypoglycemia. *Diabetes Care, 14,* 76.

Janz, N. K., Herman, W. H., Becker, M. P., Charron-Prochownik, D., Shayna, V. L., Lesnick, T. G., Jacober, S. J., Fachnie, J. D., Kruger, D. F., Sanfield, J. A., Rosenblatt, S. I., & Lorenz, R. P. (1995). Diabetes and pregnancy: Factors associated with seeking preconception care. *Diabetes Care, 18,* 157–165.

Jovanovic-Peterson, L., Peterson, C. M., Reed, G. F., Metzger, B. E., Mills, J. L., Knopp, R. H., Aarons, J. H., & the National Institute of Child Health and Human Development Diabetes in Early Pregnancy Study. (1991). Maternal postprandial glucose levels and infant birth weight: The Diabetes in Early Pregnancy Study. *American Journal of Obstetrics and Gynecology, 164,* 103–111.

Kemmer, F. W., Bisping, R., Steingruber, H. J., Baar, H., Hardtmann, F., Schlaghecke, R., & Berger, M. (1986). Psychological stress and metabolic control in patients with Type I diabetes mellitus. *New England Journal of Medicine, 314,* 1078–1084.

Kitzmiller, J. L., Gavin, L. A., Gin, G. D., Jovanovic-Peterson, L., Main, E. J., & Zigrang, W. D. (1991). Preconception care of diabetes: Glycemic control prevents congenital abnormalities. *Journal of the American Medical Association, 265,* 731–736.

La Greca, A. M., Schwarz, L. T., & Satin, W. (1987). Eating patterns in young women with IDDM: Another look. *Diabetes Care, 10,* 659–660.

Leon, R. L. (1989). *Psychiatric interviewing: A primer* (2nd ed.). New York: Elsevier.

Lustman, P. J., Griffith, L. S., & Clouse, R. E. (1988). Depression in adults with diabetes: Results of a 5-yr follow-up study. *Diabetes Care, 11,* 605–612.

Lustman, P. J., Griffith, L. S., Gavard, J. A., & Clouse, R. E. (1992). Depression in adults with diabetes. *Diabetes Care, 15,* 1631–1639.

Lustman, P. J., & Harper, G. W. (1987). Nonpsychiatric physicians' identification and treatment of depression in patients with diabetes. *Comprehensive Psychiatry, 28,* 22–27.

Mills, J. L., Knopp, R. H., Simpson, J. L., Jovanovic-Peterson, L., Metzger, B. E., Holmes, L. B., Aarons, J. H., Brown, Z., Reed, G. F., Bieber, F. R., Van Allen, M., Holzman, I., Ober, C., Peterson, C. M., Witham, M. J., Duckles, A., Mueller-Heubach, E., Polk, B. F., & the National Institute of Child Health and Human Development Diabetes in Early Pregnancy Study. (1988). Lack of relation of increased malformation rates in infants of diabetic mothers to glycemic control during organogenesis. *New England Journal of Medicine, 318,* 671–676.

Orme, C. M., & Binik, Y. M. (1989). Consistency of adherence across regimen demands. *Health Psychology, 8,* 27–43.

Peveler, R. C., & Fairburn, C. G. (1989). Anorexia nervosa in association with diabetes mellitus: A cognitive-behavioral approach to treatment. *Behavior Research and Therapy, 27,* 95–99.

Peveler, R. C., & Fairburn, C. G. (1992). The treatment of bulimia nervosa in patients with diabetes mellitus. *International Journal of Eating Disorders, 11,* 45–53.

Peveler, R. C., Fairburn, C. G., Boller, I., & Dunger, D. (1992). Eating disorders in adolescents with IDDM. *Diabetes Care, 15,* 1356–1360.

Polonsky, W. H., Anderson, B. J., Lohrer, P. A., Aponte, J. E., Jacobson, A. M., & Cole, C. F. (1994). Insulin omission in women with IDDM. *Diabetes Care, 17,* 1178–1185.

St. James, P. J., Younger, M. D., Hamilton, B. D., & Waisbren, S. E. (1993). Unplanned pregnancies in young women with diabetes: An analysis of psychosocial factors. *Diabetes Care, 16,* 1572–1578.

Shea, S. C. (1988). *Psychiatric interviewing: The art of understanding.* Philadelphia: W. B. Saunders.

Stancin, T., Link, D. L., & Reuter, J. M. (1989). Binge eating and purging in young women with IDDM. *Diabetes Care, 12,* 601–603.

Steel, J. M., Johnstone, F. D., Hepburn, D. A., & Smith, A. F. (1990). Can prepregnancy care of diabetic women reduce the risk of abnormal babies? *British Medical Journal, 301,* 1070–1074.

Surwit, R. S., & Feinglos, M. N. (1984). Relaxation-induced improvements in glucose tolerance is associated with decreased plasma cortisol. *Diabetes Care, 7,* 203–204.

Von Dras, D. D., & Lichty, W. (1990). Correlates of depression in diabetic adults. *Behavior, Health, and Aging, 1,* 79–84.

Watson, D. L., & Tharp, R. G. (1992). *Self-directed behavior: Self-modification for personal adjustment* (6th ed.). Pacific Grove, CA: Brooks/Cole.

Weatherspoon, L. J., Kumanyika, S. K., Ludlow, R., & Schatz, D. (1994). Glycemic control in a sample of Black and White clinic patients with NIDDM. *Diabetes Care, 17,* 1148–1153.

Wing, R. R. (1993). Behavioral treatment of obesity: Its application to Type II diabetes. *Diabetes Care, 16,* 193–199.

Wing, R. R., Blair, E., Marcus, M., Epstein, L. H., & Harvey, J. (1994). Year-long weight loss treatment for obese patients with Type II diabetes: Does including an intermittent very-low-calorie diet improve outcome? *American Journal of Medicine, 97,* 354–362.

Wing, R. R., Epstein, L. H., Paternostro-Bayles, M., Kriska, A., Nowalk, M. P., & Gooding, W. (1988). Exercise in a behavioural weight control programme for obese patients with Type II (non-insulin-dependent) diabetes. *Diabetologia, 31,* 902–909.

Wing, R. R., Klein, R., & Moss, S. E. (1990). Weight gain associated with improved glycemic control in population-based sample of subjects with Type I diabetes. *Diabetes Care, 13,* 1106–1109.

Wing, R. R., Marcus, M. D., Epstein, L. H., & Jawad, A. (1991). A "family-based" approach to the treatment of obese Type II diabetic patients. *Journal of Consulting and Clinical Psychology, 59,* 156–162.

Wing, R. R., Marcus, M. D., Salata, R., Epstein, L. H., Miaskiewicz, S., & Blair, E. H. (1991). Effects of a very-low-calorie diet on long-term glycemic control in obese Type II diabetic subjects. *Archives of Internal Medicine, 151,* 1334–1340.

Wing, R. R., Nowalk, M. P., & Guare, J. C. (1988). Diabetes mellitus. In E. A. Blechman & K. D. Brownell (Eds.), *Handbook of behavioral medicine for women* (pp. 236–252). New York: Pergamon Press.

Wing, R. R., Nowalk, M. P., Marcus, M. D., Koeske, R., & Finegold, D. (1986). Subclinical eating disorders and glycemic control in adolescents with Type I diabetes. *Diabetes Care, 9,* 162–167.

23

Recurrent Headache Disorders

Kenneth A. Holroyd and Gay L. Lipchik

Recurrent headache disorders have a great impact on women's lives. In this chapter we provide an overview of the two most prevalent headache disorders, tension-type and migraine headaches, with special attention given to the needs of women. We focus specifically on the role reproductive physiology plays in increasing vulnerability to headaches and in triggering headache episodes in women. Situations in which reproductive and hormonal factors influence treatment decisions are highlighted. We also review the efficacy and appropriate use of standard behavioral interventions for women and the management of problems that often lead headaches to be refractory to therapy. Although space does not permit a discussion of the medical management of headaches, good overviews of this topic can be found in Diamond and Dalessio (1992), Rapoport and Sheftell (1996), and Saper, Silberstein, Gordon, and Hamel (1993).

Epidemiology and Health Care Utilization

On average, women are two to three times as likely as men to be disabled with some frequency by migraine headaches (18% of women, 6% of men) or to experience disabling (daily or near-daily) tension-type headaches (5% of women, 2% of men). Although no sex differences in migraine prevalence are seen before puberty, after puberty there is a striking increase of migraine headaches in women. Migraine headache prevalence peaks between the ages of 30 and 45, when migraine is 3.3 times more common in women than in men. Although the female prevalence decreases after menopause, it remains more than double that of men. The prevalence of tension-type headache appears to follow a pattern similar to migraines, increasing steadily after age 12, peaking in middle age, and decreasing thereafter (for reviews, see Stewart & Lipton, 1993, and Rasmussen & Breslau, 1993).

In the United States, migraine headaches are associated with low household income. Racial differences have also been reported, with a higher prevalence among Blacks and Hispanic Americans than Whites (Stang, Sternfield, & Sidney, 1996). The higher prevalence in women with

Support was provided in part by a grant from the National Institute of Neurological Disorders, Stroke and Trauma (NS32374).

lower incomes may be related to poor diet, stress associated with living in poverty, and poor access to health care; alternatively, there is evidence suggesting that migraine disrupts functioning at work and that this occupational and social disruption may in turn exacerbate the migraine condition, leading to a downward socioeconomic spiral (e.g., Stang & Osterhaus, 1993; Stewart & Lipton, 1993).

The impact of recurrent headaches on health care utilization is substantial. Headache is one of the 10 most common reasons for visits to physicians in the United States, accounting for more than 18 million outpatient visits annually (Ries, 1986). Female headache sufferers are more than twice as likely as male headache sufferers to consult a physician about their headaches (Celentano, Linet, & Stewart, 1990). Women also are more likely than men to use prescription medications for their headaches, in part because they are twice as likely as men to receive a prescription for their physical symptoms (Cooperstock, 1976). Women are thus at greater risk for developing problems associated with excessive use or abuse of analgesic medications, such as drug-induced headache.

Psychosocial Impact of Headache Disorders

The impact of recurrent headaches on work performance, or productivity, is substantial. In the United States, women with migraine headaches spend more than 2 million days per month bedridden because of migraine headaches. Employed women suffer 18.8 million days per year of restricted activity because of migraines, with women who work during a migraine episode performing at about 40% effectiveness; housewives experience 38 million days per year of restricted activity and lost productivity because of migraine headaches (Stang & Osterhaus, 1993; Stewart, Schecter, & Lipton, 1994).

Because the incidence of tension-type headaches is much greater than that of migraine headaches, tension-type headaches probably account for a significant proportion of the population disability attributable to headaches. A Danish population study, noteworthy for its careful diagnosis of headaches, indicated that 820 work days were lost per year per 1,000 employees because of tension-type headaches compared with 270 work days lost per year per 1,000 employees because of migraine headaches (Rasmussen, Jensen, & Olesen, 1992). Although the data were not reported by gender, it seems likely that employed women accounted for a substantial portion of the lost work days attributable to tension headaches because of the higher prevalence rate of tension-type headaches in women than in men.

Family, social, and recreational activities may be more disrupted by recurrent headaches than is work performance. Although approximately 19% of migraine sufferers miss work, a larger percentage of migraine sufferers discontinue normal activities (50%) or cancel family (31%) or social activities (30%; Pryse-Phillips et al., 1992). Female headache sufferers are more than twice as likely as male headache sufferers to report that their headaches interfere with their family and social life as well as their leisure activities (Lacroix & Barbaree, 1990).

Recurrent headache sufferers also report significant impairment in general mood or well-being compared with the general population and with patients with certain other chronic diseases (Solomon, Skobieranda, & Gragg, 1993). Nonetheless, only a small proportion of recurrent headache sufferers seen in general practice settings exhibit signs of psychopathology.

Headache Diagnosis

The Headache Classification Committee of the International Headache Society (IHS; Olesen, 1988) has recently updated diagnostic criteria for all headache disorders. The vast majority of women (probably more than 95%) who seek medical assistance have benign, idiopathic headaches such as migraine and tension-type headaches, although all patients should be evaluated by a physician to rule out headaches secondary to a disease state or structural abnormality. Careful medical evaluation or reevaluation is critical for patients (a) whose headaches are of recent or sudden onset ("first or worst headache"); (b) who have experienced recent head trauma; (c) who exhibit changing or progressive symptoms or accompanying neurological symptoms (other than the focal neurological symptoms associated with migraine aura); or (d) who have fever or other signs of infection. For women older than 50, disorders that increase in frequency in older women and cause head pain should be ruled out, such as cervical spondylosis (arthritis of the cervical spine) and giant cell arteritis. Furthermore, older women's use of medications that might aggravate depression or headaches should be assessed. In addition to the excessive use of analgesics or abortive medications, attention should be paid to the use of sedatives and ataraxics (particularly barbiturates, phenothiazine derivatives, and benzodiazepines). The exact diagnostic criteria for primary headache disorders are not listed here; rather, we provide descriptions of the headache disorders most frequently experienced by women.

Migraine Headaches

The prototypical migraine headache is characterized by pulsating pain of moderate-to-severe intensity (sufficient to inhibit or prohibit daily activities) that lasts 4–72 hr, is accompanied by nausea or vomiting, and is aggravated by routine physical activities (e.g., climbing stairs). The head pain often is unilateral and frequently originates behind or around the eyes and then radiates to the frontal and temporal regions. Migraine headaches are often accompanied by a heightened sensitivity to light and sound. Thought, memory, and concentration may be impaired, and the sufferer also may experience light-headedness, irritability, anorexia, diarrhea, and scalp tenderness. The frequency of migraine varies from once a year or less to several episodes per week. For a minority of migraine sufferers, the pain is preceded by temporary focal neurological symptoms that are most often visual disturbances (e.g., bright spots or stars, a scintillating scotoma), but may include sensory disturbances (e.g., parathesias), motor weakness, or syncope. Women are more likely than men to experience neurological symptoms (e.g., visual aura, parathesias), scalp tenderness, and nausea or vomiting with their headaches. Moreover, women consistently have headaches of longer duration and report higher pain intensity associated with their headaches than do men (Celentano et al., 1990).

Tension-Type Headaches

The prototypical tension-type headache is characterized by bilateral non-throbbing (pressing or tightening, dull, bandlike) pain of mild-to-moderate intensity that may inhibit, but not prohibit, daily activities. The prototypical tension-type headache may last 30 min to 7 days and is usually not aggravated by routine activities or accompanied by nausea or vomiting. Tension-type headaches are not preceded by focal neurological symptoms. For the vast majority of tension headache sufferers, the headache episodes occur fewer than 15 days per month (episodic tension-type headache). For a small minority of tension-type headache sufferers, headaches increase in severity and occur with a frequency equal to or greater than 15 days per month (chronic tension-type headache) and may occur daily or near-daily. Patients with chronic tension-type headaches are much more likely than those with the episodic variety to seek treatment.

Headaches Associated With Substances or Their Withdrawal

The IHS system also includes a new diagnostic category: headache associated with substances or their withdrawal (e.g., analgesics abuse headache, ergotamine-induced headache, narcotics abstinence headache). Prescription and nonprescription analgesic and abortive medications (combination analgesics, opiates, nonopioid analgesics, barbiturates, ergots, and other abortive agents) have been implicated in the development of drug-induced headaches (cf. Diener & Wilkinson, 1988; Rapoport & Sheftell, 1996).

Drug-induced headaches (often referred to as "rebound headaches") may be difficult to distinguish from tension-type or migraine headaches. Although presenting symptoms vary, patients commonly report near-constant, diffuse head pain that may be accompanied by nausea or vomiting. Although patients are seldom pain-free, their pain level may vary throughout the day. These patients often awaken with a headache. Sleep disturbances, dysphoria, irritability, restlessness, and difficulty concentrating also are commonplace (Rapoport & Sheftell, 1996).

Patients with rebound headaches commonly have had a long history of intermittent headache episodes. Headache medications often provide

Table 1. Diagnostic Criteria for Headaches Aggravated by Chronic Medication Use

Headache characteristics
  More than 20 headache days per month
  Daily headache duration exceeds 10 hr

Relationship to medication use
  Intake of analgesics or abortive medication on more than 20 days per month
  Regular intake of analgesics and ergotamine in combination with barbiturates,
    codeine, caffeine, antihistamines, or tranquilizers
  Increase in the severity and frequency of headaches after discontinuation of
    drug intake

Note. Criteria are from the Second International Workshop on Drug-Induced Headache
  (Diener & Wilkinson, 1988).

only partial or short-lived relief, leading to an increase in medication intake. Over time, headaches gradually transform from being intermittent to being daily and unremitting as medication use increases. Furthermore, these headaches may become refractory to treatment (Mathew, 1990).

We suggest that health care providers consider the possibility that medication use is aggravating headache problems if an individual meets, or comes close to meeting, the criteria listed in Table 1. A patient who takes ergotamine, analgesics, caffeine, barbiturates, or codeine (as monotherapy or in combination) every day or close to every other day is probably at risk for developing rebound headaches. Unfortunately, a definitive diagnosis can be made only retrospectively when headaches improve after the withdrawal of the offending medication. Susceptibility to rebound headaches varies widely across patients, although it is claimed that rebound headaches are 5–12 times more common in women than in men (Professional Postgraduate Services Europe, 1991).

Chronic Daily Headaches

Specialty headache centers have reported that 30–40% of patients presenting for treatment suffer from continuous or nearly continuous headaches that are referred to by some as chronic daily headaches or chronic daily migraines (e.g., Silberstein, Lipton, Solomon, & Mathew, 1994). The majority of patients with chronic daily headaches report symptoms of both migraine and tension-type headaches. A significant proportion of chronic daily headache sufferers also meet IHS criteria for drug-induced headache. Chronic daily headaches typically are refractory to standard monotherapy with either drug or nondrug therapies and thus create special problems for treatment.

The Role of the Reproductive Cycle

There is good evidence to suggest that the abrupt fall of estrogens that occurs before menstruation gives rise to migraine headaches in susceptible women. Similarly, the fluctuation in estrogens that occur with oral contraceptives, menopause, and after pregnancy are believed to be related to migraine headaches in some women. It is unclear to what extent tension-type headaches are influenced by reproductive hormones. Detailed reviews of the role of reproductive hormones in headaches can be found in Bousser and Massiou (1993) and Silberstein and Merriam (1993).

Menstruation

Close to 60% of women with migraine headaches report that some of their headaches are associated with their menstrual cycle, with attacks occurring either before or during. A significant percentage of women with tension-type headaches also report that some of their headaches are associated with menstruation. Most of these women also experience headaches at other times, although a small percentage of women experience migraine headaches exclusively around menstruation.

Migraine with onset at menarche is most likely to show menstrual periodicity (Granella et al., 1993). Most menstrual migraine attacks occur either in the 2 days preceding the onset of menses or during the first full day of menstruation and are characterized by severe and intense pain lasting 2–3 days that is likely to be accompanied by prominent nausea and vomiting. Attacks without aura are most common, but attacks with aura also occur.

For women who experience a worsening of their migraines around menstruation, treatment does not differ from treatment of usual attacks (e.g., prophylactic and abortive medications, behavioral interventions). This menstrual worsening of headache also can be treated by increasing the usual amount of prophylactic medication taken before menses or by taking nonsteroidal anti-inflammatory drugs prophylactically before menses (Silberstein & Merriam, 1993). For migraines that occur exclusively at menses, percutaneous estradiol gel also may be helpful.

Oral Contraceptives

Oral contraceptives may either alleviate migraines, increase their incidence or severity, or result in no change. Oral contraceptives also can trigger the first migraine attack in a small number of women. Women with migraine headaches receiving oral contraceptives should receive a closer follow-up than those not receiving oral contraceptives. Women who experience a change in their usual pattern of headaches, such as severe headaches of sudden onset, daily headaches, neurological symptoms, or a significant increase in frequency or severity of headaches while taking oral contraceptives should discontinue their use and should receive a neurological evaluation to rule out subarachnoid hemorrhage or arterial or venous thrombosis (Bousser & Massiou, 1993). When oral contraceptives with a high estrogen content aggravate headaches, women may benefit from a trial of an oral contraceptive with a lower estrogen content.

Pregnancy

Pregnancy results in an improvement or disappearance of migraine headaches in 55–80% of female migraine sufferers, especially if the headaches had been regularly associated with menstruation. The improvement in migraine headaches is typically most pronounced after the first trimester. The majority of women with tension-type headaches report no change in headache activity during pregnancy.

For a small minority of pregnant women, migraine headaches may worsen, or even occur for the first time, often during the first trimester. Reported new-onset cases are predominantly with aura, probably because patients with these dramatic neurological symptoms are more likely to seek treatment (Granella et al., 1993).

During the postpartum week, usually between the 3rd and 6th day, approximately 35–40% of women with a previous history of migraine headaches, especially if menstrual related, suffer from migraine headaches. Patients with a definite previous history of migraine headaches tend to describe their postpartum migraine headaches as less painful than their usual attacks, although severe and repeated migraine headaches with and without aura also have been reported.

Treatment of headaches during pregnancy and postpartum (if breastfeeding) is challenging because few data are available about the risks of prophylactic or abortive medications used for migraine and tension-type headaches during pregnancy, delivery, and breastfeeding. If medication is necessary, drugs with a short elimination half-life and inert metabolites (e.g., ibuprofen, flurbiprofen, diclofenac, mefenamic acid) may be used (Bousser & Massiou, 1993). Ergotamine tartrate and parenteral dihydroergotamine, used for the treatment of migraine headaches, are contraindicated during pregnancy. Instead, behavioral treatments, described shortly, should be considered.

Menopause

Although the prevalence of various headache disorders decreases with advancing age, data about migraine headaches suggest that frequency and severity can either decrease, remain unchanged, or worsen with menopause, with some women reporting a continuation of the monthly periodicity of their headaches. Estrogen replacement therapy may aggravate migraine headaches or interfere with the effectiveness of prophylactic migraine medications and behavioral interventions. A reduction in the estrogen dose may improve therapeutic response in this situation; however, almost any change in estrogen regimen may be helpful in some instances, including changes in the type of estrogen (e.g., from an organic conjugated estrogen to a pure synthetic estrogen, or vice versa), change from interrupted to continuous administration, change from oral to parenteral dosing, or adding androgens (Silberstein & Merriam, 1993).

Behavioral and Environmental Headache Triggers

Factors identified by headache sufferers to precipitate headaches are listed
in Table 2. Stress, sleep patterns or sleep dysregulation, and dietary factors are the most frequently identified triggers and should be discussed
with patients. Headache improvement can result from teaching patients

Table 2.   Precipitating Factors for Headache Identified by Patients

Stress
  During stress
  After stress (i.e., "letdown headache")
Lack of food
  Fasting
  Insufficient food
  Delayed or missed meals
Specific foods
  Alcoholic beverages
  Chocolate
  Aged cheese
  Aged meats
  Monosodium glutamate (used in Chinese restaurants, many processed foods,
    seasonings)
  Aspartame (sugar substitute found in diet foods)
  Caffeine (coffee, tea, cola)
  Nuts
Physical exertion
Fatigue
Sleep
  Excessive sleep
  Unrefreshing sleep
  Insufficient sleep
  Sleep problems[a]
    Delayed onset
    Restless sleep
Hormones (women only)
  Menstrual period (before, during, and after)
  Postmenopausal changes
  Oral contraceptives
  Hormone supplements
  Pregnancy
Environment
  Exposure to vapors or chemicals[a]
  Weather changes
  Heat
  Cold
  Bright light, glare
  Noise
Smoking (including passive smoking)

Note. Adapted from Blau and Thavapalan (1988), Radnitz (1990), and Rasmussen (1993).
[a]More frequently reported by women than men.

to either avoid, modify, or cope more effectively with headache precipitants. Precipitants of migraine and tension-type headaches are not universal and do not cause an attack on every exposure.

Psychological Stress

The primary trigger for both tension and migraine headaches identified
by female headache sufferers is stress (Rasmussen, 1993). Close to 50% of
female headache sufferers report that they experience headaches when
rushed or confronted with difficulties in daily life (Nikiforow & Hokkanen,
1978). Women with headaches report a greater number of daily life
stresses than women who are headache-free, and they also appear to ap-
praise stressful life events, especially everyday stresses, more negatively
and cope with these stresses less effectively than women without headaches (DeBenedittis & Lorenzetti, 1992; Holm, Holroyd, Hursey, & Penzien, 1986). Although these psychological differences may be a consequence of living with headaches, not a factor predisposing an individual
to headache problems, stress-management interventions (described later)
can be helpful in managing headaches, particularly tension-type headaches.

Sleep Patterns

In female headache sufferers, the lack of refreshment after sleep may precipitate migraine headaches and restless sleep, and the inability to fall
asleep may trigger tension-type headaches (Rasmussen, 1993). Patients
that identify sleep difficulties as headache precipitants should be instructed in sleep hygiene and should be advised to maintain regular sleep
schedules. For some, headaches may arise as a consequence of a sleep
disorder that merits evaluation by a sleep specialist.

Dietary Factors

Headache patients sometimes report that their headaches follow the in-
gestion of certain foods or beverages (see Table 2), although few double-
blind studies of these triggers have been conducted and the available data
come from surveys and clinical reports. Patients often are already avoiding
obvious dietary triggers when they seek treatment. If a woman is convinced her headaches are diet related, but the offending substances have
not been identified, a diet that eliminates virtually all possible dietary
precipitants can serve as an assessment (Rapoport & Sheftell, 1996). Fluctuations in blood sugar may trigger migraines (Gallagher, 1991). Patients
who report this type of headache should be encouraged to eat meals at
regular intervals. If the patient has difficulty maintaining a regular meal
schedule, high-protein, low-carbohydrate snacks can be carried as meal
substitutes.

Environmental Factors

Patients should be instructed to avoid or restrict their exposure to various environmental factors identified as headache triggers (see Table 2). This can often be accomplished with little lifestyle disruption.

Behavioral Interventions

Description

Behavioral interventions may permit nonpharmacological management of headaches, permit the use of less aggressive therapy in women receiving drug therapy, or facilitate the management of difficult-to-treat headache problems such as drug-induced or chronic daily headaches. Three types of behavioral interventions are frequently used in the management of recurrent migraine and tension-type headaches: relaxation training, biofeedback training, and stress-management or cognitive–behavior therapy.

Relaxation training. Relaxation skills may enable women to exert control over headache-related physiological responses and, more generally, sympathetic arousal. The practice of relaxation exercises also provides a brief hiatus from everyday stresses and assists patients in achieving a sense of mastery or self-control over their headaches. Commonly used relaxation training procedures include (a) progressive muscle relaxation, alternately tensing and relaxing selected muscle groups throughout the body; (b) autogenic training, the use of self-instructions of warmth and heaviness to promote a state of deep relaxation; and (c) meditation or passive relaxation, the use of a silently repeated word or sound to promote mental calm and relaxation. These various relaxation training procedures often are combined in a treatment package.

Biofeedback training. Biofeedback devices monitor physiological responses and present information about the response in an observable display, typically an audio tone or visual display. This information, or "feedback," is used by the patient in learning to self-regulate the response being monitored. Thermal biofeedback (i.e., feedback of skin temperature from a finger, and less frequently from a toe or foot) is typically used in the treatment of migraine, and electromyographic (EMG) biofeedback (i.e., feedback of electrical activity from muscles of the scalp, neck, and sometimes the upper body) is typically used in the treatment of tension-type headaches. Both types of biofeedback training are commonly administered in combination with relaxation training.

Stress-management therapy. Stress-management therapy focuses on thoughts and emotions associated with headache-related stresses (in contrast to biofeedback and relaxation interventions, which focus primarily on teaching patients to self-regulate physiological responses). Patients learn to (a) identify stressful circumstances that precipitate or aggravate headaches and to use effective strategies for coping with these stresses; (b) cope more effectively with pain and distress associated with headache episodes; and (c) limit negative psychological consequences of recurrent headaches (e.g., depression and disability).

More detailed descriptions of these behavioral treatments as well as clinical details concerning their use can be found in Blanchard and Andrasik (1985), Penzien and Holroyd (1994), and Holroyd, Lipchik, and Penzien (in press).

Efficacy

Available clinical trials provide relatively good information about the management of headaches in women because at least 75% of the patients treated in the typical clinical trials have been women (Holroyd & Penzien, 1986, 1990). When gender differences in treatment response have been examined, women have shown improvements that were either as large or larger than those of men. Nonetheless, information about results that can be achieved when behavioral therapies are integrated into primary care or general neurology settings is limited because most clinical trials have been conducted in specialized university, medical school, or headache clinic settings. It is possible that behavioral interventions will prove more effective in managing the chronic headache problems seen in primary practice settings than in managing the chronic refractory headache problems typically found in more specialized treatment settings.

Relaxation and biofeedback therapies. Average reductions in headache activity reported with the most commonly used relaxation and biofeedback therapies are summarized in Table 3. It can be seen that relaxation training when combined with either EMG biofeedback training in the treatment of tension headaches, or with thermal biofeedback training in the treatment of migraine headaches, has yielded about a 50% reduction in headache activity. Moreover, improvements produced by these therapies have been at least three times as large as improvements reported with placebo control treatments.

Relaxation and EMG biofeedback therapies appear to be equally effective in managing tension-type headaches. Tension-type headache sufferers who fail to respond to relaxation training may nonetheless benefit from subsequent biofeedback training. There is no convincing evidence, however, to indicate that there is an advantage to beginning treatment with one, rather than another, of these interventions. On the other hand, in the treatment of migraine headaches there is some evidence to suggest that the combination of relaxation and thermal biofeedback training may be more effective than either relaxation training or biofeedback training by itself (see Table 3). With both types of headache problems, treatment can be initiated with relaxation training; more specialized biofeedback interventions then can be introduced if needed.

Table 3. Average Improvement by Type of Treatment and Type of Headache

Type of treatment	Average % improvement	Treatment groups (n)	Improvement range (%)
Tension-type headache			
Combined EMG biofeedback and relaxation training	57	9	29–88
EMG biofeedback training	46	26	13–87
Relaxation training	45	15	17–94
Placebo control (noncontingent biofeedback)	15	6	−14–40
Headache monitoring control	−4	10	−28–12
Migraine headache			
Combined relaxation training and thermal biofeedback	56	35	11–93
Relaxation training	37	38	5–81
Thermal biofeedback training	35	14	−8–80
Cephalic vasomotor biofeedback training	34	11	2–82
Placebo control (medication placebo)	12	20	−23–32
Headache monitoring control	3	15	−30–33

Note. Data are from Holroyd and Penzien (1986), Holroyd, Penzien, and Cordingley (1991), and Penzien, Holroyd, Holm, and Hursey (1985). All relaxation and biofeedback therapies produced significantly larger improvements than placebo and headache monitoring controls. Combined relaxation training and thermal biofeedback also produced larger improvements in migraine than relaxation or thermal biofeedback training alone. EMG = electromyographic.

Stress-management therapy. Stress-management therapy appears to enhance the effectiveness of relaxation training for tension headaches, but not for migraine headaches. Stress-management therapy probably enhances the effectiveness of relaxation or biofeedback treatments for certain subgroups of women: women whose psychological or environmental problems (e.g., chronic daily stress, depression, other adjustment problems) aggravate headaches or interfere with the application of skills acquired during relaxation or biofeedback training, for example. Recent reviews examining the efficacy of behavioral treatments in more detail include Blanchard (1992), Holroyd and French (1995), and Holroyd et al. (in press).

Behavioral Treatment Formats

The cost of behavioral treatment can be reduced and behavioral treatments more readily integrated into medical practice when these treatments are administered in a minimal-contact treatment format. A minimal-contact treatment format reduces the number of required clinic visits through the use of written materials and audio (or video) tapes that are designed to assist the patient in learning at home much of what would typically be taught during clinic visits. Behavioral treatments also can be effectively administered in small groups.

Implications of the Reproductive Cycle for Behavioral Management

It has often been assumed incorrectly that headaches associated with the reproductive cycle, or aggravated by hormonal preparations, are necessarily less responsive to behavioral interventions than are other headaches.

Menstrual-related migraines. Relaxation and thermal biofeedback therapies can be effective in managing menstrual migraines. For example, Gauthier, Fournier, and Roberge (1991) compared improvements in headaches associated with menstruation (occurring during the menstrual period or 3 days before or after the menstrual period) and headaches occurring at other times in women treated with either thermal or cephalic vasomotor biofeedback training. Similar improvements were observed in menstrual and nonmenstrual headaches, with about half of the women showing clinically significant (greater than 50%) improvement in each type of headache.

Pregnancy. Behavioral interventions are attractive for managing headaches during pregnancy because, unlike drugs, behavioral interventions would not be expected to pose risks to the developing fetus. Moreover, behavioral interventions also may reduce the nausea and vomiting associated with pregnancy. On the other hand, health care professionals may be skeptical about the efficacy of these therapies because headaches during pregnancy are strongly influenced by hormonal changes and often remit during the second or third trimester without treatment.

One study (Marcus, Scharff, & Turk, 1995) does suggest that behavior therapy may prove to be a promising treatment during pregnancy. In this study 31 pregnant women were randomly assigned to either eight sessions of relaxation and thermal biofeedback training and physical therapy exercises, or to an "attention control" treatment. For most women, the treatment program was initiated during the second trimester and thus completed before delivery. Women who received relaxation and thermal biofeedback training and physical therapy exercises showed substantially larger average reductions in headache activity (81% vs. 33% reduction) and were more likely to show clinically significant improvements (73% vs. 29% of women) after treatment than women in a pseudotherapy control condition. Moreover, improvements were maintained throughout the perinatal period and at 3-, 6-, and 12-month follow-up evaluations (Scharff, Marcus, & Turk, 1996). These initial findings should encourage greater experimentation with the use of behavioral intervention to manage headaches during pregnancy.

Menopause. Treatment guidelines are unavailable for postmenopausal women, and particularly for women on estrogen replacement therapy. As noted earlier, clinical observations suggest that the efficacy of both drug and behavior therapies is reduced when headaches are aggravated by estrogen replacement therapy. When the patient on estrogen replacement therapy does not respond to standard behavior or drug therapy, a reduction in the estrogen dose may improve the therapeutic response (Silberstein & Merriam, 1993).

Behavior Therapy Versus Drug Therapy

Behavioral interventions appear to yield outcomes that are roughly equivalent to those obtained with the most widely used preventive drug therapies in representative patient samples. In 60 clinical trials (involving more than 2,400 patients) in which patients were predominantly women, virtually identical reductions in migraine activity were reported with the most widely used preventive drug therapy (propranolol HCl) and relaxation and thermal biofeedback training (Holroyd & Penzien, 1990). Limited evidence also suggests that stress-management therapy is at least as effective as the most widely used preventive drug (amitriptyline HCl) in controlling tension headaches (Holroyd, Nash, Pingel, Cordingley, & Jerome, 1991). Clinical strategies for integrating drug and nondrug therapies can be found in Holroyd et al. (in press).

Special Problems

Rebound Headaches

If headaches are aggravated by analgesic or ergotamine use, effective treatment requires withdrawal of these medications (see the section Headaches Associated With Substances or Their Withdrawal). Although medication withdrawal usually can be accomplished on an outpatient basis, inpatient management occasionally may be necessary. Table 4 outlines circumstances that may require inpatient withdrawal or unusually close supervision of outpatient withdrawal. Physician supervision of the withdrawal process is necessary.

On abrupt medication withdrawal (or when medications that are being tapered reach a critically low blood level), it is commonplace to observe an initial worsening of headache and gastrointestinal upset followed by an improvement in symptoms within the ensuing 2 weeks. However, a period of 8–12 weeks may be required to fully complete the drug washout period.

A variety of medications may moderate severe rebound headaches or other withdrawal symptoms (Rapoport & Sheftell, 1996). Dihydroergotamine is frequently used to control rebound headaches. Opioid withdrawal symptoms may be moderated with clonidine; a long-acting barbiturate may be substituted for short- or intermediate-acting barbiturates to mitigate barbiturate withdrawal symptoms. Preventive therapy with prophy-

Table 4.   Considerations for Inpatient Treatment

Intractable disabling headache unresponsive to outpatient treatment
- Disabling headaches fail to respond to aggressive outpatient therapies
- Frequent emergency room visits not reduced with outpatient therapies

Withdrawal of rebounding agents risky or otherwise not feasible on an outpatient basis
- High levels of barbiturate, ergotamine, benzodiazepine, or opiate use at levels that require close monitoring of withdrawal
- Toxicity from offending medications (e.g., renal impairment, gastrointestinal bleeding, evidence of liver toxicity) necessitates close medical monitoring during withdrawal
- Patient unable to reduce the use of offending agents on an outpatient basis even after repeated attempts

Comorbid medical or psychiatric problem requires close monitoring or treatment during initiation of drug therapy for headaches
- Medical disorder (e.g., coronary artery disease, uncontrolled hypertension, ulcer disease, renal or hepatic dysfunction, uncontrolled asthma)
- Protracted nausea, vomiting, or diarrhea have produced dehydration that necessitates intravenous fluid replacement
- Psychiatric disorder (e.g., severe depression, alcohol or drug abuse, or thought disorder) renders outpatient management problematic

Note. Adapted from Rapoport and Sheftell (1996).

lactic drugs and behavioral therapy also may make withdrawal more tolerable and facilitate the management of headaches that continue to occur after the withdrawal of offending medications. To prevent rebound headaches from reoccurring, patients need to be informed about rebound headaches; clear guidelines for the use of medications that can produce the rebound phenomenon also should be provided. Individualized plans for managing severe headaches that may include a card describing appropriate emergency room headache management procedures can help the patient to obtain optimal treatment if he or she seeks emergency room care.

Chronic Daily Headaches

Even when excessive medication use is not an aggravating factor, near-daily, sometimes disabling headaches may require relatively aggressive multimodal treatment. Effective management may require the simultaneous use of two or more preventive drugs plus dihydroergotamine and symptomatic drugs for the acute control of pain and behavior therapy for longer term management.

Because patients with chronic daily headaches may only rarely experience a headache-free period, behavioral interventions focus on pain management, on the reduction of pain-related disability, and on preventing mild pain from progressing to a disabling pain. If prophylactic medication produces even occasional pain-free periods, behavioral skills for preventing headaches then can be incorporated into treatment. Unremitting pain often contributes to sleep disturbances and family problems as well as psychological distress and demoralization; when present, these problems should be addressed. Of course, when drug-induced headaches are suspected, the reduction or elimination of the offending medications becomes an important part of treatment.

Comorbid Psychiatric Disorder

Although epidemiological findings have revealed an association between migraines and both anxiety and mood disorders (Silberstein, Lipton, & Breslau, 1995), psychiatric disorders still occur relatively infrequently in the general population of recurrent headache sufferers. Brief psychological screening should be sufficient to identify the subgroup of patients who require a more comprehensive psychological evaluation.

When psychological evaluation suggests the presence of a significant psychological disturbance, numerous potential associations between headache and psychopathology need to be considered. For example, anxiety and depression can precipitate or exacerbate headache episodes in headache-prone patients. Psychological symptoms (especially depression) also can result from living with chronically disabling headaches. In other instances, headaches may be better understood as a manifestation of a primary psychological disturbance (e.g., when the headache is one of a long list of presenting physical complaints, a somatization disorder diagnosis may be warranted). Significant psychopathology also may be unrelated to the headache disorder and have little or no impact on headache treatment (e.g., when a patient presents with schizophrenia or bipolar disorder that is well controlled). Finally, personality disorders can seriously complicate headache evaluation and treatment because of these patients' difficult interpersonal style.

Significant psychopathology may contribute to a poor response to both pharmacological and nonpharmacological headache therapies. When patients exhibit significant psychological symptoms, combined psychological and pharmacological treatment should be considered. In most instances, traditional psychotherapy is not indicated; rather brief, focused attention to the specific adjustment problems that precipitate or exacerbate headache episodes, interfere with treatment compliance, or interfere with the use of self-regulatory skills often is sufficient.

Patients who present with headaches or other medical problems may not be open to discussion of mental health problems. In such instances, psychotropic medications commonly used at low doses for headache prophylaxis (e.g., amitriptyline, imipramine) may prove helpful at higher doses both in reducing pain and in managing psychological symptoms. Behavioral interventions, particularly biofeedback training, also can introduce patients to the process of psychological treatment in a non-threatening way and thus help them acknowledge psychological difficulties and accept psychological treatment.

Age-Appropriate Treatment

Treatment procedures may need to be modified to suit the needs of older patients. Mosley, Grotheus, and Meeks (1995) successfully treated patients aged 60–78 years (M = 68 years) with 12 sessions of combined relaxation and cognitive–behavior therapy; 64% of the patients showed clinically significant improvements in tension-type headache activity. In that study, audiotapes and written materials designed to assist the acquisition of self-regulatory skills were provided, and weekly phone contacts after each session to answer questions and identify problems were included in the treatment procedures. These findings suggest that by including detailed verbal and written explanations of treatment procedures, frequent reviews of the material covered, and additional time to practice elementary skills before more advanced skills are introduced, the probability that older patients can benefit from behavioral interventions can be increased.

Referral Issues

Most headache problems can be managed medically in primary practice. Referral to a neurologist or other medical specialist can be helpful when a diagnosis is not clear or when a comorbid medical disorder limits the use of standard drug therapies. Referral to a specialist also may be helpful when the special problems just noted are encountered. Medical specialists with an interest in headaches are often members of the American Association for the Study of Headache (AASH) and can be located through the AASH member directory or by contacting the American Council for Headache Education (ACHE; 875 Kingshighway, Suite 200, Woodbury, NJ 08096; 800-255-2243), which also provides patient education materials. The National Headache Foundation (5252 North Western Avenue, Chicago, IL 60625) also can provide names of headache specialists and patient education materials.

Referrals can be made to psychologists or other health care professionals in private practice who are familiar with relaxation, biofeedback, and stress-management interventions and who have experience in treating headache problems or to headache or pain clinics that typically offer these services. Patients who are uncomfortable with a referral for psychological therapies often are accepting of a referral for biofeedback because of its apparent physiological focus. The Association for Applied Psychophysiology and Biofeedback (10200 West 44th Ave., #304, Wheat Ridge, CO 80033-2840; 303-422-8436) and the Association for the Advancement of Behavior Therapy (305 7th Ave., New York, NY 10001-6008; 212-647-1890) and the ACHE have directories of appropriately trained professionals.

Conclusion

Recurrent headache disorders disproportionately affect women, causing significant occupational, social, and recreational impairment for affected women. Strong evidence implicates reproductive hormones, especially cyclical changes in estrogen levels, in triggering or exacerbating headaches in susceptible women, although this relationship is often overlooked in general discussions of headache management. We have attempted to highlight reproductive and hormonal considerations in the medical and behavioral management of recurrent headache disorders in order to emphasize topics of particular relevance to the management of headaches in women. We have also emphasized problems such as drug-induced headaches and transformed migraine headaches that are frequently seen in women and that confound the effective primary-practice management of headaches.

Despite effective behavioral and pharmacological therapies for recurrent headache disorders, most women with disabling headaches do not receive treatment, and up to 40% of the women who do seek treatment may not be treated successfully. A lack of regular access to primary care physicians and a general lack of awareness of the effective treatments that are available may account for low consultation rates. Public education concerning headache disorders and their treatment, and possibly even population-based screenings to bring women into the health care system, might help remedy this problem. The management of recurrent headache disorders in primary practice, where most patients seek treatment, might be improved by clear, empirically based primary practice treatment guidelines that are accompanied by education interventions designed to increase physician awareness and use of these guidelines.

References

Blanchard, E. B. (1992). Psychological treatment of benign headache disorders. *Journal of Consulting and Clinical Psychology, 60,* 537–551.

Blanchard, E. B., & Andrasik, F. A. (1985). *Management of chronic headaches: A psychological approach.* Elmsford, NY: Pergamon Press.

Blau, J. N., & Thavapalan, M. (1988). Preventing migraine: A study of precipitating factors. *Headache, 28,* 481–483.

Bousser, M. G., & Massiou, H. (1993). Migraine in the reproductive cycle. In J. Olesen, P. Tfelt-Hansen, & K. M. A. Welch (Eds.), *The headaches* (pp. 413–419). New York: Raven Press.

Celentano, D. D., Linet, M. S., & Stewart, W. F. (1990). Gender differences in the experience of headache. *Social Sciences and Medicine, 30,* 1289–1295.

Cooperstock, R. (1976). Psychotropic drug use among women. *Canadian Medical Association Journal, 115,* 760–763.

DeBenedittis, G., & Lorenzetti, A. (1992). Minor stressful life events (daily hassles) in chronic primary headache: Relationship with MMPI personality patterns. *Headache, 32,* 330–332.

Diamond, S., & Dalessio, D. J. (1992). *The practicing physician's approach to headache.* Baltimore: Williams & Wilkins.

Diener, H. C., & Wilkinson, M. (Eds.). (1988). *Drug induced headache.* New York: Springer-Verlag.

Gallagher, R. M. (1991). Influencing factors of headache. In R. M. Gallagher (Ed.), *Drug therapy for headache* (pp. 29–44). New York: Marcel Dekker.

Gauthier, J. G., Fournier, A., & Roberge, C. (1991). The differential effects of biofeedback in the treatment of menstrual and nonmenstrual migraine. *Headache, 31,* 82–90.

Granella, F., Sances, G., Zanferrari, C., Costa, A., Martignoni, E., & Manzoni, G. C. (1993). Migraine without aura and reproductive life events: A clinical epidemiological study in 1300 women. *Headache, 33,* 385–389.

Holm, J. E., Holroyd, K. A., Hursey, K. G., & Penzien, D. B. (1986). The role of stress in recurrent tension headache. *Headache, 26,* 160–167.

Holroyd, K. A., & French, D. (1995). Recent advances in the assessment and treatment of recurrent headaches. In A. J. Goreczny (Ed.), *Handbook of health and rehabilitation psychology* (pp. 3–30). New York: Plenum.

Holroyd, K. A., Lipchik, G. L., & Penzien, D. B. (in press). Psychological management of recurrent headache disorders: Empirical basis for clinical practice. In K. S. Dobson & K. D. Craig (Eds.), *Best practice: Developing and promoting empirically validated interventions.* Newbury Park, CA: Sage.

Holroyd, K. A., Nash, J. M., Pingel, J. D., Cordingley, G. E., & Jerome, A. (1991). A comparison of pharmacological (amitriptyline HCl) and nonpharmacological (cognitive–behavioral) therapies for chronic tension headaches. *Journal of Consulting and Clinical Psychology, 59,* 387–393.

Holroyd, K. A., & Penzien, D. B. (1986). Client variables and the behavioral treatment of recurrent tension: A meta-analytic review. *Journal of Behavioral Medicine, 9,* 515–536.

Holroyd, K. A., & Penzien, D. B. (1990). Pharmacological and nonpharmacological prophylaxis of recurrent migraine headache: A meta-analytic review of clinical trials. *Pain, 42,* 1–13.

Holroyd, K. A., Penzien, D. B., & Cordingley, G. E. (1991). Propranolol in the management of recurrent migraine: A meta-analytic review. *Headache, 31,* 333–340.

Lacroix, R., & Barbaree, H. E. (1990). The impact of recurrent headaches on behavior lifestyle and health. *Behavior Research and Therapy, 28,* 235–242.

Marcus, D. A., Scharff, L., & Turk, D. C. (1995). Nonpharmacological management of headaches during pregnancy. *Psychosomatic Medicine, 57,* 527–535.

Mathew, N. T. (1990). Drug-induced headache. *Neurologic Clinics, 8,* 903–912.

Mosley, T. H., Grotheus, C. A., & Meeks, W. M. (1995). Treatment of tension headache in the elderly: A controlled evaluation of relaxation training and relaxation combined with cognitive-behavior therapy. *Journal of Clinical Geropsychology, 1,* 175–188.

Nikiforow, R., & Hokkanen, E. (1978). An epidemiological study of headache in an urban and a rural population in northern Finland. *Headache, 18,* 137–145.

Olesen, J. (Chair). (1988). Classification and diagnostic criteria for headache disorders, cranial neuralgias, and facial pain: Headache Classification Committee of the International Headache Society. *Cephalalgia, 8*(Suppl. 7).

Penzien, D. B., & Holroyd, K. A. (1994). Psychosocial interventions in the management of headache disorders: 2. Description of treatment techniques. *Behavioral Medicine, 20,* 64–73.

Penzien, D. B., Holroyd, K. A., Holm, J. E., & Hursey, K. G. (1985). Behavioral management of migraine: Results from five dozen group outcome studies [Abstract]. *Headache, 25,* 162.

Professional Postgraduate Services Europe. (1991). *What headache? A guide to diagnosis and management of headache* [Brochure]. Worthington, England: Author.

Pryse-Phillips, W., Findlay, H., Tugwell, P., Edmeads, J., Murray, T. J., & Nelson, R. F. (1992). A Canadian population survey on the clinical, epidemiological and societal impact of migraine and tension-type headache. *Canadian Journal of Neurological Sciences, 19,* 333–339.

Radnitz, C. L. (1990). Food-triggered migraine: A critical review. *Annals of Behavioral Medicine, 12,* 51–65.

Rapoport, A. M., & Sheftell, F. D. (1996). *Headache disorders: A management guide for practitioners.* Philadelphia: W. B. Saunders.

Rasmussen, B. K. (1993). Migraine and tension-type headache in a general population: Precipitating factors, female hormones, sleep pattern and relation to lifestyle. *Pain, 53,* 65–72.

Rasmussen, B. K., & Breslau, N. (1993). Epidemiology. In J. Olesen, P. Tfelt-Hansen, & K. M. A. Welch (Eds.), *The headaches* (pp. 169–173). New York: Raven Press.

Rasmussen, B. K., Jensen, R., & Olesen, J. (1992). Impact of headache on sickness absence and utilization of medical services: A Danish population study. *Journal of Epidemiology and Community Health, 46,* 443–446.

Ries, P. W. (1986). *Vital and health statistics* (Series 10, No. 156, DHHS Publication No. PHS 86-1584). Rockville, MD: U.S. Department of Health and Human Services.

Saper, J. R., Silberstein, S., Gordon, C. D., & Hamel, R. L. (1993). *Handbook of headache management.* Baltimore: Williams & Wilkins.

Scharff, L., Marcus, D. A., & Turk, D. C. (1996). Maintenance of effects in the nonmedical treatment of headaches during pregnancy. *Headache, 36,* 285–290.

Silberstein, S. D., Lipton, R. B., & Breslau, N. (1995). Migraine: Association with personality characteristics and psychopathology. *Cephalalgia, 15,* 358–369.

Silberstein, S. D., Lipton, R. B., Solomon, S., & Mathew, N. T. (1994). Classification of daily and near-daily headaches: Proposed revisions to the IHS criteria. *Headache, 34,* 1–7.

Silberstein, S. D., & Merriam, G. R. (1993). Sex hormones and headache. *Journal of Pain and Symptom Management, 8,* 98–114.

Solomon, G. D., Skobieranda, F. G., & Gragg, L. A. (1993). Quality of life and well-being of headache patients: Measurement by the Medical Outcomes Study instrument. *Headache, 33,* 351–358.

Stang, P. E., & Osterhaus, J. T. (1993). Impact of migraine in the United States: Data from the National Health Interview Survey. *Headache, 33,* 29–35.

Stang, P. E., Sternfield, B., & Sidney, S. (1996). Migraine headache in a prepaid health plan: Ascertainment, demographics, physiological, and behavioral factors. *Headache, 36,* 69–76.

Stewart, W. F., & Lipton, R. B. (1993). Societal impact of headache. In J. Olesen, P. Tfelt-Hansen, & K. M. A. Welch (Eds.), *The headaches* (pp. 29–34). New York: Raven Press.

Stewart, W. F., Shechter, A., & Lipton, R. B. (1994). Migraine heterogeneity: Disability, pain intensity, and attack frequency and duration. *Neurology, 44*(Suppl. 4), S24–S39.

Part V

New Directions in Health Promotion and Disease Prevention

24

Individual Interventions: Stages of Change and Other Health Behavior Models—The Example of Smoking Cessation

Robin J. Mermelstein

Despite three decades of intensive public health messages about the hazards of smoking, 23.5% of female adults and 28.1% of male adults in the United States currently smoke (Giovino et al., 1994). The devastating health consequences of smoking are clear and well documented and include increased risks for a variety of cancers, coronary heart disease, stroke, emphysema, and respiratory infections (U.S. Department of Health and Human Services [USDHHS], 1989). Female smokers have the additional burden of an increased susceptibility to cervical cancer, early menopause, decreased fertility, osteoporosis, and complications of oral contraceptive use. The health risks associated with smoking also extend to a woman's fetus and children. Smoking during pregnancy has been linked to low birth weight and infant mortality, and it may adversely affect the child's long-term growth and intellectual development (USDHHS, 1980).

Given these substantial risks associated with smoking, why do so many women continue to smoke? Why can't smokers quit, and what is needed to help them to quit? The answers to the first two questions about why women continue to smoke and seem unable to quit require an understanding of the complex interplay of the social, psychological, and pharmacological factors involved with smoking. Several recent reviews of women and smoking address these questions (Mermelstein & Borrelli, 1995; Ockene, 1993; Solomon & Flynn, 1993) and highlight important considerations such as the addictive properties of nicotine, the mood and weight management benefits of smoking, and the influence of powerful tobacco advertising messages geared toward women.

In this chapter I address the third question: What are the necessary ingredients and steps for successful behavior change, such as stopping

The writing of this chapter was supported in part by National Heart, Lung and Blood Institute Grant HL42485 and National Cancer Institute Grant CA42760.

smoking? Major models of health-related behavior change that guide individually oriented interventions to provide both a theoretical and practical understanding of the essential ingredients for change are reviewed. These models can be applied to health behavior change in other areas besides smoking, such as weight control, condom use, alcohol consumption, exercise, and so on. No models, to my knowledge, specifically address and integrate the key factors uniquely related to women's behavior change, and few researchers have evaluated the relative explanatory value of these models for men and women. How each of the major models could address gender concerns is considered.

Health professionals are frequently frustrated and discouraged when recommendations to their patients to stop smoking fail to bring about change. A common assumption behind these messages is that if a smoker truly understood the damaging health effects of smoking, she would, of course, stop. In other words, knowledge should motivate and bring about change. Although knowledge is understandably one factor in the change process, most models suggest that knowledge or motivation alone is not sufficient. A strong desire to quit does not ensure a strong belief about one's ability to quit or having the skills to do so. Rather, behavior change may be the result of a combination of complex decision-making processes, attitudes about one's ability to change, one's affective or emotional reactions to change, coping skills, and how much the social environment supports or hinders change. The models reviewed in this chapter all point to the complexity of factors involved in behavior change, but they differ in their ability to consider the outcome of smoking cessation as a complex and dynamic variable in itself.

The Health Belief Model

The health belief model (HBM; Becker, 1974; Janz & Becker, 1984), emphasizing cognitive factors such as attitudes and beliefs, was originally developed to help explain why people may fail to engage in preventive behaviors. The HBM maintains that health-related behaviors are a function of (a) perceived susceptibility to disease; (b) perceived severity of the disease in question; (c) perceived benefits of the action or behavior change; (d) perceived barriers to change; and (e) cues to action. For example, a female smoker is more likely to quit if she perceives that she is personally susceptible to a smoking-related disease, such as lung cancer; that lung cancer is a serious and potentially fatal disease; that the benefits of quitting are great in terms of reduced risk for developing lung cancer; that the barriers to change are minimal; and if she is exposed to a cue to action, such as a message to quit from her physician.

In addition to the basic variables noted earlier, factors such as age, sex, ethnicity, or socioeconomic status may modify the basic variables. Behavioral differences between groups, such as between men and women, may reflect different levels or combinations of the basic beliefs. Women, for example, may feel less vulnerable to the negative health consequences of smoking or to perceive fewer benefits to quitting (Sorensen & Pechacek, 1987), or, in general, they may have lower levels of knowledge about the risks of smoking (Brownson et al., 1992). How gender differences may interact with the combination of variables is not clear, however. The HBM implies that the individual engages in a type of cost–benefit analysis, weighing the effectiveness or benefits of quitting smoking against the "costs," such as the difficulty, potential discomfort from withdrawal, possible weight gain, mood changes, and life disruption.

The components of the HBM translate directly into strategies for change. Health care providers should emphasize a smoker's personal susceptibility to a specific disease. For example, rather than giving a smoker the vague message that smoking is harmful to her, a physician might emphasize that because the woman takes oral contraceptives and smokes, she is at a much greater risk for stroke and that strokes could be disabling and life threatening. Those messages alone are not sufficient for change, however. In addition, personal barriers to change should be identified and addressed. Fear of withdrawal, for example, might be eased with accurate information about symptoms and their duration or by prescribing nicotine replacement.

The HBM is a well-researched model and has been applied to a wide variety of health-related behaviors, with varying success (Janz & Becker, 1984). Unfortunately, it has been less successful in explaining change of habitual behaviors, such as smoking, than in predicting one-time or more limited behaviors, such as obtaining immunizations or mammograms (Kirscht, 1988). It fails to take into account the frequent fluctuations in an individual's cost–benefit analysis (as the relative weights of factors change) or the frequent slips and backsliding that occur with most behavior changes, and it does not include actual skills or ability as a component in the model. Thus, despite having a cost–benefit ratio favorable to quitting, many smokers may still be unable to quit.

Social Cognitive Theory

Bandura's (1977, 1986) social cognitive theory highlights the importance of two cognitive variables in determining behavior: (a) self-efficacy expectations, which is an individual's belief in his or her ability to perform a particular behavior, such as stopping smoking or maintaining abstinence, and (b) outcome expectations, which is an individual's beliefs about whether a given behavior (e.g., quitting smoking) will lead to given outcomes (e.g., better health). Bandura emphasized that behavior is determined by a person's *beliefs or perceptions* about one's abilities and behavior–outcome links, not necessarily by one's true capabilities. Judgments of self-efficacy determine one's choice of activities, how much effort is expended, and how long one persists in the face of adversity. Self-efficacy is not a personality trait, but instead depends on contextual factors and will vary from situation to situation. For example, a woman may feel highly confident about her abilities to avoid smoking when she is around children but not at all confident about not smoking when she is socializing with other friends who smoke.

There is now a substantial body of research supporting the role of self-efficacy in achieving and maintaining abstinence (e.g., Baer, Holt, & Lichtenstein, 1988; Baer & Lichtenstein, 1988; Borrelli & Mermelstein, 1994; Condiotte & Lichtenstein, 1981). Successful interventions are often ones that foster and build a smoker's self-efficacy for quitting. Performance accomplishments, such as successfully cutting back on smoking or handling a difficult situation without smoking, are one of the most important sources of efficacy expectations. Interventions that emphasize setting and achieving proximal subgoals, that are both attainable and that provide immediate incentives to guide behavior, may strengthen self-efficacy and motivate further action. These subgoals are motivating by allowing the comparison of one's capabilities against a standard and by providing mastery control (Bandura, 1982). Thus, "cold turkey," or all-at-once quitting, may not be a successful approach for individuals who lack confidence in their abilities to quit. Individuals with low-efficacy expectations may benefit more from a stepped approach to cessation, perhaps first achieving success by limiting smoking, fading down to brands with lower nicotine content, or learning to program or delay their smoking. There is some evidence that women may prefer a more gradual approach to quitting than do men (Blake et al., 1989). However, this preference does not seem to be the result of consistent gender differences in levels of self-efficacy for cessation.

Bandura's (1977, 1986) social cognitive theory has had a major impact on other models of health-related behavior change. Although it is not necessarily meant to be a comprehensive model of behavior change, its concept of self-efficacy has had widespread application and is now incorporated into most other models of change.

Theory of Planned Behavior

The theory of planned behavior (TPB; Ajzen, 1985, 1988), like its predecessor, the theory of reasoned action (Ajzen & Fishbein, 1980), maintains that health-related behaviors are determined most immediately by reasoned intentions or decisions to behave in a given way. Behavioral intentions, in turn, are determined by (a) attitudes toward that behavior; (b) perceptions of subjective norms to engage in that behavior; and (c) perceptions of behavioral control or an individual's perceptions about his or her ability to perform successfully a given behavior. Attitudes toward the behavior are determined by outcome beliefs. Subjective norms are determined by one's perceptions of beliefs held by significant others and the individual's motivation to comply with those significant others. For example, if a smoker's spouse or children believe that her smoking is harmful to her and ask her to quit, and if the woman wants to try to satisfy their pleas, she may be more likely to attempt to quit. Perceived behavioral control is analogous to Bandura's (1977) notion of self-efficacy and has a direct effect on behavioral intentions. The TPB suggests that behavior change can be fostered if interventions attempt to develop positive attitudes toward the behavior change (e.g., by focusing on the positive changes that occur with cessation), convince people that stopping smoking is the norm and that people close to them want them to quit, and promote smokers' sense of personal control over their smoking.

Ajzen (1991) reviewed 16 studies that used the TPB to predict intentions to engage in a variety of activities, including losing weight, postpartum exercising, and attending class. In all cases, perceived behavioral control positively predicted behavioral intentions, although the relative importance of each of the key variables varied from study to study and by behavior. As with other models, it is not known how gender might interact with or influence the relative contribution of each variable.

The Theory of Triadic Influence

The theory of triadic influence (TTI; Flay & Petraitis, 1994) is a more recent theory of health behavior that integrates the constructs from previous theories, including the HBM, social cognitive theory, and the TPB, and goes beyond them by including broader cultural or macroenvironmental variables, biological and personality factors, and the social context. As such, its authors consider the TTI to be a "macrolevel" theory. The TTI starts with the basic assumption that any comprehensive understanding of behavior must integrate five factors: (a) environmental factors (broad sociocultural influences); (b) situational factors (immediate social situations around a behavior); (c) person factors (individual differences); (d) the behavior itself; and (e) the interaction among all these. The TTI includes the assumption that health-related behaviors are most immediately controlled by intentions and that decisions or intentions to perform health-promoting behaviors are a function of one's attitudes toward performing these behaviors, social normative pressures, and perceptions of self-efficacy in performing these. Up to this point, the TTI sounds much like Ajzen's (1985, 1988) TPB. However, the TTI goes beyond Ajzen's model by assuming that these health-related attitudes, social norms, and self-efficacy represent three "streams of influence" that have different origins. For example, the TTI maintains that attitudinal influences originate in the broad cultural environment, whereas social influences originate in one's current social situation or immediate microenvironment. The third stream, intrapersonal influences, arises out of inherited dispositions and personality traits and leads to health-related self-efficacy. The TTI maintains that two personality traits, behavioral control and emotional control, contribute most to one's self-concept and self-determination with regard to health-related behaviors. The model assumes that people with stronger self-determination will be more interested in health-promoting behaviors. The TTI also includes five levels of influence, cross-cutting the streams of

influence, that are bounded by the ultimate causes of health-related behaviors (which lie in the sociocultural environment and basic intrapersonal factors) and the most proximal predictors of any behavior (decisions).
In addition, the TTI incorporates feedback loops from experience with the
health-related behavior back to earlier levels of influence. Thus, as individuals engage in health-related behaviors, their experience may in turn
modify earlier influences, such as knowledge or attitudes toward the behavior.

An example of how the TTI may apply to stopping smoking may be
useful in understanding this model. Consider the case of a young woman
who is trying to stop smoking and is confronted by the immediate decision
of whether to smoke while attending a holiday party. According to the TTI,
her decision about smoking depends on factors ranging from the broad
sociocultural environment to the immediate situation of the party, as well
as on personal characteristics. As this woman prepares for the party, she
thinks about wanting to look her best and to be socially adept. Images of
the thin, glamorous women that she has seen in cigarette advertisements
come to mind. The women in those ads appeal to her—their look, their
sophistication; they obviously are having a good time, and they are not
eating. This woman lacks the self-confidence that she can feel comfortable
and enjoy herself at the party without smoking. She knows that other
smokers will be there. In addition, her recent experiences with trying to
quit have left her feeling nervous, emotionally vulnerable, and wanting to
snack a lot. She decides to bring her cigarettes with her, "just in case."
Thus, this woman's smoking is most immediately determined by her decision to bring cigarettes with her to the party, and that decision, in turn,
was influenced by a range of factors, including media influences, the immediate party environment and demands, her lack of social confidence,
and her recent experiences with trying to quit.

The TTI is a complex model of health behavior that has not been
tested empirically. However, it has important implications for interventions. For example, the three streams of influence suggest that interventions that are based on any one stream are likely to have limited effects.
Thus, interventions that provide people only with health-related information and ignore the social and intrapersonal factors that affect health-
related behavior are unlikely to have an effect on behavior. Similarly, the
multiple levels of influence also suggest that interventions that aim primarily at health-related decisions are likely to be short-lived unless they
also attempt to affect more distal factors on which those decisions are
made. Encouraging smokers to quit is a necessary final step, but it needs
to be supported by interventions that begin further up the levels of influence, such as those that change the cultural image of smoking or that
boost an individual's ability to control his or her actions or moods. Thus,
a basic implication of the TTI is that behavior change does not automat-
ically follow from providing information. Rather, many other variables
need to be influenced before behavior change is likely, including values,
decision making, motivation, behavioral control, and behavioral reinforcement.

Models of Health Behavior Versus Behavior Change

The aforementioned models attempt to explain the presence or absence of a behavior (e.g., smoking or abstinence) and are not necessarily focused on behavior change. As such, these models tend to be static (not dynamic) models, are outcome oriented (not process oriented), and are linear or uni-directional (as opposed to cyclical). One exception is the dynamic feedback component of the TTI, although this is one of the less developed aspects of the model and deals more with modifying earlier attitudinal variables, not the behavior. Bandura (1977, 1982) suggested methods for increasing self-efficacy, such as through performance accomplishments, modeling, or vicarious experience. In general, though, these models fail to account for the fact that changing health behaviors that are more everyday behaviors, such as smoking, eating, drinking, or exercising, takes time, often requires multiple attempts, and often has frequent setbacks or relapses along the way. A comprehensive model of behavior change needs to conceptualize change as a process, not just as an outcome, and allow for both missteps or leaps in progress that can occur along the way. The transtheoretical model (Prochaska & DiClemente, 1983, 1984; Prochaska, DiClemente, & Norcross, 1992) is an integrative model of behavior change that focuses on stages of change and how people change.

The Transtheoretical Model

The transtheoretical model (Prochaska & DiClemente, 1983, 1984) pro-poses that changing health-related behaviors, such as smoking, involves a progression through five stages of change: precontemplation, contempla-tion, preparation, action, and maintenance. Maintenance may branch into continued abstinence or relapse into an earlier stage. The stage model is best conceptualized by a spiral, rather than linear, progression because individuals may cycle through the stages several times, going back and forth between stages, before they ultimately exit with a maintained be-havior change.

Individuals in the precontemplation stage have no intention or plans to change behavior in the foreseeable future. Individuals in this stage may deny or lack knowledge about the adverse consequences of smoking and deny any personal susceptibility. Although precontemplators may ac-knowledge that smoking can be dangerous for some individuals, they per-sonally do not feel vulnerable or may believe that they have some protec-tion against threat. For example, precontemplators may believe that because they exercise or have a good diet, or because a relative lived until she was 90 years old and smoked all her adult life, they are protected against the negative effects of smoking. Precontemplators may want to stop smoking one day or believe that they will eventually stop, but they will state that they are not ready to quit yet, that the time is not right, or that stopping smoking is just not a priority for them at the moment. Lack of confidence in one's ability to change also may characterize the precontemplation stage. There also may be a subset of precontemplators who are committed to smoking (i.e., a group of individuals who have no intention or desire ever to quit, who see smoking as part of their self-image and who enjoy that image).

In the contemplation stage, individuals start to consider change but have not yet made a commitment to do so. This stage is often characterized by an increased awareness of the dangers of smoking and of personal susceptibility. Smokers in this stage may start to seek out or attend to information about smoking and cessation. Contemplation also may be thought of as the stage with a high level of ambivalence about change. This is perhaps the most frustrating stage for smokers. Motivation to quit wavers, the individual may still be unsure about how to change, and confidence about one's ability to change is often still low.

In the preparation stage, individuals make a commitment to change. This stage is defined by both intention and behavior. Preparation stage smokers are those who intend to quit within the next month and who have had an unsuccessful quit attempt in the past year. These individuals often have started to make small changes in their habit, such as by starting to cut down the number of cigarettes smoked, restricting smoking to certain settings, or delaying smoking. Initial motivation in this stage may be high, although confidence in one's ability could vary.

In the action stage, individuals make behavior changes, such as stopping smoking. A typical criterion set for achieving the action stage is stopping smoking for a period of at least 1 day to 6 months (Prochaska et al., 1992). Thus, cutting back on smoking may be more characteristic of the preparation stage than of the action stage. Most smokers do not stay long in the action stage, but quickly relapse.

Individuals who succeed with action go on to the maintenance stage. During this stage, individuals work to preserve the gains made in action (i.e., they work at preventing relapse). Individuals who have successfully refrained from smoking for 6 months enter the maintenance stage. There is no clear end point for maintenance (Mermelstein, Karnatz, & Reichmann, 1992), and the possibility of slips can continue throughout this stage.

Unfortunately, the most frequent outcome of a cessation attempt is relapse rather than maintenance. After a relapse, individuals may recycle back to earlier stages in the change process. Discouragement, disappointment, feelings of failure, and lowered self-efficacy are all frequent consequences of relapse (Mermelstein, Shadel, & Borrelli, 1994). Prochaska et al. (1992) reported that across several studies, the vast majority of relapsers recycled back to the contemplation or preparation stages rather than all the way back to precontemplation. Thus, those smokers were ripe for interventions.

Only a few population-based studies have examined the prevalence of stages of readiness to quit. Velicer et al. (1995) reported the results of three studies examining the stage distribution of smokers. These studies—a random-digit-dialing survey from California, a random-digit-dialing phone survey from Rhode Island, and a worksite sample from four regions of the

United States—provide good population estimates of the stage distribution of current smokers. Recent quitters were not sampled, so estimates of the late stages (i.e., action and maintenance) could not be obtained. Overall, the results were similar across the three samples: Approximately 40% of the smokers were in precontemplation, 40% were in contemplation, and 20% were in preparation. In general, there was a greater percentage of men in the preparation stage and a greater percentage of women in the precontemplation stage. Education also was consistently related to staging; as education increased, the proportion of those in the precontemplation stage decreased.

Two other recent studies of female smokers also provide stage distributions. Crittenden, Manfredi, Lacey, Warnecke, and Parsons (1994) surveyed 495 female smokers in public health clinics. In this sample, 41.2% of the women were in precontemplation, 32.1% were in contemplation, and 26.7% were in preparation. Pregnancy was positively related to readiness to quit. Warnecke, Mermelstein, Manfredi, Lacey, and Flay (1995) conducted a random-digit-dialing phone survey of female smokers with a high school education or less. In their sample of approximately 1,500 women from the Chicago metropolitan area, 74% were in precontemplation, 12.9% were in contemplation, and 13.1% were in preparation. This latter survey highlights the strong negative relation between education and readiness to quit. One striking finding from all these studies is that a significant proportion of female smokers were in the precontemplation stage, with no immediate plans to stop smoking. Health care professionals thus need to be sensitive to this staging distribution and gear their messages to smokers appropriately.

The stages of change are only one component of the transtheoretical model, representing the temporal or developmental sequence of change attempts. The second component of the model focuses on the processes of change, or understanding how individuals make progress through the stages. Prochaska, Velicer, DiClemente, and Fava (1988) identified 10 primary processes of change, including behavioral (e.g., stimulus control, avoiding or altering situations that promote smoking), cognitive (e.g., self-reevaluation, or clarifying how one thinks about oneself and smoking or not smoking), and emotional (e.g., dramatic relief, or feeling moved emotionally when confronted by warnings about smoking) activities. These 10 processes are differentially emphasized across the stages of change (DiClemente et al., 1991; Prochaska et al., 1992). As one might expect, precontemplators use the change processes significantly less than individuals in the other stages (Prochaska et al., 1992). Prochaska et al. (1992) noted that contemplators are most open to consciousness raising techniques, education, reevaluating their values, and dramatic relief experiences. Individuals in preparation may use more counterconditioning and stimulus control techniques, both of which also are important in action. Movement through the stages thus entails the increased use of the change processes more characteristic of the next stage.

As with other models, the transtheoretical model also includes the notion of the importance of decision making. Velicer, DiClemente, Prochaska, and Brandenburg (1985) developed a decisional balance measure to examine the decision-making process across the stages of change in smoking cessation. The measure contains two scales, the Pros of Smoking and the Cons of Smoking, and successfully differentiates among the stages (Velicer et al., 1985). Smokers in the precontemplation stage rate the pros of smoking higher than the cons; these smokers perceive more personal benefits from smoking than costs and, as a consequence, are not interested in quitting. In the contemplation stage, smokers identify more cons of smoking, but the pros remain high as well, thus reflecting their ambivalence about change. By the action and maintenance stages, the cons of smoking outweigh the pros, which have decreased. Prochaska et al. (1994) suggested that movement from the precontemplation stage to the contemplation stage involves an increase in evaluating the pros of quitting and that movement farther along to the action stage involves decreasing the cons of quitting or the pros of smoking. Thus, interventions should first emphasize and increase the positive aspects of quitting and then, when those expectancies are strong, focus on decreasing the perceived costs of quitting and benefits of smoking. Unfortunately, too often initial messages to smokers to quit highlight only the negative aspects of smoking without first building up a strong, positive image of nonsmoking that a smoker can identify with and find appealing.

Prochaska (1994) developed and tested two principles to predict progression from the precontemplation stage to the action stage using the pros and cons of change. His stronger principle, the one more predictive of change, reflects the importance of the pros of changing: Progression from the precontemplation stage to the action stage is a function of increasing the pros of change on the decisional balance by an amount equal to the average amount of variability of all scores on the measure. The weaker principle focuses on the cons of changing: Progression from the precontemplation stage to the action stage is a function of decreasing the value of the cons of changing by half the average amount of variability of the scores. In other words, although the cons of changing need to decrease only about half as much as the pros need to increase, movement from the precontemplation stage to the action stage is much more likely if the pros of change increase. Thus, interventions need to help individuals reevaluate the perceived benefits of quitting and make nonsmoking more appealing than smoking. Helping smokers to overcome their fears and perceived myths and costs of quitting is important too, but it is not as powerful an intervention as having them identify the positive aspects of quitting. In summary, to progress along to cessation, smokers need a positive, inspiring goal.

Tailoring Interventions to Stage of Change

One of the most important implications of the transtheoretical model is that interventions should be tailored to a smoker's stage of change. Stage of change is strongly related both to receptivity to interventions and to subsequent cessation (DiClemente, 1991; Lichtenstein, Lando, & Nothwehr,

1994; Prochaska et al., 1992). Smokers who are ready for action need more active skills training and efficacy-enhancing interventions. Educational and motivational messages alone are not sufficient for them. Smokers who are precontemplators, on the other hand, are likely to ignore the how-to and action-oriented programs and would benefit more by motivational interventions. Failure to assess adequately the stage of change is likely to lead to a mismatching of stage and treatment and to frustration, failure, or reentrenchment on the part of the smoker. Thus, interventions must not only provide change skills for individuals who are ready to take action but also must promote change, by motivating those not ready for action, and maintain change among those who have taken action. Stage of change among current smokers can be assessed easily by asking a series of questions such as the following: (a) Have you seriously thought about quitting smoking? (b) If yes, do you plan to quit smoking? (c) If yes, when do you plan to quit (in the next month, 3 months, 6 months, or further away)? (d) Have you purposely stopped smoking for at least 24 hr in the past 12 months? Precontemplators are smokers who have no thoughts about quitting or plans to quit within the next 6 months. Contemplators are considering quitting within the next 6 months, and those in preparation are planning to quit within the next month and have made an attempt in the past 12 months. Health care professionals should also ask about prior smoking in order to identify recent ex-smokers still in the action or maintenance stage. For these later-stage individuals, it is important to assess the need for continued assistance and support.

Prochaska, DiClemente, Velicer, and Rossi (1993) documented the effectiveness of matching the treatment to the stage. Prochaska et al. compared the effectiveness of four interventions: (a) a standardized self-help manual; (b) individualized manuals matched to stage; (c) an interactive expert system computer report, providing feedback on stage and processes of change, plus the individualized manuals; and (d) personalized counselor calls along with the computer reports and stage manuals. Over an 18-month follow-up period, the individualized stage-matched manuals were more effective than the standardized self-help manual. Most impressive, though, were the results of the interactive expert system. This stage-based treatment more than doubled the point prevalence abstinence rates of the standardized manual condition and did even better when comparisons of prolonged abstinence were made. As Prochaska et al. pointed out, most prior intervention materials have ignored early-stage smokers and thus have not done as well with the large majority of smokers who are not ready for the action stage. Their finding that the personalized counselor calls did not add to the effectiveness of the computer system is also encouraging for the many health care professionals who are looking for less personnel-intensive interventions.

The Role of Motivation in Stage of Change

Motivation is a key element at all stages of change and is considered a prerequisite for movement across stages. The content and strategies of motivational interventions might vary from stage to stage, but the primary objective remains the same: to help individuals make progress to the next stage. Miller and Rollnick (1991) defined motivation as the probability that an individual will enter into, continue, and adhere to a specific change strategy. Motivation is a state and not an inflexible personality trait, vacillates over time, is situationally and goal specific, and is responsive to external influence. Thus, motivation is important not only in the early stages of precontemplation or contemplation, but also in the later stages of action and maintenance, when an ex-smoker must actively work to maintain his or her desire and commitment to quitting permanently. According to DiClemente (1991), motivation involves both motives and movement.

What factors influence motivation? Motivation for smoking cessation involves two components: the reasons why smokers want to quit and the overall strength of their desire to change, or their incentive for doing so. Strength and incentive may be a function of perceived benefits and outcome expectancies (positive and negative), as well as of expectancies about the change process itself (e.g., perceived negatives, such as the stress involved or withdrawal, and "fringe benefits" of change, such as increased attention and support). Most of the HBMs discussed earlier (e.g., the HBM, TPB) point to cognitive factors (e.g., perceived vulnerability, perceived severity, expected beliefs) as variables that influence motivation (reasons why) to change. However, it is likely that these models do not apply equally well to all stages of change. For example, although perceptions of susceptibility to disease might move a precontemplator into contemplating cessation, they may not play as large a role in motivating a new ex-smoker to remain abstinent. Rather, it might be more useful to propose that at each stage of change, individuals engage in a decision-making process about adopting new behaviors. Thus, motivational interventions, although important throughout the stage continuum, should differ by stage.

Miller and Rollnick (1991) and DiClemente (1991) have outlined the key motivational tasks according to the stage of change. The primary motivational tasks in the precontemplation stage include raising doubt by increasing the perception of the risks and problems of smoking and dealing with a smoker's reluctance to change, rebellion, resignation about the inability to change, and rationalizations about why smoking is okay. The key motivational task in the contemplation stage is to tip the decisional balance toward change by evoking reasons to change and the risks of not changing. Important, too, is the need to decrease the perceived barriers to quitting and to increase the positive expectancies of change. In the preparation stage, motivational tasks include helping an individual determine the best course of action for making a change, increasing commitment to that particular course of action, and encouraging goal setting. During the action and maintenance stages, smokers must work at maintaining their commitment to nonsmoking and at reducing their possible discouragement at the difficulty involved in achieving and maintaining abstinence. Finally, after a relapse, the motivational tasks include helping the smoker to renew the processes of the earlier stages without becoming stuck or demoralized and reducing the discouragement of not succeeding.

Tailoring Interventions by Stage and Gender

Separating smokers by stage of change allows for finer tailoring of treatments by gender. Although there is no evidence that the processes of change vary by gender, the distribution of smokers across the stages may vary by gender, as noted earlier, with female smokers being more likely to be in the precontemplation stage than in the preparation stage (Velicer et al., 1995). There are several reasons why it may be useful to tailor interventions by gender. First, tailoring may help attract women to smoking cessation treatments, particularly if emphasis is placed on early-stage messages. Second, tailoring may give women extra help and attention, especially if they are not quitting at the same rate as men (Mermelstein & Borrelli, 1995). Third, tailored interventions can address the unique concerns of female smokers, such as pregnancy, weight gain, or mood management. Finally, if men and women do respond differently to treatments, then tailoring can provide the most effective treatments for women.

Each stage of change requires a different treatment focus. In the precontemplation and contemplation stages, interventions might be tailored according to a theme. Motivational messages could emphasize the family, empowerment by quitting, or women working together to better women's health and their family's health. In the preparation stage, in which a key goal is to mobilize smokers, access to treatment could be tailored. For example, information about quitting or interventions for women could be offered at prenatal care or family planning settings or in schools. During the action stage, tailoring of strategies could be important. For example, women might do better with fading versus abrupt quitting, or some pharmacological agents may be more or less effective for women (Mermelstein & Borrelli, 1995). Finally, in the maintenance stage, the content of the intervention might vary by gender. Interventions for women might emphasize weight control or mood management. There are several unanswered questions about tailoring treatments by gender. The stage of change notion, however, allows one to better formulate the following questions: "Is tailoring necessary to motivate more women to consider stopping smoking?" (a precontemplation question). "Is tailoring necessary to mobilize or attract women to cessation programs?" (a preparation stage question). "Is tailoring necessary to better match women to specific treatment components?" (action and maintenance stages question).

Conclusion

Although there are several strong theories that attempt to explain health-related behavior and change, the transtheoretical model is unique in its focus on the process of change and the spiraling, dynamic nature of change. This model is particularly useful in helping health care professionals to most appropriately match individuals to treatment. None of the theories, however, specifically addresses the possibility of gender differences in the change process, although it is also not clear that such differences exist. It is clear, though, that stopping smoking is extremely difficult for most smokers, and there are multiple influences at each stage that might determine progress to the next step. It is unlikely that any one theory can fully account for both the diversity of influences and fluctuations in their relative importance at each stage of change.

Despite the complexity of the change process, and no one guaranteed effective approach, there are nevertheless some important points physicians and other health care professionals might want to remember when discussing stopping smoking with their patients. First is the need to increase personal motivation for quitting. Tailored motivational messages that are factual, not heavy-handed, and reflect the reason for the patient's visit are useful. For example, for patients who are being seen for upper respiratory infections, asthma, or pulmonary problems, physicians could point out the link between smoking and the illness (e.g., "I'm concerned that your smoking is causing you to have more frequent colds and infections" or "I'm concerned that your smoking makes your cold/asthma/bronchitis much worse. Stopping smoking may be your best way to prevent further problems. Have you thought at all about quitting?"). For women who are being seen for prenatal care, family planning, or fertility reasons, physicians could emphasize the links between smoking and fetal health, smoking and infertility, or contraindications for prescribing oral contraceptives (e.g., "As long as you are smoking, I cannot prescribe oral contraceptives because of the increased risk of strokes or serious blood clots" or "If you continue to smoke while you are pregnant, you are increasing the chances of your baby having health problems. The smoke and chemicals from cigarettes are directly felt by your baby. I realize that thinking about this can be scary, but it might help to talk about what you can do to try to quit"). The more immediate the link between smoking and the presenting problem, the more likely the smoker is to personalize the relevance of quitting.

Beyond trying to motivate the smoker, physicians need to try to build self-efficacy. This can be done by trying to remind patients of their personal resources or ability to cope with other life problems, expressing confidence in them, or by letting them know that help is available: "I've seen you get through some difficult times. That shows me you have some good inner strengths that can help you get through quitting too. I'm confident that you'll be able to pull through quitting, but it will take some effort." Alternatively, "It seems like you've had a lot of difficulty trying to stop in the past and as a result, don't feel very sure you can do so now. I think, though, that if you try it slowly and maybe consider some help—either by joining a program or having me prescribe nicotine replacement—then you could do it."

Finally, physicians need to remember that stopping smoking does not end with the initial quitting phase. The probability of relapse remains high for at least 1 year after quitting. Supportive, reinforcing messages that point out a patient's progress are useful in helping to maintain abstinence. The focus during maintenance should not necessarily be on reminding the patients of the dangers of smoking but on pointing out the positive benefits accrued by quitting, such as feelings of pride in accomplishing a hard task, decreased blood pressure, fewer colds, improved circulation, and so on. Thus, appreciating the dynamic nature of motivational and behavior change factors along the stage of change continuum and adapting interventions to meet these different stage-based needs may be a key to successfully promoting cessation.

References

Ajzen, I. (1985). From intentions to actions: A theory of planned behavior. In J. Kuhl & J. Beckmann (Eds.), *Action control: From cognition to behavior* (pp. 11–40). New York: Springer-Verlag.

Ajzen, I. (1988). *Attitudes, personality and behavior.* Chicago: Dorsey Press.

Ajzen, I. (1991). The theory of planned behavior. *Organizational Behavior and Human Decision Processes, 50,* 179–211.

Ajzen, I., & Fishbein, M. (1980). *Understanding attitudes and predicting social behavior.* Englewood Cliffs, NJ: Prentice Hall.

Baer, J. S., Holt, C. S., & Lichtenstein, E. (1988). Self-efficacy and smoking reexamined: Construct validity and clinical utility. *Journal of Consulting and Clinical Psychology, 54,* 846–852.

Baer, J. S., & Lichtenstein, E. (1988). Cognitive assessment. In D. M. Donovan & G. A. Marlatt (Eds.), *Assessment of addictive behaviors* (pp. 189–213). New York: Guilford Press.

Bandura, A. (1977). Self-efficacy: Toward a unifying theory of behavioral change. *Psychological Review, 84,* 191–215.

Bandura, A. (1982). Self-efficacy mechanism in human agency. *American Psychologist, 37,* 122–147.

Bandura, A. (1986). *Social foundation of thoughts and action: A social cognitive theory.* Englewood Cliffs, NJ: Prentice Hall.

Becker, M. H. (1974). *The health belief model and personal health behavior.* Thorofare, NJ: Charles B. Slack.

Blake, S. M., Klepp, K., Pechacek, T. F., Folsom, A. R., Luepker, R. V., Jacobs, D. R., & Mittlemark, M. B. (1989). Differences in smoking cessation strategies between men and women. *Addictive Behaviors, 14,* 409–418.

Borrelli, B., & Mermelstein, R. (1994). Goal setting and behavior change in a smoking cessation program. *Cognitive Therapy and Research, 18,* 69–83.

Brownson, R. C., Jackson-Thompson, J., Wilkerson, J. C., Davis, J. R., Owens, N. W., & Fisher, E. B. (1992). Demographic and socioeconomic differences in beliefs about the health effects of smoking. *American Journal of Public Health, 82,* 99–103.

Condiotte, M., & Lichtenstein, E. (1981). Self-efficacy and relapse in smoking cessation programs. *Journal of Consulting and Clinical Psychology, 49,* 648–658.

Crittenden, K. S., Manfredi, C., Lacey, L., Warnecke, R., & Parsons, J. (1994). Measuring readiness and motivation to quit smoking among women in public health clinics. *Addictive Behaviors, 19,* 497–507.

DiClemente, C. C. (1991). Motivational interviewing and the stages of change. In W. R. Miller & S. Rollnick (Eds.), *Motivational interviewing: Preparing people to change addictive behavior* (pp. 191–202). New York: Guilford Press.

DiClemente, C. C., Prochaska, J. O., Fairhurst, S. K., Velicer, W. F., Velasquez, M. M., & Rossi, J. S. (1991). The process of smoking cessation: An analysis of precontemplation, contemplation, and preparation stages of change. *Journal of Consulting and Clinical Psychology, 59,* 295–304.

Flay, B. R., & Petraitis, J. (1994). The theory of triadic influence: A new theory of health behavior with implications for preventive interventions. *Advances in Medical Sociology*, *4*, 19–44.

Giovino, G. A., Schooley, M. W., Zhu, B., Chrismon, J. H., Tomar, S. L., Peddicord, J. P., Merritt, R. K., Husten, C. G., & Eriksen, M. P. (1994). Surveillance for selected tobacco-use behaviors: United States, 1900–1994. *Morbidity and Mortality Weekly Report*, *43*, 1–43.

Janz, N. K., & Becker, M. H. (1984). The health belief model: A decade later. *Health Education Quarterly*, *11*, 1–47.

Kirscht, J. P. (1988). The health belief model and predictions of health actions. In D. S. Gochman (Ed.), *Health behavior: Emerging research perspectives* (pp. 27–42). New York: Plenum.

Lichtenstein, E., Lando, H. A., & Nothwehr, F. (1994). Readiness to quit as a predictor of smoking changes in the Minnesota Heart Health Program. *Health Psychology*, *13*, 393–396.

Mermelstein, R., & Borrelli, B. (1995). Women and smoking. In A. L. Stanton & S. J. Gallant (Eds.), *The psychology of women's health* (pp. 309–348). Washington, DC: American Psychological Association.

Mermelstein, R., Karnatz, T., & Reichmann, S. (1992). Smoking. In P. Miller (Ed.), *Principles and practice of relapse prevention* (pp. 43–68). New York: Guilford Press.

Mermelstein, R., Shadel, W. G., & Borrelli, B. (1994). *Stability and predictors of recycling after relapse from smoking cessation.* Poster presented at the annual meeting of the Society of Behavioral Medicine, Boston.

Miller, W. R., & Rollnick, S. (Eds.). (1991). *Motivational interviewing: Preparing people to change addictive behavior.* New York: Guilford Press.

Ockene, J. (1993). Smoking among women across the life span: Prevalence, interventions, and implications for cessation research. *Annals of Behavioral Medicine*, *15*, 135–148.

Prochaska, J. O. (1994). Strong and weak principles for progressing from precontemplation to action on the basis of twelve problem behaviors. *Health Psychology*, *13*, 47–51.

Prochaska, J. O., & DiClemente, C. C. (1983). Stages and processes of self-change of smoking: Toward an integrative model of change. *Journal of Consulting and Clinical Psychology*, *51*, 390–395.

Prochaska, J. O., & DiClemente, C. C. (1984). *The transtheoretical approach: Crossing traditional boundaries of change.* Homewood, IL: Dow Jones/Irwin.

Prochaska, J. O., DiClemente, C. C., & Norcross, J. C. (1992). In search of how people change: Applications to addictive behaviors. *American Psychologist*, *47*, 1102–1114.

Prochaska, J. O., DiClemente, C. C., Velicer, W., & Rossi, J. S. (1993). Standardized, individualized, interactive, and personalized self-help programs for smoking cessation. *Health Psychology*, *12*, 399–405.

Prochaska, J. O., Velicer, W., DiClemente, C. C., & Fava, J. (1988). Measuring processes of change: Applications to the cessation of smoking. *Journal of Consulting and Clinical Psychology*, *56*, 520–528.

Prochaska, J. O., Velicer, W. F., Rossi, J. S., Goldstein, M. G., Marcus, B. H., Rakowski, W., Fiore, C., Harlow, L. L., Redding, C. A., Rosenbloom, D., & Rossi, S. R. (1994). Stages of change and decisional balance for 12 problem behaviors. *Health Psychology*, *13*, 39–46.

Solomon, L. J., & Flynn, B. S. (1993). Women who smoke. In C. T. Orleans & J. Slade (Eds.), *Nicotine addiction: Principles and management* (pp. 339–349). New York: Oxford University Press.

Sorensen, G., & Pechacek, T. F. (1987). Attitudes toward smoking cessation among men and women. *Journal of Behavioral Medicine*, *10*, 129–137.

Velicer, W. F., DiClemente, C. C., Prochaska, J. O., & Brandenburg, N. (1985). A decisional balance measure for assessing and predicting smoking status. *Journal of Personality and Social Psychology*, *48*, 1279–1289.

Velicer, W. F., Fava, J. L., Prochaska, J. O., Abrams, D., Emmons, K., & Pierce, J. (1995). Distribution of smokers by stage in three representative samples. *Preventive Medicine*, *24*, 401–411.

U.S. Department of Health and Human Services. (1980). *The health consequences of smoking for women: A report of the Surgeon General*. Washington, DC: U.S. Government Printing Office.

U.S. Department of Health and Human Services. (1989). *Reducing the health consequences of smoking—25 years of progress: A report of the Surgeon General* (DHHS Publication No. CDC 89-8411), Washington, DC: U.S. Government Printing Office.

Warnecke, R., Mermelstein, R., Manfredi, C., Lacey, L., & Flay, B. R. (1995). *Strategies for smoking cessation among low educated women*. Unpublished data.

25

Community-Based Prevention Studies: Intervention Lessons for Women

Carol A. Derby, Marilyn A. Winkleby,
Kate L. Lapane, and Elaine J. Stone

Chronic diseases, led by cardiovascular diseases (CVDs) and cancer, are the leading causes of death and disability among women in the United States (U.S. Department of Health and Human Services, 1988). Many of the risk factors that have been identified for these complex disease processes are a function of behaviors that act in concert with genetic and environmental factors (Luepker, 1994). The characteristics of these conditions make them suitable targets for community-based prevention strategies: The conditions are highly prevalent, risk factors have been established, both the disease and risk factors have sociocultural determinants, safe and effective interventions are available, and the social climate supports a willingness to accept these interventions (Luepker, 1994). To date, most of the major research efforts in community interventions have been in the area of CVD (Lasater, 1991). In this chapter we describe the background for the community approach to prevention and highlight the contribution of three large U.S. community-based CVD prevention studies to the growing body of knowledge on women's health. The designs of these studies are described, and findings relevant to the health of women are presented. These findings are discussed in terms of the implications for the planning and implementation of future public health programs and relevance for primary practice settings.

High-Risk and Population Approaches to Prevention

Prevention, or the promotion and preservation of health, is often defined as one of three levels: primary, secondary, or tertiary. Primary prevention involves interventions aimed at preventing the onset of clinical disease by preventing or removing precipitating causes. Secondary prevention involves the detection and timely treatment of disease. Tertiary prevention involves interventions that reduce or eliminate the development of disability among those who already have the disease. From a public health

405

perspective, the maximum benefit of prevention is derived from interventions that target the earliest possible stage in the natural history of disease by preventing the development of risky behaviors and diminishing the presence of elevated risk factors.

Prevention strategies traditionally have followed two distinct but complementary approaches. The high-risk (or medical) approach and the population (or public health) approach. The high-risk approach targets individuals who have genetic predispositions, behaviors, or exposures that place them in the upper end of the population distribution of disease risk. By contrast, the population approach targets the underlying determinants of disease incidence in a population by promoting favorable shifts in the population distribution of risk (Lasater, 1991; Oberman, Kuller, & Carleton, 1994; Rose, 1992). The choice of a prevention strategy depends on the distribution of cases relative to the distribution of identifiable risk factors and the extent to which major determinants of disease are influenced by the social and cultural environments.

Although the high-risk approach has major benefits at the individual level, from a population perspective, in general, the expected benefits are small (Rose, 1992). Conversely, small beneficial changes in individuals may translate into substantial public health benefits. This is particularly true for chronic conditions such as CVD and cancer, which are the leading causes of mortality and morbidity in both women and men in the United States (Kottke, Puska, Salonen, Tuomilehto, & Nissinen, 1985; U.S. Department of Health and Human Services, 1988).

As stated by Rose (1992), a basic principle of prevention is that "many exposed to a small risk may generate more cases than a small number exposed to a conspicuous risk" (p. 315). For example, the majority of all deaths due to coronary heart disease occur among individuals with risk levels that are average or only moderately elevated (Blackburn, 1983; Pooling Project Research Group, 1978). Clinical trials have demonstrated that small incremental changes in blood pressure or blood cholesterol levels are associated with substantial reductions in rates of coronary heart disease (Collins, Peto, Godwin, & MacMahon, 1990; Frick et al., 1987; Lipid Research Clinics Program, 1984a, 1984b). A 1% reduction in total cholesterol levels, for example, has been shown to result in a 2% reduction in mortality from coronary heart disease (Lipid Research Clinics Program, 1984a, 1984b). Prospective studies also support this principle. Estimates from the Whitehall study show that a 10% reduction in the average cholesterol level of the total population would yield twice the reduction in the rate of heart disease as would a 10% reduction in the average cholesterol level of individuals with cholesterol levels in the highest decile of the population distribution (Rose & Shipley, 1990).

Communitywide Prevention Approach

Communitywide prevention programs have evolved from the concept that a population approach is required to achieve true primary prevention

(Luepker, 1994). Underlying these programs is the concept that behaviors and lifestyle choices that contribute to an individual's risk profile are a function of his or her social and physical milieus. This concept is supported by the theoretical literature, which proposes that personal, cultural, and environmental factors interact to determine a person's behaviors (Bandura, 1977). This theory also suggests that an individual's ability to adopt healthy behaviors is a function of his or her knowledge and skills as well as confidence in his or her ability to succeed. In addition to these personal factors, an individual's behaviors are influenced by family, friends, organizations, and the geopolitical environment, including policies and regulations at both the local and national levels (Carleton & Lasater, 1994).

Community studies traditionally have included some high-risk strategies as well as the overall population approach (Lasater, 1991). The high-risk and population approaches can be complementary rather than mutually exclusive. Although the high-risk strategy aims to benefit those at the high end of the spectrum of risk, the population approach targets the underlying behaviors and environmental factors that determine the overall rates of disease (Rose, 1992). To the extent that healthy lifestyles are the social norm, individuals will have greater success in adopting healthy behaviors (Lasater, 1991; Luepker, 1994; Oberman et al., 1994). In an environment that fosters healthy lifestyle choices, the social rewards of healthy behaviors may be more immediate than the medical benefits that are remote and small from the individual perspective (Rose, 1992). Thus, some changes prompted by population prevention strategies may help facilitate behavior changes in high-risk individuals.

Lasater (1991) pointed out that it is important for community studies to include strategies for working with the medical care system to detect and treat high-risk individuals, such as assessing existing health promotion programs within the community (e.g., smoking cessation or weight loss programs) and making physicians aware of the resources available to their patients. Inclusion of the medical care system also helps to promote an atmosphere of support and cooperation for the overall communitywide program (Lasater, 1991).

Description of Three U.S. Community CVD Prevention Studies

Much of the current knowledge regarding community-based prevention strategies has been learned over the past 15 years from three U.S. research and demonstration projects for community CVD health promotion funded by the National Heart, Lung and Blood Institute (NHLBI) during the 1980s (Stone, 1991). These included the Stanford Five-City Project (Farquhar et al., 1990, 1985), the Minnesota Heart Health Program (Blackburn et al., 1984; Luepker et al., 1994), and the Pawtucket Heart Health Program (Carleton et al., 1995; Carleton, Lasater, Assaf, Lefebvre, & McKinlay, 1987). The remainder of this discussion focuses primarily on some of the lessons learned from these three U.S. community-based studies. Although future projects are not likely to encompass the scope of these three studies, the body of experience that has resulted provides information valuable for the planning and implementation of future population-based intervention programs and research projects (Elder, Schmid, & Hedlund, 1993; Mittlemark, Hunt, Heath, & Schmid, 1993; Schwartz et al., 1993). In contrast to many prior studies, which were based primarily on men, the community-based studies provide valuable information on patterns of health behaviors and on the effectiveness of various prevention programs in both women and men.

The NHLBI community studies conducted in Rhode Island, Minnesota, and California were each designed to test whether a comprehensive program of community organization and health education would produce favorable changes in the population levels of cardiovascular risk factors and ultimately result in decreased rates of CVD (Stone, 1991). Social learning theory, which states that a person's behavior is the result of complex interactions among personal, social, and environmental factors (Bandura 1977), was a major component of the multitheoretical framework underlying each of these projects. Each study used multiple channels for the delivery of health messages aimed at preventing, treating, and controlling blood pressure, smoking, obesity, consumption of high-fat and high-salt diets, and a sedentary lifestyle. The education programs were supported by community organization activities aimed at creating physical and social environments conducive to adopting healthy behaviors. These activities targeted social norms, regulations, and policies such as smoking policies, the availability of low-fat choices in markets and restaurants, improvements in recreational facilities, and institutionalization of health promotion programs in schools, worksites, and community organizations (Lasater, 1991). The end points targeted by these three studies were risk factor behavior change, the risk factors themselves, and the prevalence of CVD (Lasater, 1991, 1992; Stone, 1991). In addition, each of these studies included program evaluation components to provide information necessary for monitoring progress and revising intervention strategies as the studies proceeded (Pirie, Stone, Assaf, Flora, & Maschewsky-Schneider, 1994).

Community studies include comparison communities to evaluate whether intervention effects would exceed the effects of secular trends. Comparison rather than control populations were used because it is impossible to prevent the exposure of communities to health promotion programs from sources other than the intervention (Lasater, 1992). For example, in each of the three cardiovascular prevention studies, residents of both the intervention and nonintervention cities were exposed to national campaigns launched during the 1980s, such as the National Cholesterol Education Program (Lenfant, 1986) and the National High Blood Pressure Education Program (1993).

The Stanford Five-City Project

The Stanford Five-City Project, which began in 1978, included two intervention and three comparison communities in Northern California, with a total population of approximately 350,000 people (Farquhar et al., 1985). The 6-year education intervention (1980–1986) targeted all residents in the intervention communities. The program used concepts of social learning theory in combination with a communication–behavior change model that outlines the theoretical series of steps individuals go through as they adopt an advocated behavior (Flora, Maccoby, & Farquhar, 1989). In addition to applying community organization and social marketing principles, the program relied heavily on the use of electronic and print media for the delivery of health education. General education was supplemented by four to five specific risk factor education campaigns annually. In addition, direct face-to-face activities included classes, contests, correspondence courses, and school-based programs (Farquhar et al., 1990). Many of the educational materials were developed in Spanish. Changes in CVD risk factors were assessed by five separate cross-sectional surveys of randomly selected households and five repeated surveys of a cohort sample. Specific details of the study design have been published elsewhere (Farquhar et al., 1985).

The Minnesota Heart Health Program

The Minnesota Heart Health Program included three pairs of communities with a combined population of approximately 400,000 (Luepker et al., 1994). Each pair included one education community and one comparison community. The 5- to 6-year educational intervention promoted prevention and control of hypertension, heart-healthy eating patterns, nonsmoking, and regular physical activity. Various intervention strategies were aimed at the individual, group, and community levels (Blackburn et al., 1984; Jacobs et al., 1986; Luepker et al., 1994; Mittlemark et al., 1986). The program relied heavily on systematic populationwide multiple risk factor screening and direct educational counseling, followed by extensive community organization, school programs, and environmental change programs (Jacobs et al., 1986; Mittlemark et al., 1986; Murray et al., 1986). The intervention was based on theories of social learning (Bandura, 1977) and persuasive communications theory (Hovland, Janis, & Kelly, 1953; McGuire, 1973). This theory states that the persuasiveness of a communication depends on characteristics of the communicator, the content of the message, the groups and individuals targeted, and the responses to the message (Hovland et al., 1953). Methods of community analysis and organization were used to engage community leaders and organizations in the intervention efforts (Bracht & Kingsbury, 1990; Rothman, 1970). Compared with the Stanford Five-City Project, there was less emphasis on the use of mass media for the delivery of health education (Carleton & Lasater, 1994). Specific programs were targeted at both adults and school-age children. The program's effectiveness was assessed with data from cross-sectional surveys conducted periodically in each community. In addition, participants in the cross-sectional surveys were randomly selected to make up a cohort that was remeasured periodically throughout the study period

(Jacobs et al., 1986). Detailed descriptions of the Minnesota Heart Health Program study design have been published elsewhere (Blackburn et al., 1984; Jacobs et al., 1986; Mittlemark et al., 1986; Murray et al., 1986).

The Pawtucket Heart Health Program

The Pawtucket Heart Health Program included one education community in Rhode Island and a comparison community in Massachusetts, with a combined population of approximately 180,000 (Lasater, 1991). The Pawtucket Program originated in the local community hospital and relied on a grass-roots, community activation approach (Carleton et al., 1987; Lasater, 1991) based primarily on social learning theory (Bandura, 1977). To test the community activation approach, broadcast media were not used. People from all sectors of the community were involved, with volunteer participation in the design and delivery of programs constituting a key element (Carleton et al., 1995; Elder et al., 1986; Peterson, Abrams, Elder, & Beaudin, 1985). Cross-sectional risk factor surveys were conducted biennially in random samples of citizens in each community. In addition, participants in the first two surveys formed a cohort that was remeasured approximately 8 years later. Details of the study design have been published elsewhere (Carleton et al., 1995, 1987).

Summary of Major Results

Except for body mass index (BMI), all three community studies demonstrated strong favorable secular trends in the prevalence of cardiovascular risk factors in both the intervention and comparison cities. In general, the favorable changes occurred in women and men and across age and educational levels (Carleton et al., 1995; Lasater, Fortmann, Luepker, & Feldman, 1994; Luepker et al., 1994; Williams, Winkleby, & Fortmann, 1993; Winkleby, Fortmann, & Rockhill, 1992).

Across the three studies, treatment effects were limited and variable. In the Stanford Five-City Project, cohort data showed significantly greater changes in CVD knowledge, blood pressure, and smoking in the intervention cities than in the comparison cities from baseline to the end of the 6-year intervention period (Farquhar et al., 1990; Fortmann, Taylor, Flora, & Jatulis, 1993). In the cross-sectional sample, improvements in CVD knowledge, BMI, and resting pulse rate (an indication of physical activity) were significantly greater in the intervention cities (Farquhar et al., 1990). Cross-sectional data from the Minnesota Heart Health Program suggest a treatment effect for regular physical activity in both women and men, whereas a treatment effect for smoking was observed only among women (Lando et al., 1995; Luepker et al., 1994). In the Pawtucket Program, a significant treatment effect was observed for BMI, and for estimated 10-year risk of CVD based on observed levels of blood pressure, total cholesterol, Metropolitan Life Insurance Company relative weight, and smoking (Carleton et al., 1995). In the Pawtucket Program, the strongest indication for treatment effects occurred in the segment of the population with the least education. Among less educated individuals, there was a consistent trend for greater declines in risk factors in the intervention city than in the comparison city, although the treatment effects did not reach statistical significance (Carleton et al., 1995).

Lessons Learned for Women's Health

Despite the lack of consistent treatment effects observed in these community studies, they have made significant contributions to the body of knowledge on CVD (Winkleby, 1994). Unlike many previous studies of heart disease, large numbers of women participated in the community cardiovascular prevention projects. The cross-sectional databases alone include information on the health behaviors of more than 24,000 women. Thus, these studies provide a wealth of information specific to the health behaviors of women from diverse cultural, ethnic, and income groups and representing different geographic regions of the United States. Data from program participants provide knowledge about the types of programs most likely to reach women and which are most likely to be effective. Finally, during these studies, a substantial number of programs and materials were developed for use in community health education activities.

Secular trends. Data from the comparison cities of the three community studies provide the opportunity to examine secular trends in cardiovascular risk factors in women from three regions of the United States, and to identify gender differences in secular trends. This information is useful for determining priorities and strategies for future risk factor interventions, particularly when combined with other data from these studies, such as cross-sectional analyses and information about the characteristics of participants in specific programs within the intervention communities.

Lasater et al. (1994) examined trends in total cholesterol, systolic and diastolic blood pressure, cigarette smoking, and BMI using data from the comparison cities in each study collected from 1980 to 1990. Strong secular trends were observed in each study. Although there was some variability by region, these trends were generally favorable. The exception was BMI, which showed adverse trends. In the Minnesota Heart Health Program, for example, the secular trends exceeded the hypothesized intervention effects in some instances and were greater than previously observed national secular trends (Luepker et al., 1994).

In general, the secular trends were parallel in women and men (Lasater et al., 1994). The smoking data were, however, an exception. All three studies showed sharp declines in cigarette smoking among men, whereas the three regions differed with respect to smoking trends in women. In California, the rate of smoking declined sharply among women, whereas women in the Midwest and New England continued to smoke in nearly the same proportions throughout the 1980s. These data highlight the need for effective smoking cessation and prevention strategies for women.

The lack of a favorable secular trend among women in Rhode Island and Minnesota is consistent with national data showing that smoking cessation among women lags behind that for men (Ockene, 1993). Greater declines in smoking rates for men than women also are a function of higher smoking initiation rates for women (Ockene, 1993). Cross-sectional data from the Minnesota Heart Health Program suggest a need for gender-specific smoking cessation strategies (Blake et al., 1989). These data show that women were less likely than men to say that they wanted to quit smoking, although men and women were equally likely to report plans to change their smoking habits in the next year. Among those who reported plans to change their smoking habits, there were gender differences in the strategies selected. Men were more likely to choose quitting entirely, whereas women were more likely to cut down on the number of cigarettes smoked. The Minnesota survey data also showed that women were less likely to persist in cessation attempts, with fewer attempts lasting for longer than a week (Blake et al., 1989).

The secular trends data also emphasize the need for weight control programs targeting women. Increases in BMI were observed for women in all three studies, although the trends in California and Minnesota were steeper than in New England (Lasater et al., 1994). Cross-sectional survey data from the Pawtucket Heart Health Program (1989–1993) indicated that there are gender differentials in the rates of both attempting and succeeding in weight loss and increasing physical activity. In addition, although the prevalence of being overweight was similar for women and men, women were more likely to report weight loss attempts in the previous 12 months. This gender difference persisted after adjustment for age, education, and immigration status. However, women were no more likely than men to report that they were able to maintain a weight loss. Women, particularly those in the 18- to 34-year-old age group, were less likely than men to report exercising at least three times per week. Although women were more likely than men to report attempting to increase physical activity, women who tried were less likely than men to maintain an increased activity level.

Ethnic and socioeconomic differences in women's health behaviors. In addition to identifying specific risk factors that may require particular emphasis in women, data from the community studies provide information on the variability of health behaviors among women. The intervention communities in the Stanford Five-City Project included an ethnically diverse population of women. More than 600 Hispanic girls and women, of whom 91% were Mexican American, participated in the cross-sectional surveys. Overall, 53% of the participants in the Stanford Five-City Project were women, of whom 80.0% were White, 78.4% were high school graduates, and 64.0% were married (Williams et al., 1993).

Over the 6-year study period, the majority of women in the Stanford Five-City Project showed favorable risk factor changes (Winkleby, Flora, & Kramer, 1994). In one analysis of women from the intervention cities, more than two thirds of the women showed a positive change in a composite estimate of all-cause mortality risk based on smoking, cholesterol level, and blood pressure. The highest rate of positive change (85%) was found among the subgroup of women who were older, had higher health media use, and had higher self-efficacy (i.e., confidence in their ability to change cardiovascular risk factors). The lowest rate of positive change (50%) was for women with lower self-efficacy scores.

In the Stanford Five-City Project, women in all age and educational groups showed similar favorable improvements in smoking and blood pressure (Winkleby et al., 1992). However, improvements in cholesterol appear to be limited to women who were more highly educated. The suggestion that lower educated women are beginning to show declines in smoking and blood pressure that are equal to declines among higher educated women is encouraging, particularly in light of the high prevalence of smoking among lower educated women. In general, women who are less educated and those who are older continue to have the highest levels of cardiovascular risk factors (Winkleby, Fortmann, & Barrett, 1990).

Substantial numbers of low-income White women participated in the Stanford Five-City Project. Thus, this data set provides a valuable opportunity to examine differences in ethnic groups independent of the effects of socioeconomic status. In a matched-pairs analysis of Hispanic–White differences in cardiovascular risk factors, White women were found to have higher levels of tobacco use and higher fat diets than did Hispanic women of similar socioeconomic status (Winkleby, Albright, Howard-Pitney, Lin, & Fortmann, 1994; Winkleby, Fortmann, & Rockhill, 1993; Winkleby, Schooler, Kraemer, Lin, & Fortmann, 1995). The greatest differences in smoking between Hispanic and White women was among women with the lowest level of educational achievement (less than 12 years of school completed). In this group, White women were more than three times as likely to smoke as Hispanic women (46.1% vs. 20.6%). The ethnic difference in smoking decreased among more educated women, with the smoking rates of Hispanic and White women nearly identical in the group with a college education (Winkleby et al., 1995). White women also were significantly more likely than Hispanic women to eat high-fat foods and to have more calories from total and saturated fat as well as fewer calories from carbohydrates and fiber than Hispanic women (Winkleby et al., 1993).

These findings from the Stanford Five-City Project document poor smoking and dietary profiles among White women with low education and suggest that this group is in particular need of appropriate health education campaigns. This is especially significant to the development of future public health interventions given that poorly educated White women constitute the largest subgroup of impoverished women in America. Despite the favorable changes observed, large differences in the distribution of cardiovascular risk factors remain, with higher risk among women who are older and less educated. This highlights the need for community-based interventions to develop specific materials and programs for older and for lower educated women (Frank & Taylor, 1993). To maximize the chances that all women will be reached, these programs must consider the women's social environment, baseline knowledge, literacy levels, communication styles, and normative beliefs and values.

Emphasis on materials designed specifically for low-literacy groups may enhance the chances of reaching women of lower socioeconomic status. Data from the Pawtucket Heart Health Program provide information on the effectiveness of a community intervention in a group of primarily blue-collar women. There were 8,791 women who participated in the Pawtucket Heart Health Program cross-sectional surveys, representing 57.6% of the total adults surveyed between 1981 and 1993. These women represented many different ethnic groups, including Portuguese (28.9%), Cape Verdean (6.5%), Hispanic (4.7%), and French Canadian (19.8%). Approximately 25% of the women in the Pawtucket Program surveys were foreign born, with most foreign-born women being of Portuguese ethnicity. Many of the women who participated in the survey had attended school for less than 12 years (37.8%). Although 65.5% of the women were currently employed for pay, 55.4% of the women reported earning less than the median per capita income. Given the demographics of the target population, the program emphasized the development of materials for use by individuals with lower literacy levels (Carleton et al., 1995).

To evaluate the hypothesis that communitywide education changed cardiovascular risk factors in women residing in Pawtucket, Rhode Island, relative to those in the comparison city, differences between the baseline (1981–1984) and peak intervention (1987–1990) values were examined by gender. A favorable intervention effect on total cholesterol levels was suggested among women, although the trend was not statistically significant. In Pawtucket, the mean cholesterol level for women fell from a baseline level of 202.9 mg/dl to a mean level of 198.8 mg/dl during the peak intervention period. By contrast, in the comparison city, the mean total cholesterol level changed from 202.8 mg/dl to 201.5 mg/dl during this same period.

The intervention appeared to successfully combat an adverse secular trend in BMI in women; however, the effect was not statistically significant. In Pawtucket women, the mean BMI remained fairly stable between the baseline and peak intervention periods (mean BMIs = 25.6 kg/m^2 at baseline vs. 25.7 kg/m^2 at peak intervention). In the comparison city, there was a greater increase in mean BMI, from 26.2 kg/m^2 to 26.7 kg/m^2.

The suggestion of favorable intervention effects for BMI and cholesterol in women in the Pawtucket Heart Health Program is promising, particularly given the high prevalence of lower educated women, women with low income, and foreign-born women in the study communities. Typically, these groups are difficult to reach with health promotion programs. The results suggest that it is possible to reach these groups when special emphasis is placed on the development of health education materials for individuals with low literacy levels.

Models, methods, and strategies for community interventions. In addition to the information on health behaviors, the three community-based CVD prevention studies provide valuable models, methods, and strategies for planning and conducting community interventions. They have demonstrated successful methods for mobilizing entire communities and for gaining wide support and high participation rates in health promotion programs. The Minnesota Heart Health Program was successful in recruiting 60% of the adults residing in the educational communities in risk factor measurement, education, and counseling activities (Luepker et al., 1994; Murray et al., 1986). Thirty percent of adults in these communities participated in face-to-face interventions, and the majority of school students were involved in school-based health education activities (Kelder, Perry, Peters, Lytle, & Klepp, 1995; Luepker et al., 1994).

The Stanford Five-City Project has estimated an average total exposure for the 6-year intervention period of 26 hr per adult (Farquhar et al., 1990). Television and radio accounted for approximately 34% of the total educational exposures, and 18% was attributable to newspapers and newsletters. Booklets and self-help kits accounted for 41% of the educational exposure, and the remaining 7% was provided through classes and workshops (Farquhar et al., 1990).

During 7 years of active intervention in the Pawtucket Heart Health Program, more than 500 community organizations were involved, including public and private schools, worksites, religious and social organizations, grocery stores, restaurants, and departments of city government (Carleton et al., 1995). More than 3,600 volunteers were enlisted to participate in program delivery. More than 42,000 individuals participated in one or more programs, with more than 110,000 contacts documented for behavior change activities.

Program evaluation data obtained in the community studies are extremely useful for evaluating the types of programs women are most likely to participate in and which are most successful in promoting favorable behavior changes among women. One distinguishing feature of the Pawtucket Heart Health Program was the development of a detailed formative and process evaluation system based on a microcomputer software system for managing data associated with community-level intervention and screening programs (Assaf et al., 1992). The system maintained both individual-level and activity-level data. The individual-level data consisted of detailed program participant information for each contact an individual had with the program, including name, address, telephone number, sociodemographic characteristics, CVD risk factor values, and program participation history. The activity-level information included location, date, type of program, and the targeted risk factor. In addition, the Pawtucket Heart Health Program followed random subsets of program participants to evaluate the short-term success of the intervention efforts (Assaf et al., 1992).

Overall, the majority of program contacts in the Pawtucket Heart Health Program were older and were women. The most popular programs were those targeting nutrition, blood pressure, and weight (Carleton et al., 1995). According to the 1980 U.S. census, 52% of the population in Pawtucket, Rhode Island, was female. Yet, the percentage of program contacts that were for women far exceeded this number. Women constituted 89%

of the 13,490 exercise contacts, 76.4% of the 10,654 weight loss contacts, and 61.3% of the 4,028 smoking cessation contacts (Assaf, Lapane, Lasater, & Carleton, 1994). The average number of smoking and weight loss contacts per person did not differ by gender, but women were more likely than men to have repeat exercise contacts (Assaf et al., 1994).

Data from the first 4 years of intervention in Pawtucket show that the gender difference in participation was most pronounced for group programs. By contrast, the gender distribution of participants more closely represented the demographics of the intervention city for individualized interventions such as self-help kits and screening, counseling, and referral events (Lefebvre, Harden, Rakowski, Lasater, & Carleton, 1987). Women and men were similar in selecting primarily individualized programs.

These data indicate that women were more likely than men to take advantage of the Pawtucket Heart Health Program interventions. Unfortunately, effort does not appear to equate with success. Assaf et al. (1994) reported that although women are more likely to participate in CVD reduction programs, their success rates were equivalent to or less than those for men. In a smoking cessation campaign, quit rates for women and men were similar after a 1 month follow-up. However, after 12 months of follow-up, men were 30% more likely than women to remain smoke-free (Assaf et al., 1994). These analyses suggest that although recruiting women for preventive health interventions is feasible, there is a need to determine strategies for improving the success rate among women who attempt to make favorable health behavior changes.

Resources for communitywide interventions. The materials developed by the community CVD studies make up a vast resource for use in future prevention programs. These materials are the result of dynamic processes in which methods were developed, tested, and modified in a real-world environment. Thus, the generalizability of these methods exceeds that of methods developed in clinical trials. Numerous types of programs were developed, including Screening, Counseling, and Referral Events (SCOREs); self-help kits; contests; small-group sessions; grocery store labeling programs; labeling of restaurant menu heart-healthy selections; school curricula; and nutrition programs. The public acceptance of these programs has been demonstrated, and, for many, program effectiveness has been documented in the literature (Albright, Flora, & Fortmann, 1990; Altman, Flora, Fortmann, & Farquhar, 1987; Crow et al., 1986; Elder, McGraw, & Rodrigues, 1987; Finnegan, Murray, Kurth, & McCarthy, 1989; Forster, Jeffrey, Schmid, & Kraemer, 1988; Gans et al., 1989; Gans, Levin, Lasater, Plotkin, & Carleton, 1994; Glanz & Mullis, 1988; Jackson, Winkleby, Flora, & Fortmann, 1991; Jeffrey, Hellerstedt, & Schmid, 1990; King et al., 1988; Lando, Hellerstedt, Pirie, & McGovern, 1992; Lando, Loken, Howard-Pitney, & Pechacek, 1990; Lasater et al., 1991; Lefebvre et al., 1986; Marcus, Banspach, Lefebvre, Rossi, & Carleton, 1992; Mullis et al., 1987; Murray, Kurth, Mullis, & Jeffrey, 1990; Perry, Kelder, Murray, & Klepp, 1992; Perry, Klepp, & Sillers, 1989). These materials have been adopted by organizations within the communities and have been applied to other prevalent chronic diseases (Winkleby, 1994).

Although community intervention projects have traditionally addressed risk factors as they relate to specific disease entities, preventive interventions are unlikely to independently influence only a single disease process. Favorable secular trends in nutrition or smoking cessation are likely to affect mortality and morbidity for both CVD and cancer. Furthermore, techniques for promoting the adoption of healthy behaviors may be generalizable regardless of the particular disease context in which the interventions were tested.

For example, the experience gained in the three community cardiovascular studies was used to design and conduct the Community Intervention Trial for Smoking Cessation (COMMIT; COMMIT, 1991). This project, funded by the National Cancer Institute in 1986, targeted a single risk factor, smoking. The goal was to conduct smoking cessation activities through a diverse network of existing social organizations. Interventions were designed to help smokers quit and to maintain cessation. Unlike the three community heart disease prevention studies discussed here, COMMIT used a randomized design and included an adequate number of communities for statistical power to perform analyses using community as the unit of analysis. The major results of the COMMIT recently have been reported (COMMIT, 1995a, 1995b). Among heavy smokers, there was no significant difference in quit rates between intervention and comparison communities. However, among light-to-moderate smokers, there was a 3% excess quit rate in the intervention communities. There were no gender differences in the intervention effects on smoking cessation (COMMIT, 1995a, 1995b).

Implications

The NHLBI Task Force on Research in Prevention and Epidemiology of Cardiovascular Diseases recently has emphasized the importance of populationwide prevention strategies (National Heart, Lung and Blood Institute, 1994). The knowledge base and materials generated by the three U.S. community cardiovascular prevention studies provide an invaluable resource for the design of the next generation of prevention programs and research studies that will promote healthy lifestyles among women. As outlined next, the study findings have important implications for practitioners and their patients as well as for program planning and implementation.

Implications for Health Care Practitioners and Their Patients

The community study results suggest that health care providers would enhance their ability to promote healthy behavior changes among women if they were to do the following:

- Become familiar with local community organizations that provide effective health promotion materials and programs to which patients may be referred.
- Include assessment of lifestyle behaviors in routine evaluations and provide referrals to health promotion programs in the community.
- Provide health promotion materials tailored to the ages, educational, cultural, and social environments of the women served.
- Routinely discuss maintenance of healthy behavior changes with female patients, particularly those in the process of smoking cessation, weight loss, or adoption of a regular exercise program.
- Discuss barriers to health behavior changes that may vary for women of different age, ethnic, and socioeconomic groups.
- Congratulate patients on their healthy lifestyle behaviors and emphasize the prevention of unhealthy behaviors, particularly among young women and teenagers.

Implications for Program Planning and Implementation

To promote healthy lifestyles among all women, there is a need for future community prevention programs to do the following:

- Place special emphasis on the prevention of smoking, weight gain, and a sedentary lifestyle.
- Target the special needs of women from different ethnic, socioeconomic, and age groups, particularly lower educated and older women.
- Involve women in the design and delivery of health promotion activities.
- Emphasize strategies for the long-term maintenance of healthy behaviors among women who attempt to change.
- Target policies and regulations at the local and national levels that create an environment conducive to healthy lifestyle changes.
- Assess and make use of the resources existing within the community.
- Include health care professionals from multiple disciplines and strive to equip them with the skills and resources required for treating the special needs of high-risk women.

Conclusion

The community intervention programs discussed here provide a vast amount of information on behavioral risk factors in women and strategies for favorably changing these behaviors. One pattern that emerges from the results of community trials to date is that the community approach may be particularly effective in stimulating health behavior changes in the segments of the population not typically included in more general secular trends. Among light-to-moderate smokers in the COMMIT, individuals who were less educated were more responsive to the intervention than were college-educated individuals. The authors proposed that interventions such as those in the COMMIT added little to secular trends among the highly educated group, whereas less educated smokers might benefit more from community-based antismoking messages (COMMIT, 1995a). Similarly, in the Pawtucket Heart Health Program (Carleton et al., 1995) and the Stanford Five-City Project (Winkleby et al., 1992), the group with the lowest level of education showed the greatest evidence for a treatment effect, and, although these trends were not always statistically significant, this trend was consistent across risk factors. Although all segments of the U.S. population have benefited from favorable shifts in health behaviors in recent years, all groups have not benefited equally, and levels of several cardiovascular risk factors are no longer decreasing steadily in less educated and less affluent individuals (National Heart, Lung and Blood Institute, 1994). The socioeconomic gap in health behaviors and cardiovascular mortality is in fact increasing (Kaplan & Keil, 1993; Novotny, Warner, Kendrick, & Remington, 1988; Pappas, Queen, Hadden, & Fisher, 1993). Thus, there is a great need to expand the findings of the community studies, with emphasis on the development of interventions targeting lower educated, low-income, and older women who remain at high risk for chronic diseases.

The need to target older women will become increasingly important as the population ages. The community prevention studies conducted to date have targeted populations that were generally healthy and have not focused specifically on older people. As the U.S. population ages, increased emphasis will be required for accessing the elderly women, including those with prevalent disease and comorbid conditions. The proportion of the U.S. population over the age of 60 will increase by 50% in the next 35 years (Spencer, 1989). Currently, men and women constitute equal proportions of the population under the age of 65, but 59% of those over the age of 65 are women and 64% of those over the age of 75 are women (Ernst & Evans, 1992). The proportion of women with a history of coronary heart disease increases with age. Among women aged 45–64 years, approximately 4% report a history of coronary heart disease, compared with 10% of women aged 65–74 years and 13% of those over the age of 75 (National Heart, Lung and Blood Institute, 1994). Data from the three community CVD prevention studies support the feasibility of recruiting older women to community intervention activities. However, information about the most appropriate strategies for promoting risk factor modification in this rapidly growing segment of the population is lacking.

The community programs to date have demonstrated that community involvement in health promotion is feasible and effective. The Pawtucket Heart' Health Program has demonstrated that the use of volunteers for the delivery of health education may be one means of reaching large segments of the community while keeping costs low. Future programs and research projects may benefit from expanding these methods to involve women from diverse ethnic and socioeconomic groups in the design and implementation of programs. Qualitative data from carefully conducted focus groups provide information that is more in-depth and creative than that provided by traditional quantitative techniques. Valuing the needs and priorities of women in the community may enhance the ability to reach those not targeted by mainstream programs. On an applied level, this approach may be beneficial for practitioners striving to promote prevention among their patients. By talking with patients to determine individual women's priorities and concerns, practitioners may enhance their ability to promote the adoption of healthy behaviors.

References

Albright, C. L., Flora, J. A., & Fortmann, S. P. (1990). Restaurant menu labeling: Impact of nutrition information on three entree sales and patron attitudes. *Health Education Quarterly, 17,* 157–167.

Altman, D. A., Flora, J. A., Fortmann, S. P., & Farquhar, J. W. (1987). The cost-effectiveness of three smoking cessation programs. *American Journal of Public Health, 77,* 162–165.

Assaf, A. R., Banspach, S. W., Lasater, T. M., Ramsey, J., Tidwell, R. J., & Carleton, R. A. (1992). The Fpbase microcomputer system for managing community health screening and intervention data bases. *Public Health Reports, 107,* 695–700.

Assaf, A. R., Lapane, K. L., Lasater, T. M., & Carleton, R. A. (1994). New perspectives on the gender gap: Women try harder but are less successful at CVD risk reduction [Abstract]. *Circulation, 89,* 933.

Bandura, A. J. (1977). *Social learning theory.* Englewood Cliffs, NJ: Prentice Hall.

Blackburn, H. (1983). Research and demonstration projects in community cardiovascular disease prevention. *Journal of Public Health Policy, 4,* 398–421.

Blackburn, H., Luepker, R., Kline, F. G., Bracht, N., Carlaw, R., Jacobs, D., Mittlemark, M., Stauffer, L., & Taylor, H. L. (1984). The Minnesota Heart Health Program: A research and demonstration project in cardiovascular disease prevention. In J. D. Matarazzo, J. A. Herd, N. E. Miller, & S. M. Weiss (Eds.), *Behavioral health: A handbook of health enhancement and disease prevention* (pp. 1171–1178). New York: Wiley.

Blake, S. M., Klepp, K. I., Pechacek, T. F., Folsom, A. R., Luepker, R. V., Jacobs, D. R., & Mittlemark, M. B. (1989). Differences in smoking cessation strategies between men and women. *Addictive Behaviors, 14,* 409–418.

Bracht, N., & Kingsbury, L. (1990). Community organization principles in health promotion: A five stage model. In N. Bracht (Ed.), *Health promotion at the community level* (pp. 66–88). Newbury Park, CA: Sage.

Carleton, R. A., & Lasater, T. M. (1994). Population intervention to reduce coronary heart disease incidence. In T. A. Pearson, M. H. Criqui, R. V. Luepker, A. Oberman, & M. Winston, (Eds.), *Primer in preventive cardiology* (pp. 285–292). Dallas, TX: American Heart Association.

Carleton, R. A., Lasater, T. M., Assaf, A. R., Feldman, H. A., McKinlay, S. M., & the Pawtucket Heart Health Program Writing Group. (1995). The Pawtucket Heart Health Program: Community changes in cardiovascular risk factors and projected disease risk. *American Journal of Public Health, 85,* 777–785.

Carleton, R. A., Lasater, T. M., Assaf, A. R., Lefebvre, R. C., & McKinlay, S. M. (1987). The Pawtucket Heart Health Program: I. An experiment in population-based disease prevention. *Rhode Island Medical Journal, 70,* 533–538.

Collins, R., Peto, R., Godwin, J., & MacMahon, S. (1990). Blood pressure and coronary heart disease. *The Lancet, 336,* 370–371.

COMMIT Research Group. (1991). Community Intervention Trial for Smoking Cessation (COMMIT): Summary of design and intervention. *Journal of the National Cancer Institute, 83,* 1620–1628.

COMMIT Research Group. (1995a). Community Intervention Trial for Smoking Cessation (COMMIT): I. Cohort results from a four-year community intervention. *American Journal of Public Health, 85*, 183–192.

COMMIT Research Group. (1995b). Community Intervention Trial for Smoking Cessation (COMMIT): II. Changes in adult cigarette smoking prevalence. *American Journal of Public Health, 85*, 193–200.

Crow, R. S., Blackburn, H., Jacobs, D. R., Hannan, P., Pirie, P., Mittlemark, M., Murray, D., & Luepker, R. (1986). Population strategies to enhance physical activity: The Minnesota Heart Health Program. *Acta Medica Scandinavia, 711*(Suppl.), 93–112.

Elder, J. P., McGraw, S. A., & Rodrigues, A. (1987). Evaluation of two community-wide smoking cessation contests. *Preventive Medicine, 16*, 221–234.

Elder, J. P., McKenna, C., Lazieh, M., Ferreira, A., Lasater, T. M., & Carleton, R. A. (1986). The use of volunteers in mass screening for high blood pressure. *American Journal of Preventive Medicine, 2*, 268–272.

Elder, J. P., Schmid, P. D., & Hedlund, S. (1993). Community heart health programs: Components, rationale, and strategies for effective interventions. *Journal of Public Health Policy, 14*, 463–479.

Ernst, N. D., & Evans, M. A. (1992). Cholesterol and heart disease in women. *Clinical Applications in Nutrition, 2*, 18–34.

Farquhar, J. W., Fortmann, S. P., Flora, J. A., Taylor, B., Haskell, W. L., Williams, P. P. T., Maccoby, N., & Wood, P. D. (1990). Effects of community-wide education on cardiovascular disease risk factors: The Stanford Five-City Project. *Journal of the American Medical Association, 264*, 359–365.

Farquhar, J. W., Fortmann, S. P., Maccoby, N., Haskell, W. L., Williams, P. T., Flora, J. A., Taylor, C. B., Brown, B. W., Solomon, D. S., & Hulley, S. B. (1985). The Stanford Five-City Project: Design and methods. *American Journal of Epidemiology, 122*, 323–334.

Finnegan, J. R., Murray, D. M., Kurth, C., & McCarthy, P. (1989). Measuring and tracking education program implementation: The Minnesota Heart Health Program experience. *Health Education Quarterly, 16*, 77–90.

Flora, J. A., Maccoby, N., & Farquhar, J. W. (1989). Communication campaigns to prevent cardiovascular disease: The Stanford Community Studies. In R. Rice & C. Atkin (Eds.), *Public communication campaigns* (pp. 233–252). Beverly Hills, CA: Sage.

Forster, J. L., Jeffrey, R. W., Schmid, T. L., & Kramer, F. M. (1988). Preventing weight gain in adults: A pound of prevention. *Health Psychology, 17*, 129–133.

Fortmann, S. P., Taylor, C. B., Flora, J. A., & Jatulis, D. E. (1993). Changes in cigarette smoking prevalence after five years of community health education: The Stanford Five-City Project. *American Journal of Epidemiology, 137*, 82–96.

Frank, E., & Taylor, C. B. (1993). Coronary heart disease in women: Influences on diagnosis and treatment. *Annals of Behavioral Medicine, 15*, 156–161.

Frick, M. H., Elo, O., Haapa, K., Heinonen, O. P., Heinsalmi, P., Helo, P., Huttunen, J. K., Kaitaniemi, P., Koskinen, P., Manninen, V., Maenpaa, H., Malkonen, M., Manttari, M., Norola, S., Pasternak, A., Pikkarainen, J., Romo, M., Sjoblom, T., & Nikkila, E. A. (1987). Helsinki Heart Study: Primary prevention trial with Gemfibrozil in middle-aged men with dyslipidemia. *New England Journal of Medicine, 317*, 1237–1245.

Gans, K. M., Lefebvre, R. C., Lasater, T. M., Nelson, D. J., Loberti, P. G., & Carleton, R. A. (1989). Measuring blood cholesterol in the community: Participant characteristics by site. *Health Education Research: Theory and Practice, 4*, 399–406.

Gans, K. M., Levin, S., Lasater, T. M., Plotkin, B., & Carleton, R. A. (1994). Implementation and institutionalization of heart healthy programming in schools: The Pawtucket Heart Health Program experience. *Journal of Health Education, 25*, 89–97.

Glanz, K., & Mullis, R. M. (1988). Environmental interventions to promote healthy eating: A review of models, programs, and evidence. *Health Education Quarterly, 15*, 395–415.

Hovland, C. I., Janis, I. L., & Kelly, N. H. (1953). *Communication and persuasion.* New Haven, CT: Yale University Press.

Jackson, C., Winkleby, M. A., Flora, J. A., & Fortmann, S. P. (1991). Utilization of educational resources for cardiovascular risk reduction in the Stanford Five-City Project. *American Journal of Preventive Medicine, 7*, 82–88.

Jacobs, D. R., Jr., Luepker, R. V., Mittlemark, M. B., Folsom, A. R., Pirie, P. L., Mascioli, S. R., Hannan, P. J., Pechacek, T. F., Bracht, N. F., Carlaw, R. W., Kline, G. F., Blackburn, H. (1986). Community-wide prevention strategies: Evaluation design of the Minnesota Heart Health Program. *Journal of Chronic Disease, 39,* 775–788.

Jeffrey, R. W., Hellerstedt, W. L., & Schmid, T. L. (1990). Correspondence programs for smoking cessation and weight control: A comparison of two strategies in the Minnesota Heart Health Program. *Health Psychology, 9,* 585–598.

Kaplan, G. A., & Keil, J. E. (1993). Socioeconomic factors and cardiovascular disease: A review of the literature. *Circulation, 88,* 1973–1998.

Kelder, S. H., Perry, C. L., Peters, R. J., Lytle, L., & Klepp, K. (1995). Gender differences in the Class of 1989 Study: The school component of the Minnesota Heart Health Program. *Journal of Health Education, 26*(Suppl.), S36–S44.

King, A. C., Saylor, K. E., Foster, S., Killen, J. D., Telch, M. J., Farquhar, J. W., & Flora, J. A. (1988). Promoting dietary change in adolescents: A school based approach for modifying and maintaining healthy behavior. *American Journal of Preventive Medicine, 4,* 68–74.

Kottke, T. E., Puska, P., Salonen, J. T., Tuomilehto, J., & Nissinen, A. (1985). Projected effects of high-risk versus population-based prevention strategies in coronary heart disease. *American Journal of Epidemiology, 121,* 697–704.

Lando, H. A., Hellerstedt, W. L., Pirie, P. L., & McGovern, P. G. (1992). Brief supportive telephone outreach as a recruitment and intervention strategy for smoking cessation. *American Journal of Public Health, 82,* 41–46.

Lando, H. A., Loken, B., Howard-Piney, B., & Pechacek, T. (1990). Community impact of a localized smoking cessation contest. *American Journal of Public Health, 80,* 601–603.

Lando, H. A., Pechacek, T. F., Pirie, P., Murray, D. M., Mittlemark, M. B., Lichtenstein, E., Nothwehr, F., & Gray, C. (1995). Changes in adult cigarette smoking in the Minnesota Heart Health Program. *American Journal of Public Health, 85,* 201–208.

Lasater, T. M. (1991). Community-wide prevention of chronic disease: Theory and application. In *Conference proceedings—Primary care research: Theory and methods* (PHS-AHCPR Publication No. 91-0011, pp. 189–196). Rockville, MD: U.S. Department of Health and Human Services.

Lasater, T. M. (1992). Designs employed in community heart disease and cancer prevention projects. In H. D. Holder & J. M. Howard (Eds.), *Community prevention trials for alcohol problems: Methodological issues* (pp. 77–93). Westport, CT: Greenwood Press.

Lasater, T. M., Fortmann, S. P., Luepker, R. V., & Feldman, H. A. (1994). Secular trends through the 1980s for CVD risk factors [Abstract]. *Circulation, 89,* 933.

Lasater, T. M., Sennett, L. L., Lefebvre, R. C., DeHart, K. L., Peterson, G., & Carleton, R. A. (1991). A community-based approach to weight loss: The Pawtucket weigh-in. *Addictive Behaviors, 16,* 175–181.

Lefebvre, C. R., Harden, E. A., Rakowski, W., Lasater, T. M., & Carleton, R. A. (1987). Characteristics of participants in community health promotion programs: Four-year results. *American Journal of Public Health, 77,* 1–3.

Lefebvre, R. C., Peterson, G. S., McGraw, S., Lasater, T. M., Sennett, L., Kendall, L., & Carleton, R. A. (1986). Community intervention to lower blood cholesterol: The "Know Your Cholesterol" campaign in Pawtucket, Rhode Island. *Health Education Quarterly, 13,* 117–129.

Lenfant, C. (1986). A new challenge for America: The National Cholesterol Education Program. *Circulation, 73,* 855–856.

Lipid Research Clinics Program. (1984a). The Lipid Research Clinics Coronary Primary Prevention Trial results: I. Reduction in incidence of coronary heart disease. *Journal of the American Medical Association, 251,* 351–364.

Lipid Research Clinics Program. (1984b). The Lipid Research Clinics Coronary Primary Prevention Trial results: II. The relationship of reduction in incidence of coronary heart disease to cholesterol lowering. *Journal of the American Medical Association, 251,* 365–374.

Luepker, R. V. (1994). Community trials. *Preventive Medicine, 23,* 602–605.

Luepker, R. V., Murray, D. M., Jacobs, D. R., Mittlemark, M. B., Bracht, N., Carlaw, R., Crow, R., Elmer, P., Finnegan, J., Folsom, A. R. Grimm, R., Hannan, P. J., Jeffrey, R., Lando, H., McGovern, P., Mullis, R., Perry, C. L., Pechacek, T., Pirie, P., Sprafka, M., Weisbrod, R., & Blackburn, H. (1994). Community education for cardiovascular disease prevention: Risk factor changes in the Minnesota Heart Health Program. *American Journal of Public Health, 84,* 1383–1393.

Marcus, B. H., Banspach, S. W., Lefebvre, R. C., Rossi, J. S., & Carleton, R. A. (1992). Using the stages of change model to increase the adoption of physical activity among community participants. *American Journal of Health Promotion, 6,* 424–429.

McGuire, W. J. (1973). Persuasion, resistance and attitude change. In I. DeSola & W. Schramm (Eds.), *Handbook of communication* (pp. 261–252). Chicago: Rand McNally.

Mittlemark, M. B., Hunt, M. K., Heath, G. W., & Schmid, T. L. (1993). Realistic outcomes: Lessons from community-based research and demonstration programs for the prevention of cardiovascular diseases. *Public Health Policy, 14,* 437–462.

Mittlemark, M. B., Luepker, R. V., Jacobs, D. R., Bracht, N. F., Carlaw, R. W., Crow, R. S., Finnegan, J., Grimm, R. H., Jeffrey, R. W., Kline, F. G., Mullis, R. M., Murray, D. M., Pechacek, T. F., Perry, C. L., Pirie, P. L., & Blackburn, H. (1986). Community-wide prevention of cardiovascular disease: Education strategies of the Minnesota Heart Health Program. *Preventive Medicine, 15,* 1–17.

Mullis, R. M., Hunt, M. K., Foster, M., Hachfeld, L., Lansing, D., Snyder, P., & Pirie, P. (1987). Environmental support of healthful food behavior: The Shop Smart for Your Heart Grocery Program. *Journal of Nutrition Education, 19,* 225–228.

Murray, D. M., Kurth, C., Mullis, R. M., & Jeffrey, R. W. (1990). Cholesterol reduction through low intensity interventions: Results from the Minnesota Heart Health Program. *Preventive Medicine, 19,* 181–189.

Murray, D. M., Luepker, R. V., Pirie, P. L., Grimm, R. H., Bloom, E., Davis, M. A., & Blackburn, H. (1986). Systematic risk factor screening and education: A community-wide approach to prevention of coronary heart disease. *Preventive Medicine, 15,* 661–672.

National Heart, Lung and Blood Institute. (1994). *Report of the Task Force on Research in Epidemiology and Prevention of Cardiovascular Diseases.* Washington, DC: U.S. Public Health Service.

National High Blood Pressure Education Program. (1993). *The fifth report of the Joint National Committee on Detection, Evaluation, and Treatment of High Blood Pressure* (NIH Publication No. 73-486). Bethesda, MD: National Institutes of Health.

Novotny, T. E., Warner, K. E., Kendrick, J. S., & Remington, P. L. (1988). Smoking by Blacks and Whites: Socioeconomic and demographic differences. *American Journal of Public Health, 78,* 1187–1189.

Oberman, A., Kuller, L. H., & Carleton, R. A. (1994). Prevention of cardiovascular disease: Opportunities for progress. *Preventive Medicine, 23,* 727–732.

Ockene, J. K. (1993). Smoking among women across the life span: Prevalence, interventions, and implications for cessation research. *Annals of Behavioral Medicine, 15,* 135–148.

Pappas, G., Queen, S., Hadden, W., & Fisher, G. (1993). The increasing disparity in mortality between socioeconomic groups in the United States, 1960 and 1986. *New England Journal of Medicine, 329,* 103–109.

Perry, C. L., Kelder, S. H., Murray, D. M., & Klepp, K. I. (1992). Community-wide smoking prevention: Long-term outcomes of the Minnesota Heart Health Program. *American Journal of Public Health, 82,* 1210–1216.

Perry, C. L., Klepp, K. I., & Sillers, C. (1989). Community-wide strategies for cardiovascular health: The Minnesota Heart Health Program youth program. *Health Education Research, 4,* 87–101.

Peterson, G., Abrams, D. B., Elder, J. P., & Beaudin, P. R. (1985). Professional versus self-help weight loss at the worksite: The challenge of making a public health impact. *Behavioral Therapy, 16,* 213–221.

Pirie, P. L., Stone, E. J., Assaf, A. R., Flora, J. A., & Maschewsky-Schneider, U. (1994). Program evaluation strategies for community-based health promotion programs: Perspectives from the cardiovascular disease community research and demonstration studies. *Health Education Research, Theory and Practice, 9,* 23–26.

Pooling Project Research Group. (1978). *Relationship of blood pressure, serum cholesterol, smoking habit, relative weight and ECG abnormalities to incidence of major coronary events: Final report of the Pooling Project* [Monograph]. Dallas, TX: American Heart Association.

Rose, G. (1992). Strategies of prevention: The individual and the population. In M. Marmot & P. Elliott (Eds.), *Coronary heart disease epidemiology: From aetiology to public health* (pp. 311–324). New York: Oxford University Press.

Rose, G., & Shipley, M. (1990). Effects of coronary risk reduction on the pattern of mortality. *The Lancet, I*, 275–277.

Rothman, J. (1970). Three models of community organization practice. In F. Cox, J. L. Erlich, & J. Rothman (Eds.), *Strategies of community organization: A book of readings* (pp. 20–36). Itsaca, NJ: Peacock.

Schwartz, R., Smith, C., Speers, M. A., Dusenbury, L. J., Bright, F., Hedlund, S., Wheeler, F., & Schmid, T. L. (1993). Capacity building and resource needs of state health agencies to implement community-based cardiovascular disease programs. *Journal of Public Health Policy, 14*, 480–494.

Spencer, G. (1989). *Projections of the population of the United States by age, sex and race: 1988 to 2080* (U.S. Bureau of the Census, Current Population Reports, Series P-25, No. 1018). Washington, DC: U.S. Government Printing Office.

Stone, E. J. (1991). Comparison of NHLBI community-based cardiovascular research studies. *Journal of Health Education, 22*, 134–136.

U.S. Department of Health and Human Services. (1988). *Disease prevention / health promotion: The facts* (Public Health Service, Office of Disease Prevention and Health Promotion). Palo Alto, CA: Bull Publishing.

Williams, E. L., Winkleby, M. A., & Fortmann, S. P. (1993). Changes in coronary heart disease risk factors in the 1980s: Evidence of a male-female crossover effect with age. *American Journal of Epidemiology, 137*, 1056–1067.

Winkleby, M. A. (1994). The future of community-based cardiovascular disease intervention studies [Editorial]. *American Journal of Public Health, 84*, 1369–1371.

Winkleby, M. A., Albright, C., Howard-Pitney, B., Lin, J., & Fortmann, S. P. (1994). Hispanic/ White differences in dietary fat intake among low educated adults and children. *Preventive Medicine, 23*, 465–473.

Winkleby, M. A., Flora, J. A., & Kramer, H. C. (1994). A community-based heart disease intervention: Predictors of change. *American Journal of Public Health, 84*, 767–772.

Winkleby, M. A., Fortmann, S. P., & Barrett, D. C. (1990). Social class disparities in risk factors for disease: Eight-year prevalence patterns by level of education. *Preventive Medicine, 19*, 1–12.

Winkleby, M. A., Fortmann, S. P., & Rockhill, B. (1992). Trends in cardiovascular disease risk factors by educational level: The Stanford Five-City Project. *Preventive Medicine, 21*, 592–601.

Winkleby, M. A., Fortmann, S. P., & Rockhill, B. (1993). Health-related risk factors in a sample of Hispanics and Whites matched on sociodemographic characteristics. *American Journal of Epidemiology, 137*, 1365–1375.

Winkleby, M. A., Schooler, C., Kraemer, H. C., Lin J., & Fortmann, S. P. (1995). Hispanic versus White smoking patterns by sex and level of education. *American Journal of Epidemiology, 142*, 410–418.

Index

Abortion, 239
Access to care
  for alcohol problems, 85–86, 88
  for breast cancer screening, 5, 19–20,
    299
  cardiovascular health outcomes and, 262,
    263–264
  goals, 9
  for infertility treatment, 188, 197–198
  recurrent headaches, 382
  socioeconomic status and, 18, 19–20
Access to information, 9
Activities of daily living, 226
Adoption, 189
Advocacy
  for battered women, 52–53
  for employed mothers/wives, 170–171
Age-related differences
  activities of daily living index, 226
  in AIDS risk assessment, 280
  alcohol abuse among women, 76, 77
  alcohol abuse risk, 79
  anorexia nervosa onset, outcomes related
    to, 99
  breast cancer risk, 17
  breast cancer screening behaviors, 296
  breast cancer screening effectiveness, 298
  cohorts of older women, 224–226
  dementia, 231
  demographic trends, 222–223
  depression in elderly, 230–231
  discrimination against elderly, 221–222
  economic issues in aging, 232
  gender differences in aging, 222–224
  headache treatment, 380–381
  health care issues for older women, 226–
    228
  health care system for elderly, 233
  identification of battered women, 48
  physical activity patterns, 141–143
  risk of domestic violence in pregnancy,
    44–45
  senescence, 222
  sensory loss, 227
  sexual interests/behavior, 228–230
  sociocultural context, 221
  stigmatized health issues, 228–230
Agency for Health Care Policy and Research, 178
AIDS/HIV
  barriers to testing, 284–285
  cultural considerations in risk assess-
    ment, 279–280

  delivery of preventive services, 278–279,
    281–282, 288–289
  disclosure to loved ones, 286–287
  epidemiology, 273–274
  mortality, 16, 274
  national health objectives, 278
  needle exchange programs, 276
  postinfection care, 287, 288, 289
  posttest counseling, 283–284
  pretest counseling, 282
  psychosocial assessment of women with,
    285
  psychosocial mediators of disease pro-
    cess, 286, 288
  psychosocial needs of women with, 285–
    287
  reporting requirements/confidentiality,
    275, 279
  risk for victims of abuse, 44
  sexual behavior as risk factor, 274–275,
    276–277
  socioeconomic status and, 16, 278
  source of exposure, 274, 275
  substance use-related, 274, 275–276
  support groups, 287
  testing, 279
  trends among women, 273
Alcohol abuse
  anxiety disorders and, 81–82
  barriers to treatment, 85–86
  brief interventions, 88–89
  childhood victimization as risk factor,
    80–81
  cognitive-behavioral interventions, 89
  comorbid drug use, 85
  continuum of, 77
  current clinical conceptualization, 90
  demographic risk factors, 79–80
  depression and, 81, 82
  eating disorders and, 106
  effective treatments for women, 88–91
  etiological conceptualization, 75
  gender differences, 35, 77–79
  genetic risk, 79
  identification and screening, 78, 83–85
  indicated research, 91
  as learned behavior, 79, 89
  marital status and, 80
  physiological outcomes, 82–83
  prevalence, 75, 76
  sexual dysfunction and, 81
  treatment delivery, 75–76

Depression
  after myocardial infarction, 260–261
  alcohol use and, 81, 82
  among battered women, 46
  cardiovascular health and, 260–261
  clinical features, 238–239, 244–245
  comorbid anxiety disorder, 242
  comorbid medical disorders, 240–241
  diabetes and, 359
  differential diagnosis, 239–241
  dysphoria in menopause, 211–213
  eating disorder-related, 105
  in elderly, 230–231
  epidemiology, 237–238
  gender differences in risk, 25, 31, 238,
    336
  generic counseling for, 245
  medical basis, 240–241
  in obesity treatment, 120
  pharmacotherapy for, 245, 246, 247,
    248–249
  postpartum, 177, 180, 183, 239
  psychiatric comorbidity, 241
  psychosocial treatments, 247–248
  rheumatic disease and, 336
  risk in menopause, 211
  treatment adherence, 246
  treatment strategies, 245–249, 251–252
  work-family strain and, 164–165
Diabetes, 107
  comorbid depression, 240
  depression in, 359
  diet and, 354
  eating disorders and, 354–355
  exercise and, 353
  glycemic control in, 349
  insulin administration, 351–353
  insulin-dependent, 349, 350–355
  non insulin-dependent, 349, 355–357
  obesity and, 117, 118, 355–357
  outcomes, 349
  physical activity and, 133, 137–138
  pregnancy and, 349, 359–360
  prevalence, 349
  psychological stress in, 358
  self-monitoring of blood glucose, 350–351
  treatment formulation, 360–361
  treatment nonadherence, 355
  very low-calorie diet, 356–357
Diet and nutrition
  cancer and, 7
  community prevention programs for car-
    diovascular health, 412, 413
  diabetes, 354–355, 356–357
  headaches related to, 373
  menopause and, 216
  obesity interventions, 120, 122
  osteoporosis and, 228

  socioeconomic considerations in interven-
    tions with, 19
Dissociative disorders, 46
Doctor-patient communication
  AIDS risk assessment, 278–281
  on breast cancer screening, 297, 300, 310
  cultural sensitivity in, 279–280
  female practitioners, 58, 59
  gender differences in, 29–30, 57–58, 66–
    69
  to improve compliance, 322–324, 327
  limitations of research, 59
  notification of test results, 321–322
  patient bias in, 59
  patient gender as variable in, 65–66
  physician gender as variable in, 61–65
  practitioner bias in, 58
  as quality of care issue, 57
  research findings, 60
  rheumatic disease treatment adherence
    and, 338–339
  significance of, 57
  stigmatized health issues, 228
  See also Therapeutic relationship
Domestic violence
  assessment for, 37
  coping responses, 43
  documentation, 53
  emotional abuse and, 43
  failure to diagnose, 43
  HIV and, 44
  incidence and prevalence, 41
  interventions, 51–52
  legal advocacy, 52–53
  legislative action on, 6
  pharmacotherapy for victim of, 43–44
  pregnancy-related, 44–45
  as psychological abuse, 49–50
  referral network, 53
  safety planning, 51–52
  sexual abuse in, 49
  suicide and, 44
  woman as aggressor, 42
Dysthymia, 239

Eating disorders
  anxiety disorders associated with, 105
  assessment, 107, 108–110
  associated psychopathology, 105
  bone pathologies related to, 104
  cardiovascular problems related to, 104
  clinical course, 108
  dental problems related to, 104
  depression associated with, 105, 241
  diabetes and, 354–355
  electrolyte imbalances in, 104–105

About the Editors

Sheryle J. Gallant, PhD, is an associate professor of psychology at the University of Kansas. In her research she has focused on conceptual and methodological issues in the assessment of mood and behavior changes during the menstrual cycle and biopsychosocial correlates of premenstrual syndrome. In her most recent work, she examined problematic aspects of diagnosing premenstrual dysphoric disorder (PMDD), and the role of stress, coping, and relationship factors in the experience of PMDD. Dr. Gallant was chair of APA's 1994 national conference "Psychosocial and Behavioral Factors in Women's Health: Creating an Agenda for the 21st Century."

Gwendolyn Puryear Keita, PhD, is the Director of Women's Programs and Associate Executive Director of the Public Interest Directorate of the American Psychological Association. Her work has focused on issues affecting women and ethnic minorities, especially violence against women, mental health of ethnic minority women, and occupational stress and workplace wellness. Dr. Keita was project director of APA's 1994 and 1996 national conferences, "Psychosocial and Behavioral Factors in Women's Health: Creating an Agenda for the 21st Century" and "Psychosocial and Behavioral Factors in Women's Health: Research, Prevention, Treatment, and Service Delivery in Clinical and Community Settings," respectively.

Reneé Royak-Schaler, PhD, is an Associate Professor in the School of Public Health, Allegheny University of the Health Sciences, and a Research Associate at the Lineberger Comprehensive Cancer Center, University of North Carolina–Chapel Hill. Since 1988, her research has focused on perceptions of breast cancer risk, risk knowledge, and the process of making informed screening decisions among women who have family histories of breast cancer. A current project, the PARTNERS in Breast Cancer Education Program, will evaluate the effectiveness of an intervention conducted through the African American churches in promoting risk understanding, prompt symptom care, and communication with physicians among 40–49 year old women. Dr. Royak-Schaler served as Program Chair of APA's 1994 Conference, "Psychosocial and Behavioral Factors in Women's Health: Creating an Agenda for the 21st Century."